Splendour, Misery, and Possibilities

Historical Materialism Book Series

The Historical Materialism Book Series is a major publishing initiative of the radical left. The capitalist crisis of the twenty-first century has been met by a resurgence of interest in critical Marxist theory. At the same time, the publishing institutions committed to Marxism have contracted markedly since the high point of the 1970s. The Historical Materialism Book Series is dedicated to addressing this situation by making available important works of Marxist theory. The aim of the series is to publish important theoretical contributions as the basis for vigorous intellectual debate and exchange on the left.

The peer-reviewed series publishes original monographs, translated texts, and reprints of classics across the bounds of academic disciplinary agendas and across the divisions of the left. The series is particularly concerned to encourage the internationalization of Marxist debate and aims to translate significant studies from beyond the English-speaking world.

For a full list of titles in the Historical Materialism Book Series available in paperback from Haymarket Books, visit:
https://www.haymarketbooks.org/series_collections/1-historical-materialism

Splendour, Misery, and Possibilities

An X-Ray of Socialist Yugoslavia

Darko Suvin

Foreword by Fredric Jameson

Haymarket Books
Chicago, IL

First published in 2015 by Brill Academic Publishers, The Netherlands
© 2016 Koninklijke Brill NV, Leiden, The Netherlands

Published in paperback in 2017 by
Haymarket Books
P.O. Box 180165
Chicago, IL 60618
773-583-7884
www.haymarketbooks.org

ISBN: 978-1-60846-801-0

Trade distribution:
In the US, Consortium Book Sales, www.cbsd.com
In Canada, Publishers Group Canada, www.pgcbooks.ca
In the UK, Turnaround Publisher Services, www.turnaround-uk.com
All other countries, Ingram Publisher Services International, ips_intlsales@ingramcontent.com

Cover design by Jamie Kerry of Belle Étoile Studios and Ragina Johnson.

This book was published with the generous support of Lannan Foundation and the Wallace Action Fund.

Entered into digital printing February 2018.

Library of Congress Cataloging-in-Publication data is available.

This my last book is for those who shaped my stance under the stars:

– Truda and Miro, my parents;

– SKOJ (The League of Communist Youth of Yugoslavia), pars pro toto of the young Yugoslav Revolution that encountered and accepted me, 1945–8;

– the interpellations in the works of Karl Marx, Friedrich Engels, Miroslav Krleža, V.I. Lenin, of William Shakespeare and Bert Brecht and so many more poets in verse and prose, of Ernst Bloch and Walter Benjamin;

– the other teachers named in this book;

– last not least, Nena, the companion of my life.

All of them shape and are contained in the ideal image of The Foam-Born, eternal like the sea and the yearnings of humans.

∴

Jean(?) Kerleroux, We Have To Start All Over Again ('Il faut tout recommencer')
REPRODUCED FROM LE DESSIN D'HUMOUR OF MICHEL RAGON (POINT-VIRGULE, SEUIL)

'Do you compare yourself with them?'
'All my life I've compared myself with them'.
    adapted from SAMUEL BECKETT

•••

Not being (non-being) is admissible, ... but once something has already been, then it must have been so, and its not being (non-being) is inadmissible.
    MASTER MO DI, Fifth Century BCE

•••

It ain't necessarily so.
    THE GERSHWIN BROTHERS, 1934

•••

I mourn my homeland, 'Che mi fu tolta, e il modo ancor m'offende' [Of which I was bereft, and the way of it still offends me – Dante]
    UGO FOSCOLO, 1798

•••

A further consequence is here that we are not dealing with the past but with the present. Only the outer aspect has passed away, people, their destinies, etc. ... Thus we do not deal with historical data but with a presentness, in which we ourselves are present ... We are dealing with a concept which is our own.
    G.W.F. HEGEL, 1827

•••

The philosophy is that ensemble of questions in which the one who poses the question is identical to the one who is put into question.
    MAURICE MERLEAU-PONTY, ca. 1949?

•••

[U]nless the past and the future were made part of the present by memory and intention, there was, in human terms, no road, nowhere to go.
URSULA K. LE GUIN, 1973

∴

I insist that the colonial reinvention of Yugoslavia has so far advanced and is so dangerous that we must conceive it as our duty to take Yugoslavia in hand again, maybe not as a political project but certainly as a research problem ... In a certain sense the crisis of capitalism helps us to revise viz. reconceptualise Yugoslavia.
SVETLANA SLAPŠAK, 2010

∴

Contents

List of Figures and Tables XIII
Acknowledgements and Thanks XVI
Foreword to Darko Suvin, *Splendour, Misery, and Potentialities: An X-ray of Socialist Yugoslavia* XIX
    Fredric Jameson

Introduction: Pro Domo Sua 1

PART 1
Fundaments: Freedom and Accumulation

1   Radical Emancipation and Yugoslavia: On the Founding Singularities of SFRY 23

2   Accumulation and Its Discontents 36

PART 2
Class Interests and Politics as SFRY Dominants

3   On Class Relationships in Yugoslavia 43

4   On a Hidden Ruling Class and Central Conflict 72

5   What Has Been and What Could Have Been 81

6   15 Theses about Communism and Yugoslavia, or the Two-Headed Janus of Emancipation through the State (Metamorphoses and Anamorphoses of 'On the Jewish Question' by Marx) 105

7   The Communist Party of Yugoslavia 128

PART 3
Self-Government vs. Alienation: A Tractate on Yugoslav Economics and Politics

SECTION 3.1
On Self-Management in S.F.R. Yugoslavia: A Critical Stock-Taking (1945–72)

8   Anatomy: Macro-Political Economics, or the View from Above   162

9   Anatomy: Micro-Political Economics, or the View from the Workers   180

10 Physiology: The Interests and Stakes behind the Macro-Events   206

SECTION 3.2
On the Horizon of Disalienation in S.F.R. Yugoslavia: Self-Government and Plebeian Democracy

11 On the Politics of Disalienation, Inside and Outside Economic Production   247

12 In Production: Rise and Fall of Self-Management   253

13 In Civic Life: Dis/Alienation and Oligarchy Monolithism   264

14 Conclusion: On Failures and Potentialities   279

APPENDICES
The Socialist/Communist Discourse about Bureaucracy

Appendix 1: Bureaucracy: A Term and Concept in the Socialist Discourse about State Power (Upstream of Yugoslavia)   323
Appendix 2: The Discourse about Bureaucracy and State Power in Post-Revolutionary Yugoslavia 1945–72   345

References   388
Index of Proper Names of Historical Persons   421

List of Figures and Tables

Figures

Jean(?) Kerleroux, *We Have To Start All Over Again* ('Il faut tout recommencer') IV
1   Walter Benjamin (1930)   6
2   Ernst Bloch (1956)   7
3   In lieu of Brecht's photo, wearing his leather jacket, from the mid-20s   10
4   Drawing of Karl Marx as a student (1836). Detail from a lithograph of D. Levy(-Elkan)   13
5   Portrait of Josip Broz, by Moša Pijade (Lepoglava penitentiary, 1931)   29
6   Portrait of Miroslav Krleža by Petar Dobrović (1926)   32
7   Drawing of Vladimir I. Lenin   38
8   Rosa Luxemburg (1915)   38
9   Antonio Gramsci, prison mugshots (ca. 1930)   46
10 Branko Horvat, age 18+   62
11 Branko Horvat, drawing in the 1960s   62
12 Women partizans (ca. 1944–5)   69
13 Boris Kidrič (liberated territory of Kočevski Rog, Spring 1944)   94
14 Gaussian Bell Curve of Yugoslav Self-management   102
15 Youth Working Brigades 1948–50: Andrei, Yovo and Mića in front of the British barracks in Sremska Mitrovica camping, Highway of Brotherhood and Unity Zagreb-Belgrade 1948   159
16 Youth Working Brigades 1948–50: British brigade at evening meal in Sremska Mitrovica camping, Highway of Brotherhood and Unity Zagreb-Belgrade 1948   159
17 Youth Working Brigades 1948–50: Dutch brigade on the building site of University City just outside Zagreb 1950   160
18 Youth Working Brigades 1948–50: Dutch brigade on the building site of University City just outside Zagreb 1950   160
19 Youth Working Brigades 1948–50: assembly of Dutch brigade at the building site of University City just outside Zagreb 1950, DS sitting second row right with dark glasses   161
20 Orographic Map of Yugoslavia. Orographic and agricultural zones (above) vs. political subdivisions (below)   172
21 Spatial Distribution of Employment Growth outside Agriculture 1948–65   173
22 Mihajlo Arsovski, *IFSK 66* (1966, title page and poster)   192
23 Rudi Supek (1987)   226

24	Gajo Petrović (1978)	233
25	Vjekoslav Brešić, ['Yugoslavia for Kids'], illustrated map from the youth encyclopedia 'Svijet oko nas', Zagreb 1967	240
26	Ivan Picelj, 'Untitled (Galerija suvr. umjetnosti – Djela iz fundusa)', Zagreb 1961	241
27	Milan Vulpe, 'Chromos ...' ['we too are solving the housing question'], Zagreb 1953, poster	242
28	Josip Vaništa, *Columbus's Stormy Ship*, illustration from D. Suvin, *Od Lukijana do Lunjika*, 1965	286
29	*Ianus*	318
30	Edvard Kardelj at UN (1951)	355
31	Walter Crane, *The Angel of Socialism* (1885, as reused by Russian émigrés 1902) awakens labour lying prostrate under the vampire of capitalism	378

Tables

1.1	Annual pro capita revenue 1939	23
1.2	Some key data of economic growth	34
3.1	Population	51
3.2	Social origin of federal government 'employees' 1960	61
3.3	Lazić's quasi-class division 1984	64
4.1	A class pyramid, 1971	72
7.1	Prewar class provenience of the 'elite'	130
7.2	Class provenience of CPY leadership 1948	131
7.3	Flux of membership	132
7.4	Women party members in mid-60s	135
7.5	Social groups in party in 1968	135
7.6	Breakdown of 'employee' membership 1969	136
7.7	Trajectory of membership by class 1946–68	137
7.8	The party apparatus	140
8.1	Division of national cake	167
8.2	Growth of some key indicators, 1953–61	168
8.3	Comparative social product per capita	169
8.4	Socioeconomic indicators, 1950–1970	170
9.1A	Number of worker-managed enterprises	183
9.1B	'Workers' Universities'	185
9.2	Membership of WsC and managing board, 1960	187
9.3	Self-management in social service organisations	190
9.4	Division of work-force in socialised sector, 1970	194

9.5	Issues at WsC meetings	203
9.6	'Klek' qualification structure	204
10.1A	The horizons of Yugoslav economy	208
10.1B	Yugoslav mainstream ideological debate	208
10.2A	Decline of the social sector, 1960–85	211
10.2B	Change in labour productivity and incomes 1956–75	211
10.3	Source of fixed capital in economic enterprises	224
10.4A	Social sector employment and job-seekers	227
10.4B	Employment status of labour force	228
11.1	Politics inside (1) and outside (2) economic production	250
12.1	Growth of Yugoslavia in different historical periods	257
14.1	Forms of class and economic hegemony	316
1	Active population of SFRY	370

Acknowledgements and Thanks

Earlier versions of some chapters, parts or groups of chapters in English have been published as:

- 'On Class Relationships in Yugoslavia 1945–72, with a Hypothesis about the Ruling Class' in *Debatte* 20.1 (April 2012): 37–71, www.tandfonline.com/doi/pdf/10.1080/0965156X.2012.747473.
- 'Bureaucracy: A Term and Concept in the Socialist Discourse about State Power (Up to 1941)', *Croatian Political Science R* 47.5 (2012): 193–214.
- 'Splendours and Miseries of the Communist Party of Yugoslavia, 1945–72', in *Socialism and Democracy* 27.1 (2013): 161–89, www.tandfonline.com/doi/abs/10.1080/08854300.2012.754213 (with special thanks to the comments of Victor Wallis).
- '15 Theses about Communism and Yugoslavia, Or the Two-Headed Janus of Emancipation Through the State', in *Critical Q* 57.2/3 (2015): 90–110.

My thanks go to the editors and publishers of the journals of original publication. Almost all these essays have been somewhat or significantly expanded or modified in the book.

The author has researched for all illustrations contacts for possible copyright owners, but in some cases has not succeeded. If any illustration not listed below is copyrighted, the author would be glad to receive information of how to contact the (C) owner. Thanks are due for permissions to use: the photo of Rudi Supek (1987), to Prof. Božidar Jakšić, Belgrade; of Gajo Petrović (1978) to the late Ms. Asja Petrović and Prof. Ante Lešaja, Zagreb; of the colour graphics by Ivan Picelj, Milan Vulpe, and Vjekoslav Brešić (1953–67), to Mr. Dejan Kršić, Zagreb, as reproduced in the publications *Socijalizam i modernost – umjetnost, kultura, politika 1950–1974 /Socialism and Modernity – arts, culture, politics 1950–1974* (ed. Ljiljana Kolešnik, MSU & IPU, Zagreb 2012) and Mihajlo Arsovski, *Type & Design* (HDD, Zagreb 2015, forthcoming), and for 'Ivan Picelj, Galerija suvremene umjetnosti – djela iz fundusa, exhibition poster' also to Ms. Anja Picelj-Kosak, Zagreb; for the photograph and drawing of Branko Horvat, to Ms. Branka Horvat and Mr. Siniša Cyrille Lohinski, Saint Genis Laval, France, with thanks also to Prof. Lino Veljak and Prof. Branko Despot, Zagreb.

Working on this book I incurred large debts to people who generously helped an author residing outside ex-SFR Yugoslavia and faced with great difficulties (such as the incommunicability of the National University Library of Croatia) to get the statistics and the secondary materials. Two of the most important

ACKNOWLEDGEMENTS AND THANKS   XVII

readers and constant dialogue partners have been Boris Buden and Mladen Lazić, pioneers in the field, who sent me their works and tried, not always with success, to rein in some of my speculations, and to whom parts of the book are dedicated. For the whole, I am first beholden to: in Uppsala to the Carolina, Dag Hammarskjöld, and Karen Boye libraries; in Montreal, to the Inter-Library Loans Dept. of McGill University, its English Dept., and my long-time and constant friend Marc Angenot; to librarians of Pisa and Belgrade universities, with special thanks to the anarchist library Agora in Pisa. Other helpers inside ex-SFRY are detailed in the earlier Belgrade version (*Samo jednom se ljubi*, Rosa Luxemburg Stiftung, 2014); for the Appendices, chronologically written first, I had indispensable help from Srećko Pulig, Matko Meštrović, and Vjeran Katunarić, and especially from discussions with Dragan Lalović – all from Zagreb. Beside the above, Goran Marković, the late Olivera Milosavljević, Rastko Močnik, Catherine Samary, Krunoslav Stojaković, Branimir Stojanović-Trša, the late Dag Strpić, and Vladimir Unkovski-Korica kindly sent me their writings, and Mira Šuvar works of her late husband and my long-ago colleague Stipe, which left traces. Much help on the Women subsection and AFŽ came from Novi Sad women comrades, primarily Gordana Stojaković and then Andrea Jovanović and Maja Solar, on other materials from Richard Gebhardt, Nils Matzner, and Ivan Zlatić, while the Basso Foundation in Rome sent me the Magri essay from the legacy of my late friend Luigi Cortesi. Božidar Jakšić, himself both an important piece of *Praxis* history and its historian, was exceptionally generous about putting his huge store of materials at my disposal.

I derived many insights from comments by colleagues and friends in Ljubljana, Belgrade, Berlin, and on the internet, often accompanied by protracted debates and sometimes disagreement, many of whom are thanked in the Belgrade edition. This holds also for electronic discussions with Ronnie Davis, Rada Iveković, Slobodan Karamanić, Gal Kirn, Todor Kuljić, C. Douglas Lummis, Ivana Momčilović, later also with Gloria MacMillan and Slobodan Šnajder, and to wonderful weekends debating the draft with Boris Buden and then Michael Stöppler, who also helped much with materials for my final rewriting. For the Conclusion in particular, I must add my exchanges with Saša Hrnjez, Gianni Maniscalco Basile, Tom Moylan, Stan Robinson, and Lino Veljak. All of them saved me from egregious errors and stimulated my thinking through queries and disagreements. My first reader was, as always, Nevenka Erić-Suvin, without whom this book would have been either a different or a non-existent animal. It will be apparent how much I have learned and reused from the insights of Ozren Pupovac and Marko Kržan. Rich D. Erlich volunteered a heroic colour-coded line-by-line reading of the book to clarify the style. All this help sustained me in an otherwise rather lone endeavour. It is acknowledged with deep gratitude, but those thanked are in no way to blame for any particular statement, opinion, and argument (or stylistic idiosyncrasy) the author has stubbornly refused to abandon.

Finally, two friends and colleagues from USA, too well-known to be here evoked, spurred recalcitrant me on to a substantial recasting of the order of arguments for non-specialist readers. It is probably not linear enough for them, but I did what I could, unwillingly yet gratefully.

Without such considerable remnants of the innate communist solidarity of intellectual scholarship, the book and I would have been very much poorer.

Thanks to all: *sine vobis ita non*!

Foreword to Darko Suvin, *Splendour, Misery, and Potentialities: An X-ray of Socialist Yugoslavia*

Fredric Jameson

Socialist Yugoslavia has many lessons for us, and they are different from those we might learn either from the problems of the Soviet Union or those of the other East European states. It is no secret that it is primarily the failure of all these experiments in socialism that has determined the current anti-statist or anarchist mood on the world Left today. Yet ultimately it is hard to see what form a radical movement might take in late capitalism – a movement that would be capable of unifying a host of separate protest actions against the variety of abuses the latter's operation involves – without some serious reconsideration of the successes as well as the failures of the once famously 'actually-existing socialism'.

But those successes are far clearer in the case of socialist Yugoslavia, and our neglect of its lessons even more culpable: for this was the country of so-called 'workers' self-management' as well as of a uniquely effective federal system, about which the only thing that seems to interest people nowadays is its disastrous breakdown (to be sure, itself a historical issue of the greatest importance).

It should be noted that the 'sacred' obligations of objectivity are ruled out in advance, as signs of reified disciplinary convention and prejudice. The very choice of a history of this or that aspect of socialism is a partisan one, for it asserts the latter's importance in the face of some more general academic acquiescence to the status quo and its unexamined assumptions. Of course, the 'embedded' intellectuals also work with unformulated presuppositions: counterfactual history is willing enough to take on punctual events such as this or that seizure of power. But an ideological figure like François Furet worked hard to divest the name 'revolution' of all its complex social and political overtones, so as to turn 1789 back into another event among others in a continuum in which it no longer had any privileged claim on the present.

When we have to do with even more complex events such as the socialist revolutions, the meaning of the historian's periodisations becomes an even more acute philosophical and political issue. One of the omnipresent debates in so-called bourgeois revolutions is that of their termination: Napoleon, for example, took great pains to declare that the revolution was over, that things were back to normal, that the new state was legitimate and no longer open to question. Perhaps this can never be the case for a socialist revolution; but the latter always seem haunted by the specter of Thermidor, and the present work is no exception. To be sure, we can clarify the problem by distinguishing the revolution as a punctual act and a seizure of power (itself probably neverending and plagued by treason, counterrevolution, and paranoia) from what has no analogy in the aftermath of a bourgeois revolution, namely the *construction of socialism*. This is then the fundamental subject of Suvin's study here. The issue is discussed in depth, with a wealth of both data and critical comments, as strategically relating to a 'plebeian' upsurge of the lower classes resulting in a State power and apparatus both liberatory and dictatorial, with the proportions between the two shifting in favour of the second pole after the 1960s. In Suvin's account, the event most indicative of this shift came when the struggle inside the Party (League of Communists of Yugoslavia) resulted in diverting the striving for a full plebeian or workers' democracy onto the fateful path of 'decentralisation'. But the book does not treat these developments as merely an intra-party affair. It presents a many-sided account of Yugoslav socialism as a living if compromised possibility; and it would be a meaningless topic for any bourgeois scholar who has no commitment to socialism nor even any belief in the possibility of such a radically new social order.

The author is a distinguished theatre scholar for whom theatre is itself a microcosm of society as such; a Brechtian committed to the training of the famous 'estrangement-effect' on all those phenomena we take to be natural (and eternal) rather than historical and man-made. He is also a student of Science Fiction and that Utopian form of which he has memorably shown that the enduring monuments of our imaginary futures and worlds are sub-sets of Utopia itself. He is thereby well-qualified to identify the Utopian even in its 'broken promises' in the real. In addition, he lived through a good part of these years and has had access to the fundamental statements, documents, and debates which were unknown to even those few Western scholars with an interest in a period in which the Yugoslav experiment enjoyed a worldwide prestige we have forgotten. His book, which ranges from the philosophy of self-emancipation to the political economy of socialist planning, and from the micro-sociology of workplace management to the macro-analysis of international loans, is in a way a witnessing, but it is primarily a critical Utopian intervention in and for present-day discussions.

But we must insist on theoretical and methodological dilemmas which even the most sympathetic historian can scarcely avoid. History versus sociology: this is the age-old dilemma with which reality as well as its analysis confronts us: events and their causes, or structures and their component parts, diachrony versus synchrony, narrative versus concepts. And across this tension, which can never really be resolved, there passes the equally ancient problem of representation. Suvin's solution is to write that difficult text which might be characterised as 'reflexive history', or in other words a consideration of events and developments which at every moment reexamines, problematises, challenges the categories in which we seem condemned to think those events and to tell their story. And nowhere is this form as urgently required as in the study of the most complex event human history offers, namely social revolution as such, which promises absolute novelty and innovation and must therefore somehow invent its own categories as well.

Marx did not theorise all these: his experience of modern revolution was after 1848 limited to the short-lived Paris Commune, he would only have been able to imagine the Leninist party in the limits of Blanquism, and as for bureaucracy, he certainly did not conceptualise it as a class. Lenin necessarily produced new concepts for the unique situation with which he was faced; as did the Yugoslav revolutionaries themselves, such as Edvard Kardelj, whose zigzagging thought, little known in the West, is here extensively discussed, but even better Boris Kidrič, who theorised a self-governing economy, and the outstanding economist Branko Horvat as well as some philosophers from the *Praxis* group, who fought for it unsuccessfully after Kidrič's death. Unfortunately, caught between the menaces of Stalinism and capitalism, the Yugoslav revolutionary impetus faltered when it lost the strong basis in the plebeian masses that it possessed in the first fifteen postwar years or so and the promised self-management was, as Suvin puts it, 'ghettoised'. Reflexive history must both disengage such new categories and weigh and judge them in the light of their results. But such judgement is not a one-way street: the Utopian thinker will want to follow Hegel's maxim, that it is not only the concept which must be adequate to reality, but reality itself must rise to the level of its concept!

Finally, although it is beyond the scope of this work, no reader will be able altogether to think away the bloody dissolution of the system it describes; Suvin mentions that he was moved to write the book looking backward, in the approved Utopian fashion, from that collapse in order to find its enabling causes and possible, but too feeble, counterweights. We now know enough to disregard the mythic propaganda of the time, which evoked age-old enmities and deep-seated or ancestral rivalries between the peoples of the federation. The influence of the capitalist outside world, in particular the IMF and some political centres in Europe, played a decisive role in encouraging the independence of the federal republics from one another and the break-up of the system as a whole. The now former Yugoslavia has then also something to tell us about capitalism, as well as about the unique socialism memorialised in this indispensable book.

Introduction: Pro Domo Sua[1]

> The impartial historian, even if he personally hates somebody, will hold the common interest to be more eminent and prefer truth to enmity; and if he loves somebody, this won't keep him from blaming his mistakes.
> LUCIAN FROM SAMOSATE

> Io sono il Prologo:// ... Ma non per dirvi come pria/ 'Le lacrime che noi versiam son false,/ Degli spasimi e de' nostri martir/ non allarmatevi!' No! No!/
>
> [I am the Foreword ... But I don't enter to tell you, as earlier, 'The tears we shed are fictitious, don't get upset at our throes and sufferings'. No, no!!]
> RUGGERO LEONCAVALLO

> The knowledge of what is still future, not taken to its end, in the past, is necessarily remembrance (*Eingedenken*), namely of the One that is lacking and needful.
> ERNST BLOCH

∴

---

1 In the whole book I write State as *état* with a capital letter, to differentiate it from state as *condition*, also utopia as condition and genre in lower case as opposed to More's Island/State and title. I prefer 'etatist' to 'statist' for a belief in or devotion to the State. The terms 'republic' and 'republican' are in this book mainly used, in conformity with SFRY practice, to mean the six federal republics, to which after the mid-60s Kosovo should de facto be added. I write 'partizan' with a zed to mean the Yugoslav 1941–5 movement and its spirit. Unattributed translations are always mine, also tacit corrections from extant translations into English where I had the original in Yugoslav languages. Italics in all citations are by the original author, unless otherwise stated.

   Disliking 'God-words', I wrote in my first essay – now Appendix – on the 'Bureaucracy' debate 'party', 'communist', and 'revolution' in lower case. After I wrote those two essays, and to the end, I realised that when writing not only about the single party in SFRY but also a largely sanctified one (rightly or wrongly), I would create misunderstandings unless I used, for brevity and somewhat reluctantly, Party with capital P for the Communist Party of Yugoslavia – including the later League of Communists (LCY) – whenever 'communist party' was not preferable.

   The various available German and English versions of the works of Marx are all imperfect, so that, pending the Berlin edition now in progress, I have opted for using those available

0.1 To Begin

0.1.1

When night falls, there flies the divine owl of Athena, cognition. It sees more and more clearly the mysterious ruins of empires and dominations. They are all built on the inextinguishable strivings of humans for survival, sense, and happiness. Disappointed and alienated, nonetheless the strivings recur and will keep recurring.

How is it then with those who built those dominations and empires, lived in them, believed in them? What do the surviving have to show to the owl? Was there life before and after the ruins? Can they if not echo at least comprehend the skylark's song from the once bright day? Perhaps even adumbrate the once and future wild Western Wind, bringing the tang of immense oceans?

Or, advancing from Hegel to Marx and Bloch, cannot a hungry owl hunt also at the end of the night, in the grey of early morning?

Hegel's Owl and Shelley's Skylark are the totem-birds of this book's cognition and hope. May they embark on their fraternal flights while I tell this collective love-story, bitter-sweet: *mentre che 'l vento, come fa, si tace*, while the winds are for the moment silent (Dante).

0.1.2

In this book about the Socialist Federative Republic of Yugoslavia (as I shall for brevity's sake call the 1943–91 society of Yugoslavia, further SFRY) I am attempting to account for some questions arising from its (our) utter defeat, which can be put into a list:

- How come SFRY (and indeed, in its background, the USSR) started out – given the most violent destructions of imperialist world wars – very well and ended up most badly?
  This led to my 'oligarchy as ruling class' hypothesis.
- How come the Communist Party was, when properly used, such an effective organisational form in armed seizure of power but afterwards proved in general (and particularly in SFRY) prone to degeneration?

---

to me on internet or in print, in no particular order. When using the internet I abbreviate www.marxists.org/archive/marx/works as WAMW. In view of the differing and often anonymous translations of Marx into English, I have checked all with the German text and tacitly emended some translations, especially from WAMW.

In bibliographies, I use a slightly emended MLA Style. I number the notes in each part of the book, while the Works Cited are grouped at the end of the volume according to thematic need.

This led to my 'need of plebeian civic democracy as second leg to self-management in production' hypothesis.
- Correlative to both: what in the Marxian, and then Leninian, tradition ought to be more or less radically changed in order to cope with such grievous deviations leading to defeat?
I have in some places entered upon this, but it looms implicitly in much of my text.

I was not persuaded by the extant – often panicky or gloating – answers to all three, some of which I nevertheless learned much from and build upon. Thus I wrote also a lot of collateral meditation on both the latter points.[2]

The *Haltung* (stance or bearing)[3] of the text is one of looking backward from the mostly scandalous years 1972–89 and Yugoslavia's fully scandalous downfall

---

2   Beside what can be found in this book I have explicitly reached, building on work by many others, towards a Marxian thinking for our age – Marx as revisited primarily by my holy B-trinity, Bert Brecht, Ernst Bloch, Walter Benjamin, but then also Gramsci and many others, in these English essays (omitting some written in Croatoserbian):
   - *For Lack of Knowledge: On the Epistemology of Politics as Salvation*, Pullman WA: Working Papers Series in Cultural Studies, Ethnicity, and Race Relations [No. 27], 2001.
   - 'Living Labour and the Labour of Living (2004)' and 'Inside the Whale, or *etsi communismus non daretur* (2006–07)', in my *Defined by a Hollow: Essays on Utopia, Science Fiction, and Political Epistemology*, Oxford: Peter Lang, 2010, pp. 419–502.
   - 'Brecht and Communism (2008)' and 'Death into Life: For a Poetics of Anti-Capitalist Alternative (2009)', in my *In Leviathan's Belly*, pp. 119–24 and 149–60.
   - 'From the Archeology of Marxism and Communism': Part 1, 'Phases and Characteristics of Marxism/s'; Part 2, 'On the Concept and Role of the Communist Party: Prehistory and the Epoch of October Revolution', *Debatte*, 21.2–3 (2013): 279–311. [Part 1 also in *The Montreal Review* (February 2013) www.themontrealreview.com/2009/Phases-of-Marxism.php].
   - 'Communism Can Only Be Radical Plebeian Democracy' (forthcoming in *International Critical Thought*).
   Also in much of my poetry.
3   I have written on Brecht's most fertile redeployment of the term *Haltung*, constitutive of his whole work, in:
   - 'Haltung', entry in *Historisch-kritisches Wörterbuch des Marxismus*, vol. 5 (Hamburg: Argument, 2002), col. 1134–42.
   - 'Brecht and Subjectivity', in my *Darko Suvin: A Life in Letters*, ed. Ph.E. Wegner, Vashon Island WA 98070: Paradoxa, 2011, 107–32.
   - 'On Stance, Agency and Emotions in Brecht', in my *In Leviathan's Belly: Essays for a Counter-Revolutionary Time*, Baltimore MD: Wildside P for Borgo P, 2012, 23–64.
   Some previous essays may be found on https://independent.academia.edu/DarkoSuvin/Papers and http://darkosuvin.com/.

in the worst imaginable variant of mutually embattled dwarfish classes leading brainwashed mini-nationalisms into warfare. The auroral beginning and the pitch-dark ending have both to be explained.

This is not a handbook for an already well-cognised disciplinary area but a kind of large essay, that protean and conjectural genre hospitable to wide-ranging discussions, point-like analyses of particular matters, and, within reason, digressions – but then accommodates also one formal tractate (Part 2 of Chapter 6). What Jameson brilliantly says about capitalism holds here too, if not more:

> Every ... possible representation is a combination of diverse and heterogeneous modes of construction or expression, wholly different types of articulation that cannot but, incommensurable with each other, remain a mixture of approaches that signals the multiple perspectives from which one must approach such a totality and none of which exhaust it. This very incommensurability is the reason for being of the dialectic itself, which exists to coordinate incompatible modes of thought without reducing them to what Marcuse so memorably called one-dimensionality.
> 6–7

I deal with large and complex materials, subject not only to professional but above all to politically over-determined approaches. Though I fortunately found a dozen valiant pioneers to rely upon in this jungle trip, I do not provide a simple overarching theory in the proper full sense but only one central hypothesis in various guises.

A blow-by-blow chronology is not found here. I recommend consulting a good historical overview (say my late friend Fred Singleton's *A Short History of the Yugoslav Peoples* and the more diffuse and rich works by Dennison Rusinow *The Yugoslav Experiment 1948–1974* and *Yugoslavia: Oblique Insights*), while meeting with much suspicion the deafening screech of axe-grinding after 1989.

0.2   On What, Why, and How

'Some books present fresh evidence; others make arguments that urge the reader to see old problems in a new light' (Skocpol xi). Neat books for a good reason rarely mingle both: the task is too large for the talents and energy (time, money) available to a single person, and results in more or less glaring omissions and simplifications, if not outright mistakes. However, in the present book I was forced to combine the pertinent and available evidence with an attempt to see the very significant but rarely treated problem of SFR Yugoslavia as a historical and dialectical, that is contradictory and not predetermined, trajectory. In times of much smug self-satisfaction by the rulers, dialectics spots seeds of probable change and possible reversal.

For, my writing was done in the age of a dominant, leaden and smothering, counter-revolutionary pall. Ideologically, it enforces a demeaning of the whole history of SFRY – as not only a botched job, which would be an easy (if undialectical) extrapolation backwards from its end, but as even from the very start a misconceived or indeed pernicious enterprise. Yet considering the project of an emancipated Yugoslavia I think of the poet Attilio Bertolucci's 'absence, an acuter presence' (in *Sirio*), and of the Italian proverb 'When the tree has fallen, there is no more shadow': we are exposed to the full desertifying glare of capitalist desiccation. The book's premise is thus twofold: first, *that a critical overview of salient aspects of SFRY is urgently needed*; as Benjamin put it, I write books I'd much like to read but cannot find. Second, *that a critical utopian horizon is the proper way to judge alienation and disalienation* (concrete dystopia and concrete utopia – and I had been writing about both for more than 50 years). Further, I am one of the few people left who have intimate experience of both the polar discrepancies – of the true novum of revolutionary Yugoslavia and the fake novum of its demise. In the terms of classical historians: I have seen Livy's Founding of the City but am living in Machiavelli's time, When the Republic Was Lost. Therefore I felt it incumbent upon me to buckle down and attempt this overview.

The book deals with what I take to be the fateful aspects of SFRY. Contrary to present ideological hegemony, nationalisms were to my mind for a long time not such (cf. Calic 215–16), and when they became such it was because of class necessities; this book does not deal with national conflicts. Nor does it deal with the foreign relations of SFRY, and Tito's other great invention of the 'Non-aligned' movement. Nor obversely with the strong pressures SFRY was under, especially from the USSR. As Kuljić notes (58) it is an axiom that the degree of democracy in a country is inversely proportional to the foreign threats; and it explains in particular the treatment of Milovan Djilas and others who trod on Russian corns (Mihajlo Mihajlov, Dušan Makavejev, etc.) Finally, I could not enter in-depth into anthropological explanations about patriarchy and cognate matters, which I merely suggest in the Conclusion. It is therefore possible to hold that the range here is too wide for effective coverage by one person and too narrow for sound explanation; about the first possibility, it is inappropriate for the author to say more than that at times he would have heartily agreed.

FIGURE 1

Walter Benjamin (1930)
IMAGE IN THE PUBLIC DOMAIN

Within these limits, the book proposes a discussion and clarification of the SFRY Where To? and also its What For? This requires probes, employing both a wealth of materials and also a cognitive method relying on a latent and possible – provisional and strongly changing – totality in Ernst Bloch's sense. It is a discussion that can be friendly to but cannot be reduced to witty points; and it abhors a scheme bereft of horizon. I further found like Barrington Moore – who was dealing with the even more mystified subject of the first 30 years of USSR – that

> it is advisable to plunge into the data with only the simplest and most flexible hypotheses, together with some ideas about the way in which one might examine them, ... [which meant] continually modifying the theories on the basis of new information or newly perceived relationships, and turning to the facts with fresh insight and renewed curiosity ... If such is the case, more fruitful and more tenable hypotheses should emerge at the end of a study than at the beginning.
>
> 4–5

In the language of the 60s, I could not deal with the historical course and the underlying structure or logic separately, but had to tack and veer between them. To the nearly 500 items I read for this book, I have applied two overriding criteria: first, as Molière wisely observed, I take what's good for me wherever I

FIGURE 2

Ernst Bloch (1956)
PHOTOGRAPHER: QUASCHINSKY,
HANS-GÜNTER, BUNDESARCHIV, BILD
183-27348-0008 / CC-BY-SA. 3.0

find it, so that I have merrily pillaged whatever I could of the material found, and used it where I could as a quasi-Benjaminian montage. Second, to radically doubt the classifying principles of the enemy – I like to think of this as a theoretical version of Epicure's swerve and Fourier's *écart absolu*, which was also Marx's resolute deviation in view of and authorised by a possible, and desperately needed, radical betterment. My form here rather attempts to thematise and put into a tendential order a richness and multiplicity not bound by academic turfs (history, sociology, political science, economy, etc.) with their partial methodologies and huge unsaids (*non-dits*). As Bloch concluded, 'Without consciousness of a whole (*Totum*) there is no concrete theory or practice; the whole of our freedom and of its furthering and hindering objects is not fixed, it is in process through dialectical contradictions. And any cognitive discussion of note will include unanswered questions, unfinished attempts, unsettled knots' (11–12).[4] Most important, a philosopher is – as almost all of them from Plato to Husserl tell us – always an absolute beginner, astounded at what her epistemology turns up: like poetry, philosophy is astonishment in and at the world.

---

4 In the wake of Marx and Bloch, the reified and arbitrary wholes of such disjointed 'particular sciences' are to be seen as strongly diminishing the possibilities of critical reflection, of making sense of an (always provisional) historical totality. Many of their findings can and must be used, but they do not suffice.

The argument in this book identifies the main contradiction of Yugoslav social life as one *between revolutionary disalienation of humanity and a continuation or indeed rebirth of alienations*, in a chain whose central link is a budding, and by the 1970s closed and static, oligarchy in power. If such inimical intrusions happen into a system striving for disalienated human relationships, Bloch noted, then

> [the foreign bodies] prevent for the sake of *safety* the courage for *liminal questions*, for the sake of the idealist *proper arrangement* [or *good order*, *Wohlgeordnetheit* – the Chinese leaders might call it *harmony* – DS] they prevent materialist *interruption*, for the sake of closure by means of an ontologically hypostatised principle they prevent the figure and finally the praxis of a historically processual *openness, the frontline* and *the novum*.
> Subjekt 468–9

As opposed to the liberatory singularities articulated from Chapter 1 on, the system dominated by the social body opposed to emancipation closes upon itself, it ceases advancing into cognitive space and finding solutions in an imagination open to the future. Bloch's reference to a schematic, 'idealistically closed construction of dialectical materialism' targets quite clearly – as does my book, and Petrović's fastening in the 70s on this passage of Bloch's (57) – the incarnation of an alienated structure of power in a new ruling class that needs a closed construct. In this travesty of Marxian theory and communist horizons (see Chapter 6), 'reason becomes nonsense, the blessing a scourge' (Bloch, *Subjekt*, 25–6).

It turned out that it was not only possible but in a way mandatory to work upon data stemming mainly from 1950 to 1972. The gap of 1944–50 is regrettable, for many fundaments were decided and for better and worse cast into granite then, and the strange mixture of revolutionary freshness and Comintern harshness leading to the epochal break with Stalin presents idiosyncrasies which deserve a book of their own. But the influence of events from this period upon the ensuing history can be in a first attempt dealt with through their results, the main one being the formation of two strong currents in the population and the Party: emancipatory and autocratic. The gap of 1973–89 is of course for a historian also regrettable and worth a book of its own, but it would have been for me obligatory only if an a priori tenet of Cold War ideology were accepted: that a plebeian communist revolution must necessarily end in catastrophe. Since I do not accept this premise, this epoch presents to a political epistemologist no novel elements, only a most painful involution and devolution under full oligarchic dominance, riding for a fall. I have therefore concentrated on developing hypotheses about the beginning, end, and essence of SFRY as sufficient for my purposes of an initial X-ray.

The book arrives at an explanation, validated by the scandal of SFRY's demise, and pressed upon me by the weight of evidence. However, I cross-checked Descartes's fertile analytical method, that ascends from empirically salient effects to causes, with what my data were telling me. This was constructed slowly and to a good part inductively: up to the end of the very early investigation on classes in SFRY (now Chapters 3 and 4) I really had not decided whether a ruling class had come to exist in SFRY. The immanent logic is here not a predetermined *telos* but an initially open-ended choice for the permanence or for the decadence of the plebeian revolution. The wrong choice in the 60s led to the bad end. This is scarcely a teleology, since it was an alternative and therefore avoidable one: it is a tension between potentialities. However, it approaches a discourse about essence. Can one still talk of essences? I have argued (in 'Two') one not only can but also inevitably must in order to say anything of larger relevance, on condition that one dialectically historicises all such essences in feedback with particular social existences.

The chapters or groups of chapters in this volume were originally written as essays in Brecht's sense of *Versuche*, attempts assaying at cognitive exploration – which was also Montaigne's and Bacon's sense – and partly published separately. But they were from the start intended as cumulative and only relatively independent probes into the same matter. For the Anglophone reader, much of the text has been rewritten to enhance sequentiality, though this obscures the author's path from most patchy knowledge to – still provisional – theory (the path can be seen in the Croatoserbian translation of the first version) as well as his inclination to spiral argumentation.[5]

The vector of desire and astonishment, pleasure and outrage, remained, I trust, constant, yet the dimly apprehended horizon towards which it pointed grew clearer, and the locus of a society turning from concrete utopia to concrete dystopia richer and, I hope, more precise. The procedure gropingly arrived at and illuminated by the above Moore quote made impossible monographic neatness, but it has the advantage of foregrounding, in the proper Brechtian way, the historicity of my own slowly developing understanding. This entails that, when arguments (as often) are further developed in the new light of,

---

5 A section on the chronology of this book's writing may be found in the Foreword to the Croatoserbian translation of its first version, *Samo jednom se ljubi* (Beograd: Rosa Luxemburg Stiftung, 2014), and more data in its Acknowledgements.

FIGURE 3

In the editions of this book published by the Rosa Luxemburg Stiftung,[6] a photo of Brecht wearing his leather jacket from the mid-1920s, leaning on the left elbow was here included. Due to copyright restrictions this image is not included here but can be found at http://goo.gl/dwrlPk.

for example, economics, I have opted for cross-references to earlier and later mentions which allow the reader to verify the continuity and variation.

The unifying subject-object and the ways in which chapters lean upon each other will be, I hope, more or less evident. However, more should be said about how the book came to be written. It arose as collateral damage to writing my *Memoari jednog skojevca* (Memoirs of a Young Communist), the first part of which was published in 2009, and thus must have been written in 2008.[7] Earlier, around 2002, I had, after a third of a century of life outside SFRY plus thirteen years of refusing to set my foot into ex-SFRY, begun to get again in touch with somewhat or much younger colleagues from Zagreb, initially Srećko Pulig, Matko Meštrović, Vjeran Katunarić, Srećko Horvat, and Marijan Krivak. Krivak generously took it upon himself to translate half a dozen of my essays written

---

6 Samo jednom se ljubi: Radiografija SFR Jugoslavije 1945.–72., uz hipoteze o početku, kraju i suštini, Belgrade: Rosa Luxemburg Stiftung, 2014, 406pp., transl. by M. Mrčela and D. Suvin, ISBN 978-86-88745-08-6; 2. edn. 2014, 408pp., ISBN 978-86-88745-09-3.

7 The three parts so far written are:
   - 'Slatki dani, strašni dani' [*Memori jednog skojevca*, Part 1]. *Gordogan* no. 15–18 (2008–9): 25–54; available on www.gordogan.com.hr/gordogan/wp-content/uploads/2011/10/2009-Gordogan-15-18-25-54-Suvin-Memoari-manji.pdf.
   - 'Poslijeratni Zagreb: Cuvier i suhe kosti' [*Memoari jednog skojevca*, Part 2]. *Gordogan* no. 19–22 (2011): 26–92, www.gordogan.com.hr/gordogan/wp-content/uploads/2011/10/G_4_02.pdf.
   - 'Poslijeratni Zagreb, književnost, Savez studenata: plodne doline' [*Memoari jednog skojevca*, Part 3]. *Gordogan* no. 27–8 (2012/13): 111–57.

in a vein of political epistemology (on turbo-capitalism) and publish them in a philosophy journal of which he was deputy editor; I participated actively in correcting and debating the translations, which finally appeared as a book in 2006. These colleagues and comrades led me further to a remarkably talented group of researchers mainly resident in Germany, to begin with Boris Buden, then Gal Kirn, Ozren Pupovac, Slobodan Karamanić, and the peripatetic Ivana Momčilović. I was interviewed several times in maverick Croatian periodicals and began collaborating in a few of them; and I gave lectures on parts of this book both in Ljubljana 2010, at the Delavsko-punkerski univerzitet of young left-wing colleagues such as Marko Kržan, mainly pupils of Rastko Močnik, and in Beograd 2012, at the Centar za kulturnu dekontaminaciju of Borka Pavičević and Branimir Stojanović and at Professor Mladen Lazić's doctoral seminar in the Institute for sociological research. These interactions strongly facilitated my writing of the *Memoirs* – which I much hope to finish after this book. In so doing, I was transported back into both the war years of immediate fascist (Croatian Ustaše) threat to my psychic and physical survival as a small but conscious boy, and to the wondrous years after 1945 when as schoolboy and student I became a Titoist activist. The aura of those days was in some ways harshly black-and-white but bracing and overwhelmingly hopeful and bright. The dire discrepancy between that epoch and the same locus two generations later, with the ignominious and bloody demise of SFRY in between, prompted rankling and cutting reflections: *how was this devolution from rosy to black horizons possible?!* Behind this, an even more disquieting reflection went on: *was there any sense in the revolutionary horizons and therefore my youthful activism?* I had no clue, and said to myself (copying Brecht's Galileo): *Ich muss es wissen!* – I have to understand it!

Not to wax too autobiographical, but to put last things first, my conclusion in this book is: *yes, there was a strong emancipatory sense* in them, even if always threatened, and later betrayed.

Since I am a life-long admirer and reader of the cognitive poet Milton, the urge of writing this book is, in a different lay atmosphere and a much smaller compass, much like his in *Paradise Lost*: to justify the ways of God to Man after a revolution retracted. But instead of his beautiful yet mythically unhistorical Arcadia or Earthly Paradise, my 'god words' and loci of communism or Yugoslav socialism turn out to be internally contradictory: so I need to find what was justifiable and what was not. The horizon remains that of a Supreme Value. However, though what I take to be the theoretically most rounded and perhaps innovative Chapter 6 deals, as the young Marx did, with politics and the State within a salvational horizon, another thematic field beside nationalism I do not deal with, in an already overburdened book, is religion, or if you wish belief. I certainly regret this much more than my first omission, since so much remains to say about what that chapter posits as the decisive tension between the ideal or heavenly horizon, which I there call Communism 1, and the pragmatic or earthly alienation into class politics and rule of Communism 2. They cannot be reduced to the pairs theoretical/practical nor ideal/real, since these orientations participate in different ways in both poles of these opposed pairs. I shall try to say more about implications of belief and creativity for emancipation and communism in the Conclusion.

Many significant matters had to be dealt with in one sentence, so that not only nuances but also some important secondary contradictions could not be spelled out. A good example is the 1966 fall of the system of secret police infiltration into all pores of social life: I book it in Chapter 7.22 as a last victory of the partizan democratic spirit, but of course Ranković and his secret services were also (alas!) the only efficient force working on strengthening central government as against the disintegrative tendencies of the 'republican' partitocracies, as a tertiary contradiction they were mainly Serbian and Montenegrine, and perhaps most important, they were the spearhead of a large group of patriarchal power-wielders in the Communist Party unwilling to relinquish the positions acquired between 1943 and 1953 and often sincerely suspicious of urbanised modernity (cf. Rusinow, *Oblique* 54–57). All such recomplications had to be resolutely avoided or left for a subsequent section in what I might perhaps claim as a pioneering overview, where you hew out a trail through the jungle with a machete and cannot look left or right too often.

I think of my ***approach*** as being a 'political epistemology', in the sense so well insisted on by Marcuse from 'Foundation' on: that in Hegel and then Marx, as heirs to the French Revolution, history and society enter into the theory of knowledge – and into the very structure of knowledge; this might be akin to the very sympathetic notion of an odyssey of dialectical reason (Kosík 60, 110, and *passim*). Simultaneously however, I have since my student days been deeply impressed with the long duration unity (as least as long as class society) of human imagination and strivings so well recorded in culture. I think it was 1970, or maybe one year later, when I initiated an informal graduate seminar, eventually held with two graduate students, me, and an English Department colleague, called *Aristotle after Brecht and Marx*. A life-long wrestling with this stance crystallised in my long essay, 'On the Horizons of Epistemology and Science'. I much hope I could count as my patron saint, together with the other two, Aristotle's study of a *pragmateia* or field of inquiry by way of an inspired mixture of editorial *bricolage* and a path of research (*meth'hodos*), leading to a marriage of empirical data and history with prodigious flights of abstraction. Within such an approach, the purpose of the book – to tease out and define the

FIGURE 4

Drawing of Karl Marx as a student (1836). Detail from a lithograph of D. Levy(-Elkan)
IMAGE IN THE PUBLIC DOMAIN, REPRODUCED FROM HTTPS://WWW.MARXISTS.ORG/ARCHIVE/MARX/PHOTO/MARX/IMAGES/36KM1.JPG

good and bad singularities of SFRY – necessitated a running reconsideration of much Marxist theory and inoculation of new cuttings upon its sufficiently sturdy branches. I had been consistently practising this reconsideration in literary, theatre, and generally cultural studies following the example of Brecht, and had now to learn how to do it on fresh fields and pastures new. Only partially, in truth, for I found that in this variant of social critique Marx's great insight that 'theory becomes a material force when it enters the consciousness of masses' (or only when it is incarnated in the dominant social forces) still holds in spades – both for valid and for mystifying theory. I only hope I can approximate what he meant by a 'critique': which is in this case largely also a self-critique of my ignorant young self, though by no means a retraction of the emancipatory horizon of that phase. I have endeavoured to keep the first person singular mainly out of the text after this Foreword, but I hope the horror, desire, wrath, loyalty, and auroral astonishment of the young communist have been carried over into this reconsideration of a senile age.

I further heeded Wright Mills's identification of two 'research ways' or 'working models of inquiry'. There is the macroscopic one (from Marx, Weber, Simmel), dealing with 'total social structures in a comparative [world-historical] way' (553–4) and the molecular one, dealing with small-scale problems, still abstract but 'on a lower level of abstraction' – 'isolating from larger contexts a few precisely observed elements' (558); and it was best to 'interpenetrate more neatly molecular terms and macroscopic conceptions', as the propositional meaning of many macroscopic statements is ambiguous and unclear while the conceptual meaning of many molecular statements is often barren (566).

Finally, I would not have known how to propose unexceptionable proofs, but attempted to formulate useful and productive errors – since in the present state of our knowledge we can do no other. This means I wished to go for a writing of the ionosphere, not outer space type (where Badiou and Nancy, not to speak of the earlier Derrida, mostly reside). Outer space has to be reached for interplanetary flights of the mind, exhilarating and far-off, at the esoteric frontiers of the known. Ionosphere bounces back the radio waves and is thus essential to communication: it is two steps in front of the wished-for or target reader, not three. Half a century of writing mainly for academic colleagues was not of great help in this endeavour, especially since I proposed to pull no punches which might be of cognitive help. Two steps will have to be made.

0.3 Definitions, Delimitations, and Caveats

In the body of the book, I arrive at some terms which are in places defined and often used. I shall review a few key ones here, striving for usefulness rather than for philosophical exhaustion.

Freedom is the possibility of people's conscious choice and activity between alternatives in a given situation. In capitalism, those who live by selling their labour power have restricted opportunities: uncounted proletarians of all our globalised countries are hungry or otherwise helpless to prevent physical and psychic lesions. Politically and economically, freedom has to do with self-determination of the conditions of life for individuals but also large social classes and communities. The process of gaining freedom is liberation or, metaphorically richer, emancipation. It should lead to personal and collective self-determination and self-government.

Whoever exploits, oppresses or humiliates other people is himself (usually it is a male) not free but fixated on that relationship. I believe that Marx was right insofar as our only hope lies in those who suffer. They too are (we are) alienated but we are the only social segment whose vital interests mandate an end to the pernicious fixation, and demand a thoroughgoing radical democracy. I use as a shorthand for people whose interests and practice are opposed to the exploiters and power-holders two terms. The term and notion of *plebeians* comes from a historical conflict, through Brecht with a pinch of Bakhtin and Babeuf. It means here all social classes who live by means of their physical and/or mental work –

and are today dominated and exploited by capitalists – rather than through wealth and privileges from capital or power, and today constitute about 95% of the population. I could also have used Marx's term and notion of *proletarians* from the same Roman history, although, strictly speaking, this term should perhaps be reserved for those plebeians who have little or no possessions except the labour power they procreate – plebeian paupers, workers largely excluded from gainful work. More important, it seemed to me that 'plebeians' was not only less abused in enthusiastic propaganda and less tied to the industrial workers of the nineteenth-century type, but that it also stressed the element of civic opposition to pernicious State power of a ruling class rather than the equally important position within the capitalist production process, the global work-cum-finances system which is today fully interlaced with politics. Since both terms are in modern times largely metaphorical, I prefer the connotations of plebeians, though I sympathise with proletarians also and will not be debarred from occasionally using this term if it fits better. In a wider sense, I would mean by either of these terms a congeries of social classes – in propitious cases a historical block – defined as working for their subsistence and not having had political power: *the working people (radni narod)*.[8]

It will be apparent that, from the imperfect Golden Age of Athens to the present, the only real or worthwhile *democracy* is the one truly based on common decision-making by the majority, and therefore difficult to subvert by the power of violence and money or capital. Some friends of mine believe the term is irretrievably damaged but, being a conservative in culture, I think that by firmly wedding it to the adjective plebeian or proletarian, it can be redeemed.

All class societies are, except at their revolutionary beginnings, opposed to the search for freedom (emancipation) as universal self-determination. A long duration constant of that kind is *patriarchy*. In my too scant use I attempt to dovetail the ancient definition whereby it is a social system (family, community) in which a male is the head of the family and men rule over women and children, with the materialist feminists' stress upon social practices and ideologies that are based upon a systemic bias against and exploitation of women;

---

8   In my readings of the documents from 1941 on, I have found the term 'plebeian' used for the Yugoslav insurrectional ideology only in Boris Kidrič's 'Report of the CC of CP Slovenia from the Second Half of Dec. 1941 to the CC CPY ...' (353).

   As to 'working people', this term of mine fits into what many people from the 1950s–60s on have called 'an extension of the working class to include (as sources of surplus value ...) a very large part of the "middle classes"' (the quote is from one of the best attempts, in Marcuse, 'Cultural', 127). Today, their commonalty in pauperisation is obvious.

this then means exaltation of warrior mores and chieftain power or monocracy in all social institutions and relationships.

Disalienation or the undoing of what Marx found as alienated humanity[9] is a complex matter: I cite in Chapter 11 his approximation to it as 'The absolute working-out of peoples' creative potentialities ..., which makes ... the development of all human powers as such the end in itself' (see more there and in the Conclusion). This is not simply a moral resurrection but primarily a revolution in the role of labour force and existential time for one and all. It is rendered possible by disalienation in economics, defined by Marx as beginning with the abolition of private property over the means of production, and by disalienation in politics. As to the latter, I limned it in Thesis 14 of Chapter 6 as: 'Only when real, individual people re-absorb in themselves the abstract citizen of the State and when individual human beings have become in their empiric day-to-day life, work, and relationships integrally human beings, only when people have recognised and organised their own powers as social powers, and, consequently, no longer separate social power from themselves in the shape of State power, only then will human emancipation have been accomplished'. Marx refers to this in his praise of the Paris Commune as 'the self-government of the producers' (cho5.htm). It is my overarching end and 'concrete utopia' (Bloch). At any rate, homo sapiens being a social animal, real freedom and disalienation can only be found when each person as well as people together are *self-governed*; *self-government* is logically and politically super-ordinated to self-management in production, and I recur to this key relationship often.

I worry at (and about) *socialism* at many places in the book, finally in the Conclusion. I have strong reservations about the term when used as a historical epoch, both because of the confusion with the ideal and practice of socialism in the nineteenth century and – more neuralgically – when the epoch is thought of as a rounded-off, monadic social formation, on a par with feudalism and capitalism (cf. Suvin, 'Marksizam'). This second meaning is nowhere to be found in Marx but is a neologism dragged decisively to the forefront by Lenin in *The State and Revolution*, thus initially used in quotes and with a capital letter (I discuss this in Appendix 1). It seems to have come from Kautsky, and I have argued elsewhere it is not aptly named (Kautsky's ideology was nearer to Bernstein than to Marx). Lenin was however quite clear that it would mean

---

9   For a first approach to Marx's concept of alienation, I recommend Bloch 'Entfremdung', Calvez, Dunayevskaya, Mészáros, and Ollman. A more articulated discussion of alienation would have to take into account the enormous psychophysical consequences of fetishist *reification*, to which an excellent introduction is in one of the teachers of my youth, Lucien Goldmann.

a society and State with initially strong remnants of bourgeois and capitalist ways, mindsets, and stances, which would run much wider and deeper than the 'remnants' of private peasantry or initially remaining capitalist enterprises, and hold for the whole national life.

I tried to use the term in quotation marks, but the overwhelming straight reference to it in and out of SFRY made this impracticable. However, I mean by socialism a radical class reorganisation in view of justice, a revolutionary attempt to do away with exploitation of people, with the horizon of direct cooperation between self-managed associations that follow a 'politics of use values' (Elson 6). It is a transitional period (which may last for generations) between exploitative capitalism and communism – with communism defined as a society putting into effect both a full feedback democracy and Marx's full slogan, *Jeder nach seinen Fähigkeiten, jedem nach seinen Bedürfnissen*: 'From each according to his ability', but then emphatically including 'to each according to her needs' (*Critique* 388). If this is correct, socialism is 'the historical practice of communist interventions into material and productive [as well as moral and imaginative – DS] presuppositions of the bourgeois world' (Divjak 13).

Thus, the term 'socialism' is useful only if understood as a field of forces polarised between a congeries of class society alienations and communist disalienation, connoting dynamic and fierce contradictions on all levels. In that sense socialism is not simply an economistic alternative to capitalism but also, and primarily, a cultural alternative – the coming about of a different civilisation, with radically better relationships between people as well as of people with nature. Socialism can never be finally 'built' as a house, especially not 'in one country': if it ever were finalised, it would no longer be socialism but democratic communism. The corruptions are then marked by various adjectives and/or quotation marks, such as 'State socialism', 'market socialism' or 'really existing socialism'.

An *oligarchy* is a relatively small social group or class (here sometimes also called politocracy from its locus of power) which decides the key affairs of the community. To the extent it sunders itself from the working people, from whom it has as a rule arisen in revolutions, it becomes a ruling class with interests independent from, eventually opposed to, the working people. This syndrome is a permanent tendency after revolutions in class societies, but I do not at all believe in its stemming from God – that is, in Michels's 'Iron Law' of parties degenerating as they become successful. It depends on what countervailing forces are mobilised in concrete situations.

Perhaps I should here add *comprador*, an adjective denoting a capitalist grouping or bourgeoisie subaltern to and intermediary for a foreign capitalism.

The term arises from early capitalist penetration in southern China – hence the Portuguese word – and has been reactualised in this globalised age.

At times I recur to the term ***mindset*** rather than use 'ideology', which is caught in the uneconomic denotational bind between unavoidable class consciousness and false consciousness (the two sometimes coincide and sometimes do not). My term is translatable as 'way of thinking', and the delightful internet example from the Oxford English Dictionary is 'the region seems stuck in a medieval mindset'.

Concerning method, a discussion of my favourite terms for orientation, which recur in the book, is in 'Locus, Horizon, and Orientation'.

Three final caveats: First, my early versions treated, in the wake of several other writers, the year 1975 or 1974 as the *terminus ad quem*, after which the game was up and an overview could stop. After further reading and reflection, I think that this remains perhaps economically true but that the dominant political aspect had clearly jelled by 1971–2. I have accordingly tweaked the text.

Second, I have not attempted a proper theorisation of my subject (though I have indulged in the exception of Chapter 6), preferring to shuttle between induction and deduction. Many theoreticians to whom I turned for illumination, and often received some, remain unmentioned in this book; others are mentioned too cursorily. My Central European speculative side regrets this, my Anglo-American empirical side rejoices in it. Nor is the time at all ripe for even a first full judgment: we need at least a dozen Ph.D. theses using archive materials, and then an international debate of scholars shunning the uncritical extremes of adoration as well as damnation.[10] Rather, I think of this book as a first step in undoing the odious obliteration of memory, best visible in President Tudjman's dynamiting 700+ – possibly 3,000, cf. Hrženjak XII – memorials of the People's Liberation Struggle 1941–5 in Croatia, sometimes sculptural and/or architectonic masterpieces, following the same Talibanic rage and theological hatred as in the dynamiting of the Buddhas of Afghanistan (but not incurring the same liberal disapproval). Even when phrased apodictically, this book necessarily deals in hypotheses rather than in a theory.

Third, I am achingly aware of at least two additional approaches this book lacks, and I sense some more (but I lack materials, time, and space for them).

---

10   The first such work, so far as I know, was the excellent dissertation by Olivera Milosavljević, 'Država i samoupravljanje 1949–1956' (The State and Self-management 1949–56), Beograd Univ. 1987, whose theme ran into such a rigid taboo at the end of ex-Yugoslavia and in 'democratic' Serbia that it could not be published. I stumbled on it by chance (there is no proper bibliography of the field), and was able to use its insights because the author kindly sent me a photocopy.

These would be a modern economic geography of Yugoslav spaces, right from the beginning fettered by 'republican' boundaries and powers – (see the excellent approach by Hamilton, especially 131–53); and then depth soundings into class psychologies in different regions, where we have at least for earlier Serbia a great pioneer in Radomir Konstantinović's *Psychology of the 'palanka'*, and where to my mind nationalism would belong.

Fu vera Gloria? Ai posteri l'ardua sentenza – 'Was it a true Glory?' Manzoni asked about Napoleon: 'To those who come after us the difficult decision is left'. To begin with, to you, dear reader, my human brother and sister: *Hypocrite lecteur – mon semblable – mon frère*!

PART 1

Fundaments: Freedom and Accumulation

The main subjective difficulty into which I bumped at every step was that the author – coming himself from that environment, knowing it as one knows his homeland, embroiled in its hopes and disappointments, having taken part in its impetus and its aberrations, truth and error – had to force himself to forget what he believed he knew, to detach himself from what hurt him, to establish between him and the facts the distance indispensable for understanding. The reader should judge whether he has succeeded.

    FRANÇOIS FEJTÖ, 1969 (free translation)

CHAPTER 1

Radical Emancipation and Yugoslavia: On the Founding Singularities of SFRY

No socialism without freedom, no freedom without socialism.
Slogan of student demonstrators, Belgrade 1968

∙∙

1.1 The Yugoslav Founding Singularities

Yugoslavia before World War 2, though very rich in natural resources, was one of the poorest countries in Europe, a semi-colony economically not even halfway between the Asian colonies and metropolitan countries of Europe:

TABLE 1.1 *Annual pro capita revenue 1939*
FROM FEJTÖ 1: 368

Country	Revenue in $	Country	Revenue in $
USA	554	Czechoslovakia	134
Germany	520	*Yugoslavia*	96
UK	468	Egypt	85
France	283	India	34
Austria	166	Indonesia	23

For one thing, Yugoslavia had a surplus village population estimated at between 4 and 6 million out of 11.4 millions peasants ...

When Tito (Josip Broz) was in the mid-30s appointed by the Comintern first organisational and shortly thereafter general secretary of CPY, he insisted that the leadership must be inside the country. Aided by the world economic depression, the ideological bankruptcy of the monarchist regime and legal political parties, as well as a new Comintern anti-fascist policy, he succeeded in forming a tightly disciplined, illegal communist nucleus. As Edvard Kardelj, one of his main helpers, remembered, in that situation 'a serious impact [was only possible] through a well-organised and conceptually monolithic revolutionary organisation' (*Tito* 187). Though the communist parties had under Stalin totally lost 'the early traditions of dissent and debate', and their model both for internal and outward use was 'a social dictatorship ... that was master of all public life' (Ali 149), this did not much matter under illegal and revolutionary conditions. In the 1930s the Party began putting roots (as it had already after World War I, before being outlawed) into 'a mass revolutionary movement, but without depriving its consolidated underground organisation of its distinctively cadre features' (Kardelj, *Tito* 188). The uprising and military struggle 1941–5 against the Nazis and their followers added much flexibility in the necessarily autonomous local guerrilla movements – communication was only by courier through multiple enemy lines – that everywhere flanked the partizan HQ moving between Bosnia, Montenegro, and Serbia, and the monolithic hierarchy served it well.

The Party's proclaimed aim in the war was liberation struggle upward from the roots. A People's Front grouping of everybody willing to fight the occupiers and local quislings was developed, while class struggle was taboo. In each locality, liberated or occupied, a People's Liberation Committee (*Narodnooslobodilački odbor, NOO*) was instituted, from which wealthier peasants were not excluded – in some cases they were more militant than the poorer ones – but they were not allowed to govern without the poor: 'Many well-to-do peasants and ... members of the bourgeoisie joined our struggle and [remained] with us to the very end' (Kardelj, *Tito* 149). In order to draw the population into the uprising, the partizans 'kept insisting on their vital social and political interests', while key positions were kept in CPY hands as the only alternative to failure (150–1, and see 149–54). The partizans' fight turned into an unacknowledged class conflict, overtly initiated from above when the monarchist *četniks*, in defence of their power base and privileges and spurred on by the refugee royal government in London, attacked the partizans at the end of 1941, '[preferring] a civil war even at the cost of overt collaboration with the [Axis] occupier' (153). The war could thus be conducted as the people vs. the traitors.

Yugoslavia after World War 2 therefore issued from a vast, communist-led popular or plebeian war-cum-revolution unique in Europe (except for the satellite case of Albania), and in some ways much more similar to the Chinese and the first Vietnamese revolution (cf. Fejtö 225–8 and *passim*, Johnson). All of these were revolutions rooted in Leninist anti-imperialism and national sovereignty, carried by the peasantry, and organised by a handful of tightly knit professional revolutionaries with a considerable input by urban intellectuals. They were outside of Stalin's reach, distrusted and resented by him. The strong partizan tradition of solve-it-yourself-on-the-spot (*snađi se druže* – also translatable as 'comrade, find your bearings [on the spot]') applied not only in the fighting units but also in the network of territorial power from below and in the political organisations. Hence, there was in-depth experience of self-determination in the People's Liberation Committees and in country-wide organisations such as the Anti-fascist Youth League (USAOJ – with a prestigious nucleus of Young Communists [SKOJ]), the Antifascist Front of Women (AFŽ), and others. They were all initiated and supervised by the Communist Party but allowed extensive autonomy; in the words of the excellent monograph on women by Jancar-Webster, each was 'an original creation' and 'a remarkable expression of political acuity on the part of the Party leadership' (on the AFŽ, 122–5). Inversely, after 1944 all these autonomies kept shrinking, perhaps because they were too successful: the Women's Front was dissolved in 1953 and the Communist Youth in 1949, as remarkable examples of political blindness (I shall return to the reasons for this).

Due to the huge productive and cultural backwardness of Yugoslavia and the absence of a rooted working-class culture, this revolution was necessarily at least as much a 'bourgeois-democratic' as a 'proletarian' one. It took equally seriously the guiding slogans of the French Revolution 1789–94 and its propagations to the 1848 'Spring of the peoples' – that is, *liberté, égalité, fraternité* – and the somewhat less pithy but nearer slogans of the Russian Revolution and the ensuing civil war 1918–21 – that is, 'land to the peasants' (which could be extended to 'factories to the workers'), 'turn the imperialist war into civil war', and 'all power to the Councils [of direct democracy]': in a stroke of genius, these two horizons were fused. The impulses denoted by the slogans of the former two revolutionary epochs were reshaped in a *bricolage* fashion in the great partizan slogans 'Death to fascism, liberty to the people' (*smrt fašizmu – sloboda narodu!*) and 'Brotherhood and unity' (*bratstvo-jedinstvo*) – backgrounding Lenin and adding 'unity', which denoted the Yugoslav focus (as different from the universal pretensions of both the previous revolutions, as well as against the fascist territorial division and chauvinist alienation) and connoted the Communist Party component. This original do-it-yourself fusion, most appropriate to the situation, is the matrix that underlies and works within all the other singularities and stances I shall posit in this book.[1]

---

1 Not knowing it at the time, Tito and their comrades acted upon the same impulse as Marx when analysing the 1848 revolution, who stressed that the next indispensable step was the

While these two slogans may not explain all that happened during the war, and even less after it, some of their implications seem central for the history of Yugoslavia and its peoples. I have called them great because they express the agential system at the root of the 1941–5 'struggle for liberation of the people' (*Narodno-oslobodilačka borba*, NOB), destroying the old class system materially and morally. This *first and founding singularity*[2] issued in a strong libertarian and emancipatory mindset in the people it touched during the ensuing decades, who confronted as best they could the later fall into class rule. Self-management of the people, as producers and as citizens, was in the 1950s and 60s the central rung, achievement, and battleground of this confrontation.

The deep structure of human relationships, I found out when working on dramaturgy, can be thriftily presented in terms of agential functions, forces or 'actants' which evidence the central terms of an epoch's (or of its major social forces') imaginary encyclopedia, of how it understands its constellation of historical long-range forces in mutual relations of power and value.[3] This is predicated on a semiotic conflictual arrangement shaped as a triangle between a Protagonist (P) contending with an Antagonist (A) for a commonly coveted supreme Value (V). The Protagonist is validated by a Mandator (M), and each of these four actants may have secondary but often also decisive helpers (H):

---

  alliance of the city revolt with the peasants, who would (as Mike Davis reads his insight) 'either insure the victory of the revolutionary-democratic insurrection or be its gravedigger. Such an alliance must be built on the terrain of a revolutionary nationalism and against foreign intervention ... [Marx argued] that martial nationalism was an essential fuel for social revolution, as well as a precondition for socialist leadership of the peasantry and the lower middle classes' (Davis 54 and 61).

2 I am indebted for the term of 'singularity' to Ivana Momčilović and Slobodan Karamanić from our email debates and the materials swapped in 2011. I was also stimulated by Gal Kirn, who calls this 'politics of rupture': he fuses the rupture with Stalin and self-management, while introducing as the third one the Non-aligned movement: cf. 'From the Primacy', and 'Conceptualisation' 229–36 and *passim*.

   I found an interesting forerunner to this concept in Bobrowski's pioneering discussion of 'two particularities' of the Yugoslav communist party: its rootedness in the living past of the national anti-fascist resistance and in the peasant masses (49).

3 I proposed a semiotic hypothesis of agents in the 1960s–70s (cf. Suvin 'How'); see further in Conclusion. Within it, 'actant' is a term from Greimas's model in theory of narratology, which I much modified with inputs from Propp and Souriau; it is a depth structural role or element – such as antagonist, protagonist or value – indispensable for all narrative.

Actantial Scheme

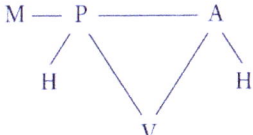

The agential system here reposes upon the category of '*the people*' (*narod*), in whose name the 'People's Liberation Struggle' was fought and the 'People's Liberation Army' was eventually brought about out of the partizan units. As Engels wrote about the Chinese reaction to the British 1857 invasion, 'this is a war *pro aris et focis*, a popular war for the maintenance of [the identity of a people]'. In diachronic terms, The People meant here the subaltern filiation stretching from, say, Roman plebeian struggles against the patricians to the bourgeois revolutions against feudalism and foreign interventionist armies up to 1848; this historically includes the traditional Balkan subversive brigands (*hajduci, uskoci*) as well as Rousseau's, Robespierre's, and Marat's *peuple*, and Mao's simultaneous *renmin*. Though probably the most popular brief Marxist tract in the wartime Yugoslav Party was *The Communist Manifesto*, reprinted by the agitprop departments of various partizan divisions, this movement was 'proletarian' (and claimed that name in its first shock units) only in the wide sense of the original Latin, 'people without possessions except for the work contributed by its young' (*proles*). The proletarian or plebeian People was an inclusive category based on a simple and trenchant exclusion: 'Whoever fights against liberation, is the enemy of the people'.[4] Therefore the partizan struggle could use, and also be shaped by, generally humanist, ethical, and bourgeois-democratic ideas and ideals, combined with the patriarchal virtues of rectitude and loyalty unto death. On the other hand, as different from the tradition of Marx and Lenin, this revolution was not theoretically analysed before, during or immediately after its course, the current slogans arose directly from improvised practice. This People was *not* a Herderian ethnic set united by language and historic tradition (cf. Buden), though the partizans drew on the deeply rebellious aspect of the tradition, but a set of subaltern classes united

---

4 The term 'enemy of the people' is of acute revolutionary provenience, first of the French Revolution (Robespierre 1793: 'The revolutionary government ... owes nothing to the enemies of the people but death') and then of the Bolshevik one, where it was often backstaged in favour of 'class enemy' or similar. In the meantime it became apparently a well-known democratic swearword, sarcastically used by Ibsen as the title of his 1882 play.

by denial of intolerable social injustice (in Roman terms, a radical secession in arms and across the whole land against patrician usurpation). This made for lack of clarity in peacetime, even when the category of 'the working people', of Second International coinage, was substituted for the wartime 'the people'. In particular, the necessary turn from a denying or negative to an affirming or positive horizon or slogan, the 'relation between anti-fascism and socialism' (Hobsbawm 307 and *passim*), remained unclear among improvisations for at least five postwar years, until the invention of self-management.

In a pioneering essay, 'Projekt Jugoslavija', Pupovac proposed that the people is here the political subject of historical creativity, defined and formed by the dialectics of emancipative negativity (as identified by Hegel and Badiou). This central protagonist was by means of a total mobilisation articulated into organisational forms for its components: the partizan units as the combatant spearhead embodying both the negativity of armed fighting and the positivity of protecting all other actions, the network of local People's Liberation Committees in each village or town, the youth and women's organisations, etc., 'in brief, the forms of mass direct democracy which flow out of the liberation struggle' – all of them organised, coordinated, united, and dominated by the Communist Party, which infused it with 'the internationalist and militant spirit of the workers' movement' (Pupovac, 'Projekt' 5, cf. also his 'Why'). Tito picked up practically the only inspired moment of the Communist International after Lenin, its 1935 call for anti-fascist 'popular fronts' (see the magisterial Hobsbawm 261–313). The array of new organisational names which interchangeably used 'people's' and 'anti-fascist' testifies that the whole impulse was born out of and defined by ***denying*** in thunder the intolerable old world of repression and injustice, which was culminating in brutal and genocidal international fascism but included the obviously failed monarchist and semi-colonial dictatorship of 1918–41 bloodily preserving national and class inequalities (cf. also Denitch chap. 3 and 4) – and the two very soon allied against the popular movement. In Herman Melville's words:

> [T]he man who, like Russia or the British Empire, declares himself a sovereign nature (in himself) amid the powers of heaven, hell, and earth ... may perish; but so long as he exists he insists upon treating with all Powers upon an equal basis ... [H]e says No! in thunder ...

The struggle against fascism and for sovereign liberation, NOB, is the people-protagonist's mode of existence as well as reason for existing. And a sovereign emancipation does not stop at ridding itself of foreign occupiers, its obverse is what a few years later was identified as 'The People's Revolution'.

FIGURE 5   *Portrait of Josip Broz, by Moša Pijade (Lepoglava penitentiary, 1931)*

As to the relationship between the Party and the People, I shall recount here an anecdote narrated to me in the early 60s by the great poet Jure Kaštelan, who worked in the agit-prop team (I think of a division) during the war. The partizans had an improvised guerrilla theatre consisting of short forms, with much singing and dancing but including also brief skits such as the following one:

> The Peasant is sleeping deeply, heedless of the hints of destruction around him. Allegorical representatives of alternative armed forces come to awaken him. First the Croat fascist Ustasha, then the Serbian monarchist Chetnik, and then various other grotesque quislings (this 'epic' form could be at will shortened or lengthened as well as embellished according to the local situation), but he sleeps on. Then comes the Partizan and says: 'Comrade, wake up!' He does, shoulders the offered gun, and exits following the Partizan. Stormy applause by the audience!

The most significant Croatian and Yugoslav writer of the century, Miroslav Krleža, interpreted this situation in his keynote speech at the Writer's Union Congress in 1952, quite properly, as a lay version of Christ awakening Lazarus: 'Lazare, veni foras!' In this scenario the Partizan (or the Party) is the auxiliary but crucial salvational agent, and the life of the People, the chains of which – the sleep as lacking consciousness, equivalent to moral and material death – are burst, is both Protagonist and the supreme Value to be saved: the Value is People's Power, and the vector leading from the People to it (in bold below) is emancipation, putting into effect the mandate of historical Liberation:

Yugoslav Actantial System 1941–1945

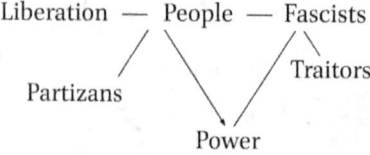

In such scenarios, however, the Communist Party was at the time as a rule not overtly posed – except for Tito's wartime speeches to partizan brigades or the AVNOJ gathering (see for example 'Development' 143) – but only implied. I think the reason was threefold. First, having undergone the bloody school of 20 years of illegality and a dozen years of assassination of its members on sight, it was understandably reluctant to insist on and theorise its leadership of the partizan struggle – though this was to boomerang in peacetime as the habit of secrecy and opaque decision-making. Second was the international situation within which Tito and the partizans had to manoeuvre, between the conservative Western Allies and the suspicious Stalin. But third and most consequential for the future, the innovation or novum of 'People's Liberation' had fully sublated and replaced the straightforward class-against-class agenda of the Stalinist early 1930s, which undoubtedly existed in the minds of some top cadres; whenever it briefly surfaced, as in the extremist practice in Montenegro 1941/42, it was catastrophic and firmly squelched by Tito and the headquarters. The revolution which was happening here, in quite un-Leninist ways but inspired by the October Revolution and paradoxically helped by the Stalinist idea 'just come to power, and then we'll go on from there', was *a plebeian revolution*. In synchronic class terms, glossed over at the time, it was a peasant revolution (see Bakarić 2: 305) led by that combination of dissident intellectuals and internationalist working-class traditions as channelled by Stalinism which was the small but tight and rapidly expanding CPY and its youth wing.

'[T]he axiom inscribed in Project Yugoslavia ... was the end of all forms of domination and exploitation' (Pupovac, 'Projekt' 5), and its horizon was a classless society. But the corollary to this constellation was that the leaders in war came to power in peace: as Gramsci says arguing for a long duration necessity of politics, there has always been a difference between leaders and led (cf. Hobsbawm 330). The passage from leading the fluid partizan movement in the open air of forests and mountains to leading the State as a solidified apparatus from inside city offices magnified the powers and institutions at the disposal of the Party but presented hitherto unknown snares (see for example Đilas 120 and passim). I shall return to the main one: how Lenin drew in *The State and Revolution* from his readings in Marx and dialectics the fulgurant conclusion that the 'socialist' transition period would have a semi-bourgeois State, indeed that in it 'there remains for a time not only bourgeois law, but even *the bourgeois State – without the bourgeoisie!*' (/ch05.htm#s4, emphasis his). But this means also, we have learned, '*the bourgeois economic framework – without the bourgeoisie!*' (emphasis mine).

Of all such snares the Party's revolutionary optimism was blissfully unaware. They had to be discovered by struggling through them and finding entirely new tools and institutions. The central one, and *the second important Yugoslav singularity*, was Boris Kidrič's 1949–50 introduction – with input, it seems, from Kardelj and Djilas, and final agreement by Tito – of Workers' Councils. It was a direct continuation of the creative imagination from the partizan war, now redefined in terms of *the protagonist's do-it-yourself political economy* (see more in Chapter 5). The problem was to define the Antagonist: who was

FIGURE 6

Portrait of Miroslav Krleža by Petar Dobrović (1926)

it that, after the immediate post-war reconstruction, blocked The Working People's attainment of the Value or emancipation? How to give a face and class habitation to Backwardness? I return to this at the end of the book.

Thus the first Yugoslav singularity was that the revolution 1941–5 was fought as an anti-imperialist war for national liberation and social justice. While sparked by fascist mass killings and oppression and led by the Party's hierarchic network, the struggle was conducted from below upwards, for freedom and against the Axis occupiers and their monarchist and fascist collaborators, and it resulted in a people (or group of peoples) freeing itself by its own forces. A second revolutionary singularity came about in 1948 with the successful refusal by Tito and the great majority of the Party of Stalin's attempt to impose rule by Russian stooges. While up to Stalin's death it was touch and go whether Russia would not invade, Tito and the CPY could in the event claim a unique double, albeit local, victory: over Hitler's and Stalin's most oppressive and murderous social systems. The singularity culminated by fusing the national and the plebeian (much as Gramsci recommended) in sketching out a possible road to a real socialist democracy and self-management from below.

Retrospectively it is clear that:

> [Yugoslav self-management] had vigorous roots in the partizan movement that routed the fascist invaders in World War II and brought the new society into being ... Partizan strategy ... rises from the ranks ... The

partizan system, decentralised and enormously complex, turned out to be more stable than the relatively simple and highly centralised military system ... The partizan system is economical. There are no overhead expenses and no supervisory costs ... [T]he partizan system was a self-management system applied to war – and it worked in Yugoslavia as it later did in Algeria, in Israel as in Vietnam, and in Malaysia as in Latin America.

MANN BORGESE xx–xxi

Kardelj said much the same: 'The original partizan detachments were already an expression of the self-manag[ing] revolutionary wish of the people ... The management of economic resources on liberated territory was another form of self-management' (*Reminiscences* 236). He repeated this often and concluded that without such a revolution 'we would probably never have initiated the self-management later' (ibidem 238, and cf. 233–42).

1.2   A Brief Prospect

The criteria for my further interpretation will have to be twofold, as the post-revolutionary historical trajectory depended on yoking together two aspects: how to produce the cake and how to distribute it.[5] The first one is *economic performance*: how a given class alliance has mastered enlarged social reproduction in a very backward country, exposed to fierce pressures from other States and international constellations (such as the capitalist market). The second is *class reorganisation in view of justice*: socialism as a revolutionary attempt to steadily diminish exploitation of the 'working people'. The presupposition for both was the State's independence and security. This particular history was also happening within a federation of half a dozen ethnic groups with a common historical interest in emancipation from semi-colonial status, yet with legitimately strong desires for autochthonous development, which was blocked primarily by economic backwardness; the latter was not only absolute but also, and most sensitively, relative to each other, so that an additional criterion, beyond the above two, was whether economic inequality between the constituent republics is being diminished or not.

I shall argue later that a useful division of SFRY history would be one into the periods of 1945–52, 1952–65, 1965–72, and 1972–89. More simply, the first

---

5   I acknowledge an important stimulation for this consideration from Kržan's 'Nacrt' lecture.

two phases could be called *les vingt glorieuses* (the twenty glorious years), as they are clearly positive in all essential respects. These are: full independence of Yugoslavia and its growing stature in international affairs; rapid growth of productive forces and (in the second period) of the living standard; very rapid urbanisation and development of both working class and intellectual class; a diminution of relative economic inequality between the republics; and a most imaginative deployment of self-management inside and non-alignment outside the country. From 1949 to 1961, the country underwent a Great Leap from a very undeveloped agrarian to a middle-income industrial society, for which capitalist Western Europe had needed a much longer period with much deeper suffering of subaltern classes. The downsides were a political and for a long time economic neglect of the peasantry (still one half of the population) and a blindness to gender problems and the authoritarian mindset, both arising out of a strong patriarchal tradition in daily life and culture. Still, Phyllis Auty could as late as 1970 conclude: 'No one could doubt that the Yugoslavia of today is a far more prosperous, more equitable, more estimable a society than that of [Tito's] youth' (291).

TABLE 1.2 *Some key data of economic growth*
FROM BILANDŽIĆ 386–94

- *Rate of growth of industrial production* **1969/1953**: 10.5 % (officially fifth highest in the world)
- GNP *due to industry vs. agriculture*: **1947**, 18 vs. 42.6 %; **1972**, 38.1 vs. 18.8 %
- *Growth of pro capita* GNP **1969/1953**: 259 %; yearly average 6.1 %
- GNP *pro capita*: **1953**, ca. 300 US$; **1971**, ca. 800 US$ [this may be optimistic] Still, having started as one of the poorest economies of prewar Europe, devastated by war to boot, this meant Yugoslavia was in the 70s only entering into the ranks of economically middling countries: its *pro capita* GNP remained roughly half of Italy or Czechoslovakia, though more equitably distributed.

The second two phases, which could be called *les vingt minables* and finally even *déshonorantes* (the twenty inglorious and finally even disgraceful years), are divided into 1965–72, a decisive battle lost by turning towards a planless market and a Party territorial polyarchy, and the decay into repressive stasis after 1972 (which I shall not deal with).

Glossary

quisling = collaborator with Axis occupiers (from the name of a Norwegian traitor)
pro aris et focis = for one's own home and its deepest values (literally, for hearth and home)

CHAPTER 2

Accumulation and Its Discontents

> Accumulate! Accumulate! That is Moses and the prophets.
> MARX, 1867

∴

2.1   Politics and the Crux of Accumulation

Societies attempting to organise themselves in the aftermath of a modern plebeian revolution, especially those following the indications of a necessarily reinterpreted Marx, seem to oscillate in their policies between a development as quantitative well-being – bourgeois life without the capitalists – and the utopian horizon of a classless just society.[1] Both for pragmatic success as well as for steps towards utopia, all countries not having undergone a thorough bourgeois revolution found it imperiously necessary to rush into industrialisation as the engine of urbanisation and of a general rise in the standard of living. But whence was to come the indispensable 'primitive accumulation of capital'? In capitalism, it draws on three possible sources: exploitation of the working people, canonically analysed in *Das Kapital*; exploitation of other countries; and foreign loans. Socialism historically as a rule did not have the second source.

A first sharp debate about accumulation arose in the USSR immediately after stabilisation in the mid-1920s between Preobrazhensky, a Trotskyite who favoured extracting 'socialist primitive accumulation' from the peasants, and Bukharin, who objected that this would mean destroying the worker-peasant alliance upon which Lenin founded the Soviet power, and bringing about 'parasitary and stagnant monopolism' (Foa ed. 100 – the booklet handily translates the whole debate; cf. Samary, *Marché* 33–42). Preobrazhensky also theorised a priority of 'producers' goods' over 'consumer goods' (Erlich 140–1), that is,

---

[1] The terms 'development' and 'utopia' for the competing horizons are taken from Löwenthal who was generalising from two communist revolutions: the semi-peasant one in the USSR and the peasant one in China, both possessing important parallels and as important differences with Yugoslavia. Cf. for SFRY Woodward 21–2 and *passim*, the best work on SFRY political economics extant.

of heavy industry over light industry and consumption. After liquidating both these 'wings', Stalin finally adopted the former stance, and reaped the consequences predicted by the latter; in a characteristic obfuscation, the term itself of 'primitive socialist accumulation' was consigned to oblivion.

The Yugoslav rulers and theoreticians drew heavily on both Leninism and Stalinism. After 1949 they attempted (with notable but less than full success) to get rid of the officially execrated Stalinism, deeply rooted both in the old Party cadre, and the widespread peasant-cum-patriarchal petty-bourgeois (*palanačka*) mentality, as well as to go back to the radical Lenin, whose libertarianism also struck a deep chord in the traditions of popular self-government and of partizan self-reliance (cf. Buden, Denitch 153, Woodward 52, and for Yugoslav mentalities Chapter 4 and later). More than a pinch of Bukharin's stress on market production was, unbeknownst of the source, added later; these three were, in an analogous economic situation, the only available options (cf. Woodward 74–5, for Bukharin also Cohen).

Yet in a system where all means of production (except perhaps a few remnants, and in the case of Yugoslavia and Poland also most agriculture) have been taken over by the State run by a single party that also had a political and organisational monopoly, the Party-State, power is wielded – unless counteracted by strong democratic pressures from below – by a relatively small oligarchy. It drew its legitimacy first from the revolutionary achievements of plebeian upward mobility, which changed the life of millions for the better, and the attendant defence of independence (the latter was absent from the Soviet satellites), but then, as emancipatory horizons waned, increasingly from the population's standard of living – in Hungary this was popularly dubbed 'goulash socialism'. The system therefore had, unless it were to rely largely on police repression, to achieve a noticeable and ongoing economic surplus and to have it distributed in a way that appeared just to the majority of the population, especially the industrial working class and other city dwellers. This is where both the increase and disposal of the surplus value arising from labour-power, to be balanced between industrialisation, defence, and living standard, became a crux; in Yugoslavia, as in the USSR, 'the source of rapid capital accumulation [was left unresolved]' (Woodward 75).

This coincided with a long-duration dilemma, first theorised by Rosa Luxemburg: that in order to continue at all, capitalism needs an ongoing, permanent 'primitive accumulation', dispossessing millions and devastating further regions of geography and social life, up to the women, virtual space, genome, and intellect (Harvey 304–5 and *passim*, Amin, Meillassoux, De Angelis chap. 7 and 10–11, Benanav et al.) – while socialism was set up to counteract such devastations. To anticipate my conclusion, capital accumulation in Yugoslavia

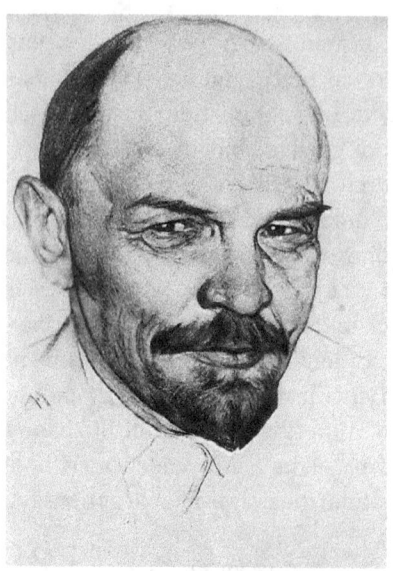 

FIGURE 7   *Drawing of Vladimir I. Lenin*
IMAGE REPRODUCED FROM
L. LIH, LENIN

FIGURE 8   *Rosa Luxemburg (1915)*
PHOTOGRAPHER UNKNOWN,
BUNDESARCHIV, BILD 183-
14077-006 / CC-BY-SA

was unable to proceed for two reasons: negatively, because of cultural (including technological) backwardness; but then positively, because it meant an all-round disempowerment and alienation of people that the revolution – like all such great plebeian uprisings from the French through the Russian to the Chinese revolution – had originally been expressly designed to strongly limit by means of 'elements of solidarity, social responsibility, [and] control over the market mechanisms, worked into its institutional frame' (Močnik 149), and to begin abolishing.

2.2   Accumulation and Singularity in SFRY

Thus, the new State power in Yugoslavia embarked on a rapid industrialisation of the country as the quite inevitable precondition for its independence, well-being, urbanisation, and cultural modernisation. The capital for this had to be found from the only source available in the absence of a modern working class or of foreign plunder: the peasantry. All industrially undeveloped countries have striven to do so, whether the ideological justification be, say, Bismarckian or Leninist. After 1945 Yugoslavia followed the Soviet road in the State organisation of economics and power, but fortunately not the worst facets of Stalinist practice. What was singular is, to begin with, that this organisation was in 1945 rooted in popular enthusiasm for reconstruction of a devastated but now liberated country. This allowed a strong recovery (*obnova*), by which transport and most branches of production were by 1950 above the prewar level (CIA 4: 51). Singular in Yugoslavia was, further, both the secession from Stalin and some top leaders' rediscovery after it of the Paris Commune and of their own partizan roots in Marxian self-government. They set the Party out on the road of both strengthening the local centres of power down to the basic territorial units and of slowly introducing self-management in the nationalised enterprises. My second SFRY singularity (Fejtö calls it a second revolution, 2: 225 ff.) sketched out a zigzagging road to a real socialist democracy from below. Furthermore, Tito as of 1950 found a second source of financing which permitted him to dispense with forced collectivisation of land and subservience to Moscow: foreign loans (US and international capitalist loans amounted in 1950–61 to around 2.5 billion US$).[2] Because of overriding US interest in the strategic role of the Yugoslav army during the Cold War, these loans were not accompanied with the usual foreign ownership and domination turning the recipient into a semi-colony. This allowed the Yugoslav social experiment a quarter century (roughly 1949–73) of breathing space before the world market and the Western powers began to squeeze the windpipe.

On the international scale, this singularity allowed that further remarkable experiment of the Non-aligned movement, working for peace and independence against both Cold War camps. It resulted in a real independence of Yugoslavia, until the ruling class involution made it economically and politically vulnerable.

The attendant major social shift in SFRY 1950–72 was the move of between 1.5 and 2 million peasants to the cities in an unstoppable tide. Another major social change was the rapid mass production of the first modern proletariat and intelligentsia in this part of the world. This set the stage for a new conflict in the 60s, when it was officially admitted that there was sharp friction at the highest and middle Party and State levels between tendencies which were then termed bureaucratic vs. self-management 'forces'. The top federal level was eventually reconstituted as a papered-over unity, but just below the top, at the

---

2 US economic aid – without other countries or private banks – amounted in 1950–9 to 1,158 million dollars (Hoffman and Neal 348); later data have it amount for the period 1950–5 to $1.2 billion, half of it military (Rusinow 46), and it seems that in 1955–61 as much more was given (Auty 170). Lampe claims the total US aid to Yugoslavia 1949–67 amounted to $2,465 million, of which a growing third were loans and the rest grants; Heuser adds 128 million in UK and French aid 1949–53 (219). Direct military aid ceased in 1957.

middle and higher middle level of key executives, the hidden conflict remained virulent. At issue was, in Marxist terms, the quite central problem of division of surplus labour while ensuring a growing income pie to be divided. I shall enter upon the economic data and their complex ramifications in Part 3 of the book, but I suggest that the conflict theoretically or ideologically, at least in good part, hinged upon the attitude toward an optimum balance between planning and commodity production for the market. In brief, enforceable planning, a key plank of the original Kidrič economic system in 1950–1 (see Chapter 5), was simply dropped. The opposition between planning and market was then sidetracked into interminable debates about centralism vs. decentralisation.

Finally, the Party 'reformers' reached a compromise with the middle-of-the-road against a return to Stalinism on a platform of Party monolithism and politocracy rule, and became 'decentralisers', which meant to one group power to the republican and local leaders, and to the other, smaller one, power to the self-managing working people. Only the first meaning and power was implemented, with verbal and smaller material sops for the workers, and much consumerism for the middle classes on an only partly controlled market. This resulted from the mid-60s on in a disempowerment of the 'investment funds' (mainly federal ones) that had until then disposed of three quarters of all investments. The top leaders' and the people's revulsion against centralised 'State socialism' was mainly channelled into liberal market idolatry.

Behind the scenes of this anarchoidal polyarchy, the World Bank and IMF were untiringly pushing capitalism in Yugoslavia, its teams insisting on ever more 'decentralisation as a Trojan horse for marketisation', so that each IMF loan programme was followed by further decentralisation (Woodward 169–70); these political aims successfully culminated in 1989. In the meantime, the self-interested ideological confusion resulted in a kind of confederacy of the six constituent 'republics', allowing the local rulers – especially in Slovenia, Croatia, and Serbia – sufficient power to block unwelcome federal initiatives. Top Party leader and official theoretician Kardelj even estimated in a fit of despondency that conditions for the rise of capitalism or, more probably, of managerial-technocratic monopoly or a central State bureaucracy were better than for the success of self-management (Bilandžić 316–17). Since even he could not bring himself to delve into the class interests determining such chances (cf. Chapters 4 and 10.4), this became a self-fulfilling prophecy.

To understand the springs of such later conflicts we need to look at the SFRY class system.

PART 2

Class Interests and Politics as SFRY *Dominants*

∴

We should know what there ought to be in order to judge well what there is.

ROUSSEAU, 1762

CHAPTER 3

On Class Relationships in Yugoslavia

> [T]he function of the historian is not to establish permanent truth (except about what the evidence can establish), but to advance a discussion which must, inevitably, sooner or later, make his or her work obsolete ...
> ERIC HOBSBAWM, 1984

∴

3.0   Introduction

This chapter searches for a general hypothesis to explain the development and eventual collapse of SFRY by way of an analysis of classes and their interests. It segues into a further chapter which concludes that the key factor was the rise of a ruling class which eventually fractured, and its decisive fractions decided that their interests were better served by fracturing the State too and constituting themselves into legally independent neo-comprador classes (in the case of Slovenia and Croatia) or gambling for a Greater Serbia. This hypothesis was by no means certain in my mind, so that I tried to have it unfold from an as 'thick' as possible analysis of the overall Yugoslav class structure, and passed a judgment only at the end.

At the beginning, I encountered such a cacophony of stances about what class is (if anything) that I had to clear this up for my further use, and I hope that of the reader's. This first section feeds into the next two chapters in many subterranean ways, but I have not tried for an overt linear connexion between them.

3.1   On the Concept of Class

3.1.1   *Discussion*

The basic point of why bother about classes can be supplied by Hegel: 'When we say that man must be a "somebody", we mean that he should belong to some specific social class, since ... [a] man with no class is a mere private person and his universality is not actualised' (addition to § 207).

A working hypothesis on how to use the concept of social class today can be derived from a debate that begins with Marx's indications. I propose to retain from it the following six points, which seem reasonably certain and indispensable for further work.

1. After the tribal community, human societies are divided into multifarious struggling groups of more and more differentiated kinds. Some of these groups determine so strongly the position and behaviour of their members that they compete in importance with the overall society, and that membership in one excludes membership in other groupings on the same level (Gurvitch 105 and 116–20). From an array of terms for such groups, such as caste, stratum or layer, and – before capitalism – estate (*Stand, état*), I shall use only '*class*' and '*class fraction*': Poulantzas (see *Pouvoir* 77–100, especially 99 – cf. also his *Classes*) acknowledges only those two constitute a social force, and Marx could be read that way too (Ollman, 'Marx's' 576).

I shall sidestep the problem whether classes can be said to exist in a rather different form before the rise of capitalism – and a certain bourgeoisie – though I believe that they did. I shall use the Weberian tradition of approach to social groups where necessary for the discussion of Yugoslavia, but it will not be prominent. Two major advantages of the Marxian approach seem that (a) it relates to the economy as a whole (though his analytical stress was mainly on production) while Weber relates only to distribution, and (b) it can encompass the Weberian 'elite' as a class fraction, while the 'elite' approach as a rule tends to analytically deal with elites plus invidious biosociological 'masses'. However, it will be useful where the Marxist tradition has refused to face problems and degenerations after its own coming to power.

2. Classes are distinguished from other supra-local social groups not only by their importance, multiple functions, and an inner articulation. Most important is that classes are *legally open* to anybody; in reality they are halfway closed.

3. As many other groups coterminous with society as a whole, classes do not exist alone but are *relational* animals: there is no bourgeoisie without aristocracy or proletariat (see Thompson, also Bensaïd, Resnick & Wolff, Ritsert, Roemer, and Wright). Each class is not only different from other ones but its interests are often incompatible to those of other classes (Ossowski 120 and *passim*). Nonetheless, class differences and antagonisms as well as their alliances may vary considerably, and their boundaries are often '[obliterated by m]iddle and intermediate strata' (Marx, *Capital* 3, /ch52.htm).

Classes practice simultaneously a certain solidarity, stimulated by common opposition against other ones, and internal competition, with frequent inner and outer conflicts (see MEW 3: 54). Thus, opposition and furthermore *tensions and collisions* are included in the very concept of social class. Class conflict is as a rule a zero-sum game: what is *monopolised* by one dominant class is denied to the dominated classes (Lazić, *Čekajući* 47), though if necessary a fraction of the monopolised power and affluence can be allotted to keep the dominated classes from rebelling.

4. Classes are multi-functional, and insofar too compete in importance for its members with the national unit of which they are parts, or with gender. A central factor of class unity is the individuals' common *power-position* in the mode of production and similar financial share of the social wealth, which can be in capitalism called their *economic* conditions of existence, 'that separate their mode of life, their interests, and their culture from those of the other classes, and put them in hostile opposition to the latter' (Marx, *18th Brumaire*, /ch07.htm). In this vision, classes are primarily organised around the axis of '*a relationship of exploitation*', that is, 'appropriation of a part of the product of labour of others' (Ste. Croix, 'Class' 99–100 and *passim*, and see his *Class Struggle*). A second factor reinforcing class unity is *professional* condition. Both of these conditions, taken in the largest sense, mean that members of a class belong to the same layer of the social pyramid. Thus, an individual's membership in a class is relatively stable, and, except in politically and/or economically revolutionary times, classes themselves are relatively stable.

5. Classes are, unlike most other groups, 'partially conscious and partially unconscious' of some important aspects of themselves (Gurvitch 111). In the Marxist tradition, 'Class in the full sense only comes into existence when classes begin to acquire consciousness of themselves as such' (Hobsbawm 16, and see the foundational case-study by Thompson); Gramsci calls it – as Lenin did – an advance from economic to political consciousness (181). The attribution of such consciousness often led to wishful thinking, based first on revolutionary impatience and later on dogmatism. Marx's and Engels's initial, somewhat monolithic conception of a stable class consciousness seems to me subject to conjunctures in real micro-history, apparent in their own later writing and the tormented theory and practice after them, and paradoxically clearest in Lukács's 'imputed consciousness' (126 ff.) A class's consciousness is a 'potential ... rooted in a situation' (Ollman, *Dialectical* 157), it is constructed by various existential pressures upon existing, often alienated, presuppositions and inclinations and depends on actions. Therefore, independent of concrete micro-

FIGURE 9   *Antonio Gramsci, prison mugshots (ca. 1930)*
            IMAGE IN THE PUBLIC DOMAIN, REPRODUCED FROM HTTPS://DARKOSUVIN
            .COM/GRAMSCI-PRISON-MUGSHOT/

historical situations, 'it is wrong to suppose that *any* particular class ... is subjectively and incorruptibly revolutionary *per se* ...' (Hobsbawm 222). As of the rise of industrial capitalism, the degree of class consciousness clearly rises, and becomes more exclusively economic beginning with nineteenth-century western Europe (cf. Hobsbawm 17–18 and Lukács). Finally, the same class's relation to social reality, and thus consciousness, often changes drastically, sometimes even in the short term.

In conjunction with point 3 on classes as relational, this means they are (especially before fascism) organised only partially, in flexible and changing ways. They have many subordinated fractions, overlapping functions, and fuzzy fringes. Nonetheless, classes are 'powerful centers of spontaneous collective reactions' (Gurvitch 133), articulated in current ideologies and long-duration cultural artefacts and traditions. Each class shares an everyday *culture*, more or less estranged from the culture of other classes – in some cases, for example England, Ceylon or Haiti, speaking different dialects (Ossowski 152).

6. Polanyi supplies some important reminders of matters forgotten in the Marxist vulgate, which often envisaged practically isolated entities. First, 'the relation of a class to society as a whole' (163), which defines a class's role and prospects, includes major overarching factors – such as a war or climate change – that affect different classes in different ways. Second, alongside deep-

seated class enmity in some cases, there exists in other cases an irrefragable need for complementary roles, which was recognised by all theoreticians who were also practical politicians, such as Lenin or Weber; indeed, the success of any major class interest depends on alliances with other classes, and thus on the ability of formulating a common wider interest for society as a whole (Polanyi 159). Third, 'interests' should be interpreted not only – though always also – economically but they significantly include factors like comparative status and security (161–2; cf. Hobsbawm 222); Adler defines class by means of 'the vital life interests (*Lebensinteressen*) of a human economic group' (101–2), for which 'economic exploitation is only the initiating or constitutive (*klassenerzeugend*) impulse' (104).

3.1.2   Delimitation

I would opt for an operative use of the following elements from Gurvitch's definition (116): Classes are really existing, large, supra-local social groups characterised by strong determination of their members' lives, partial openness toward new members, exclusiveness toward and opposition to other classes in the same spacetime, multi-functionality focussed on and by their members' economic plus professional condition as well as other needs of status and security, that is, interests which crystallise in a spread of changing class consciousnesses.

This needs three crucial additions. The first one, from Lenin, uses the relationship to surplus labour – though with a stress on its political aspect – and also has the pragmatic merit of being applicable to all the connotations of class in Marx and Engels (Ossowski 82). His definition of classes is 'large groups of people differentiated by their position in a given historical system of social production, by their relations (in most cases fixed and sanctioned by laws) to the means of production, by their function in the social organisation of labour, and consequently, by the way and the measure in which they enjoy the share of riches of which they dispose. Classes are groups of people of which one can appropriate the labour of the other according to the distinct place occupied in a given system of social economy' (Lenin 472).

Second, elements from Polanyi and Gramsci: As classes are fully relational entities, they are, especially at times of threat and rapid change, organised in hegemonically structured alliances based on the hegemon's ability to interpret society's strategic goals.

A third crucial addition has to do with an evaluation of class society today, and it is a paraphrase of the constant horizon shared by Marx and all the people and movements that claim this filiation: class society, especially after the full development of capitalist industrialisation, is an increasingly violent, decisive fetter stymieing not only social justice but threatening the very existence of humanity. True, that type of society eventually attained in capitalism, amid horrendous sufferings, a rise in overall wealth which can finally make exploitation and domination unnecessary for a decent life by one and all; but in the last two or three epochs, say after 1848, class societies are a root cause of psychophysical destructions, a hugely growing threat to the existence of society and indeed of the genus Homo.

The resulting overview may be too loose for a definition, but the term 'class' has probably an inherently polysemic character (cf. Aronowitz). At any rate I need a guideline for further work:

- Synchronically, *classes are large, supra-local social groups differentiated by their position in a given historical system of social reproduction, which means their power and function in the exploitative organisation of labour and their position within the distribution of the fruits of production, including for the upper and middle classes the appropriation of labour from the lower ones. Classes are characterised by strong determination of their members' lives, partial openness toward new members, exclusiveness toward and opposition to other classes in the same spacetime, multi-functionality focussed on and by the individuals' economic plus professional conditions as well as other needs of status and security, and a spread of changing class consciousnesses.*
- Diachronically, *classes are as a rule, especially at times of threat and rapid change, organised in hegemonically structured alliances based on the hegemon's ability to interpret society's strategic goals. However, class society, especially after the full development of capitalist industrialisation and wars, is an increasingly destructive fetter stymieing not only social justice but threatening the very existence of humanity.*

3.1.3 Toward Application

For individuals, the above delimitations mean that class is a grouping to which members do not belong by birth (as in caste) nor by explicit choice (as in voluntary associations) nor by any command of a precise social power. On the other hand, the members' overriding common interests make for a tendency toward attaining class consciousness, especially in situations that threaten the whole class – as was the case with the bourgeoisie before the French Revolution or the industrial proletariat of nineteenth-century Europe. Marx's category of *interest*, itself based on 'need' (MEW 3: 28) but larger, seems to me of strategic importance, for it unites collective and personal levels, while at the same time allowing one to factor in people's material circumstances. It is accompanied by the terms of 'orientation' and personal 'motivations' (Ritsert 69–71).

The focus of Marx's opus, however, grew to be the critique of 'economics', a branch of sapience or science which arose with capitalism and bourgeois quantification in seventeenth- and eighteenth-century Britain, and in which classes are for the first time established exclusively on the basis of ownership and/or labour, rather than military or political-cum-religious roles as in feudalism or preceding ages. In this tradition classes are strategic nodes for understanding a society, since they determine relations between, on the one hand, the key production, circulation, and consumption of goods needed for life, and on the other hand everything else in the human production of life. These relations arise on the basis of unequal appropriation of surplus labour, thus of 'objective' (that is, tendentially dominant) economic and psychological interests of large groups of people whose individual interests are decisively shaped by their common situation within a social division of labour.

If we want to find some simpler common denominators for classes as forms of interdependence between people, that is, of how some groups of people depend from other groups, the debate after Marx gives us three main criteria: dependence on basis of *power*, of *social function*, and of *economic position*. The best Marxians, such as Gramsci, have also retained Marx's original anthropological bent by stressing the *cultural practices*, in the widest sense, of the reproduction of social life. These four criteria are not exclusive but usually combined in various ways. Therefore, paraphrasing what Lazić points out, the reproduction of classes is not exclusively economical, but tied to human productivity in the domains of material production, of social control, and of the symbolic imagination, three different forms of praxis themselves differently integrated in different social formations and concrete societies (*Čekajući* 47).

From times immemorial, the dominant metaphor of spatial opposition in politics was based on heaviness or labour of those below and lightness or privilege of those above, often mediated by metaphors from engineering construction (base and superstructure) and from geology (strata). This can be used in a *binary* (digital) or *graded* (analog) way, resulting in the opposition of only two or of more – usually four to eight – classes. The first way is the sturdy plebeian or popular cognition of 'us' vs. 'them' (oppressed/oppressor, powerless/powerful, the have-nots/haves); Marx uses it in his didactic overviews such as *The Communist Manifesto*, modifying the last opposition after his work on *Capital* into exploited/exploiters, and adding to this a 'middle' class oscillating between the upper and lower one. The second one is the scholar's work on an actual society; Marx uses this richer articulation in his historical investigations such as *The 18th Brumaire*, and Lenin at various points from *The Development of Capitalism in Russia* to his characterisation of early Soviet society. The unresolved question of class (self-)consciousness, which has vexed the Marxian approach from

Marx and Engels through Lukács and Gramsci to Lefebvre and the present day, is so difficult to resolve because it is at the crossroads of Marx's revolutionary didactics and scholarly punctiliousness; I shall approach this too in concrete Yugoslav discussions.

It has been pointed out that Marx's work sometimes uses the term loosely (Ollman, 'Marx's' 576), and furthermore fuses three approaches to class structuring: the dichotomising one, the gradational, and the functional, while occasionally introducing a flexible but inductive fourth one, the interaction of two or more dichotomies (Ossowski 93), which became the central Marxist procedure. In sum, class was never explicitly defined by Marx or Engels but used in flexible ways, with various connotations according to the investigation at hand. Nonetheless, the nucleus of the concept of social class, to which I have pointed above, is – together with the one of surplus labour – a kind of emblem and metonymy of Marx's doctrine and of all Marxist political programmes. Marx's theory of class is foundational: 'simultaneously rich in possibilities, in some ways rather contradictory, and insufficiently worked out ...' (Gurvitch 6). Yet, owing to the reluctance of non-Marxists to found it in exploitation of labour and to various misconceptions among Marxists, this powerful tool has given rise to multiple and incompatible interpretations.

3.2 Data about and Categorising of Classes in Yugoslavia 1945–72

3.2.1 *Problems of Yugoslav Statistics*

As anyone knows who has used the official statistics of Yugoslavia (FPRY/SFRY), it is extremely difficult to disentangle its rubrics of public vs. private 'workers' and the myriad subdivisions, based on an economistic and productivistic Soviet modelling, not only for class statistics but even for a full articulation of the population. Macesich looked askance not only at the divergence of its economic nomenclature of activities from the International Standard Classification, but also at the changes of weighting in the indices of physical production which were retroactively corrected and resulted in 'a very hazy picture' of industrial output (151).[1] Bakarić rightly called its categories 'State capitalist ones' and

---

1 This was the 'Material Product System' taken from Soviet (Stalinist) economics, which 'aims to measure the annual output of *material goods*, in contrast with services' (see http://en.wikipedia.org/wiki/Material_Product_System, with further bibliography), or levels of aggregate output – regardless of efficiency or per capita productivity. Its main indicator was the

complained it lent itself to ignorant misreading (3:127), while Moore noted 'services' were in the Soviet model deemed unproductive and excluded from the data on national income, and yet in the USSR of 1952–71 an average of 30% of the 'social product' was paid to them (22 and *passim*). Most important, research about the intertwined economy and politics of Yugoslavia has provided us with no satisfactory apparatus 'to cope with socialist historical reality' (Kovač 446 – the complaint is from 1987, but I think still valid). True, there have been some sterling and very valuable efforts, yet to a large extent all of us have to provide intelligible pictures ourselves: any work in this field must at present be considered highly provisional. This holds in spades for my attempt, written outside ex-Yugoslavia with many personal limitations.

Nonetheless, macro-proportions seem generally clear, and I shall proceed by constructing some estimates of social classes in SFRY, all rounded off to nearest 100 or 50 thousand. I propose to speak here only about the situation from 1945 to the mid-70s; we could maybe call this period Yugoslav Socialist Fordism (a very incipient and low-grade one). A first approach shows the total population and its most salient divides: the agricultural/urban, the female/male, the 'active'/'supported', and the minors/adults:

TABLE 3.1 *Population (in thousands)*
FROM SG81: 80, 83, AND 99–101, WITH 1981 FROM
WOODWARD, SOCIALIST 192

Year	Total	Agricult.	Female	"Active"	>15 yrs
1950	16,350	10,500	8,400	7,750	5,150 ['53]
1961	18,600	9,200	9,500	8,350	5,700
1971	20,550	7,850	10,450	8,900	5,500
1981	22,000		11,200+?		

A preliminary but central problem visible from Table 3.1 has to be faced here. It pertains to the ubiquitous chief subdivision in Yugoslav statistics, 'active [pop-

---

Net Material Product. It was analogous to but ca. 15 percent lower than Gross National Product in the UN or the capitalist System of National Accounts, because it adopted Adam Smith's definition of services as non-productive and thus unfit for developed economies (cf. Simon 51–2, Lampe et al. 76). A useful critique, in spite of the one-sided stress on 'money totem', is in Kurz, chap. 'Das Strukturdilemma …' (99–132), and the titles by Aganbegian and Zaslavskaia quoted there.

ulation]'. It is a weird patriarchal or Adam-Smithian-to-Stalinist productivist category which counts all those publicly employed outside private ownership plus the male and a part of the female peasants, while a large part of peasant women are lumped with children and oldsters as 'kept' or 'dependent' (cf. the complaint by Bakarić 2: 195). Most though not all 'active' people are between 15 and 65 years, while dependants comprise the young, the old, the invalids and sick, students, and all the non-publicly employed women which could be in the rubric 'housewives' (that classification, however, does not exist).

I propose rather, first, to constitute a more realistic category of *working people.* This means that, to begin with, we need to add to the 'Active' all the *female peasants + urban not otherwise employed housewives.* This can be calculated keeping in mind, as concerns gender, that the ratio of female to male agriculturists was consistently ca. 53:47 % (while in the population as a whole ca. 51:49 %); and second, as concerns age, that the total population over 15 years of age was in 1950 = 11,200, in 1961 = 12,900, and in 1971 = 15,050. The difference to the so-called active population would be: 1950 = 3,450, 1961 = 4,550, 1971 = 6,150. From this should then be subtracted the elderly (between 1,000 and 1,600 in those years, of which ca. one third was in agriculture counted as 'active', see SG81: 100), and those 'privately employed' (ca. 300). It then becomes clear that in 1950 roughly ca. 2.5 million, in 1961 ca. 4 million, and in 1971 ca. 5.5 million actually working people are not accounted for in these statistics.

Second, in that number the categories of invalids, students, and self-employed artisans grew between 1961 and 1981 from ca. 0.5 million to above 1 million. I do not see what else the rest *from 2 to above 4 million* could be except: (a) the **working women** in village and town officially not counted as 'active' by the above definition, of which, for the not counted adult peasant women, indications from SG81: 101 are that they could be 1 million or somewhat over, while the number of urban housewives remains unknown; (b) increasingly, **workers not permanently employed**, mainly male, including those who failed to register for statistics (say migrant construction workers), those officially unemployed (in 1971 = 290 thousands, ca. 3 %); and (c) some other marginal strata. I shall return to this in section 3.2.2.2.

3.2.2   An Attempt at a Survey and at Class Statistics
3.2.2.1   Initial Hypothesis
In a complex and unsatisfactorily theorised society, the problem is to hypothesise which classes and/or class fractions may be said to exist, and what was their dominant relationship. My hypothesis is that (besides the small and vanished, mainly comprador, bourgeoisie of Serbia, Croatia, and Slovenia), the classes were:

(1) *peasants* (who were officially, as producers based on private property, in the cities flanked by urban *artisans*, from 1945 to the mid-60s a numerically smaller group oscillating between 0.8 and 0.3 million); in time, the number of peasants would fall significantly, while the numbers of all other classes would rise. In percentages, only peasants would fall heavily, roughly from one half to one third, and all other percentages would rise (except perhaps for housewives, in 1953 35% of all women! – Sklevicky, 'Emancipacija' 104). All Yugoslav averages would have distinct republican deviations.

(2) *fully employed manual workers*, rising between 1945 and 1975 from less than 0.5 to almost 3 millions, thus composed largely of migrants from villages plus some from artisans, and subdivided into class fractions.

(3) as of the early 1950s, an ominously swelling group *of partly and precariously employed workers* outside the official system, later to a good part employed in western Europe or for long stretches unemployed, coming from peasants and manual workers. If women working as *housewives only* are counted as an analogously marginal group, this quasi-class congeries, in the margins of the system but important to it, is numerically comparable to category 2, and lacking a better name I would call it mainly *sub-proletarian* (though some housewives were well-off, and even had domestic help).

(4) the *dominant class*, later probably several class fractions, perhaps best named (as in Horvat, see 3.2.2.3) the *politocracy*, but out of which probably a new 'technocracy' arose; it was composed of a ruling core, a subordinate secondary outer circle, and a merely executive but still privileged auxiliary fringe. Their numbers and roles are a matter for further study.

(5) the *'middle' classes* of employees and non-manual workers, divided at least into the fractions of **white-collar workers**, both in industry and outside it, then **engineers and technicians**, and **the intelligentsia**, mainly in human sciences, initially a mainstay but then an increasingly doubtful ally of the politocracy (I can speak out of personal experience here).

(6) at some point in the 70s and 80s, thus outside my brief here, one could perhaps find a true potential *bourgeoisie* of the comprador variety (representatives of foreign firms, top banking and foreign trade personnel, etc.)

There are not only grey zones between the classes and their fractions but up to ca. 1960 the classes were unusually fluid and upward mobility frequent. But by the end of the 1960s, Šuvar estimated that 2% of the Yugoslav population had reached the living standard of the capitalist 'middle class' and another 10% were close to it, while 20% – that is, around 4 million people! – lived on an 'existential minimum' (*Sociološki* 165).

3.2.2.2 An Approach to Actual Classes: The Working or Lower Classes

What is a proletariat depends on its definition. While it was no doubt useful for Marx to focus primarily on industrial workers, so that in his wake they became practically synonymous with proletarians, Lenin no longer could do that, and today it seems much more useful to use Engels's elastic definition: 'By proletarians we understand the class of modern wage-labourers who have no means of production of their own and therefore depend for livelihood on selling their labour-power' (Bensaïd 47, as a condensation of Engels's 'Principles'; Marx sometimes spoke this way too). If by labour-power we mean – as we should – both the manual and intellectual one, I count here my hypothetic classes 1–3 and a part of 5 from 3.2.2.1. The official discourse was of a united 'working people', immediately after the World War composed of 'workers, peasants and honest intelligentsia' and later of 'working people'; the workers were, especially often from the 70s on, belatedly and inconsequentially, promoted to 'working class'. In my own discourse I call working people (or workers) all those who produce or create new values (see Suvin 'Living'), so that I shall call Marx's proletariat – without any doubt a class – manual non-agricultural workers.

Peasants

In pre-1941 monarchist Yugoslavia the agricultural labour surplus was estimated at ca. 60%, or perhaps around six million people out of a population of 15.5 million, and was the central economic issue (Woodward, *Socialist* 67); in a backgrounded way it remained such in SFRY too, as it supplied an unending stream of immigrants to cities. Furthermore, productive forces in the village were abysmal: in 1945, 44% of households had an iron plough, 18% a wooden one, the rest none ... The later trajectory of the peasantry was paradoxical: immediately after the 1941–5 Liberation War peasants constituted ca. 70% of the Yugoslav population, around *10 millions* (Bilandžić, *Ideje* 156, ELZ5: 8). The partizan army had been composed mainly of peasants, largely young ones. As to wartime differentiations among peasants, Dedijer believes a specificity of the Yugoslav revolution was the mass participation of middle and even richer peasants in the Partizan struggle, while he is rather jaundiced about the corruptible peasant poor (562–64). The most active and politicised became professional Party workers, civilian or military, and later a part of the dominant class(es); their small relative size can be gauged from the 1945 Party membership of 141,000, in overwhelming majority of peasant provenience. The immediate post-war years included the 1945 land reform, when more than half of the confiscated 1.5 million hectares was distributed to individual peasants, and the resettlement of 43,000 families, mostly Serbian, from the poorest parts of Croatia and Bosnia to Vojvodina plains (Singleton 216–17). In 1948, of

483,000 Party members 49% was by provenience peasant, 30% worker, and 21% other – mainly intellectuals or employees – while membership of Party committees included 23% of peasant provenience locally and 5% in the federal central committee (Barton et al. 47). But after 1949, when the Party organised a huge drive for collectivisation of agriculture, the majority of peasants clearly switched to a mainly passive opposition – a brief revolt in Cazin 1950 seems to have been exceptional – that contributed to scuttling the much premature collectivisation (cf. Horvat 'Jugoslavenska' and both titles by Tomasevich). After a few years, the collectivisation was repealed, the work cooperatives promptly disbanded themselves, and the peasantry remained as very small landowners with an average of three people working on one holding (SG81: 83), and with a smaller number of State farms in the plains (amounting in 1957 to 9% of the arable land). In sum, 'Extensive land reforms had cut down the most market-oriented top layer of the old peasantry, curtailed the forces of proletarianisation operating in pre-war Yugoslav villages, and created a numerous stratum of highly homogeneous peasant households predominantly oriented towards subsistence agriculture' (Schierup 81).

The peasantry was after the early 50s politically more or less forgotten and for a long while 'left to get modestly along on their smallholdings' (Bilandžić, *Ideje* 156), with the assumption that industrialisation would thin its ranks (which did happen) and solve all other problems. The government did later provide tax and technical help, for example with fertilisers, high-yield grain seeds, and similar. Yields and earnings in agriculture rose considerably around 1960 through cooperation with distribution cooperatives and State farms, villages were well on the way to complete electrification, the cooking range was taking the place of the open hearth, and the standard of living – radically better in SFRY than between the World Wars, cf. Calic 103–6 – improved, first sharply and after 1969 slowly; household investments on farms rose from 16% of incomes in 1959 to 30% in 1972, while self-consumption of peasant production fell from almost half of the earnings at the end of the 50s to one quarter toward the end of the 70s (Stipetić 185–7, 190–1, and *passim*). Yields of main crops per hectare also rose spectacularly: for 1978, in wheat they were higher than in USA, Argentina, and most of Europe except France and the UK, and similar holds for corn with a yield lower than in France and USA (idem 194–9). However, since the average family holding was under four hectares while 39% of the 2.6 million holdings in 1969 were under the market-production limit of 2 hectares (Kontetzki 423, Fiamengo et al. ed. 63), problems remained. According to SG81: 236–7, in 1974 agriculture supplied the country abundantly in meat, fish, milk, and eggs, but by value two thirds of grain products and over half of fruit and vegetables were imported. Horvat noted that 4 million Yugoslav peasants feed 20 million people, with a productivity of about 1/6 of the US agriculture; peasant illiteracy was in 1961 still near 29% (*Essay* 181), and even by 1971, one third of the village population had less than four years of elementary schooling (Kontetzki 26, based on SG74), meaning they could sign their name, recognise numbers, and cope with brief texts. Further, there are indications the bigger holdings were again employing more seasonal land workers, perhaps around 300,000 per year (Šuvar, 'Srednji' 89). The peasantry's role as a political subject was unimportant.

Nonetheless, it was an epochal change when by 1959 the peasantry, with ca. nine million members, fell under one half of the total population for the first time since the Neolithic: in less than a quarter of a century more than 1.5 million had moved to smaller or bigger townships, though not all to full employment. Reducing the rural population from 70% to 30% took in SFRY 30 years, as compared with 90 years in Sweden and the USA and ca. 70 years in Japan (Stipetić 197). In the mid-70s the agricultural population was probably around 7.5 million, or ca. 36% of the total population, with a continuing large flow from almost half of all holdings to the urban, expatriate, as well as 'irregular' workers. By the early 70s the growing number of part-time workers fluctuating between industry and agriculture, called 'peasant workers' – or vice versa – but statistically unrecognised, reached ca. 1.5 million (cf. Denitch 64, Kontetzki 384–5, Stipetić 182–3, also articles by Puljiz and Cvjetićanin in Žuvela et al. eds., 144–50 and 243–55, and their books), while of the *Gastarbeiter* workers in West Europe, whose number swelled from two thirds of a million to a full million, 45% came from the villages (Kontetzki 395 – of which one third were women, mainly young peasants, Tomšič 87–8). By the end of the 70s private peasantry was estimated to be only 20% of the population (Šuvar, 'Radnička' 34) and less than one third of the total employed labour (Schrenk et al. 32), and since over half of the families had at least one member, as a rule male, permanently employed outside agriculture, the percentage of women in the rural labour force kept rising (Stipetić 170–1): two thirds of the labour time in fields belonged to women. Further, by 1972 rather more than half of rural income came from outside agriculture (industrial work by men, tourism, cottage industry – Tomšič 107). Economically, this means that income in the industry could be lower since about half the workers received a 'free rent' or hidden subsidy from private agriculture (cf. Korošić, *Jugoslavenska passim*).

Manual Non-agricultural Workers

In the 1939 statistical rubric of 'salaried' there were ca. 900,000 people, but this included a good deal of white-collar employees. The precise number of the pre-war industrial plus mining workers is unknown but estimated between 240 and 350 thousands employed plus their families (Calic 107, Hamilton 10, Lampe

153, 188, and 190), mainly in small enterprises, and in 1945 about half of them remained (Bakarić 3: 52–3). During the 1941–5 war and revolution an estimated 90,000 skilled workers were killed (Rusinow 19): even if we assume skilled workers were in the small pre-war workshops much more frequent than after the war, in my view the workers' overall participation in the partizan struggle was proportionately rather significant (see also Bakarić 2: 426–7, Badovinac 60, and for a contrary opinion Bilandžić, *Ideje* 91). But the workers were numerically swamped by the peasants, also not so well represented in the higher echelons of the Party as the intellectuals, yet still several times higher than the percentage of workers in the population. In 1948, the Party membership was by (claimed) provenience 30% workers, while among committee members, from local to the topmost ones, people of worker provenience constituted ca. 40% right up to the federal central committee (Barton et al. 47).

The working class officially did not exist in any statistics or published studies of my chosen period (only 'the working people' or 'self-managers'), therefore everybody must infer how matters stood. In 1945 there were 460 thousand wage-earners in Yugoslavia, and the number of such 'self-managers in production' leapt in 1955 to 1.5 million, by 1961 to over 2 millions, and by 1971 to over 3.2 millions. The statistics as a rule conflate them with enterprise 'experts' (engineers plus other university graduates from 'soft' sciences) and managers, and often also with enterprise employees, under the rubric 'active' or 'productive'; that group rose by 1971 to 4.3 and by 1976 to 4.8 millions, of which one quarter to one third were women (*Situation* 109 and 137, SG81: 80), while industrial workers in it are estimated at 60% or in 1971 to **2.6 millions**. The CPY officially had by the mid-60s as members 346,000 workers or 34%; however, a virtuous working-class 'origin' was often substituted for present occupation even for people who advanced from the ranks: 'Those members of the working class who took a place in the hierarchy of social power ... cut off ties with their class as regards their condition, interests, way of life, and ideology' (Bilandžić, *Ideje* 93). Probably the percentage of actual manual workers in the Party was by that time not higher than the 30% of them in the active population, itself a considerable achievement. From 1963 to 1970 their proportion fell steeply in the Federal Assembly from 5.5% to 0.6% (4 people in all ...), in the 8 republican assemblies from 7.5% to 1.3%, and in the communal assemblies from 14.6 to 13.1% (Tozi-Petrović 1591, and cf. Jovanov 80). In sum, it remains to be discussed whether the government of Yugoslavia was, to use Lincoln's language, 'for the workers' but it was not 'of the workers' nor 'by the workers' outside the domain of actual productive enterprises, where the workers had some real if circumscribed power.

The increase in worker numbers was a result of very rapid Yugoslav industrialisation, only rendered possible by strong pressure from above for extensive use of a growing new labour force, with a forcible accumulation of surplus labour from mainly unskilled or semi-skilled labourers (Bilandžić, *Ideje* 91) who had as a rule neither a working-class nor an urban and civic tradition. This first of all meant that the working class was young: as late as 1965, 56% were under 35 years of age and employed for 10 years or less, while only 9% were over 50 years, that is, probably working before World War 2 (Bilandžić-Tonković 84). Further, in 1953 out of 1.6 million manual workers 36% were 'unskilled' (ELZ 4: 601), mainly fresh out of lower schools and/or villages, indeed often 'peasant workers' who shuttled between land and factory, coming mostly from larger families with smaller holdings, and growing in relative numbers up to the mid-70s (see for the 50s Schleicher 364–7, and in general Cvjetićanin et al.) The proportion of at least one quarter of workers with less than 4 years of elementary schooling was unchanged as late as 1971; even illiteracy was by 1961 still over 5% (Horvat, *Essay* 181). On the other hand highly skilled workers rose from 4.7% in 1961 to 9.7% in 1976, when the 'skilled' ones were 29.5% and the rest had low skills or were unskilled (Bilandžić, *Historija* 393, cf. Tonković 439). The average net income of the highly skilled was in 1966 and through the 70s higher than that of the 'skilled' by 38%, than the 'semi-skilled' by 65%, and than the unskilled by 84% (Novaković 42–3). Distinct ideological strata or working-class fractions (Bakarić 2: 449) emerged, based on qualification, income, and permanence of employment. Probably, as in other countries, the 5–9% of highly skilled workers in the 60s had a distinct consciousness, which led them to participate more actively in politics and self-management, while on the other end the unskilled ones were more rebellious but 'less politically conscious and far less organisable than the skilled' (Hobsbawm 222, see also 215–16 and 232). The unskilled plus semi-skilled fraction was in the 70s–80s still estimated at 30–40% of all workers (Šuvar, 'Radnička' 34), and possibly it was near or over one half since it comprised also a growing number of sometimes semi-legal and statistically unacknowledged non-permanent workers with one foot in industry and another in the village (cf. Cvjetićanin et al., Puljiz, and Simić). Šuvar judges this oscillating amalgam harshly:

> *A significant mass of unskilled or semi-skilled workers*, with low or non-existent education, from undeveloped peasant milieus, exposed to heavy and repetitive labour, repressed out of self-management ... *still exists on the margins of society*, in peculiar ghettoes of seasonal and *Gastarbeiter* work, captive to boot of a parallel economy on smallholdings, possessing traits not only of peasant ... but also of lumpenproletarian consciousness.
> 'Radnička' 47

I'm not sure what is 'lumpenproletarian consciousness', but it is well-known that the peasant who gets a job in town is at the beginning a more or less pure *homo oeconomicus*, seeing in industrial work no other value but a monetary one.

In sum, if unskilled-cum-peasant workers are a class fraction, then there were at least four fractions in the working class, and women workers might have been a fifth one.

When incomes of workers are compared to those of employees at an analogous level of fourfold stratification (see Chapter 4.2), the official income minimums were from the beginning in 1952 at least 10–20% lower for the workers, and the gap kept growing; the relation between lowest and highest incomes – those of the unskilled workers vs. top officials and professionals – which was in the austere 1950s perhaps as low as 1:3.5, had in 1968 reached 1:10 (Bilandžić, *Ideje* 131 and 260). A major difficulty was lack of proper housing for the rapidly rising number of newcomers to towns, which was supposed to be provided by the enterprises hiring them. On the other hand, beside practically lifelong employment, health insurance, pensions, and many other facilities (cheap and extensive holidays, for 'highly skilled' workers cheap housing, etc.), the living standard of the fully employed working class was certainly much superior to the pre-war one and kept modestly rising until 1980 (Tonković 448 and 453), so that this 'socialist primitive accumulation' was much less cruel than the capitalist one described by Hogarth, Engels, and Marx, which meant for the masses in Britain three centuries of utter misery and alienation.

The attitude of this class toward the politocracy and the government is poorly documented, but it was in great majority clearly not hostile. Findings are scant and contradictory up to the mid-1970s. An inquiry about mobility in 1963 found that 80% was satisfied to be workers and 70% believed they were being respected and valued by society, yet 85% wanted their children to be office workers (cited in Horvat, *Essay* 179). Some years later, a part of the most industrious and skilled workers largely fuelled the outflow to western Europe: the *Gastarbeiter* lived in horrendous circumstances there, but their average monthly wage was 3.5 times as large as at home.

The 1981 census showed that *out of 13 million people* in Yugoslavia aged 19–60, *7 million were in employment* (*radni odnos*) – this comprises in industry manual workers, engineers, technicians, white-collar employees, and managers, and outside of industry the last four professions plus professionals; *1 million* were registered in unemployment bureaus; nearly *1 million* (that number was reached in 1971) were abroad; and a remainder of *4 million* is not fully identified (Woodward, *Socialist* 191–2, 199). Who composed this remainder? As suggested in 3.2.1, these people fallen between the meshes of statistics were, on the one hand, peasant women, full-time housewives, 200,000 unable to work, over 300,000 students, ca. 800,000 urban self-employed, mainly artisans; and on the other hand an unknown number of unregistered, extra-legal workers. They were a seasonal, largely unskilled workforce shifting from job to job, often in short-term construction, who stemmed mainly from the poorer regions south of the Danube-Sava-Kupa divide. These final 'precarious' workers formed, together with the Yugoslav unemployed and the workers employed in western Europe, a heterogeneous sub-proletariat unrecognised by theory or public opinion, which became a permanent threat both to the fully employed workforce and to democracy or socialism in general. Counting the housewives as 'workers' too, we might by then get to over 20% of the 'active' labour population living under super-exploited conditions. This tallies with Šuvar's 20% of the population at the existential minimum.

Finally, all the independent investigators see the worker-bearers of self-management as an atomised class by its objective economico-psychological position, who because of its inexperience, fragmentation by enterprises, lack of trade-union tradition, and other factors did not become 'a class for itself' (Marx, MEW 4:181). Even the strikes, more and more frequent after the 1960s, were almost always caused by income demands and confined to a single enterprise (cf. Jovanov, also Arzenšek 59–82).

3.2.2.3   An Approach to the Ruling Class (Actual or Potential)
It was genuinely unclear for the first post-war decades whether there was in Yugoslavia a ruling class and, if there was, what its composition and nature might be. Both for this reason and because of self-censorship and political prudence, it remained tricky how to name it. The pioneering Branko Horvat – who knew it from experience as a top expert, but whose data go from the 50s to early 60s – began by describing it vaguely as on the one hand the 'State apparatus (bureaucracy)', defined as those relying on physical power, and comprising 'the government administration, the judiciary, the police, armed forces, and professional politicians'; he calculates them in 1953 at 220 and *in 1961 at 257 thousand people* (*Essay* 170–1, 176, and 184). On the other hand, using official statistics, he calls them leading (*rukovodeći*) cadres, comprising in 1961 ca. 60,000 people, half of them having a secondary and half a university education (179–80), while ca. 26,000 more were a kind of middle bureaucracy. A ranking by salary reveals that in 1963 there were 213,000 people receiving over 70 thousand dinars (which however included also top university teachers and some other professionals). A very rough division into a top and a middle *core governing group* might be effected, which in the early 60s, following these

rather fuzzy statistics, might be guessed to comprise respectively 60 and ca. 80 thousand each, though the middle stratum was destined to rapidly expand with the shift of power to the level of federal republics and partly to the local one. There would then remain less than half of Horvat's 257,000 as the lowest or auxiliary 'politocracy'; the three groups together might be called at least a *potential ruling class.*

The 1953 revision of Party statistics from using provenience to using present profession resulted in 45,000 peasants and 93,000 workers being declassified as such (Filipi 762); most probably, a great majority of these 138,000 people comprised – together with a smaller number of 'professional' provenience – my upper plus middle ruling group. A 1960 statistic on the *social origin* of full-time government 'employees', presumably comprising everyone on the salary rolls of the central government (it is reproduced by Horvat only as to percentages), can be simplified into three groups, in good part identifiable by means of education: Workers, Peasants, and 'Other' (meaning here mainly intellectuals, possibly other petty bourgeois such as white-collar employees, and indeed, especially in the middle stratum or class fraction which comprised the top co-opted experts, some bourgeois; 'Lower employees I' were those with secondary education, II with primary education):

TABLE 3.2   *Social origin of federal government 'employees' 1960*

Father's occupation	Peasant	Worker	Other
Leading cadres	36.7	24.9	38.4
Middle employees	27.2	21.7	51.1
Lower employees I	31.9	33.0	35.1
Lower employees II	55.1	29.1	15.8

Horvat's overall hypothesis accords well with the later statistics in SG81: 110, which finds in 'Societal activities [meaning the political organisations] and State organs' in 1965 183,000 people, the number then falling until 1969 and after that rising to 210 for 1974. This number does not comprise the army, exempt from statistics, nor the rapidly rising 'technocracy', of which more below.

The well-informed insider Bakarić (see Appendix 2) had already in the 60s noted the existence of an important and privileged group in positions of federal and local power, though he consistently shied away from identifying it as a

FIGURE 10 *Branko Horvat, age 18+*
REPRODUCED WITH KIND PERMISSION OF THE HORVAT ESTATE

FIGURE 11 *Branko Horvat, drawing in the 1960s*
REPRODUCED WITH KIND PERMISSION OF THE HORVAT ESTATE

class. This etatist enemy of direct democracy was by him *in 1971* identified as roughly *a quarter of a million* active people, including by then the new centres of financial power in banks and other credit institutions – that is, free-floating capital. A couple of years later, he also noted that fractions of this new and ubiquitous class power were not quite yet capitalists but represented capital and were repristinating capitalist relationships (of exploitation), leaning on the international capitalist market. They needed only military and political power to grow into a classical capitalist bourgeoisie (3: 604).

One key predicate for a ruling group is its monopoly of power. The Yugoslav one officially possessed this, including in the final instance the organising of commodity production and in general the reproduction of social life, however this may have reposed on balancing between its interests and the pressures from the manual workers, and however it was later modified into a polyarchy between the federal centre and lower levels. Since the power of deciding reposed on political command not only of the armed forces but also of macro-economic decisions, I would in a first approximation accept Horvat's term of ***politocracy***. This group enjoyed material privileges which were much lower than either Soviet or post-Welfare-State capitalist privileges, yet probably, especially toward the top, much larger than the salaries found in public statistics, since they included free and generous transport, apartments, holidays, and many other perks. The politocracy also had a high, in the first 20 years almost hieratic but from the 1970s on rapidly falling, consensual prestige as leader toward a better future for all. Bilandžić, who was himself a part of it, makes a heartfelt plea for its having in the first post-1945 years sacrificed all of its personal time and energy to collective social interests (*Ideje* 74), and I can testify that was to a large degree true up to, say, the mid-50s. Yet it is equally true, as another inside observer noted, that 'officials in the government, as wielders of power and living in strictly hierarchical social structures, are exposed to fearful conservative and antisocialist pressures' resulting in 'tendencies to deformations in consciousness [and] behaviour' as well as to despotism, as publicly admitted in the secret police infiltrations denounced in 1966 (Horvat, *Essay* 171)

In sum: **was this a class** – which would have major interests of its own not identical with a function necessary for the society as a whole – or was it, as the official Party *doxa* later had it, a stratum? The criteria for deciding what it was are more than usually vague. However, I shall use three: a theoretical one, a deductive one, and an inductive one. The first criterion flows from two observations by Marx: (a) that a class can exist in relation to another class while it still doesn't exist 'in relation to itself', and (b) that the condition for the liberation of the working class is the abolition of all classes (cf. Gurvitch 23 and 22) – which wasn't even beginning to take place in SFRY. The second follows the Marxian method of explaining the hand of the ape by the hand of man by looking backward or 'regressively' (term from Lazić, *Čekajući* 60; cf. Ollman, *Dialectical* 133–79) from the last two decades of SFRY, when I believe it was a class – or in fact several classes: for this can most economically explain the break-up of Yugoslavia. For the third, I use Lazić's most encompassing retrospect based on data from 1984; he devised an 'Index of Overall Society Position', based on location in the social pyramid, material status, education, type of job, and site of residence, which can for the final phase of SFRY – serving for the look backward – be summed up in somewhat modified terms and presented as the following table of 'strata', which to me approximate classes:

TABLE 3.3 Lazić's quasi-class division 1984 (by % of belonging)
SISTEM 81

	Highest	Higher middle	Middle	Lower middle	Low
Politicians	31	63	6		
Managers	5	79	16		
'Experts' & w-cw*		2	78	20	
Workers Sk			1	70	29
Workers Unsk				17	83
Peasants				24	76

* *w-cw* means white-collar workers, *Sk* skilled or highly skilled, *Unsk* lower skilled or unskilled

While one could fault some premises of these findings, conducted within what was possible to envisage in however tolerant an SFRY, the overall picture is indicative of a class system.

Thus the original ruling politocracy – up to, say, the middle of the 1960s – is best called ***a class in statu nascendi (being born)***. It had two horizons and interests: first, beside wielding power it was the collective controller of all major investment funds for social production and reproduction; second, it developed a major interest in its own positions, in a collective State 'capital'. It corresponded to the Weberian category of an elite through its concentrated control over resources indispensable for, and active participation in, the reproduction of a given social structure (freely paraphrased from Lazić, *Čekajući* 43), though I have indicated above how Occam's razor leads me not to use this terminology. As Hobsbawm notes anent the USSR, 'a process of this kind was implicit in the "proletarian revolution", unless systematically counteracted' (30).

One indirect measure of the closure at the top was ***upward social mobility*** in Yugoslavia. It seems to have been very high in the first decade and considerable in the second one, but falling fast after it. For example, in the 1961/62 school year, secondary schooling (from 15–18 years) was undergone by virtually all children of employees, one third of workers' children, and one seventh of peasant children. The chance of a worker youngster to enter university was 1/8th, and of a peasant one 1/13th of the chance of an employee youngster (see Horvat, *Essay* 151 and 237–8). Lazić concluded that by the 70s vertical social mobility was significantly restricted, though some sons of peasants and manual workers could still rise into the 'middle' classes (cf. *U susret* 77–148). From the above Table 3.3 it follows that the ruling class was self-perpetuating, absorbing the highest managers and a few experts.

The class equivalent of these large power shifts was not, as Marxist theory and the original plebeian perspectives demanded, the vertical extension of self-management by the 'working people' up to the federal power-level, but the rise after 1965 of a supposedly 'technocratic' class fraction centred in the republics and constituted by the top enterprise and financial managers. How to evaluate this *'technocracy'*? Its rapid rise to a share in power was based on triangular balancing between the working classes, the Party politocracy – on which it leaned while competing with it – and the world market, reproducing what came openly to be called 'the capital relationship' or even 'financial capital' inside Yugoslavia (see Bilandžić, *Ideje* 295–7 and 300, and Bakarić *passim*). The statistics to be found in Horvat's *Essay* (cf. Table 3.2 above) show for 1972, among 3.4 million employed in production and commerce, *154,000* with 'high professional education' (SG81: 114), though many were in somewhat subordinate positions of engineers or accountants. Horvat characterises the early technocracy through its central figure metonymically as 'managers' – that is, directors of economic enterprises – and observes that their function was, among other things, to represent the interests of society, so that they were co-nominated by local governments; within the self-management system theirs was early on a hybrid role, stressing more the political than the professional status (*Essay* 164). The enterprise directors, at least, participated also in a generational shift: in 1966, of a population of 1,270, one fifth were newly elected and among them almost half were 30–9 years of age (Rusinow 144). Bilandžić's later definition of this technocratic fraction (*menedžeri*) is 'business people from the productive economy, banks, insurance societies', as well as from systems combining several enterprises (*Historija* 411), he dates their swift rise to the 1965 reform, and believes the politocracy in the strict sense began to take second place to them in power and reputation. This meant, I would guess, the transfer of some former 'bureaucrats' to this fraction and their confluence with younger and better schooled newcomers (not only engineers). It was thus a complex rearrangement amid a power struggle within the ruling class. I discuss this in more detail in Chapter 10.4.

If 'bureaucracy' can only be governmental, they might be called technocrats (idem 184). However, after a lengthy consideration I concluded in the Appendices that 'bureaucracy' was finally a wrong term, and to my mind technocracy too was an unfortunate designation taken from Western discourse, and used by this sub-class as 'expert' alibi.

3.2.2.4 Others
'Middle Classes'

This only partly meaningful term is here not used, as in much sociology, as a synonym for the bourgeoisie or the petty bourgeoisie, but for groups in an analogous 'middle' position between manual workers and the ruling class, for which a better term does not seem available. It could be, in inevitable simplification, called *the professionals*, that is to say – in my terminology – non-manual workers who were neither within the politocracy nor directly competing with it (as the 'technocrats' were). It was often metonymically called the intelligentsia as in the French, German or Russian uses of the term, though it was clearly a congeries of various 'professional' or 'expert' (*stručni*) fractions, an existentially and politically somewhat heterogeneous spread united by university graduation (cf. both articles by the Ehrenreichs). It may be useful to divide it at least into three wings: first, the classical humanist intelligentsia, social scientists, and teachers as well as the rather distinct scientific and medical intelligentsia (more easily bought off); second, engineers in production (officially an 'expert' part of workers' self-management); and third, a large wing of white-collar workers ranging from production enterprises to all other administrative labour (differentiated into upper and lower by the divide of university degree). Numerical data are obtainable mainly for the university graduates, 79,000 in 1948, while 220,000 more graduated between 1945 and 1965 (Horvat, *Essay* 184). Thus the professionals were in Yugoslavia, except for the traditional priests and pen-pushers (lower bureaucrats), a creation of socialism. Much work remains to be done on the subdivision, evolution, and relation to power of these 'middle classes'. Their upper reaches, both in industry and outside it, were often officially suspected to be an embryonic 'new class' (that is, bourgeoisie – see Bakarić 2: 8); though their consumerism and ostentation tended to reinforce this view, they mostly remained either subordinates or on the outskirts of the truly rising new class within the politocracy. How are all these fractions to be subdivided is again unclear, though one main indicator would be the level of schooling. Debray proposes for developed capitalist societies a division into a minority of 'organic' mercenaries, the reproductive or distributive intellectuals – the admen and 'design' professionals, the new media clerisy, most lawyers and engineers – vs. a majority of increasingly marginalised humanists and teachers (95 and *passim*): if we only knew how to quantify this (see Suvin 'Where').

The intellectuals were prominent equally in the pre-war Party and in the 1941–5 struggle, during which an estimated forty thousand intellectuals, a high percentage of that small class, were killed (Rusinow 19), mainly fighting with the partizans. They remained prominent in the ruling Party after 1945: as shown above, Party membership in 1948 – the core of the budding politocracy – was by provenience around 20% intellectuals or professionals. Tens of thousands joined the Party in the 'heroic' 1945–52 years, when this did not simply guarantee better career chances but more work and danger. Horvat rightly concluded that the intellectuals were in the first two decades of SFRY 'one of the mainstays of the system' (*Essay* 168); but he also acknowledges that – if we except those who became a part of the politocracy – they were often considered as poor cousins, since Marxist and socialist parties paradoxically had an inbuilt anti-intellectual strain (183). Lineaments of this 'mainstay's' disaffection can be exemplarily and exasperatedly followed in the 'bureaucracy debate' which I have analysed in Appendix 2.

Women
This is an adjunct to class analysis, but to my mind indispensable to and intersecting with it. Before the war, women's position was, except in a very few major cities, one of patriarchal subordination; employed women were mostly unskilled and paid two thirds of the male salary or less. Both at work in the household and out of it, women were often treated abominably. Jancar-Webster's indispensable survey, from which I take much data in this paragraph, shows that between the World Wars women's share of the employed rose from 20 to 28%, with a maximum of around 200,000 (19). The most resolute among the exasperated young women from the working and other classes found their way into SKOJ, the illegal and at the time direly persecuted youth wing of the Party, of whose 30,000 members in early 1941 one third were women (101). The Party programme adopted in 1940 was full material protection of maternity and full legal equality for women, including equal pay for equal work; both were decreed during the 1941–5 war, and a host of associated democratic legal and economic measures followed. 'The official figure for women's participation in the partisan cause is 2 million', of whom over 100,000 were soldiers (25,000 were killed, 40,000 wounded) and 282,000 were killed in the concentration camps of the various fascist governments (46). It is unclear what proportion of the partizan units this represented before the 1944 mass mobilisation, but in some brigades it reached 10–12% (in Montenegro 1943); much larger was the participation without gun in hand, so that in Croatia women NOB participants were estimated at 34% and female war invalids represented 46% (Kovačević et al. 92 and 135). This means that, by tradition, choice or lack of opportunity, two thirds of women stayed on the sidelines, but it nonetheless represented a huge breakthrough, and made of the partizans the first bi-sex army in Balkan history. Of the women fighters, 70% seem to have been under 20 years of age, and as with the men, they were predominantly young peasants (48); during the war,

more than 2,000 women became army officers (Kovačević 25). There is a dearth of articulated statistics for SFRY as a whole, but the female 'active participants' in the partizan cause from the federal republic of Croatia for whom occupation is known are divided thus: 249,000 peasants, 202,000 students, intelligentsia, and 'white collar', 86,000 workers, 91,000 'housewives', plus 217,000 'unknown' (Jancar-Webster 54); I would think most of the last two categories can be allotted to peasants, who would thus account for about half of the women included. As fighters, the *partizanke* (women partizans), though at first often admitted grudgingly, were very capable, tough, determined, and immensely devoted. A huge number of younger women, whether fighters or supporters, were taught literacy and self-confidence; the percentage of illiterate women fell from 56% in 1939 to 22% in 1971.[2]

The Antifascist Front of Women (AFŽ) had a key role in that as well as in aiding the fighters during the wars, so that women were represented in all the local authorities: Tito even called them, at the AFŽ founding congress in 1942, 'the right hand' of the anti-fascist insurrection (Petranović & Zečević eds. 586). He stressed their two tasks as participation in the liberation struggle and in organising a final emancipation of women (Božinović 147). However, tensions between these two were to persist – even among the partizans and in the Party there were deep resistances to women's equality. A full network of AFŽ committees, from local to regional, was during the war given autonomy, but key posts were appointed by the Party as a whole. Women in their hundreds of thousands dearly loved the AFŽ, where they were part of a nascent active sisterhood – not only at consciousness-raising meetings but at work through the various 'actives': for child care and raising, for press reading and writing, for nutrition, for stitching and tailoring ... I have cited Jancar-Webster's characterisation of it as not only 'an original creation' but 'a remarkable expression of political acuity on the part of the (ca. 1944–45) Party leadership', and she is rightly very critical of the Party's turn to AFŽ's subordination from early 1944 on, which culminated in its eventual dissolution in 1953 (122–5; cf. Božinović, Sklevicky, and Stojaković). The ensuing League of Women's Societies – there were about 2,000 of them at all organisational levels – and then as of 1961 the

---

2 The illiteracy percentage is from Tomšič 113. Until this book manuscript was finished in early 2015, I have unfortunately not known of the book by Batinić, by now the standard work supplementing Jancar-Webster, nor of the sources she cites in her note 18 on p. 10, by Mary E. Reed and Barbara Wiesinger, earlier unknown also to all my contacts and informants in ex-Yugoslavia. In view of its importance and the new data, this section is to be considered a rudimentary sketch.

FIGURE 12A&B *Women partizans (ca. 1944–5)*

Conference for Women's Social Activity still did some sterling work, but was eventually left with no power.

Parenthetically, a quite parallel judgment should be made relating to the *youth*, who were together with women overwhelmingly the main demographic force of partizan victory 1941–5, and a pillar of loyalty and potential against the patriarchal tradition immediately after the war (cf. in general Erikson 22–3).

But the obverse of that parallel is the remarkable example of political dullness or blindness conveyed by dissolving the highly active Communist Youth League in 1949 (cf. Schleicher 385–7), even before the AFŽ. Young workers up to age 24 were in the 50s over 30% of all employed, and there was a burgeoning of middle professional schools for apprentices, who however often lived in difficult circumstances. About half the membership of Workers' Councils and Managing Boards in 1956 enterprises were aged 35 or younger (idem 387–94). If there were more data at hand, youth might be an additional category of 'Others'. The always more or less independent Union of Students became strongly New Left in the 60s, with rabid fringes of nationalists in a few republics, and was dissolved in 1971.

After 1945 a full panoply of laws for equality in family and at work was passed (cf. Božinović 152 ff. and Sklevicky): women could divorce, they could abort if 'socio-medically indicated' (Tomšič 142–4, and abortion was further liberalised in the 60s), those officially employed had the same health and social insurances as men, and protection at work was enforced. The high mortality of babies fell constantly toward the European average. However, the material bases for equality, such as kindergartens, came about only in the cities, slowly and partially, and the political role of women fell after the war. The percentage of women in the labour force oscillated and eventually settled in the 1970s on a level of ca. one third, though most of them were, as before the war, in the lower-skilled occupations (Jancar-Webster 164–5), so that women's average income was less than the male average. In 1979 employed women represented ca. 54% of their age cohort – 20 to 55 years, the pensionable age – but again almost half of them were still unskilled (167). They were employed primarily in manufacturing, especially the traditionally low-income textile industry, and then in culture and education, in health and social welfare, and in catering and trade, including the lower clerical occupations. In the village, and to a good part in town too, 'the family remained the locus of production and organizer of labor' (Woodward, 'Rights' 250). Illiteracy among women fell from the prewar heights – reaching peaks of 84% in Bosnia and 94% in Kosovo – to 29% in 1961 (Ramet 95–6). Weighty factors for their position were the 'second shift' of employed mothers, estimated at 30–5 hours per week, and patriarchal attitudes (Woodward, 'Rights' 241–2, 249, and *passim*); as a result, many women were confined to domestic work, while in industrial enterprises women were rarely leaders, and their promotion to the coveted 'highly skilled' category in 1961–71 hit a clear 'glass ceiling' (Novaković 57). In 1979 women were 54% of the official 'job seekers', including 63% of those with secondary or higher education, and in industry they were liable to be laid off first: all these were clear indications of gender bias. In politics, women's membership in the Party stagnated in 1946–66 at between 15.5 and 18%, though, due to the general massification of the Party, it quadrupled in absolute terms, reaching 186,000, of whom 1.5% were peasants, 17% workers, 23% pensioners and housewives, 5% students, and about half from the middle and ruling classes (using my terms – data in Filipi 748, 752, 781; see for women in the Party also Chapter 7.12). In 1970, women comprised 10% of the upper chamber of the Federal Assembly, while in the republican chambers they comprised 3.5–9%, and in the municipality committees 6.7% (Denitch 44–5). At the end of the 70s, women were ca. one third of the delegates from the 'basic organisations of associated labour' (OOUR), but only 12% of the workers' councils and 6% of its managing boards (Jancar-Webster 170), a fall-off in comparison to 1966 when the proportions were ca. 18% and 12.5% (Roggemann 122). On the positive side, by the 70s some 40% of the hugely burgeoning university student population was female, disproportionately concentrated at first in arts and humanities, pharmacology, and social work (Jancar-Webster 168–9), but later also in medicine, 'soft' and natural sciences; the proportion of women in high school (ages 15–18) rose to almost half (Kovačević 28). However, the encroachment of the market economy meant that as of the mid-60s many more women were pulled or pushed out of full-time employment (cf. Woodward, 'Rights' 247–9, and data in *Žena*).

I have to ruefully concur with Jancar-Webster that much of the development from the later 60s on, and indeed earlier, amounts to a reassertion of many patriarchal biases and usages, though there were also several unretractable gains in legal equality, higher education, and employment: certainly the position of women was up to the crash of the 80s better than in the successor States today. However, the Party never allowed public discussions of its members' gender prejudices and of women's power status, and from the 70s on acquiesced in horrendous yellow-press degradation of women. The upshot of the economic and psychological devolution was lack of power and rising political apathy among most Yugoslav women, while a few went their own ways into feminism.

CHAPTER 4

On a Hidden Ruling Class and Central Conflict

'Ex-Yugoslavia' (the term itself is eloquent) ...
ÉTIENNE BALIBAR, 1994

∴

4.1   A Hypothesis: The Involution of the Ruling Class

4.1.0
Here is a compressed summary of the class data found in Chapter 3.2.2 for 1961–71, adjusted for the 1971 total population of 20.5 millions – of which women 10.5 million and under-fifteens 5.5 million – and adding family members. The average household in 1971 had 3.8 members (SG81: 80 and 102), so I had to guess how many family members in each class were 'non-active'. I'm uncomfortably aware that (except for the peasants) in this statistical mess all numerical conclusions are tentative; but they are preferable to nothing, and as relational proportions defensible. It is a pyramid with a broad base and steep slope:

TABLE 4.1   *A class pyramid, 1971*

- Ruling class/es: 0.5 to 0.8 million
- Middle classes (including technicians): 4.5 to 5.5 million
- Peasant smallholders: 7.5 (+ private artisans 0.5) million
- Manual workers (industry, transport, building, services): around 7 million (the 1 million workers abroad were partly from this class and partly from peasantry)
- [*Total population: 20.5 million*]

4.1.1
My approach is Marx's anthropological one: emancipation of all persons through emancipation of humanity from classes (cf. Draper). This means that each class society – which is what SFRY remained, though class antagonisms

were quite muted for the first two decades – should be judged by the criterion of how much it contributes to this emancipation.

A central presupposition for anything else is society's self-preservation. This meant for Tito and the Party, and later for the politocracy (but also for a great majority of the population): independence plus industrial development with rising disposal of material goods. The function of the ruling class being born was to organise strong and permanent drives towards these two horizons. Both of them zigzagged through important difficulties but at the end of the first two post-war decades had met with impressive success. However, as of the 60s harmonious development of the whole economy needed radical democracy through self-government, which did not happen. When the economy faltered, so did all else. I shall return to the reasons for its faltering, which were in my opinion both exogenous (the world capitalist market and big powers) and endogenous.

On what basis should classes be differentiated in historical societies? As discussed in Chapter 3, classes are groups with different positions within the exploitative appropriation of the product of labour or natural resources. Different classes and class fractions had different strategic shares of political power, economic production, and cultural hegemony or legitimacy (cf. Lazić, Čekajući 30), the latter pertaining, I think, mainly to knowledge and prestige. In all class systems, the ruling ideas, norms, and horizons for the whole society are those of the ruling class (usually with pockets of deviation, mainly in the proletarian classes and the intelligentsia). In socialist societies, as in many pre-capitalist ones, the politocracy had a leading role in all three domains. Furthermore,

> It is always the direct relationship of *the owners of the conditions of production* to the direct producers – a relation always naturally corresponding to a definite stage in the development of the methods of labour and thereby its social productivity – which reveals the innermost secret, the hidden basis of the entire social structure and with it the political form of the relation of sovereignty and dependence, in short, the corresponding specific form of the State.
>
> MARX, *Capital* III, /ch47.htm, emphasis DS

I shall begin with a closer theorisation based on this approach and the data in Chapter 3.

Did a ruling class exist in Yugoslavia? There was a group possessing a monopoly of power, control of the conditions of production, material privileges, and a collective consciousness. Further, there was a class of manual workers: since classes are relational entities, *yes, a ruling class existed.* (Neither class was officially recognised, though Party ideologists rinsed their mouths with the working class from the 60s on.)

The denial that there existed a ruling class was, if at all argued, usually argued on the basis it did not *own* but only administered the 'strategic heights' of the economy, as manifested in the fact the members of this 'stratum' could not alienate any part of it, say through personal inheritance (cf. for example Pečujlić, cited in Appendix 2). Even the less monochromatic Šuvar, who boldly talked about a 'counter-class' juxtaposed to the workers, denied there could be an antagonistic opposition because the appropriation of surplus labour was used for 'socially useful work' and thus was not exploitation (cited in Kerševan, 'K vprašanju' 1469–70). As opposed to such prevarications, the 'Marx sequence' of concepts for property (Ritsert 33–7) reposes upon ***appropriation*** of things, goods, and services (though after the industrial revolutions, cognitive entities also grow in importance) effected by classes in power through violence, which entails the exclusion of other classes and lesions – in a wide sense – of its members. The result of these appropriations is exclusive possession (*Besitz*), that is, ways of 'factual disposition over the means of appropriation, respectively the really appropriated shares of products and services by the excluded others' (34; see Hegedüs 94–7). When the appropriation is legally sanctioned, a given form of 'ownership' (*Eigentum*) comes about which is 'exclusive possession, justified by cultural contents and norms', in Weber's term a domination (*Herrschaft*) based on obedience (Ritsert 34). To speak with Hegel, 'possession is the subsumption of a thing under my will' (cited in idem 36). Most pertinent here is that in the Marxian optic 'class relationships are relationships of appropriation' (37) – that is, they are simultaneously relationships of production and of possession (65). Marx explicitly condemned collapsing relationships of production into their legal form; as he put it in the italicised part of the above quote, the crucial point is who decides 'the conditions of production'. In Yugoslavia, it was the ruling class, being born or actual.

Thus, while legal justifications and sanctions are no doubt important, they do not determine the central power relationships inherent in all possession, in whichever ways these be justified; in ancient societies often in religious ways, which partly carried over into feudal ones, and – as I argue in Chapter 6 – in masked ways also into socialist ones. As Trotsky noted in *The Revolution Betrayed* about the USSR of the 1930s, 'The means of production belong to the State. But the State, so to speak, 'belongs' to the bureaucracy' (ch09.htm). In Ritsert's terms, the SFRY ruling class did not individually own any means of production, but it collectively possessed them all (this is also the thesis of Lazić's works), and administering the economy implied considerable economic advantage. However, the politocracy ruled – at least up to the divide of the early 70s – by making not inconsiderable economic concessions to the middle class and manual workers. And as to socially useful application of the surplus labour, the criterion would be: did the direct producers have a significant say in determining what and how much was useful where and how (cf. Kerševan, 'K vprašanju' 1476, Visković in Žuvela et al. eds., 97–104)? On the whole, they did not.

Was there exploitation of the working class – and other working people – in SFR Yugoslavia? In Marx's terms, which envisage a daily dynamic compulsion (*Zwang*) for appropriation of labour's surplus value (MEW 26.2: 409), clearly yes, there was. This is temporally and axiologically prior to and underlying all the ideological and territorial quarrels within the by now polyarchic politocracy about distribution of this surplus. The surplus remained constant at 2:3; that is, ca. two thirds of the surplus labour ended up outside the enterprise – a level identical to those of the Maya statelets, as Bakarić noted (2: 7). Here too, Weberian 'domination' terminology proves insufficient (see Suvin 'Terms').

However, did a ruling class spring full-blown from the 1941–5 revolutionary war? No, it did not. Justice should be done to the complexities of a contradictory revolution, a two-headed Janus bearing simultaneously huge liberations and a threat of counter-revolutionary re-subordination if the revolution did not, after coming to power, permanently continue by other means (I develop this at length in Part 3). I do not believe even that the early nuclei of this class noted by Djilas in 1954 deserve to be called more than a class being born. When did a ruling class fully constitute itself, in Marx's terms as 'a class for itself', that is, with a core of class consciousness arising out of a 'diffuse' one (Gurvitch 103)? Some crucial determinations can be found by historical investigation of the declining cognitive solutions and economic success in Yugoslavia. The turning point for these factors, its original sin so to speak, can be found in the mid-60s as the politocracy's fierce resistance to further experimentation with direct democracy – that could have sprung from, but surely could not coincide with, the limited self-management in the factories and then other workplaces. This indicates that the ruling class's aims at that time became 'raised to a political level', which is the standard Marxian definition of class consciousness (say by Gramsci, or here by Polanyi 183). The period of about 1965–72 would then be one of the lost final battle – or two battles – against this involution, waged by an insufficiently decisive minority at the top, supported by but never really allied with the working class and a part of the middle class (the subterranean battle was theorised by the Praxis group and up to a point by Horvat and Kardelj, see Appendix 2).

This complex field of forces might be illuminated by turning to the very important ideological conundrum of 'class struggle' in the Leninist vulgate.

4.1.2 An Excursus on Classophobia

The Yugoslav politocracy and society lived with three major denials or Freudian repressions: of the peasantry, the women, and the not fully employed workers. The most pertinent ones were 'the women question' (as suggested earlier) and the denial of class.

How can lifelong Marxists deny the existence of classes in a still fairly backward society? I shall take as my *exemplum* the second-ranking person in the Party and State, and its main theoretician, Edvard Kardelj, who did so (he is discussed at greater length in Appendix 2). How and why did he get to this classophobia?

Having read most of his voluminous opus, I shall take as a sufficient example key passages of his 1967 article the title of which translates as 'The Working Class, Bureaucratism, and the LCY'. It is on the one hand, within its peculiar *langue de bois*, remarkably frank and clear – the bureaucracy is a lawful phenomenon when the revolution has shattered the bourgeoisie but the working class is too weak to enforce self-government: 'Therefore, an independent administrative stratum had to come about, politically very strong, which could have an essential influence on the regulation of social relationships and contradictions ... Because of such political power, this stratum can and does come into collision – sometimes a progressive and sometimes a conservative one – with the central mass of the working class or with some of its parts'. On the other hand, he claims this bureaucracy is *not* a class: 'But because of such a position, the bureaucracy in the professional sense [notice the prevarication – DS] does not become such a new class that would be the main obstacle to the social influence of the working class'. And further '[We are not dealing with a struggle of] class against class, because finally the long-range interests of all these strata are the same. Therefore the class struggle is in such circumstances expressed ... primarily as an ideational and political struggle' (all 45–8). I must sadly say that this mishmash of Weber and Lenin without Marx can only be called a refusal to think the matter through, to the end.

Two contextual matters are also implied here. First, an argument was frequently made in other places by Kardelj and other supporters of the system, of whom I mentioned above Šuvar (*Sociološki*, cf. Kerševan, 'K vprašanju' 1476), that there are over-riding social needs – such as independence and development of industry – which must be met, and which in situations of dire stress must take precedence. I believe this is a correct argument, but it comes maybe 15 years too late: no socialist society can be developed if a permanent siege mentality is fostered beyond necessity. This was proved to the hilt by the Stalin experience, and Kardelj was – in one of his favourite terms – 'subjectively' an anti-Stalinist. Second, Kardelj was the highest representative of the wing inside the

Party favourable, within limits, to self-management. But his argument shows, *a fortiori* for most other leaders, that finally the politocracy behaved like all other ruling classes: there can be no fundamentally threatening contradictions in *our* society. In a banal misreading of Hegel, it believed that the real is also the rational and moreover the only possible state. It would have been a better argument, and a step toward seeing reality, to say (like many bourgeois sociologists in capitalism and the fully revisionist Stalin) that classes exist and they can all be friends together. Why not admit that?

It is because we are here at a theoretical dead-end. To a Leninist, calling a group an opposed *class* with which the working class is in conflict means that this group has to be dispossessed by all means at hand (I found this expressly confirmed by Bakarić 2: 486). Yet the theorem that if classes exist, there must automatically and unceasingly be an intense overt and strategically purposeful struggle between them, is Stalinist obfuscation: 'Class *conflict* ... is essentially the fundamental relationship between classes involving exploitation and resistance to it, but not *necessarily* either class consciousness or collective activity in common ...' (Ste. Croix, 'Class' 100; cf. Mills 309–10). That is, the ambiguous term of 'conflict' can be stretched to mean anything between actual insurrectionary fighting and latent opposition or inherent contradiction. Only in a rather wide sense is class conflict all that a class does or suffers insofar as it affects its power in relation to other classes (see Ollman, *Dialectical* 164 and *passim*), so that 'class conflict is the way class relations and classes themselves exist' (Kerševan, 'Razredni' 129). However, the logical obverse to Stalinism, that if there is no intense overt struggle there are no classes, is liberal and social-democratic obfuscation. Both strongly influenced Kardelj's waffling between bureaucracy 'in the professional sense' and in the Leninist sense.

And finally, who were these politically highly important strata or social groups with economic interests opposed to the producers' self-management, alluded to oh-so-circumlocutorily by Kardelj, how many people? We have no clear data, but, based on the indirect statistics mentioned above, I would argue this might have comprised maybe one third of the politocracy, including at least about one half of the middle and just-below-the-top Party cadre, and thus many, if not most, professional politicians. To call them enemies would mean that they should be removed from positions of power. In difficult economic and international circumstances, and without a democratic socialist civil society based in the lower and middle classes and to be nurtured as an ally, such a radical split in the politocracy was too much to envisage even for its (very moderately) 'left' wing, and was therefore transmogrified into 'ideological struggle': an avowal of impotence that solved nothing.

4.2 The Hidden Central Conflict

To understand the political oscillations in SFRY, we have to postulate a permanent – though carefully hidden – clash between the warm and the cold currents in Yugoslav communism (as in all radical movements): that is, between the orientation on plebeian democratic power from below versus the orientation on elite or vanguard domination from above (I theorise this in Chapter 6).

In the brief but brilliant introduction to his *History of the Russian Revolution*, Leon Trotsky posited a 'law of combined development' for the post-revolutionary period in industrially and socio-economically backward countries. It amounted to the constraint of jumping from pre-capitalist or indeed archaically patriarchal economic and technological forms to the most advanced socialist forms. This entailed not only the necessity of accelerated development but also of leapfrogging over some historical phases, and it could only be done by constantly using the key State power. It was accompanied by a deluge of collateral effects, and first of all, in Lewin's words, 'the coexistence and reciprocal maiming between the most advanced forms and the huge queue of vastly backward forms' (14–15): the backward patriarchal, petty-capitalist, and autocratic forms were pulled vertiginously forward, but the advanced socialist forms of equality and fraternity – not to mention liberty – in production and distribution were subject to a similar contamination and pull backwards. Specifically in Yugoslavia, as Dedijer remarked, the 90% of Party cadres which in 1945 came from the peasantry 'left an imprint on the institutions into which they grew ... by manifesting the old tradition that the warrior should enjoy the fruits of his victory, while in such conceptions of rule the personal good was identified with the general ...' (565–66); this peasant generation, newly arrived into the unfamiliar cities to which they had to urgently adapt, often reached for narrow careerist conformism. Today we could add to Lewin that not only was it an open question which pull would be stronger, but also that using the State as a direct administrator of the economy, while needful at the beginning and thus understandable in the most backward Russian 1920s (cf. Suvin 'On the Concept'), would certainly help the backwards pull by entailing a loss of democratic initiative from below, the only force which could, in the difficult economic plus threatening political situation of the world, make for the revolution's success.

This issues into the question of what is ***the central conflict*** in a State ruled by a communist Party of the Leninist type. It must of course keep in mind the undying enmity of the world capitalists and their barely restrained eagerness for the rollback of revolution and seizure of its riches, and is thus forced to keep the State's ideological and material defences honed. However, after the first few years the principal conflict obtains not between internal 'capitalist remnants' or émigrés and the revolution but between forces internal to the original revolutionary seizure of power – *the budding oligarchy*, always in favour of dictatorship from above, *vs. the budding self-government of the masses*. The oligarchy was formed by the 'institutional separation of the function of supervision, command, control, and management from other functions' (Hirszowicz 90) and had dual interests, representing the State and/or society as a whole and itself as a ruling class, while the plebeian classes rightly felt that communism should be a step by step democratic disalienation in the workplace and in political life. If the Party oligarchy wins, an impasse and stasis results which sooner or later leads to ideological and economic collapse.

The founding two singularities and the ensuing history of SFRY were in my view imbued with and determined by such a central tension between the impulse of the emancipatory plebeian revolution, begun in the partizan liberation struggle, and the impulse developing after 1945 in the Party/State core to turn its essential and successful initial function of centralised leadership into the permanent class status of an oligarchic politocracy. Insofar as this succeeded, Yugoslavia tended towards the Soviet type of 'really existing socialism', where 'exploitation flows ... from the full dependence of the work-force from the totalised right by the State to dispose of the means and conditions of work ...' (Golubović, 'Novije' 83). Such societal systems strangely resemble Hegel's constellation (§ 201 ff.) of three classes, a substantial peasant one, the 'business class' of workers and merchants, and, on top, the 'universal' class dealing with general interests which must be financed either by the State or by private wealth. And as the cold current came to dominate toward the end of the 1960s, a *third singularity* came to the fore: the full inversion, around the pivot of the 1960s, from going toward to going away from socialist justice and communist emancipation as well as from economic well-being. To anticipate a detailed argument in Part 3: this can only be explained in terms of a conflict of class interests between the growing oligarchy and self-government of the people. Slowly but surely, the oligarchy turned from an alliance, however tacit and dictatorial, with the working class and the intellectuals to their marginalisation; since the fulcrum of this alliance was self-management, its ghettoisation ensued. From the breakdown of the progressive alliance there follow the lack of imagination and the reintroduction of 'firm hand' repressive policies, together with the catastrophic slump in all economic indicators, including a yawning gap between republics, and the barbarisation of impoverished human relationships. Its tell-tale manifestations were the huge rise of credit capital and unemployment.

The plebeian classes – peasants, workers, and much intelligentsia – being neutralised and rendered powerless, a *secondary but eventually dominant conflict* came to the fore: the unbelievable rise of regional oligarchies, which became nationalist and chauvinist as against the federal power top; their veto power led to its increasing powerlessness and to impasse. The once revolutionary Party partly ate its children (the repressed 1968 students), but mostly turned them into monsters. As in nineteenth-century Germany, this made for political impotence and intellectual *misère*; as in eighteenth-century Poland, the State was bound to be carved up as soon as its enemies stopped cancelling each other out. Together with the fostering of runaway consumerism as an alternative to democracy from below, this resulted in a resurgence of nationalist middle classes in various republics, increased foreign leverage, and finally indeed in the *tertium gaudet** victory of capitalism. The internecine struggle between the ruling class's disoriented factions began evolving toward a comprador bourgeoisie waiting for the best Western bidder.

CHAPTER 5

What Has Been and What Could Have Been

> Here I need to pour out my heart: you need to hear the truth.
> The counter-revolution is in the management of the finances.
> We shall perish because we did not want to seize the moment marked in the history of humans to found liberty.
>
> ROBESPIERRE, fragments from the last speech before the Convent, 8th Thermidor Year II (26/7/1794)

∴

5.1   Theorising the Macro-Events

5.1.0   On Method

The reflections of this book should not be looked at as a sufficiently thick presentation of SFRY development, a matter so formidably complex and protean it would require a fat tome. I suggested in the Foreword that I would like it to be a methodologically oriented first introduction to the study of some key groups of facts (*facta*, inexorably co-created by the student) and to making sense of the whole. I am faced – to wax rather immodest, but all comparisons to inspiring ancestors are needs such – with the same problem Marx had in *Das Kapital*: how to simultaneously articulate a new continent and evaluate it. He has for a long time been roundly condemned for it by one (rationalist) school of thought. But I have this defence for his, and my, ensuing twists and turns: the matter demanded it.

I have to face a further (huge) complication: socialist or communist revolutions against capital have in their first historical round, identifiable with Hobsbawm's 'short twentieth century', failed. There were heaven-storming hopes, even great and memorable successes, but the revolutions finally did not overcome the formidable internal and external obstacles of capital. Thus there is no vigorously thriving progeny, with historically palpable power, to claim Marx as a Great Ancestor, though he remains quite indispensable, and I write in his wake. Putting my cards on the table, I consider integral self-government from below in all human affairs our only hope to oppose the barbarously violent neo-fascist turn of capitalism in which we are presently living. I have approached this thoroughly radical democracy or democratic communism in essays about utopianism and political epistemology (collected in *Defined, Darko*, and *In Leviathan's*) and can only marginally suggest its theory in this book, but I hope it will be mostly self-explanatory. The positive and negative lessons of Yugoslav development, centring on self-management, are indispensable for working out lineaments of such self-government.

Obviously, in such cases the continent is in a way not unknown: many people have sketched in preliminary mappings, sometimes very useful, but an outline of its coastline and significance isn't yet understood: *bekannt* yet not *erkannt* (Hegel). Marx himself did a thorough review and judgment of his predecessors, whom he read with immense zeal and persistence. However, I have been working on this subject for only four years as opposed to his forty, and at that outside ex-Yugoslavia, so I cannot pretend to have exhausted or superseded my predecessors anywhere near to the same degree. My defence is my mortality – I am at the end of my life and must hurry as much as decently allowable in an intellectual endeavour, knowing full well that I too shall at the end leave a torso. Finally, Marx to my mind succeeded in explaining the central significance of his continent, while I would be happy if I managed to suggest some central ways how to go on explaining the significance of mine, having perhaps formulated some inroads on which further research is to be done by others. My ambition is simultaneously huge and modest.

I have therefore adopted a form which allows for different ways to delve into my matter, but all bear in mind concrete social alienations opposed to simultaneous potentialities of disalienation. I believe verbal indicatives are indispensable but insufficient unless faced with at least some suggestions of inherent alternative possibilities as optative conjunctives of desire. There is no critical stance to social history without the foil of utopia as *eutopia*, the good place (see Suvin *Defined*; I say more about it toward the end of the book) – and at that what Bloch calls 'concrete' utopia, in constant feedback with reality, not a legitimation myth of imaginary achievement. Success has meaning only as opposed to failure and degradation to advancement.

And briefly, are in an overview of Yugoslavia and the plebeian strivings for self-government such hypothetical questions epistemologically allowable? Once and for all, I believe they are when a prevailing social form has come into open contradiction with its potential horizon or 'demands of its own contents', so that it 'can be successfully attacked by thought' (Marcuse on Hegel, *Reason* 51, and see 130–9). I shall expand upon this in my Conclusion.

5.1.1 *Three Horizons*

Any stock-taking inevitably contains a yardstick and stance, implicit in choosing and organising the factual data and descriptions and leading to their critical interpretation. I have occasionally, where the argument demanded, briefly explicated or at least suggested my stance and criteria. I shall here, and later, attempt to explore the depth events – what Brecht called the events behind the events – in socialist Yugoslavia. I argue that the ruling class's counter-offensive against associational democracy based on self-management develops after 1968 into political disorientation, papered over by a feverish proliferation of measures and laws, and institutes elements of vigorously developing capitalist relationships. Such judgements hinge, dialectically, on what were the alternatives. For if there were none, one could assume the politocracy was doing the best of a bad job; since that had to end as it did, in the downfall and destruction of both socialism and Yugoslavia, it would follow that this State and society experiment was doomed from the word go. Having lived through the glorious years of the Yugoslav socialist wager, and then reflected upon its later decay from afar, more intensely after 1989, I refuse to believe it. To my mind there were three possible, theoretically exclusive horizons: Stalinism, capitalism, and communist associative democracy.

The years from 1948 on were marked by the rejection of the first one, a *Soviet-style police State* with totally centralised detail planning, as intrinsically abhorrent, wastefully inefficient, and achievable only by full submission to Stalin.

The second horizon might just as well be called by that dubious name, *market socialism* (as opposed to firm socialist planning using the market). It was rendered ever more urgent by what was in my judgement a necessary opening to the capitalist market and therefore to a confrontation with its evolving ideologies. I cannot pass in review the many improvisations beginning in the 60s, the logical horizon of which was a kind of co-operative plus State capitalism – in the Yugoslav case, a confederation of major republican State capitalisms – but I shall use some of the most important ones as clarifying examples. I do not see to what else could this horizon, which jettisoned the communist project morally and materially, lead but what historically happened, a potential division into comprador bourgeoisies and mafias actualised as soon as the Cold War confrontation was definitely dissolved.

This alternative could be urged as the only possibility to avoid the police State only insofar as it was wilfully denied and occulted that there existed an already partially mobilised and quite well functioning sketch of a third, properly plebeian socialist horizon. This third possibility was a *fully associational democracy*, consciously assuming the conflict between the old (capitalism and patriarchal power) and the new (democratic communism) as its orientation.

This would have meant both accepting the consumer market as a reckoning device, that is, in a rather prudent and hedged about way, and denying the capitalist law of value in key sectors affecting the people's well-being in favour of a supple planning.

I do not propose to focus on the (real enough) tensions between various territorial wings of the politocracy but on the underlying macro-decision between 'market socialism' and associational democracy. The economic politics or politicised economy crucially meshed with failures of imagination: economic events were most intimately interwoven, or in feedback, with the epistemological horizons. Later on, I shall examine how this meshed with the tension between Party monolithism and a development of integral plebeian rule.

5.1.2   Periodisation of SFRY

I have suggested earlier the reasons for stopping at ca. 1972 as the last moment the vector of degeneration might perhaps still have been inverted. For a crucial example, after this date self-management was perhaps still helping thousands of workers and other people but it was a devolving caricature of the original idea, so that investigating its sorry course would yield abruptly diminishing cognitive returns. I also neglect the regional nationalisms which were gathering force but not decisive before my cut-off date, and in general particular political events, even important ones (as in 1968 and 1971), where they are not immediately pertinent to my purpose.

My historical hypothesis for Yugoslav political phases – I propose to factor in economics and surplus labour later – is then:

(1) *Upward development*
   – ca. 1945–52: swift post-war reconstruction and consolidation, centralist fusion of Party and State, command economy from top down.
   – ca. 1952–61: introduction of limited self-management, monolithic unity of Party and State continues, high economic growth.
(2) *Plateau stall*
   – ca. 1961–65/66: growth of self-management and a small critical public sphere but also counter-offensive of the conservative majority of politocracy, by the end of this period a self-conscious ruling class centred to a large part in the republics, against a wavering federal centre.
   – ca. 1966–72: the lukewarm battle for direct democracy through extension of self-management to the power top is being lost; the ruling monolith has fragmented into a polyarchy of republican power-centres, which with the turn to a not systematically contained profit principle mostly slide into nationalism; beginning of significant economic decline.

(3) *Downward slide*
   – post-1972: stagnation and ad-hoccery, sharp economic decline. This Brezhnevism could be perhaps divided by Tito's death, that is: up to 1980, stronger role of politocracy as a confederal polyarchy; after 1980, crisis and weakening in all respects.

This periodisation tallies with world history after 1945 insofar as the major break occurs in the early 70s. Signalled by the oil crises, it was characterised by the exhaustion of the propelling impulses arising out of victory against fascism: the militarised Welfare State, the separation of the 'Soviet bloc' into a fenced-in subsystem of centralised State planning, decolonisation and the Non-aligned movement, as well as depth tectonic movements from Fordism to Post-Fordism and to a return in force of private corporation capitalism. I shall return to what this means for Yugoslavia when discussing self-management in Chapter 8.

The ups and downs of the SFRY experiments will be treated in more detail later. Let me here stress two points. First, though the upward phase did not lead to worker control of enterprises or a genuine democracy from below, it did generate much input by workers and intellectuals and much civic enthusiasm, reflected in the remarkable economic success 1950–60, with a levelling off in the 60s. Second, such plebeian self-management threatened members of the new ruling class. The oligarchy that had monstrously supplanted the anti-imperialist revolution clung in the USSR to a full monopoly of economic and political power, which was in its ideal form of full Stalinism at a greater class remove from the rest of society than the bourgeoisie of the Welfare State. In SFRY, while allowing significant but finally minor compromises, it refused a direct democracy from the basis to the top of power, and regrouped from the end of the 60s on as partly a financial 'technocracy' and partly as three major and three or four minor ruling groups in the constituent republics, introducing a lot of waste and a slide towards nationalism.

5.2   What Might/Ought to Have Been and Was Not

5.2.0   *Introduction*
The diverging class interests of the split oligarchy fractions grew increasingly at odds with the major premise of socialist Yugoslavia: **unity**, based on amity between the constituent republics, ***and independence***, based on growth of both ***production*** (and pro capita productivity) ***and living standards***. Was 'the chance of the alternative' (Marcuse, *One-Dimensional* 301 ff.) possible?

I hold that at least until the mid-70s, before world economics started influencing heavily the inner events, an opposed economic and social model clearly was feasible. I shall in this sub-section present two arguments for it. First, Kidrič's astoundingly radical horizon in 1949–53 deserves to be analysed at some length. After this, attempts in his wake by Horvat and others will be briefly mentioned (I refer to general political perspectives of that kind by Horvat and the Praxis group in my Appendix 2).

5.2.1   The Economico-Political Prospects of Boris Kidrič

> O violet-curled Muses, give me the best truth, the Unforgetting.
>
> SIMONIDES, *Elegy for the Battle of Platea*, ca. 470 BCE

⁂

I wish to draw out here the significance of Boris Kidrič's approach to political economy and a radical democratic perspective for the incipient socialism in Yugoslavia.[1] It was in a way decisive for the creation of the SFRY as well as for its aporias – which also means for our glance at the horizons of that society, and what we can learn from them today. I start from the axiom that any intelligently argued emancipatory alternative is worth careful consideration, and especially indispensable today, in the age of a savage and misanthropic capitalism. Thus I am not here dwelling on objections one could today have to some of Kidrič's terms or notions, but on his horizons and argumentation. His second major and most significant field of activity, the organisation and implementation of the

---

1   See further Suvin 'Death'; also, in this book Chapter 6, Appendix 2, as well as longer discussions of notions such as 'the working people'.

I have not been able to check the Slovene edition of Kidrič's essays and so do not know whether the Serbo-Croatian or the Slovene variant was the 'original'. Unless otherwise indicated, citations in section 5.2.1 are by number of page in Kidrič's *Socijalizam* (1979).

Perhaps a brief biographical note might be of use: Following his crucial role in the antifascist struggle in Slovenia between 1941 and 1945, Kidrič was between 1945 and 1946 the first Prime Minister of a self-governing Slovenian Republic within federal Yugoslavia. After 1946, he was called to Belgrade as the chief responsible for the creation of SFRY economics, and became a member of the CPY Politburo in 1948. At his death, Djilas rightly called him 'the most daring mind of our revolution'.

People's Liberation struggle and revolution in Slovenia by means of founding and leading the Liberation Front, shall remain wholly outside my purview. Therefore this first approach to a largely forgotten figure does not pretend to a rounded off conclusion about the significance of the revolutionary and statesman Kidrič.

5.2.1.1   The Plan
I shall begin by focussing on Kidrič's 'Theses on the Economy of the Transitional Period in Our Country' ('Teze o ekonomici prelaznog perioda u našoj zemlji'), which appeared at the beginning of 1951. It can be inferred that the text was written at the end of 1950 as a *summa* of Kidrič's experiences as the leading official in charge of economic policy in the Party and the government of Yugoslavia from the beginning of 1948. That period was one of a sudden turn from State to self-managing socialism, and he was one of the main champions of this turn.[2] The 'Theses' constituted a theoretical self-understanding for Kidrič – and most probably for a crucial portion of top members of the Communist Party of Yugoslavia and the overlapping State leadership – and provided a basis for significant action.

The essay consists of four parts, each part having five to eleven theses. Bearing in mind the length of single theses, which – particularly in the first part – encompass two or three printed pages or 1000 words each, we would today probably call his work rather a tractate, in the wondrous Arabic and Jewish tradition reactualised by Spinoza and more recent writers. The name of the genre is of course not essential, but one can feel in this text an oscillation between the tradition of brief theses and of an article. A second general characteristic and permanent method of Kidrič's writing is a fusion of scientific argumentation,

---

2   At the time of Kidrič's first works on economics in 1946–7, on pp. 1–54 of his *Socijalizam* book, the only and unavoidable set of sources for ideas on 'building socialism' was an application of the Soviet model (see on this Stalinist context Bilandžić 95–131). The official theory of Soviet practice (after Lenin) held not only that the State plan determines prices, salaries, and quantities of produced goods; it also implied that politics can more or less fully determine economics. Under Stalin this – never argued – voluntarism was equated with the abolition of commodities and all possible exploitation. The only exception on the left to such theorising was Oskar Lange's *On the Economic Theory of Socialism* in 1938 (which Kidrič may not have known). Very early on, Kidrič began modifying the Stalinist traditions; nonetheless in the speech at the Fifth Congress of CPY in 1948 he still claimed that 'there is no surplus value in the socialist sector [the State-run enterprises]' (*O izgradnji* 24). His works from that period are of interest because they point not only to key issues in the social history of the SFRY and USSR – and beyond – but also to the gigantic turn in Kidrič's stance which he swiftly and radically effected in 1948–9.

radical democratic communist horizons, and orientation towards immediate applicability. I shall limit myself here to a discussion of the first part, which is of fundamental theoretical importance; the other three parts are 'Planning', 'Prices', and 'Money'. The first part is untitled but we might call it 'General and Basic Considerations'. I shall here follow the order of his theses, while at times using some of Kidrič's later work.

The first brief thesis begins with the definition of 'a socialist enterprise' (*poduzeće*), an entity that acts 'within the socialist commodity exchange ... as an economic and legal individual under the legal regulations of the State of the working people (the dictatorship of the proletariat). These regulations ought to correspond to objective economic laws ...' (79) The single *enterprise* is here both an empirical and an axiomatic agent, 'a fictive person' refunctioned from bourgeois legal jargon into the basic cell of socialist production. It is important as the nodal point for action, yet it acts only within a definite and defined frame or field of force in the polity. Already this first step is a decisive notional breakthrough, because it proceeds inductively from the working collective – that is, from below upwards – as opposed to the Soviet way of proceeding from the State apparatus of titanic central ministries and their branchings downwards. In other words, for Kidrič the socialist enterprise is no longer an object of State administration and State acquisition of accumulation from surplus work, which in the USSR took the place of profit. On the contrary, the enterprise is the *subject* of creating income for the whole society; within that income the largest part will still be 'accumulation' withdrawn by the State for planned distribution. The accumulation itself is not determined *a priori* but to a large part *a posteriori*: it depends on the success of the enterprise's work and is defined by a prescribed percentage of State withdrawals. The enterprise's success thus does not increase the percentage but only the total size of the accumulation withdrawn (cf. Lipovec 269–70). This represents an axiomatic or fundamental stance of orientation towards the popular initiative from below – as in the wartime Liberation Struggle – as against the Stalin-type command system of monocracy from above (*odinonachalie*). Kidrič situates Yugoslavia within the horizon of *plebeian creativity* as an alternative to the horizon of *command power* (Gramsci would have called this a hegemony based on consensus rather than on naked coercion).

The field of social forces within which the enterprises' self-initiative operates is 'socialist commodity exchange', discussed in Theses 1.2 to 1.6. It proceeds as regulated by a State that Kidrič has no qualms in calling a 'dictatorship of the proletariat'. This was rather unusual among the CPY leadership of the time, as the term was backgrounded in the Popular Front strategy before, during, and after the war. It testifies to Kidrič's deeper understanding both of Lenin and of the history of Soviet struggles after Lenin's death, within which Stalinism arose. This strategy indicates that he was striving for a democratic communism led by a conscious vanguard, and not at all for a 'market socialism'. His socialist commodity exchange flows out of 'objective economic laws' and is seen as the best realistically available variant of material life in 'the State of the working people' as defined in postwar Yugoslav practice and theory. Socialist exchange is opposed, as Kidrič constantly stresses, not only to capitalist commodity exchange but also to Soviet-type totalised administrative planning which pretended to do away with commodity and value. However, that practice has shown that the liquidation of commodity exchange led not only to violent oppression and exploitation of the working people, but also to poor results in production: to shortages of goods, their abysmal quality and limited variety, etc. (80–1). The USSR example shows that 'State socialism', while necessary immediately after the revolution, necessarily grows into 'the strengthening of a privileged bureaucracy as a social parasite, the throttling ... of socialist democracy, and a general degeneration of the whole system', so that there comes about 'a restoration of a specific kind ... a vulgar State-capitalist monopoly' (84).[3] In other places, as in Kidrič's long article 'On the Drafts of the New Economic Laws' ('O nacrtima novih ekonomskih zakona', 116–42), he explicitly stressed that the Yugoslav experience in the years 1945 to 1950 was of the same type: it was then still necessary 'to throttle the law of supply and demand as well as the law of value'. It is clear now that these laws, though being 'an avowed remnant of the past', must necessarily operate, albeit within the limits of social planning, on the 'present-day level of material productive forces, which is relatively still very low' (124).

At the same time Kidrič manages dialectics well and does not shy away from the inner *contradictions* of his system.[4] Both 'the socialist enterprise' and 'the commodity' represent, on the one hand, social property as against private property, first as 'socialist State property, and then increasingly as all-people's property managed by freely associated direct producers, only under [general] control and protection of the State' (80). On the other hand, within

---

3   I shall not deal here with the vast, and to my mind inconclusive, theoretical debate on the real economic character of the USSR after the victory of Stalinism. It suffices here that Kidrič correctly identified both the economic and political consequence of the Stalinist system.

4   Kidrič's stress on the central role of contradictions within socialist development precedes by seven years Mao Zedong's speech on 'contradictions within the people'; to my mind, Kidrič's treatment is deeper though rather less systematic. Mao's two articles on practice and on contradiction from 1937 were at the time unknown in Europe.

this large novelty there exist four 'elements of the past' (or 'remnants of capitalism', 82): 'commodity exchange as such'; the 'socialist enterprise as an economic and legal individual'; 'economic measures of a State-capitalist character in the socialist sector' (which he however holds to be transitory and optimistically believes are on the whole subsiding); and 'the appearance of the socialist State and its enterprises on the world market' (80–2). It should also be stressed that he clearly characterised the accumulation taken (taxed away) by the State as the 'alienated' part of the surplus labour, and defended it as unavoidable at a time of primitive accumulation. Still, here as well as later, Kidrič stresses that 'The law of value and commodity production still bear within themselves the danger of some tendencies towards restoration' (113). Kidrič meant here primarily a restoration of capitalist relationships, but he was quite clear in his own thought, and made quite clear to his readers and in his policies, that dangers could also nestle in the federal administration and that of the constituent Yugoslav republics. This understanding and contemning of 'restoration' was later accompanied by the harshest attacks on Stalinian 'bureaucratic counter-revolution, which anti-dialectically denies that within the socialist sector itself … there necessarily exist contradictions and a struggle between the objective … elements of the capitalist past and the communist future' (128). He even postulated that 'the economic and social role of the Soviet bureaucratic caste was quite similar to the role of the capitalist class' – if the role played by the USSR rulers was not worse (230). So radical a position was rare in Yugoslavia, and it was totally forgotten after the leaders of CPY were reconciled with Khrushchev in 1955.

His conclusion from the first five theses in Part 1 is that '*Socialist commodity exchange is … a dialectical contradiction valid for a given time in the transitional period between capitalism and communism*'. And further: 'It appears as the basic inner contradiction of the whole social economy … It certainly gives rise to contrary interests but does not necessarily lead to class antagonism' (82–3).

Thesis 1.6 then discusses the character of an 'economic association' of enterprises that represents a 'higher association of the producers' and comes about by transferring certain rights of the enterprise to the association's 'planning and operative administration'. And Thesis 1.7 proposes, very radically, that the State can immediately begin a transfer of certain planning and operative rights to the enterprises through such 'higher associations'. In Thesis 1.8 this is articulated, in what Bloch would call a perspective of concrete utopia, as the possibility that such an association 'covering an entire economic branch in the whole of Yugoslavia' could be run by a superordinated or highest workers' council elected by the lower councils of the local 'higher associations'. This highest council of the whole branch 'would consist of workers from the enterprises; the only payment would be given to its chairperson with a small apparatus of two to six people ...' – presumably specialists hired for planning and coordination purposes. Each full or highest branch association and its council would, on the one hand, be subject to the general rules of the State organs nominated by the Federal Assembly, and on the other hand, the branch association would have the right and the duty to participate in the 'federal councils for individual economic branches [the equivalent of ministries – DS]' (87). In a later article, Kidrič defends this hierarchy of plebeian democratic authorities by citing at great length the measures, documents, and rules of the Paris Commune of 1871 (148–52).

As far as planning is concerned, the 'Theses' insist at length on the necessity of only basic planning on the federal level, that is, the determination of some key economic proportions for distributing resources among branches and regions, while micro-planning is left to the enterprises and their higher associations on the basis of market supply and demand. Kidrič broaches here the whole problem of 'market socialism' which was to become dominant in the 1960s and later – unfortunately bereft of his careful framing within a plebeian and planned horizon. He insisted, however, that even the basic planning ought to be speedily de-etatised, so that the branch associations and their articulated organs 'gradually grow from purely State organs into mixed ones with the participation of direct representatives of associated producers' (90). In a lecture from 1951, he foresaw that the State – the federal government – would then immediately leave 50–70% of investments to the planning by direct producers and their associations (104): the same percentage was aimed at by the apparently sincere but lukewarm proponents of the 1965 socio-economic reform (such as Kardelj and Bakarić).[5]

The macro-economic independence of enterprises was accompanied by a second permanent novelty that characterised the history of socialist Yugosla-

---

5 It should be added that in 1946 Kidrič formulated, as one of his first orientations in his capacity as head of the Federal Planning Commission, a highly interesting ideal communist model for the dynamics of republican economic development, having as its presupposition an equalisation of per capita income in the future. It foresees that when the average income will in year N (its number is not specified) be tenfold as compared with the present base level, then the per capita income of all republics will be equal; this would mean that the income of Slovenia would grow 6.75 times, Croatia 9.5 times, Bosnia 13.25 times, and Kosovo 18.75 times (adduced in Hamilton 138–9, who cites *Ekonomist* no. 3–4 [1963]: 608–9). As I debate at length in this book, such a truly revolutionary horizon was sadly and foolishly forgotten after Kidrič's death.

via, the micro-economic *division of salaries* into a fixed component – that is, the mandatory part which corresponds to a minimum use of productive capacities – and a variable component, proportional to the rise of labour productivity, up to a federally prescribed maximum (by percentage of salary, 105). Within such given parameters, salaries are not fixed by State regulations but set by the enterprise itself – through the workers' councils system Kidrič was just introducing – as a function of their sales, where the prices are again (within given limits and regulations) determined by each enterprise. This new way of operating led at the beginning of the 1950s to an exceptionally high rise of production and productivity, while competition among enterprises led also to lower prices. However, this could be managed only by technologically better equipped enterprises, which led to a quest for better technologies; to this end, Kidrič introduced a new 'Law on Inventions and Technical Perfecting' (cf. Puharič), a policy that ingloriously perished in the 60s in favour of uncontrolled import of foreign licences.

Within the enterprises tensions lessened between the director, nominated by the municipality, and the workers, since the management and the workforce had more interests in common. Historically speaking, the division of income into a fixed and a variable component was potentially a step towards abolishing the exploitative wage relationship. In fiscal terms, Kidrič's system meant passing from direct (that is, administrative) financing by the State to lending, to a system of credits. All of these actions opened the door to additional processes and further contradictions that characterised the Yugoslav economy from that time on.

In his Theses and policies, Kidrič envisaged a synergy of two processes. The first one, thoroughly discussed in his Part 2, is to continue the centralised planning of certain basic proportions, starting from the necessity of 'a single centralised plan' for the country (91), but a de-etatised or democratised one (a detailed project is in Thesis 2.11). The second process is to use within such a centralised plan the good aspects of the market which possesses, within limits, the capacity of automatic adjustment between supply and demand, that is, of correcting the planning errors. Should the overall plan not be fulfilled, 'be it because of newly arisen conditions, or because of a low degree of consciousness in the working collective, or because of still slack socialist relationships', the central administration might introduce supplementary planning instruments. However, their 'every detail shall have to be minutely justified', with a right of appeal by the direct producers to be adjudicated by mixed panels of the two parties, the panels being required to consider both the appeal and the mandatory justifications by central administrators of their supplementary instructions (106). The mixed top councils with a strong participation by the direct producers and all such attendant proceedings were never instituted; instead, the economic instruments, proportions, and regulations were arrived at without public participation, by means of behind-the-scenes struggles between the federal and the republican authorities.[6]

The conclusion of Kidrič's first part in Thesis 1.9 clearly sums up his main thrust:

> It is necessary to introduce as soon as possible workers' councils in each economic branch for the whole of Yugoslavia ... Without introducing at the same time a centralised and a democratic association of working collectives, that is, of the direct producers, the decentralisation of operative management away from the State does not lead forward but leads inexorably back to State capitalism – in fact, to several State capitalisms [in the republics] which would be particularistic in relation to the whole [of Yugoslavia] and bureaucratic-cum-centralist towards below, in relation to the working collectives.
> 88

A few months later, this was supplemented by the general statement that the discussion of the economic system deals with the basic question 'of exploitation of man by man in ... the system born of the socialist revolution, that is ... who disposes of the surplus labour – and behind these questions sooner or later the even more fateful one arises of who in fact appropriates the surplus labour' (122).

Beside using a kind of bridled law of value, an initial development of 'socialist social relationships needs', Kidrič insisted, 'two further measures'. First, all levels of the SFRY had to respect and adopt 'at least some elements of management by the direct producers of the basic productive means', and second, the society had to intimately incorporate 'at least some elements of socialist democracy in the content and character of power' (128–9 – I speak further to his political

---

6   The early historian of SFRY Bilandžić allows that Kidrič took an important step by using 'the socialist enterprise' as the keystone of his economic theses (instead of a small cog in the centralised machinery), but faults him for insisting on firm planning proportions that limit the enterprise's independence (172–3). However, economics is based on interdependence, and the end result of the jettisoning of federal regulations (which Kidrič wanted to be decided by panels where representatives of citizens meet with representatives of workers' councils) has been demonstrated by the ensuing chaos in SFRY history. Bilandžić was a member of a republican oligarchy, so that for him any federal organisation or rule is automatically reactionary; this is dead wrong.

FIGURE 13

Boris Kidrič (liberated territory of Kočevski Rog, Spring 1944)
IMAGE IN THE PUBLIC DOMAIN, REPRODUCED FROM HTTP://WWW.WIKIWAND.COM/SH/BORIS_KIDRI%C4%8D

and class stance in Appendix 2). Kidrič also identifies as the most dangerous enemy of socialism the important category of ***monopolism***, strongly denying that it is identical with a planned economy but educing it from 'a blind empiricist adoption of Soviet practice', and even deeper from 'monopoly capitalism ... brought to a peak in Soviet bureaucratic centralism' (70; on monopolism – especially as exercised by the banks! – cf. 229). Socialist democracy is for Kidrič 'most deeply connected with ... the process of abolishing monopolies' (200–1). I assume the category of monopoly was borrowed from Lenin's *Imperialism*, where it plays a major role not only as the hallmark of that phase of capitalism but especially as a source of blockage and decay in economy. 'The socialist democratic rights of the direct producers' cannot at all be reduced to territorial self-government (Kidrič 201); for them 'basic is – the right of the working masses to self-management at all levels of socialist State power' (221–2). It might be remarked that integral dismantling of monopolies, in particular, cries out for further development, but Kidrič was not granted time for it.

'To have conceived the idea of workers' management and to have sketched in its realisation amid an acute economic and political crisis is an act of intellectual courage worth noticing', concluded Bobrowski's excellent early overview (121). Further, these propositions by Kidrič were deeply prophetic for the future and fate of SFR Yugoslavia. The disposition of surplus labour was clearly the central social and political problem for the development of workers' self-management, and indirectly for socialist democracy from below. I do not see how, even today, both the rise of republican State capitalisms and the need for a strong interaction between self-government in production and in civil society could be formulated more clearly and pithily. Thus, the failure to adopt Kidrič's bedrock principles of democratic socialism and a corresponding planning led by steps to decentralisation without democratic association of working collectives, 'several State capitalisms' in the republican mini-fiefs, economic failure, and finally to the dissolution of Yugoslavia and the horrors of the Yugoslav Secession Wars.

5.2.1.2   The Lessons

After Kidrič's death, his approach to planning and in general to the economic system was forsaken. It was in force from September 1951 to 1954, less than three years. In my view, Kidrič's insistence on a single centralised plan of developing Yugoslavia, in constant feedback with the direct producers, was fully right, whatever additions and corrections would need to be incorporated into it by experience. Like all proper cognition and science, Kidrič's system possessed built-in possibilities for self-correction (cf. Lipovec 273 and 275). Without such a firm yet flexible plan – which is the central, potentially fertile project of all communist economic horizons – the Yugoslav economy necessarily found itself in a blind alley. Jettisoning democratic de-alienation of socio-economic structures in favour of incompatible stresses on profit and on full employment exacerbated friction between the federal centre and the republics, and finally led precisely to that economic and political anarchy that Kidrič proposed to avoid.

In SFRY Kidrič's set of proposals and horizon, clear in the 'Theses' and other cited works, did not have time to be tested and developed in practice. To the contrary, the dark alternative which he so well foresaw came into force. Kidrič's detailed counter-proposal formulated very clearly, at the beginning of the Yugoslav self-managing trajectory, the overriding need for an integral self-government as not only an economistic or productivistic measure but as a political and organisational one. As opposed to local self-government and self-management in production, victory fell to the conservative current in the Communist Party and the power centres, which brought about an ossified oligarchic monopoly in politics and a slow but sure *de facto* (and at the end also *de iure*) return to the capitalist profit principle. I shall examine in Part 3 how an atomised self-management confined to the enclosure of basic enterprises – which had even so raised great hopes and led to great economic successes – had by the latter 1960s become a minor economic sop to working people in compensation for their disempowerment, for the denial of effective and permanent democratic control from below. SFRY thus fell prey, in spite of all the difference between it and the USSR, to a variant of Brezhnevian stasis, leading to an equally inglorious end.

After Kidrič, there remain some cognitions to be treasured and some open problems. I shall mention only one, which appeared also in the USSR and PR China after the revolution and coming to power of the Communist Party, so it might be a central one. In all Leninist revolutions, the mainspring for the great majority of participants was the slogan with which the Italian partizan song *Bandiera rossa* ends: 'Evviva il comunismo e la libertà!' (Long live communism, long live freedom!). In the Yugoslav popular uprising this mainspring was encapsulated in the omnipresent slogan 'Smrt fašizmu – sloboda narodu!' (Death to fascism, liberty to the people!). For communism as liberty for the people, the post-revolutionary system clearly had to break down the official but hypocritical capitalist sundering of economics and politics into water-tight compartments. The huge concentration of economico-political power ensuing upon Party/State control of the economy was initially necessary both for a revolutionary conquest of power and for the material reproduction and development of a backward society. But how was that seizing of power to be harmonised with a political democracy that would not be a fraud in the interest of the ruling class – as is mostly the case in indirect (parliamentary) democracy and in all 'socialist' imitations of such parliamentarism? How might a revolutionary movement avoid the fateful split between communist theory and practice, or between communism and the plebeian democracy it was supposed to usher in (cf. Lenin's *State*)?

I mentioned earlier that Kidrič quickly arrived at the central question which will incessantly plague SFRY and any other would-be socialist polity: 'who in fact appropriates the surplus labour?' In Marx's terms, we are speaking about de-alienating the real decision power about central questions of life in society, about their quick and decisive transfer into the hands of a fully articulated vertical system of associated producers (which Kidrič strongly urged). In China, for example, there were serious discussions during the 1960s and 70s and before Deng's turn towards capitalism – that is, just before and during the so-called Cultural Revolution – about the expropriation of the workers' decision power and their surplus labour by the commanding political heights. Even more important, on the agenda was the structurally perhaps deeper problem about *the incompatibility between the interests of working people and the oligarchic management of economy within which the reproduction of capital still reigns*. In Leninist terms, the question is: should the revolution, made in the name of the proletariat and led by the Communist Party, only carry out the failed bourgeois revolution while topping it up with a dispossession of the bourgeoisie – that is, by abolishing private exploitation – or does this revolution have deeper aims? Does not the first alternative, in conditions of economic and cultural backwardness, usher in a new type of etatist exploitation and alienation? Is socialism only an economistic and productivistic alternative to bourgeois society or is it also a cultural alternative in the widest sense of this term – the coming about of a different relationship between people as well as of people with nature? Does the revolution lead to a new Leviathan or to the replacement of Leviathan with a society of all-sided citizens as Marx imagined it?

Decisive for these processes are depth economic and psychological currents that can be theoretically identified as the 'law of value' and an economy based on commodity exchange. Kidrič was the giant pioneer of a protracted discussion about these processes in SFRY, which in the decades after his death came to no satisfactory conclusion. The theoretical and highly practical question remains: does Marx's opus equate commodity production with capitalism, or does commodity production, once begun, continue forever, that is, after capitalism too? In SFRY theoretical thought there were conflicting stances about this question. One group, the official view whose main spokesmen were Edvard Kardelj and, among social scientists, Miladin Korać, held that Marx does not criticise commodity production *per se* but only its capitalist 'form', so that a socialist political economy whose object is 'socialist commodity production' is possible. A second group, mainly composed of *Praxis* collaborators, such as Gajo Petrović, Vanja Sutlić, Ljubomir Tadić, and Žarko Puhovski, but including the pioneering book by Bavčar, Kirn, and Korsika, held that in a truly Marxist analysis only a socialist *critique* of commodity production, as well as a *critique* of political economy, is possible. I hold that in a careful Marxian analysis, and in fact, capital is not merely an economic category but a given historical way of producing a human community and its metabolism with nature – the regulative principle of a specific way of life. That capital has been taken to be only an economic category flows out of a historically unique constellation, a hegemony of capitalist thought in which it is believed that 'the economy is not a means for developing other human activities; on the contrary, other human activities become a means for developing the economy' (Divjak 67). Thinking in dialectical opposition to such hegemonic ideas leads, I argue, to the realisation that socialism is not a historical monad-epoch but a longer transitional period between exploitative capitalism and a full, communist associational democracy.

We cannot know of which camp the realistic Marxist and statesman Kidrič would have approved. He was certainly for the horizons of the second camp, but also for a realism of transitional measures which the first camp often advocated (or took as an excuse). Still, I finally hold that the first group's stance is untenable, since commodity exchange is not at all simply a legal or technical activity but a way, as Kidrič understood, for people to live together that determines their lives.[7]

5.2.2 A Betrayed Disalienation

After the descent into unbridled 'market socialism' and the failure of the 1965 reform (about which more later), an opposed development model for SFRY, dissenting from the dominant Party *doxa*, was proposed in a *White Book* drafted for the central government around 1971 by a group of economists headed by Branko Horvat, but it was blocked by opposing forces at the top (*Jugoslavensko* 34–5). While I have not had access to it, here is what to the best of my knowledge was possible – and after reading much Horvat I suppose the *White Book* must have had similar horizons. In economics a radical turning meant a melding of the Kidrič model of vertically integrated self-management, which would have supplanted the bourgeois parliamentary system, with the following **macro-economic** measures, as worked out by the Polish school (see Brus 74–7, but the whole tradition from Lange through Kalecki should be taken into account), managed at the centre through wide feedback from lower levels:

– Retention of decision-making for long-term directions on the horizons and the speed of development, for general proportions of income consumption (personal vs. public), and on priority objectives and resources such as energy, agriculture, transport, education, housing.
– Setting the rules of behaviour of decentralised sub-systems, including material incentives and the market.
– Working out a set of economic instruments (prices, interest rates, tax rates, exchange rate) which permits both monitoring of and effective influence on their application through market competition, since in socialism we are dealing with commodities.
– Organising an inspection apparatus with strong legal powers, active in the whole country, to monitor and enforce the above decisions.

---

7 I have not found thorough discussions of Kidrič on economics, but a first approximation may be found in the well-balanced Milenkovitch 55–9 and 77–89, also in Lipovec. Boffito rightly writes that of nine essays between 1949 and 1967 in his anthology about socialism and the market in Yugoslavia he chose three by Kidrič, 'because he clearly had the main role in introducing the new economic system based on self-management' (19 – see also 21–2 and 26–7).

Such both centralised and decentralised planning would be able to quickly correct harmful oscillations due to either an uncontrolled market and/or oligopolies. Consonant with this, direct allocation of resources by the State would have to diminish in favour of their determination by the associated producers at both plant and higher (branch, area) levels. But there should be no question in socialism of dispensing with planning in the sense of '[vertical] economic coordination above the level of individual enterprises' (Horvat, *Towards* 225–6) – the question would be who would do it how, besides and above (as was in Yugoslavia eventually agreed upon) the horizontal coordination of the market. In that sense, the market would then be used as a non-bureaucratic method of micro-planning, instead of as the ridiculous panacea it was, against all rhyme or reason, widely believed to be (so that for example the railway system of a small country was finally split into six republican ones, which led to the same chaos in maintenance as in the post-Thatcher U.K.).

Horvat spelled out his position in a paper on the 'market as instrument of planning': 'there is today no so-called free market; it can be proven that planning is absolutely needed for its functioning well'. However, *the market could be one of the possible planning types*, and one among the instruments for ... the allocation of resources needed for consumption' – especially for short-range plans and consumption goods. This can be brought about by planning control of market forces and prices. Yet drawing up the plans should be the prerogative of the people, that is, all economic subjects, with full feedback flow of information ('Der Markt', 108–12; cf. Markuš 147–51). It is of interest that Trotsky blamed Stalin for abolishing the market in 1929, thus depriving the State of an indispensable barometer in planning (in Dallemagne 107).

The system of Workers' Councils appeared here as the ideal possibility of reconciling central planning with both democracy from below and efficient economic development. Kidrič envisaged already in 1950 such a development: for example, in foreign trade 'real decentralisation will [come about] when ... [industrial] branches, factories and producers, ... not the republics, will buy and sell goods. Then we will reach the mutual association of individual branches' (cited in Unkovski-Korica 23). This was reaffirmed in the LCY 1958 Programme (see *Yugoslavia's Way passim* and Korošić 257). For Kalecki, however, this move would be inseparable from central planning not only for emergencies such as initial industrialisation (in which case capitalism also abundantly uses it, as in the World Wars and permanently in military investments) but also when a higher level of economic growth is reached: 'because, in such circumstances, contradictions arise between the standard of living in the longer term and the share of consumption in the national income in the short term'. The rejection of central planning implies 'either abandoning rapid economic development, or dependence on permanent foreign assistance' (62). Alas, Yugoslavia after the 60s managed to combine both these negativities.

In official Yugoslav theory, the Workers' Councils were in the 1960s supposed to be fully compatible with a planning subject to two conditions: (1) that it is effected by organs that themselves emanate from a vertically prolonged self-management, where State organs truly become internal to a free association of producers (as in Marx or Lenin), and (2) that plans be reduced to forecasting and general guidance, to correction of market allocations in case of glaring imbalances or monopolism, and to supplementing what market processes obviously could not do, such as development of backward regions or coping with short-term acute social problems (cf. Brus 81–5). But in practice point 1 never happened, and even theoretically point 2 unduly reduced the necessity of active central planning 'based on the supremacy of macrocriteria and long-term economic calculation extending far beyond any market criteria and signals' (Brus 88); this was due to an ideological constellation more sensitive to a crude anti-Stalinism than to capitalist elements in the market mechanism. And we can today stress that it would have been necessary not only to posit disalienation from productivism, capitalist technology, and ecocide as the main goal (cf. Harvey 218–21), but also to make coherent sense of the already major practical 'communist corrections' of the Law of Value (Tripalo 31; cf. Horvat, *Political* 277–9) – I return to this later. At any rate, this and point 2 hinged on point 1, a radical democracy from below that was never permitted to develop. This led to a central aporia of Yugoslav economics: when long-term strategic decisions and the attendant strong regulation of the market are abandoned, 'the function of the self-managing enterprise becomes maximisation of net income per employee ... at the price of a lower degree of utilisation of productive capacity or more capital-intensive investment' – a stance sustainable only during a shortage of labour and surplus of capital, whereas actual conditions were the reverse (Brus 89)

Thus, despite Kidrič's early model, and despite Party programmes (from the 7th to the 9th Congress) and proclamations, an integration of plebeian democracy and workable economic planning was not what happened. Instead, systematic planning by a central instance unifying planning from below and market stimuli, with the attendant control of income distribution parameters, was simply jettisoned – and had then to be resorted to, in an unceasing series of smaller and larger crises, piecemeal, ad hoc, and without a chance of durable success (see Chapter 10.2.2). This abolition of a unifying centre was officially, and with uncanny unconscious precision, called 'depoliticisation'; while possibly a good thing when countering the economically untenable, arbitrary centralism of the Stalinist type as well as arbitrary communal parochialism, planlessness as a general principle cut also – and primarily – against legitimate political interests from within the self-management system. It showed a deplorable lack of awareness that every economy is politically framed. An eminent student of self-management concluded bitterly in 1966:

> For self-management is essentially a problem of democratic planning ... Even in Yugoslavia, the problem is so far from being solved that it is not impossible we may yet regard that country as an object-lesson in pitfalls, rather than the brave pilot which it looked like being in the beginning.
> COATES 108

5.3 The Upshot: Suicidal Class Singularity

> All depends radically on politics.
> ROUSSEAU, *Confessions*

∴

The involution of the ruling class halted further emancipation of labour and of the public sphere, which had coincided with maintaining an independent and reasonably prosperous federal Yugoslavia (cf. Suvin 'Pogled'). It allowed a more or less unhindered development of endogenous and exogenous factors militating against such a State. It destroyed all credibility in a vanguard communist leadership. I called it in Chapter 3 *a final, suicidal singularity*. Halting emancipation, Yugoslavia – very late – joined the other 'socialist' countries from Poland to Bulgaria in unresolved stasis.

The endogenous factor can be initially described as a fattening of the arteries in the split and quarrelling ruling class, which turned exclusively towards its class interests. This meant abandoning its victorious historical block with the workers, peasants, and middle classes. When it forsook this alliance, it lost the working classes' horizons which borrow solutions for the society's major problem from the future (Polanyi 162, echoing Marx). A sociopolitical counteroffensive against the forces in favour of self-management by a strong conservative faction of the ruling class began in opposition to the very interesting Programme of the League of Communists passed in 1958 (see *Yugoslavia's*). The politocracy's ideological helplessness and confusion led to a stalemate at the decisional top in the mid-60s which allowed only piecemeal solutions. Of

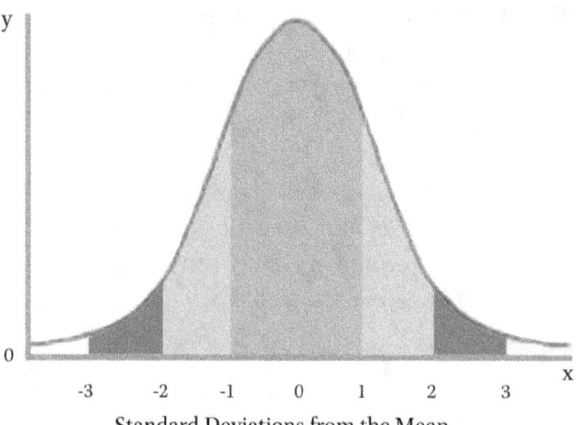

FIGURE 14 *Gaussian Bell Curve of Yugoslav Self-management*

the other classes, the two large proletarian ones, peasants and manual workers, were politically and economically neutralised and sociologically atomised. So was the majority of the middle classes, mired in consumerism, while a radical wing of the humanist intelligentsia was by itself too powerless to seriously count (cf. Žvan 463–4). This led toward a politico-economical paralysis after the 1965 reform, and more acutely in the less favourable international economic climate of the 1970s (cf. the titles by Samary).

The economic situation that resulted was neither theoretical 'market socialism' (for 'the market did not apply to factors of production – labor, capital ..., raw materials, credit') nor planned economy: after 1952 plans became unenforceable policy goals or indeed forecasts (Woodward 169–71 – see more in Chapter 10.2). This was a confession of failure, but it tided ruling interests over for the next couple of years at a time. Economic growth, the basis of the Party's legitimacy, stalled and eventually reversed. By 1979 Yugoslav foreign debt had in three years levitated from 4–5 to 17–19 billion US$, and in the 1980s the capitalist world politics and market interests became increasingly unfavourable. Politically, the 'capital functions concentrated [in the Party/State apparatus] ... could never fully lose their status of "worker representatives"' (Kerševan 1485), so that they had to enter into some compromises with the workers or producers. But the politocracy shifted central economic functions to the six federated republics, which meant the rise of six (in fact seven, with Kosovo) local ruling classes. At some point this doubly hybrid status became increasingly irksome to some of them and the economic sops to working classes impossible. Having refused a full economico-political democracy where they would lose some of their central prerogatives, the only course available to dominant class/es was a sharp political change by which their economic class interests might be largely safeguarded (it turns out this belief too was mistaken). This safeguarding was attainable at the price of supporting nationalism and dismantling the Yugoslav Federation.

With due cautions about oversimplifying matters which did not appear in solid chronological blocks but with quicksilver tides back and forth, my hypothesis is that we have a process approximating a Gaussian bell-curve from error theory (see previous page).

At −3 to −1 there is a first slow and then quicker rise (ca. 1952–7) to a middle plateau (ca. 1958–68); there follows a fall towards zero, at first a bit slower (to 1974) and then precipitous (1974 to the 80s). On the upward curve, the Workers' Councils were created as a politico-ideological project to elicit a renewal of enthusiasm from below, that is, a renewal of the Party's alliance with at least the urban lower classes, and they were of decisive help in bringing about what the Chinese would have called 'walking on two legs' – the political and the economic one. On the downward curve, the politico-ideological impetus from the Party and State, by now polyarchic and divided, failed, and so did the economic leg.

This process could be analysed, as the best Yugoslav theories of the time attempted, in terms of a possible move away from the wage relationship and workshop alienation by having the associated direct producers increasingly control how the surplus labour extracted from them is used. As the lucid Bakarić acknowledged in 1964, in the post-war nationalisations 'the basic relationship in capitalism, that between the worker and capital, was essentially unchanged, though the capitalist was removed'; they were accompanied by 'State capitalist or, if you wish, State socialist planning'. These relationships were first changed with the introduction of Workers' Councils and significantly continued in the 1960s by decentralising central State investment funds. However, the situation still contained 'elements of a wage relationship ... somebody else decides how the real worker will produce'. Eventually it was attempted to accompany the organisation of society based on ruling from the top down with 'a parallel social system going from below ... [a] process now underway'. He went on to explain that a long period of direct State command over expanded social reproduction creates 'a bureaucratic stratum ... which can become an independent class, deciding the people's destiny ... Such a process even today resists ... further development of direct democracy and direct management of economy [from below]' (2: 138–43). Against his hopes, the 1965 reform and later measures did not continue in this direction but reversed it.

To get ahead of my analytical limits here, this means that as of the early 80s the capitalist powers were in a position to bring Yugoslavia economically crashing down simply by stopping IMF loans. Practically, the SFRY became a peripheral dependency of global capitalism (a position prefigured from the 60s on, when it had become a supplier of cheap labour to the West European economies), left for the moment to stew in its own sauce but with a prospect of full integration into capitalism by a fire-sale of its whole economy. This was actualised when the USSR withdrew from world politics after the mid-1980s. The USA preferred a united subservient Yugoslavia. The German banks and the Vatican, with longer memories of painful defeat, preferred dismembering it; they won out.

Very few ruling classes in recent history have opted for dismemberment. This was a true negative singularity, as extreme as the earlier, positive ones: the experiments in self-management and peaceful international coexistence.

Glossary

doxa = current prevailing opinion, often manipulated by the hegemony, as different from systematic cognition

CHAPTER 6

15 Theses about Communism and Yugoslavia, or the Two-Headed Janus of Emancipation through the State (Metamorphoses and Anamorphoses of 'On the Jewish Question' by Marx)

In memory of my *Praxis* colleagues and comrades at the Faculty of Philosophy, Zagreb: Rudi Supek, Gajo Petrović, Branko Bošnjak, Predrag Vranicki, Veljko Cvjetičanin, Milan Kangrga

For Boris Buden, who fought for truth and justice

∴

6.1   Introductory[1]

The State everywhere presupposes that reason has been realised. But in this very way it everywhere comes into contradiction between its ideal mission and its real preconditions.

MARX, 1844

∴

---

1 Footnotes don't go well with Theses, I have avoided further ones, except for two afterthoughts. This goes for the apparatus too, so that from the large library on the subject treated here I have cited only the indispensable Kouvelakis and Zolo, also the best treatment of the polysemic minefield of civil society in Hegel that I found in Bobbio 143–50, 185–7, and *passim*, though I do not agree with his stance on Marx. On religion and the 'reoccupation' of its terrain I was much influenced not only by Marx but also by the tradition of Curtius, Löwith, and Blumenberg.

6.1.1 *The Basis of Theses*

I have taken over the basic epistemological approach to people, the State, and emancipation from the first part of *On the Jewish Question* (*Zur Judenfrage*, publ. 1844, MEW 1: 352–61) by Karl Marx. He counterposes – in the terms of his age, which at times do not correspond to today's historical semantics – political and legal emancipation to complete emancipation. Marx's approach here uses Feuerbach's term 'species-being' (*Gattungswesen*, that is, the natural being of the genus Homo sapiens), to which I shall return. This way to speak about human potentials rather than about privatised individuals has however much deeper roots, in the French Revolution and in Spinoza's discovery that human freedom is primarily threatened by a belief in a predetermined, holy teleology, consubstantial to power and rule. I take it that this approach transcends Marx's epoch, and that at its core would in today's semantics be: what is the relationship of special political (primarily State-building) alienation to general social alienation as well as to 'species-specific' de-alienation or disalienation as the individuals' emancipation or classless freedom? The relationship between emancipation and alienation remains a constant horizon for Marx. True, he still lacks here the key field between theory and practice: the economy, where commodity reification and fetishism will appear as the antagonists of freedom. But this is no Althusserian *coupure épistemologique*, as the new terminology will be a more precise reformulation of the old one from which it evolved.

Its absence means however that my theses do not address economic relationships: this is their limit. Their conclusions would have to be supplemented (and perhaps significantly re-metamorphosed) with further considerations, starting primarily from Marx's rich considerations about alienation and exploitation of living labour, which I approached in my essay 'Living Labour': I would have to advance from its conclusions. But the State and politics must be dealt with first.

My attempt does not deal in Marxology, although I take it into account in 6.1.2. It is a ***reworking***, a genre of its own. This is a quintessentially Marxian stance: he starts with reworking Hegel, and then continually and gluttonously reworks himself and other incomplete and new cognitions (for example, Adam Smith or the experience of the Paris Commune). Since Marx's argument in the 1840s is literally inapplicable today – who cares about the State of King Frederick William IV? – I am violently tearing out, assembling, and re-functioning ten segments from Part 1 of *The Jewish Question* for today's purposes. I completely or partly metamorphosise them using specified operators, and the resulting metamorphic text then demands to be supplemented with other considerations. This makes the whole of this chapter anamorphic in relation to that of Marx: rotated into the dimension of Post-Fordism, the new Leviathan. The text is therefore mine, written because of Yugoslavia after the 1941–5 revolution, and uses Marx as an indispensable stimulus and catalyser – because his style is consubstantial to some fundamental methodological insights into philosophical anthropology and epistemology that I would like, *mutatis mutandis*, to preserve.

As his red thread for orientation, Marx's essay poses the problem of emancipation from the fiction of 'the religious State'. True, such an official fiction testifies also to the strong presence of pre-bourgeois 'estate' and feudal elements in the Prussian State; however, this has the paradoxical advantage of allowing the ideological contradiction hidden by full bourgeois hypocrisy to palpably emerge. My hypothesis is that, regardless of great differences between the Europe of early capitalism in 1844 on one hand, and on the other the world after 1945 – a situation of full imperialist capitalism and after the first anti-capitalist revolutions – I can usefully apply the following basic operator to post-revolution Yugoslavia: replacing Marx's official 'religion' with 'communism (official)' everywhere and seeing what comes out of this. Of course, I do not claim that communism is simply a religion – although it is an annunciation of *this-worldly salvation* (see Suvin, 'Inside') and its organised professional avant-garde easily translates into an analogue of the Church. But it is a sufficiently robust analogy, the basis of which is the hegemony of an explicit and articulated doctrine that contains all central values for the orientation of humanity in the present historical moment. The justification for its use can only be its fruits.

For the analogy to work, subsidiary metamorphic operators should also be used: replacing 'religious' with 'ideological', and then 'political' (in Marx's lay meaning of opposition to the religious State and government) with 'social': through society or the social, humanisation or disalienation is achieved. The reigning alienation is not to be understood looking backward, as a Fall from Earthly Paradise (neither Eve and Adam's nor the Noble Savage's), but looking forward to the natural possibilities of the human generic being – the disalienation draws its poetry, as Marx will say, from the future. (Today we could formulate the alienation as three interlocking alienations: that of labour, that of language, and that of freedom and sense of life – but this transcends the brief of the present Theses.) Finally, I arrive at the focal image and concept of the two-headed Janus.

Contextual tact and flexibility should also be applied. First, in selecting only some passages, which are not just crucial but also roughly applicable to Yugoslavia after the revolution. And then in translating between epochs and contexts; for example, Marx's early chiasmic rhetoric (if A : B then NonB : NonA), which is nice, but not always efficient as real – not only rhetorical –

proof, should be used in supple ways and cautiously. I quote the passages according to the English translation, available in Spring 2011 on WAMW/1844/jewish-question; this translation is useful because, among other things, it is itself (unavoidably) a half-step towards a reworking of Marx's speculative historiosophy into the discourse of English empiricism and thus dovetails with my epistemological purpose. In the following multiple translating, before metamorphosing it into my own text, I often corrected the English text using the German original, which has been identified after each passage. (I debated whether to quote the German text too, but since it can be readily found, I preferred not to overload the apparatus.) Through the discussion of these passages, the method and argument will gradually crystallise.

Just as Marx distinguished between the earthly and heavenly reality of religion, I start with 'communism' in the sense of official, 'State' communism in SFR Yugoslavia as a belief – as an ideological vulgate on and of the State. The obverse of 'religion', Marx's 'atheism', for him the true orientation towards complete human emancipation unlike illusory religion, is emancipatory communism (to which Marx will explicitly arrive immediately after the *Jewish Question*). One should take care here to discern whether this denotes theory, practice or both (to Marx this was not a problem since he had not got that far yet).

I was thinking about naming this little tractate 'Sing Me a Song of Translation'. It involves not only shuttling between three languages (German, English, and the Croatoserbian in which it was originally written), but also among three time epochs, translating Marx's discourse from the time of the already tottering Sacred Alliance into our own discourse of looking backwards from 2011 to post-revolutionary Yugoslavia from 1945 to the mid-1970s (the possibility for subsequent degeneration is based on the consideration here, and is dealt with explicitly in other chapters).

6.1.2   *An Excursus on Marx and His Evolution*

Though the following theses are not an exegesis, they presuppose an exegesis of some essential parameters of Marx and his evolution, and therefore of the specific weights and significance (*Stellenwert*) of the short text excerpted here, the first part of *On the Jewish Question*. The Theses develop the basic dichotomy and opposition of *bürgerliche Gesellschaft* against *Staat* from early Marx.

6.1.2.1   *'Bürgerliche Gesellschaft'*

Marx started with this opposition in his 1843 *Critique of Hegel's Philosophy of Right* in: 'The general law is[:] the *bürgerliche* society and State are divided. Therefore the *Staatsbürger* as well as the *Bürger*, member of the *bürgerliche Gesellschaft*, is divided' (MEW 1: 281). I am here faced with the fundamental and already metamorphic problem in the form of the classic translator's dilemma of how to translate *bürgerlich*. The central denotation is 'civil', the adjective derived from *civis*, citizen, but does this aim at 'the citizen as a subject, that is member of the State' or 'the citizen as a member of the bourgeoisie or the middle class'? As in the above quotation, Marx occasionally uses the term *Staatsbürger*, which is the first denotation, but he also has to add in apposition the member of the *bürgerliche* society. While by this we might today mean the whole of the people minus the State apparatus, this second term also participates in and oscillates between both poles of the translator's dilemma: is it something like 'civil society' or like 'bourgeois/ middle class society'? The terminology here expresses Marx's persistent probing around the not yet completely clear joints of reality. A few months later, precisely in *On the Jewish Question*, Hegel's not yet fully differentiated opposition between the *citoyen* and the ambiguous and limited *bourgeois* (cf. Rehmann 5–6 and *passim*) becomes Marx's brilliant and deeply significant, though undeveloped, dichotomy where the *citoyen* bears the values of the French Revolution while the *bourgeois* is the bearer of every political counterrevolution from 1794 to 1848 as well as of anti-feudal capitalistic development of production and the corresponding miserable human relationships. Since Marx's texts were at the time only beginning to push toward clarity on this convoluted but also crucial issue, each individual instance of *bürgerlich* should be examined to see which of the two above translations, or of their contaminations, may be more correct (Rehmann 6–7 argues for the dominance of 'société civile', which Marx uses when writing in French). In English and Italian, *bürgerliche Gesellschaft* is unambiguously translated as 'civil society', *società civile*, perhaps also because in the Hegel of 1821 it is a translation of the 'civil society' by eighteenth-century liberals (as Marx explained in the 'Preface' to *A Contribution to the Critique of Political Economy*), such as Adam Ferguson and Adam Smith. I have no French translation at hand, but the 'orthodox' Labica & Bensussan dictionary explains that *société civile* is Hegel's term, *société bourgeoise* being Marx's (see 182 and 414), which is, to put it very mildly, insufficient.

Each of the above solutions has significant flaws. Those associated with the use of 'citizen' I have suggested above. 'Civil society' does not have those flaws, but has two other major ones. First, in the major European languages, 'civil' means civilian (as opposed to military, and in English 'civil law' as opposed also to criminal), then public-spirited (as in French *civisme*), and finally civilised, cultured, with a connotation of a narcissistic national, even class-oriented, self-praise. Second, 'civil society' has been taken over from English around the 1980s as a propagandistic term used by advocates of parliamentary (hence bourgeois) democracy to denote lack of freedom in officially 'communist' countries of the

Soviet bloc or Yugoslavia, with the purpose of wringing from the regime a return of opposition parties and the restoration of private ownership over central means of production.[2] However, no matter how abhorrent some of us might find this one-sided, ideologised abuse of both Hegel's and Marx's perspectives, which are richer and deeper (if often mutually contradictory), a plebeian and associational concept of civil society seems to me utterly indispensable in a discourse about what was missing in 'really existing socialism'. We therefore cannot leave this category in the hands of its kidnappers but must use it, cleared of abuse and properly articulated, within Marx's radical perspectives of direct democracy. Binoculars do allow a better view of artillery or sniper fire at, let's say, Sarajevo, but I doubt that is reason enough to discard binoculars.

I would therefore propose to use 'civil' for Marx's *bürgerliche* in most cases.

6.1.2.2   Marx 1843–75: Political Emancipation and the State

Thus, in the *Critique of Hegel's Philosophy of Right* Marx uses Hegel's terms in order to identify – contrary to Hegel – the opposition between the 'holy' State apparatus interests of governance, coercion, and ideology, and the profane social and economic interests of the rest of society. The latter are ruled by bourgeois individualism and egotism (as in Hegel), yet they are opposed to the State as real life to abstract universalism. Further, Marx was an avid reader of Rousseau and the Jacobins as well as 'the modern Frenchmen' (MEW 1: 232 – meaning utopians and communists such as Babeuf and Buonarroti, Saint-Simon and his school, Fourier, Proudhon, and Cabet) and supporters of radical popular sovereignty; thus, Marx diametrically opposes Hegel's allotting of priority, rationality, and absolute importance to the State. Hegel's topology of *bürgerliche Gesellschaft* is in Marx first overturned, becoming a precondition for the State; and then this antithesis as a whole has to be transcended by a total politicisation of civil society which would abolish both itself and the separate State (compare MEW 1: 326–7 and *passim*).

On the *Jewish Question* is a big step forward because it introduces **the theme of 'false holiness'**, which was to culminate in the theory of commodity fetishism in *Capital*: false, but extremely important as it dominates the mind of the masses. On both sides of Hegel's dichotomy of social life between State and civil society, man is a 'plaything of alien powers', under 'the rule of inhuman elements and relationships' (MEW 1: 355 and 360), human 'species-being' is alienated; in particular, 'civil society' is Hobbes's war of all against all (MEW 1:

---

2   This is explicitly recognised by, for example, Miller (1) and implicit in almost all the writings of and about the 1980s. For a better use of 'civil society' after Gramsci see Suvin, 'Communism'.

356). Marx's reading of Feuerbach and his *Gattungswesen* terminology about the species or generic essence of man resonate here, but he reaped the maximum benefit out of this single-minded focus on human sensuality (MEW 1: 345). First, Feuerbach's anthropology, although applied to religion only, was and remains revolutionary in its view from the bottom up, that is, basing and centring the creation and understanding of social beliefs and relationships in material and sensuous ***humans***. His stance was a useful topological device of separation and rupture, opposed to Hegel's view downward from the height of the Absolute reconciliation (here the State). Marx aspired to such a radical anthropology even before he read Feuerbach, and it remained his absolute and fixed guiding star throughout, including his work on *Capital*. Furthermore, the epistemological limitations of Feuerbach's humanism have been largely evaded in the last quotation from Marx in this chapter (see MEW 1: 370), which stresses power in society: he transfers the notion of species to politics, where instead of reposing upon the intersubjectivity of sexual love, it reposes on the Hegelian 'life of the people' (cf. Kouvelakis 289). The limits are fully transcended a year later, in the essay on 'Alienated Labour' from *Economic and Philosophical Manuscripts of 1844*, with the laconic formula '*Gattungsleben* [the species or generic life of man] is productive life': the direct usefulness of Feuerbach for the transition into the critique of political economy comes here into view (MEW Ergänzungsband 516 – see Zolo 122, and a bibliography on the relationship Marx–Feuerbach ibidem 90). In *On the Jewish Question* civil society stands for all economic and ideological aspects under the political State's and the ruling class's structure of power (see also Thesis 10 on Feuerbach, MEW 3: 7). And I shall further suggest that this focus on the emancipation of people and their productivity – in the widest sense of all creativity – is not only constant in Marx's thought but also very pertinent to later contradictions, after the proletarian revolution, between that emancipation and the socialist State.

I shall here briefly deal only with the perhaps most important stages in his development of this emancipatory or libertarian opposition. In the seminal *German Ideology*, within the 'civil society' in ***all*** social formations there is an ongoing conflict of classes, which depends on material production relationships; still, the 'civil society' itself remains the 'true hearth and arena of all history'! Here this society is resolutely liberated from the narrow context of the bourgeoisie and Hobbes – although it is from the bourgeoisie that both the term for as well as the first full form of such a society come: 'civil society [*bürgerliche Gesellschaft*] comprises the whole material traffic [that is, all relationships – DS] of individuals within a given developmental stage of the relationships of production' (all MEW 3:36). Moreover, it is here, I think, that Marx for the first time proposes the thesis according to which the precondition for a free development of personalities is their rule over contingency and reified relationships, namely, a communist organisation of society (MEW 3: 424–5, and cf. 69–70).

Similar positions are to be found in the *Communist Manifesto*, with the important addition of discussing class economic interests protected by the State. But in *The 18th Brumaire* further developments can be found in the analysis of Bonapartism and its complete subordination of legislative to executive power. The deep structure is that of the youthful critique from the 1840s, with the State as the antagonist and negation of the civil society, but now also as an apparatus for regulating the economic class conflict. Marx induces from historical experience that, in a stalemate between classes, the executive can appear completely autonomous in relation to civil society (MEW 8: 197); after a further historical experience of 150 years I would add that in our 'hot' society this may be inherently unstable and last no longer than one generation. This horizon is clarified and developed in two other vital writings: Marx's admiring analysis of the Paris Commune, and his critique of the German Social Democratic Party. In *The Civil War in France*, written in English, he rejects the earlier assumption that the proletariat should form a non-bureaucratic State centralism after the fall of the bourgeois State apparatus, and most resolutely advocates a federation of communes, therefore decentralisation, the reason being that – as in *On the Jewish Question*! – the quasi-religious sacralisation of the State, which has replaced medieval Heaven and Church, must be smashed. In the note 'The Character of the Commune' (drafts/cho1.htm#D1s1), Marx dismisses the State, 'this supernaturalist abortion of society', and its 'Holy State Power', and praises the Paris Commune counter-project of 'the reabsorption of the State power by society as its own living forces instead of as forces controlling and subduing it'. As Zolo's research has cogently argued, Marx's analysis of revolutionary changes in the Paris Commune opposes the economic and social element to the political and bureaucratic one: this historical overview 'matches the opposed pair "civil society" – "political State" that Marx has ever since the *Critique of Hegel's Philosophy of Right* used to express, even though with partly diverse and tentative semantic values, the basic contradiction within that formation' (176–7). This stance is in Marx the presupposition for his focus on the organisation of associated labour in the Commune and the organisation of the entire nation on the basis of self-government (which is what this chapter and book of mine also wants to be).

Finally, in the *Critique of the Gotha Programme* (*Randglossen zur Programm der deutschen Arbeiterpartei*) from 1875 it can be seen, by contrast, how important it was for Marx to resolve his youthful dichotomy of State vs. civil society through communism, as the only possible way out and horizon. In this perspective the State is no longer simply power over society, but – contrary to the anarchists – it becomes after the proletarian revolution the executive organ of universal social functions. Such a project can be approached, he avers, only in a scholarly way, which suggests his conclusions from *Capital* about gradually but resolutely abolishing 'the commodity form', that is, the production of commodities for the market. The goal or *telos* of the process is to make it possible, 'after the enslaving subordination of the individual to the division of labour ... has vanished', that 'the narrow horizon of bourgeois right be entirely transcended and [that] society inscribe on its banners: From each according to his ability, to each according to his needs!' (/ch01.htm)

I conclude that the term 'civil society', in opposition to the State as apparatus, recurs in Marx's political thought. After the *Critique of Hegel's Philosophy of Right*, it was gradually but surely liberating itself from its Hegelian matrix, where civil society meant the corrupt egotism of private interests, and approaching the meaning of interaction between politics and the sphere of social and economic relationships, the relationships which ultimately co-determine production. Civil society becomes co-extensive with those activities where social decision-making is not taken over into the State as apparatus. The central oscillation remaining in Marx is then whether civil society is necessarily also co-extensive with class struggles, as is clearly the case in both absolutism and capitalism. His notions tending to abolition of class society, such as proletariat and communism, do not fit into the opposition between civil society and State but represent its utopian and scientific supersession (*Aufhebung*). Let me add that I would today doubt this 'annulment of politics' aspect of Marx's oscillation, which was then exclusively developed by Lenin in *The State and Revolution* (I develop this in other chapters of the book).

6.2 The Theses Developed

> [It would be easy to prove] that, first, no State was ever founded without Religion functioning as its basis, and second, that christian law is finally rather harmful than useful to the strong establishment of the State.
> ROUSSEAU, 1762

∴

– ENGLISH TRANSLATION OF MARX, PASSAGE 1 (MEW 1: 352): 'The question of the relation of political emancipation to religion becomes for us the question of the relation of political emancipation to human emancipation'.

– COMMENT: Since politics has become a substitute of religion as self-awareness by the government, Marx's relationship *lay politics : religion* should be metamorphosed into our relationship *social : officially political.* But a further complication arises: social or complete human emancipation (soon to centrally include for Marx economic emancipation from misery and exploitation) is identical to Marx's vision of communism, which I shall awkwardly, but I hope clearly, call 'true communism' here. To my mind, this is a horizon of total social justice and disalienation, politically implemented through free self-determination of every person in independent working and territorial communities with no State. This means that the relationship of such complete human social emancipation to the official political emancipation is also a relationship of true communism, or of the original Marxian project (we may call it c_1), to official Party and State communism (we may call it c_2). True – partizan, plebeian – communism with direct democracy is homonymous to, but very different from, actually existing Party and State communism. Here then is the beginning of my reworking of Marx for the chronotope of SFR Yugoslavia.

– DS METAMORPHICALLY:

Thesis 1. **The problem of the relation of complete social emancipation of people to official State and political emancipation is the problem of the relation of real plebeian, directly democratic communism that liberates and empowers people vs. official State and Party communism, partly very real but emancipatory only to a degree and beset by temptations to repression.**

Gloss to 1: It follows that the problems of emancipation in Yugoslavia were a version of constant conflict and permeation between two currents within the socialist and communist tradition from the Industrial Revolution on: should sovereign democracy, and even organisation, flow from bottom upward or from top down? On the first extreme of the spectrum are both Marx and the anarchists, on the other Stalin, while Lenin, perforce, moved from the first pole in his theory up to 1917 toward the other one in his extremely endangered application after 1918. This dilemma is explicated in Mao's harsh initial slogan of the first Cultural Revolution in a communist State: 'Bombard the headquarters [with criticism]'.

∴

– ENGLISH TRANSLATION OF MARX, PASSAGE 2 (MEW 1: 353): 'The limits of political emancipation are evident at once from the fact that the state can free itself from a restriction while man is not really free from this restriction, that the state can be a free state [pun on word *Freistaat*, which also means republic] without man being a free man ... It follows from this that man frees himself through the medium of the state, that he frees himself politically from a limitation when, in contradiction with himself, he raises himself above this limitation in an abstract, limited, and partial way'.

– DS METAMORPHICALLY:

Thesis 2. **The limits of social emancipation are evident at once from the fact that the State can free itself from a restriction while people are still not really free from this restriction, that the State can be politically free or a parliamentary republic without people being free. It follows that when people free themselves** *through the medium of the State*, **they free themselves only in a limited way.**

It follows also that when the State freed itself from the restrictions of capitalist class rule while preserving, in Marx's encompassing anthropological sense, a capitalist organisation of production and bourgeois law, the working people or plebeians were not really freed from the restriction of the 'capital-relationship', that is, the exploitation of labour and all particular egotisms that arise from it in the exploiters and the exploited. This was accompanied by other class alienation factors: the legacy of patriarchal despotism, gender discrimination, city vs. country, intellectual vs. manual labour (readers can supply additional factors).

Gloss to 2: But in this entire chapter it is indispensable to factor in that the actual chronotope of Yugoslavia is doubly philosophically 'impure' in comparison to Marx's orientation. It is first impure in general, as any praxis in comparison to theory, since it involves practical politics with all the necessary compromises, anachronisms, etc. It is also impure, second and especially, since it involves a 'transitional period' from capitalism to communism like the one that Marx – only initially, but fundamentally – characterised much later, in the *Critique of the Gotha Program*. Consequently, we are not dealing with a largely closed and stable historical chronotope, such as the early 1840s, but with tempestuous ebb and flow on a much more complex terrain. An example: the revolutionary enthusiasm and plebeian tradition of the Yugoslav Liberation War 1941–5 were in the beginning able to completely neutralise the capital-relationship (note for example the economically ridiculous radicalism of nationalising small family-owned stores and taverns after 1946/47). Contrariwise: this initial enthusiasm abated naturally somewhere around 1960, for biopsychological reasons of the revolutionary generation's wear and tear, and it was not being continually reinvigorated by a permanent revolutionising of human relationships, both in production – because of a ghettoisation of self-government at company level while blocking its ascent to the summits of power – and in public life or civil society (in the sense of citizen, *citoyen*, participation).

∴

– ENGLISH TRANSLATION OF MARX, PASSAGE 3 (MEW 1: 353): 'It follows, finally, that man, even if he proclaims himself an atheist through the medium of the state – that is, if he proclaims the state to be atheist – still remains in the grip of religion, precisely because he acknowledges himself only by a roundabout route, only through an *intermediary*. Religion is precisely the recognition of man in a roundabout way, through an intermediary. The state is the intermediary between man and man's freedom. Just as Christ is the intermediary to whom man transfers the burden of all his divinity, all his *religious constraint*, so the State is the intermediary to whom man transfers all his non-divinity and all his *human unconstraint*'.

– DS METAMORPHICALLY (I use an additional operator: Marx's 'atheist' = today 'true communist'):

Thesis 3. It also follows that when people proclaim themselves socialist/communist through the medium of the State – that is, when they proclaim the State to be socialist/communist – they still remain non-communist, because they acknowledge themselves only by a roundabout route, only through an intermediary. Non-communism is precisely the recognition of people through an intermediary, by an indirect and not a direct route. The State is the intermediary between people and their freedom, just as religion (a Christian would say Christ) is the intermediary to whom the working people transfer all their communism and all their unconstraint.

It further follows that belief in the State is in a sincere (not Stalinist and counter-revolutionary) communist government a homologue of religion in Marx's Prussia and the like: it replaces further communist emancipation of the working people by a supernaturalist principle of emancipation.

It finally follows that a sincere (not Stalinist and counter-revolutionary) *Communist Party* is to be understood as a key instrument for neutralising the deleterious effects of this etatist intermediary after the revolution. However, for this purpose it needs to change from an instrument primarily of violence to an instrument primarily of learning and education (including educating the educators) for the most complex task of permanent revolutionising.

Gloss to 3: This mediation is not, and cannot be, seriously undermined by a *representative* (parliamentary, essentially class) democracy, but only by *associative plus direct* democracy. I shall worry at this in the following chapters.

∴

– ENGLISH TRANSLATION OF MARX, PASSAGE 4 (MEW 1: 355): 'Political emancipation is, of course, a big step forward. True, it is not the final form of human emancipation in general, but it is the final form of human emancipation within the hitherto existing world order. It goes without saying that we are speaking here of real, practical emancipation'.

– DS METAMORPHICALLY ('political' vs. 'human emancipation' is State vs. human emancipation here):

Thesis 4. Political and legal emancipation through the State is, of course, a big step forward. It is the final step of human emancipation possible in the hitherto existing world-order and macro-framework of States and classes.

∴

– REFLECTIONS ON THE FIRST FOUR THESES METAMORPHOSISED FROM MARX

Thesis 5. What are the *limits of applicability* of this entire metamorphic transfer of Marx from the 1840s to Yugoslavia after 1945? Two clusters of arguments indicate that these limits exist.

5.1 The first cluster is that after all there are limits to the analogy religion = communism (Marx's 'politics' is consequently 'society' for us, and what is called politics in our chronotope is not affected by this since it is the zone of tension between the State and the rest of society – the civil society). Other lengthy but secondary distinctions would be needed here, which I shall avoid simply by using scissors: by dealing only with those passages from Marx that I need; for this brilliant text of his is anyway just a crucial incentive, catalyst, and indispensable base for a reworking.

Gloss to 5.1: A large-scale forgetfulness of one's object would be a very questionable practice, but since this is not a text about Marx but through him, I would vigorously defend this method.

5.2. The other cluster is that, in a largely differing historical reality, similarities to Marx's chronotope walk hand in hand with significant differences. The knot of Yugoslavia and the world in the time of many-sided revolutionary dynamics in productive forces and production relationships is much more convoluted than the static Prussian-European one when Marx wrote his diatribe. Neither the economy nor the government nor ideology were in the 1940s what they used to be in the 1840s.

Thesis 6. The reflections so far lead to a thesis fundamental for understanding SFRY: *the Party/State government was a two-headed Janus* (at least in 1945–72). Diametrically opposed to Marx's State in the 1840s, the Party/State government of Yugoslavia was not only a factor of alienation, but *concurrently* also the initiator and lever of real liberation – up to a certain important limit (the liberation is important and the limit is important!).

Liberation: banishment of occupiers and collaborators – capitalists, bureaucrats, and mercenaries – hence the independence of the country (Tito) as a prerequisite for all other moves toward self-government; nationalisation and creation of a unified planned economy (Kidrič); realisation of a bourgeois revolution in a patriarchal-comprador and despotic country. Such liberation included equality for all before the law including women and the young; mass rise of young peasants (to power during the revolution, to urban employment after the revolution); mass creation of industry and of working class as well as of intelligentsia; realisation of even a Welfare State with social security (employment, education, health-care, electrification, a serious although inadequate attempt to build housing and urban infrastructures, etc.) It opened the doors to full freedom or disalienation, its emblem was *policy* (to adapt Rancière). It was a road to C1.

Limit: at the same time, the Party/State government was an intermediary, custodian, and protector of a liberation that, with numerous zigzags, increasingly turned towards oppression; that is, the oligarchy became a class *in statu nascendi*.* It closed the doors to the freedom of Marx's 'final human emancipation', its emblem was the *police* (to adapt Rancière). C2 was fossilising and fencing in C1.[3]

---

[3] Two years after writing this I stumbled upon two cognate matters:

6.1. These two principles, horizons, and currents clashed within the leadership of the Yugoslav Communist Party and the State: so far so good. But their potential dialectics was suffocated by a 'bureaucratic' tradition (in Marx's sense) of monolithism and non-transparency, here of Stalinist origin. Add the economic, as well as ideological, pressures of capitalism from outside, and then increasingly from inside as well (as per the immensely popular song 'Tata, kupi mi auto' – 'Daddy, Buy Me a Car'), stir and shake well in a closed vessel, and there's the SFR Yugoslavia for you.

∴

– ENGLISH TRANSLATION OF MARX, PASSAGE 5 (MEW 1: 359–60): 'Criticism is, therefore, fully justified in forcing the state that relies on the Bible into a mental derangement [*Verrücktheit*, pun on craziness vs. displacement – DS] in which it no longer knows whether it is an illusion or a reality, and in which the infamy of its secular aims, for which religion serves as a cloak, comes into insoluble conflict with the sincerity of its religious consciousness, for which religion appears as the aim of the world. This state can only save itself from its inner torment if it becomes the police agent of the Catholic Church. In relation to the church, which declares the secular power to be its servant, the state is powerless, the secular power which claims to be the rule of the religious spirit is powerless.

It is, indeed, alienation which matters in the so-called Christian state, but not man. The only man who counts, the king, is a being specifically different from other men, and is, moreover, a religious being, directly linked with heaven, with God. The relationships which prevail here are still relationships dependent on faith. The religious spirit, therefore, is still not really secularised.

First, data about the fourth-century theologian Ticonius, according to whose commentary upon the *Apocalypse* the Christian Church is a 'bipartite body', divided into a black and a clean aspect (*fusca* vs. *decora*), the first of which belongs to the Antichrist and the second to the Saviour. He was clearly influential on Augustine of Hippo's concept of Earthly and Heavenly City – which Marx may have remembered in the *Jewish Question*. This encounter was no big surprise, I dealt with the salvational parallels as well as differences of communism and religion already in 'Inside', but the exasperated split into two notional bodies is a pleasing boomerang.

Second, a sentence in Engels's letter to Bracke of 30 April 1878: '[W]e should not forget that all transfer of industrial and commercial functions to the State can today have a double meaning and double effect, according to the particular circumstances: a reactionary one, a regress to the Middle Ages, and a progressive one, a progress to Communism' (Marx-Engels, *Briefe* 236).

But, furthermore, the religious spirit cannot be really secularised, for what is it itself but the non-secular form of a stage in the development of the human spirit? The religious spirit can only be secularised insofar as the stage of development of the human mind of which it is the religious expression makes its appearance and becomes constituted in its secular form. This takes place in the democratic state. Not Christianity, but the human basis of Christianity is the basis of this state. Religion remains the ideal, non-secular consciousness of its members, because religion is the ideal form of the stage of human development achieved in this state'.

– DS METAMORPHICALLY (taking Thesis 6 into account!):

Thesis 7. Criticism is, therefore, fully justified in forcing the State that relies on Holy Writ to understand that it is in a deranged and crazy position in which it no longer knows whether it is a fiction or a reality, and in which the dubiousness of its *empirical* aims, for which ideology (c2) serves as a cloak, comes into insoluble conflict with the sincerity of its *communist* (c1) consciousness, for which communism appears as the purpose of the world. This State can only save itself from its inner torment if it becomes the *police agent* of the institutionalised Party.

Gloss to 7: In the two-headed Janus perspective from Thesis 6 above, the idea of the State as the police for the Party is true only for one completely negative – monolithic and despotic – face of government in SFRY: this was completely and 'purely' striven for by the Party conservatives, who are therefore non-Stalinist Stalinists. But with this reservation and to that extent (which is yet to be determined) – it is true. The only alternative: the State should – gradually but steadily – wither.

7.1. In the etatised, oligarchic, police face of the so-called communist State, what prevails is *alienation*, and not *people*. The only people who count are those of 'a special mould' (Stalin), moreover directly linked with ideology (with Heaven). The relationships here are still relationships of *faith*. The religious horizon of official communism is, therefore, still not secularised or laicised.

But the 'State communist' (c2) horizon cannot be really secularised, for what is it itself but the *alienated* form of a transitional stage in the potential development of human emancipation from millenary State power, patriarchal violence, and class exploitation? These alienations *demand* a schism between the earthly and the heavenly horizon, operative also in the period of potential transition from class society to communism. The State-communist stance can be realised and abolished [*aufgehoben*] only insofar as the stage of development of human emancipation of which it is the ideologically alienated expression is radically and permanently revolutionised in a this-worldly, *disalienated* spirit. This may take place in such a socialist society where direct plebeian self-government would prevail over etatism and other alienations. The basis of this cohabitation would then not be State communism but human emancipation or communism (C1).

∴

– ENGLISH TRANSLATION OF MARX, PASSAGE 6 (MEW 1: 360–1): 'Political democracy is Christian since in it man, not merely one man but everyman, ranks as *sovereign*, as the highest being, but it is man in his uncivilised, unsocial form, man in his fortuitous existence, man just as he is, man as he has been corrupted by the whole organisation of our society, who has lost himself, been alienated, and handed over to the rule of inhuman conditions and elements ... That which is a creation of fantasy, a dream, a postulate of Christianity, that is, the sovereignty of man – but man as an alien being different from the real man – becomes, in democracy, tangible reality, present existence, and secular principle'.

– DS VERY METAMORPHICALLY (but within Marx's vocabulary):

Thesis 8. Real and integral political democracy is communist (C1): it restrains and humanises the necessary State. State communism (C2), however, empirically knows man in his uncivilised, unsocial form, man in his fortuitous existence, man as he has been corrupted [*verdorben*] by the whole organisation of our patriarchal and capitalist society, alienated, handed over to the rule of inhuman conditions and elements. Official communism may dream of and postulate the sovereignty of man as the highest being, but that is an alien being, different from the 'really existing' man. In real communism (C1) this creation of fantasy and dream would however be tangible reality, present existence, material principle – carrier of self-determination and self-awareness. Marx's 'transitional period' is the growth of people from C2 to C1. This is the criterion for any measure and institution in it.

∴

– ENGLISH TRANSLATION OF MARX, PASSAGE 7 (MEW 1: 354–5): 'Where the political state has attained its true development, man – not only in thought, in consciousness, but in reality, in life – leads a twofold life, a heavenly and an earthly life: life in the political community, in which he considers himself a communal being, and life in civil society, in which he acts as a private individual, regards other men as a means, degrades himself into a means, and becomes the plaything of alien powers'.

– DS METAMORPHICALLY (this alienation is not transferrable to Yugoslavia *tel quel*, at least not before the 1970s):

Thesis 9 (alternatively to Thesis 8). Where the communist State government has developed into a closed ruling elite or politocracy, people lead – not only in thought, in consciousness, but in reality, in life – a twofold life, ideal and real (heavenly and earthly). They live in a community in which they consider themselves communal beings, and also live in a civil or bourgeois society in which they consider themselves private individuals, regardless of all other individuals that are being treated as a means, and in which they become degraded and playthings of alien powers.

∴

– ENGLISH TRANSLATION OF MARX, PASSAGE 8 (MEW 1: 357–8): 'The so-called Christian state is the Christian negation of the State, but by no means the political realisation of Christianity. The state which still professes Christianity in the form of religion, does not yet profess it in the form appropriate to the state, for it still has a religious attitude towards religion – that is to say, it is not the true implementation of the human basis of religion, because it still relies on the unreal, imaginary form of this human core. The so-called Christian state is the imperfect state, and the Christian religion is regarded by it as the supplementation and sanctification of its imperfection. For the Christian state, therefore, religion necessarily becomes a means; hence, it is a hypocritical state. It makes a great difference whether the complete state, because of the defect inherent in the general nature of the state, counts religion among its presuppositions, or whether the incomplete state, because of the defect inherent in its particular existence as a defective state, declares that religion is its basis. In the latter case, religion becomes imperfect politics. In the former case, the imperfection even of consummate politics becomes evident in religion. The so-called Christian state needs the Christian religion in order to complete itself as a state'.

– DS METAMORPHICALLY (with a supplement):

Thesis 10. Similarly to a State which professes religion, the so-called communist State is the communist negation of the State, but by no means the social realisation of communism. The so-called communist State is the imperfect State, and communism is regarded by it as the *supplementation* and *sanctification* of its imperfection, so that communism necessarily becomes a *means*, and the State – a *hypocritical* State. The so-called communist State needs communism in order to complete itself *as a State*.

Gloss to 10: In that case, the official Party-State communism (c2, although the official interpretation in Yugoslavia avoided the term 'communism'!) becomes an ideology in the negative sense of an alienated view of reality. Since it still invokes the original communism of Marx and of Lenin at his best (c1), c2 becomes hypocrisy as well, like to the Christian Pope preaching evangelic love for fellow-man (to stay with Marx's parallel) from the opulent St Peter's Cathedral and the State enclave of the Vatican to masses gazing at the megalithic colonnade. The closing of doors to Marx's integral emancipation (lineaments of which were becoming visible as an integral self-determination in economics and politics) transforms even the very real contributions of the first Janus head increasingly into hypocrisy. Yet that hypocrisy remains 'a tribute which vice pays to virtue' (La Rochefoucauld).

c2, the 'religion' of government, is in comparison to c1 always a partial – and eventually becomes a fake – achievement. It is within this discrepancy that the Zagreb magazine *Praxis* appears, as an example of the conscience of communism (c1) – which itself is also one-sided, being oppositional and militant instead of sovereign and triumphant.

Thesis 11. In (important!) contrast to other-worldly religion, this-worldly communism understands the second sentence of Thesis 10 as a *temporary postponement* of perfection – until the productive forces of a people are developed and outside threats eliminated (which practically means *sine die* or, so far as we can see in ever-worsening capitalism, when hell freezes over). I suppose that this aporetic gap gives rise to important strategic modifications for the future to Marx's political horizon itself, which are to be based on philosophical anthropology and very costly experiences. Centrally, the necessary orientation towards the role played by economic production and consumption in disalienation – albeit in the long term pivotal – must be conjoined with the role of democratic power outside direct production.

Gloss to 11: In fact, communism has no sense whatsoever unless it preserves the horizon of a radical this-worldly salvation, namely mass production of a qualitatively better life, and not only social-democratic reformism. But how? C1 is **politically** a matter of developing, within communism and as the essence of communism, efficient and intertwined forms of both associative and direct democracy, in the interaction of State and the rest of society, and *economically* a matter of developing efficient and intertwined forms of many-sided and pyramidal planning on the basis of critical feedback from such a democracy. **Philosophically**, it is a matter of resisting all pretences to the One Final Truth, and all attendant corollaries of Oneness from top down; these are best seen in Stalin's monolithism and his ubiquitous vertical chain of the 'single command' system [*odinonachalie*], but are well and thriving in all Churches and capitalist corporations.

Religion (monotheistic) is beyond repair; Marxism and communism (C1) are not.

Thesis 12. Communism cannot abolish politics, that is oppositions within civil society between citizens of a State or other community. Marx gave to politics the exclusive sense of antagonistic collisions, in the final instance based on class interests; this strand runs from the passages discussed earlier to, for example, *The Misery of Philosophy*, and culminates in the *Communist Manifesto* conclusion that 'Political power, properly so called, is merely the organised power of one class for oppressing another' (Tucker ed. 353). After the twentieth-century revolutions, however, we know also of 'non-antagonistic contradictions within the people' (Mao). Without civil-society politics to resolve them, only the State remains for that job – a necessary, but very one-sided politics from above. This became the major fault of Leninism, growing out of a backward patriarchal reality.

Today we may redefine politics as existing outside class antagonisms too, so that its germs could well be present in and intertwine with class politics (what else is C1 in the 'transitional period'?). The State cannot really be abolished until its necessary functions are taken over by associations of producers as well as associations of citizens – civil society – in manifold institutions of direct democracy from below (see more in Suvin 'Communism' and other chapters).

Gloss to 12: We are talking here about *the self-determination and self-awareness* of individuals interacting within the social totality (according to Hegel at his best). These terms are derived from individuals, as active and reflexive aspects of their sovereign being, and they can be understood as *self-government* of oneself and of human collective affairs against the horizon of mortality.

If self-government is understood solely as a translation of these terms into the language of mass administration (self-*management*, as in Kardelj), this remains a necessary but not a sufficient step.

⁂

— ENGLISH TRANSLATION OF MARX, PASSAGE 9 (MEW 1: 357): 'In periods when the political state as such is born violently out of civil society, when political liberation is the form in which men strive to achieve their liberation, the state can and must go as far as the abolition of religion, the destruction of religion. But it can do so only in the same way that it proceeds to the abolition of private property, to the maximum, to confiscation, to progressive taxation, just as it goes as far as the abolition of life, the guillotine. At times of special self-confidence, political life seeks to suppress its prerequisite, civil society and the elements composing this society, and to constitute itself as the real species-life of man, devoid of contradictions. But, it can achieve this only by coming into violent contradiction with its own conditions of life, only by declaring the revolution to be permanent, and, therefore, the political drama necessarily ends with the re-establishment of religion, private property, and all elements of civil society, just as war ends with peace'.

— DS METAMORPHICALLY (and, in the end, totally different but within Marx's vocabulary):

Thesis 13. **In periods when the State government is born violently out of society, when liberation through the State is the form in which people strive towards their liberation, in this time of special self-confidence, the State seeks to smother (*erdrücken*) its prerequisite, the society of citizens, and to constitute itself as the real fullness of man, devoid of contradictions. But the State can achieve this only by coming into violent contradiction with its own conditions of life, only by declaring the revolution to be *permanent*, and the drama necessarily ends with a change in the character of the State or a change in the character of the society.**

Gloss to 13: I think this corresponds to the ongoing dilemma of SFRY. Extraordinary: although Marx cannot be literally applied to it, he formulated the dilemma of its government as coercive power brilliantly indeed! As we know, the drama ended with a change in the character of the State (in the worst possible version of the Yugoslav Secession Wars between feuding mini-classes and captive peoples), *because* no change had come about in the character of the citizens' civil society (no full direct and associative democracy) in order to empower a full vertical association of producers.

∴

I have two conclusions, one based on Marx and the other on experiences from the October Revolution onwards:

– ENGLISH TRANSLATION OF MARX, PASSAGE 10 (MEW 1: 370): 'Only when the real, individual man re-absorbs in himself the abstract citizen, and as an individual human being has become a *species-being* in his everyday life, in his particular work, and in his particular situation, only when man has recognised and organised his "own powers" [Rousseau, *Contrat social*] as *social* powers, and, consequently, no longer separates social power from himself in the shape of *political* power, only then will human emancipation have been accomplished'.

DS METAMORPHICALLY:

Thesis 14. Only when real, individual people re-absorb in themselves the abstract citizen of the State [*Staatsbürger*] and when individual human beings have become in their day-to-day life, work, and relationships integrally human beings, only when people have recognised and organised their 'own powers' (Rousseau) as *social* powers, and, consequently, no longer separate social power from themselves in the shape of *State* power, only then will human emancipation have been accomplished.

AFTER MARX, WE TODAY:

Thesis 15. However, whenever C2 suppresses C1 (Stalinism, today PR China), this is a counter-revolution that annuls the beginnings of disalienation (Enlightenment, Welfare State, attempts at self-government). The metamorphosis of Luxemburg's slogan 'socialism or barbarism' in conditions of hegemonic world capitalism is: 'Communism (C1) or counter-revolution into savagery'.

In sum, as Rousseau well saw: if the Ruler (ruling class) kept a will separate from that of the Sovereign (the people), eventually the interests of the former towards self-preservation might (or had to) collide with the preservation of the State (Book III, chap. 1, also II.3). This shall be further discussed in the rest of this book.

Glossary

coupure épistemologique: epistemological break
mutatis mutandis: having changed what needs to be changed
in statu nascendi: just being born
tel quel: as is
sine die: without defined or any deadline, irony for 'never'

CHAPTER 7

The Communist Party of Yugoslavia

> Certain citizens of the City we just founded possess some knowledge that doesn't judge about any particular matter but about the City as a whole and the way it should best comport itself, both internally and toward other Cities ... Thus, a whole City ... would be wise because of the smallest group and part in it, namely the governing or ruling one. And to this group ... belongs a share in the knowledge that alone among all others is to be called wisdom (*sofia*).
> PLATO, *Politeia*, ca. 380 BCE

> *post res perditas* (after all was lost)
> MACHIAVELLI after the fall of the Republic

> *felix qui potuit rerum cognoscere causas* (Happy is s/he who can get to know the causes of matters)
> VIRGIL on Lucretius

∴

7.0   Introductory Overview

The Communist Party of Yugoslavia (under its various names) was the backbone of holding SFRY together and developing it. It is indispensable to explore its trajectory in the roughly 30 years from coming to power to settling into a sterile crisis around 1972.

Section 1 attempts to ground what follows in the statistics of Party membership and its evident turning from the initial peasant bulk, led by some radical workers plus professionals or intellectuals, to an employee and white-collar bulk presided over by a politocratic oligarchy. Section 2 discusses the main Party problems and achievements, which I group under the concept of singularities and resistance to them. Section 3 concludes with an assessment looking backward from its final failure.

My thesis in this book is that in the 1960s the Party 'reformers' reached a compromise with the middle-of-the-road against a return to Stalinism on a platform of politocracy rule, and became 'decentralisers', which meant more power to the republican and local leaders plus verbal and smaller material sops for the workers and much consumerism for the middle classes on an only partly controlled market. The ruling monolith fragmented into a polyarchy of 'republican' power-centres. But the Party's historical block or tacit alliance with the plebeian classes forged at the end of the 1930s and during the Liberation War was waning, while no possibility of open pressures by these classes was being developed.

In Chapter 4.2 I argued that a State ruled by a Leninist party, under permanent threat of world capitalism, must look to its ideological and material defences. However, I read its principal conflict after the first few years as one between the budding oligarchy and self-government of the masses. In Yugoslavia, because of its singularities, a small part of the Party tried to think about a disempowerment of oligarchy. But since its professional core, out of class interest, shied away from bottom-up democracy, it could not allow it inside the Party either. An impasse resulted in the form of a veto power by the regional oligarchies, which became nationalist and chauvinist as against the power top in Belgrade. In an unfavourable international political and economic climate, the split oligarchic classes became as a rule ready to turn into neo-comprador bourgeoisies at the service of foreign financial capital. The inglorious downfall of its last 15 years and collapse into a congeries of feuding dwarfish classes leading mini-nationalisms is the final, suicidal Yugoslav singularity.

7.1   Some Central Data

First we must get to know who – in the sense of typical or representative groups – we are speaking about.

7.1.1   *The Party Top*

In the early 1970s a team headed by Barton and Denitch analysed 'Opinion-Making Elites in Yugoslavia'. It tabulated the ***top 120 people*** (bar some at the very top who didn't have time to participate) by prior occupation (45); I shall consolidate and rename their findings as follows (followed in parenthesis by % for the 'elite' 1918–41):

TABLE 7.1 *Prewar class provenience of the 'elite' (in %)*

	Comm. party early 70s	Old elite 1918–41
Ruling class (financial, military, State officials, professional politicians)	0	(45)
Professional and white collar	59	(56)
Workers	37	(0)
Peasants	5	(0)

This 'communist elite' was roughly, I surmise, the top surviving professional revolutionaries from 1941 plus 10–15 top experts recruited into the government administration at the end of the war. (Characteristically, the only comparable proportion among professionals in the 'elite' between monarchist and socialist Yugoslavia was of lawyers, 16% after the war and 22% before! In a wider group of over 1,500 top 'opinion-makers' in 1969, a huge 29% had completed law studies: and in federal administration every second person had a law degree [137] ...)

Immediately below this apex of maybe 150 people there was – as I argued in Chapter 3.2.2.3, following Branko Horvat's necessarily fuzzy statistics (170–1, 176, and 184) – a top and a middle governing group which in the early 60s might have comprised respectively ca. 60 and 70 thousand each, though the middle stratum was destined to rapidly expand with the shift of power to the federal republics and partly to the local level. One would assume that they were almost all in the Party, and that this 'leading cadre' group remained in the 1960s between 150 and 250 thousands; the numbers tally with the Party membership at the end of World War II and up to the 1948 expansion (see Table 7.3 below). Horvat's hypothesis accords well with the later statistics in SG81: 110, which finds employed in 'Societal activities [meaning the political organisations] and State organs' in 1965 183,000 people, the number then falling until 1969 and after that rising to 210 for 1974 (this number does not comprise the rapidly rising 'technocracy').

As to the class composition of the Party and its centres of power, Barton et al. (47) cite data which I again summarise (with % of the class in 'economically active' population added at the end):

TABLE 7.2   *Class provenience of CPY leadership 1948 (in %)*

Level	Workers	Peasants	Others[a]
Top leadership[b]	39	7	54
Local leadership[c]	40	23	37
Total membership	30	49	21
Share in population	13	73	14

Note (a) Intellectuals, students, salaried employees, others
Note (b) In federal and republican Central Committees
Note (c) In district, town, and local Party committees

The Party Central Committee confirmed at the crucial 1940 Fifth Conference had 18 workers, 16 intellectuals, 3 employees, and 1 peasant (Cohen 119). The prewar leadership was thus composed of professionals/intellectuals and workers in equal proportion; the urban/rural divide of the 'elite' (Barton et al. 54 and 109) shows that less than one-third came from communities of over 5,000 people, so that it can be concluded that both these groups were largely first-generation descendants of peasants. This should be compared to the Central Committee of 109 members elected in 1948, after the purge of 'Cominformists', which had 38% of (ex-)workers, 5% of peasants, and 57% of employees plus intelligentsia, with an average age of 35 years; of the last group 59% came from middle-class or petty-bourgeois families, 38% from peasant ones, and 5% from worker ones, so that over two-thirds of the leadership was of peasant or worker origin (Cohen 119, 125, and 123).

7.1.2   *The Party as a Whole*

Before the mid-6os the statistics on Party membership were published on the occasion of Party congresses and only rarely and unsystematically in between, so the situation was unknown to everybody except the inner circle of rulers and some top administrators. But it can now be approximately reconstructed (from *Pregled*, Filipi, and *Situation*) as follows:

TABLE 7.3 *Flux of membership (in thousands, rounded off)*

Year	Total	Women	Notes
1941 (April)	12	not available	Note (a)
1945 (end of WW2)	141	not available	50 died in war
1946	258	43 (estimate)	
1947	285	47 (estimate)	
1948	483	84	Note (b)
1949	531	96	
1950	607	109	
1951	705	123	
1952	773	132	
1953	700	121	
1954	655	113	
1955	625	106	
1956	649	108	
1957	755	124	
1958	830	138	
1959	936	157	
1960	1,006	167	
1961	1,035	171	
1962	1,018	169	
1963	1,019	172	
1964	1,031	178	
1965	1,046	184	
1968	1.146	not available	
1972	ca. 1,000	not available	
1976	1,400	not available	

Note (a) 9,000 of the 1941 CPY members died during the war and 3,000 survived. To this should be added the important SKOJ (Communist Youth) with 30,000 members (by July 1941, the beginning of guerrilla warfare, the number had rocketed to 50,000, see Petranović & Zečević 507), without whom there would not have been the necessary cadres for the partizan movement in 1941. The population before World War II was 15.5 million.

Note (b) At the end of the year the category of 'candidates' (probation members of CPY), then numbering 52,000, was abolished, so the 1949 number includes most of them.

I am not aware of detailed statistics about the class composition of Party cadre 1945–8 beyond Table 7.2 above, but Dedijer believes that in 1945 ca. 90% came 'from peasant or semi-peasant environments' (565 – 'semi-peasant' might count in either small market towns or first-generation descendants of urbanised peasants).

There were two early crucial years in this flux. The first was *1948–9*, the conflict with the USSR and the Cominform, when between 50 and 60 thousand members were expelled (and a quarter of those arrested) on suspicion of siding with Stalin. This was statistically swallowed up in the unannounced but ample recruitment drive in the first half of 1948 in view of the brewing conflict, which accounts for at least 80,000 of the 1948 members (Bilandžić 158); the 'Cominformists' were thus ca. one seventh of the early 1948 Party membership. It can be assumed that in 1949 one third of the Party were new members, presumably less prone to the cult of Stalin.

The second is the obvious dip in the years *1953–6*, with 187,000 members expelled (Filipi 749 – as of this period there were significant oscillations also in the number of members resigning of their own accord, which must be inferred because it was not systematically published; for example, in 1957–64 it was around 200,000, cf. *Izveštaj* 32). It was due first to the debacle of the village collectivisation campaign in 1953 (Barton et al. 100) and immediately thereafter to the ouster from power of Milovan Djilas and his sympathisers. After the patchy results of the first Five-Year Plan – which were partly hidden and partly attributed to the USSR/Cominform imposed blockade – the collectivisation was a first obvious defeat of the Party. It was mismanaged in a moderately Stalinist fashion both during its course and in the lack of explanation for backing down, which also meant the lack of a perspective for village politics. As mentioned in Chapter 3 and confirmed by further statistics, this marks the divorce of the politically awake part of the peasantry from the active enthusiasm for Party-led politics which had lasted for a decade, from 1942–3 on. But I suspect, though cannot prove, that a final factor for the alienation of somewhere around one quarter of the 1952 Party membership was also weariness after a decade of huge psychological strain, where all the hours and sinews were devoted to the armed revolution and then to organising a largely destroyed and hugely threatened country. The climb down from collectivisation, and the immediately following, inevitable delimitation from Djilas's abstract utopianism of simply abrogating Party power, were certainly much less bloody and more dignified than the diametrically opposed course embarked upon by Stalin at the analogous period in the USSR after 1927, with the disastrous collectivisation and brutalisation, but they took a toll.

To the contrary, the rise in members *1957–61* can be attributed first to the threat after the Soviet put-down of the Hungarian uprising of 1956, and more lastingly to years of economic growth, decentralisation to the federal republics plus the refurbished communal system, and a cautious but significant expansion of self-management, while the stagnation or fall in *1961–5* is strictly homologous to the economico-ideological difficulties of the time, such as the growing disunity among the Party leaderships in the various constituent republics (see 'Nedovoljno'). Tito rightly remarked that workers joined the LCY in greater numbers 'when it was uncompromisingly engaged in putting the socialist program of development into effect' and conversely left it when it was vacillating (speech at Tenth Congress of LCY, in Comisso, 'Can' 71–2).

Beyond the above statistic, Carter points to a large number of people leaving the Party in *1970* amid the apathy after the turn to the market and the repressed student demonstrations of 1968. Anyway, the rise of the market economy and technocracy as well as the fixation on education degrees meant that as of this time 'the membership of the Party was much less important than it had been earlier, or than it was subsequently to become' as a stepping stone to a socially privileged position (30).

The percentage of **women** oscillated during 1946–66 between 16 and 18%, it was highest in 1949 (data for 1946–7 are estimates based on the number of women in the partizan forces during the war). Prior to World War II there were practically no women in legal politics, so that their large wartime involvement – 100,000 women were in the partizans where they constituted ca. 1 in 8 fighters, many more were in the often just as dangerous supporting organisations (Cohen 126) – constituted a decisive watershed. An additional cause for their dip 1953–8 and permanent stagnation thereafter was the productivist dogma that industrialisation will solve everything, which also meant the downplaying of particular organising for women. A further factor was widespread patriarchal attitudes: female membership was in Slovenia down from 32 to 27% and in Croatia from 28.5 to 21%, while in Macedonia it fell from 14 to 11%, in Bosnia, the epicentre of partizan warfare, it fell from an astounding 22% in 1946 to 14–15%, and in the professional armed forces it was 4% (in 1965 perhaps 3 out of 76 thousand people). Furthermore, the percentages were much lower in the top leadership, where they oscillated between 3 and 9% (Cohen 127). As to the social composition for the mid-1960s, Table 7.4 shows that the main groups of women members were either in the factories (ca. 32,000, probably ca. one tenth of the worker members), or in various offices including those of the ruling class (ca. 104,000), or in 'territorial' Party units (41,000 pensioners and housewives); of the scanty handful of peasant members, women were 1 in 9 (*Izveštaj* 38).

TABLE 7.4   *Women party members in mid-60s (in %); others' make up the small gap toward 100 %; professional army members not counted*
ADAPTED FROM FILIPI 781

Class	1964	1965	1966
Workers	18.3	18.0	17.1
Peasants	1.9	1.5	1.4
Professional, white-collar	52.9	52.9	53.1
Students	3.9	4.4	4.9
Pensioners, housewives	22.7	22.9	23.0

More articulated data about *Party social composition* are available for a few years later, at what was near to the apex of LCY popularity, in Table 7.5:

TABLE 7.5   *Social groups in party in 1968 (numbers in thousands)*
ADAPTED FROM BARTON ET AL. 113

Social group	No. in LCY	In population	% of group in LCY
Leading cadre or personnel	83	107	77.2
Professional army		not available	
Technical intelligentsia	50	112	44.4
Security personnel	31	84	36.5
Non-technical intelligentsia	129	443	29.1
Students	37	143	25.8
Administration employees	140	900	15.5
Workers	357	2,439	14.6
Pensioners	90	1,256	7.2
Unemployed	16	327	4.9
Private peasants	84	4,420	1.9
Private craftsmen	5	292	1.2
Housewives and 'others'	34	2,700	1.2

Comment (by lines, where needed): All data are estimates; the data for the army are unclear and to my mind unreliable, but the % of the professional armed forces in LCY would have been near to the first line. 'Technical intelligentsia' meant primarily the engineers, while 'non-technical' meant the humanist, medical, and similar intelligentsia; their % in the Party is strikingly high, as is the case with students. The pensioners include a great number of former partizans given preferential options for retirement due to war service. The small number of peasants is an example of the Leninist bias against and lack of understanding for this class, recently the bulk and mainstay of Tito's partizans. The full number of LCY members was then 1,146,000, and of the Yugoslav population 20,154,000, with those over 18 years 13,140,000.

In 1948, the Party membership was 'by provenience' 30% workers (see Chapter 3.2.2), but probably around half of them had left the working class for the partitocracy. After the early 50s, the proportion of workers stagnated, so that by 1954 it was overtaken by members in administrative jobs (Filipi 755); only highly skilled workers rose from 5% in 1961 to 9% in 1965 (idem 775). Also, a higher than usual proportion of workers were being expelled from the Party (Filipi 766, Horvat 231). In 1962 workers and peasants accounted for 20% of the local Party committees and 13% of the district ones (Horvat 202); the numbers decreased in higher committees, and as time went on. By the mid-60s I calculate that the percentage of the actual manual workers in the Party was smaller than their 30% in the active population.

The best breakdown I found of the 'professional and white-collar' group in the Party, officially called Employees (Carter 260), gives a clearer picture:

TABLE 7.6 *Breakdown of 'employee' membership 1969 (in %)*

Group	Number	% of party
Managers (leading cadre)	67,250	6.1
Engineers and technicians	54,765	4.9
In education, health, science, and culture	132,853	11.9
Administrative staff	138,217	12.4
TOTAL	393,085	35.3

It ought to be stressed that a great, often inordinate attention was paid in the Yugoslav system, and therefore in statistics too, to formal qualifications and degree of schooling. It was the key to the economic and ideological division of the working class into perhaps five fractions (as analysed in Chapter 3). Technical and other intellectuals are defined by their university degree, without which one is a simple technician or employee, and further divides obtain between high-school and elementary school graduates. This was also a way to avoid class analysis, while simultaneously constituting a pointer (often the only one extant) to it. An example might be the statistic about mid-60s women in the Party used in Table 7.4 above, where my category of Professional and White-Collar is in the original divided into university, high-school, and elementary school graduates (respectively ca. 9.8, 25.7, and 17.5%, in all 52.9%). After the 1960s practically everybody aspiring to prominence had to obtain a graduate degree; a case in point may be Franjo Tudjman, who seems to have politically browbeaten professors into it.

A telling overview of Party membership % 1946–68 (that Barton et al. 116 take from Nikolić ed.; cf. Carter 260), divided into Workers, Peasants, White-Collar, and Others, which I abbreviate even further, may serve as a summary:

TABLE 7.7   *Trajectory of membership by class 1946–68 (in %)*

Workers rose from the 1946 fictitious % of 27.6 to a high of 36.7 in 1962 and then fell to 31.2, and in 1971 to 28.8 (Carter 32); there was a clear shift towards more highly skilled workers. In 1961 workers comprised only two thirds even in the industrial Party cells (*Izveštaj* 35).

Peasants fell precipitously from the 1946 % of 50.4 to 42.8 in 1952, 22.6 in 1954, and 7.4 in 1968 (not all counted as such were actually working in the fields).

The misleading category of ***Others*** includes pensioners, students, housewives, and a few others; it fell from the 1946 % of 11.7 to 6.1 in 1962 and then rose to 18.7.

The even more obfuscatory category of *'White-Collar Workers'* or ***employees*** hides, of course, the ruling class, its direct administrators, the technical and humanist intelligentsia, and all other employees. It rose steadily from the 1946 % of 10.3 to the 43.8 of 1968.[1]

As noted earlier, the major demographic and social shift in the first phase of SFRY was the movement of more than 1.5 million peasants to the cities, and the flow continued unabated. Barton et al. note that this shift 'from peasant to worker or white-collar-cum-administrator, was spearheaded by the Party members, who were also the most mobile. [This meant] that the most active,

---

1   See for the seven categories of 'occupational background' statistics in the Party Cohen 173.

articulate, and talented activists in the villages left' (117). In 1953 Party statistics were revised from counting provenience to counting present profession, which resulted in 45,000 peasants and 93,000 workers – out of 700,000 members – being declassified as such (Filipi 762); it can be inferred that most class composition statistics 1945–52 should be analogously revised. As of the mid-1950s, 'the LCY had ceased to be a predominantly peasant party without becoming a working-class one' (Rusinow 96–8); it had in fact become predominantly a party of employees and office-holders, who by the mid-60s even had an absolute majority (Horvat 199–204). By that time there were 77,000 peasants in the million-strong LCY (Filipi 754–55, cf. Rusinow 144–5), mainly functionaries of the trading cooperatives and suchlike institutions in the countryside. The Party aged: after SKOJ (the Communist Youth League) was abolished in 1949, the People's Youth organisation grew increasingly bureaucratic and irrelevant (Carter 34). In the 50s *youngsters* up to age 26 were 40% of the members; however in 1966, when the 26–40 age cohort comprised 59% and the over 40 cohort 30%, young Party members were only 12% (cf. Rusinow 137 and 144–5, *Izveštaj* 37). In fact, by the mid-60s the average age of the Party leadership was the same as their prewar antagonists in 1940 (Cohen 126). The young came back in great numbers in the 1970s (*Situation* 72), but then for career purposes (see for worker members Lazić 128, 196, and *passim*). Horvat's summary in the late 60s was that instead of the major admittance criterion being 'sociopolitical commitment' (that is, carrying out Party decisions), it should have after the first decade rather been moral stature and work (227).

7.1.3   Concluding Pointers
Writing in the mid-60s, the well-informed Horvat concluded:

> In 1963 workers and peasants made up 20% of communal [Party] committees, and 13% of the district committees ... [T]he percentage must be still lower for the higher echelons ... [Thus] employees dominate the organisation, and especially its leadership ... If we add that relations in the Party were 'hierarchical and semi-military' (as M. Todorović stated), it becomes clear how dangerous the pressures toward bureaucratisation were in the LCY.
>
> 202–3

After the first post-war decade the LCY was predominantly a party of people working (or not) by sitting down, rather than of the manual labourers standing up. At this point, no value judgement is implied, except that official ideology clung to the vehement affirmation that it was ruling in the name of the workers.

And a careful foreign observer living in Yugoslavia summed it up for 1965:

> Generalisations based on such statistics are hazardous ... [B]y 1965 over 70% of the rank and file and most middle-grade officers had not been adults during the war; 75% of them had not been members ... before the break with Stalin; [and] the top leadership by virtue of longevity in power had survived and might be presumed to have learned from a greater variety of revolutionary and post-revolutionary experiences than in any other socialist State except China.
> RUSINOW 145

The central point to remember is that the Party was, at least from 1950 to the beginning of the 1970s, 'not a homogenous self-identity but the battleground of progressive and conservative forces' (Petrović 22) – that is, of those for self-management and expanding plebeian democracy vs. those for monolithic and opaque Party rule.

7.2 Main Party/State Politico-economic Problems

I am not writing a (however potted) history of the CPY/LCY, but an overview of what seem its essential historical features with a view to explaining its great successes, its tergiversations, and later symmetrically great failures. As Lukács rightly remarked about Leninism, in it the Party's role is even more decisive after the revolution, so that 'every turning point in [mass history] is always simultaneously a critical internal Party matter' (86). It involves articulating economic problems with political decisions. I have therefore chosen to give a sketch of the main politico-economic developments and central problem clusters in this chapter. However, the transfer of focus from the whole population to the Party means that I shall group the problems a bit differently than heretofore.

7.2.1 *1945–65: Successes and the Creeping Third Singularity*
In 1945, as realistic foreign commentators noted, Tito, the partizans, and their whole programme were outright popular in all parts of the country (Auty, cited in Fejtö 1:70), and won the elections hands down. The Party, by now 141,000 members hardened by war, in majority young peasant men and women but with an important leavening of intellectuals and professionals, took over the key positions in the government, as it already had in the army and in the developing security apparatus, busy fighting counterrevolutionary guerrillas in the

mountains for years to come. Thus began a period of enthusiastically reconstructing the almost totally destroyed country, mainly by manual labour led by Party members and voluntary youth 'brigades' (cf. Calic 184); Fejtö rightly calls it also the period of democratic reforms (universal suffrage, agrarian reform, democratisation of education, and much more) – in fact the first Enlightenment government in the Balkans (1: 127–9).

After 1948, the lesson from the 'Cominform conflict' with Stalin was to shun 'the deformation of any communist party which identified itself with the State and with the police apparatus' so as to avoid its fallout, where 'the working masses had been isolated from government and separated from the execution of power'. The only way out was in reviving the people's power of partizan days – that is, self-management (Kardelj, *Reminiscences* 122–3); the privileges of the 'bureaucratic caste' were in good part revoked (cf. Fejtö 1: 305). Between 1950 and the end of 1952, professional Party functionaries were reduced from 11,900 to 4,600 (Lilly 23), and ever after their number stayed at a low level of ca. 3 per thousand of the membership (given that the Party did not much trust outside institutions, probably too low a level):

TABLE 7.8 *The party apparatus (f. = functionaries, e. = employees)*
EDITED FROM COHEN 400

Year	Central f.	Central e.	Republican f.	Republican e.	Total
1950	(unknown)	(unknown)	(unknown)	(unknown)	11,900 (f. only)
1965	58	146*	1,311	2,026*	3,482*
1972	15	213*	796	2,364*	3,373*

Note *: of the employees only 22 % were 'specialised political workers', the rest staff.
If we do not count the latter category, the Total for 1965 = 1,847, for 1972 = 1,378.

But then, economic needs and problems, always threatening, loomed increasingly large: as in all countries east of Germany or south of the Gulf of Mexico, '*industrialisation was an imperious necessity*' (Fejtö 1: 299). Whence was to come the absolutely needed 'primitive accumulation of capital' for industrialisation, urbanisation, and economic development in general? As suggested earlier, self-governing from below and foreign threats eventually made impossible a Stalinist dispossession of small private peasants, of dubious immediate help anyway. Further, after the secession from Stalin, some top leaders' rediscovery of the Paris Commune and of their own partizan roots in Marxian self-government set the Party out on the road of both strengthening the local centres of power down to the basic territorial units and of slowly introducing *self-management* in the nationalised enterprises. As of 1950, Tito found beyond domestic surplus from labour a second source of financing which permitted him to dispense with forced collectivisation of land and subservience to Moscow: *foreign loans*. I argued in Chapter 2 how 'Western' strategic interests during the Cold War did not mean these loans turned SFRY into a semi-colony – this can be followed in detail in Lampe et al. – but allowed its social experiment roughly a quarter century to develop. That space-time became meaningful on a world scale when it was used for an experiment in self-management, first through workers' councils in industrial enterprises, and then extended to all 'societal service' workplaces from education and culture to health, as well as an experiment in global peaceful coexistence through the Non-aligned movement (see Kuljić 132 and *passim*). A '*second revolution*' (Fejtö 2: 225 ff.) sketched out a zigzagging road to socialist democracy from below (cf. Buden, Denitch, Kardelj 'Snaga', Lilly 3, 250, and *passim*), which I shall follow.

The strength and overriding novelty of a communist social remodelling lay in *centralised economic planning* for wider production and greater productivity – if wisely and democratically managed. Simultaneously and contradictorily (it is the contradiction between the models of fake and genuine communism, C1 and C2, of my Chapter 6), this necessitated in historical practice a capillary broadening of central Party power. The Party had historically acquired – from Marx and Engels through the illegal struggles and finally World War I and the Russian civil war – a dominant military metaphorics and a siege mentality, which in a real (and later in part imaginary) siege fostered strong tendencies towards oligarchy, hierarchy, ridiculous meddling in details, and allergy to democracy: the bind that spawned Stalinism was ceaselessly reproducing it. The way out can retrospectively be seen as, first, the use of the best available data and models from both experts and the concerned 'working people', second and concomitantly, an open and level playing field for their competitive confrontation. The Yugoslav Party set up some economic institutes but their work was strongly counteracted (and eventually, certainly by the early 70s, nullified) by behind the scenes pressures from segments of the oligarchy – local, sectional, finally nationalist – intent on aggrandising their bailiwick; already in the mid-50s they had demoted Kidrič's central planning to unenforceable 'forecasts' (cf. Chapter 10.2.2). The Party had also inherited from Stalinism and its own illegal past a total aversion to public scrutiny (cf. Carter 89–92), constantly counteracting the 'partizan' mass openness. In theory, this led to a political organisation in two concentric circles: at the centre the Party, in the outer circle the People's Front, the local authorities from the communes upward, and eventually self-management by workers' councils. Between them, a constant feedback of stimuli and opinions was supposed to obtain. In practice, a fully hierarchical Party, where all the main decisions were arrived at by a few people and their intimate collaborators, meant that the outer circle, while allowing much minor grassroots initiative, was for major decisions a voting machine and propagandist adjunct, a Stalinist 'transmission belt' downwards. In short, 'the party was not ideologically prepared for all the complexities of peacetime construction from a position of power' (Horvat 195). The cultural level of its core cadre was on the average rather low: the spotty statistic for the Party committees in 1948 found the schooling background for ca. 70% to be four years of elementary school or less, for 15% 5 to 10 years of schooling, and for less than 5% a full high school or – very rarely – a university degree (Ranković 39). The cultural level of its core cadre was on the average rather low: the spotty statistic for the Party committees in 1948 found the schooling background for ca. 70% to be four years of elementary school or less, for 15% 5 to 10 years of schooling, and for less than 5% a full high school or – very rarely – a university degree (Ranković 39). The stifling Russian apathy was avoided in the experimental climate of the first 20 years; thought was free but propagating it in the press and then the rising media met not only with some understandable taboos, present in any society (cf. Carter 199), but with a generalised suspicion by Party cadres against rocking the boat and 'anarchy'. The best diagnosis extant at that moment, the one by Horvat cited in Appendix 2, clearly blamed the centralised and hierarchical Party organisation for a strong tendency towards 'dictatorship over the proletariat' and an oligarchic practice barring the road to real self-management (196–7 and 238).

Nonetheless, the need for mass support, the Party's own roots in the desire for justice, and economic imperatives combined to push in the 50s and 60s for a more or less democratic reform. Politically speaking, the battle was borne by a good part of the Politbureau, now dubbed Executive Committee, cautiously enlisting support from urban working people against the Party middle cadre in effective executive power:

> ... the process of decentralising party control from the top but not transferring power to the lowest levels created a middle layer of State and party officials, who were very anxious to preserve their positions and therefore became pillars of dogmatism and the establishment.
> BIĆANIĆ 69

But the battle was hidden, shadow armies fighting on a darkling plain beyond the public's understanding, so that support from the people could only be half-hearted. This was much complicated by a situation in which the vanguard Party was just creating the working class in whose name it purported to speak. Thus it see-sawed, based on contingent economic and macro-political pressures (Soviet stances, world market, and inner regroupings): in 1950–3 democratisation was advancing, culminating in the 1952 Sixth Party Congress with a remarkable attack by Tito on the USSR social system – expunged from his *Works* after the 1955 reconciliation, see Lalović – and in abolishing immediately afterwards the agitation-propaganda and the cultural departments of the Central Committee secretariat, practically the Party watchdogs and norm setters in these fields (Hoffman-Neal 180). The Constitutional Law of January 1953 introduced 'social self-management' also outside industry as well as a new Council of Producers in the federal parliament. But the Djilas affair of early 1954 entailed a clampdown of several years, the direct Party control then leading to much economic inefficiency (see on membership the comment on Table 7.3 above).

Then the wind began veering: in 1957 the first Congress of Workers' Councils was timidly held, against stout opposition of the Party middle level; in January 1958 the first workers' postwar strike occurred in Slovenia; in February 1958 the Executive Committee issued a sharp and public Circular Letter attacking bureaucracy and dictatorial, corrupt, even chauvinist practices by communists (Hoffman-Neal 201–3). This sequence culminated in the 1958 Seventh Party Congress and the remarkable LCY Programme adopted at it, which a group headed apparently by Kardelj and Party stalwart Veljko Vlahović was entrusted to write. Though Soviet protests against an early draft resulted in amputating a theoretical characterisation of Stalinism, enough remained to make this supreme articulation of Titoism quite indigestible to Khrushchev, and to Mao (Fejtö 2: 153–4). I cannot discuss here its imposing bulk and in places unmistakably Kardeljian prolix discourse: it had clear strong and weak sides, the latter (cf. for them Lalović, and on Kardelj Appendix 2 and Chapters 4.1.2 and 10.4) including too much optimism about world politics and too much scientism. However, I remember well the euphoria caused at the time by the conclusion: 'Nothing that has been created must be so sacred for us that it cannot be surpassed and cede its place to what is still more progressive, more free, more human' (*Yugoslavia's Way* 263). The prospect of such a permanent humanist revolution, alas, never materialised.

The properly economic aspect of the postwar development and the battle around self-management cannot be followed here in any detail; I am doing so in Part 3. Suffice it to say that after the ambiguous half-success of the first Five-Year Plan in 1947–51, the economy boomed from 1953 for most of that decade, indeed officially the industrial growth of Yugoslavia was among the highest in the world; the Five-Year Plan starting in 1957 was fulfilled in four years. Rusinow (98–100) summed up the result as better supply of raw materials and better infrastructures, but not better allocation of resources or control of prices, nor smaller disparities between the Northwest and the Southeast regions, since the social product gap grew (from 110:71 against the country average of 100 to 116:67). Again, in theory it was decided as soon as 1955, at a Brioni meeting of the Executive Council with experts, to abandon extensive for 'accumulative' industrialisation, which also meant a higher share of investment for agriculture and consumer goods (Rusinow 101–2), but in practice the extensivity lasted well into the 1960s. There was a recession in 1961–2, 'exposing the weaknesses of the compromise economic model of the 1950s' and inaugurating a polarisation within the oligarchy (idem 112). Both factions wanted to keep a political monopoly for the Party, but the 'conservatives' wanted to keep self-management penned up to manage the 30% of revenue allotted them in industry with the State disposing of the rest, whereas the 'democrats' proposed to build up self-management into a complete politico-economical system, up to the federal parliament and possibly government, as Kidrič had originally planned (see Chapter 5.2.1).

The logical end-horizon of the democrats would have been a return in the economic key to Lenin's 1917 horizon of 'all power to the Soviets', which had turned practically into 'all power to the Party' under the pressure of economic chaos and the civil war. This would have meant not primarily less power to the Party, which would still be hegemonic and in control of army and security forces, but less practical privilege – moral and material – to the Party cadres, from lowest to highest. Since Tito did not much like this idea and nobody except some intellectuals dared to propose that it be practically implemented, people like Kardelj and Croatian Party leader and economic theorist Vladimir Bakarić hesitated to propose it even to themselves, never mind publicly. (We still don't know what happened at the famous explosive March 1962 Central Committee meeting, except that Kardelj's position on top was seriously threatened and was saved only by compact Slovene Party support and threat of secession; one can surmise he learned the limits of what could be fought for, and concluded that a slow march through the institutions would have to suffice.)

In this bind, we must assume the 'democrats' reached a de facto compromise with what one could call the middle-of-the-road and became 'decentralisers', since this meant to one group power to the republican and local leaders, and to the other power to the self-managing working people.[2] The unreconciled

---

2 I differ here from the great majority of the otherwise useful Western commentators, such as Carter and Lilly, including the most deserving Rusinow, insofar as they were entirely innocent

hard-line conservatives took good care that only the first meaning was ever implemented; the façade of unity was kept. The 1960s' rise of a 'polyarchy' (Rusinow 192 ff.) in the ruling class and Party, including the six power centres in the federal republics, bolstered mainly pressures from lower echelons of Party and power, but very little directly from the working people. Most important, inside the Party, both at the federal and at the republican levels, half a dozen people in each Executive Committee or even just its Secretariat in fact decided all important matters (cf. the interventions, including Tito's, at the Central Committee 1966 session, in *Četvrti, passim*). Still, this meant that '[a]n impressive number of autonomously organised and institutionally legitimised forces ... [represented] diverging interests and values ...'; this was to a sympathetic observer an interesting and suggestive case of political democracy evolving without a multi-party system (Rusinow 347) – for one example, the youth press alone had 68 newspapers in 1969 (Carter 196). There was also a high turnover in the membership of the federal and republican central committees: in the federal one elected in 1964 the rate of renewal was 47% and in 1969 56%; and to the permanent core of professional politicians were at that time adjoined the 'politicised professionals' – coming from managerial and other part-time political careers (Cohen 152–4). But there was no possibility of open pressures on key choices by the still young and inchoate working class, as well as by intellectuals and youth, the forces which had (together with the long ago backgrounded peasants) carried the partizan spirit. In terms of the Party this meant that it was no longer only a cadre party, but it was confused and unable to tap mass energies from below (cf. Carter 31). The compromise shifting of power to the constituent republics and its territorial oligarchies could finally rely, against the power top in Belgrade, only on alliances with nationalism, which therefore made a remarkable comeback in the 1960s, buoyed on the wave of consumerism and a pervasive re-emergence of both native patriarchal and Western bourgeois mores.

7.2.2   *1965–72: A Half-hearted Battle Lost*

The mid-60s seemed to be a time of changes. In Russia not only the Stalin but also the Khrushchev destalinisation era was over, the apparatus settled into stasis. The Vietnam War had largely neutralised the USA as far as intervening

---

of both Leninist and 'new class' psychology and cut everything down to the Procrustean bed of liberals vs. conservatives (a canny exception is Comisso, *Workers'*, cf. 120). A clear differentiation should be drawn between 'liberals' in the sense of pro-market and unchecked development of bourgeois attitudes, and in the sense of pro-self-government and plebeian democracy from below.

elsewhere went. The first generation born in the post-war Welfare State was of student age and eager to flex its wings against the gerontocracy reigning everywhere. The economic development of the 'people's democracies' could only go on by means of trade within the world capitalist market, which meant exposing its production to foreign competition. As for Yugoslavia, though its problems were for the moment smaller, its economy was faltering at the beginning of the 1960s, and it too decided to go the path of increased foreign trade, which meant asking for increased foreign aid (around $350 million in 1961 alone) and for the future either reaching a favourable trade balance or huge problems of indebtment. At that point the unresolved minefield of the police within LCY exploded.

In Stalin's USSR, the Party had become dominated by the political police, and he exported this model to all the communist parties in the 1930s. In the 'people's democracies' of east-central Europe, '[t]he first acquisition of the revolution, its first base, was the police' (Deutscher 534). The exception was Yugoslavia, where the CPY organisational secretary Aleksandar Ranković was deputised by Tito to form an autonomous one – *Uprava državne bezbednosti*, the Bureau of State Security, popularly called Udba. It relied inevitably on the Russian strong-arm model, however tempered: instead of a whole archipelago of gulags, there were two main ones, and the number of prisoners seems to have been in the lower five digits; still, in 1951 Ranković admitted half of the arrested were finally exonerated (*Sednice* 522). The Udba eventually began capillarising through the whole society, but it was at this heady time of opening met with such vehement protests in the Party leadership that Tito sacrificed his close collaborator at a public Central Committee session in June 1966, and the incipient police State-within-the-State was reduced to something approaching normality. In the meantime inflation and unemployment had worsened and a 'great economic reform' was planned (Fejtö 2: 231), eagerly theorised and pushed by Kardelj and Bakarić.

The lingering spirit of partizan democracy and autonomy prevented descent into a police quasi-Stalinism. Yet the way this was done, by secret backstage manoeuvres using army intelligence against the police, testifies that the problem had itself arisen from the lack of a clear alternative – and principally: just what was self-management supposed to politically mean, for society as a whole and the decisive Party cadre nucleus? The long stalemate at the top meant that even steps in the right direction were arrived at late and piecemeal, and that the middle generation now arriving to power as well as the Party members (in 1964 71% of them were under 40 years of age! – Rusinow 144–5) did not have a clear horizon. There was no real democratic centralism in the Party: even for major decisions, the Central Committee met very rarely, and then only to affirm monolithism (cf. Miloslavlevski 248–9 and *Četvrti*). The status of leaders – professional politicians – was quite different from that of rank-and-file members, and what is worse this was quite unquestionable and bordered on semi-feudal subject loyalty. The Yugoslav singularity was singularly slow to unfold. In fact, the change of atmosphere in the Party itself seems to have been remarkable; a fully embedded but dissenting intellectual phrased it thus: 'The [Party] collectives were transformed into aggregates of private individuals, frankness and openness gave way to reserve and calculation, egoistic opportunism took the place of comradeship, principle was replaced by conformity, courage by careerism' (Horvat 195). Social mobility, as seen for example in the schooling figures by class (Horvat 238), slumped. Ideologically,

> Marxism ever more obviously split into dogmatism and pragmatism ... The waning of social mass activity was accompanied by growing institutional activity, ... [with] endless reorganisations on all levels ... founded on the illusion that through [these] social inertia can be prevented ... Hence a condition ensued which we called 'bureaucratic optimism'; our leaders frequently spoke of a reality not experienced by the masses ...
> RUS 278–9

The key plank of the 1965 reform was very promising: to empower production enterprises – the 'direct producers' – by raising the share of the produced income at their disposal from 30 to 70%. This would have not only delighted the workers, the more active trade unions under the leadership of Svetozar Vukmanović Tempo, the critical intellectuals, and the new educated managers (misleadingly called 'technocracy' in Yugoslavia), but would have also meant a major boost for financing economical *and* political initiatives from below. But it was impossible to put into effect without a parallel full democratisation of the Party as not simply a transmission apparatus from the top down (its ossification was best analysed by Cvjetičanin). This finally needed an empowerment of sustained loyal minority dissent inside it, cautiously advocated by dignitaries like Miloslavlevski and Crvenkovski (in Nikolić ed. 240–7, cf. Carter 76–9) but shunned like the plague by the top, including Kardelj and Bakarić (cf. for the latter 2: 288). Instead, the compromise of allowing a more or less unchecked market economy to co-exist with self-management was reached.

As a result of this knot, the income share of the direct producers leaped in the first two years after 1965 but then slumped back to 30%; the problem began to fester amid much friction and inefficiency. The etatist monopoly on disposing of surplus labour was not diminished or disempowered but decentralised into seven or eight semi-State apparati plus a burgeoning financial system based on the local republics (banking, insurance, foreign trade). The republics were rapidly becoming a power on a par with the central State administration, run by separate fractions introducing classical capitalist relationships in its key domain (cf. among many such diagnoses Bavčar et al., Divjak, Dyker 64–76, Kardelj *Subjektivne* 313–17 and *passim*, and Rus). Real income, which had almost doubled between 1952 and 1965 and further advanced to 1970, stalled; worker emigration grew by leaps and bounds and reached one million by 1973, when a reflux was imposed by the slumping West European economy (SG81: 18, 83, 95–6, Woodward 191–200 and *passim*, Baučić). By 1970 bank funds were 51% of all investments in production and housing, while the share of the 'Organisations of Associated Labour' fell to 27% (Rusinow 206)!

At that still undecided point of balance, Stipe Šuvar drew the best available picture of the politocracy top:

> Today in our country there are around 7,000 political professionals in socio-political organisations, and around 5,000 elected individuals in representative assemblies. That is the group which still adopts all major decisions ... which revolves in its own circles, which is connected hierarchically by an identity of interests and views notwithstanding struggles between cliques and despite the fact that it is no longer a monolith but formed of relatively independent centers of political power ... It has the right to higher personal income, to earn more outside the workplace, connections for influence and representation, honours, awards, etc. Its standard of living is guaranteed at the top and never falls to the bottom ... One enters this group according to criteria of loyalty and conformism and falls only ... as the result of excommunication in the settling of accounts between cliques.

Šuvar goes on to estimate the personal income among the top 50 people as 6,000 new dinars monthly each (ca. US$ 6,000 annually, compared to the average income of ca. $700), not including 'extra income for travel ... [and] many indirect privileges (office and staff both in Belgrade and the home republic, permanent car with driver, small plane for distance travel)', and so on ('Srednji' 92).

For a while it had seemed the interests of the direct producers could prevail 'by means of a major mobilisation of "factors of socialist consciousness", often outside the Party (trade unions, the student union, intellectual groups and institutions)' (Lalović 154). When this hit a dead end, and the politocracy stopped at 'half a step in self-management, and, what is worse, without a new concept of social planning matching the self-management system' (Kardelj,

Subjektivne 313), the resulting frustration erupted first as a 'new left' egalitarian one in the student demonstrations of Summer 1968, most sustained in Belgrade, which proved how large potential energies were available from below – and was spurned. The quarrelling Party, by now predominantly a white-collar organisation, drew itself together, as it did in the face of the immediately following Soviet invasion of Czechoslovakia, which sounded the death-knell of libertarian communism in Europe. But no problems were solved; Kardelj, reputedly the second man in the Party, acknowledged in 1970:

> The League of Communists of Yugoslavia has in some essential ideologico-political matters become almost impotent to keep to a common course of action in practice. Within ... our economic system and self-management, the pressure of ... various ways of sundering the working people from decisions about the conditions, means, and fruits of their work has effected serious inroads into our system and our revolutionary orientation. There are serious tendencies toward the expropriation of people's self-management rights ..., especially by way of an inadequate integration, the banking system, etc.
> *Subjektivne* 205

Therefore, the problems erupted again in much uglier ways in the nationalist 'Croatian Spring' of 1971, and had again to be put down by a show of force and personal demotions at the expense of the middle generation; this was unnecessarily repeated a year later in Serbia on the old Stalinist principle to preserve power by striking once at the Right and then at the Left. The Party, discreetly in the background from 1958, came back into direct command in 1972, parallel with the cumbersome and unenforceable, thus irrelevant, constitutional amendments at the time. Thus it became clear that 'the programmatic perspective of the emancipation of labour was quite given up, that the LCY had ossified into a bureaucratic apparatus falling apart internally, unable to see the real situation ...' (Lalović 154). Truly a vanguard from 1941 to the 1960s, the Party became in a more differentiated society the main brake upon further development of both self-governing democracy and economy (cf. Kuljić Ch. 6). Internally, it fell prey to the deradicalisation Michels had well described for the German Social-Democratic Party: how a stable professional elite of proletarians and intellectuals gets detached from its class origins and assimilates values of earlier elites.[3] The vanguard had become the Old Guard, and many in

---

3 See Michels 365–76. Interestingly, his reader Bukharin allowed Michels had shown that such

it 'embraced the Revolution as a profession and the Republic as a prey' (Robespierre 300).

In the Party statistics this can be seen in the startling reshuffle of the Central Committee elected in 1974 with 75% of new members and – more importantly – a mass re-emergence of the conservative wing of war veterans, the military (11%), plus tame sympathisers from workers (19%) and managerial staff (Cohen 156–9). The Party's insistence on the 'commanding heights' went hand in hand with the *embourgeoisement* inside and outside it.

At the end of the present inquiry, the Yugoslav economic model relied on the one hand on a largely uncontrolled and never examined profit motive and, on the other, on a largely piecemeal and inefficiently decentralised 'command economy' of the Soviet type in an ad hoc patchwork with a more or less free consumer market which led to a stall. Within it, 'Generational cleavages [we]re reinforced by the unselective, wholesale use of West European social models of behaviour, pushed by the mass media, particularly the popular journals and television' (Denitch 27). There was no organised public sphere 'to put pressure on the outrages of the [unregulated] market and on the arbitrary tendencies of the State institutions' (Rus 280). Further, 'republicanisation of money and finance ensured that the fundamental problems of macro-economic monetary policy would remain unsolved' (Dyker 89). Rusinow's judgment on it (345–7) seems to me fair: in this economy nobody could come close to rational allocative decisions. The laissez-faire element meant that traditional capitalist economic and political problems recurred, such as monopolies and misdistribution of riches without real regard to unequal ability or diligence. As in many Welfare States, the government then intervened to tamper with the economy, which here meant a return to the political 'strong hand', wielded by a fully careerist, State Party.

7.3   Looking Backwards

7.3.1   *Ending*

In Yugoslavia, the singularities discussed earlier nudged a part of the Party toward thinking about a disempowerment of oligarchy. But since its Stalin-

---

a '"degeneration", that is the excretion of a leading stratum in the form of a class-germ' was 'a tendency' within the transition from capitalism to socialism, which will however be counteracted 'first by the growth of the productive forces; second, by the abolition of the educational monopoly' – but he further allowed that the outcome 'will depend on which tendencies turn out to be stronger' (310–11).

ist genotype had an inbuilt distrust of democratic rule from below outside of the Party, it could not allow it inside the Party either. Tito had believed it was enough that the Party should return after 1972 to a leading role in order to ensure economic coordination and national unity. But an ideologically confused Party beset with multiple fissures, including a strong 'technocratic' fraction of financial institution leaders balancing between the politocracy and the world market and capitalist financial institutions, could not do more than paper matters over for another 15 years. The upshot was that it proved unable to resist the hurricanes of history, which smile at trapdoors to ramshackle shelters.

These world-wide hurricanes or shifts of tectonic plates may be summarised as follows:

> From 1975 onwards the pace of economic growth in the developed countries ... fell by at least half ... In some years there was virtually zero growth ... Unemployment became omnipresent and structural. The growth model ... had been based on various factors: very cheap energy supplies; importation of foreign labour; cheap raw materials; virtual full employment; fixed exchange rates between currencies; [etc.]. This growth was underpinned by a very rapid salarisation of an originally agricultural population, an abundant supply of family dependents and a demand that was driven first by postwar reconstruction, and then by wars taking place in the Third World ... This model finally ran out of steam more or less abruptly in all countries ...
>
> MOULIER BOUTANG 11; I tried to wrestle with this much less concisely at the end of the 1990s in three essays collected in *Defined*

The oil crises after 1973 and 1979 were additional catalysers and welcome excuses for not understanding what was an incipient mutation of Fordist industrial capitalism (and socialism) into globalised financial capitalism at its most unrestrained. It entailed the collapse of the USSR and its camp, driven into bankruptcy. The ending of tensions between the two camps in the high 80s cut out the economic prop of relatively easy loans from the West as well as its interest in a strong Yugoslav State (that is, army). It needed only a push, supplied by the German banks-cum-government and an eager Vatican, for the divided oligarchy to commit suicide as a class, and thereby to unleash the necessarily murderous, mutually exclusive nationalisms and tear apart Yugoslavia.

7.3.2 *What Remains?*

What then remains of the Federative Socialist Republic of Yugoslavia? Nothing can erase the inglorious and injurious downfall of its last 15 years and its collapse into the worst possible alternative: a congeries of mutually embattled dwarvish classes leading brainwashed mini-nationalisms. This is the final Yugoslav singularity, which pragmatically erased the founding ones. Together with the repressive and unintelligent course of events that led to it, it remains a lasting blot and regret. But of the original concept and practice, I think a lot remains – despite the *damnatio memoriae** enforced by the hatred, much of it self-hatred, of the 'successor' governments and statelets. Not only the various brilliant achievements of culture and cohabitation, its mass production of the first modern proletariat and intelligentsia in this part of the world – and, if I'm correct, in a bitter irony of history, of a new ruling class, perpetuated in its born-again successors in the seceding statelets – but furthermore a lesson for the future: since the only viable future for the Balkans is some kind of formally instituted peaceful coexistence and economic interchange, eventually perhaps even amity.

And what remains of the Communist Party of Yugoslavia? Again, not primarily a memory but a historical lesson. It is what I have called the singularities. They should be understood and meditated. The *external or power key* may here be the relationship of the Party to the State: the State's liberatory role cannot be but ambiguous and precarious (see my Chapter 6). This is mirrored in the Party's internal functioning; in Wang's witty inversion, the Party-State becomes the State-Party – shedding communism as plebeian democracy in the process.[4] An oligarchy falls under the curse of Montesquieu's aristocratic government, as it finds it easy to repress other social groups but difficult to repress (or discipline) itself: 'Public crimes can be published here, because they concern everybody; but particular crimes [that is, intra-oligarchic ones – DS] will not be punished because it is everybody's concern that they not be' (1: 146). The *internal or ideological key* may be the relationship of disalienation or emancipation to economism or productivism; that means accepting a non-manipulative version of Lenin's insistence on 'politics first' – with the strong proviso that politics is to be understood as open confrontation of legitimate 'socialist' interests, which then crystallises as criterion for everything else. In both economics and politics, the key was a development of the self-management system vertically up to the

---

4 The formulation is from Wang 8. There is by now a considerable list of disregarded modern proposals advocating democratic communism, for example by Merleau-Ponty, Gorz, Lefebvre, Bahro, Althusser, Magri, and Medvedev, perhaps the best initial articulation being in Anderson 98–100; I have approached it in a Marxian philosophical key in Chapter 6.

'republican' and federal power levels, replacing parliamentary democracy by delegation (delegation was then confusingly tried in the 70s–80s but without integral self-management, therefore piecemeal and too late). This would have meant changing the Party's role, no doubt through intense requalification and regrouping, from commander to trainer for consent: not necessarily with much less power, but with a power that interacts with an encouraged political as well as economic democracy going from the ranks upwards (I reflect further on this in the Conclusion).

The precondition for all that was a radical political and ethical change of the mindset inherited from Stalinism. Yet the professional Party core had totally forgotten Marx's and Lenin's eager life-long pursuit and acquisition of new knowledge. Indeed, they fell prey, from the 1960s on, to the worst intellectual sin possible: *they didn't want to know* – to face the radically new problems of the times.[5] A revolutionary politician must also be an intellectual: on pain of pursuing death.

Glossary

damnatio memoriae = ritual physical erasure of all public memory traces of an unpalatable former ruler, described by great Roman historians

---

5 At the end of the 1960s, Horvat bitterly complained that no major central body, including the Party Central Committee, had any long-term arrangement with a scientific body to investigate whatever fundamental problem, despite initiatives from the scientific side (Cohen 254). The situation was similar at the beginning of the 60s (also later, see in Appendix 2), when Horvat himself was fired as government advisor. Cf. Gorz 102–3.

PART 3

*Self-Government vs. Alienation:
A Tractate on Yugoslav Economics and Politics*

In memory of Tommy Asimakopulos, who first talked to me about Kalecki at McGill in the 1970s

⁘

This matter has a large scope. In this mass of ideas that come to my mind, ... I must discard left and right, I must break through and emerge.
　　MONTESQUIEU, 1748

Well, don't forget, Scott, that a great writer is not only a leaver-outer but also a putter-inner, and that Shakespeare and Cervantes and Dostoievsky were great putter-inners – greater putter-inners, in fact, than taker-outers and will be remembered for what they put in ...
　　THOMAS WOLFE, letter to Scott Fitzgerald 1937

⁘

I proceed here in two parts. Part 1, consisting of chapters 8–10, attempts a stock-taking of Yugoslav self-management and economics. Part 2, chapters 11–13, examines how what is presented in Part 1 meshed with the tension between Party monolithism and a development of integral plebeian rule.

SECTION 3.1

*On Self-Management in S.F.R. Yugoslavia:
A Critical Stock-Taking (1945–72)*

∵

The form of association, however, which if mankind continue to improve, must be expected in the end to predominate, is ... the association of the labourers themselves on terms of equality, collectively owning the capital with which they carry on their operations, and working under managers elected and removable by themselves.

    J.S. MILL, 1865

FIGURE 15

Youth Working Brigades 1948–1950: Andrei, Yovo and Mića in front of the British barracks in Sremska Mitrovica camping, Highway of Brotherhood and Unity Zagreb-Belgrade 1948, photo by them
AUTHOR'S COLLECTION

FIGURE 16   *Youth Working Brigades 1948–1950: British brigade at evening meal in Sremska Mitrovica camping, Highway of Brotherhood and Unity Zagreb-Belgrade 1948, photo by them*
AUTHOR'S COLLECTION

FIGURE 17   *Youth Working Brigades 1948–1950: Dutch brigade on the building site of University City just outside Zagreb 1950, photo by them*
AUTHOR'S COLLECTION

FIGURE 18

Youth Working Brigades 1948–1950: Dutch brigade at the building site of University City just outside Zagreb 1950, photo by them
AUTHOR'S COLLECTION

THE COMMUNIST PARTY OF YUGOSLAVIA 161

FIGURE 19   *Youth Working Brigades 1948–1950: assembly of Dutch brigade at the building site of University City just outside Zagreb 1950, DS sitting second row right with dark glasses, photo by them*
AUTHOR'S COLLECTION

CHAPTER 8

Anatomy: Macro-Political Economics, or the View from Above

> The more backward the country which, owing to the zigzags of history, has proved to be the one to start the socialist revolution, the more difficult it is for it to pass from the old capitalist relations to socialist relations.
> RICHARD LÖWENTHAL, 1970

∴

8.0 Introduction

The sequence of historical events embodies the only clues as to their essence (cf. Suvin 'Two') and their possible causal systems: 'the way to truth is not only an epistemological but also a historical process' (Marcuse, *Reason* 99–100). I have discussed how the tradition of the partizan popular revolution – an orientation towards plebeian power from below – made the Party shy away from Stalinist parasitary and stagnant monopolism with its unbearable cost in terror and people's blood. From the start, Tito and his comrades hoped for 'fraternal aid' by the socialist countries of the Soviet bloc; instead, they got exploitation and attempts at takeover rammed down their throats. Ironically, Tito then found in the Yugoslav Army and its unique strategic value a source of both military and civilian US and West European aid. This was considerable, around US$ 2,600 million (see Chapter 2.2), and – together with the surrender of their surplus labour, at first patriotic and enthusiastic and then customary and institutionally enforced, by most Yugoslav city dwellers – tended to solve for a good while (say for 20 years) the pressing problem of accumulation source.

I further proposed in Chapter 5.1.2 that Yugoslav history strongly suggests a subdivision into the 1945–61, 1961–72, and post-1972 phases, where the boundaries are not quite abrupt but could be easily moved two or three years in most cases, and that its events can be readily accommodated within a periodisation of world history after 1945 where a first major break occurs in the early 1970s (cf. Amin, *Empire* Ch. I–II and *La gestione* 21). This break or turn, I argued, was characterised by the exhaustion of the major impulses arising out of victory against fascism: the militarised Welfare State, the separation of the 'Soviet bloc' into a subsystem of centralised State planning (leading to Cold War and US roll-back strategies), and the decolonisation as formalised in the Bandung conference and then in the Non-aligned movement. This seems verified by my research into Yugoslavia, in which these three factors intersected. Before my *terminus ad quem* of 1972, revolutionary political pressures allowed economic growth outside the capitalist metropolitan areas, violating exclusive profit logic. It is followed by a period of erosion, crisis, and breakdown of the 'anti-fascist' phase and eventually the return to 'pure', savage and unbridled, profit capitalism, to all of which Yugoslavia became a prime example. It is possible this second period itself breaks down in the great economic crisis of financial capitalism in our years, the late Oughts and Tens, but it is too early to tell.

8.1 Foundation of Yugoslav Self-management

At the end of the insurrectionary war, the country was devastated: the average age of the over one million people who died in the war (7% of the population) was 22 years, 3.5 million were homeless; the Allied Reparations Commission estimated the war damage at 50 times the pre-war annual national income; the living standard in 1945 was estimated at about half compared to the already low one in 1939, with clothing and medical care at less than one quarter; the retreating Germans ploughed up all rail ties, and the whole country counted 200 trucks. Yet, with the important and welcome help from UNRRA – which supplied in two years $415 millions' worth of goods, including 1.2 million tons of food, 4,000 tractors, 237 locomotives, 15,000 trucks, etc. (see data in Fejtö 1: 127–9, Bobrowski 66–8, Hoffman-Neal 138–9, Lampe et al. 20–3) – the reconstruction rapidly attained, by 1947, much of the pre-war situation and overtook it in industrial production.

The reason for a small group in the Party Politbureau hitting after 1948 upon a system of Workers' Councils (*radnički savjeti*, further WsC) was, I believe, twofold. First, economically, there were two major problems that could not be solved by State centralisation and administrative fiat: (1) a remuneration according to work, that is a differentiation of pay required to stimulate productivity while preserving social justice; (2) a conflict between long-range planning and the limited horizon of an enterprise manager who is a public official appointed for a given period, and who is to boot often imbued with the patriarchal and Stalinist stance of authoritarian command. And in fact self-management was introduced at the time of very difficult economic battles to increase output and productivity (cf. Milosavljević, 'Država' 83–106 and *pas-*

sim, Woodward 145–52). It was meant to harness 'the popular consent and participation ... glimpsed in the industrial consultations, youth or volunteer brigade efforts, and shock-work' (Unkovski-Korica 20). In a longer view, self-management may engage the interest of the whole workforce in long-term results, if (and only if) the creation of elites in enterprises is prevented and a proper system of economic incentives for planning is created. Such an effective self-management should have enormous educational significance for socialist attitudes to work and ownership (cf. Brus 70–1). Its horizon would be both a noticeable rise in productivity, entailing a rise in workers' income, and a major beginning of disalienation in the workplace; both would translate into political support.

Second, at the time Yugoslavia was isolated in the world, realistically fearing a Soviet invasion, and needing a renewal of political enthusiasm from below. Symptomatically, the first public signals of such a course were given in the first half of 1950 by Kidrič's interventions, and by Kardelj's speech in the Federal Assembly when introducing the law about People's Committees (municipal authorities), sharply denouncing the 'bureaucratic apparatus': 'Socialism can only grow out from the initiative of millions of common people together with the leading role of the proletarian party, and by means of their ever larger participation in the State apparatus from its lowest to the highest forms' (*Reminiscences* 233). In the speech he expressly argued that such a 'principle of self-management' should be developed 'in every organised unit of our social life ... in the enterprises and the institutions, etc.' and specifically in factories (cited in Unkovski-Korica 11, and cf. Kardelj, *Samoupravljanje passim*). The WsC were supposed to supply an essential part of this renewal, as a potentially democratic way of running independent entities producing commodities, perhaps approaching 'a planned economy using a regulated market mechanism' (Brus 74, and cf. Kornai 334–40) – though after 1965 things got much more complex and less neat.[1] Due to pressure from below, the self-management organs gradually gained greater influence over some key decisions, so that, after a first period with emphasis on centralised command, the director (general manager) was selected by a parity commission of the enterprise WsC and the commune (lowest territorial unit) through public competition. The WsC issued their own internal regulations, including decisions about workers' income after subtraction of State taxes. Further, the area of self-management was in 1953 extended

---

[1] I use Brus (72–4 and *passim*) also for the WsC development since the 1950 law setting them up, with further data and evaluations from Bilandžić, *Historija* 175–8, 184–5, 215, 223, my Chapter 7, and others as noted. A retrospective survey of problems and opinions on the Yugoslav use of the market and then of the plan is in Korošić, *Jugoslavenska* 250–9 and 271–9.

from industry to State agriculture, trade, construction, transport, and communications, and then also to education, culture, health services, banking, and insurance (it was not applied to the army and security services, public administration, and the administration of justice, where the Party cells were supposed to provide the necessary balances). Soon self-management was timidly introduced to the 'parliamentary' or electoral system at the levels of commune, district, republic, and federation; in the latter first one and then at times several 'producers' chambers' were to represent self-management organisations in production, education and culture, health services, and social policy.

Crucial to all, and the source of major battles, was the attempt at creating economic foundations of self-management – a variant of the 'socialist accumulation of capital' conundrum. This concerns decisions about dividing the earned surplus between, on the one hand, workers' incomes and enterprise investment, and on the other, the general investment allocations, taxed away and then distributed by the State. The proportion between the two hands measures the balance between elements of etatism and of self-management in the society.

The 1945–52 years I have called the double Yugoslav plebeian singularity: first of partizan victory, with political centralisation and speedy economic reconstruction of the country following, and then of the successful break with Stalinism, resulting in the breakthrough of the workers' self-management idea as against 'bureaucratisation'. From 1950 to 1960 self-management and the first elements of decentralisation were introduced into the organisation of Yugoslav economy; in 1961–5 self-management powers were extended to distribution of incomes earned in enterprises, with the State retaining the dominant role in investment, and systematised outside of direct production as 'social self-management'; I shall here treat both of them together as a first stage. A second, see-saw stage, 1965–72, proposed to transfer expanded reproduction to enterprises, while leaving to the State authorities (federal or republican) resources for some defined general purposes, including reduced subsidy funds for backward regions, but this ran into the sand. Possibly the post-1972 degeneration could be divided into two, with a final phase from 1980 to 1989 (Močnik, 'Workers''), but this period introduces nothing new 'except phraseology' (Horvat, 'O socijalnoj' 54), and I do not deal with it (the sad tale is covered in Comisso, *Workers'* 124–35 and many later works).

8.2 Political Economics

8.2.1 *1950–65: The Lift-off*

Decentralisation was from this time and until the end of SFRY a key watchword and slogan, often resulting in more obfuscation than light (I shall return to this). In the first stage of 1950–3 the top-heavy system of central economic ministries was dismantled and its functions reassigned either to central planning or to the republican level; over 100,000 employees were let go from the central government and political organisations, so that the central State apparatus shrank by about half (Bilandžić, *Historija* 175–6). All enterprises henceforth depended on the republics, the federation retaining only rail, air, and river traffic as self-managed economic associations, and all had to depend on income from a combination of subventions and market sales. I explained in Chapter 5.2.1 how the remarkable statesman and theoretician in charge of economic affairs, Boris Kidrič, envisaged a system of self-management which would soon combine central planning with democratic control from below at all levels, up to the federal government. The salaries of all employed were ranged on a scale whose maximum spread was 1:5.5. At the same time, the Party changed from a cadre to a mass one, and changed its name at the Sixth Congress of 1952 to League of Communists, signalling the horizon of returning from Stalin to Marx. A rough estimate of major post-war wealth redistribution was that the average consumption of industrial goods changed from 100 in 1938 to the following indices in 1952 (Bobrowski 208; for a similar statistic up to 1955, by which time the gap inside 'employed people' seems to have shrunk, see Schleicher 335):

– Employed manual workers: 167
– Employed office workers: 75
– Poor and middle peasants: 137

Finally the Constitutional Law of 1953, in fact a new constitution, introduced 'social self-management' outside industry too, and instituted Councils of Producers from the local to the federal level indirectly elected by those working in production, transport, and commerce according to their group's share in the gross social product (cf. Schleicher 59–77). In 1953, the Yugoslav economy took off after years of scarcity, and at least one factor of the boom was the enthusiasm created by the WsC and the horizon of democratisation; in the seven years after 1950, WsC had had 1,129,000 members, of which 75% were supposed to be manual workers from the shop floor (*Pregled* 535).

At this point, a beat of arrest in social reorganisation followed, which saw the alienation of one quarter of the 1952 Party membership. It was and is often attributed to the shock of the early 1954 Djilas affair, and there is no doubt his ouster from power was a detonating factor. However, I have argued in Chapter 5 that other factors were weariness after a decade of huge success and huge psychological strain, the climb-down from collectivisation, a slow rapprochement with the USSR, and strong resistance to disempowerment inside the higher reaches of the Party. Crucially, however, the protagonist status of producing enterprises was firmly established. Many industries reoriented themselves towards consumption.

Up to 1961, central State administration determined the salary mass of each enterprise and retained ca. two thirds of all incomes. In 1958 the whole national cake was divided thus:

TABLE 8.1 *Division of national cake*
(out of 1,683 billion dinars in current prices)
BILANDŽIĆ, HISTORIJA 227–8

Rubrics	10^9 dinars	%
Investments into production	574	33
Investments for social standard	118	7
Other investments + refunds & subventions	23 + 39	4
State administration and defence	197	12
Other 'social standard' consumption	51	3
Personal incomes	663	40

At the time, investments were financed 39% by federal government, 31% by enterprises themselves, 7% by republican governments, 17% by lower territorial units, 7% by others (ibidem).

However, the most daring discussions of the 1950s, for example at a First Congress of Workers' Councils in 1957, did not go further than to ask for a larger share in net income – in 'surplus value', or gross receipts minus costs (which were material expenses, depreciation, capital tax, interests paid on credit, etc.) and minus local, turnover, and other State taxes (Horvat, *Towards* 117). This net income was to be given to enterprises rather than to the federal or republican governments and lower territorial units. The larger share did not happen; instead, the enterprises were entitled to distribute the income remaining after taxes without State interference (except for rules about minimum personal incomes according to qualification), but with strong input from the commune. All other matters – prices and subventions, foreign trade, planning, such as it was – were left as before; in fact, the 'surplus' managed by various political levels outside the enterprise grew in 1962 to 84% (Bilandžić, *Historija* 282). All energies were taken up by such limited debates and rising production-cum-consumption; the latter may be measured by real earnings which rose by 52% from 1952 to 1960 (Vanek 80).

The 1957–60 Five-Year Plan had on the whole a resounding success. Some results of those years can be seen in the Tables compiled from official statistics; the first is adapted from Wachtel 3, with 'motor power' added from Bićanić 88:

TABLE 8.2 *Growth of some key indicators, 1953–61*

Real social product per capita [analogous to GNP, in 1960 dinars]	Literacy %, age 10 and above	Population % in cities above 20,000	Motor power, kW / employed person
947	74	13.8	1.7 [1951]
1,636	82	22.4	2.12

If we divide the structure of households' expenses into two departments: (A) essential necessities (food, drink, and smoking, clothing and footwear, lodging and heating) vs. (B) 'sociabilities' (health and hygiene, mail and traffic, education, entertainment, and cultural consumption), then department A occupied in 1952 ca. 93%, and in 1965 ca. 77%. The large jump in 'traffic' from 1.6 to 6.3% was due to private cars – see Table 8.4 below – and in 'culture and entertainment' from 0.7 to 3.3% to TV sets (all Tonković 431). It should be noted that group B was always smallest in peasant households, and then in working-class ones, as compared to white-collar ones, and that this gap in class expenses for civilising 'superfluities' grew rapidly after the mid-60s (cf. Macesich 27–8). Agriculture also forged ahead in 1957–65, with large investment both in the State farms and in items such as mineral fertilisers and tractors even for individual holdings, so that the net material product jumped in 1957–75 almost by half while persons employed fell by one third (Simon 128 and 114, cf. Stipetić 329–33 and *passim*).

Finally, the gap to most other countries had been narrowing up to the mid-60s:

TABLE 8.3 *Comparative social product per capita (in constant US$ of 1970)*
FROM BILANDŽIĆ, HISTORIJA 287

	1954–6	1968–70
USA	905	515
West Germany	431	318
Italy	234	192
YUGOSLAVIA	100	100
Hungary	168	139
Poland	176	139

The Gini coefficient, a measure of inequality of income or wealth in which 0 means perfect equality of income and 1 maximal inequality, was in 1963 0.32, better than the rich capitalist countries. In Comisso's fair judgment, 'data ... do indeed show a high rate of growth, industrial expansion, an increase in the standard of living, and a shift of employment from the primary into the secondary and tertiary spheres of the economy' (*Workers'* 56). Further, 'labor productivity rose on an average of about 4% ... a surprising achievement when employment was also rising' (Dirlam and Plummer 158). Yet Yugoslavia was still 'a relatively underdeveloped, and extremely unevenly developed, economy, with an inadequate infrastructure ...' (Prout 5), with a per capita social product about half that of Italy. Furthermore, it had insufficient raw materials for some varieties of textile, fuel, and industrial chemicals, notably crude oil, and a permanent problem with foreign exchange (CIA 4: 52); also, the improving productivity was still low. And trouble was brewing because of some central structural contradictions.

A strong harbinger of possible openings toward plebeian democracy was, despite its many compromises, the Party programme promulgated in 1958 at the Seventh Congress – also notable for the all-time high of 32% worker members – which envisioned an ongoing revolutionary de-alienation (I cite from it in 7.2.1). However, real processes were more ambiguous. In the 1950s, two momentous changes had grown to be unquestioned. First, 'however intimately the economy, the State and the Party might remain interconnected and controlled by the last, ... these three basic "sub-systems" had been definitely disaggregated and given separate formal structures with inherent capacities for autonomous growth' (Rusinow 80). Second, as mentioned in Chapters 3–5 and

7.2, decentralising without empowering the plebeian classes created a middle layer of State/Party officials anxious to preserve their positions who became pillars of conservatism; economically, these local rulers 'came to exercise great discretion in economic matters and invariably used their power to pursue the interests of their own region, which ... amounted to obtaining investments for the construction of industry and then protecting that industry at any cost' (Paul Shoup, cited in Rusinow 49). This 'commune' oligarchy level, for which power was synonymous with opening jobs and extensive economic development – that often meant creating unnecessarily huge plants – was well integrated with the republican level, and also paid out of taxes on production. These two levels or oligarchic class fractions became the main drags on self-management and democratisation (cf. Bakarić 2: 398); the republican administrations busily poormouthed federal centralism but practised it in extreme forms towards the communes (cf. Milosavljević, '"Centralizam"' 369).

TABLE 8.4   *Socioeconomic indicators, 1950–1970*
FROM LAMPE 295

	1950	1960	1970
GDP per capita (in 1966 prices)	216	333	520
Infant mortality (per 1000 live births)	119	88	55
Illiteracy (% of population 10 and above)	25	20	15
Population per doctor	3,360	1,474	1,010
Radio receivers (per 1000 persons)	21	78	166
Automobiles (per 1000 persons)	0.4	2.9	35
Urban population (%)	21	28	39

An economic slowdown in 1961–2 exposed the weaknesses of the existing compromise model, which had not much mattered during the lift-off from deep backwardness, and made it clear that a rethinking of Yugoslavia's economics was urgent. For one example, as can be seen from the energy column in Table 8.2 above, industrialisation was 'extensive', based on cheap raw materials and cheap labour: economic growth in the above period was 59% due to an increase in the number of employed and 41% due to an increase in the productivity of labour (data in Bićanić 144). For a second example, the production of raw materials and fuel began substantially lagging behind the production of consumer commodities as of 1962 (idem 78–9), so that many plants operated well below capacity. The economico-political system was torn between development demands from all areas and all levels of power. However, it was blocked by the split inside the Party/State at the federal centre, pressured by the increasingly assertive republican administrations. Again an ad hoc compromise was adopted, which did little to impede proliferation of what were popularly called 'political factories': 'to everybody a little of everything. This method of *decentralisation without specialisation* [emphasis DS] was the least economical and the most expensive policy of development, second only to centralisation without liberalisation. The consequence was the creation of enterprises which were too small, too diversified and non-economic' (idem 198). In particular, the export-import gap widened threateningly: whereas in 1953 the foreign trade deficit amounted to 2,616 billion of new dinars, in 1961 it grew to 4,268 (idem 166), in 1964, to over 5 billion n. d. (over US$400 million), and except for 1965 continued rising every year up to 1983, making for a cumulative and dangerous indebtedness.

Together with high growth, a key economic goal had been to reduce the huge disparities in regional living standards by transferring much capital to poorer areas through a central General Investment Fund. However, despite significant investments, the gap was not closing. In my opinion, one of the key problems was that boundaries of the federal republics, which determined investments, necessarily disregarded natural economic areas. One example is the following juxtaposition of orographic-cum-agricultural zones with political zones (from Bobrowski XIV):

The political and ethnic compromises disregarded important features of Yugoslav economic geography: the *distribution of economic activities by regions* was not identical with the federal republics. Hamilton's pioneering, and so far as I know untranscended, survey from the mid-60s found a historical heritage of the country in a very unbalanced relationship between not only the 'Austrian' and the 'Turkish' part – that is, West and East of Drina river, with Bosnia hesitating in the middle but inclined to the 'Turkish' side. The deeper problem was different implantation of not only industrial capitalism but of the whole infrastructure for civil and civic life – beside railways and other communication lines which all went North-South instead of West-East, let me mention the seemingly different cases of electrification and gender relationships. The following map clearly points out the situation and its complexities.

The employment outside agriculture, by district per 1,000 of population, is evidenced in the map by different shadings: white for 30–69 new employments (70 is average for the whole country), cross-hatched with intervals for 70–109, cross-hatched densely for 110 and more. New employment is marked by a black 'proportional pillar', over a white pillar standing for the 1948 level of employ-

FIGURE 20 *Orographic map of Yugoslavia. Orographic and agricultural zones (above) vs. political subdivisions (below).*
IMAGE REPRODUCED FROM C. BOBROWSKI, LA YOUGOSLAVIE SOCIALISTE

ANATOMY: MACRO-POLITICAL ECONOMICS, OR THE VIEW FROM ABOVE 173

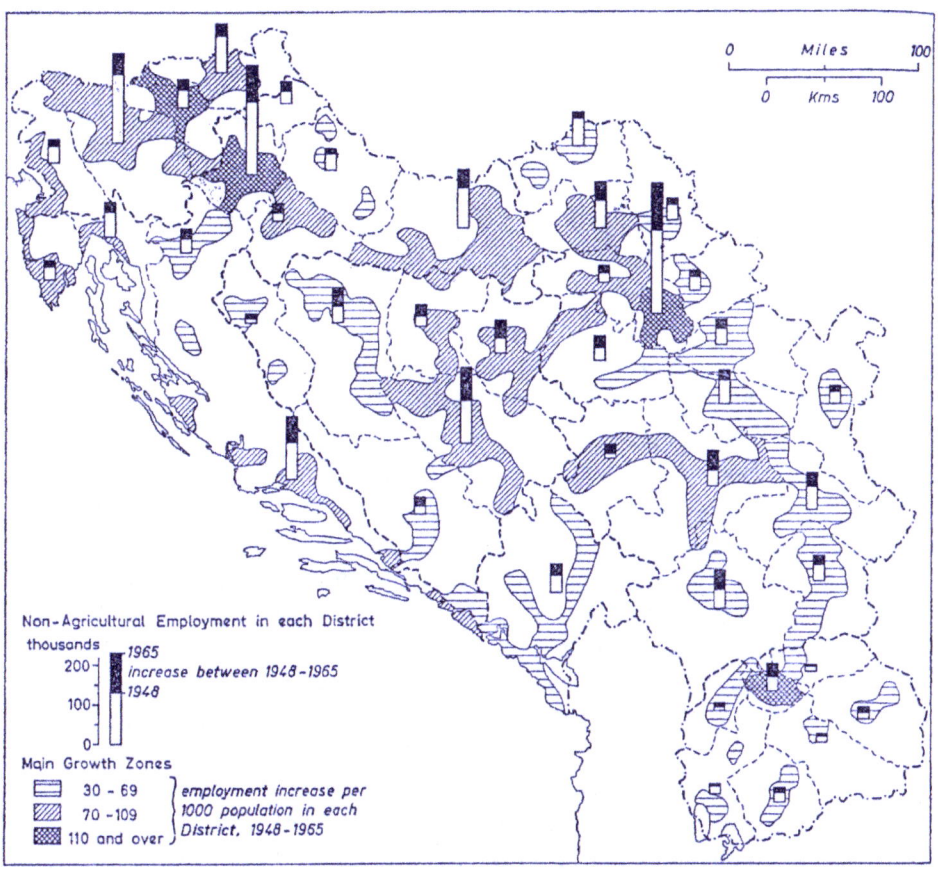

FIGURE 21   *Spatial Distribution of Employment Growth outside Agriculture 1948–65*
IMAGE REPRODUCED FROM I. HAMILTON, YUGOSLAVIA: PATTERNS OF
ECONOMIC ACTIVITY, 134

ment. But it is obvious from this and from Hamilton's following comments (134–7) that the republican boundaries cut across his *five significant growth areas* in which two thirds of all new employments are found, although the population of these areas was less than one half of Yugoslavia. They are: (1) 'Belgrade with south-west Vojvodina and eastern Slavonia; (2) west Croatia and Slovenia; (3) east-central Bosnia linking with west-central Serbia; (4) Dalmatia; (5) the Skopje region of Macedonia'. The growth in employment happens in and around the political-cum-administrative centres; in general, the new industries and services in districts that earlier did not possess them latch on to towns and their tributary areas well served by communications, including river valleys, toward other regions. The white areas mark stagnating regions –

mainly mountainous and 'pasturing', see Map 1 – where quick demographic growth accompanied by significant youth emigration led to a higher proportion of employment in agriculture.

This estranged view of an outside economic geographer shows up, first, the limits of the reigning exclusive political (thus also ideological and statistical) concentration on the republics: not only are they found to be multiply dependent upon each other but the real geo-economic regions largely cut across them. Second, as opposed to the power-wielders in the western republics who kept arguing that investment in 'backward' regions was unprofitable, Hamilton found that in all areas the levels of per capita investments basically account for the growth in per capita social income, so that high income stems from high investments and low income from low investments (see 141). Planning by economic sectors, necessarily leaning on an expansion of existing industries and communications, sometimes 'missed the greater benefits which could be derived from greater infrastructural investments into backward areas by integrated sector and spatial planning' (142). In brief, Hamilton convincingly argues that there was bad investing for quick effect, and he cites approvingly a study by Gorupić in 1962 according to which 'Yugoslavia really has no long-range, logical, and systematic development policy, not even at the Federal level' (Hamilton 143–4). This central failure led to inefficient use not only of labour power but also of educational resources in the country as a whole (cf. 145–7); it was never corrected.

No doubt, there was in poorer areas a goodly amount of waste – for example, bad choice of building sites in relation to supplies – but that often happened in the richer republics too. Thus the argument of the richer republics' leaders, principally from Slovenia and Croatia, that investment should be based on market profitability so as to get better results, was met by a justified outcry from the poorer regions (cf. Milenkovitch 179–80 and *passim*). Yet, in one of the fundamental political mistakes of SFRY history, the federal General Investment Fund was abolished in 1963 and replaced by a compromise, smaller Fund for Accelerated Development (see note 1 to Part 3, Chapter 12).

The root cause which held up a rational rethinking was 'a non-existent and increasingly evasive ideological and political consensus' (Rusinow 112; cf. Horvat, *Essay* 75) within the ruling oligarchy and therefore also the whole Party. The dilemma was, as always, whether to carry out further the democratisation from below – which would inevitably begin spilling over from economics to politics, and include narrowing the income gaps – or to return to central rule from above. The compromise solution, which no insider expected to last very long, was to do neither but to give more power to the republican administrations – 'that is, the creation of a federation which cannot rule over the bureaucratic elements in the republics' (Bakarić 1: 627). The republican governments, which tended from the very beginning to centralise all in their hands, were eventually left to grow by default into separate 'State capitalisms'.

8.2.2   1965 and After: 'Market Socialism'

The loss of clear goals by 'agencies of economic policy' became worrisome, though known only to the top, in 1961, when the first moves toward a new economic system functioned poorly and led to a breakdown in planning (Horvat, *Essay* 241). As noted, between 1963 and 1965 the social investment fund system was abolished. In mid-1965 the Federal Assembly passed new guidelines for the economic system, usually referred to as the Reform with capital R. The main reasons given were that many industrial enterprises were inefficient and technically backward and had to be subsidised, and as they grew that burden grew too; that protectionism meant there was little incentive for change in a monopoly market; that many branches of industry (textiles, metal, tobacco, food processing) had excess capacities amounting sometimes to two-thirds; and that participation in burgeoning world technologies could only be obtained by imports and world-market competition. Credit for unnecessary investment had to be restricted in favour of an 'intensive' rather than extensive economy, and cost of labour increased (both eventually proved impossible, the first because of inter-republican competition and the second because of the staunch and unanimous refusal of WsC to fire people: see Chapter 9 below). Kardelj spelled the objectives out in his fifty-page paper from that year ('Problems and Objectives of Socioeconomic Development', *Integration* 5–54): the aim was 'to develop forms of production and economic relationships which will require fewer coercive measures for their maintenance' (7) – from which laudable premise he proceeded to propose decentralising even the railways in little Yugoslavia.

In such a bind, the Western type of market appeared to most as the new saviour: industries which could compete in it had to be favoured, and internal administrative boundaries, especially the republican ones, transcended (cf. Bićanić 81 and 88). The currency was devalued to 12.5 new dinars to 1\$US (in 1971 this rose first to 15 and then to 17 n.d.). The economic objectives of the 1966–70 Five-Year Plan were stabilisation of the currency and prices and rise of efficiency and technological modernisation; a key political plank in it was that the share of enterprises in the net social product should rise to 70% (Bakarić 2: 173). Bakarić's retrospective justification for the Reform, in 1970–1, was that Yugoslavia could not economically stand alone, so that, having failed to find support in the socialist camp, it had to open up to the world market; yet its foreign trade was small and structured in a 'quasi-colonial' way, exports being mainly raw materials and imports goods to develop productive forces, and later also consumer goods since they sold well (3: 157). This is dubious: the export structure jumped from 7% of finished manufactures in 1952 to 43% in 1962 and kept rising (Macesich 187, Simon 78, Lampe et al. 99), so that in 1965 raw materials accounted for only 17% of exports (Hamilton 127): metal goods or textiles sold very well abroad. Perhaps more important, Bakarić was confident that new laws then in preparation would reverse the downward trend, for example by subjecting bank and other credit to efficient control (3: 243–4): this did not happen.

There were some successes, such as a 25% rise in workers' productivity in four years (Bilandžić, *Historija* 314), which was in Bićanić's judgement largely due to the extension of self-management downward to the 'economic units' (144); a possible benign influence was also the reduction of the working week to 42 hours in 1965. Further, private farms in the lowlands immediately used the credit now available to upgrade production: the number of tractors rose from 5,000 in 1965 to 39,000 in 1970, and fertiliser consumption increased by one half, so that production rose by 6% each year and reduced food imports to roughly the pre-1939 level (Lampe 288). However, the Reform failed to reach most of its objectives: gross national income growth, planned at 7.5–8.5%, achieved only 5.6% (as compared to 12.6% in the halcyon 1957–61 days and 6.6% in the reform-causing 1961–5 period), the efficiency of investments fell drastically and the trade deficit soared (Gnjatović 60–2, 135, and 152–3), passing from 14% of GNP in 1964 to 30% in 1971 (Samary, *Marché* 184–5). Though 10% of the enterprises were officially 'inefficient', toting up deficits, practically no consequences ensued: by 1971 only 1.1% were under provisional receivership (Drulović 103, cf. Comisso, *Workers'* 87). Processed export goods remained most diverse, in a scattershot way, while overall growth, and in particular industrial growth, remained heavily import-dependent (cf. Prout 210–11). The general trend of excess of consumption over production, which had already in 1960 reached 65% of the GDP, continued escalating (cf. Simon 50–1). Earnings per head in various sectors began to pull apart, rising most quickly in oil, electricity supply, shipbuilding, and chemicals; equally, payments by skill groups were increasingly skewed towards the top categories of both manual and office workers, though the range was still narrow by capitalist standards (cf. Estrin 131–2 and 138). Finally, the simultaneous reform of financing burdened enterprises with huge debts, which not only led to a wave of strikes after 1971 due to lower incomes but also much smaller – or zero – new investment by enterprises (cf. Dyker 63–7). The precarious balance of payments prevented lower prices and the proper development of processing industries, not to speak of electronics.

In brief, as in 1961, the major reform around 1965 was after much debate finally done in haste by the central bureaucracy, rejecting input from below, and failed to reach its objectives. In the best informed summation of Horvat, there was no international reason for the ensuing Yugoslav economic backsliding: 'Only in the oil crisis of 1973 were we for the first time more strongly affected, and by 1973 we had already prepared our inflation well, ... with built-in ... [and] in fact accelerating trends ... We did not create what a self-governing society ought to have created – the initiative from below' (*Jugoslavensko* 31 and 34). As a result: 'The 1965 Reform not only introduced a liberal laissez-faire policy of market relationships, its effect of growing differentiation between the republics and the social strata, of unemployment etc., led to the awakening of latent nationalism' (ibidem 36; see also 94 ff. and 41). Worst: the reform was tacitly abandoned and never seriously analysed, beyond slogans about excess liberalism (ibidem 31). The federal apparatus continued churning out literally thousands of new laws and regulations, to little or no avail. Power was handed over to a combination of financial capital in some banks and feuding republican hardliners.

The economic situation that resulted was well described by Woodward as not being the theoretical 'market socialism' à la Lange and Taylor: while there was substantial price and other regulation, there was no set of legally binding commands, quantity controls or directed allocations, so that the central government resorted to ad hoc quantity controls where immediate results were needed (169–71). The uncouth hybrid 'market socialism' (cf. Comisso, *Workers'* 72 ff.) should therefore probably be called 'market-cum-administrative' – that is, the socialist aspect was reduced to administrative fiat. The ad hoc interventions were a confession of failure, but they tided ruling interests over for one or two years at a time. This mishmash economic model did not fuse the capitalist 'law of [exchange-]value' with communist planned production for use-value, or indeed subordinate the former to the latter, but insured that neither could fully operate.

The three main consequences were, first, conspicuous *economic instability*. Most worrisome for social solidarity and the whole fabric were, first, rising unemployment at a time when the better schooled post-war generation was looking for work, to which I shall return, and second, inflation. The latter was caused by high import costs and by domestic factors such as low productivity, both in industry and in agriculture, which henceforth became a fixture and led to marked inefficiency of Yugoslav investments as compared to other countries of European periphery, from Ireland to Turkey (Bajt 13). The inflation came to average 22% by the early 1970s and began affecting the real wage (cf. Woodward 227–8 and *passim*, Simon 86–91, and generally Hanžeković in Bićanić

211–15); in the 1970s, it was by far the worst in Europe, together with Portugal (Tyson 76).

Second, *the balance between the federal centre and the republics* was drastically and permanently altered in favour of the latter; the federal government and political bodies lost heavily in prestige and efficiency, since going to work in Belgrade was, paradoxically, no longer a good career move (Bilandžić, *Historija* 354). To the contrary, the 1968–9 and later constitutional amendments ratified the growing authority of the republics and raised a refurbished Chamber of Nationalities into the key power point in the legislature; this was later also applied to top relationships inside the Party. The transfers of responsibility for social services from the federal centre to the communes, and then increasingly to the republics, both entailed a transfer of loyalties by those served and reduced funds.

The 'republicanisation' was one more factor of the third consequence, increasing social *polarisation* reversing the post-war trend. Income rates of the upper 10% grew in the late 60s more than twice as fast as those of the bottom 40% (Comisso, *Workers'* 96); this meant that a majority of young and unqualified workers could scarcely make ends meet each month. On the one pole, there was an exodus of workers to western Europe with a peak at around one million people by 1973; on the other, a lightning concentration of capital in the reformed banks which could now be founded not only by local communities but primarily or exclusively by business enterprises; I shall return to both in Chapter 10.3. The banks soon accounted for a whopping 45–50% of all fixed-asset investments and, in cahoots with republican authorities, disposed of foreign currency earnings. The government could only resort to ad hoc zigzagging by means of 'administrative' monetary policy, some remaining federal subsidies and investments, as well as temporary extraordinary fiscal measures. While this meant that its remaining redistributive role up to the 80s 'helped to keep differences in the social standard of living from growing intolerable', it also meant that federal intervention was done without long-range planning and 'not surprisingly created more problems than it solved' (Comisso, *Workers'* 91 and 80). The educational system was in middle schooling – from ages fourteen to eighteen – always split on strict class lines as between 'gymnasia' and trade schools, but in 1971 the 77% of peasants and manual workers in the population were represented even in such split middle schooling by only 57% and in universities by 42%, while the 15% of 'employees' were represented by 30% and 45% (Novaković 88–9, and see the whole section on vertical mobility and education 86 ff.). Finally, industrial production fell in the 1970s to the fourth source of currency revenues by value, after remittances from workers abroad, tourism, and agriculture. This marked a resounding defeat of the industrialisation political plank.

The federal State was economically and ideologically indeed withering away – there were no federal radio or TV programmes! – and without coordination so was rapid economic progress in production and standards of living; a 'development of non-development' came about (Bavčar et al. 118). In particular, hidden from official statistics was the tendency to crass inequality of incomes in the growing 'private sector', which included in 1969 nearly 5,000 small shops and 12,500 small restaurants and boarding houses (Dirlam & Plummer 79, and cf. 86 ff.; the tax system was undeveloped and lax), as well as to corruption. The economic consequences came to a head much later, but the political instability and polarisation were immediate – the student revolt in 1968 and the Croatian Party's slide toward nationalism interrupted in 1971[2] – and ominous, especially since their root causes were not addressed; these in turn persuaded the ruling class to supplement 'market socialism' with central interventions. Just as ominous was the turn to IMF loans, with Yugoslavia becoming in 1965 their first 'socialist' receipient.

---

2 See on the student revolt, especially articulated in Belgrade, the materials in Petranović & Zečević eds. 1122–33, Pervan, and more richly in Kanzleiter-Stojaković eds. I cannot enter here into its role and consequences; however, one clear consequence was the Party oligarchy's rejection of their radical Left demands for socialist pluralism, which left only nationalism as the basis of future mass support.

CHAPTER 9

Anatomy: Micro-Political Economics, or the View from the Workers

> Denn die einen sind im dunkeln
> Und die andern sind im licht
> Und man siehet die im lichte
> Die im dunkeln sieht man nicht.
>
> [Some in light and some in darkness/ That's the kind of world we mean/ Those you see are in the light part/ Those in darkness don't get seen. (Transl. J. Willett and R. Manheim)]
>
> BRECHT, 'Mack the Knife' song, 1930

∴

9.1   Workers' Councils in the 50s–60s

Marx's central stance, theorising centennial plebeian outrage, is an indignation against alienation and exploitation, the strategic knot of which he saw in the treatment of the industrial proletariat, and the overcoming of which lay in the associated producers taking the power into their collective hands, as against the State and the ruling class. This meant organising all social life around its new mode of production and reproduction, including circulation and consumption. The stance was affirmed by all socialists and communists before Stalin's etatist revision, for example by Lenin: 'The socialist State can arise only as a network of producers' and consumers' communes ... Every factory, every village is a producers' and consumers' commune whose right and duty is to apply the general *soviet* (council) laws in their own way'.[1] It entails a thoroughgoing self-determination of associated people on all levels and in all

---

1   Lenin, 'Immediate'. The history of workers' control in various countries, which is not the subject of this book, is well sampled by Ness and Azzelini eds.; the ups and downs of its fate in the early USSR can be seen in Bettelheim 1: 147–52, Brinton, Carr 2: 60–74, and some contributions in Mandel ed. The WsC came up spontaneously in most plebeian insurrections,

fields. In SFRY this would comprise territorial associations, from municipalities and 'communes' upwards, and association in direct or indirect production. As Marcuse suggests in various places (cf. *One-Dimensional* 251–2, also his paper published in *Praxis* 1–2 [1969]), **self-determination** is broader than the somewhat bureaucratic term of self-***management*** (*autogestion, Selbstverwaltung*) which does not clearly connote the radical liberatory aims and horizon of collective emancipation for one and all.

Within this spectrum, the central strategic cell and stance of ***workers' control*** is distinguished from ***workers' participation*** in that the highest authority rests with the workers, who decide, among other things, on the appointment of managers. In capitalism, there is no question of workers' control except perhaps in some cooperatives or a very few worker-owned factories. In Yugoslav practice it is not always easy to decide about the shadings between the two: at the beginnings the control exercised through the WsC was shared between workers, defined as ***all*** employees of an enterprise but with a sizable majority in elected bodies reserved for the manual workers, and the manager appointed by the commune, with a strong input by federal rules, which for example in 1950–7 set down the basic structure of wages or incomes; a somewhat reduced input was exerted later by various other bodies such as the tax authorities, the Social Accounting Service, and Economic Chambers for various industrial branches. The proper pragmatic term here, as Zukin remarked ('Representation' 267), would have been the British one of 'Work's Council', stressing the entrepreneurial aspect, but that would lack the utopian political aspect.

---

thus Hungary and Poland in 1956 and Czechoslovakia in the 60s, also China in 1956 and after 1967, Cuba in 1965, Chile, Portugal, Mozambique, Iran, and Nicaragua, while in response to popular pressures they were briefly introduced from above, sometimes directly stimulated by the Yugoslav experiment, in Algeria, Tanzania, Peru, Turkey, and Egypt; and there were surely myriads of unrecorded instances of such plebeian soviets in earlier history, for example when former slaves took over plantations in South Carolina during the 1867–77 Reconstruction (Blackburn 152). The theory will be mentioned in later sections, but see overviews in Bourdet and Guillerm (on definition 22–32, and a bibliography in French 267–86), Pannekoek (with a bibliography by R. Barsky, updated to 2001–2, on 209–19), and Vranicki, the latter reprinted in a large two-volume anthology of international writings dealing with *Self-governing Socialism*, from Owen and Proudhon on. A strategic survey of the participatory theory of democracy and its application to the workplace, from the French Revolution to Guild Socialism (but before the impact of Gramsci was felt) and with a chapter on Yugoslav self-management, is found in Pateman. An approach using the Yugoslav example for general discussion of industrial or economic democracy is in Mann Borgese and Adizes eds., with a useful select bibliography up to 1973. The distinction between workers' control and workers' participation is generally agreed to in English and French literature, for example in Pateman and Gould.

The notional basis of Yugoslav self-management was a sharp distinction between steering or governing and execution (*upravljanje* and *rukovođenje*), the first being the prerogative of the elected WsC and its committees, and the second of the Director and his appointed managerial hierarchy. This founding and initially inevitable idea, with its aporia of a self-management not supposed to have overall management, was, alas, later never questioned. Thus, as of the constitutional amendment 15 (operative in 1969), the Managing Board, later often revealingly called Business Board, had no class composition strictures, it began to be filled with executives and to overshadow the WsC; after that, outside of the incomes' differentials and firing, 'the worker had almost as much influence over the means left to the enterprise as he had over the means [collected by] the central government – that is none' (Tripalo 26; cf. Comisso, *Workers'* 110). In between, ***ca. 1958–68 is the Golden Age of Yugoslav self-management***, which I shall be focussing on.

In it, the self-managing collective was composed of manual workers, technicians, professionals, and clerical staff with equal rights of decision. The collective had exclusive managerial rights in the enterprise but no property rights in the net worth, which could not be alienated. New members were recruited when desired, existing members could leave when they wished, but no one could be expelled except for a clear reason and following detailed statutory procedures. Each enterprise formulated its plans, policies, and daily decisions independently, under the laws and regulations of the land. 'It may associate with others, operate mergers, set up new enterprises or divide itself if so desired ...' The enterprise was given initial assets, whose value had to be maintained through depreciation provisions. The results of its activity were disposed of through the market. The self-managing collectivity could share the resulting income among its members directly or in the form of common services, or retain parts for expansion of activity and a reserve fund. Theoretically, 'If [the enterprise] runs into deficit and cannot secure a loan, it will be wound up or reorganised and the workers' collectivity as such will cease to exist' (Vanek xv–xvi).

In 1966, there were 14,237 'worker-managed' enterprises, of which 4,458 were artisanal or 'Others', mostly small. The rest were of the following distribution and number of workers:

TABLE 9.1A *Number of worker-managed enterprises (end of 60s)*
FROM VANEK 94

Branch	Total	5–60	61–500	Over 500
Industry & mining	2,467	316	1,468	683
Agriculture, fisheries, forestry	2,890	1,072	849	169
Construction	706	248	308	150
Transport, communications	397	75	227	95
Commerce, catering, tourism	3,319	1,878	1,342	99

Of these ca. 10,000 enterprises, about half had less than 250 employees, but there were 201 with more than 2,000 employees; by number of employed, the Yugoslav enterprise was larger than its average Western counterpart (Vanek 105). There was a relatively very small number of firms and especially few with less than 100 workers – around 1958 SFRY had ca. 40% (and in 1965 only ca. 23%) of such small firms as against 73% and 91% in the UK and USA – so that 'the large hinterlands of small firms' from established capitalist countries was lacking (Estrin 83–4 and 117). The larger enterprises, those with over 1,000 workers and with 5 million dinars or more of capital, accounted for most of the country's economic activity (Macesich 154, Dubey ed. 120). This concentration kept growing: in industrial manufactures, the average number of employed rose from 372 in 1958 to 553 in 1966 and 643 in 1971, while the respective fixed assets in millions of dinars rose from 20.2 through 40.2 to 61.6 (Estrin 109). There were very few new firms from the mid-50s to 1964, then practically none until 1968 when the numbers soared, probably because of 'nominal changes' (idem 90); and there were virtually no liquidations. It resulted in 'a considerable proportion of [product] markets [being] monopolies or oligopolies' (idem 86).

All employees of an enterprise were deemed 'producers', including those under 18 and trainees, and elected a non-remunerated WsC as the supreme management body, with a size of between 15 and 120 members according to the number of employed (in enterprises with 30 or less people they were also the WsC); until 1959 the elections were annual, after that biennial. No elected member could serve more than twice in succession, which was an option for education in breadth, and in 1950–8 out of 1.7 million workers at least 600,000 members were elected to management bodies; since of them 30–50% were re-elected for a second mandate, I calculate that membership in management involved ca. 1 in 8 workers (ILO 303, Roggemann 115, and cf. Singleton and Topham 9 and 24 – from this last pithy overview stem many formulations here); indeed, in 1964, membership in WsC and its commissions rose to 23% of the employed population (Bilandžić-Tonković 82). The ratio of voters to one member of WsC was around 1960 the very favourable one of 14:1 (Roggemann 74). The election took place usually at the beginning of the year, after the yearly accounting statement of the enterprise. Its procedure was sufficiently democratic: a list of candidates was presented by the Trade Union, but other lists could be freely added, names could be added at a general meeting, and electors voted by names not by lists. The practical outcome was, not surprisingly, that the most skilled and most active members were over-represented at the expense of the less skilled, who included a good proportion of 'peasant workers' teetering between employment and work at home; the percentage of Party members varied considerably, with an average of 35%, but investigations did not notice much difference between their and the other workers' attitudes (cf. the excellent explanation in Comisso 'Can'). Members could be recalled, which in 1956 happened to 0.8% of them – one thousand out of 125,000 – of which one third was initiated by the Director or communal organs and two thirds by the WsC or the enterprise membership; interestingly, members of the Managing Board were recalled more frequently: 1.2%, or 480 out of 40,000 (Schleicher 434). The council met monthly, most often after work, it was responsible for the enterprise's basic rules or by-laws (*Statut*), the annual plan and financial statements, large purchases and disposal of fixed assets, the methods of determining personal incomes, and enforcement of disciplinary rules. Any member of the enterprise could be present at its meeting. On their own initiative, the WsC began forming subcommittees, and a law of 1957 made two of them mandatory: the commissions for industrial discipline and for hiring and firing.

Notoriously, '[t]he automatism of *laissez-faire* never worked properly in [training and "skilling" of labour]. It broke down because it is not profitable for a private entrepreneur to invest in [this]' (Rosenstein-Rodan 204–5). The training was especially acute in SFRY, where of the over-10 population in 1953 92% had less than eight years of schooling, and in 1969 still 55%. Therefore, an important programme of **adult education for workers** was launched during the first 15 years and mainly entrusted to the Trade Union organisation, often through so-called Workers' Universities (WU) and the general adult-education People's Universities, which provided both public lectures and courses ranging from some weeks to two years (I have found no data about the type of courses). The People's Universities were older, and their number fell from 808 in 1956 to 442 in 1960 in favour of workers' education, which received generous financing from the Trade Unions and from the enterprises that used them for training their workers; the richest report in Seibel notes there were by 1967/68 236 WU

ANATOMY: MICRO-POLITICAL ECONOMICS

and 230 People's Universities, while in 1970–2 (that is, in two years) 210 People's Universities held 4,200 courses and seminars for 116,000 people plus 5,200 public lectures for 400,000 people (Seibel 180–2). Singleton and Topham note from direct observation that the WU 'do not lack for buildings and equipment, but they are still very short of trained personnel. Many of the teachers ... engage in adult education as a spare time occupation ... It would appear that teaching techniques are behind those of similar bodies in Western Europe', relying much more on mass lectures than on tutorials or student participation (22). Education could be contracted for on the basis of an enterprise's (or a group of enterprises') needs. Workers could thus complete their primary education, vocational schooling, obtain higher qualifications, learn a foreign language, and even prepare for entrance examinations to universities (Drulović 146).

TABLE 9.1B *'Workers' universities'*
SEIBEL 180–2

Year	WU no./ no. of courses	No. of publ. lectures	Participants at courses	Participants at lectures
1967/68	236/9,769	20,465	311,000	2,000,000
1970–2 (yearly average)	217/5,350	7,750	200,000	400,000

From the above Table it is clear that the WUs' activity fell abruptly around 1970.

In the 60s the emphasis shifted to subsidising workers' leaves for attendance at regular technical schools and universities, with scholarships from enterprises where the State ones were not available; there is ample evidence that companies often supported promising workers (see the case of Rajko in Adizes 91). Županov and Tannenbaum analysed in the mid-60s the opinions of 56 workers attending a two-year course at the WU in Zagreb, probably the cream of the crop, of whom 22 were first-line supervisors and almost 90% Party members (95). It was found that 'prolonged education for workers, including special courses for members of WsC, considerably increases their participation' (Marković, *Affluence* 235). At its best, 'self-management was ... a major national educational project. If they are compelled to manage, workers have to learn to read, to compute, to account, to forecast ... The peasant of yesterday has to learn for a good reason: his paycheck will grow as he shares the results of the company's efforts. Hence, self-management may be a desirable management for developing countries undergoing the industrialisation effort' (Adizes 223).

Further, 1,200 enterprises – mainly those with over 100 employees – had their own newspaper with data, proposals, and decisions; inquiries or surveys were frequently used, referendums sometimes (Drulović 146; Roggemann 70–1, in whom see more on WsC 72–81). The law obligated all enterprises to make their activities accessible to the public, including 'interested citizens and organisations', while 'business secrets' had to be spelled out in the enterprise's Statute (Roggemann 101–2).

Vanek's summary is: 'In the area of training and skill, significant results are undeniable. In a country where 30 years ago [that is, before World War II] there were, for all practical purposes (and outside the railway system), no industrial, managerial or scientific skills available, the deployment of over 3 million workers in a modern sector of the economy, under the sole responsibility of nationals, is in itself no mean achievement' (279). I do not dwell in this book on Yugoslav general education policy, beginning with the introduction of the eight-year obligatory basic schooling after 1945, where the number of pupils per teacher fell in the period 1945 to 1975 from 59 to 22, and with the huge expansion of the university system. It achieved great quantitative and partially also qualitative results, while remaining in the bourgeois and scientific mould: from 1961 to 1971 the percentage of the population over 10 years of age who had high schooling rose from 1.4 to 2.8%, middle schooling (12 years) from 9.3 to 15.2% and 8 years' elementary schooling from 7.3 to 15.1%, while two thirds of the youngsters remained with 4 years' schooling or less (Novaković 163; see also Chapter 8.2.2). Thus, 'it was the worker-managed enterprises which bore the brunt of responsibility in this field. They provided their own training, set up training schools and systems, financed technical and university studies, developed their own upgrading programmes and, generally speaking, prepared their own members for the job to be done. In most firms the necessary funds were readily forthcoming for this most profitable form of investment ... Of course only in worker-managed enterprises is there basic identity between those who require skills for production, those who finance their acquisition, and those who benefit from such training and can repay its worth as members of the same work collectivity ... In many areas of applied technology, such as telecommunication, civil engineering, building, shipbuilding or agriculture, the results achieved, mostly *ex nihilo*, by the former worker-trainees are quite astounding' (Vanek 280).

The formal qualification structure of the Yugoslav manual workers therefore rose steadily: in 1961–71 95,000 people successfully stood for exams to gain the most coveted skill rubric, 'highly qualified', doubling its share from 4.7% in 1961 to 9.7% in 1976, when the 'skilled' ones were 29.5% and the rest had low skills or were unskilled (cf. Chapter 3.2.2).

The WsC elected a Managing Board (*upravni odbor*, further MB) of 3 to 11 members as executive organ for current decisions. Its members did not have to come from the WsC but it was normal for a majority to be such. Besides dealing with current commercial matters and appointments, it prepared proposals for the WsC, including the annual plan, balance sheet, and income schedules. To guard against this body becoming isolated managers, its members had a limit of tenure, they continued at their normal occupation, and by the law of 1950 three quarters were supposed to be direct production workers, but this kept sinking. Their activities brought them into closer contact with the Director and the technical and administrative staff, who were usually well represented on the Board anyway. From the beginning, WsC and MBs were dominated by the two highest qualification strata or class fractions within manual workers and employees.

TABLE 9.2   *Membership of WsC and managing board, 1960*
FROM SINGLETON AND TOPHAM 10, BASED ON SG 1961

	WsC nos.	WsC %	MB nos.	MB %
Highly skilled[a]	23,133	15.0	9,762	19.3
Skilled	62,785	41.0	17,718	35.0
Semi-skilled	20,805	13.6	4,537	9.0
Unskilled	11,242	7.3	2,157	4.3
Total workers	*117,965*	*76.9*	*34,174*	*67.6*
Highly skilled	6,299	4.1	5,594	11.0
Skilled	17,967	11.7	7,463	14.8
Semi-skilled	10,306	6.7	3,126	6.2
Unskilled	917	0.6	173	0.4
Total 'staff'[b]	*35,489*	*23.1*	*16,355*	*32.4*
GRAND TOTAL	*153,454*	100.0	*50,529*	100.0

Notes: (a) There was a lot of scrambling for the status of 'highly skilled', both by job experience replacing formal degree and by classifying lower technical personnel as 'staff' (Comisso, 'Can' 70).
(b) For 'staff' or white-collar workers, the above 4 categories mean, from top to bottom: university degree; 2-year colleges, high-school (gymnasium) or equivalent trade school degree; 8-year elementary school degree; less than that (usually auxiliary employees).

The above proportions were similar from 1956 (cf. Schleicher 329–30) to 1968 except that top management with university degrees early on had a smaller share; however, by 1976 they had more than doubled in WsC to 9.2% (Drulović 67), while the MBs were almost entirely in their hands if not abolished in favour of entirely 'professional' Collegiums. Decisions such as that of the large textile combine Varteks to abolish the central MB 'in order to prevent its bureaucratic sway' (Roggemann 179), presumably in favour of ones in economic units, remained isolated.

The key post of manager or *Director* was since 1952 appointed for four years by a parity commission of the WsC and the municipality. He (rarely she) could be dismissed by petition of the WsC and agreement of the municipality, but the agreement was practically always granted. He was up to the mid-60s usually a partizan fighter of peasant origins, and until the 70s usually came from Party work, while after that the specialist candidates found it in their interest to enter the Party. His role and that of his staff was very influential, both for his political connexions outside the enterprise and increasingly for his (and their) rising professional expertise, so that a good part of WsC decisions followed his proposals, but as a rule after lively debates and clarifications: 'It was noticeable that [WsC] members were on much surer ground in making decisions over personal matters than over investment and marketing, where in the absence of documented alternatives ... the workers' representatives accepted [the suggestions of the Director and other "staff"] almost from necessity' (Singleton and Topham 23, referring also to Kolaja). Discussions of personal incomes or work rules led to greater participation of self-management bodies, 'in a more egalitarian fashion, and with more influence shared among all occupational strata' (Wachtel 91). Though the situation was rather nuanced, outside of job description and remuneration 'the directors and the representatives of the specialised services play[ed] the first fiddle' (Supek, 'Problems' 234), especially as concerns investment policy: they had the only primary access to information – unless a very assertive WsC insisted that it be shared – and could manipulate it. On the other hand, many observers recorded that detailed accounts of monthly and quarterly accounts circulated amongst the collectives, and about enterprise matters in general 'in most cases more information [was provided] to the employees than is supplied to their counterparts in Britain or the United States, or in the Soviet Union' (Kolaja 76). In 1957 the Director's prerogative of hiring and firing was transferred to the WsC and later to the constituent units, with approval at monthly meetings of the whole unit. On the whole, with major variations in individual cases, WsC had some real power in decisions about what and how to produce within existing frameworks and how to distribute the revenue under the prevailing macro-strictures, and in case of conflict whether to approve the work of managers. 200 directors were fired in 1958, while from those whose mandate ended re-election was denied to 19.8% in 1966 and 13.3% in 1968 (Roggemann 116).

It should also be stressed that out of 2.6 million industrial workers in 1971 probably well over 90% had entered employment after 1945, so that Kolaja (17) found the average age of the Managing Board members in the two factories he investigated in 1958/59 was 33.5 and 37.9 years, in which situation both the Director and some 'masters' (foremen) might have been older (and in a permanent employment context all ages would rise steeply in time). Situations differed much from place to place: from his account it can also be calculated that in Factory A verbal participation in 17 sessions was per session 18 interventions each by management personnel and only 3.5 each by other members of WsC, whereas in Factory B (a much smaller one) the numbers in 22 sessions were 16:18 each; that is, we have a rather passive WsC and an active one, the latter explained by the membership of three university graduates who were in research and therefore not counted as management. The Director and his dependent staff not rarely curtailed the rights of WsC by means of top-heavy reports, informal cliques, and similar, and then intimidated workers into silence on macro-decisions. Certainly their bonuses often raised the highest-to-lowest income ratio above the normal 4:1 spread (Kolaja 32). Complaints about some aloofness of these institutions from the workers led to legal and political encouragements of meetings with the whole collective, usually very well attended, as well as to elected departmental or economic unit councils to decide on production and finances, especially in larger enterprises. Nonetheless, the trend in the 60s was to circumvent the exclusion of top executives from WsC by inclusion of more junior economists, technicians, and engineers under the rubric 'foremen' (Adizes 223). I shall return to the vexed charge of technocracy separately.

In the later 60s Supek concluded – as did most other investigators – that workers ranked the power and influence in the enterprise, from the most important down, as: (1) managers, (2) MBs, (3) professional staff, (4) WsC, while the Party, the workers, and the TU were way below ('Some Contradictions' 271). Thus, from the statistics and reports of the 1960s, it can be concluded that power was usually up to a point shared by the Director and his technical staff with the highly skilled and skilled workers; women and lower ranks only counted in case of general dissatisfaction. There is little doubt, however, that the Director and other white-collar planners and overseers, together with eventual allies, as a rule exercised preponderant power in the WsC. Among other matters, the Director was the only person legally responsible for the enterprise and for guarding in it interests of society as a whole, as well as de facto the link to the political power structure in the local community – and the higher levels – that had co-appointed him in the first place (cf. Comisso, *Workers'* 111 and 56–64). He had thus to serve two masters, often resulting in lesser efficiency. In 1965, the Director's final appointment was ceded to the WsC but the background role of the commune, and in important enterprises of the republic, remained very strong, in spite of legal provisions for appeal by the enterprise to courts against its decisions (see for these Roggemann 107).

From 1965, self-management was legally systematised in all non-industry working units or '*social service organisations*', in health, education, culture, science, etc., though it had existed in them in some form for a dozen years (an attempt at consumer councils fell quite flat, while councils in public housing were stymied by lack of funds):

TABLE 9.3   *Self-management in social service organisations*
FROM SEIBEL AND DAMACHI 175, BASED ON SG 73: 79

Institutions in:	Councils	Council members	Man. board members
Primary & secondary schools	4,718	128,871	18,810
Higher education	232	6,719	3,711
Science	309	6,091	1,374
Culture, art, entertainment	1,428	21,726	2,441
Health	980	20,845	6,310
Social welfare	974	18,591	2,500
TOTAL	*8,641*	*202,843*	*35,146*

The problems of this rather successful public service wing, lamely called 'social self-management' as different from workers' self-management, were threefold. First, almost all of them wholly depended on a percentage of the State, and then increasingly the commune, budget, with some additional special funds, for example for cadre training, and were thus dependent on the authorities' economic success and political will; ways to arrange financing directly from associations of users and thus give them a stable financial basis independent of the State apparatus were not found before the capitalist marketisation cyclone hit in the late 60s (cf. Gerškovič 19–21 and *passim*). The varying percentages were set aside from the national income; in 1970 they amounted to 41%, divided as follows: education 5.2%, science 1.4%, the arts 2%, health service 5.7%, social welfare 0.8%, child allowances and child welfare 1.3%, veterans' and invalids' welfare 0.6%, housing construction 7.9% (Drulović 101 – science is obviously underfinanced). Second, the difficulty of 'measuring work' in them was compounded by the traditional hierarchies where power was increasingly in the hands of little groups clustering around the highest rank: the 'primarius' (chief doctor) in medicine, full professors in universities, stage directors in theatre. Third, according to much the best Yugoslav constitution of 1963, 'citizens and representatives of organisations concerned' had the right to be represented in this 'social management' (Roggemann 221), but in practice consumers' associations never developed and public opinion had little or no input into the top-down TV stations, major newspapers or professional theatres, so that these institutions easily floundered into sensationalism and kitsch (see Supek, 'Problems' 236–7), later into nationalism. To the contrary, until the reimposition of censorship in 1972 there was a golden age of book publishing, with 13,000 new titles yearly, of a wide spectrum of newspapers with over 1,500 titles (circulation of press peaked in 1964 at 10 million), of 1,150 periodicals, and of the ubiquitous radio with 3.5 million sets and ca. 180 stations which had interesting and popular programmes including special ones for culture and for children; TV sets exploded in the 1960s and by the 70s reached one per 10 inhabitants (cf. Robinson 20–1, 49, and *passim*). Especially, student theatres and amateur cinema clubs in the 1950s–60s (see both titles by Janevski, Žilnik 153–5, and Kirn, 'A Few Notes') grew into independent and fully self-managing production units, vibrant nurseries nudging all of culture towards a rich freedom.

A kind of hybrid between 'workers' self-management' and 'social self-management' was practised in railway and postal communications, electrical power systems, and similar, which soon fell prey to 'republicanisation'.

Nonetheless, in the branches deemed less vital for political power, say in health (or education or science), the bipartite committees representing the patients – through the intermediary of a health insurance group – and the medical staff usually worked well.[2] In the judgement of Catherine Samary, a critical left-wing commentator, 'practical self-management in publishing and the university ... were certainly superior ... than in most parliamentary democracies' ('Autogestion', electronic p. 13). Mihailo Marković's disenchanted view from the early 70s was that the 'interest communities' for education, science, and culture (for example in theatres, publishing houses, museums and galleries) – organised vertically through local councils and regional and republican assemblies

---

2 Basic data about the health insurance system: in 1950 4.9 million people were insured and in 1969 12.8 million or 63.3%, including those 'temporarily out of work', pensioners, and family members; the total expenditures rose in the above period from 4.4% to 4.9% of national income, peaking at 5.8% in 1965 (Dubey ed. 110).

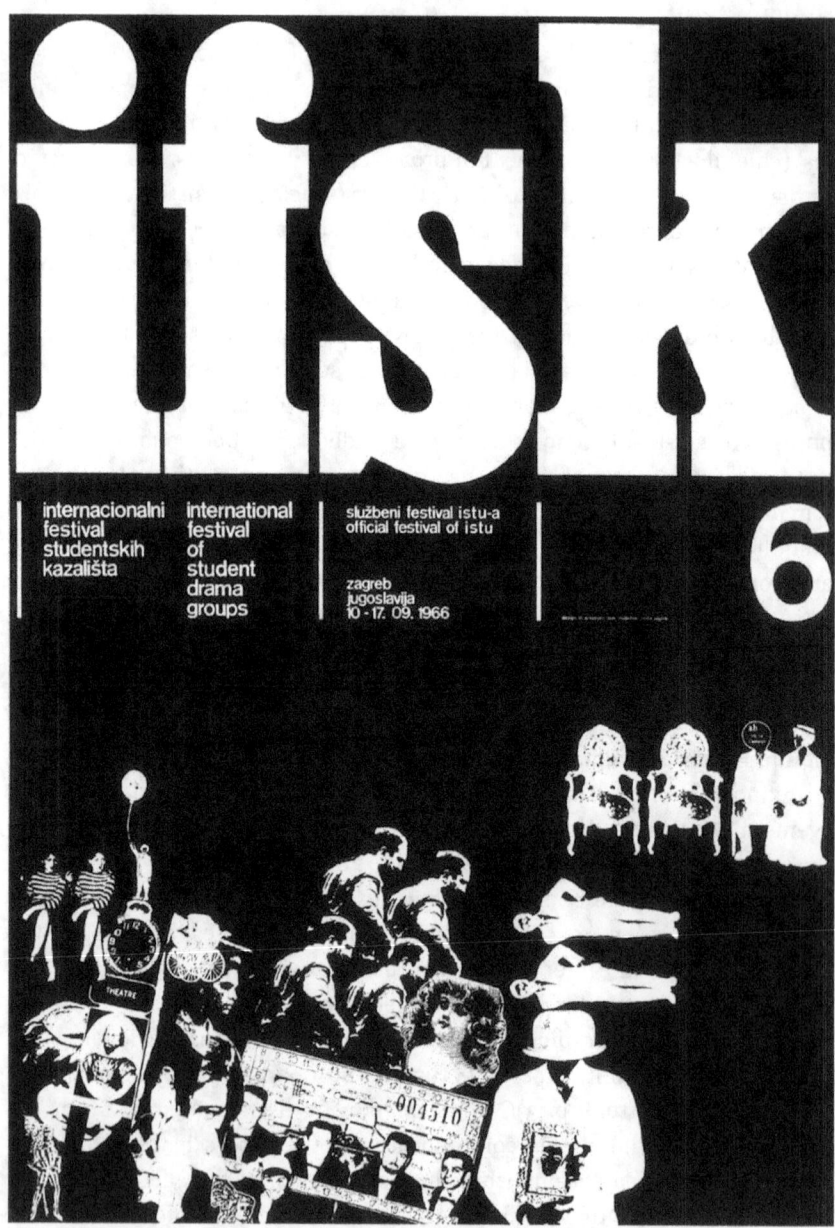

FIGURE 22   *Mihajlo Arsovski,* IFSK 66 *(1966, title page and poster)* (IFSK 66 *was the publication of the Zagreb International Student Theatre Festival for 1966.* DS *was its artistic director up to and including that year and commissioned the cover.*)
PHOTO REPRODUCED WITH KIND PERMISSION OF DEJAN KRŠIC

'which make final decisions on all matters of ... policy and also take full responsibility for distribution of available funds' – were often stymied because the politocracy kept the legally fixed budgets low so that it could intervene when further allocations were needed (*Affluence* 238–9). Whether this was not due in good part also to economic problems rather than to malice prepense remains to be investigated. Finally as of the 70s the oligarchy's counter-offensive took the form of packing its boards with loyal appointees supposedly representing 'consumers'.

The third area of potential self-management were the local communities which numbered 9,000 in 1972, each of them run by a council, the members of which can be estimated at 100,000, and 500 larger 'communes' with 41,000 councillors (Seibel and Damachi 184), a preponderance of which were administrators and professional politicians. All organs were elected but in the absence of watchful public opinion they had a strong tendency to constitute themselves into little power cliques and to override the 'social' but especially the workers' self-management in key areas such as investments and nomination of directors (cf. Gerškovic 17–21 and 41–2). Finally, general agricultural cooperatives had in the early 60s ca. 200,000 members (Singleton and Topham 24).

However, the central and crucial question remained: will self-management be decisively built up both horizontally (outside of industry) and vertically (up to the real seat of power, the Party/State centre in Belgrade), into an all-encompassing plebeian associative democracy? This was not simply an ideological demand, it was the precondition for existing initial forms of self-management functioning properly by controlling the social accumulation of surplus labour and its strategic distribution. It was also from the beginnings on a spontaneous, albeit inchoate, urge of the self-management organs themselves (Milosavljevic, 'Država' 116 and *passim*). A gesture in this direction was the introduction of four Councils of Producers in the federal assembly in the 1963 constitution but, characteristically for the ongoing cooptation, they were filled largely by trade union functionaries and enterprise managers (Bakaric 3: 86). Even this bothered the Party monocracy, for it 'did not take into account the liquidation of the working class as a class' (sic! – ibidem 87), so that it got taken back in the next round of constitutional changes, after the regressive 1965–8 reforms. Faced with diminishing economic results, the Party top decided in 1971 on a reform of the self-management system, which culminated in the new constitution of 1974 with mammoth laws about planning and 'associated labour'. The intricate reorganisation had some interesting features, such as the idea of 'interest communities' outside industry (public health, say, would be run by a roof organisation in each territorial unit with delegates from the unit, industry employees, and the public health employees), and of associations between industry enterprises in which Močnik sees an attempt at Post-Fordist outsourcing ('Nismo' 146). The enterprises were further articulated into 'Basic Organisations of Associated Labour' (BOALs) and central enterprise bodies. However the change resolutely affirmed and perpetuated the 'Indian reservation' of WsC as 'productive' micro-structures only; to the contrary, the role of the Party was strengthened and talk about dictatorship of the proletariat returned after 30 years of taboo. The negative consequences of these measures culminated in the rapid growth of 'alienated social capital ... in technocratic-administrative centres which began to develop into a specific political power over the workers' (Bošković and Dašić 224, and see their documentation). I shall return to this key point.

On the whole Yugoslav self-management in its heyday hesitated between workers' control, which it did not fully achieve, and strong workers' participation. In its stagnation and decadence after 1968 it retained workers' safeguards against firing and a certain amount of participation in the distribution of earnings.

9.2 Workers' Incomes: The Ins and the Outs

TABLE 9.4   *Division of work-force in socialised sector, 1970 (out of 3,853 thousands, SG 1973: 367)*

Skill (kvalifikacija)	In %	Skill (kvalifikacija)	In %
University degree	6.62	Highly skilled	9.32
Two-year college	5.01	Skilled	28.73
Secondary or technical school (12 years)	16.01	Semi-skilled	14.73
Primary school (8 years) or less	4.53	Unskilled	15.01
Total office workers (ca. 1,250,000)	32.2	*Total manual workers* (ca. 2,600,000)	67.8

'Wages in Yugoslavia are not merely a means to an end. They are also a symbol, a slogan, a social goal, and an individual preoccupation' (Zukin, 'Beyond Titoism' 17). No aspect of self-management was of more immediate concern to the workers and had such unceasing and lasting input by them as remuneration. Scores of titles have been written on it, but Wachtel's seems the only book in English dealing with this period to give equal prominence to self-management and workers' 'wages' (108–10). The term 'wages' was officially spurned in Yugoslavia in favour of either *dohodak*, 'income', or later *dobit*, which meant 'gain' but could also mean 'profit'. The wages/incomes were established starting from the federal legal minimum, distinguishing four categories of skills (*kvalifikacija*) within both the office and the manual workers; the minimum usually changed each year but it was well below the lowest average wage of any industry branch as well as of the lowest skill-group. Up to 1961 the income consisted of a fixed part and a part varying with the enterprise's income (cf. for the mid-50s the detailed overview in Schleicher 103–53). The variable income for the office workers was 8–20% above the fixed income, while for the manual workers it was 5.5 to 17%. The 'highly skilled' manual workers always received a variable percentage larger than the two lowest skills in the office group but smaller than office workers with secondary school or above, while the 'skilled' manual workers had a lower percentage than all levels of office workers. The full income differentials, with the average for all those employed as 100, was for the two groups in 1956 123:97, in 1961 199:95, and in 1967 117:85; in the same years, the incomes of university graduates vs. highly skilled workers related as 191:151, 201:155, and 177:134. After 1961 these statistics were no longer kept because the variations were left to each enterprise (!).

In the commune Meister studied in 1960 the unskilled workers' incomes were between 6,500 and 9,000 dinars whereas the highest ones (engineers, directors) were around 35,000, so the spread was around 1:4 or 5, while in the big cities such as Belgrade the spread was rather 1:6; in the mid-60s the minimum-maximum spread was rising (69–70). Singleton and Topham (17) found in 1962 enterprises officially varying the maximum fixed-income spread from 3.75:1 to 7:1. However, when large groups (that is, entire class fractions) are compared, the income differentials in the Yugoslav economy were in the 60s 'quite narrow when compared to other economies, especially in light of its lower economic development, which would normally herald wide differentials. By 1967, the highest-paid skill-group [that is, office workers with university degree, DS] was earning only 2.5 times the lowest-paid group (unskilled blue-collar workers)' (Wachtel 146). Wachtel further argues that in an economy glutted with a labour-force with lower skills, the bias toward higher skills and education was due to competition for specialists who could, and did, switch enterprises. In absolute numbers, the real income for manual workers rose by 48% from 1956 to 1961, when the monthly average income was 18,860 dinars, while for employees it rose by 67% and the monthly average income in 1961 was 27,850 dinars (my calculation from data in Comisso, *Workers'* 57).

Widespread benefits such as transportation, children's allowances, etc., were not included in the above statistics. Nor were some hidden perks for the highest group, comprising travel allowances, expense accounts, payment for overtime, prizes, refunds for use of a private car and for meals, etc – a constant source of great irritation to manual workers. Furthermore, the growth of a grasping private sector, the introduction of a 42-hour working week, and labour laws which made it more difficult to hire people for short periods, 'all gave highly trained individuals an incentive to hold down second jobs' (Comisso, *Workers'* 109). Dunlop believed already in the 50s that the non-wage compensation in Yugoslavia was higher than in any other European country (304).

By the late 60s, Adizes found distributing the income 'cake' into workers' incomes was fully decided by the enterprises studied, whether by the central WsC or by the economic units. The cake itself was brought about, as indicated in Chapter 8, by interaction with the great outside forces of official laws and financial regulations as well as of the market, national and then increasingly international: all the WsC decisions were to a great degree determined by 'the relationship between nominal and real income, which depends on monetary policy and the price of agricultural produce ...; and [on whether there was] equality of treatment in economic policy' (Bićanić 116). At Adizes's enterprise ABC (see 9.3 below) the maximum full fixed-income spread between the Director and a janitor was frozen at 5:1. Everybody else fit into the intermediary scale determined by job hardship, responsibility (functional contribution to the collective), level of education, and years of seniority. For each job the WsC determined the minimal education and training needed; after 1970, the rule was that people without these minimums would be automatically transferred. For jobs with a norm, bonuses were given based on quantity of output, cost of production, and quality. For executives, bonuses depended on total enterprise profit and sales under their control; according to the company manual, the percentage of basic income to be given for each % of enterprise income above 95% of the planned (or under 95% for cost of production) was between 7.2 for the Director and 5.2 for the procurement manager. The rest of administrative staff received bonuses according to the financial results of the enterprise. There was also an intricate distribution between economic units, each of which then distributed the income realised to variable personal income or to funds (for reserve, homes, recreation, etc.). The monthly pay check thus fluctuated. Adizes describes in detail such distributions of revenue 'according to results', which meant that almost every process output and input had to be quantified. The system fostered competition, also ceaseless debates both horizontally between workers and vertically between them and the executives as to what were proper benchmarks for norms and plans (50–60). There was also a strong tendency towards social justice, which led to a country-wide minimum guaranteed income of 55% in relation to last year's average personal income in industry, and for example in SR Croatia to fixing the maximum income (president of the Republic's Presidium) at no more than four times this average (Tonković 421) – perks not figured in.

Besides direct personal retribution, each enterprise had a Fund for Common Spending (*zajedničke potrošnje*), amounting in the 70s to 6–10% of income (Korošić, *Ekonomske* 74), and providing meals in 90% of them at no or minimal cost, assisting in yearly holidays (cf. Duda), usually by building workers' resorts on the seaside or in the mountains, etc. The latter, as well as the daily and weekly recreation and sports activities, were usually coordinated by the TU. The main rubric in this fund – in the 1970s over one third – went for lodging, either by building enterprise apartments or by giving credits for individual apartment purchases. Though 784,000 apartments were built from 1953 to 1984 in Yugoslavia, at a rate of 6.1 apartments built per 1,000 of population with an average of 64 square metres each, the unceasing influx into cities meant there were never enough, and in the 1980s it was calculated there was a need for 90,000 more. The apartments were allotted for a lifetime and rents were frozen at a low rate, so that in 1965 they took below 5% of a household's expenses; attempts at raising them to allow for full repairs and upkeep were successfully resisted to the very end of SFRY (Tonković 424–6 and 431). A perpetual bone of contention was that, according to research after the mid-70s, the manual workers, who were 71.5% of those employed, got only 49% of 'social property' housing. Furthermore, with the strengthening of capitalist market influences not only did the rhythm of creating new housing stagnate after 1965, but the number built by factories and communes fell (Horvat, *Jugoslavensko* 96).

Vanek summarised the situation well for the 1960s: 'What the Yugoslav firm offers in lieu of wages is a (known) part of, or share in, the future (hence unknown) income, as well as many other known and unknown benefits in terms of career prospects and employment security, training, welfare services, etc' (277).

On the whole, the impression arises that, in the 1960s and early 70s, the workers' incomes were decent for those who had an apartment, whereas for the skilled workers and the upper half of staff they were good, and for the top staff at times opulent. Later, the tension between profitability and equity became acute, and opinion surveys from 1968 on 'consistently show that wages occupy first place in people's concern' (Zukin, 'Beyond' 18). I probe the muddle around 'reward according to work' further in Chapter 10.4.

As of 1958 the first strikes came about in Yugoslavia. It speaks well for the government's acumen and for the balance of class forces at the time that they were not repressed by violence, but grudgingly acknowledged under the bashful name of 'work stoppages'; indeed, the Second Congress of WsC in 1971 discussed allowing a legal right to strike, but this foundered on the political tensions in 1971 and the subsequent turn towards a 'firm hand' (Zukin, 'Representation' 300). In the 1958–69 period there seem to have been 2,000 or possibly 2,500 mainly small strikes (Meister 173, Zukin 'Representation' 298, Novaković 118). All commentators cite the data from Jovanov's *Radnički štrajkovi*, commissioned by the TUs, who surveyed 56 months in 1964–9 and found 869 strikes with an average of ca. 90 people per strike (cf. also his *Sukobi* for second thoughts). The wavelet seemed related to the economic development of the republics and the workers' expectations: it started in Slovenia, continued in the middle republics, while in Kosovo the first strike occurred only 10 years later. The strikes were exclusively centred on income demands, most frequent in industries with low income levels, and directed mostly against the enterprise administrators: most important was income distribution, and after that low absolute amounts; in 75–80 % of the cases only the shop-floor workers took part, sometimes only from part of the enterprise, in which case it was directed most often against the top management and the WsC too went on strike, but in one fifth to one quarter of cases it was also directed against the WsC. However, when the perception was stronger that low incomes were due to exogenous factors such as government decisions, in ca. 10 % of the cases, mainly early on, everybody participated. Seibel, following Jovanov, pinpoints as the main cause of strikes the low evaluation and rewarding of shop-floor work, that is, a class conflict between the manual workers and the enterprise 'technocracy' (169–72). As a rule the strikes were brief, 374 of them one day or less, for both the local authorities and the political organisations would immediately rush to the enterprise and patch up an ad hoc solution, while the workers were fragmented into sub-classes and the leadership improvised and hesitant. Meister's conclusion is that 'all in all the strikes were in small numbers ... the system has succeeded in integrating the workers' (173).

However, all of the above held only for those fully (which also meant permanently) employed. I shall approach the growing sore of unemployment in Chapter 10.3.

9.3 Three Case Studies Astraddle the 1965 Reform (Tornquist, Adizes, Comisso)

9.3.1 *David Tornquist*
Tornquist analysed around 1964 the large Galenika pharmaceutical company, founded in 1945 in Belgrade and employing 2,000 workers (174–94, cf. Hunnius ed. 303–5). It had a major share of the Yugoslav market, but after the introduction in the early 60s of a handling fee for prescriptions the sales fell sharply and the company had to look to exports. It decided to merge with two other Belgrade enterprises, after which management concluded 10 % of the employees

should be cut. This most sensitive matter occasioned tough bargaining between management, the WsC, the economic units, the LCY branch, and the TU branch. When faced with the proposal of firing 160 people, many workers, supported by the Party, felt that other factors beside economic considerations should be weighted. Most prominent were: other sources of income in the family; job evaluation, the number of work-days missed, and discipline in general; the status of war veterans, political activity, and participation in self-management. The Party, uncharacteristically prominent in this case, held that good workers cannot be laid off but only shifted to other departments. The most important decisions were made by the basic economic units, and Tornquist gives the decisions of one which had 13 employees to lay off as typical (177 – note they were as a rule not core production workers):

> M.C. Superfluous but good clerk. We'll find a place for her.
> O.P. Messenger. Good discipline. Should be kept.
> R.V. Charwoman. Has something to fall back on. Should be laid off.
> J.M. Messenger. Allergic to drugs [produced in the plant]. Has chance of another job. Should be laid off.
> D.B. Janitor. Has other income. Should be retired on his pension.
> L.T., G.S., R.M., and A.O. Hired only for three months. Should be let go.
> T.V. Janitor. Vote on his case split. Should stay.
> T.J. Janitor. Ailing, veteran, no one to take care of him. Should stay.
> E.F. Janitor. Vote on his case split. Should stay.
> I.K. Watchman. Tends his farm and comes to work tired. But is wounded veteran with four children. Should be transferred to another unit.

Another economic unit in Galenika with no surplus workers agreed to lay off six unsatisfactory workers to take up the surplus from this and other units.

Two further stages after the economic units were a review by the TU and Party, 'to be sure friendship and enmity played no part in the decisions' (ibidem), and the final decision by a five-person commission of the WsC which fired 97 of the 160 proposed by management. Those fired had the right of appeal to the MB, and 12 of them were reinstated. Finally, the WsC granted 20 million dinars (official exchange was $2.66 million but the purchasing power was perhaps double) to the Director for helping the dismissed find other jobs together with the local employment security office: 50 jobs were found in return for Galenika loans to two other companies, and other jobs found for 17 people. In the end only 18 office workers were left without employment, though there were vacancies outside of Belgrade and they were promised help in finding them, if needed after their severance pay ran out.

I should interject here that a whole range of possibilities to prevent firing was developed by the Yugoslav basic economic units after 1958/59: 'availability' (surplus from one unit to be employed in other units), 'temporary lending' from one unit to another, 'substitution' (when a worker with diminished capacity is found a less demanding job), and similar widespread though mostly informal expedients, often directly negotiated between the units. The plant Statutes themselves foresaw special protection for employees with more than 8 years' seniority, invalids, those who fell sick while employed, women and youth who live in families with less than a given income per capita, women who are the only support of one or more family members, and war orphans: if the unit fires them, they are put into the group for 'temporary jobs and reskilling', with an obligation to undergo professional education as directed (Hadžistević et al. 129–35).

9.3.2 Ichak Adizes

In Spring 1967 and Autumn 1968 Adizes studied two Yugoslav companies in depth, and observed a dozen others at the time, within an 'open systems approach' which factored in the environment. The two textile companies on the outskirts of Belgrade, each with two non-contiguous plants, were alike except for their leadership, at the opposite ends of the authoritarian-permissive spectrum. They had 2,600 or 2,900 workers, and similar age, technology, workers' provenience from villages around the city, ratio male/female (not given), markets, and distribution channels; Adizes focussed on their decisions about modernisation, preparing annual plans, and disciplinary actions (6–8). Of the official steering or governing organs in company XYZ, the WsC of 54 members had six permanent committees with 26 members, and the MB had three with 20 members, plus six ad hoc committees with 54 members; of the 100 committee members, 15 were in the WsC or MB. In the plant studied there was also a local Council with 34 members and 11 plant-level committees with 73 members, plus the level of the Economic Units into which the plant was subdivided, each with an elected council of 11 members and numerous committees. Even the foremen were elected by those units and had limited authority. Thus 'representative decision-making positions are available to about 40% of the membership'; given the obligatory rotation, 'virtually no member of the organisation can escape ... participation in the decision-making process' (36); also available were referendums, and a full company meeting [*zbor*] called for elections and all main decisions. The company was strongly production-oriented, much less toward marketing, its financial department employed less than 20 people.

The executives in each company were composed of the company Director, directors of plants and departments, and foremen; each coordinated an organisational space, with powers specifically delineated by the governing bodies. However, there is also a non-elected *kolegij* composed of the top executives and presided by the Director, and an 'extended collegium' convened as need arose, to which plant, shop, and shift foremen as well as the staff (economists, planners, analysts) were added; the collegiums formulated proposals for decision by WsC. There was also a 'political *aktiv*', which met when need arose; it included top members of both the executive and the workforce as well as of the Party, the Trade Union, and the Youth Brigades (for younger workers); the latter had their own steering bodies, formed clubs (e.g., for chess, mountain climbing or 'book of the month') and contributed to the decisions. These three socio-political institutions are not mentioned in federal economic laws or company by-laws, and Adizes explains them as arising from the need for a centripetal force in organisations highly segmented by authority (46–7). A very interesting account of how decisions about a proposal are arrived at is to be found in Adizes 82–7, postulating a 'Phase a' starting with external factors (government and the market) and a 'Phase b', in XYZ with internal democratic pressures and a 'ripple effect'.

Company ABC was more centralised and with fewer governing bodies and committees, no component plants' MB, and its Director was a man in his 30s with a university engineering degree, 'aggressive, strong in the Party, and with a most phenomenal ability to convince people' (67). He had worked in ABC as a technician, studied at night, become first production manager and then Director. The company was strongly marketing-oriented, it contained a large economic planning department and a financial department that employed 54 people, it even had mechanised accounting equipment. By 1967, they produced 20 million metres of fabric, from a beginning of 2.6 million in 1951 which was equal to the 1940 production under an absentee owner. As in XYZ, most workers travel to work and may get up anytime after 4 a.m., though some live in small company-built apartments or in old derelict city dwellings. The company was destroyed in the World War and rebuilt by the workers themselves in overtime efforts between 1945 and 1951; after minor modernisations, in 1960 the company built a new spinning plant, again by voluntary overtime labour from the workers, producing at full speed by 1962. After that, new automated equipment was introduced in the weaving department, and in 1963 ABC was formed by merging it with a supplier of cotton. As in all such cases, it is claimed not a single worker was fired by cause of modernisation or merger (62–5).

I insert here the XYZ's WsC debate (188) of the suggestion of an Economic Unit to fire Vera, who was punished by the disciplinary commission of the unit several times: once for absenting herself one day and for not wearing the protective overcoat, and several times for coming to work drunk. *A worker* (not member of the WsC) said she has difficult conditions at home, but she had disregarded several promises to stop drinking. *A social worker* from the staff reported Vera was mentally retarded, but after working in XYZ for 10 years she should not be thrown out and become a problem for society. She was good at work and should be transferred away from machines so she could get medical aid more frequently. *A junior executive*, member of the WsC, said he would be uncomfortable firing an unhealthy person, she should be cured in the company. *Another worker* (not member of the WsC) said she is really a problem in the spinning unit, other workers protest, but her domestic life is tough, her sexual life not normal (I take this as a euphemism for promiscuity), and 'we should not leave her on the street'. *The WsC* unanimously voted to reject firing Vera and mandated the health unit to cure her, after which she would be transferred to another unit so nobody would be in direct danger of getting hurt.

Both companies had in the 60s to embark upon modernisation of very obsolete equipment, rendered necessary by a buyers' market and competition from abroad. In XYZ it went through long, sometimes explosive debates from below, involving much of the workforce, in order to raise productivity per person (see 90–100 and 111–16), and the cautious approach brought about long stalemates. In ABC it was conceived by the Director and his senior staff on the basis of purchasing Italian machinery, discussed at all the official and unofficial forums, and after the Director wrote a 50-page report voted on by the WsC: 'ABC's meetings were calm, short, and efficient'. The ABC growth rate of average income per worker was higher because of earlier investment, but XYZ distributed a greater proportion of earnings as personal income (76–7). The price to pay in ABC was the instauration of an elite: the WsC met around tables set in a horseshoe pattern, with the Director, the Council president, and the top executives at the head table, and when coffee was served they got special gold-rimmed cups; the Director insisted that new offices for the marketing and production managers 'were built with luxurious interiors resembling the latest Park Avenue executive suites' (127). There was no open opposition but human and labour relations turned sour, goods began to be returned from Italy because of low quality, average incomes began falling, and eventually there was a strike; Adizes attributed this to failure in digesting the new machines and methods (128–9). His conclusion was also that the legal structure of self-management and the pressures for decentralisation encouraged long discussions to develop a democratic consensus, and this was 'incongruous with the new market needs introduced by the economic aspects of the reform' (201). Nonetheless, with all the dysfunctional behaviour described, 'self-management generally yielded amazing functional results in the long run': it absorbed the shocks of decentralisation and created collective commitment (222).

In sum, the picture emerges of a real if somewhat unwieldy and not too market-savvy plebeian democracy in XYZ, a 'bottom-up strategy' (119), as opposed to a fast adaptation to the market with more 'technocracy', a 'top-down strategy', and a power gap between top and down in ABC, leading to an at least momentary stumble.

Adizes does not give a breakdown of the main issues on the agendas of his two WsC, but the official statistic of all WsC meetings in manufacturing and mining in 1962 and 1964, before the major economic reform of the mid-60s, looks as follows:

TABLE 9.5   *Issues at WsC meetings*
            FROM WACHTEL 68, % OF TOTAL

Agenda items	1962	1964
Distribution of net receipts and personal income	15.4	13.8
Vocational training	8.1	7.7
Benefits; housing, vacations, etc.	12.0	11.1
Total 'direct worker issues'	*35.5*	*32.6*
Labour productivity	22.0	26.9
Sales	13.4	12.3
Investment	13.5	14.4
Cooperation with other enterprises[a]	5.7	5.7
Work of Director and MB	9.7	9.7
Total 'general management issues'	*64.3*	*67.4*

Note (a): arrangements for intermediate goods, mergers, etc.

After 1965, sales and finance items would have been more prominent.

9.3.3   Ellen T. Comisso

I shall mention more briefly **Ellen Comisso**'s excellent study of the pseudonymous machine-producing company Klek (*Workers'* 135 ff.). Since it was done after the full force of the post-1965 reforms came to be felt, it shows the trend which was to continue. Her most interesting finding is that during the company expansion the manual workers lost much ground to the white-collar ones, whose status was in the peasant tradition always higher, and especially to the executive staff, as mentioned earlier à propos the constitutional amendment 15: 'the center of gravity began to shift off the plant floor and into the offices' (151). Part of this was no doubt inevitable with the advent of higher technology and emphasis on quality of production in view of export as well as of the more complex financing environment, but part was not:

> ... Klek practically doubled the number of highly paid university graduates in its employ between 1972 and 1974 [see Table 9.6]. Whereas in the past, the few university graduates Klek employed were by and large engineers and supervisory personnel who worked directly with the production workers on a day-to-day basis, the new employees were primarily economists, sales representatives, and research engineers who rarely ventured onto the plant floor. The social distance between manual and mental labor thus appeared to increase, and the various incentives offered the new employees, such as housing and more flexible job definitions, certainly did not help to diminish it.
>
> 151–2

TABLE 9.6 *'Klek' qualification structure*
ADAPTED FROM COMISSO, WORKERS' 152

Sub-classes	Nos. 1966[a]	Nos. June 1972	Nos. Sept. 1974	% rise 1974/72
College or university degree	27	17	30	82
Secondary or technical school	46	55	80	45
Primary school (8 years)	4	19	16	n.a.
Total employees	*77*	*91*	*126*	*38*
Highly skilled	105	37	44	19
Skilled	112	235	252	7
Semi- or unskilled	57	99	116	17
Total workers	*274*	*371*	*402*	*8*

(a) Data before 1972 refer to the official job description, which the job holders in many cases did not match; the 1966 numbers are thus quite considerably higher than the real qualifications involved, especially in the uppermost bracket of each half.

Thus while the total workforce expanded 50% in the above 8 years, the white-collar subset expanded by 65% or 1.3 times as rapidly. This trend was underway from the beginning of the 1960s but now came into full force. Further, 'The impact of the market and the modernisation plan also brought a sharper distinction between upper management and the rest of the work collective, a distinction that affected white-collar and blue-collar workers alike' (153). Thus on the whole a three-tiered stratification seems to have been developing: upper staff – white-collar – manual workers, probably with some exception for a better status of the small number of highly skilled workers remaining after reclassification.

CHAPTER 10

Physiology: The Interests and Stakes behind the Macro-Events

> Swimming against the stream is stupid, but one needs wisdom to recognise the direction of the stream.
> BRECHT, ca. 1929

∴

10.0 Introduction

This chapter studies at more depth the underlying dilemmas of the economic politics or politicised economy and how they crucially meshed with failures of imagination. It focusses on the underlying macro-decision between 'market socialism' and associational democracy. Economic events were most intimately interwoven, or in feedback, with the epistemological horizons involved. I shall proceed in a zigzag between the two, from the pragmatic debates about the decentralisation and the market to a discussion of productivism, economism, and the abandonment of planning, and then resume shuttling from capitalisation and unemployment to the growing oligarchic blindness of power, presented in a discursive analysis of some works by Kardelj. My first idea was to confront what was really happening in each case with what might/ought to have been and how come it was not, but in the interests of clarity I desisted from this, trusting the reader will understand the confrontation from previous discussions, especially Chapter 5, and Chapters 13–14 following. However, I did add a sting in the shape of Section 4 at the chapter's tail.

10.1 Decentralisation, the Market

The foreground of debates in the most fertile years of Yugoslavia, roughly 1955–70, was occupied by the *centralisation vs. decentralisation* dilemma and quarrel. Accompanying it as a mostly rhetorical *basso continuo* was a dilemma about more or less *industrial democracy* (decision-making by direct producers from below), implying both by analogy and necessity more or less political democracy (decision-making by citizens from below). A first decentralisation came about in the 1950s, when the share of public expenditures by the local governments rose from 12.6 to 29.5 %, a level never to be reached again because of the counteroffensive of republican oligarchies, recentralising on the level of the constituent units of SFR Yugoslavia. A second huge wave came about at the beginning of the 1970s, and left 80% of fiscal means subject to regulations of the by then eight federative units (Begić 70).

Self-management and the whole society demanded, to the contrary, a supportive breathing space. As Brus phrased it:

> Yet decentralisation of the system of functioning of the economy, which is a precondition of self-management, cannot go beyond certain limits defined by the economic and social reality of central planning, by the growing need in the modern world for internalisation of external costs and benefits, by the requirements of maintaining the supremacy of the 'system' as a whole over the 'sub-systems'.
> 95

There existed at the time at least the lineaments of a possible democratic political evolution and planning, based on the partizan tradition and leaning on Lenin's *State and Revolution*, on Marx's articles about the Paris Commune and his critique of the Gotha Programme of German Social-Democracy, as well as on the more developed hypotheses of Gramsci's about workers' councils and hegemony (cf. Comisso, *Workers'* 1–41). I shall call this strand utopian communism, in the positive sense of utopia, and it entailed a vertical expansion of self-management at the expense of the State apparatus (cf. Žvan and Chapter 6 here) as well as effective democratic competition of ideas. True, Gramsci had just begun to be known at the time and Lenin's democratic aspect was overshadowed by the Civil War and expunged by the Stalinist vulgate, but even the Yugoslav experiments in democracy from the roots, acknowledged as a desirable horizon say in Bakarić (2: 117–18 and *passim*) and more hesitantly by Kardelj, and the work of economists like Horvat would have sufficed to begin building upon:

TABLE 10.1A *The horizons of Yugoslav economy*

	Centralised	Decentralised
Democratic	Utopian Communist	Proudhonist
Oligarchic	Stalinist	Nationalist

However, such a properly rich consideration of alternatives came up against the taboo that posited, in the vein of a bureaucratic optimism, that central political problems have for the foreseeable future been solved, so that only Saint-Simon's and Engels's 'management of things' remained. This is why problems of political and class power, the vertical dimension of the above Table, remained invisible and the debate was posed in the crassly misleading oppositions of autarchic decentralisation vs. total centralisation. 'Campaigns of artificial disintegration have yielded to campaigns of forced integration' (Stojanović, 'Social' 120), and economic reform was doomed to failure. Table 10.1B shows these Yugoslav mainstream ideologico-political and epistemological horizons at the time, as a thought-experiment *ad absurdum*. In it, once questions of political power within socialism were expunged, the dilemma of centralisation vs. decentralisation became a dead-end or false categorisation (cf. Chapters 3–5, also Brus *passim* and Milenkovitch 3, 104–9, 176–7, 282–99). To boot, the terminology was steeped in the stale and increasingly inappropriate rhetoric about bureaucracy, which I found to be ultimately meaningless (cf. Appendices 1–2 – it was hiding and obfuscating precisely the issue of communism as democracy):

TABLE 10.1B *Yugoslav mainstream ideological debate*

	Centralised	Decentralised
Democratic	?	?
Oligarchic	Stalinist ['Centralised']	Nationalist ['Decentralised']

If one means by democracy a real power of the plebeian masses from below rather than the putative parliamentary power at the mercy of elements in control of the economy and capital, that is of the bourgeoisie in the capitalist and the politocracy in the 'socialist' countries – then democratic centralism is a very good option for a State having to defend its independence, and a decentralised democracy another very good one for easier times (say in Rousseau's small community or in Jeffersonian USA). Obviously, decentralisation was indispensable and meaningful in dismantling the centralised command economy, say in 1949–52. But SFRY was faced with the crucial problem of self-management as a potentially associational large-scale democracy starting in economics, with 'direct initiative and direct responsibility [by the] direct performers of the tasks' (Horvat, *Towards* 117). Such self-management makes political and economic sense, that is, it can properly function, only if it is integrated vertically upward – from the basic enterprises, through their various branch associations, and up to federal decision centres – by means of delegates controlled by and recallable from below, as hypothesised by Kidrič at the beginning of self-management in the wake of Lenin and the Paris Commune (see Chapter 5.2), and as untiringly proposed by the socialist 'loyal opposition' of the Praxis group and Horvat. Within it, ***the stark opposition centralised-decentralised is meaningless***: some subsystems and functions need to be decentralised, some must not be – the system would solve this problem internally, by feedback. (In modern hi-tech economies one finds sectors which are necessarily highly centralised alongside some decentralised features.) As Marković put it, it is essential to distinguish between interventions from the centre 'which are [and which are not] necessary either for economic rationality or for socialist humanism' (*Affluence* 143). Or Golubović: 'decentralisation [turned] from de-etatisation and democratisation (as suggested in the 1950s) to a renewal of etatisation by means of a multiplication of centres of State power, which meant a significant narrowing of democracy' ('Novije' 32).

Thus, the mainstream decentralisation debates remained wholly inconclusive cognitively (arguments in the vein of Table 10.1A by the loyal opposition were marginalised), though not at all inconsequential practically. Total centralisation is only achievable by means of police terror, total decentralisation in a complex industrial society is Proudhonist delirium;[1] both are economi-

---

1 Several authors of the Praxis circle, for example its co-editor Supek ('Some Problems' 253–5), mentioned Proudhon when criticising some horizons of self-management. Comisso's book, balancing successfully between sympathy, a rich survey of both macro- and micro-developments, and sophisticated theory, is subtended by the opposition between the Gramscian and the Proudhonist model of self-management; see for the latter also Horvat et al., *Self-governing Socialism*, and Bourdet and Guillerm 65–9. While this might be of some theoretical use, I have found no evidence that anybody in Yugoslav politics was meditating on Proudhon (cf. the debate in Golubović ed. 58–61). The Praxis people mainly followed Marx's treatment of Proudhon in *The Communist Manifesto*, where he was identified with 'conservative or bourgeois socialism', and used his name as a safe shorthand for this rubric.

cally unworkable. In a system with a ruling politocratic oligarchy, if economic decision-making is totally centralised, it is etatist, necessarily accompanied by strong-arm politics of the police type, with a final horizon of Stalinism; its rejection was sealed by the ouster of Ranković in 1966. If it is totally decentralised and bereft of vertical integration, it is either impelled toward disintegrative chaos (cf. Brus 203) and/or necessarily accompanied by reliance on republican nationalism, with a final horizon of separatism. Both of these in fact happened. At stake in this whole mystifying opposition of centralism vs. depoliticisation was, as Bakarić regretfully noted in 1964, the concept of a united federation more important than the sum of its parts: 'not insofar as it is a sum of separate units but in itself, insofar as it is the cohesion factor of precisely those units' (1: 590). He hoped this would be rectified as a priority; but it never was.

My hypothesis for the root cause of the debate in these years, and of the eventual deadlock it caused, is that both the federal or centralising and the republican or decentralising factions of the ruling oligarchy had one overriding interest: to avoid endangering their power – that is, ***to ward off introduction of full economic democracy***, which would be necessarily accompanied by political democracy (a budding civil society within socialism, as theorised by Gramsci) and a management of open conflicts within the most interesting 1963 Constitution, though not a multi-party system. While their 'bureaucratic optimism' probably did not allow them to envisage the baneful results of a national economy incapable of making 'a strong, concentrated effort [in any field]' (Marković, *Affluence* 104, writing in the early 1970s), this took second place to keeping power. The compromise arrived at was to liquidate federal planning and funding (except for the armed forces and foreign policy). The resulting stasis continued for a quarter century:

See however Gurvitch's testimony about Proudhonism in Russia at the time of the October Revolution, cited by Supek, *Arbeiterselbstverwaltung* 224.

Many commentators understood the need for intelligent and supple centralisation in some key matters, in which light the 1965 reform was (at best!) a botched beginning. Among them was Kardelj, who rightly concluded that a reform must also include a new form of democratic centralisation on the basis and within the framework of social self-management (*Integration* 22, cited in 10.4), including a new concept of planning so far stymied by ignorance and resistances (Kardelj, *Subjektivne* 312–13); however, nobody in power did anything about it.

TABLE 10.2A *Decline of the social sector, 1960–85*
FROM LAMPE 323; CHANGE IN %

	Average per annum 1960–70	Average per annum 1970–9	Average per annum 1979–85	Total 1979–85
Social product	6	4.5	−0.5	−3.1
Consumption per person (1972 prices)	5.7	4.5	−1.3	−7.7
Real product (per employee in social sector)	4.3	1.8	−3.5	−19.5
Real net income (per employee in productive social sector)	6.8	2.1	−4.7	−27.9

TABLE 10.2B *Change in labour productivity and incomes 1956–75*
FROM SIMON 90

	Average % per annum 1956–60	Average % per annum 1961–5	Average % per annum 1966–70	Average % per annum 1971–5
Labour productivity (per person in material production)	7.2	5.9	5.9	6.1
Cost of living (per employee in social sector)	5.4	13.6	10.4	19.4
Real net income (per employee in social sector)	7.7	5.4	7.3	1.5

In other words: while labour productivity remained high 1961–75, though not so high as earlier, after the cost of living had risen above the rise of personal income by almost 18% in the early 70s, all indicators tumbled into red.

The market was from the 1960s on the one hand needed both as an economic control instrument to supplement insufficient credit and fiscal policy and as a political alternative to a quasi-Stalinist centralism. It was the minimum common denominator of an intra-oligarchy compromise, and '[its] use as the basic coordinator of Yugoslav economic life was ... more a decision by default than an act of positive policy' (Comisso, *Workers'* 75; cf. Samary, *Marché* 155)! Given the opprobrium awakened by seeing Stalinism in practice in the USSR and the People's Democracies, as well as by elements of their way of ruling present in the Yugoslav experience 1945–50 and in some ways even beyond, the Stalinist wing was forced to acquiesce to a system that opposes economic centralisation and central planning; yet they were ideologically, economically, and politically unable to envisage this without, unwillingly, conceding an accompanying market as a minor evil compared to integral self-management and major loss of power. The republican oligarchies were *a fortiori* in the same position, and the Slovene and Croat ones believed to boot that decentralisation and the market would strengthen their economic superiority (whereas the oligarchies in Bosnia and Macedonia feared this comparative loss of advantages, and were thus less enthused about decentralisation accompanied by market relationships).

A market could, on the one hand, pinpoint and puncture several major myths of etatism, to begin with that of full employment – which often turns out to be inefficient – and that of rising production – which often turns out to mean stockage of useless products (cf. Stojanović, *Kritik* 114 and *passim*). Yet on the other hand the market was also mystified within this system of false categorisation because it was used as a panacea, 'a socialist invisible hand' (Milenkovitch 285), disjoined from and opposed to federal planning – to what Brus proposes as 'the model of a planned economy using a regulated market mechanism' for better economic accountability (74).[2] If not corrected by and subordinated to strong planning and fencing-in measures, the market had potential elements of a reintroduction of capitalism. It also brought to a head 'the weakness of capitalist rationality and profitability in structuring accumulation in Yugoslavia' (Pienkos 56). And in fact 'the Yugoslav market did not follow the path foretold by neoliberal capitalist ideology, from a market regulated by the Party/State to a free market, but to a regulated market broken away from any democratic control and ruled by international centres of financial capital' (Buden, 'Gastarbajteri').

---

2 A number of Western Marxist commentators sharply opposed the economic policy of SFRY from the 1960s on. One group was around the New York *Monthly Review*, and was represented by Sweezy and Huberman's 'Peaceful Transition from Socialism to Capitalism?' The other group was a number of French-language Marxists writing about Yugoslavia, most prominently Ernest Mandel, and in his wake Albert Meister and Catherine Samary, to whom is due the first overall Left-wing critique of the Yugoslav trajectory. They made many pertinent critiques, and history has proved them prescient, though to my mind before the early 70s they fastened only on the negative side of a fluid situation. Theoretically the best answer to Mandel as well as to the market idolaters is the brilliant article by Diane Elson which I pass in review hereafter. There is by now a whole little library of debates about socialism and the market, all influenced by Polanyi (both titles), of which I list only Hodgson's and McNally's books, and by Lange's argument that the market could be used to find relevant consumer preferences while maintaining social and State control over economic development.

The illuminating discussion of Elson richly argues the hypothesis that Marx's 'commodity fetishism' arises from sale and purchase 'under conditions which enable them to take on an independent life of their own', and that such conditions can be changed by 'the socialisation of buying and selling and the price formation process' (4). If one starts from the production and reproduction of labour power, which is wider than the needful attention to workers in paid labour, then a 'politics of use values' could use a dialectical approach to the market. With Marx, the useful aspects of market coordination ought to be recognised, negatively as against the personal subalternity in feudalism and positively as helping the mutual satisfaction of needs, but also the enforcement of atomised profit mentality and massification of exploitation it necessarily carries. Not only do people not at all matter in the cash nexus, occulted behind a social relation between commodities, but their interests are a priori defined and strictly enforced as isolated, and information is valuable and used only insofar as it contributes to antagonistic competitive advantage:

> Information flows are fragmented; there is a lack of open access to information networks; there is waste of resources as information-gathering activities have to be duplicated in the interests of secrecy. [As Marx expresses it] in the *Grundrisse*, cooperative attempts to overcome the alienation of the market do not, in a market economy, transcend that alienation.
> ELSON 15

Probably even more important is the fact that 'no economy can adjust solely through a market-led adjustment process because *there are key resources which cannot be fully commodified. The most important are labour and the environment*' (emphasis DS). In families and households, 'labour power ... is not produced as a commodity' but as a mainly 'altruistic collective behaviour, ... [in] a resource allocation pattern that is not wholly determined by [market prices]' (Elson 17). In sum,

> A socialised market is one in which the market is made by public bodies, which are financed out of taxation of enterprises and households, rather than out of sales. It is also one in which the 'invisible handshakes', the relations of good will and reciprocity, ... are made into public information networks with open access ... A socialised market permits the dispersal of initiative, which is an essential feature of a society which liberates people, but creates new channels and incentives for individual initiatives to serve the common good.
> idem 32

Such an approach puts paid to scholastic debates, rife in Yugoslavia from the 1960s on, about whether the Law of Value[3] operates in socialist commodity production or not (cf. Chapter 5, the pioneering overview in Bavčar et al. 11–16 and *passim*, also Bakarić in Zović-Svoboda 96–7). This sterile dilemma should have been replaced by efforts to articulate how to use the market only as an auxiliary instrument and simultaneously counteract its potentially virulent dissemination of dominant capitalist ideology by means of overall economic planning (to which I come below):

> But it would take the form of a guiding strategy, a vision of the future, not a detailed allocation of material inputs. The planners in the Central Office of Economic Planning would draw upon the information networks of buyers and sellers of key resources in formulating alternative scenarios, of which one could be chosen by some democratic political process. Fiscal and monetary policy would play an important role in plan implementation, but so also would relations of reciprocity, good will and persuasion, as happens in Japanese economic co-ordination.
> ELSON 42

---

[3] The problem can be theoretically phrased as: does Marx's 'Law of Value', that is, the production of commodities for a however modified market, hold after a socialist/communist revolution? All such revolutions so far have come about in industrially very backward countries, from Russia through China to Cuba and Vietnam, which – as Lenin first and best theorised – could not dispense with this 'law' and with the indispensable primitive accumulation of capital, having to do the work of both a bourgeois-capitalist and a socialist anti-capitalist revolution (on which bind see more in Chapter 1 and at the end of the book); the question therefore becomes, just how far and how fully does and should commodity production hold? This feeds into the most crucial consequence for any socialist rule: how does commodity production relate to State planning?

Personally, I confess that after 50 years of on and off reading *Das Kapital* I have not understood what Marx means by value, though the opposition between use and exchange value is crystal clear and I still find the labour theory of value persuasive (even if today the weight of nature – of husbanding negentropy, cf. Suvin 'Introductory' – would have to increase). I'm comforted by Marx's clarification in the late *Notes on Adolph Wagner*: 'for me neither "value" nor "exchange-value" are subjects [of capitalist economics], but *the commodity*'. See for a beginning discussion in Elson ed., *Value*, especially her own essay, and Graeber (on Marx 54 ff. and 66 ff.).

I would be in favour of Baslé's proposal to split Marx's Law of Value into LV_1 and LV_2: the first relating to allocation of labour in various proportions for various purposes, which must exist in any society (except Cockayne), the second being the capitalist alienation of LV_1 in a commodity economy with profit, competition, etc. *ad nauseam* (see Nove 14 and *passim*).

10.2 Ideology and Planning

10.2.1 *Excursus on Productivism and Economism*

The Yugoslav Party/State politocracy dealt at first very successfully with economic politics, in an alliance with the working class and the intelligentsia and a tacit stand-off with the private peasantry. But after the first 15 years, most rapidly after 1965, it lost its way because of the economist and monolithic mindset and horizon, returning to semi-Stalinist repression and finally Brezhnevian stasis. To understand this, it is indispensable to factor into the considerations so far the 'idols of the tribe' or ideological dead-ends dominating the mentality and imagination of this politocracy throughout its rule. I shall here deal with the politics affecting only the economy, and leave the overarching problem of Party monolithism vs. associational democracy for later consideration.

The first idol was *productivism*. By productivism is meant a strong primacy allotted to developing industrial productive forces in the crassest sense of building the maximum possible number of possibly huge industrial plants. It is situated within the horizon of *economism*, and in order to understand how this came about a brief historical excursus is needed.

Economism or economic determinism was a pragmatic caricature of Marxism which held that all politics and class struggle is 'the direct and immediate result of economic contradictions [which] are thus supposed to be able by themselves to "engender" social changes' (Bettelheim 1: 34, and see the whole discussion 32–41). It pervaded the European labour and socialist movement throughout the Second International phase (1880–1914), spearheaded by the huge apparatus of the German Social Democratic Party, and was if anything strengthened in the Third International and the communist parties from the early 1920s on. This was diametrically opposed both to the liberatory stance of Marx, which started from the alienation of humans and especially workers and analysed how to work for its abolition, and to Lenin's revolutionary insistence that Marxism was *not* an 'economist' theory in which all other factors, especially political consciousness and organisation, ought to be backgrounded – on the contrary, he fiercely struggled to ground the indispensable build-up of productive forces in such factors. Stalinism only had to graft upon economism total State control of economic development (and therefore everything else) in order to complete the shift away from the actual efforts and interests of the manual workers' class and its anti-capitalist allies.

After the October Revolution, Lenin held that an efficient State capitalism under the control of the Party, which would therefore work for socialism, was the only possible way of survival. In the 1917 *State and Revolution* he had glossed carefully Marx's work on direct democracy in the Paris Commune and his *Cri-*

tique of the Gotha Programme. From the latter he drew the fulgurant conclusion that the 'socialist' transition period would have a semi-bourgeois State, indeed, as he provocatively put it, 'there remains for a time not only bourgeois law, but even **the bourgeois State – without the bourgeoisie!**' (*The State* /ch05.htm#s4). In devastated Russia he did not much speak about the relationships inside economic production except to refuse immediate workers' control (cf. Brinton), so that it was later easy for Stalin to proclaim total monocracy (*odinonachalie*) from the plant upward. I suggested in the Foreword that we can today conclude socialism would mean a society with initially strong remnants of bourgeois and capitalist ways, that do not consist only in private property by the peasantry or remaining capitalist enterprises but pervade the whole State and national life. In 1922 Lenin theorised this by drawing up a wondrous inventory of five modes of production or 'economic structures' existing within the USSR: 1. Patriarchal village economy (in the Asian tribes); 2. Petty commodity production, that is, the peasants selling grain; 3. Private capitalism; 4. State capitalism; and 5. Socialism. The last economic structure being still very weak, even after the expropriation of most private capital, the dominant one was petty commodity production, from which it followed that strong doses of State capitalism were the central remedy devoutly to be wished for (cf. 'Five Years').

Stalin violently simplified these dialectics to the effect that State capital really represented State socialism, which had by definition nothing in common with capitalism, and made out of Lenin's contingent and supple treatment of the 1918–22 situation the inexorable 'objective law' of socialist society. Socialism is by Stalin treated not as a struggle between old class models and communism but as a separate and independent type of society, rounded off unto itself as an Aristotelian species within the genus of social modes of production, or indeed as a Leibnizian monad. Within such socialism, beginning with the USSR, planning was the major knot of theoretical and practical considerations, encompassing the whole of economy, down to the smallest detail, and vested in the central Party/State apparatus (cf. Chapter 5.2, Appendices 1–2, also Suvin, 'On the Concept' and further bibliography there). This type of planning on the one hand did have considerable success in laying fundaments for earlier non-existing heavy industry, but on the other hand was most wasteful and inefficient, also subject to gross manipulation of figures and, most important, required a huge apparatus to enforce it – a police by whatever name it went. Its ideal was capitalist productivism crasser than in Adam Smith. All communist horizons for human relationships, all indignities that drove Marx, Lenin, and millions of their followers to devote their lives to doing away with them, were simply irrelevant to this economism, they were shunted off and embalmed in a separate watertight compartment of ideological theory called 'agitation and propaganda' with ever lessening bite on reality. And when Party politocrats wanted to find a way out from productivism, they mainly opted for its complementary obverse, an equally economistic consumerism (cf. Stojanović, 'Social' 129).

In the Stalinist aberration, power was not only the first but the *only* central problem: once the Party is in power, economic development in the productivist vein will solve all. This meant that theory, in Marx's sense of going to the roots rather than explaining the surface flow, was the privilege of the Party top (if not the Leader); and that politics, in the sense of who determines the economic development of a given kind and the class appropriation and distribution of what is produced and consumed, was held to have ceased with the successful revolutionary control of the 'commanding heights' of society – a simplification of which Marx too was guilty in his revolutionary optimism, and Stalin erected into a dogma. Politics was swallowed up in economic policy, and the rest reduced to police: how to enable the Party and State to neutralise and liquidate the enemy groups and saboteurs hindering economic progress; in Gramsci's terms, hegemony was held to consist only in coercion. This also meant that the class alliance of workers and peasants – and other unacknowledged groups such as a fraction of the intelligentsia and the patriots opposed to foreign domination – which had brought about the revolution was to be discarded in favour of the rule by an ostensibly workers' party; however, without feedback from a democracy at the roots it inexorably grew into an office politocracy (cf. Chapters 3–4, 7, and Suvin 'On the Concept', Comisso 'Can'). Such a severely mutated genome of 'socialism' was transmitted to all Third International parties, including the Yugoslav one, fiercely purged by Stalin's liquidations in the 1930s. The 1940s' CPY cadre was educated on and indoctrinated with Stalin's *Short Course of ACP/b/* (apparently translated in good part by Tito while in Moscow) as holy writ.

While I do not think every orientation toward developing industrial productive forces and downplaying all other (redistribution) politics is necessarily positivist, and in fact socialists came to this through a highly critical attitude to bourgeois failures, this type of economism and productivism clearly became positivist when it grew into a not further questioned or questionable common sense of socialist societies: 'Positivism, the philosophy of common sense, appeals to the certainty of facts, but, as Hegel shows [also Marx – DS], in a world where facts do not at all present what reality can and ought to be, positivism amounts to giving up the real potentialities of mankind for a false and alien world' (Marcuse, *Reason* 113). What remained was accelerated industrial modernisation and unheard of shifts of plebeians, mainly peasants, into the working class and middle classes, with remnants of the communist horizon visible in schooling and social services. But the existing concepts of socialist political economy remained quite insufficient, and in each country after a revolution led to more or less open debates between totally centralised budgeting for economy, accompanied by propagandist moral suasion, and autonomy for enterprises with material stimulation according to results; the debate was unduly simplified as the plan vs. the market. I have dwelt on it for the USSR in Appendix 1.

However, I know far too little, for example, about the practical fall-outs of the debate after the Cuban Revolution, in 1963–4, between Che Guevara, flanked by Ernest Mandel, and Alberto Mora, flanked by Charles Bettelheim, which ascended from these practical knots to theoretical considerations about the Law of Value. The Guevara-Mandel wing insisted that this law could be by degrees (but rather soon and much) modified through conscious human intervention, that is by 'socialist planning' – treated as a dialectical contradiction uniting these two terms, but also as 'the category defining socialist society and the point where the human conscience finally manages to direct the economy toward its goal, the full liberation of man in communist society' (Guevara, in Lowy, *La Pensée* 53). The Mora-Bettelheim wing stuck to Stalin's formulations, according to which the scientific Law of Value could in this phase not be modified but used – it was not clear just how – in planning (cf. also Tablada Pérez *passim*, Lowy, *La Pensée* 40–1, 50–4, 58–9, and 62–7, and Lowy, *Dialectique* 80–2). The problem seems to have been that Guevara went from the above fertile alternative – within which he rightly observed that subventions for key items such as food, schooling, lodging, health care, and social help violated this 'law' – into the extreme of refusing commodity relationships between State enterprises since they could grow into forces making for inhuman relationships between people. His apodictic summation is: 'To build communism people have to be changed at the same time as the economic basis' (Lowy, *La Pensée* 62), and he even began talking about a looming progressive extinction of categories such as money, the market, and material interests (Tablada Pérez 89, 82–3). Perhaps his most pregnant formulation is 'You cannot defeat capitalism by using his fetishes' (Lowy, *La Pensée* 64), not so dissimilar from the radical feminism of Audre Lorde, 'The master's tools will never dismantle the master's house'.[4] Similar oscillations could be found in the USSR before and after Stalin

---

4 Two matters deserve to be noted. First, this is – after the halfway house of the fairly acrimonious but still fair Preobrazhensky-Bukharin discussion – the first and I think only fully free and dignified example of a debate between these opposing standpoints, yet with mutual respect, within a post-revolutionary country (but Mora committed suicide in the less tolerant year 1971). Also, both sides had studied not only the Soviet experience but also Lange,

or in China. The Yugoslav system of self-government was designed by Kidrič and the original godfathers, a small group at the politocracy top, precisely as a radical (if not fully articulated) way out of this dilemma. As a main advocate cautiously phrased it by contraries: 'What was characteristic for capitalism, and perhaps up to a point for our system immediately after the war, was that principal care was devoted to the introduction of machines ...; the human being was here I won't say neglected but in the second place' (Bakarić 2: 135).

10.2.2 *Planning*

It should first be clear that modern technology, as it has been shaped by the needs of capitalism and warfare, cannot exist without extensive planning; all the mass media heavy drum-fire against planning for the last century is merely a smoke-screen for leaving planning to the large corporations and their divisions of the market as well as to governments controlled by them spending taxpayers' money (cf. Best and Connolly 32–40 and 207: US government spending rose from 8.2% of GNP in 1913 to 38.1% in 1977, while in World War II it peaked at nearly 50%). In other words, a socialist/communist political programme would at some not too distant point have to plan also reshaping technology for its own needs, to make it as far as possible disalienating inside each single plant and eco-sustainable outside of it; this did not at all happen in SFRY, swamped after the 60s by licensed Western technology. I propose to deal here only with planning within early socialism. In fact, Lenin took his cue for improvising largely from the central planning introduced in all major capitalist States during World War I, especially the German one whose efficiency he much admired, and 'the war economy remained the basic model of the Soviet planned economy' (Hobsbawm, *How* 9). However, this super-productivist economism determining politics had the downside of being totally unfit for industrial democracy; rather than a planned it deserves to be called a 'command' economy (Markuš 124).

Early 'State centralist' planning, as introduced by Kidrič, was legally enforced and monitored through the State and Party apparati. What happened in Yugoslavia under 'market socialism' was, as I suggested in previous chapters, a growing momentum of jettisoning coordinated planning. Yet intelligent planning

---

and used the insights of prominent Marxist intellectuals even though one of the latter was a Maoist and the other a Trotskyist. Second, Guevara had visited Yugoslavia at the beginning of the 60s and was horrified to find 'something like capitalist competition between enterprises as units, not as groups of workers', though he liked the workers' councils, which he tried to introduce in Cuba (Lowy, *La Pensée* 58–9). Beside the three books I list, a handy presentation of the debates is in Bettelheim, Castro, Guevara, Mandel, Mora: *Wertgesetz, Planung und Bewusstsein*, Frankfurt: Neue Kritik, 1969, which I have not managed to consult.

was the key to solving the major social contradictions and aporias of what happens during industrialisation after a revolution that dispossessed the – largely foreign – capitalist class, including planning's hidden twin and political analogue, the place and extent of democracy from below as its indispensable partner (cf. Elson in 10.1 above). The early 1960s book by Waterston caught the central Yugoslav trend: 'As the decentralisation movement gained momentum after 1952, the Federal Planning Commission was progressively stripped of its executive and administrative powers over the economy ... [and renamed] as the Federal Institute of Economic Planning ... [Its] powers are only technical and advisory ...' (31) It submitted plans, often overruled, to the federal government and the central parliament, analysed how the plans were accomplished, and worked on further prospects and methods. From 700 employees before 1952 it had 10 years later retained 180, about half of which had university degrees, including 40 economists, while the rest were in clerical or other work. Besides it, the six republican planning offices had between 30 and 70 employees each. True, in the early 60s the overall production targets for the economy were legally binding, but 'the practical significance of this position is hard to understand', noted this International Bank expert wryly, for 'the growing importance of the market has converted the federal plan into a forecast' (39–40; cf. Milenkovitch *passim*). In fact, if the intentions and goals of lower economic actors (republics, funds, etc.) were altered, 'it was the plan which changed, not the behaviour of the economic unit' (Comisso, *Workers'* 77, cf. 92–3 and *passim*)! The annual plan for 1962 had a scant 25 pages in the *Official Gazette*, and was in four parts: a short qualitative statement of basic aims and tasks; proposed directions for the economy, including quantitative expectations for gross national income, production, personal consumption, federal expenditures and foreign trade, employment and productivity; expected growth of production by sectors; and finally, implementation instruments, such as the budget and the investment funds. The same applied to the 1957–61 Five-Year Plan, which took up only 40 pages (Waterston 46–7 – for comparison, the USSR 1927/28 Five-Year Plan had 1,600 pages). The planners elaborated also 10-year plans for main sectors.

While the 'market' for capital goods was before 1965 still mainly determined by allocation of investment funds, which became a hugely growing bone of contention, consumption was largely determined by market demands for its quantity and quality. This produced a 'happy contrast with the mediocrity and standardisation of monopolistic enterprises' (Waterston 57) during Stalinist centralism; prices did not decline, since reduced costs of production were offset by inflation, but this did not much matter as long as real income was rising steadily. Furthermore, price control at that time was still imposed for more than one quarter of domestic production for items in short supply and for keeping costs in line with incomes (housing rents, electricity, transportation), though it began to be dismantled when Yugoslavia joined the GATT in 1959, and was then reimposed by fits and starts in the 70s and 80s. A new law on planning was even passed in 1976, but it was too late and wrongly conceived.

The very sympathetic account by Vanek concluded that, if planning includes instruments for implementation of targets rather than simply research and forecasting, then planning was abandoned after 1965; he believes it was because consumer and investor behaviour was becoming unpredictable (83). However, this could be (to my mind better) argued the other way round: the unpredictability was the result of political disorientation and lack of planning.

After 1965, planning by basic proportions was replaced by even vaguer 'indicative planning' (Schrenk et al. 22), and federal plans became largely political pious wishes. Yet '[s]tandard economic reasoning tells us that, in a typical underdeveloped country, the market mechanism can produce inferior investment decisions' (Milenkovitch 294). The major argument against market reliance, developed in both titles by Polanyi, was handily summarised by Joseph E. Stiglitz in his 2001 'Foreword' to *The Great Transformation*:

> [Polanyi clarifies] how free market ideology was the handmaiden for [bourgeois] industrial interests, and how those interests used that ideology selectively, calling upon government intervention when needed to pursue their own interests ... Today, there is no respectable intellectual support for the proposition that markets, by themselves, lead to efficient, let alone equitable outcomes.
> vii–viii

The ad hoc government countermeasures that took the place of planning ensured neither market nor planning would work properly. Finally, 'Once investment planning is abandoned, an entrepreneurial agent becomes truly necessary' (Milenkovitch 297). This could have theoretically been the WsC of each enterprise or their pools, the later horizontal 'self-management agreements' and vertical 'social compacts' (*samoupravni sporazumi i društveni dogovori*, cf. Tyson 5–7 and *passim*, Dyker 85–7), but since they were legal fictions without teeth (for example the necessary funds), it became the major lenders: banks. In such a situation, WsC devolved back to decisions about internal enterprise matters: hiring and firing, and minor adjustments on the shop floor.

10.3 At the Poles: Capitalisation and Unemployment

10.3.1 Independent Capital Lenders

The new Banking and Credit Law passed in 1965 (cf. Simon 32–4) had far-reaching consequences, possibly in part unintended by the lawgivers, but it reveals as an acid test the power reconfiguration going on at the politocracy top. Ca. 480 well-functioning communal banks were virtually abolished in favour of a much smaller number of larger regional institutions. The law provided that investment and commercial banks can be founded by any group of 25 enterprises and/or political units. Though the lending institutions had 'assemblies' that represented the founders, practically they needed the consent of the republican top – this was even spelled out in a further 1976 law, see Lampe 316 – and up to a point of the communes (Zukin, 'Beyond' 15–16); the incongruous WsC of the bank represented only the bank employees. This meant that, while the banks were supposed to extend credit anywhere within Yugoslavia, they did so within the republic where they were sited. The founding law was hastily conceived and represented a signal victory of those who opposed even the principle (however unclear) that income must be derived from work performed – that is, within the system of WsC.

There was a very good reason both for intervening into the untenable concentration of investment capital in the federal government and for not distributing it simply to existing enterprises, as these were unable to generate sufficient fluid capital, thus blocking further circulation and investment: 'For an efficient use of investment funds, there must be capital mobility in some kind of a socialist capital market' (Milenkovitch 177; cf. ample data on finance in SFRY up to 1972 in Dimitrijevic & Macesich, and on the dead-end USSR debates Chavance). If we accept the persuasive, if heretic, views of Bakarić, the transitional period called socialism is economically based on commodity or capitalist production relationships, with suitable changes by the new State power, such as backgrounding the profit motive, thus changing some regulative norms of production. The role of workers was changed by the huge rise in their number, the upgrading of their skill level and their pro capita income, and by having this income keep pace with the cost of living (in Zović-Svoboda 96–7, also Bakarić 3: 60–1 and generally 52 ff.). A central State investment bank necessarily grew into a strongly 'bureaucratic' institution – in fact, State capitalist without the bourgeoisie – exposed to all possible political pressures of powerful groups (cf. Horvat, 'Der Markt' 113). Further, one of the aims of the 1965 Reform was to restrict credit: there were superfluous investments galore, for example multiple capacities in the same branch due to republican insistence on self-sufficiency – usually below the technological and economical rentability level –

and to create jobs and/or profits. Thus little Yugoslavia had six steel plants, five oil refineries, five car assembly plants, eight ports with little specialisation, and, most scandalously, 80 independent electrical power firms (Drulović 177, Prout 159–63)! However, the credit law was shaped within a clash between sharply disagreeing approaches (Bilandžić, *Historija* 342). On the one pole were people who wanted to introduce a full and unhindered set of 'commodity and financial' – that is, Manchester capitalist – tools including bank bills, securities, etc., as well as shares issued by enterprises and citizens. On the other pole were ideologists who rightly remarked this was against the principles of socialism, but were unable to offer a third way.

The resulting compromise was characteristic of the 1965 Reform: a substantial loss of self-management and advancement of capitalist relationships, stripped of their full panoply and decorated by a few curlicues of associational democracy and quasi-Marxist language which proved unimportant and misleading. For one example, in the banks' 'assemblies' the investing economic organisations had in 1969 78% of votes, but since their debt to the institution was larger than its initial investment, the vote outcome, as in capitalism, always followed the recommendations of the MB (Bavčar et al. 102, Bakarić 3: 254). For another, capital came to be referred to as 'elapsed labour' (*minuli rad*), a Jesuitical ennoblement officially adopted by the 1974 constitution (cf. Woodward 167). For a third, the banks and cognate institutions paid de facto dividends (Comisso, *Workers'* 76; cf. Dirlam and Plummer 161–99), but did not call them such. Simultaneously, charges for the use of social property, natural if these were deemed to have been leased by enterprises from the community as a whole, were simply abolished, prompting Milenkovitch to ask, 'Can socialism decentralise and still remain socialist?' She does not propose an answer but tentatively sides with 'the humanists' within socialism – what I have in Appendix 2 called the loyal opposition – who saw here a new class establishing property rights (Milenkovitch 297–99; cf. Bakarić 3: 17). This may have been a bit premature, but it delineated a horizon gradually coming into its own – especially since the banks embarked in a quite capitalist way on a wave of mergers (Comisso, *Workers'* 83), so that their number shrank from 567 in 1960 to 29 in 1971 (Dirlam and Plummer 178), while a number of export-import enterprises expanded horizontally into conglomerates (Comisso, *Workers'* 107).

Since there was no formal capital market, enterprises could by law recur to indebtment only from loans or credits. The banks exercised more and more capillary control over indebted enterprises, such as refusing loans until the management was changed (Adizes 225). Beside them, loans were also given by insurance companies and remaining state funds, and – especially in fast expanding tourism – by ***import-export houses*** licensed for foreign trade by the federal government. They had privileged, indeed oligopolistic ownership of foreign currency and could lend it to enterprises depending on purchases of materials or equipment abroad, or 'employ it toward imports they themselves could directly market via retail enterprises in Yugoslavia' (Comisso, *Workers'* 84–5).

The result was a huge shift of fixed capital source in the economy:

TABLE 10.3 *Source of fixed capital in economic enterprises (in %)* FROM DENITCH 171

Year	Enterprise	Territorial gov.ts[a]/	Banks
1960	37.4	61.6	1.0
1965	36.8	31.5	31.7
1969	34.8	19.8	49.4

(a) Federal, republican and communal administrations and/or their planning agencies

In the years after 1969, the share of banks and other credit institutions showed no sign of diminishing. Thus, already in 1968 Bakarić opined that practically the whole 'surplus labour' of many enterprises (beyond modest income distribution to employees) went to paying the credits they had taken, and that beyond some good results such credits had a strong capitalist aspect, though he thought the big foreign trade conglomerates were the main culprits (cf. 3: 233 and 13–14). Kardelj judged by 1971 that more than 70% of the economic enterprises' business fund went to repay the capital investment loans (*Integration* 145); by 1980 the much touted new 'self-management association of [financial] means' through horizontal and vertical agreements of the enterprises themselves contributed to 'the credit potentials' a mere 0.7% (Bavčar et al. 118). The banks claimed they were returning the profits gained to 'the economy', but that meant merely widening the circle of the indebted: 'the most mobile and fertile part of surplus value was not in the hands of the direct producers but of [groups in the banks]' (Bakarić 3: 155). This also entailed huge disruptions in financial policy and foreign exchange. 'By 1971, federal authorities had lost all control over credit policy'; the federal investment funds were from the 70s on replaced in part by household savings – buoyed by the rise of a middle and then crypto-capitalist class and the revaluation of the German mark – but mainly by Western capitalist loans, mostly by the World Bank, which in turn dictated key items of economic policy: an example would be agricultural investments as of

1973, available only to the private sector, another the 1976–80 Yugoslav 'social plan' which followed World Bank parameters (Woodward 236 and *passim*). Foreign investment sources – including workers' remittances from abroad – rose from the 1961–4 level of 18% to 28% in 1971–5 (Gnjatović 129).

In such oligopoly the banks became the most profitable economic branch, merrily transgressing the legal maximum return rate of 12% up to the double, and with an annual increase in gross income two to three times higher than the rest of economy (Zukin, 'Beyond' 13). Its higher echelons became leading power-brokers and a veritable seedbed for the new privileged stratum or class fraction, tightly intertwined with autarchic politics in the major republics (among others, a certain Slobodan Milošević began his career that way), and favouring luxury imports which both served and enriched it. To the extent that capital became more mobile it was also 'republicanised': 'and it was not just finance capital, it was **State** finance capital, or something very near it ... "for now everyone has his own local State, partial towards him, with full powers, but not with full responsibility". [In the 1970s the banks] became *sui generis* finance ministries of para-State political structures ...' (Dyker 88, the inside quote is from Gavrović 1979). Together with constitutional amendment 15 voted in 1968 (see 9.1 above), the credit system in the late 60s practically dispossessed self-management (cf. Hanžeković, in Bićanić 220–4, and Adizes 225). A Federal Assembly report cited by Supek calls it 'a brutal exploitation ... assuming infantile usurious forms that astound even businessmen from contemporary capitalist economies'; most dangerously, the credit institutions followed the purely speculative logic of quick profit which blocked 'the development of modern technology (which works with shortened amortisation cycles and cannot successfully progress without subsidies, in other words an overall developmental strategy)' ('Some Contradictions' 258).

In sum, 'in the later 1960s, usurpation of investment funds, credits, and foreign exchange by banks occurred, and with dire consequences for working class interests and ethno-nationality relations' (Pienkos 65). Even Tito's keynote speech at the Party's 1974 Tenth Congress acknowledged that in the credit institutions huge means were concentrated, on whose disposal the workers that created them had the least influence (Bošković & Dašić 330–1). Kardelj repeated this in the same year at more length, and added that this was 'the economic basis for linking our techno-structure in the economy' with bourgeois nationalism (*Subjektivne* 317). Some measures for 'resocialising' the banks were passed in the 1970s, making them more dependent on a compromise between the partitocratic and the technocratic wing. However, it was forgotten that 'capital is not a sum of money but a definite social relationship' (of command over labour – Lenin, 'Immediate' 249), and it continued to dominate over self-

FIGURE 23

Rudi Supek (1987)
PHOTO REPRODUCED WITH KIND
PERMISSION OF BOZIDAR JAKŠIC

management – for the most part uneconomically to boot. The *nouveaux riches**
class set into motion a full consumer society with unbridled petty-bourgeois
values including pornography and much kitsch.

An alternative would have been to base the capital market too on associational democracy and nation-wide planning, that is, on a corresponding rise of vertical and savvy roof organisations of self-management, with their own research institutes etc. In such a system banks would have been much more tightly controlled both by federal antitrust rules – that existed but were not applied – and by the associated WsC of the founding and borrowing enterprises (cf. Horvat's proposal, *Towards* 226–7 and *passim*). In its absence, the dispossession of Soviet-style centralised bureaucratic planning meant that the remaining, very partial and toothless 'planning' necessarily led to disaster in an environment based on political and market improvisation. The home banks and other credit institutions, and then the international ones, took the vacant place of the central government and became just as (if differently) alienated and alienating: an independent outside factor allied with the republican politocracies and determining the life of the 'self-managing' enterprises.[5]

---

5   Also, in 1967 legislation was passed which permitted foreign investors to become partners of Yugoslav enterprises up to a share of 49%. This did not develop in major ways, but it was to begin with mainly German: 'by 1971 German capital represented 25% of the $93.5 million

10.3.2 Unemployment

The political and economic stalemate beginning in the second half of the 1960s meant there were more and more unemployed, official and unofficial. Indeed, one of the purposes of the Reform was the shift to an 'intensive' rather than extensive economy, with higher productivity and less workers (it was unclear what should then happen to them). Both the restriction of credit, with attendant strictness in repayment, and the higher taxation of enterprises were supposed to prod them into releasing all surplus workforce. However, as seen in Chapter 9, the WsC stood quite firm and tended to insert a formal no-retrenchment rule into their by-laws: employment expansion was indeed arrested, except for higher staff, but 'no significant release of workers ensued' (Vanek 277). I cannot render justice here to the magisterial study by Woodward, which deals with much more than unemployment, but it shows that even before 1965 the steady growth of ca. 4% in the 'social sector' employment failed to compensate for the huge outflow from the peasantry. A growing group fell between these two stools and found no steady employment in either.

The following unemployment table is based on the official registration of job-seekers:

TABLE 10.4A   *Social sector employment and job-seekers (in 000s, at year end)*
ADAPTED FROM SINGLETON 243

	1962	1968	1974	1982
Registered workforce in social sector	3,400	3,660	4,600	6,100
Registered job seekers	274	326	449	888

The numbers of registered job seekers oscillated primarily in function of worker migration abroad, which subsided abruptly with the economic downturn in the West from 1973 on; in 1962–73 they were between 6.5 and 9% of the whole workforce, but they reached 9.7% in 1974 and grew inexorably to 14.5% in 1982. This statistic only partly shows what really obtained, since there were two additional large groups: workers abroad, and unregistered workers with low

---

which had been invested. In addition there were licensing and marketing agreements entered into by Yugoslav firms, which increased the dependence of the economy on foreign partners' (Singleton 243).

skills and low incomes shifting seasonally around the country (especially in the building trade); yet the worsening tendency is clear even before the crash of the 1980s. By 1970 almost half of all unemployed were under 25 and the percentage kept rising (Veljko Rus in Jerovšek et al. eds. 210)

A better approximation can be found in the World Bank report by Schrenk et al. according to which those not employed inside the country reached 14.7% in 1973, though even there I would assume the unregistered workers, camouflaged here mainly as peasants, amounted to several hundreds of thousand more:[6]

TABLE 10.4B *Employment status of labour force (in 000s)*
ADAPTED FROM SCHRENK ET AL. 85

	1969	1973	1975
In social sector	3,622	4,222	4,667
In private agriculture and artisans	4,385	3,479	3,256
Temporarily abroad	572	1,100	900
Registered unemployed	198	229	324
Total labour force	*8,777*	*9,030*	*9,147*

It appears that this outflow of migrant workers abroad (mainly to Germany, but practically to all of affluent capitalist Europe and Australia) had two components, especially after the mid-60s: the most highly skilled, and the unskilled or semi-skilled. Drulović (187–8) counts the 'highly skilled' in 1971 as 3% of the migrants, evenly divided between intellectual and manual workers. They were joined by a mass of unskilled workers – over 76%, of which 60% fresh from the farm – and a middle-sized group of lower-skilled workers; for this great majority, it should be kept in mind that in 1971 the average Yugoslav worker abroad was estimated to earn US$4,500, while earnings in private agriculture were about $700 (Schrenk et al. 266). The small but important group of the most highly skilled including technicians, engineers, and university graduates

---

6 Cf. Suvin, Chapter 3 and later discussions in the book. Problems with the unemployment statistics are mentioned by Allcock (95): they may be on the one hand overestimated, as a high proportion of registered 'job seekers' were employed, and on the other hand underestimated, as benefits could be claimed only after a lapse of time, so that in the mid-60s only one in eight received them (Parkin 316), and many peasant workers went temporarily back to their smallholding. The relative figures seem safe.

constituted a brain-and-skill drain – 1.5% of 1 million equals 15,000 university graduates, thence the 1973 regulation of migration planned to prevent their unchecked outflow. This failed: Rus (in Jerovšek et al. eds. 210) cites a study by which the share of job-seekers from two upper skill levels rose from below 20% in 1957 to over 50% in 1982. Research agrees that ca. two thirds of workers left because of too low earnings, especially to afford an apartment, and a bit above one third because of unemployment. Most of such *Gastarbeiter* lived abroad as a rule in horrendous circumstances, but their average monthly income was in the mid-60s 750 West German marks (236,000 old dinars), as compared to the ca. 210 marks at home. At that time, about 40% of workers had monthly incomes below 60,000 o.d. or 190 marks (Bilandžić, *Ideje* 260); a survey in 1967 found out the workers would have stayed in Yugoslavia had their income been 350 marks, that is almost double (ibidem 252).

In sum, I interpret Woodward to indicate that the ghettoised system of self-management necessarily turned inwards and by protecting those already 'in' at the expense of hiring new workers contributed to unemployment. As she notes, normal 'frictional' unemployment in developed capitalism was 4–5%, in Yugoslavia as of the first statistic in 1952 it was above 7% (4); it can be seen in Tables 10.4A and 10.4B that, counting both those abroad and registered job-seekers, in the 60s it hovered near 10%, in 1969 it was de facto 13.5%, in 1973 24%, and in 1975 20% (though in Slovenia it was practically non-existent and in Kosovo or Macedonia much larger). From Table 10.4B it would appear the average proportion of the secure vs. insecure fractions between 1969 and 1975 was roughly 4:1. But if we subtract from the securely employed total the non-manual – white collar – workers and add to the non-officially employed the invisible seasonal workers, not to forget the rural and urban housewives who would in better times be seeking employment in the social sector, I would in the absence of any data speculate the proportion was close to 3:1, that is, three parts of the working class protected by the system (at least until the wild inflation and economic breakdown), one part not protected. Yet, as Woodward rightly stresses, Yugoslavia was officially designed around community through labour, so that unemployment meant exclusion from full membership and social rights, moral and material marginalisation. The political macro-economics divided the working class and other employed into those with what the Chinese have called 'the iron rice-bowl' – a permanently secure job – and those we have since come to know as the 'precariate': people oscillating for a long time between stay-at-home unemployment and unsure and insecure employments, badly paid and badly policed, therefore sites of heightened exploitation. Solidarity, the central plank of all workers' movements, socialist or communist, was not extended to them. Instead, 'The ostensible freedom of self-managed firms with respect to labor, revenues, and individual incomes focused political energies on the firm rather than the State ...' (Woodward 329).

The ultimate political conclusion of *Capital* is that a society relentlessly organised around value-creating labour not controlled by the associated workers *necessarily* lurches into a polarisation between the rich appropriators of surplus labour and a permanent mass of under- and un-employed: '[N]ot the least terrible [union of opposites discovered by Marx] is that indispensable function of capital to create what is blandly known as the reserve army of the proletariat' (Jameson 576). Thus the simultaneous appearance of what was in Yugoslavia officially called 'the capital relation' and mass unemployment signalled that this terrible union of opposites had again been activated. Exploitative class society was raising its head.

10.4   On the Blindness of Power: Oligarchic Utopianism, Neither-Nor-ism, Technocracy

10.4.0

I refer elsewhere, in Chapter 4 and Appendix 2, to ideological illusions of the Yugoslav politocracy as represented by its central and very articulate protagonists Kardelj and (at best) Bakarić, reputed to have been the representatives of the pro-self-management wing and anti-Stalinists. However, the matter is so central that it will bear articulating here in order to understand, this time, the economistic fixations of this class, which underlie its decisions and which fit well with voluntarist, ad hoc interventions. I shall consider Kardelj's abstract utopianism, his axiom of 'income according to work', and his treatment of the 'capital relation'. For the first two themes, I shall focus on key indications in his essays from 1965 to 1972 collected in *Integration*. At the end, I postulate two discursive templates for this turning away from revolutionary politics, a bourgeois optimism of progress and a petty-bourgeois 'neither-nor-ism'.

10.4.1   *Oligarchic Utopianism*

As in the earlier instances, Kardelj begins in his defence of the 1965 Reform from a, to my mind, correct refusal of Stalinist practice and theory, even in the attenuated form (stripped of full police terror) of 'the mentality of State paternalism', defined well as 'the role of the [Party] and the socialist State is to manage things, which is to say, promote production and economic development through good technocratic management, State control and inspection, and take reasonable care for the material advancement of working people' (6). The alternative is to accept intimate cooperation with foreign economies, which means setting sights 'on the achievements and levels of [their] labour productivity'; he totally brackets out a possible negative influence of such cooperation, arguing that 'insularity and an exaggerated fear of foreign economies is a sure method of preserving backwardness, low productivity of labour and a permanent deficit in the balance of payments, while maintaining the need for increased State intervention in the shape of premiums, subsidies and bonuses'. This premise, accompanied by assurances that '[appropriate] measures of planning, coordination and guidance ... will have to be taken' (all on 10) seems to me acceptable, especially as he stresses that 'The working man, and the work community of which he is a part, *should be in a position to influence the conditions of their labour, from the elementary decision-making in the actual process of labour, to the system of expanded reproduction, to the social plan and other decisions of a general significance*' (9). He even posits that, as I argued above, decentralisation 'must also include *a new form of democratic centralisation on the basis and within the framework of social self-management*' (22). Nonetheless, this was both leaving out a great deal and out of gear with what was really happening.

For, Kardelj goes on to discuss just to whom should the formerly centralised State resources be allotted, and soothingly assumes that 'territorialisation at a lower level' (their transfer in part to communes but mainly the constituent republics) will happen within 'the sphere of self-management at all levels' (*Integration* 42). It is unclear what this means beyond ritual obeisance to a general principle, for self-management did not really exist at any level beyond the basic enterprises. His triumphant horizon about the introduced economic reform is: 'Such integration is the present and future of mankind. It transcends all frontiers and all languages. But the condition of its development is that it should be a true product of the needs of production relations in each nation, and that it should never be imposed from outside' (ibidem). Here one rubs one's eyes and asks: on what planet are we? The one of the Vietnam War and Cold War? Is international economic cooperation based on socialist brotherhood or on the self-interest of capitalist corporations and States? The splendid anti-imperialist end of his peroration forgets his beginning.

In other words, Kardelj, and other top decision-makers, had by the mid-60s succumbed to the fatal illness of considering all furthest utopian horizons of a major set of measures as identical with its pragmatic moment. Almost as in Borges's revealing story 'On Exactitude in Science', the map of the momentarily dominant Party theory is supposed to reproduce the territory on which the changes happen, or at least all of its strategically relevant features: it fully corresponds to reality (on the direct roots of this deviation in Stalinism cf. Bettelheim 2: 546–7). The best critics inside Yugoslavia have noticed this was a hidden but normative Idealism,[7] and we could have seen from Borges that it ends in the imperial map rotting over its territory. I would call it, pillaging Bloch, triumphalist *abstract utopianism* – a belief that if the theory is sound enough and corresponds to 'the needs of production relations in each nation', then the idea's quality and force shall necessarily carry the day. However, even the theoretically soundest measures can only mark a certain stage of flowing reality and begin orienting it toward given horizons, within which it will encounter not fully foreseen obstacles and counter-tendencies. Without factoring them in, it may (and did) turn out that both Kardelj's internal presupposition of integral self-management and external presupposition of a level playing field remained pious wishes. Miko Tripalo, an intelligent man at the top of the Croatian establishment before he descended into nationalism, referred to this obliquely, I think, when he complained about the financial situation after 1965: 'Our whole self-managing system is becoming questionable due to the material relationships in distribution. And let us not even mention that many documents, theses, position papers, etc., show a certain self-managing society which is in Yugoslavia absolutely non-existent ... [U]nfortunately, we claim that there exists what we would wish to exist' (340). And even stronger: 'A realistic picture of the true situation of our working enterprises and their associations is stymied either by bureaucratic optimism or by an interest of the etatist structures to safeguard existing relationships within distribution [of the surplus]' (351).

10.4.2   'Income According to Work'

Within such a largely deluded system Kardelj not only popularised but also in good measure set the terms of official discourse in its various phases. An earlier keystone upon which to build his discursive edifice was his axiom of 'reward (or: income) according to work' (*nagrađivanje* (*dohodak*) *prema radu*), that is, a worker's emoluments or – more politically correct – income must be derived from work performed. This was a Stalinist adaptation of Marx's much richer slogan, of Biblical and utopian-socialist origin, 'From each according to his abilities' ('Jeder nach seinen Fähigkeiten'); Mandel notes this economistic turn dates in the USSR from 1932, a time of growing social inequalities. It became

---

7   See Divjak 97, Močnik 'Od historičnega' 151, especially Rus 279. By the way, this quote is a good example of Kardelj's not so rare non-Marxian use of Marx's terms; another one is 'association of free producers' instead of Marx's 'individuals'. I do not pretend to have fully unravelled his templates, one would need a small book; cf. for the only sustained overview I found Černe, *Jugoslovansko* 197–319, who stresses on 200 his 'imperative and normative' (that is, command) turn.

FIGURE 24

Gajo Petrović (1978)
PHOTO REPRODUCED WITH KIND
PERMISSION OF ASJA PETROVIC AND ANTE
LEŠAJA

an obsessive slogan in Yugoslavia dating from the 50s, at the forefront in the 60s, but lasting into the 70s too. Kardelj's inimitable inflated style presented it emphatically as: '[A]t the present stage of development of labour productivity, [it] brings out the essence of social ownership and the working man's economic status in socialism ... The working man's labour should benefit him, his work collectivity, his commune, his nation and community as a whole, and should encourage creativeness, ability and initiative in each person' (*Integration* 14–15). Its positive aspect was supposed to militate against emoluments being due to one's hierarchical position, as in feudalism and Stalinism (or in capitalist profits). But, leaving aside matters of communist humanism incompatible with this slogan, well explained in Petrović (*Filozofija* 161, and see Appendix 2), just what did it practically mean for daily measuring? Since the ideologico-political debate centred on industry, I shall leave aside the even more complex problem of who else was a worker or 'working man' (*radni čovjek*) – how do you measure performances in school or hospital? (Never mind working women who were included under the generic 'man'.)

A whole slew of dilemmas arises here. To begin with, should one measure quantity (in pieces or hours), quality, or a combination of both? The inclusion of 'measuring quality' was in USSR an alibi for oligarchic arbitrariness, where it covered up a strong stress toward rewarding hierarchical status (cf. Golubović ed., *Staljinizam* 47–8 and 65). Furthermore, as Zukin notes, the water was thoroughly muddied when in the 60s reward according to work gave place in official discourse to 'reward according to *results of* work' in line with the emphasis on the market. Originally starting from surplus labour in Marx, which is fairly clear, the category may now mean not only some combination of work quantity and quality but also, and increasingly, a share in the profit that the enterprise realised from that work. The latter is mediated by many factors internal and especially external to the enterprise: 'product placement, world market prices, or advertising budget', and I would add Yugoslav macro-economic factors such as taxes and credits, so that, say, 'a gain in productivity may ultimately be registered – according to "the results" – as a loss' (Zukin, 'Beyond' 22, and cf. Brus 78–80). In other words, to splice Marx's quite general Labour Theory of Value with 'market socialism' – where conditions for earning of income were rarely equal, so that for the same work a worker in different enterprises could be paid two or three times as much (Supek, 'Some Contradictions' 259) – results in much confusion. If the results are based on top-down control of productive forces, exploitation seems clearly involved (Korošić, *Jugoslavenska* 257). Let us generously assume this may have been the price to pay for bold innovation: however, at a minimum it should then have been brought to the forefront of attention as a problem to be remedied – but Kardelj never considers it.[8]

Historically, the French revolutionary *égalité* became either a call for equal status of commodity producers (cf. Bakarić 2: 136), that is a level playing field, or in a literal interpretation – say by Babeuf and the Equals – a retrogressive yearning for a kind of 'barracks communism'; in either case it had little to do with full justice in a complex division of labour. A clear indication of the limits of 'distribution according to work performed' was penned at the time in Gajo Petrović's essay '"Birokratski socijalizam"' ('So-called Bureaucratic Socialism', 1971), which I review at more length in Appendix 2.

He points out this is a caricature of Marx's idea that it will in the transitional period be temporarily necessary to use the bourgeois right, which is

---

8 See for some unresolved theoretical and practical knots in 'income according to work' Černe, 'Raspodjela'. A serious consideration of the *Critique of the Gotha Programme* by top people like Kardelj, including the fact that it was written as an internal memo for a few people, would have helped.

A frightening parallel to the Stalinist rise of piece-work – which applied to 29% of workers in 1930 and 65% in 1931 – was pointed out by Cliff (19): it is the Nazi doctrine of 'performance wage' (*Leistungslohn*). Hitler explained it as their 'iron principle ... not to permit any rise in the hourly wage but to raise income solely by an increase in performance'. This meant practically a full sway of piece-work, and Neumann judges it to be 'consciously aimed at mass manipulation' (352–3; see for much more Rabinbach). This ought to have made emancipatory communists – as Kardelj believed himself to be – pause.

essentially unjust because it applies equal measurement to different people and situations. He noncommittally allows the slogan may be 'relatively progressive' when applied to people able to perform productive work but 'it grows inhuman if applied to old people, the sick, the invalids, pregnant women, children, and others who cannot work or who have no occasion to work' (486 – this would obviously apply to the unemployed!). Nonetheless, in Yugoslav practice there was no discussion at all whether, when, and how this should coexist with distribution 'according to need', though there have always been significant 'communist corrections' in the social security network, health, apartment allocation, and so on (see 10.3 above).

And when banks became dominant, their loans had no relation to the 'work' of the original fund-investors and even less to that of the bank bosses. Theoretical patches were put into place by abusively applying Marx's notion of work accumulated in the past (*minuli rad*), but the huge problems of 'proportion of "current" labour to "dividends"' (Brus 80–1) was never properly faced.

The banks were only the top of the iceberg of burgeoning private and privatising appropriation. 'These other earnings constitute an "invisible", socially uncontrolled and usually untaxed portion of income, which accrues mainly to functionaries and other experts' (Comisso, *Workers'* 109); together with more or less allowed items, this comprised rising, sometimes shamelessly huge, bonuses and outright swindling. It was estimated that in 1971 they added to personal incomes 5,100 million dinars or US$340 million (Atlagić and Milanović eds. 45). Assuming from Table 9.1A that we are here talking about the larger 3,500 enterprises and that there could not have been more than 20 people per enterprise with such perks, plus an unknown number in the politocracy which I have calculated at ca. 250,000 people (Chapter 3.2.2.3), the average statistically invisible addition to income would have been at least US$1,250 or 19,000 dinars per year per person, a handsome sum which rose steeply as one went toward the top. The whole system of 'distribution according to work' was therewith denied.

10.4.3 *'The Capital Relationship', and an Explanation*

Finally, I shall consider Kardelj's frequent euphemism 'the capital relation' – implying that capital is and is not really such, that is, capitalist (*lucus a non lucendo**). I believe he began talking about capital in his keynote speech at the Second – and last – Congress of Self-managers in 1971 (*Samoupravljanje* 213–80). He straightforwardly defined State capital as 'the part of social accumulation which up to 1965 the State seized and channelled into the central investment funds' (240) and about the post-65 situation he stated: 'I use the expression social capital lacking a better term ... we are talking about the *economic* functions of "capital" in the domain of expanded reproduction, not about capital in the sense of a social force that reproduces capitalist social or property relationships' (in Bošković & Dašić 238). Emphasised 'economic' means here that this capital in scare quotes has no *political* function, and the revealing reference to property invokes the standard denial that a ruling class exists in socialist Yugoslavia since politocracy members do not possess the right of alienating or inheriting the property they command (see Chapter 4). Again, I do not complain here about the use of the term or indeed the real presence of capital but about the cognitive muddle stemming from the avoidance of foregrounding and scrutinising it: the only explanation Kardelj gave was the apodictic, typically Stalinist, affirmation that 'under the workers' control (sic!) capital has lost its class nature' (cited in Bavčar et al. 14). This led to a quite anachronistic market ideology of the nineteenth-century type, and to unconscious oxymorons in blithe use such as 'socialist commodity-money relationships' and 'socialist capital' (Supek, 'Some Contradictions' 256 – the best inside overview I know of). As to 'the capital relation', Kardelj concluded in 1974 that some of its forms were dangerous but no more so than one of the most dangerous, the whilom '"socialist" primitive accumulation, based on simple usurpation of worker income' (*Subjektivne* 314–15), thus dodging the question of whether a third option was possible.

One should duly respect Kardelj's tireless dedication to finding categories for a new socialist common sense based on labour. Yugoslav post-war discourse began here felicitously, by formulating – however initially and insufficiently – the experience of the 1941–5 revolutionary war and power as based not simply on a very small, undeveloped, and culturally mainly non-existing working class, but on a broad alliance whose mass basis was the peasantry and (unacknowledged) leaven the radical intelligentsia, that is on the new concept of *the working people*. This is why the fledgling self-management was to be carried by the managerial, white-collar, and technical strata with equal rights to the very young manual workers' class (Denitch credits this with 'the assumption that organic changes were occurring in the composition of the working force which will substantially reduce the proportion of blue-collar workers' [179], but I see no evidence that this was present in the politocracy's flying by the seat of their pants). Allegorically, the working people were embodied in the image of *the working man*: overt reference to class agents inside and outside the country was conspicuous by its absence until revived by Tito around 1971/72, while gender discourse remained permanently and grievously absent, in the tradition of the two Internationals. By the mid-60s the imaginative energy inside the Party had been dissipated by the crushing pragmatism of daily difficult struggles for independence and economic build-up as well as by its budding status as a ruling class, so that it did not know how to reach out and incorporate fresh views, say by the most loyal Party intellectuals outside the politocracy from my Appendix 2, or indeed by the workers: in Kardelj they revealingly often become *the working masses* (cf. Černe, *Jugoslovansko* 291 and *passim*). Thus his exceptionally voluminous effort follows, it seems to me, two templates. The first, considered so far, consists of leaving out elements obnoxious to abstract utopianism, or perhaps one should call it oligarchic *optimism of progress*, of obvious high bourgeois or ruling class origin ('we have problems but we shall prevail' – in contrast to Lenin's usual template of revolutionary sobriety 'if we don't do so-and-so, we are lost'). The last mentioned essay, called 'For Democracy ...' (*Subjektivne* 301–42) is written following his second template, which I shall call, adapting Roland Barthes (*Mythologies* 241 and *passim*), **petty bourgeois 'ninisme'** – neither-nor-ism, on the one hand but on the other. For an example strictly analogous to that of capital, the frequent and tolerated strikes are and yet are not really such, since they are 'work stoppages' within the self-management system (Kardelj, *Proprietà* 130–2; cf. Samary, *Marché* 244–5, Černe, *Jugoslovansko* 200); I shall return to them in the following section on Technocracy.

Finally, in the 70s Kardelj's plan was the illusory one of 'maintain[ing] socialist production relations continuously, automatically, without political intervention from above ... *on the basis of joint and mutual investments of social capital by work organisations*' (*Integration* 101). Yet as is evident from Table 10.3 above and its comment, the investment by work organisations (that is, enterprises) was quite insufficient and dwarfed by the stranglehold of credit capital from banks and similar institutions. This article, titled 'Self-management Integration of the Yugoslav Social System', is an excellent example of the first template, and underscores what I would judge to be the principal taboo and *non-dit** of this whole theoretical opus after 1965: the **systematic avoidance of a qualitative heightening of self-managing powers up to the governmental level** (irritatingly garnished by unceasing invocations of self-management). This is of a piece with the universal identification of all centralised macro-economic decisions with etatism and the 'absence of a critique of the political system' (Samary, *Marché* 241).

What is striking in both templates of Kardelj's discourse is the absence of an intimate sense of necessary contradictions lurking within each significant process, with the negative intimately shaping every positive – that is, of dialectics. It was a real epistemological obstacle, which Bachelard defines as arising when rupture in a hegemonic organisation of thinking threatens.

This type of ritualised discourse, numbingly dominant in the final quarter century of SFRY, did not only discredit the Party, in power but obviously out of touch with steering economics. It should be stressed that it mightily contributed to hollow out and pre-empt for the future the otherwise, to my mind, fertile and quite central concepts of self-management, working people, social capital, and many others by using them as ad hoc justification for badly articulated and catastrophically unworkable schemes. For example, in the original of Kardelj's above title the 'Self-management' was an adjective (*Samoupravna*), the substantive being counterfactually assumed to be both fully present and fully explained. Instead of supple clarity, Kardelj's discourse repeatedly lists at pedantic length elements strictly separated into positive and negative, and therefore cannot deal with the sudden jump he is announcing (striving to clone the starry moment of the 1941–5 revolutionary war). He often calls them contradictions but they are not dialectical but either-or, or neither-nor, ones. His horizon was mainly a contamination of Second International – at best, Austro-Marxist – and Third International positivisms. The epistemological revolution most clear in Einsteinian physics but simultaneously present in Modernist culture – including communist heretics such as Eisenstein, Picasso, Brecht, Benjamin, and in a most cognate way Gramsci and Marcuse – passed Kardelj by. As Bakarić confessed about modern physics, this revolution was totally unknown in the rather provincial 1930s' Party (3: 118–19) – and when glimpsed, it was treated in the Stalinist vein as heretic deviation to be purged, for example in the famous 1930s 'conflict on the literary Left' (*sukob na književnoj ljevici*) as well as later.

Importantly, Kardelj was also the political head of a relatively large and extremely productive federal **legal bureaucracy** which, especially after 1963, tirelessly churned out the most diverse rules, regulations, and laws, whose endless bulk necessarily contained gaps and contradictions. In particular, economic enterprises were buffeted by their unceasing flow ('Corruptissima re publica plurimae leges', noted the great historian: the more corrupt a State, the more laws it passes). Adizes found that federal laws pertaining to economy (not counting the also numerous republican and local ones) numbered 753 in 1963, 718 in 1964, 983 in 1965, and 800 in 1966, with 250 new laws being passed each year 1965–70; furthermore, in 1966 the Secretary of the Treasury issued 630 regulating orders (23)! Necessarily, such four-digit numbers were on the ground often simply disregarded in favour of back-room deals. Furthermore, the federal Institute of Statistics reported for 1965 that the cost of the information flow for planning purposes was 150 billion dinars, or US$ 32 per worker family of four, comparable to 5% of their annual income (Adizes 154). By the end of the 1970s, State administration, presumably federal plus republican, had grown to be 8 to 11 times larger than in countries of comparable size (Calic 259). In the vein of abstract utopianism 'juridical over-regulation … was paradoxically meant to facilitate the "withering away of the state"' (Močnik, 'Workers'' 3). While the number of laws was even bigger in FR Germany or France (cf. Pusić 266–8), much fewer of them applied to the economy. Wachtel commented that '[Yugoslavia's] Central European heritage is evident in the enormous proliferation of laws governing enterprise affairs. Its Turkish heritage is manifested in the uneven enforcement of the laws by the government and in the absence of obedience to law' (63). Often what was proclaimed in the law was taken back by explanations and implementation paragraphs; occasionally high government officials acknowledged there was an inflation of measures. The constitution of the 1970s, including the 20-odd new constitutional amendments, was reputed to be the longest in the world, and was probably also the least understandable one: its potentially useful and interesting aspects could thus have little impact.

10.4.4 *Technocracy*

Instead of furthering a full democracy and self-management extending from below upward to the level of federal government, the diametrically opposed return of oppressive hierarchy in the economy began a few years after 1965 to be officially, with much alarm, called ***technocracy***. It was never clear which social groups were meant by that, but the grab-bag spread was supposed to include on the one end the younger generation of the always important managers in basic enterprises (cf. Vanek 287) and on the other end the newer capital-lenders. I would guess they came mainly from some former 'bureaucrats' together with younger and better schooled career newcomers: in 1966, one fifth of the enterprise directors were newly elected and among them almost half were 30–9 years of age (Rusinow 144). The technocracy took up the only social space available, an arrested, stunted, and thus emptied framework of self-management, but its cohesiveness was guaranteed by what Kardelj's heavy lingo called 'the techno-bureaucratically oriented parts of the political structure [that is, of the Party State] in the republics' (*Subjektivne* 317). It was a complex rearrangement amid a power struggle within the ruling class between different orientations and what increasingly looked like different class fractions. The matter was dealt with in Kardelj's speech at the Party Executive Committee in 1970 (ibidem 195–219), and I shall take as *pars pro toto* his discussion of intra-Party 'democratic struggle of ideas' (214–15). On the one hand, he argues, leading communists may participate in forming public opinion. But on the other, when this causes 'disunity in the working masses', then it leads to 'fractional activity' (*frakcionašenje*, a simon-pure Stalinist term and concept), and is better done behind the scenes and at the same time 'under the maximum possible control of public opinion'. I shall leave aside the denial of the elementary dialectics that any fertile unity must arise from disunity, and only ask how can a strong clash

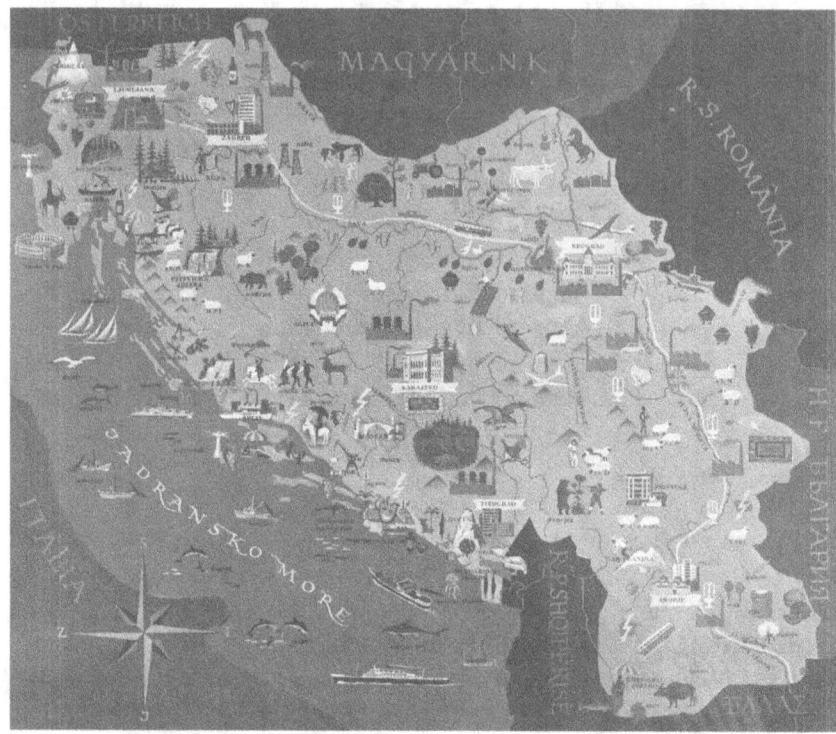

FIGURE 25   *Vjekoslav Brešić, ['Yugoslavia for Kids'], illustrated map from the youth encyclopedia 'Svijet oko nas', Zagreb 1967*
IMAGE REPRODUCED FROM THE YOUTH ENCYCLOPEDIA 'SVIJET OKO NAS', ZAGREB 1967, REPRODUCED WITH KIND PERMISSION OF DEJAN KRŠIĆ

of opinions be at the same time confined to 'party forums' and under control of public opinion. This is understandable only as an oscillation between 'on the one hand' and 'but on the other'. On the one hand public discussions are a good thing, but on the other it is quite another matter 'if public polemics are waged by members of the leading Party forums' – that is, of the federal and the republican Executive Committees, and perhaps secondarily of the Central Committees. It is thus impossible to fathom who would be exempt from such a prohibition: a glorious example of *ninisme*. In other words, the increasingly self-emasculated federal central structures of the Party were warning the republican 'techno-bureaucratic trends' not to go too far.

Three years later, the moral and political suasion having been counteracted by macro-economic trends initiated by the same centre, Kardelj penned in an essay about current constitutional changes, which he supervised and theorised, a section on the 'Class Nature of Technocracy' (*Integration* 124 ff. – by then,

FIGURE 26

Ivan Picelj, 'Untitled (Galerija suvr. umjetnosti – Djela iz fundusa)', Zagreb 1961
PHOTO REPRODUCED WITH KIND PERMISSION OF
DEJAN KRŠIC

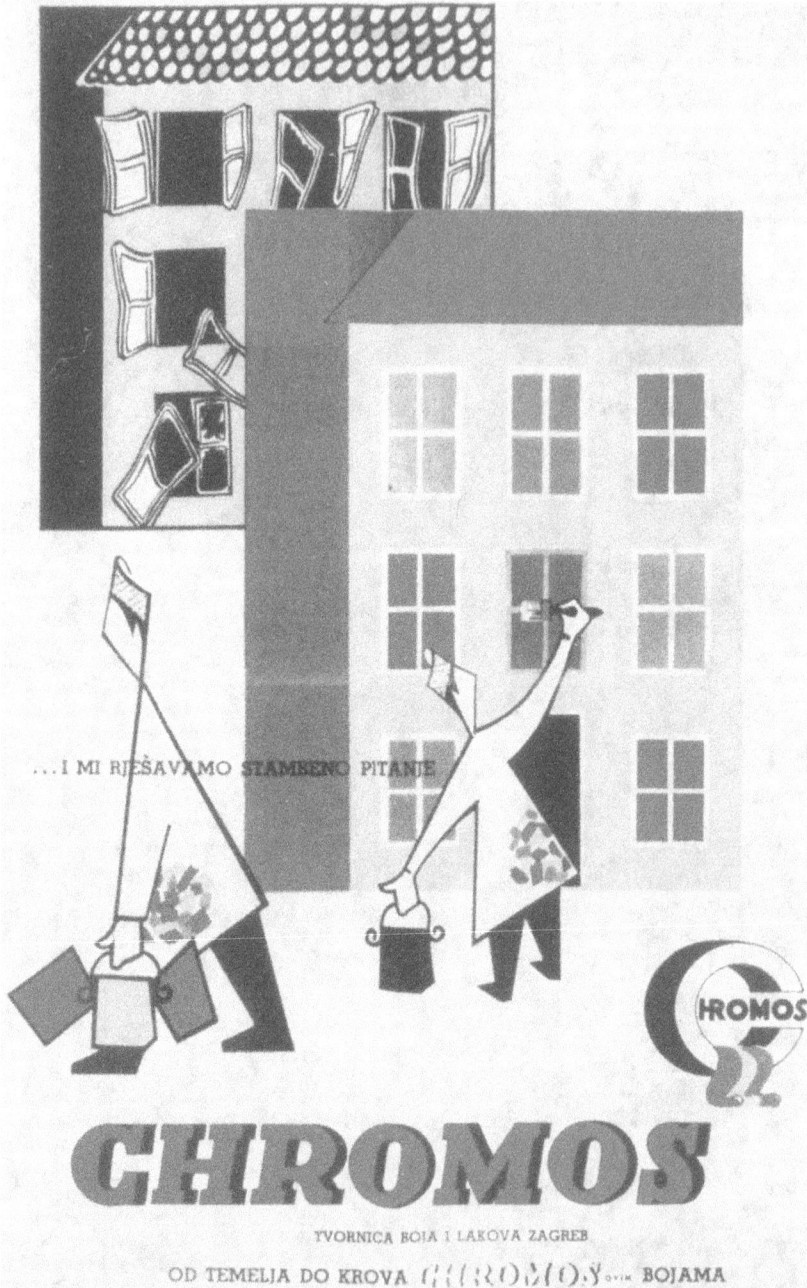

FIGURE 27   *Milan Vulpe, 'Chromos ...' ['we too are solving the housing question'], Zagreb 1953, poster*
PHOTO REPRODUCED WITH KIND PERMISSION OF DEJAN KRŠIC

rehabilitation of talk about class, absent for three decades, was in full swing), thundering against 'the resurgence of technocratic-monopoly relations and tendencies'. Against it he brought out the heaviest artillery:

> The funds of social accumulation [alienated from the self-management control of the workers] have gained ... much independence in the hands of certain managerial top circles in production, foreign and internal trade, banks, and in other economic organisations ... Any monopoly in controlling social capital unavoidably brings in its wake elements of class relationships between the workers and the holders of these monopoly rights.
> 124

Having after 1965 'uprooted the economic and political power of the State ownership bureaucracy', that power had now moved over to 'the managerial top echelons of the centers where society's capital stock was concentrated'. This resulted in the threat of 'the nascent technocratic-managerial monopoly' merging with the State power in the republics but this time 'playing the first fiddle' (all 125). In conclusion, 'the professional-managerial establishment' must keep to 'its specialised function in the management of things' while being subordinated to 'the workers' interests' and to 'their economic and political power' – meaning the Party centre (146).

In brief, the politocracy had identified a rival monopoly, a class of people who very quickly established solid, if competitive, mutual alliances (as opposed to the working class atomised into enterprises), and did not intend to cede the first fiddle to it, but rather to use it as a convenient whipping boy for all failings in the economy. The technocracy's rapid rise to a share in power was based on balancing between the politocracy – on which it leaned while competing with it – and the world market, reproducing what came openly to be called 'the capital relationship' or even 'financial capital' inside Yugoslavia. For Lazić, the technocracy's approach was based on the mediation between the world and domestic market (*U susret* 47–8), so that it had to be counteracted by politico-administrative measures suspending the market whenever needed. The politocracy counted on its role as representative of workers, but having enclosed them into competitive atomic units it did not have its pre-1965 strength. True, it mounted a counter-offensive by means of the Constitutional Amendments of the early 70s, legally culminating in the Law on Associated Labour of 1976. In them, new powers in the enterprises, meant to limit the technocracy's influence, were given to the basic production units (the BOALs) and a complex system of representative 'delegations' to communal and republican assemblies was created, but it was too little and too late: the downward spiral of the economy and the oligarchic blindness prevented by then any proper decisions about enlarged reproduction and productivity (cf. Županov 34–7 and *passim*). Its main effect was, I think, a stand-off within a more and more unfavourable economic climate. Since the economy proper was as of the 70s increasingly subject either to the market or to the technocracy, the politocracy was left only overall political decisions (cf. Lazić 46–7), while the new stratum or class fraction was allowed to develop as a second but indispensable fiddle until the collapse of SFR Yugoslavia showed it for what it was – the main kernel of the new comprador class, which easily absorbed the increasing defections from the politocracy proper. (Only in Serbia did the born-again politocracy after 1989 still attempt to wield power and had to be bombed out by NATO.)

What was the technocracy had by the 1980s become, at least in the most developed Slovenia, rather clear. That republic's Assembly called it 'an enriched stratum standing before the doors of our system with a powerful primitive accumulation of capital' (cited in Bavčar et al. 99), while Bavčar, Kirn, and Korsika identified it straightforwardly as 'a new fraction of capital', indeed its 'possible ruling fraction' (78–9; cf. Bakarić 3: 523). Their conclusion is more or less that the developing enterprises coping better or well were in its hands, whereas the backward branches and regions stuck with the politocracy as they depended on its aid (Bavčar et al. 88, 117 ff., and *passim*). This fraction of political and economic cadres, 'gearing revenues to "contribution" (that is, deepening income inequalities)' finally led to the centre being more and more dependent upon the republican oligarchies, which in the 70s began to fuse with the 'cultural bureaucracies ... always more or less nationalist', that 'provid[ed] ideological support for the transfer of power' (Močnik, 'Workers'' 6). This technocracy had thus little to do with either engineers or specialists from soft sciences (for example economists), it was entirely managerial. The name itself first fulfilled the function of comparing it positively with the universal outcry against 'bureaucracy', which was supposed to be governmental. However, I concluded in Appendices 1–2 that bureaucracy was finally a wrong term, and to my mind technocracy too was an unfortunate designation taken from Western discourse. It served this sub-class as an 'expert' and 'modernising' alibi against the Party centre's political meddling (much as in the neo-liberal discourse of the last 30–40 years in Europe), while they developed as proto-comprador classes. The true problems of capitalist technology and its technocratic fetishism were not mentioned, except by the 'loyal opposition'.

In the final instance, the rise of these proto-comprador classes is therefore a prominent example and illustration of the same blindness of power I was analysing earlier.

SECTION 3.2

*On the Horizon of Disalienation in
S.F.R. Yugoslavia: Self-Government
and Plebeian Democracy*

∵

For Mladen Lazić, who fought for truth and justice under all regimes.

∴

Hope deferred maketh the heart sick, but when the desire cometh, it is a tree of life.
    Proverbs 13:12

∴

CHAPTER 11

On the Politics of Disalienation, Inside and Outside Economic Production

– Are you comparing yourself with Jesus?
– All my life I've been comparing myself to him.
    BECKETT, 1949

∴

The aim of Part 3.2 is to conclude about self-management in production, collocating it within a process of possible disalienation through full civic self-government – that is, a plebeian democracy. The possibilities of radical emancipation present in Yugoslav history after 1941 began when they were actualised as the singularities of refusing both fascist imperialism and Stalinism. When new social forces succeeded to block emancipation, this finally brought about the downfall of both self-management and SFR Yugoslavia, which are thus revealed as being consubstantial.

I ground myself in the Archimedean starting point of Marx's anthropology of labour and alienation, handily summarised by Gajo Petrović:

> The alienation of the results of man's productive activity is rooted in the alienation of production itself. Man alienates the products of his labor because he alienates his labor activity, because his own activity becomes for him an alien activity ... [A] consequence of the alienation of man from himself is the alienation of man from other men ... As the worker alienates the products of his labor, his own activity and his generic essence from himself, so he alienates another man as his master from himself. The producer himself produces the power of those who do not produce over production ...
>
> In his *Economic and Philosophic Manuscripts* Marx speaks about communism as a society which means 'the positive supersession of all alienation' ... Such a conception of communism as a negation of alienation forms the basis of Marx's later works.
>
>   'MARX'S'

It ought to be acknowledged that Marx and Engels did not work out a theory of politics grounded in disalienation of labour (cf. Feenberg, especially 51–60). After his early writings, Marx focussed on the analysis of labour and capital as the strategic way of understanding emancipation, but in so doing he assumed that the necessities of associational democracy – which he never doubted – would follow the lead of an emancipated labour process, and relegated politics explicitly to class society. Still, he did indicate briefly they would have to be based on what might be called the organisation of use-value politics:

> In fact, however, when the limited bourgeois form is stripped away, what is wealth other than the universality of individual needs, capacities, pleasures, productive forces, etc., created through universal exchange? ... The absolute working-out of [people's] creative potentialities, with no presupposition other than the previous historic development, which makes this totality of development, that is, the development of all human powers as such the end in itself, not as measured on a predetermined yardstick? Where he does not reproduce himself in one specificity, but produces his totality? Strives not to remain something he has become, but is in the absolute movement of becoming?
>
> MARX, *Grundrisse* 488

Thus, Marx's key category of 'productive forces' ought to be looked at, against economism, as 'the term designating the sum-total of the resources for liberation available to a given society' (Marcuse, *From* 213) – and the most important 'machine [or] instrument of production [is] the working class itself' (Gramsci, *Ordine* 134, reprinted in Horvat et al. eds. 232). This further means that Marx's 'realm of freedom' is only approximated to the extent that the workers as integral personalities are furthered, whereas labour as toil is minimised (cf. Marcuse, 'Über' 19 and *passim*, Morris). In that vein, Burawoy rightly notes that 'the creative transformation of nature (labor) and the collective self-regulation of society (politics)' are firmly linked, so that the disjuncture of production and politics is counterproductive (83). Their separation is a quintessentially capitalist move, a new thing under the sun of history stemming from the desire to evade any and all social regulation in order to ensure their parochial quest for profits; this is taken over by socialist productivism which reduces socialism to the labour process and relations within it, isolated from the democratic control of society.

Furthermore, we have learned that political emancipation is within the process of overcoming class society just as necessary, and must proceed at the same time if the reorganisation of production is to come fully about. Unfortunately, the practice of an endangered and then ossified USSR belied the strongly emancipative aspect of Lenin's theory and abandoned politics exclusively to the domain of Party/State rule. Inside the European Left this stance was countered only by the 'council communism' of Pannekoek and Korsch, best developed by Gramsci's uniting it with post-Lenin political struggle in the new Fordist age, to which I come below. Even Lukács's reappropriation of Marx for the analysis of production as reification (in *Geschichte*) shared the messianic illusion, as he later phrased it, that the revolution in power will automatically abolish social alienation. 'Western Marxism' then stressed the reification, having learned from experience that messianic confidence in the Revolution, the Party or even the industrial proletariat is by itself insufficient and can turn pernicious: as Ernst Bloch once phrased it, behind the *citoyen* came the *bourgeois*; god help us, who is coming behind the comrade?

Thus we cannot be exempted from theorising here not only the aspects of 'relationships of production' present within production but also how they complexly intertwine with the aspects outside production: both of these aspects participate, in different ways, in what we categorise (often wrongly) as economics or as politics, and to call either only economic or only political leads to grievous error. This is true even for capitalism, but it holds in spades for 'socialist' societies where '[a] *defining feature ... is the fusion of the apparatuses of the workplace with those of the State*' (Burawoy 113).

Within such a fusion, I have throughout argued that *self-management poses central questions for a radical democracy*. The first one is not so much why did it degenerate in SFRY, which seems clear after foregoing considerations though it will be brought to a point here, but: could it work better than capitalist enterprises? However, I shall first deal with a second question: can the relation between economic enterprises and the State be rethought around disalienating *self-government* (Marcuse's self-determination, see Chapter 9.1) by tying economic into political democracy, in the manner of a double helix?

I shall approach the Yugoslav experience by turning to a mildly reorganised version of Burawoy's table of the relationships of politics inside and outside economic production, where some terms have been changed but his central historical insight retained (119–21):

TABLE 11.1   *Politics inside (1) and outside (2) economic production*

Intervention of politics (2) into politics (1)	Separation	Fusion
Indirect (civil soc.)	Market Despotism	Collective Self-Government
Direct (State)	Welfare-Warfare State	Politocratic Despotism

Of the four historical types here, Burawoy's 'market despotism' refers to 'pure' capitalism without much or any State intervention inside economic production, as known to Marx in the nineteenth century and reborn from the 1970s to the Great Crisis which began in 2008. The Welfare-Warfare State is what came about through both lower-class militancy and upper-class concessions out of fear of communism and revolution in Roosevelt's New Deal and the social-democracy between the World Wars, and was supreme from 1945 to the mid-70s. 'Politocratic' despotism is what came about under Stalin in the USSR and was exported into all other countries ruled by communist parties and faced with the task of primitive accumulation of capital, though first Yugoslavia and then China attempted to find ways out of it; it was substituted here for Burawoy's "bureaucratic" which I find obfuscating. Finally, I substituted an encompassing 'self-government', in all domains, for the original (and the Yugoslav) 'self-management' belonging to economic production only.

'Indirect intervention' comports a refusal of etatism and a possibility of avoiding police despotism. 'Fusion' of politics inside and outside economic production without etatism then comports, if it really occurs, a decisive refusal of economism and the possibility of full release of plebeian energies moving upward from the social basis to the ruling top. Both together would be an eminent case of democracy as defined by Aristotle for the Hellenic City-State (*polis*): 'the citizen must know and share in both ruling and being ruled' (*Politics* 1277a31–2 in *Selections* 470; see also 1275a). This is squarely within the historical horizon and problem of what I suggested was the agential system from the partizan Liberation War, based on the sovereign and constitutive People, and which I further develop in my Conclusion. But for a vector toward this horizon I need first of all to explore how the ancestral Paris Commune or Petrograd Soviet were (or were not) translated into daily and lasting mechanisms of an expanding 'collective self-government' or associational democracy.

Here Gramsci is indispensable, and I shall approach him as brought to the point by Hobsbawm, and put into feedback with Yugoslav WsC by Comisso. Hobsbawm argues that politics is for Gramsci 'the central human activity, the means by which the single consciousness is brought into contact with the social and natural world ...', since in it 'understanding the world and changing it are one', and emphasises: 'This applies to the construction of socialism as well as – perhaps more than – anywhere else'. In other words, socialism is (becoming) classless insofar as it is a just society of producers. It is based on socialisation not only in the indispensable economic sense, 'that is the socially owned and planned economy ... but [on] socialisation in the political and sociological sense', that is the formation of 'habits in collective man which will make social behaviour automatic, and eliminate the need for an external apparatus to impose norms; automatic but also conscious' (321–2). However, Gramsci does not see the division of labour *per se* as alienating, but on the contrary as the fundament for qualitative equality (since everybody is equally necessary) and for solidarity. Nor does he envisage doing without authority, hierarchy, and management as professional skill in a plant, but proposes to disperse and politicise them, eliminate the unproductive 'policing', and subject them to constant worker control from below.

Significantly, politics was for Gramsci tied to his study of **who functions as intellectual** and who has hegemony in the State; I shall discuss this in the Conclusion. Last not least, Gramsci never succumbed to the temptation of leftist policy, so visible in all post-revolutionary periods, to envisage 'not ... the real working class with its mass organisation but ... a notional working class, ... a sort of external view of the working class or any other mobilisable group' (Hobsbawm 329).

Gramsci is thus the Marxist 'who most clearly appreciated the importance of politics as a special dimension of society, ... because he recognised that in politics more is involved than power' (Hobsbawm 331) – that is, social **production**. True, it is comprehensible that socialist societies have lagged behind the bourgeois attention to political frameworks and mechanisms, concentrating first on power and on planning the economy. However, because of this (and later most probably because of the rise of a new oligarchic class which feared openness and democracy from the roots), from Stalin on

> the major political decisions which affect the future of the country appear to emerge suddenly from the struggles of a small group of rulers at the top, and their very nature is unclear, since they have never been publicly discussed. In such cases, something is clearly wrong ... [H]ow can we expect to create a socialist society (as distinct from a socially owned and managed economy), when the mass of the people are excluded from the political process, and may even be allowed to drift into depoliticisation and apathy about public matters?
> idem 332

Still, though in reality workplace-cum-production and State-cum-civic-life must be seen as constantly interacting in a feedback, for purposes of analysis they will be considered separately – self-management at work in Chapter 12 and civic life in Chapter 13.

CHAPTER 12

In Production: Rise and Fall of Self-Management

> Yugoslav socialism will stand or fall with self-government.
> HORVAT, 1967

∴

12.1   Its Fortunes

The fortunes of self-management, its significance and impact, were shaped at least as much – usually more – by political macro-economics as by input from below, so that they changed radically in different periods. I am here somewhat modifying the 2 + 2 chronological division worked out in Chapters 5 and 8–10. The important difference is that inside production I believe the twilight of self-management set in earlier, as the basis and harbinger of matters fully brought to a head in the country only by and after 1972, since production was still rising and the cumulative effect of the good trend 1953–68 still continued for some years. From the copious data, I found in Chapter 9 that the most useful of self-management's achievements and potentialities is to be found in the central 'golden age' of ca. 1958–68: before, there is a promising and hopeful incubation period, culminating perhaps in 1957, when the hiring and firing of workers was taken in hand by the WsC, while afterwards there is a period of strangulation and decay. But even within the most successful decade there were both inbuilt problems, and new fissures that appeared in the early 60s, much strengthened after 1965 by the uncontrolled capitalist market which radically shrank what a plant council could influence.

The Yugoslav WsC and self-management system had its pros and cons. On the positive side, I found that self-management could, and up to 1968 often did – where the creation of dominant elites in enterprises was prevented – engage the interest of the workforce in long-term results. Effective self-management had a great educational significance for socialist attitudes to work and ownership, clearly manifested in the commitment to further education through the Workers' Universities, during the heyday, of ca. 200–300,000 people per year, where worker-managed enterprises set up training schools and systems, developed their own upgrading programmes, and not rarely financed full technical and university studies (though obligatory teaching of book-keeping and other administrative and technical matters, as proposed by Samary [*Marché* 179] and Lebowitz [77], never became part of the paid workday). Together with the rise in productivity and in the more skilled workers' income, this made for a tentative beginning of disalienation at the workplace. Dunlop found for the 1950s that self-management helped to commit workers coming from farms to industrial discipline, it reduced barriers between groups in factory, and decisions concerning incomes taught workers to envisage larger social issues (294–6).

On the negative side, the most visible remnant of bourgeois law, ideology, and power in production remained the unbridged gap between blue collar and white collar. This was especially acute at the two class extremes. On the one extreme, manual workers were at first interested in immediate financial gain, understandable when arising out of penury, and the mass of unskilled and semi-skilled workers with a peasant acquisitive mentality more or less remained such (cf. Milosavljević, 'Država' 445–6). On the other extreme, there was the untouchable and untouched position of the 'specialists' with a university degree, at first in technical sciences but later also in 'soft' ones such as economy and law; they were also, increasingly often, paid more than the supposed ceiling of five times the unskilled workers' income. This was of a piece with the unquestioned, indeed sanctified, status of science and technology, as if they were extra-historical. Following the tradition of the Second and Third Internationals, it was totally forgotten that Marx believed the real subsumption of labour was the worker's subordination to the instruments of production and to the division of labour (cf. Burawoy 97–8), so that he treated 'the technology of capitalism ... with cautious reserve, and the organisation and administration of labor ... with passionate hostility' (Braverman 12).

More particularly, within the doctrine of 'atomised' self-management – in which individual enterprises (later the BOALs) were to boot not situated in a clear and constant system of rules – its function was reduced to maximisation of net income per employee. However, it is the ABC of economics that this tends to lower output and employment and to demand higher capital investment, so that it cannot work in the dearth of capital situation that obtained in Yugoslavia (as in all other post-revolutionary countries). Thus time and again the central authorities had to return to direct managing instruments, such as price freezes as well as regulation of personal incomes and of the enterprises' foreign currency earnings. Since these interventions were not systematic but ad hoc treatments of 'acutely inflamed conditions', they could not be effective. The doctrine contradicted objective needs and possibilities (Brus 89–91).

In the mid-60s the very optimistic Horvat struck this balance from extant investigations (among others, by A. Todorović, S. Možina, V. Rus, and J. Županov with A. Tannenbaum):

> ... on the basis of the influence on the work and decisions of the workers' council, three groupings appear, with a clearly hierarchical differentiation: (1) the managers of firms and economic units, and experts; (2) the foremen, [white-collar] employees, and skilled workers; (3) the semiskilled and unskilled workers ... [F]oremen, [white-collar] employees, and skilled workers have equal influence, which means that the classical gap in the capitalist factory has been eliminated.
> *An Essay* 163

My stance is that there was an unresolved tension between hierarchy and horizontal integration, rather different from place to place, and promising insofar as it was evolving toward real participation in decisions by the shop-floor workers.

This translated into political support by most of the working class for socialism and the Party: the all-time high of worker membership in it (see Chapter 7), almost a full third, was in 1958; the 357,000 people involved made up one seventh of the workforce at the time. The WsC in 1950–68 had perhaps two million members, of which a comfortable majority was supposed to be manual workers from the shop floor; we do not know how many of them were re-elected after the legally enforced interval, but the number of people who became WsC members could be approaching one million, that is up to 25% of the workforce, and more if members of sub-committees are counted. Their experience in such voluntary and unpaid work, equally about the bright and the dark sides of organising production and human relationships, was certainly unique, and where the self-management was genuine, probably rather satisfying. True, as I described at some length, there was much frustration, self-serving, and sheer cussedness involved among hundreds of thousands of people without a working-class tradition; and in the 60s, a growing tiredness with involvement seems to have been on the rise among the workers.

12.2   Its Performance

Qualitatively, workers' self-management was the only way towards disalienation of labour. Theoretically speaking, if private ownership of means of production is a relationship of class dominance which, when the direct producer is legally free, takes the form of hired labour, then both capitalist ownership and simple nationalisation, that is State ownership of means of production, are class relationships. In this essential sense supposedly public ownership can still be called private in the original sense of *privatus*, that is, **depriving** direct producers from disposing of the products of their labour (cf. Brus 17 ff.) Ironically, and presciently, Engels had warned against expropriation and nationalisation of means of production by the State, since in that case 'the power of economic exploitation and political subjugation of the worker would be in the same hand' (letter to Bebel 1891, MEGA 22: 596–7)!

As Broekmeyer concluded, in a largely melancholy look backward from the end of the 70s:

> [D]uring the period of self-managed industrial relations, considerable parts of Yugoslavia have been industrialised. This transition ... has occurred without severe convulsions. There have been no famines, no bloody clashes between workers and the police, as for example in Poland, and no widespread misery as in so many other countries. On the contrary, Yugoslavia has managed smoother transition to industrialisation than either Western or Eastern Europe. Moreover, the transition took place more rapidly than elsewhere.
>
> 139

Quantitatively, in comparison to what capitalist enterprises might have done at the same technological level, most commentators who engage in it seem to judge Yugoslav self-management enterprises before 1968 as, at worst, performing just as well and some (including myself) think they performed on the whole better. Certainly there was waste, largely determined by macroeconomic forces. However, '[w]e should then compare the waste built into the self-managing system with the waste built into a centralised economy. Also, ... there can be no doubt that the self-managing system produces values which cannot be measured in terms of money alone' (Mann Borgese, in eadem and Adizes eds., 125). Seibel, whose Chapter 6 concluded that self-management and economic growth are compatible, devoted his Chapter 7 to this comparison and assembled there seven opinions, of which I cite three representative ones (with minimal editing of his references):

> Jan Tinbergen (119–20) noted: 'A rate of growth of *per capita* real income of about 6%, together with a considerable degree of democracy in the everyday environment of the mass of producers, is not easily found elsewhere'. And even Albert Meister (365), who has been most critical ..., admits that

Yugoslavia has, 'in only 15 years, managed to bring about basic industrialisation of the country, which it took us [Frenchmen] nearly a century ... And, despite some abuses, Yugoslavia attained this result in a much more human fashion ...'

And Jenkins (110–11) ... sums it all up by saying '... Just as kibbutz industrial management in Israel seems to lead to acceptable economic results, so companies under self-management in Yugoslavia seem to survive in a satisfactory fashion – even though neither of these peculiar ways of running companies quite fits in with traditional beliefs about the omniscience of the men at the top of the pyramid'.

SEIBEL 119–20

The sympathetic but rather critical Bourdet and Guillerm register 'the historical achievement of Yugoslav self-management ...: during a long period, handing factories over to the workers, far from leading to economic decline, managed a growth "Japanese style" ... The abolition of taylorism [and strict surveillance from above] has not depressed production. – Thus, self-management did not fail in Yugoslavia' (174–5).

The bluntest conclusion was drawn by Branko Horvat, both insider and dissident 'loyal opposition', in a table based upon research in his institute that intriguingly compares the unique spread of Yugoslav economic growth 'under capitalism, State socialism, and self-management':

TABLE 12.1   *Growth of Yugoslavia in different historical periods (in %)*

Period	GNP	Employment	Fixed assets	GNP growth due to increased efficiency [a]
Capitalism 1911–32	3.28	1.87	3.52	0.71
Capitalism 1932–40	4.67	0.72	2.59	3.16
Etatism 1946–54 [b]	5.91	4.76	9.99	−1.04
Self-government 1956–67	10.31	4.44	7.84	4.44

(a) efficiency is defined as growth of output attributable to *technical progress*, obtained after subtracting the contribution of labour and capital.
(b) I'm not sure why just these years, probably based on changes in planning.

Horvat's summary runs:

> Central planning [1946–54] expanded output and employment fast, and capital formation even faster, as compared with the private capitalist pre-war economy. But it also reduced overall efficiency. Self-government accelerated the growth of output and technical progress beyond anything known before while preserving fast employment expansion.
> Essay in *American Economic Review* [1971], 91–2, cited from SEIBEL 122

It should retrospectively be added that if the supposedly self-governing economic periods of SFRY were 1956–68, 1969–73, and 1974–88, the decline of nominally still existing self-management in all rubrics for the last two periods would have been equally abrupt. And of course the comparison is with colonial or semi-colonial capitalism.

Nonetheless, a number of researchers have pointed out that self-management generally yielded amazing functional results in the long run: it absorbed the shocks of rapid urbanisation and of decision decentralisation by creating collective commitment and comradely care (evident in the revealing WsC discussions about firing cited in Chapter 9). A special praise is due to the excellent and vertically organised, truly self-managed and independent, 'interest communities' for education, science, and culture, neutralised in the 70s. Močnik rightly underlines that even after 1972 such 'self-managed interest communities – including health, pensions, and social services – successfully regulated democratic mechanisms of non-commodified social solidarity, and resulted in health and education systems among the best in Europe' ('Workers'', electronic p. 7).

In a mixture of quantitative and qualitative criteria, Ichak Adizes elaborated eight reasons for 'advantages [of self-management] over other sociopolitical and economic systems', of which I mention six: it creates a learning environment favourable for coping with new conditions; it precludes monopolisation of power, involving all in setting goals; it enhances capital formation through sacrifice, also encourages group entrepreneurship and management, both important for 'developing nations'; it 'encourages the search for objective truth, [based on] full disclosure in information'; finally, it is humanistic – it might restore in people the sense of fulfilling their own purpose (Mann Borgese and idem eds., 149–61). No doubt, I add, this applies to its ideal horizons.

So, did self-management perform well? In micro-economics odds are that yes, in macro-economics only if and when certain macro-knots, which were at least glimpsed in Yugoslavia (see Horvat), were smoothed out – and after 1965, they were not.

12.3   Its End

Finally, as self-management was created from above, so it was also deconstructed from above. In order for the associated producers to have a chance at functioning properly in the more complex circumstances two factors were needed. First, that they dispose of a big enough cake: quite properly, the key political plank of people like Kardelj and Bakarić in the 1965 Reform was to reverse the ratio of the surplus labour (the net social product) at the enterprises' disposal as against what is taxed away from 30:70 to 70:30 (Bakarić 2: 473). Second, that a mechanism of obligatory planning, incorporating a feedback between planners and associated producers, be created and enabled not only by legal but also by sweeping politico-ideological measures. The second was never attempted, while the first, left on its own, was swamped in the move to a planless market and failed ignominiously: a slight rise in the first few years after 1965 was soon taken back by the attendant loss of planning and reliance on a not systematically controlled market. '[Enforced commodification crippled] both self-management in the enterprise (with greater power passed to the management – that is, technocracy) and planning in the economy as a whole' (Kržan 'Some', electronic p. 5). As of 1962 the material basis of WsC stagnated and then began shrinking (Cvjetičanin 246), at the beginning of the 70s it was no longer a living and developing organism. The percentage of workers in WsC fell from 76.2 in 1960 to 67.5 in 1970, of which only 55% were direct shop-floor producers; even more important, the percentage in the Managing (or 'Business') Boards fell from 67.2% to 44.2%, of which only 32% were direct producers (Marković, 'Struktura' 813). In the productively most developed Slovenia, WsC members considered by 1974 that the 'top managers' plus 'experts' decided long-range planning, investments, production norms, and even most of the criteria for workers' incomes: no wonder that the workers felt powerless and alienated within the returning wage relations (Arzenšek 10–14, 16–18, and 22), and socialism began to mean for 80% of them – 90+% for unqualified, semi-qualified, and women workers – simply a 'higher living standard' (idem 54–6). The Party members in production consisted more and more of executive staff and less and less of workers (see the impressive Comisso 'Can'). In a nutshell, the self-management vector to the future got smothered by the dirty present.

A parallel turn in the stepmotherly treated agriculture, which came to receive the lowest subsidies in Europe, meant that in 1964–71 the number of cooperative members fell from 1,261,000 to 883,000 members, while the number of tractors in the 'socialised' sector fell from 45,000 to 26,000 (Samary, *Marché* 210–12).

The best analysis spanning Yugoslav macro-economics and the WsC, that of Wlodzimierz Brus, sums up the results of the key 1965 reform as having given more legal power to the 'basic associations of labour' but also enhanced the role of banks to compensate for weaker State control over accumulation, which 'removed the centers of decision further from the workforce and compelled resort to frequently multi-level systems of indirect representation of self-management units' (84–5) without opening up clear lines of political democracy to determine such delegation of powers, and without competing programmes within socialist horizons but based on open information flows (cf. 191–211). The division of the surplus value earned in production into workers' incomes plus enterprise investment vs. allocations taxed away by the State remained a permanent *measure of ruling-class seizure of capital away from self-management* (cf. Brus 72–3). The cited ambition of the reformers to slash the power top's disposal of national income from 70 to 30%, but without putting the difference under the direct producers' control, failed totally. Without political democracy from below, the necessity of meso-economic mergers and other vertical cooperation fell under the sway of banks and analogous uncontrolled and alienated centres of financial power.

Thus, from the 70s on, all the wondrous legal forms of 'self-managing negotiations' (*dogovaranja*) proved inefficient within toothless 'indicative planning' and a profit-bent capitalist market. It spawned unbelievable logorrheas, for example in the norms occasioned by the 1972–80 laws about the new 'delegate system' of elections (see the judgement of Zukin and the data by Adizes in Chapter 10.4.3 above). The hardnosed conclusion by Prout seems correct: 'Apart from the innovations in the capital market, the [mid-60s] reform measures are significant, institutionally, not for what they created but for what they removed' (47) – which was, crucially, impediments to the rise of the capital market! The end result was a '*hybrid system*', combining elements of etatism in politics and ideology, elements of capitalism in the commodity and market economy as well as in mass culture, and 'elements of self-management – as co-management – on the lowest level of enterprise, and in ... cultural activities (except politics)' (Golubović, 'Novije' 38).

The central and crucial question remained: *will industrial self-management be built up both horizontally and vertically into an all-encompassing plebeian associative democracy, realising practically the withering away of the State as apparatus?* The answer was no. While nobody dared to argue openly against workers' management, its proper functioning became all but impossible. In class terms, this excluded workers' influence on economic macro-structures. The power of WsC fell sharply in favour of MBs packed by executives; the best enterprises were successfully taken over by the 'technocracy', an ambiguous class fraction wavering between the partitocracy and (increasingly) the international market pressures and culminating in the rise of powerful homegrown financial capital which became dominant in the best developed parts of the economy. Self-management grew increasingly to be executives persuading workers to accept 'necessary sacrifices'; this is palpably clear in Comisso's exemplary early 70s' conflict at 'Klek' factory: 'the workers, wanting their version of "self-management now", reacted ... with anger and dismay' (*Workers'* 178–9 and *passim*). The stagnant, and eventually falling, living standard (cf. Novaković *passim*, Vidaković 226–7) and loss of political horizons neutralised the young and inexperienced working class, which turned to increasingly bitter passivity, as seen also in the rise of strikes which seem in 1968–73 to have involved almost every second manual worker in industry (Samary, *Marché* 215). A startling example may be found in Lazić's late 70s' research among workers in Croatia, Serbia, and Bosnia, in which to the question 'What profession do you desire for your children?' from almost 800 people only 5.9% answered 'worker'! The choice of 12.1% was foreman or technician, 18.1% white-collar worker, 10.3% political or economic manager, and a whopping 41.4% 'specialist' (with a university degree); the researcher commented: 'To become a worker means the end of all desire' ('Radništvo' 193). True, the research was carried out in 1978, so the bitterness might have been smaller earlier. But clearly, 'nothing is less effective and more demoralising than apparent participation' (Brus 189). It is quite remarkable that, despite all this, the workers were still in favour of 'a State of self-managing councils' with 74.2%, as opposed to 'a State managed by professional politicians', in which 16.5% believed (Lazić, 'Radništvo' 274): the working class kept the faith in self-management a dozen years after the oligarchy had proved it lost it, and protested *en masse* in the wave of strikes after 1983 (cf. Lowinger).

Did the experiment of self-management succeed? It showed much promise in the seven years of incubation, and the eight to ten years of maturation before it was strangled. However if 'the essence of self-management is that the worker should simultaneously work and fulfil those functions which were in capitalist society exercised by the capitalist and in etatist society by the State' (Kardelj, cited in Bavčar et al. 46), self-management definitely failed some years after 1965. The reason was, as I indicated in Part 2 and as Brus concluded, that a true socialisation of means of production needed '*not "depoliticisation of the economy" but "democratisation of politics"*' (91–2, emphasis mine; cf. also Flaherty). The limited autonomy of the self-management system 'proved insufficient to bring about a deeper change in the ... Yugoslav political system [which] does not admit opposition, does not give the opportunity for presentation of an alternative solution [on] the socialist road of development or for soliciting social acceptance of any such alternative ...' (Brus 93–4).

The withering away of lower-class powers in self-management was accompanied by an economic downturn after 1965. It was at first slow, but not only was Yugoslavia starting to progress slower than most neighbouring countries but, most ominously, for the first time its backward regions grew slower than the relatively developed ones and the spread between them widened henceforth unceasingly – that is, ethnic differences could now be mobilised as claims for economic justice. The gap between incomes within the same skill level also grew, which testified to destruction of a countrywide level playing field. As Kržan stresses in 'Nacrt', trade between constituent republics fell drastically in favour of their inner market or of exports, which meant the republican oligarchies in the North of the country were orienting themselves toward isolated development. Finally, employment even officially stagnated as of 1963, and unofficially it probably relatively fell. This means that the young peasants could not be sure they could find a job in an urban environment and started going to work in capitalist countries and later in extra-legal jobs, and that the army of unemployed workers turned into a permanent feature of the system, even though the average skill level had risen appreciably. All of this continued accelerating and exacerbating after 1972.

The shelving of a coherent and enforceable economic politics meant that, after a series of world financial shocks, the highest per head 'social product' of Slovenia when compared to the lowest one of Kosovo had by 1981 opened a gap equal to the one between the UK and Algeria (Horvat, *Jugoslavensko* 37); Kržan's example in 'Nacrt' is the gap between New Zealand and Pakistan – though in all these cases social welfare meant the Yugoslav lower classes would have been better off. True, both these regions were extremes and the rest of Yugoslavia had a maximum gap between highest and lowest below 2:1 (Gregory 214), but it is clear that in SFRY there came to coexist a shear between the European or Northern and the African or Southern vector of (under)development: no country can at length stand such a strain.[1]

At the opposite ends of society the upper perhaps 5% got noticeably richer – and a clear class mentality of the capitalist kind developed both in the private sector and in the 'socialised' sector where top incomes reached, already by 1971, 15 times the lowest one, and in shady deals between the two sectors (see

---

1   The key politico-economic goal of reducing the disparities in living standards between republics by transferring capital to poorer areas by means of the Fund for Accelerated Development (FAD), mentioned in Chapter 8.2.1, and the story of its degradation after the mid-60s can be gleaned from Comisso, *Workers'* 69–70, 74, 79, and 101–3; Močnik 'Nismo'; Prout 41–2, 117–21, 145, and 245; Samary, *Marché* 167 and 248–9; Gregory *passim*; also in Bakarić 2: 130 and 132, Bakarić 3: 14–19 for a general approach, and Tripalo 296.

Atlagić and Milanović eds. 9–11, 45–8, 53–4) – while both unemployment and immiseration burgeoned in the lower reaches of the working class. Bases for an exploitative class system were put into place not only with the rise of credit capital but also among the 210,000 people in private construction and catering by the mid-70s (Horvat, *Essay* 138–9, Prout 143). In the summation of Horvat, the reason for the Yugoslav economic slowdown was ('possibly', he cautiously put it) 'a crystallisation of class interests ... The political system became the chief brake of social economic development' (*Jugoslavensko* 9).

I now turn to the political system, or civic life.

CHAPTER 13

In Civic Life: Dis/Alienation and Oligarchy Monolithism

> Hence arises a possible conflict between what is and what ought to be ...
> HEGEL, 1820

∴

13.0   Introduction

I proposed in Chapter 10.2.1 that productivism was the first idol to ceaselessly dominate the mentality of Yugoslav partitocracy. Yet eventually, say by the beginning of the 60s and increasingly through the following dozen years, it became clear that its twin (if older) fetish, supposedly essential for all production and productivity, was *monolithic unity* in the Party.[1] This proved incompatible with democratic communism and disalienation.

13.1   Horizons of Self-Government

I have argued in this book that the only reasonable hypothesis for the decline and stagnation of SFRY and then its dramatic downfall is the existence of *a ruling Party/State oligarchy*, which as of the 1960s split into republican ruling classes increasingly at odds with each other, a decisive part of which then grew into the role of secessionist compradors. The loyal opposition of Praxis and Branko Horvat, as well as some perspicacious but not practically followed insights of a few Party/State leaders, understood that this was the obverse

---

1   The totem and taboo of monolithism was relentlessly built up by Stalin for 10 years, endorsed in Party documents of the 1924 Congress, and achieved by 1931 (see Appendix 1, also Moore 152 ff. and Golubović, *Staljinizam* 119–22). It was fully espoused by Tito, see for example the references in Perović 24, 285, and 364. Illuminating discussions of it may be found *en passant* in the lucid Magri 25–6, and an interesting opposition between it and a necessary utopian vision of the future society is found in Rus, 'Participativna' 715.

of (and reason for) the refusal to let self-management develop from within industry and social services into a fully self-governing system across the board.

Veljko Cvjetičanin wittily posed that such a development ideally would have expanded into three dimensions, relating to the horizontal, the vertical, and depth ('Entwicklung' 252–4; cf. Supek 'Problems' and 'Some'). By *horizontal* is meant the very neglected dimension of broadening it into the territorial communities, from the basic 'communes' to the republics and then the federation as a whole. This would have been important for de-alienating the rapidly growing 'lonely crowd' of the urban centres as well as for de-provincialising the rural communities. However, the transfer of power to republican mini-States – a harbinger of huge troubles to come – effectively put paid to such grassroot democracy, while the interesting organisational form of residential or housing community (*stambena zajednica*) was unfortunately never given sufficient funds nor attention to develop. 'The *vertical* dimension of self-management is most sharply opposed to the State apparatus and is therefore the least developed one'. It could develop in two ways: either as an integration filling the gap between the enterprise plans and the local community as well as central planning; or by economic branches, including 'social services' such as health or education, in the form of several permanent central councils, each 'a self-management congress or working people's parliament, relying on scientific analyses and planning. In this case the State organs would truly become [as envisaged by Lenin and Kidrič – DS] auxiliary organs of this workers' parliament'. The *depth* dimension means a direct associational democracy, which is a key to socialism. It would mean creating presuppositions in all social units for overcoming the division into leaders and led.

As of 1958, that halcyon time when the Party Programme (*Yugoslavia's Way*) called for 'the transformation of all State organs into organs of self-government', this vision was a widespread horizon, a Blochian 'concrete' – that is, possible – utopia. It is then that to the republican and federal Assemblies, beside two chambers composed of professional politicians, three chambers were added (for economic policies, for social services, and for education and culture) composed from delegates of basic organisations in the field, and having no financial privileges (cf. Marković, 'Self-governing' 165–7). The vision started from *creative labour* and envisaged full control of the labourer-creators over the fruits of their labour, personally and in association within 'interest communities'. Though the oligarchy halted the threatening proletarian or plebeian thrust in 1965, and the vision broke down by 1972, we might today use it to construct a model with full respect both for a right to individual self-determination against any collective and for the right of an open society to survive and cherish supra-individual values. No primacy obtains here but an empowering feedback: 'an association, in which the free development of each is the condition for the free development of all' (Marx, *Manifesto*) – and vice versa – and where labour is no longer exploited toil. I have identified it earlier as a plebeian utopian communism.

I shall concentrate on Cvjetičanin's horizontal level, which was just as neglected, for power reasons, as the other two. To my mind it opens up the whole problematic of a thriving Gramscian civil society, the 'living community' which is in the context of high technological production 'interlaced and mutually conditioned' with productive communities (Supek, 'Problems' 228) as a precondition and strategic site of decision-making from which organisation and humanisation in production depend. Self-management in production is an essential political element of it, but only 'in conjunction with political democratism ...' (Brus 92), which I interpret as an open expression of legitimate interests within a socialist framework by different and sometimes clearly opposed political groups – and I would claim by real or potential classes or at least class fractions (territorial, professional, etc.). The economics of this democracy would be based on the US revolutionary principle, well-known in Yugoslav debates too (see Woodward 153), of 'no taxation without [effective] representation'.

An indispensable additional thematic field and way of understanding social totality, not present before materialist feminism but convincingly demonstrated in it, is to link production strongly with the reproduction of labour power (including consumption), which Elson calls 'the nexus between enterprises and households'; in socialism, the direct cooperation between self-managed associations in these two fields would follow a 'politics of use values' (6).

The horizon of such self-determination, where people are 'the authors and actors of their own drama' (Marx, *Poverty* ch02.htm) seems to me indispensable for establishing what was missing in 'really existing', and eventually really suicidal, 'socialism'. In historical terms it means first of all that the logic of classes and subordination can be overcome, that oligarchic power in production and in States is not inescapable (see Badiou *passim*). In ideological and ethical terms it is based on the great lower-class principle of **solidarity**: and a warm and hospitable personalised solidarity means *fraternité*, brotherhood, the partizan *bratstvo*.

That also means that socialism as a historical transitional phase could and should have as its centrepiece nothing else but the struggle to advance toward Marx's horizon for distributing the fruits of labour: 'From each according to his ability, to each according to his needs!' (*Critique* 388). The precondition for success was **to see socialism as a political society**, rather than to see the just society forever directed by the State. Workers' self-management raised great hopes among both manual workers and intellectuals that the objects of social change could also become its subjects (see Milosavljević, 'Država' 414 ff.), which is roughly Aristotle's definition of democracy. However it also came up against the unresolved aporia of an ossified political 'vanguard' or Party core: the hopeful horizon was abandoned in favour of oligarchic class rule. So after 1965 things kept going from bad to worse.

I stressed in Chapter 1 and later the importance of *unity* for the Titoist partizan innovation: it was the glue that kept together the disparate regions, partizan units, and indeed classes and interests, rendered possible by focussing on fighting the enemy, then on reconstructing the destroyed country, and organisationally guaranteed by the iron discipline of the Party. But even a unity arising out of negative fission, out of repulsion against the fascist Antagonist, lives on and changes, often drastically, in new circumstances: the times and enemies change, and so do people (*tempora mutantur, nos et mutamur in illis*). The only stable unity is one that allows internal dialectics, the expression of maturing contradictions as the inescapable prerequisite for a possible resolution. This did not happen in Yugoslavia, and crucially inside the Party. For – except for foreign threat, which Tito most efficiently kept at bay from 1945 on – there was no obvious social group or class inimical to the original revolutionary programme. The first possible antagonist was ca. 1970 the 'technocracy', and even this turned out to be secondary, an enemy brother that could be incorporated with some concessions, that is, a piece of the cake. In the *doxa* shared by Tito, Kardelj and practically everybody at the top, there only remained 'subjective' failings inside the Party, thus called to tie it to single members rather than groups, confronted with 'objective' conditions – a crude Kantian or indeed vulgar materialist (Plekhanov's and early Lenin's) dichotomy shedding no light and giving no guidance.

13.2   On Odious Secrecy as a Root of Failure

> Finally it is no wonder that the plebeians do not know any truth or judgment, when the principal affairs of domination are being kept secret from them, so that they can conjecture about it only from the few elements which were not possible to hide.
>
> SPINOZA, 1676

∴

I am embarking here upon a subsection about open information (by contraries, through bureaucratic secrecy, against which the young Marx was at his most scathing),[2] because it seems to me intimately tied with what I suggested in Chapter 10.4 was a basic and fateful failure of the top people in the Party to *renew their thinking* in the altered material and ideological circumstances, especially beginning with the 1960s. I see in this one of the main reasons for the failure of the whole Yugoslav revolutionary experiment. Renewal would have meant learning much but also, crucially, *unlearning* as indispensable precondition for acceding to a new knowledge paradigm: for a problem cannot be solved by the same methods which have in the first place created it (as happened in Yugoslav economics, and also politics). It is a matter of changing focus and categories: 'Unlearning is required when the world or your circumstances in the world have changed so completely that your old habits now hold you back' (Davidson 19).

The only way for a teacher to teach himself what he did not study in his formative years is to continually balance between not losing her central insights and agonisingly reappraising them whenever necessary through new learning. (Here should come an equally long subsection on the sad decay and class involution of the revolutionary expansion of schooling from the upward period of my Gaussian curve in Chapter 5, but the data and discussions – e.g. by Horvat in *Essay* or *Jugoslavensko* 203 – are readily available: in brief, high schooling was from the late 70s drastically reoriented and became a class 'entry ticket' for upward mobility inside the oligarchy but a barrier for the working and the middle classes; see Chapter 9.1, also Lazić, *U susret* 71–4 and *passim*, and cf. Schierup 95.) The precondition to such balanced learning is to have open information circuits with the reality you supposedly control. Knowledge as the possibility of steering social processes is the pillar of every rule. In particular, Marx's key tenet of introducing *transparency* (*glasnost'*) in social relations by means of associational and *citoyen* democracy would have in Yugoslav politics meant breaching two huge mystifications: that *the extortion of surplus value* had been transcended or at least neutralised, and that there was a need for *Party monopoly* on informations and policy. Neither breach came about: one strongly suspects they were causally related, so that the ruling class had to hide its social being.

---

2 On Marx cf. Kouvelakis 250–328; Marx must have known well Kant's view that publicness [*Publizität*] is the condition for freedom and that all actions inciding on rights of others are wrong if they cannot be rendered public, see idem 250. On Yugoslav Party secrecy cf. information in Carter 86–92 and some clues in Mićunović, Appendix 2.

Learning and unlearning go necessarily hand in hand with an unfettering of imaginative creativity that I have mentioned several times in this book as operating, and that forsook the Party as of the mid-60s. As pointed out in the 'Foreword', I take seriously and literally Marx's fulminant insight that theory (imagination) becomes a material force when it enters the consciousness of the masses – and first of all, of its supposed vanguard in the Party State. Even in its least Stalinist wing, Bakarić fell despondently silent and Kardelj went for sterile twists and turns. The situation is quite analogous to the extremely low level of inventions and patents, abandoned in favour of wholesale acquisition of foreign licenses for technology. What was needed, in strict parallel to the 1941–5 stance, was embracing the energies of the student revolt of 1968, of the workers' strikes, and of *Praxis* and Horvat as a well-meaning opposition, and then creating a level playing field for rival imaginations within socialism.

The Party power-wielders had totally forgotten that ten days after coming to power, Lenin wrote a 'Draft Resolution on Freedom of the Press' which stated: 'For the workers' and peasants' government, freedom of the press means liberation of the press from capitalist oppression, and public ownership of paper mills and printing presses; equal right for public groups of a certain size (say, numbering 10,000) to a fair share of newsprint stocks and a corresponding quantity of printers' labour'. The first RSFSR Constitution of 1918 guaranteed workers' freedom of speech, opinion, and gathering in the same way. However, Lenin's sketch remained unpublished owing to a grave shortage of paper (Bettelheim 1: 268), and this whole project of direct democracy fell victim to the civil war. The forgetfulness extended to the lesson of the French Revolution: 'The character of a people's government is to trust the people and to be severe toward itself' (Robespierre 300).

Thus by the late 50s, some deep rethinking would have been necessary in Yugoslavia. The theme of economic-cum-psychological alienation and the theme of efficiency again intertwine here, but since the former has been well pioneered by the Praxis group, let me note how hardnosed economics fully mesh with the problem of information flows, decisive in reasonable decision-making:

> [Its] cardinal condition ... is the availability of a number of variants which 'enter the lists' on equal terms ... It is clear, too, that the optimisation procedure ... must generate new information and thus have some influence on the final result ... In a socialist economy, then, there appears both a necessity for particularly well-developed and free flow of information to and from the central decision-making body and a particular possibility of restriction and manipulation of the information system.
>
> BRUS 191–2

The latter can be avoided only by democratic transparency, 'the creation of *political* pressure and control of a kind such that the decision center must base its choices on full sources of information and really comprehensively use the method of variant analysis ...' – in other words, on political pluralism within socialist horizons. This embraces 'not only freedom of expression of opinion but also the possibility of organisation in defence of one's own conception and of critical evaluation of official conceptions'; and finally, 'the selection and changing of leading teams on the basis of the programme presented and the results achieved' (idem 192 and 194). All of this applies equally to information systems inside an enterprise, between enterprises, on a socialised market (cf. Chapter 10.1), and to 'long-term links between buyers and sellers, which help to stabilise an enterprise's environment' (Elson 32).

In short, unhindered flow of information to and from all decision-making bodies, the 'socialisation of the arenas and processes of knowledge construction and information acquisition' (Pienkos 55), is indispensable both ideologically and economically. Practically, the infamous verbal crime clause (*délit d'opinion*) of the penal code should have been the first to be abolished: for, emancipation in general is not only the official ideology of socialist social integration but also the basis of the regime's legitimacy. Yet, just as in capitalism and sometimes even more so, regimes pretending to achieved harmony find it particularly easy to restrict and manipulate information flows, disallowing a possible public sphere limited only by upholding the constitution.

Therefore, a self-conscious working class would beyond better consumption and civil rights also demand, as the Gdańsk workers did around 1980, free dissemination of and a level playing field in information – in press, TV, and cognate media – and the democratisation of central planning with formalised input by workers' organisations (cf. Burawoy 117, also Mandel ed. 1: 45–6).

This whole political and cognitive knot necessarily includes the growing role of long-term strategic decisions and of experts, and thus raises the larger question of *the role of intellectuals* (clearly in the wake of Gramsci): for one example, Horvat (*Jugoslavensko* 344) rightly infers from the scarce data available that their role in the People's Liberation Struggle was a key one – and yet they were always poor cousins at the table of the ruling class. On the other hand, once economic development has jumped to a middling level and should go further, the knot at hand equally includes the change of labour process from simple manual execution and operations to skilled, largely conceptual brainwork, especially in work with computerised and automatised technology, as well as 'the aspirations of the educated worker of whom thought, independence and inventiveness are demanded' (ibidem 197). Thus it raises the question of a true cognitive alliance with the working classes in view of shrinking the gap between manual and mental labour. Radical democratic pluralism, though ideally not in the form of antagonistic political parties, is therefore indispensable both for a rational planning and for motivating the producers. It would have to use public, specialised and competing, services for collecting and analysing political and economic information (see Horvat, *Essay* 225–6).

At the end of the 60s, monolithism confessed it was not such but a congeries of half a dozen monoliths (see my analyses of Kardelj in Chapters 4 and 10 and Appendix 2), yet insisted to still appear such outside the oligarchy core. In practice this meant secrecy about the vital debates and the means of deciding them, that is about the people participating, their views, and the ways in which they decided.

Had a public sphere come about within an emancipatory horizon of democratic communism, small autonomous groups inside and outside the Party, no longer shackled by (a largely façade) unanimity, could have begun to articulate seemingly abstruse but in reality central questions suggested by my whole discussion. For example:

- What is work and production, and therefore 'distribution according to work'? Historically, 'work' (*Arbeit*) has had two main meanings: misery, affliction, and toil (as in the Judeo-Christian Fall from Eden) or productive accomplishment (*opus, opera*). The sanctification of work as 'accomplishment that provides life with significant content' began with the Protestant bourgeoisie (Löwith, *From Hegel* 264–79 and *passim*; see also Groethuysen and Marcuse 'Über'). Serious discussion begins with Smith and his reader Hegel, who exalts collective human work, which is not opposed 'to leisure or play, but the basic way in which man produces his life, thereby giving form to the world'. It is concretised in the great invention of money, and it is qualitatively different for peasants, manual workers, and merchants; it brings about culture but its 'self-activating life of what is dead ... like a wild animal demand[s] constantly to be controlled and held in check' (Löwith, ibid. 265 and 268). Marx then fully articulated the original contradiction, where dependent work is at best a necessary evil, and dialectically demands the right of creative laziness too: 'the realm of freedom actually begins only where working which is determined by misery and outer expedience ends' (*Capital* III, ch48.htm); his son-in-law, Paul Lafargue, wrote a pamphlet on *The Right to Laziness* from Marx's notes. Furthermore, in *Critique* Marx waxed very sarcastic against the 'bourgeois phrases' extolling labour divorced from nature (382–3) and noted how dehumanising it was to regard some people '*only as workers* and nothing more' (387).

- What is the socio-political role and psychological fallout of commodity production and the 'capital-relation' (Kardelj)? What about Polanyi's argument that wage-labour is falsely treated as a commodity since it is inseparable from the labourer? What about Marcuse's equation 'technical progress = growing social wealth (the rising GNP!) = extended servitude is the law of capitalist progress' (*Counterrevolution* 4)? If such alienations were still to a significant degree inevitable, what were (a) the limits of their duration on the road to communism, and (b) the Keynesian and Marxian ways of correcting them, right from the beginning and while they lasted, towards class and citizen solidarity, towards indispensable (and already existing) elements of 'distribution according to need'?
- How can capitalist technology be rethought so as to work for disalienation? This would mean, first, making coherent and systematised sense of the already major practical communist corrections inflicted on the Law of Value and profit-making in all social services and to advance from them; and second, measuring productivity in terms of energy consumption and entropy increase (cf. for example Wallis 139–40 and Suvin, 'Introductory' 338 ff.), not within supposedly 'scientific' capitalist management schemes.
- Assuming that fundamental macro-economic planning about the direction of social development remains indispensable in socialism, how and by whom should it be done, how tested and debated, and how should it use and limit the market? Can the federal level be totally emasculated without eventually losing the State? How much decision-power must there be left in a State for it to remain a State?
- How can big economic systems, absolutely needed for technologico-economic rationalisation and for increase of productivity, come about within associational democracy but without authoritarianism?
- 'What responsibility do workers in self-managed enterprises have for the unemployed and the excluded? Who is responsible for creating jobs?' (Lebowitz 79)
- If one opts to use the market, what about the markets for capital and land? Since especially the first one was de facto permitted, wouldn't the dire consequences have been diminished or fully forestalled by a (lacking) socialist investigative theory?
- How is freedom of the press and media to be positively defined in terms of obligatory right of access by civic groups and organisations arguing for a particular policy?
- When can freedom of association and assembly be declared to be anti-constitutional and using what precise criteria? Is it to be tested in courts as independent of the executive branch in socialism as they are supposed to be (and at their best are) in capitalism?

13.3 Why Did SFR Yugoslavia Fail?

> Qui si convien lasciare ogne sospetto;
> ogne viltà convien che qui sia morta.
> (Here all hesitation needs to be left behind;
> All vileness needs to wither here.)
> *Inferno*, Canto III: 14–15

∴

The exogenous forces of the world market became as of 1973 much less favourable to middling developed States; in particular, Yugoslavia lost at the end of the 1980s the trump card of its strategic role between the two Cold War blocks. The most perspicacious diagnosis so far is to be found in Woodward: 'The fundamental trap lay in the leaders' Faustian bargain between [this] strategic position internationally and access to foreign capital (both credits and trade)'. This was subject to unpredictable external shocks from trends in global capital and trade and from superpower conflict or dominance. *The logic of 'collective action' in favour of 'socialism in one country ... [was] opposed to [the] logic of capital internationally'*. Giving in to this second logic, '[i]n place of governmental guardianship over sectoral balance and infrastructural investments for sustained growth and declining regional inequality, [plans and investments] were oriented to the needs [for foreign earnings and loans] and projects [with] external financing ...' (256–9, emphasis mine). How was the first logic, utopian communism developing in a world capitalist market, to be sustained? Kržan ends his 'Nacrt' lecture by cautiously endorsing Samir Amin's thesis that socialist economic development is possible only through decoupling from the capitalist market. But the modalities and international support for doing so remain to my mind still to be worked out; in their absence, the fuller such a decoupling and inward turning would be, the stronger would grow the forces of politocratic despotism. An exogenous macro-alternative to what SFRY descended into remains an open question, a kind of Pascalian wager.

However my thesis is, as Horvat's in Chapter 8.2.2, that a chance of encountering stormy weather with a firm and steerable ship was squandered earlier, in 1965–72. The dismantling of the Welfare State began in SFRY before the world capitalist offensive of the 70s, but for analogous class reasons. Therefore I speak here only of the endogenous factor, which hinged on the behaviours of the partitocratic oligarchy.

The ideology of *monolithism* of the ruling Party – or, in practice, its permanent professional core, which I have estimated in Chapter 7 at 150,000 people after 1945, rising after a quarter century to perhaps half a million, including families (cf. also Chapter 3.2.2 and 4.1) – entailed that it must, like the virtue of Caesar's wife, both *be* and *appear* totally homogenous and impermeable to upsetting influences. This was the only appropriate way of living and thinking under the savage conditions of persecuted illegality and revolutionary warfare. But in peacetime, modernisation and economic development in what clearly still was a class society quite inevitably bring clashes of opposed group or class interests. This happened in Yugoslavia at the latest by the early 1960s, but was kept carefully masked and out of sight except for cryptic hints without naming the bearers of those interests (cf. the previous chapters). Yet since self-government needs joint decisions on many territorial and branch levels, choosing the best programme for the country as a whole demanded an open society of associational democracy, however united: without public discussions around conflicting platforms within a socialist horizon, this is finally impossible.

In Chapter 7 I concluded that in States ruled by a communist party of the Leninist type, after the first few years, the principal conflict obtains between forces internal to the original revolutionary seizure of power – *the budding oligarchy*, always in favour of dictatorship from above, *vs. the budding self-government of the working people*, who rightly felt that communism should be a step by step democratic disalienation in the workplace and in political life. To repeat, when the Party oligarchy wins, an impasse and stasis results which leads to ideological and economic collapse. In particular, '[a]utocratic and paternalistic methods lose their effectiveness not only with the growth in the complexity of the ... tasks and the professional level of the workers', but also with the rise in their material security which then foregrounds the needs for the affirmation of human personality in an overall disalienation of labour (Brus 189). Together with the fostering of runaway consumerism as an alternative to plebeian democracy, this resulted in a resurgence of nationalist middle classes in various republics, increased foreign leverage, and finally indeed in the *tertium gaudet** victory of capitalism: the split oligarchic classes were – as different from plebeian opposition, for example the wave of worker strikes in the 1980s – as a rule ready to transmogrify dissatisfaction from below into nationalism (see Lowinger) and themselves into neo-comprador bourgeoisies at the service of foreign financial capital.

It must be said in praise of the communist party in Yugoslavia that some of its leaders tried for more than two decades to extricate the Party from the State – but this failed since, as I noted, it was just below the top, in the republics and communes, that the oligarchy came to have its key sites and levers. As Kardelj felicitously phrased it at the Central Committee meeting of 1966: 'In fact all of us were often in the dilemma what should communists struggle for: a kind of *etatist paternalism*, that is, for a good government which should humanely care for the good but "stupid" people, or for a genuine socialist self-management of working people, that is, for such socioeconomic and material conditions in which the working man could care for himself by himself' (*Treći* 298). The dilemma was thus identified but never solved – because the antagonists were not identified, they remained faceless and unnamed. They were in fact a majority of the Central Committee and thus could not be fought without a strong movement from below, which was not allowed.

For the extrication from etatism – federal or local – to work, two axiomatic tenets of Leninist parties should have been unpacked and disputed. The first was that the Party as vanguard was supposed to gather round itself all the 'progressive forces' and simultaneously to remain monolithic. Yet practice always showed that between mass democracy and Party monolithism without democracy there was a contradiction that grew in strength and acuteness; as I have argued throughout, the country lacked a civil sphere subject to openness and reasonable competition. Second, a most firm conviction of the top and then the whole Party core should have been demolished, that I shall phrase as 'once we have power, and keep it monolithic, economic development will solve all and we do not need to bother too much with innovating in politics or rethinking ideology' – so that a clear variant of the economicism satirised by Marx in *Capital* became the universal First Commandment: 'Accumulate! Accumulate! That is Moses and all the prophets'. It was then in and after the 60s for too many social climbers easy to – so to speak – privatise this commandment into Guizot's 'Enrichissez-vous!' (Get rich!). Positivism without ideology and politics – that is, ridding itself of the partizan singularity – succeeded only to transfer etatism to the level of constituent republics and their associated financial centres holding capital. Add to this pragmatism: socialist governments are faced with overwhelming and unforeseeable pressures, most of all from international capitalism with its twin crushing tentacles of armed intervention and financial intervention, but then also from internal factors such as climate (for agricultural yields) and the heredity of backward mentalities. Therefore, as most other governments, they necessarily practice tactical navigating by sight. Yet if such tactics do not follow an overall strategic plan but simply trust the heavenly influences of etatism and economicism, the ship unfailingly gets off course. Once off course, the stage is set for an endless series of knee-jerk interventions, necessarily borrowing more and more from 'free market' liberalism.

This led to 'transforming the Yugoslav federation into a de facto confederation of nation-States' (Močnik 'Workers'', electronic p. 5).

I am not pleading for Mao's reputed 'politics first, economy second' idea, though much could have been learned from his mid-6os' turn and identification of the main Antagonist; certainly his injunction 'bombard the headquarters [with criticism]' would have been useful for Yugoslavia too. However, as argued in the conclusion to Chapter 7, I would understand sane politics as open but non-violent confrontation of loyally socialist interests in and out of the economy. In that sense politics crystallises as criterion and precondition for everything else, including the no doubt key economics, which is for Gramsci anyway a cultural and ethical proving ground.

Ausklang: The Consciousness of Defeat

> If the Russian Revolution were overthrown by the violence of bourgeois counter-revolution, it would rise again like a phoenix; if however it lost its socialist character and thereby disappointed the working masses, the blow would have ten times more terrible consequences for the Russian and the international revolution.
> KARL RADEK, 1918

∴

As epitaphs I can use two from the mid-70s, when sympathetic and well-informed observers began sorely doubting:

> [P]erhaps the basic contradiction in present-day Yugoslav society [is the one] between the mundane possibilities of a relatively underdeveloped, small, independent nation-State, and its heroic aspirations to solve the complex problems of multinationality, industrial democracy, egalitarianism, and social mobility in a way that has not yet been attempted anywhere in the world.
> DENITCH 27–8

As the State and the regime began their fourth decade ... it seemed more likely that Yugoslavia would become another slovenly, moderately oppressive, semi-efficient, semi-authoritarian State run by an oligarchy

of contending elites, a society in which many are free and participant and
many are not. Like most States.
   RUSINOW 346-7

This is what the Yugoslavia they described for years with such precise and I
would say loving detail was coming to. It was, to them, a sad climb-down.
   But how much sadder is what one would have to write as a proper epitaph
after the fratricidal wars, the wholesale and firesale material and moral dis-
possessions, the misery of the counter-revolutionary break-up! The trajectory
described in this chapter, and my preceding ones, can be seen as a Morality
Play or a Pilgrim's Progress, where our Hero/ine – the original People's Liberation impulse as indicated here, Enlightenment for the first time come to
power in the Balkans, Disalienation – struggles mightily not only with momentary avatars of the Antagonist, Balkan alienations, but with its long-duration
hydra heads. The biggest head may be feudal and patriarchal authoritarianism
fused with the 'heroic code' (cf. Erlich *passim*, also Žvan), powerfully recreated
in the 1941–5 war discipline, and branching on society's top into the 'winner
take all' ethos and on bottom into the Dinaric mountaineer knifing machismo,
or symmetrically into petty-bourgeois escapism of the *kitsch* kind.³ Some other
heads would be *kulak* sharking usury (*zelenaštvo*), the only known and gras-
pable form of capitalism; the untranslatable Serbian terms for ideological viz.
economic grasping closure of *palanka* and *čaršija*, the negligence (*javašluk*)
inherited from Ottoman decadence, the subaltern Croatian envy (*hrvatski jal*),
or the pedantry and narcissism of the Yugoslav Teutons, the Slovenes: and all
the other dead-alive tentacles of the past too numerous to recount. As long as
the Heroine, the original Enlightenment Yugoslavia, was vigorous and clear-
headed, heads were being lopped off and the defeated monsters retreated to
their lairs, away from the light. But when she floundered and finally lost heart,
they emerged little by little. Furthermore, the process was not like my Medieval
allegory but much more similar to Jekyll and Hyde, or the *Alien* movies: the
monster invaded the hero's interior. Thus after all, these multiple, huge, and
capillary alienations, with the decisive help of the ruling oligarchy's obtuseness,
after all they won out against the Liberation Struggle. Alas and alack.
   In a way, what I am writing is my way of doing a cognitive epitaph, looking
backward from today and because of today: for knowledge may not make us free

---

3 Cf. the quite inconclusive debates about the burgeoning mass pop culture from the 1960s
   on, and a first attempt at theorising it in Šuvar, as well as a theoretical commentary on the
   debates in Senjković and a wider approach in Dimitrijević (whom I thank for sending me his
   dissertation).

without power, but we can never attain freedom without starting from efficient knowledge. Therefore I add a third epitaph for the way-going traveller passing by Thermopylae, for me apposite: 'I carry with me the consciousness of defeat as a victorious flag'. It is by Pessoa, in *Bernardo Soares's Book of Disquiet*.

Glossary

lucus a non lucendo = a nonsensical paradox by which the same term (here its root in 'lux') may actually mean the opposite

pars pro toto = rhetorical figure in which a part is taken for or representing the whole

non-dit = literally 'the unsaid', what a certain discourse cannot say because it is based on the omission of this factor

liberté, égalité, fraternité = freedom, equality, brotherhood

nouveaux riches = the newly rich, *parvenus*

tertium gaudet = the third one rejoices (in a quarrel between two others, as in Aesop's fable)

CHAPTER 14

Conclusion: On Failures and Potentialities

'Go home and think about this' (3 Mos. 19:18): only this is the Law, all else is interpretation.
RABBI HILLEL, 1st C BC

Friend, it is enough. If you wish to take more hence,
Go and become yourself the script and essence.
ANGELUS SILESIUS, 1657

Wir stehen selbst enttäuscht und sehn betroffen
Den vorhang zu, und alle fragen offen
[We're disappointed too and see with a frown
All questions open as the curtain comes down.]
BERTOLT BRECHT, 1940

∴

14.0 Cognitions of Poetry and Philosophy: A Chronological Florilegium

'Master Mo met an old friend who spoke to him: "Nowadays, nobody in the world values *yi* [right action, righteousness, and justice]. You are only inflicting pain on yourself by being *yi*. Better you stop". – Master Mo said: "Suppose there was a man who had ten sons, one of whom ploughed while nine stayed at home. The one who ploughed could not help but work with increased urgency. Because those who eat are many, but those who plough are few. Nowadays, nobody in the world values *yi*, so you should be encouraging me. Why would you stop me?"'
The Book of Master Mo Zi, 5th C BCE

∴

'Now being is spoken of in one way as either what or quality or quantity; and in another way in accordance with potentiality and realisation …'
    ARISTOTLE, *Metaphysic*, ca. 330 BCE

'I dwell in Possibility –
A fairer House than Prose –
More numerous for Windows –
Superior – for Doors –'
    EMILY DICKINSON, ca. 1870s)

'Hegel arbitrarily improves the facts … as if all that is rational were also true. Thus he has simultaneously too much world and too little world'.
    ERNST BLOCH, *Geist der Utopie*, 1964 [1919]

'Children dice with the vertebrae of extinct beasts.
The fragile chronicle of our era draws towards an end.
Thanks for what has been:
I too erred, lost my way, got entangled in the account.
The era rang like a golden globe,
A hollow cast, unsupported,
Answering "yes" and "no" whenever touched.
[…]
The sound echoes still, though its cause has vanished.
The steed lies in dust and groans in a lather,
But the tense curve of his neck
Still keeps the memory of a run with rambling feet …
[…]
What I now say isn't said by me,
But excavated from earth, like fossil wheat kernels'.
    OSIP MANDEL'SHTAM, 'Finding a Horseshoe', 1923

CONCLUSION: ON FAILURES AND POTENTIALITIES

'Beim hungern und beim essen
Vorwärts, nicht vergessen
Die Solidarität!'
(When starving or when eating
Forward, not forgetting
Our solidarity!
　　　BERTOLT BRECHT, 'The Solidarity Song', 1930

⁘

'Je suis comme je suis/ Je plais à qui je plais/ ... Que voulez-vous en faire?/ Que voulez-vous de moi?'
　　　JULIETTE GRÉCO, Existentialist chanteuse, Paris soon after 1946; words by
　　　JACQUES PRÉVERT

⁘

'What happens to a dream deferred?

Does it dry up
like a raisin in the sun?
Or fester like a sore –
And then run?
Does it stink like rotten meat?
Or crust and sugar over –
like a syrupy sweet?

Maybe it just sags
like a heavy load.

Or does it explode?'
　　　LANGSTON HUGHES, 1951

In the case treated by this book, it was a dream 'deferred' – that is, denied – in the worst possible way: a dream begun and interrupted unfinished, a dream disappointed from the inside. No wonder it leads to nightmares.

⁘

> 'Those [during socialism] were difficult times, but full of hope. Compared with those hopes, the present seems to me sad and dark'.
>
> KAREL KOSIK, letter to Asja Petrović 2002, in GABRIELLA FUSI, *PRAXIS*, 2012

∴

> 'What if it were the failures [...] of socialists and communists which left in their wake a universal disillusionment in which only consumption and narrow fanaticism (market and confessional) seem possible, at least for the present?'
>
> FREDRIC JAMESON, *The Modernist Papers*, 2007

As Benjamin saw already in Weimar and Nazi times, the final, most radical novelty of the commodity economy is Death. The only way to prevent capitalism from wasting the planet and all our lives is 'the desire called utopia', an opposed and normative system based on use-values: but that is in its final horizons a redefined communism. I shall have much more to say about it in Section 3 of this Conclusion.

14.1 Revisiting Economics, Power, and Politics

14.1.1 *Two Premises*

First, the richest and fairest formulation I know of the post-revolutionary project and problem in an analogous, indeed ancestral, situation, as formulated by E.H. Carr:

> [What the October revolution committed Lenin and his followers to] was nothing less than to make a direct transition from the most backward to the most advanced forms of political and economic organization. Politically, the programme involved an attempt to bridge the gap between autocracy and socialist democracy without the long experience and training in citizenship which bourgeois democracy, with all its faults, had afforded in the west. Economically, it meant the creation of a socialist economy in a country which had never possessed the resources in capital equipment and trained workers proper to a developed capitalist order. These grave handicaps [the revolution] had still to overcome. Its history is the record of its successes and failures in this enterprise.
>
> *Bolshevik* 1: 100–1

CONCLUSION: ON FAILURES AND POTENTIALITIES   283

Second, it should be clearly understood that in the first two decades of SFRY the economic and political gains of the plebeian majority were huge and indeed revolutionary; let me mention only national independence, full employment, free social services – eventually extended to peasants too – and a huge upgrowth of schooling. At least up to the middle 60s, the ruling class formed a historical block with the manual workers and most middle classes in a common effort for a rapid social (productive and cultural) build-up benefiting a large majority. This Conclusion discusses such key achievements but looks backward from the later decay and crash, and thus cannot give these important life enhancements their due prominence. However, in a fair balance, especially today when capitalism is trampling all of them underfoot, they ought to be insisted upon.

14.1.2   Political Economics, the State

A decisive theme of this book may be brought to a point by two of Marx's key insights in political economics. First, that 'It is always the direct relationship of the owners of the conditions of production to the direct producers ... which reveals the innermost secret ... of the entire social structure, and with it the political form of the relations of sovereignty and dependence, the corresponding specific form of the State' (*Capital* III/ch47.hm). Second, capitalism as a system means 'divorcing the producer from the means of production' through a class struggle from above using the State on behalf of the expropriating class (*Capital* I/ ch26.htm); this is not confined to 'primitive' accumulation, we have learned, but is the ongoing underlying principle of all capitalist accumulation. Thus the capitalist legal 'separation of the economic and the political, or the transfer of certain "political" powers to the "economy" and "civil society"' (Wood 14) is the system's constitutive and defining factor, simultaneously exacerbating its division into alienated sub-systems and firmly grounding it in a unity transcending this division.

A communist revolution started, in all extant cases, by sparking an overt class struggle from below through a tightly organised political party in a predominantly peasant and patriarchal society at the periphery of the world system, backward both industrially and agriculturally, which was then further destroyed by war and civil war imposed by imperialism. Any worthwhile mode of living would have to be arrived at by doing after the revolution, almost simultaneously, ***the work of capitalism*** insofar as a 'primitive accumulation' to build up industry and tertiary services was quite indispensable, not least to eventually also achieve a technologised agriculture, as well as ***the work of communism*** by abolishing the Chinese wall between the economic and the political in order to arrive at a new unity of solidarity: this is the central rich but bewildering problem-knot at work after the revolution.[1] Millions of peasants stream into new factories and burgeoning cities, a small or non-existent working class suddenly becomes a huge mass of workers being trained on the job, professionals in teaching, health, and other services have to be created and geared towards the new mass clientele; practice puts on the agenda theoretical problems for which existing epistemology has no answers, so that novums are needed at almost every step; the Party has to supply, train, and/or absorb leading cadre both in politics and in production; and so on.

As against Marx's and Lenin's general and optimistic forecasts – or at least as an important supplement to them – 'socialism [is no] "easy" system which solves all conflicts by the act of "expropriating the expropriators". Such utopian simplifications include ... the view of the extraordinary ease of democratic government of a socialist State' (Brus, *Socialist* 187). 'It is not enough to destroy the old State's repressive apparatus ... A very long time is needed to really put in place wholly new, proletarian political, trade union or schooling systems. First one must know *what* exactly to develop, which new systems to *invent*, and how to develop them. A proper line should be found for each system, *in detail*. Finally one must form a competent staff, loyal to the revolution[, for each] ...' (Althusser, *Reproduction* 125). For a major example, it should be frankly recognised that the Yugoslav working classes in town and country were, as Marx says of the peasants in 1840s France, countrywide 'incapable of asserting their class interest in their own name', and were therefore 'being represented' (*18th Brumaire*, ch. VII) by the Party in power. The working people were poorly communicating among themselves, just emerging out of and in good part still subject to poverty, with an overwhelmingly rural or at best petty artisanal cultural tradition largely useless in urban and industry milieus. They were further isolated on the one hand by the Party/State's neglect of peasantry and its fragmenting stress on the individual competitive enterprises and on irrational republican economic areas, and on the other by its firm suppression of horizontal civic associations whenever they threatened to impinge upon general politics or ide-

---

1   I have suggested in Chapter 1 the overwhelming economico-cultural necessity of tackling this knot in Yugoslavia. The relationship of bourgeois-democratic to socialist revolution, especially in the paradigmatic case of Russia/USSR, was widely debated in the international Left movements before and after the October Revolution, and awaits further clarification. The most important pieces of this uncompleted puzzle were the interventions of Lenin and Trotsky; for the latter this ranges from *The Year 1905* to 'Trois conceptions de la révolution', in his *La révolution* 21–4 and *passim*, and indicative excerpts may be found in the handy anthology by Bongiovanni, 185–99 (see there also the generous but to my mind muddled Gorter, 120–5).

ology, and especially between classes. All of this, and centrally the exigencies of the dual, proto-bourgeois and proto-socialist, revolution made for a strengthening of the State apparatus: the particular ruling group that led the revolution necessarily begins by using the State to expropriate the expropriators. I shall therefore make a brief excursus into the emergence of the State before capitalism, in a parallel situation lacking the separation of economic and political power.

Historically, the State came about, inaugurating class society, as 'the complex of institutions by means of which the power of the society is organised' (Wood 32, citing Morton Fried), that eventually arrogated to itself the monopoly of legal coercion – though plebeian bandits and competing mafias abounded. It was centrally 'a means of appropriating surplus product ... [and] a mode of distributing that surplus', at times also a means of intensifying production to ward off emergencies and increase the surplus (ibidem). In 'Asiatic' social formations it was also a dominant and direct means of surplus appropriation. A remark about them by Marx is directly applicable to socialist States if one substitutes – as I do here – for his example of land the general term of 'means of production': 'Sovereignty here consists in the ownership of [means of production] concentrated on a national scale ... [and] no private ownership of [means of production] exists' (*Capital* III: 791; cf. *Grundrisse*, also Wood 4–36). A further aspect analogous to sovereignty after communist revolutions is that the 'Asiatic' mode of production is also a transitional mixture of classless (tribal) and class elements, where inequality went hand in hand with social diversification and collective safety (cf. Godelier 111 and 118–21). In fact, the European development from the Greco-Roman slave-owning system through feudalism to capitalism is a minority case faced with a welter of 'Asiatic' systems from Bronze Age Greece, Egypt, and West Asia through South and East Asia to South America, not to mention More's *Utopia* and a number of its imaginary successors. We should get rid of either exalting or vilifying this majority of social formations: to my mind, it comprises – *pace* Wittfogel – both benign and malign cases. The twentieth-century socialist parallels to this mode are to a certain extent benign (during the revolution and the first 10 or so years after it, say in Lenin's time) but then in most cases (say in Yugoslavia beginning with the 1960s) develop a malignancy; I debate this in Chapter 6, '15 Theses'.

The historical horizon and *telos* of the communist revolution is for Marx and Lenin, as well as for the plebeian tradition, **direct rule by the associated producers**, where the State should dwindle as the locus of power and decision. '[T]he proletariat needs only a State', concluded Lenin, 'which is ... so constituted that it begins to wither away immediately, and cannot but wither away' (/cho2.htm#s1). But in the conditions of backwardness plus inimical encir-

FIGURE 28 Josip Vaništa, Columbus's Stormy Ship [*This was one of the illustrations by Josip Vaništa commissioned for my book* Od Lukijana do Lunjika *(Zagreb: Lykos, 1965). It accompanied a fragment from Krleža's early play* Kristofor Kolumbo *and represents his ship voyaging on stormy seas to an uncertain goal. I wrote under it a note reading Krleža's early opus – which I had at the time discussed at length – as representing the sharpest conflict between the class actuality of our times vs. a utopian and necessary, humanised reality; that opus's magical asymptote toward the stars was a programme of the still inchoate Croatian plebeian consciousness.*]
ILLUSTRATION FROM D. SUVIN, OD LUKIJANA DO LUNJIKA, 1965

clement, the State apparatus remains indispensable for some crucial functions of protection and coordination, and beyond that tenaciously clings to dominance by absorbing the executive energies of the revolution. What is more, as Bukharin, Lenin, and Trotsky realised during and immediately after World War I, the imperialist Warfare State (to which the Welfare State was later, for a time, added) had changed the rules of the international power and indeed survival game by coordinating the whole economy under the sign of coercion and warfare. It co-opted all significant professional and political organisations, most prominently the organisations of the workers 'transformed into serfs, attached ... to the plant' (Bukharin 13.htm), forging a monolithic embattled nation, covered by the spurious veil of organic corporatism and nationalism. Willy-nilly (in Lenin's case with enthusiasm) the Bolsheviks explicitly latched on to the best known variant, the German State: in Bukharin's terms, they 'nationalised ... all mass organisations of the proletariat' to become the cells and agents 'of the collective reason of the working class, which finds its material embodiment in the highest and most encompassing organisation, in its State apparatus'.[2] In this Platonic statolatry, which under Stalin became if not more efficient certainly more monolithic than the World War I economies, economy overrode democracy. Even the utopian Lenin, fully submerged after 1917 into the grim business of surviving, opined that democracy had no business within production, and little outside it: 'Industry is indispensable, democracy is not', was his pithy if brutal conclusion in the brutal Civil War (*Collected Works* vol. 32: 27, cited in Harding 28). From 1915 on, Lenin's article of faith was that a full-fledged monopoly capitalism needed only political seizure of power by communists in order to turn into socialism (see e.g. 'Impending', 11.htm#v25zz99h-360); this everywhere turned out to be insufficient for the indispensable withering away of the State.

The only brake on the State's immense ruling appetites is the development of a strong democracy from below by politicising both economic production and a 'civil society' – in Gramsci's sense of the decisive bearer of politics after the revolution (cf. Suvin 'Communism') – to which I shall return. While parallels to the first 10 years of the USSR and to Mao's attempts to 'bombard

---

2 The quote is from Bukharin's following book on *Economics of the Transition Period*; I was led to his imprudently enthusiastic sincerity in this matter by Harding 16–18, 24–9, and *passim* (quote from 25), for which I'm grateful, while dissenting with the author's take here and elsewhere on both Marx and Lenin.

   A confession about this Conclusion: at times I could not find a way of formulating certain knots better than I did in the book, and I repeated the formulations. I hope they are, however, within a more precise and conclusive overview than in their original places (which are noted).

the headquarters' are relevant, in Yugoslavia between 1950 and the mid-60s a full-scale start was made toward direct democracy in economic production (and then in important social services). The thesis of this book is that this *self-management could not fight the unholy Party-State union without developing a direct democracy in civil society too*. This was disallowed and quashed by the coercive force of the State, most clearly manifested in suppressing the student revolt in 1968, so that the self-management system inside production was not allowed to evolve vertically towards the power top but fenced in and disintegrated into atomised units. The relations of domination came back with a vengeance. The central lesson to be drawn here is that there is no full socialisation of means of production without a socialisation of the State (that is, massive reduction of its power and ongoing control from below).

Where could both hardware and software for the key industrialisation come from? Again, only from the capitalist experiences, slightly modified in benign cases by earlier working-class struggle against its excesses. In fact, in the seminal USSR of the early 1920s 'measures of productivity as well as the techniques of production were imported from the capitalist countries; ... industrial designers were brought from the United States to plan factories; ... and competition, like incentive, became compulsory' (Zukin 400) – there was no other way. 'Labour mobilisation, economic exchange mechanisms, and the role of the State [had to be improvised] in the absence of the direct economic coercion of capitalism' (ibidem 411), but also – significantly – in the presence of an economic and power encirclement by capitalist States and markets. The central choice was between physical coercion by a hugely burgeoning State with its organs for violence (Stalinism) and a measure of workers' self-management plus material incentives (attempted in SFRY).

In these straits, what becomes of class relationships and struggles? What of economic development and success? And what could and should be the role of an integral plebeian democracy in such socialism anyway?

14.1.3 *Classes*

If class consciousness and salient class actions exist only in relation to other social groups, as I argue in Chapters 3–4, then, for concrete historical societies, Marx's shorthand of defining class in relation to the means of production ought to be interpreted in the sense that 'economic exploitation is the initiating impulse that constitutes classes; but they then form sociological structures which have ... a specific reality and stability' (Adler 104). Classes must therefore be integrated – as Marx did in his splendid historical interventions – into all the pertinent mediations of political power and economic exploitation, in order to richly show the main lines of social development; and furthermore, for SFRY, into the initially fluid relationships of potentiality and choice, where all classes were *in statu nascendi.** The society was pregnant with choices, classes, paths, alternatives, often coexisting as different lures in the breast of each separate yet tightly interrelated and co-defined group. A focus on the Party top, evolving by its symbiosis with State power into an **oligarchy** (rather than a bureaucracy, as I argue in Appendix 2, 'The Discourse on Bureaucracy'), and on the junior partner of an eventually evolving managerial '**technocracy**', by itself cannot provide a satisfactory explanation: the role and interests of at least the peasants and the various sub-classes of manual workers, plus those of women and the 'middle' classes such as the intelligentsia, have to be integrated into the explanation. This is a daunting task for which I have been able to provide at best some suggestive probes. On their basis I shall here sketch some conclusions.

Radical revolutions eliminate whole huge power complexes, such as the monarchy, the mandarinate or the private corporations, but what they create in their place grows out of a legacy of centuries: from a long-duration culture of human behaviour, of divisions of labour, age and gender relations, taboos and myths. These are in continuous feedback with endogenous and exogenous structural constraints of economic and power (often military) survival. There is to begin with a wholesale promotion of the revolutionary generation to positions of power and prestige, that is, rapid upward class mobility from peasantry and a small working class to the middling executive and to a minor degree even to the ruling class. But this rupture is, first of all, historically due to 'nonrepeating causes' (Moore 244, cf. Skocpol *passim*) such as heavy war casualties, primitive accumulation of capital, and building up a new politico-economical machine in lieu of the smashed one. Second, this no doubt new history is, semiotically speaking, susceptible to becoming a change of surface agents rather than a permanently revolutionising change of deep-seated types (Marx called them *Charaktermasken*): of actors and not roles.[3] As a corollary, the peasants very soon devolve from the revolution's main armed and ideological support to a sidelined class, often actively harassed by accumulation necessities and ideological prejudices; and yet, the patriarchal peasant culture is immensely powerful in countries where almost every family – except in part for the numerically slender immigrant petty bourgeoisie – is, or was one or two

---

3 The semiotics of agents I derived in the 1960s–70s is much richer than the actantial level presented in Chapter 1 and picked up later in this conclusion, for it comprises two more levels: of 'types' and 'characters' (Suvin 'How'). For the historical aspect, see Moore *passim* – the quote is from 244 – on the paradigmatic USSR, and Skocpol *passim*.

generations ago, a peasant smallholder family. In parallel, the upward mobility of manual workers to the 'middle' classes (to technicians and lower managers) slowed after the early 1960s to a trickle.

My conclusion from Chapter 4 on was that by 1971 a proper class pyramid had developed in SFRY. Of a total population of 20.5 million, it reposed on two large lower classes: first, 7.5 million *peasant smallholders* (to which in the statistics ca. 0.5 million private artisans in cities were adjoined); second, ca. 7 million *manual workers* (in industry, transport, building, services). I calculated the *ruling class*, including families, at 0.5 to 0.8 million, and the various *middle or intermediary classes* (including technicians in production) at 4.5 to 5.5 million (all urban statistics are approximate as the SFRY ones lumped all employed people, from unskilled worker to top manager, into one group). Swift upward social mobility for workers and peasants was in the first 20 years a mass phenomenon, and the original nucleus of the ruling class was of worker and peasant provenience, though with an important share of intellectuals and employees. Even if after the first dozen years the invocation of moral superiority of the proletariat and of manual labour (cf. Tamás 112–13) became hypocritical, it still remained, as long ago La Rochefoucauld put it, a tribute paid by vice to virtue.

Furthermore, several classes or class fractions were at the time still 'in relatively undefined or even contradictory class locations' (Zukin 401). Considering both vertical mobility trends (up and less frequently down) and horizontal solidarity connexions, in my judgment the situation was as follows:

The 'manual workers' or non-agricultural working classes were clearly subdivided, I argue in Chapter 3.2, by earning and status, and then gender and age, into perhaps five fractions. At the bottom were the 'unskilled' workers, mainly fresh from lower schools and/or villages, often 'peasant workers' shuttling between land and factory. Then the 'semi-skilled' workers, as a rule commuting from villages or from shanty suburbs around the town but no longer working on the land. Women workers, approximately 30% of the whole, were legally equal but burdened with the second job of housekeeping and thus, except in the branches where they constituted a majority (such as textile industries), rather sidelined, paid on the average clearly less, and with promotion to the coveted 'highly skilled' category usually hitting a glass ceiling. These three fractions constituted probably more than half of the employed manual workers (indeed, together with young workers and apprentices I would think 60–75%), and from the first two plus peasants were recruited most of the *Gastarbeiter* abroad, mainly in central Europe. After the mid-60s, and especially after the return of many *Gastarbeiter* following the 1973 recession, SFRY saw the rise not only of statistically visible unemployment but also of a class fraction of seasonal workers and similar sub-proletarian groups from the 'southern' republics, increasingly outside the legal payment and representation norms, that is, subject to surplus exploitation. To the contrary, the 'skilled' and especially the 'highly skilled' workers were those most active in self-management and most upwardly mobile to 'middle' managerial or Party jobs, or alternatively most likely to engage in strikes for better compensation.

However, the contradiction between the ideologically highest status of 'working class' and its much smaller economic and political weight has not yet been properly explored. It will not do to take seriously either the official Party and State propaganda or Post-Modernist cynicism about it all being window-dressing. The element of class alliance between the ruling oligarchy and fully employed manual workers led to a situation where 'Yugoslav workers now [ca. 1970 – DS] enjoy a degree of control over the job situation much greater than that available to their peers in other societies, capitalist or communist', as Parkin observed (305). To my mind there was a social alliance comprising also most fractions of the middle class, though as concerns the workers (and the humanist intelligentsia) the alliance attenuated at the end of the 60s and probably lapsed during the 70s. A good index of this may be the contrast in the handling of strikes: in the first dozen years, up to roughly 1972/73, they were hastily ended by granting the monetary demands; at the end, as in the famous Labin mine strike of the 80s (see Kuzmanić), they were repressed. If we had better statistics for the whole SFRY which would confirm those of the Split region (Vušković 36), it might be found that by the mid-70s, with a politically blocked self-management, the fractions below the 'skilled workers' were near to or under the poverty line, while the skilled and in part even the highly skilled workers were getting perilously close to it. In this situation, unimaginable 10 years earlier, the only politics of a majority was one of hedgehog survival – that is, they ceased to be active in politics, just as the peasants had a quarter of a century earlier. On the other hand, indications from studies such as Lazić's, and from the Vukovar and Labin strikes in the 80s applauded across SFRY public opinion, point to a loyalty of the working class to the original idea of self-management.

The intermediate classes comprised, as noted in Chapter 3, rather different fractions: the humanist intelligentsia, to begin with strongly loyal but potentially most deviant from orthodoxy; the technical and medical intelligentsia, jealous of its status and privileges but willing to follow the ruling class insofar as these were not touched; the lower technicians and employees, recently risen from the two lower classes, differentiating themselves from them by life-style and economically by the spouse's employment (Vušković 35), but with smaller prestige than other intermediate classes; and finally, the higher administrators in production (the upper reaches of engineers and white-collar workers, and the managers), with far greater financial incentives – especially the partly hidden perks – and real executive powers within workplace limits. The apices of this last group already constitute, together with the lower power-wielders in politics, the lower and middle reaches of the ruling class.

As to the ruling class, the eventually frozen Party/State establishment, I found (see especially Chapter 10.4.4) that the post-1965 differentiation into politocracy and technocracy was of secondary importance for SFRY problems at the time, though perhaps crucial for its demise. The 'technocrats' had little to do with either hard or soft sciences, rather they were the republican and high local managers in alliance with local politocrats. This alliance kept snipping away at the federally centred politocracy, and eventually evolved in the richer republics into secessionist proto-comprador classes. The rulers were not a capitalist class, since they did not possess the means of production, and could neither destroy nor personally inherit any. However, 'social ownership ... is not at all the same as social appropriation' (Magri 1091): except for the personally minimal private property of peasants and artisans, the disposal over both the means of production and the surplus from labour was in the hands of a *sui generis** ruling class. When fully constituted, as of ca. 1972, it was ***a politocratic oligarchy***, defined by being professional politicians and having these decisive powers, which also involved material and prestige privileges. Its class interest was to have a full monopoly of public leadership and domination, or negatively that self-management should never become a vertically integrated plebeian self-government.[4]

It should be clear from discussions in the book that social consciousnesses were of great, sometimes decisive weight in specifying class. The two major plebeian classes, peasants and workers, showed no full class consciousness but let themselves 'be represented'. Further, understanding the role of consciousness is complicated by the importance explicit – but often misleading – theorisation plays in socialist societies (cf. the pioneering hints in Zukin 395 and *passim*). The 'Party line', as well as attempts to change or indeed transcend it, often became explicitly integrated into immediate or long-range material and political practices. Real dilemmas of interests and choices were encoded in such often leaden, but sometimes also surprisingly auroral, debates; the latter are to be found in Yugoslavia in the 1941 'national liberation' slogans and in the work of Boris Kidrič on economico-political organisation, both developed at some

---

4 I acknowledge a stimulus for this final definition from criticisms and analyses of the Praxis group, in this case primarily of Marković's 'Socijalizam'.

length in Chapters 1 and 5. The leaden caution is to be explained by what was at stake – no less than the life or death of the social project: writings theorising a revolution while it lasts are a kind of trek on a small path high upon the watershed, where abysses threaten right and left, and both deviations and hesitations may be deadly. Explaining does not mean condoning: for the dominant mentality, closer to the pole of false consciousness, I have used semantic critiques, mainly of the very revealing Kardelj, in order to advance hypotheses about the otherwise hermetically sealed debates within, and insoluble contradictions of, the oligarchy and the social system for given touchy matters.

14.1.4 *A Brief Balance of SFRY Socialism*

It follows from the longer arguments about economics vs. self-government and disalienation in this book that economic success was the animating force for and at least one of the decisive factors in the life and death of 'socialist' systems in Europe, here including SFRY except where it is expressly exempted. In the next paragraph I paraphrase – and supplement – the best balance of 'socialist' economics I know of, Wlodzimierz Brus's final word (with Kazimierz Laski) in 1989:

The strategy of economic modernisation had for its pivot rapid industrialisation through massive investments in new capacities, prioritising heavy industry and extractive industries (partly because of military necessities, which were a heavy burden). This resulted over a period of two to three decades in impressive rates of overall industrial growth, accompanied by most rapid urbanisation and full employment (job security) in towns, a more equitable income scale and lack of enormous wealth differences, and in general a degree of social security only approximated in a few capitalist Welfare States. However, planning based on material bulk had, together with clear initial successes, two fatal drawbacks. First, it failed in respect of the cost of growth: inputs of labour, material, and capital in relation to output vastly exceeded those in capitalist countries at a similar economic level; in other words, productivity often fell, at some points after ca. 1965 more quickly. Second, a command economy from top down meant an oppressive command polity or State dictatorship (Stalinism), which left little room for spontaneous activity from below. Foreign trade remained in part semi-colonial, exporting mainly primary commodities and importing high technology plus licences. Environmental costs were not at all factored in, though socialism was supposed to do exactly that. Homegrown technology and innovations never took off: 'there is not a single case of leapfrogging into frontier technologies (like electronics, plastics, man-made fibres or new pharmaceuticals)' (32, and cf. 23–4, 32–5, and 38–9). Thus, a number of countries starting from a low level reached a welcome but modest middle affluence, yet 'catching up' with affluent capitalism never happened, and was anyway probably a wrong economistic idea. Finally, the misguided turn in the 70s to 'import-led growth' was a sign of loss of nerve and severely exposed the deficiencies of the economic system.

This hard-nosed approach by Brus and Laski renounces all talk of ideals and ethics. But people are not Benthamite robots, and the perennial lower-class rebellion against intolerable oppression and yearning for a just society *before* the revolution together with the ongoing need for people's motivated participation *after* the revolution – that is, the horizon of disalienation of labour as well as of politics – can only be satisfied by the maximum self-government possible. To the contrary (as Engels warned, see in Chapter 12.2), in monopolistic public ownership the dominance 'can be far more relentless', as it disposes of an 'instrument of *economic coercion*' which 'the State can directly link to further *political coercion*', sometimes including a de facto liquidation of freedom of speech and right of assembly (Brus, *Socialist* 17–18). Marx's critique directed at private ownership of means of production thus applies to all subordination and exploitation of labour. This is of a piece with a critique of monocratic State power (here: State/Party power) as the other face of the Stalinist coercive model. I speak to politics in other parts of this Conclusion, but even concerning only economic efficiency it becomes obvious that no information feedback will be forthcoming within planning unless people below the top are motivated by enthusiasm and incentives, and free from the dread of police reprisals. No socialist country or communist party managed to understand that as of the World Wars we crucially live in a 'knowledge economy', which ought to be consciously assumed in tandem with associational democracy from below.

Nonetheless, self-management in SFRY led during a dozen years to a 'Japanese style' growth, expunging the inefficiency of command planning through social solidarity and technical progress, clearly superior to pre-World-War-2 comprador capitalism (see the argument in Chapter 12 and its Table 12.1). True, this happened with favourable worldwide presuppositions:

> the miracle years of ... roughly 1950–73 ... depended not only on a world war and an enormous uptick in state spending, but also on an historically unprecedented transfer of population from agriculture to industry. Agricultural populations proved to be a potent weapon in the quest for 'modernization', since they provided a source of cheap labour ...
> BENANAV et al. 1

However, such possibilities could be exploited largely or not at all. In SFRY, they were exploited very usefully.

A sympathetic foreign researcher studied in 1967–8 a number of Yugoslav industrial enterprises and concluded that self-management had the following potentials: it precludes monopolisation of power, involving all in setting goals; it creates a learning environment favourable for coping with new conditions and thus 'encourages the search for objective truth, [based on] full disclosure in information'; it enhances capital formation through sacrifice, also encourages group entrepreneurship and management, both important for 'developing nations'; finally, it is humanistic: it might restore in people the sense of fulfilling their own purpose (Adizes, in Mann Borgese & idem eds. 149–51; cf. more from him and others in Chapter 9.2). However, after the failed reforms of the early 1960s, the embryonic self-management was shut into an 'Indian reservation' in favour of an unworkable hybrid system which combined strong elements of etatism in politics and ideology, expanding elements of capitalism in the commodity and market economy as well as in mass culture, co-management on the lowest level of work organisation and cultural activities (but not in politics), and a sad decline in fostered, and soon even in permitted, public theorising about the bewildering changes.

The etatism was, not so slowly but quite surely, shifting from federal centre to constituent republics. In an unholy spiral of particularist and protectionist economics and politics, SFRY was falling apart long before the 1990s, as 'elites in individual republics ... were opting for a fragmented integration into world capitalism' (Schierup, 'Prelude' 90, and more in it *passim*). Even the common PTT, rail, and energy systems fell apart into shards. The 'new regimes' in the republics in the 1970s–80s led to 'a ruling combination of neo-Stalinist voluntarism and patriarchally territorialized corporatism', subordination to the loans and technology of foreign capital, and in the end to closed, separate republican economies and to Yugoslavia's 're-peripheralisation' (Strpić 32, and cf. both titles by Ocić). The increasingly sundered republican sub-economies were more and more dependent upon foreign capital and isolated from each other. This led not only to a full withering away of plebeian powers in self-management, but also to a full paralysis of State-wide (federal) planning and any consistent federal policy, accompanied by huge economic waste (cf. Horvat's thorough *Business*). The common SFRY market for commodities and services fragmented while organisational and infrastructural ties, such as inter-republican capital transfers, and economic integration in general languished: 'the Yugoslav economy lost the effects of increasing economies of scale and of ... functional specialization ... [The enterprises] and political power structures [would] fiercely guard their own local "home" markets while fighting and undercutting one another ... on the world market' (Schierup, ibidem 95–6, cf. also Korošić and Schierup, 'Quasi'). When each republic had its own, jealously protected foreign currency account, no common stance towards the world market but competitive antagonism prevailed. True, in the 1970s the GNP in industry continued its considerable growth on inherited strong bases, but this was, first, made possible by foreign loans and remittances from workers abroad, and second, it led to rampant capitalisation and ideological privatisation – evident, for example, in the hypertrophy of competition for private cars while basic elements of collective welfare such as public transport and public housing were neglected. The downturn after the mid-60s was a 'reorganization as destructuration' (Schierup, 'Prelude' 109) that gradually jettisoned any socialist horizons and developed into utter economic disaster, evident in huge outlays for repaying loans and in inflation. Finally, '[t]he republics manoeuvered the State [as a whole] into the deadly trap of [foreign] debt' (Calic 256).

In particular, from the mid-60s on any rational approach to the transfer of technology from capitalism collapsed, shedding all considerations of its consequences: there was no inkling that technology is frozen productive relations, only wholesale acceding to the capitalist conditions for its use and repayment. As opposed to the efforts towards a coherent domestic technological system fostered by Kidrič (see Chapter 5), this reduced domestic innovation to practically zero and led to 'outspoken technological dependency, stagnating autonomous development of technology in Yugoslavia and decreasing competitive power on foreign market' (Schierup, ibidem 97, also 119, and see Černe, *Jugoslovansko* 414 and Đurek) – in fact, a falling back into full, if not yet fully apparent, semi-colonial economic status.

The reason for the Yugoslav economic slowdown and political disaggregation was a crystallisation of class interests, by which the oligarchic system became the chief brake of social economic development. The ruling class/es and the new bourgeoisie got noticeably richer: a clearly capitalist mentality was developing in the private sector, in the 'socialised' sector by 1971 a 15:1 gap obtained between the highest and the lowest incomes, and shady deals proliferated between the two sectors, while unemployment and immiseration began to burgeon in the lower reaches of the working class. By the mid-70s, bases for an exploitative class system were put into place with the uncontrolled rise of credit capital in the 'republicanised' banks as well as of private construction and catering. Subalternity to the wrong IMF recipes of cutting budget deficits and tariffs was the final nail in the coffin.

To conclude: 'the "self-management" reforms of the 1970s, and their unintended aftermath of bureaucratic resurrection at the republican level, merely intensified some of the more negative consequences of the economic reforms of the 1960, locking and petrifying them into a stagnant bureaucratic iron grip ...' (Schierup, ibidem 117). In the catastrophic 1980s, 10% of the richest people in SFRY possessed more than did over 40% of the poorest people, no better than in capitalism (Calic 279–80). Should anyone have purposed to ruin the Yugoslav federation and the whole idea of SFRY, politics and economics should have been developed exactly as they were from 1972 on – or already from 1965.

Yet the hopes, the early achievements, and the potentialities were great. Even from a quasi-Keynesian point of view, it is quite clear that the only way of raising the living standard in Europe East of Germany was a 'Russian style' rate of planned capital investment for more than 10 years or 'Big Push' (cf. Rosenstein-Rodan 203, 211, and *passim*) – which was done. It led to 'an Industrial Revolution in one generation' (Dirlam & Plummer 15). I believe there was a good chance that intelligent cooperation of all plebeian classes in an open-society atmosphere could have coped with the never solved problems of capital flow coupled with fair employment opportunities (cf. Brus & Laski 117–31), and other conundrums of economics. And the disappointment is correspondingly huge.

Montesquieu put it precisely:

> In a people's State, another resource [beyond the force of laws and the force of arms] is needed, which is *Virtue* ... When it ceases, ambition enters into the hearts which can aspire to it, and avarice into all hearts. The desires change their object: what was loved once is loved no longer ... In the past the good of individuals made for public treasure; but as of now, public treasure becomes the heritage of individuals. The republic becomes a spoil (*dépouille*); and its force is no more than the power of some citizens and the licence of all.
> 1:145

Does my argument solve whether 'socialism in one country', anyway much smaller than Stalin's one sixth of the world, was feasible? No, it does not, for this is a wrongly posed question. It conflates, as Löwy argues (even though I do not completely share his terms), 'two different sets of questions ... first, the possibility of an isolated workers' state surviving for some extended historical period; and second, the potentiality for achieving a completed socialist society in a single country' (71–2). Since for Marx the second set involves the disappearance of commodity production and money, such perfectly 'achieved socialism' is unfeasible in one country or indeed any group of countries depending on exchange with capitalism. To the contrary, the first set is to be answered in terms of contingent power relations, so that I do not see why it would be a priori unfeasible; it is a subset of the problem of 'future sea-battles' (see Chapter 5.1 and note 9 below).

14.2   Human Creativity as Emancipation

Though it is indispensable to clarify matters of political economics, power, class conflicts and regroupings, and ideology, these are to my mind **means** to the goal of human liberation. All are crucial mediations in the emancipative disalienating of human creativity – an exodus from bondage that alone confers full sense upon the means. I therefore collocate their further treatment, and in particular the stress upon self-determination and self-government (leading to direct communist democracy), within the horizon of creative disalienation.

I have argued at length (at the beginning of Part 3.2) how Marx, though focussing on the analysis of labour and capital, never doubted that full associational democracy would necessarily follow the lead of an emancipated labour process. While understanding fully that 'Power ... itself is an economic potency' (*Potenz* – *Capital* 1/ ch. 24), he brushed off politics as bound with class society. We have however learned that, within the process of overcoming class society, assuming and developing the glorious *citoyen* tradition is just as necessary – in other words, that the conscious assumption of capillary participation must proceed at the same time if the reorganisation of production is to succeed, so that the insufficient bourgeois 'formal' freedoms have to be transcended while observing them fully. As Luxemburg advocated, the proletariat must 'walk with both feet', namely undertake both the economic and the political struggle (cited in Supek 45). Politics cannot be confined exclusively to Party/State rule and hidden internal squabbles, as in the ossified USSR and finally also SFRY, but ought to continue Lenin's confidence that the Party can be a ruler because the masses will control it from below. Yet even Lenin never managed '[to link or integrate] his doctrine of the party with his account of the soviets' (Anderson 116). Thus we must today speak about not only the aspects of 'relationships of production' present **within production** but also how they complexly intertwine with the aspects **outside production**. This is true even for capitalism, but it holds in spades for 'socialist' societies, which always began with the fusion of the apparatuses of the workplace with those of the State.

Self-management in production is not enough nor can it succeed on its own. After all, nobody is only a worker without also being a member of several overlapping communities: consumer, family member, citizen (*citoyen*), and most important a person with given needs and desires. In all such roles humans have a creative potential which is not to be confined to Adam Smith's – and often, but not always, Marx's – narrow definition of what is economically productive, i.e., that it bring capitalist profit: one can produce, or create, both chairs and love, observed Brecht.[5] Or Preve: the steam machine is a 'productive force', but

---

5 See a discussion of Marx in Suvin *Defined*, esp. Section 15, and of Brecht in Suvin 'Living'

so are Enlightenment and Marxism (*Passione* 138). The central historical contradiction in our time between forces and relationships of production is not simply one between capitalists and proletarians, albeit this to my mind remains an essential component, but the much wider and deeper one *between human creativity in the working people vs. the alienating fetters laid upon them in dominated relationships both within production and within civil society*, increasingly enforced by the capillary State in the service of sterile capital. Can the relation of people to State-cum-capital in order to liberate Prometheus be rethought around a disalienating *self-government* by tying economic into political democracy, in the manner of a double helix? For, 'there will be no democracy at all, if the freedom of the producer is not accompanied and underpinned by the freedom of the citizen' (Bobbio 45). This self-government can only properly function when built vertically up from below – by economic branches, and where needed also territorial areas not necessarily identical to the existing federal republics – so that its highest federal organs would replace or be the ministries of a liquefying State, when they would begin by disposing of 70% of national income, as foreseen by the failed 1965 reform, and when the delegates in Workers' Councils as well as in all higher units would work for a skilled worker's income without further material privileges (cf. Kidrič in Chapter 5.2 and Marković 61–2).

The fusion of politics inside and outside economic production yet without State domination comports, if it really occurs without state domination, the possibility of a full release of plebeian political energies moving upward to the ruling top. Here I in part repeat the lessons of Gramsci developed in Part 3.2, and in particular that politics is 'the central human activity, the means by which the single consciousness is brought into contact with the social and natural world', since in it 'understanding the world and changing it are one', and that '[t]his applies to the construction of socialism as well as – perhaps more than – anywhere else' (Hobsbawm, *How* 321). The 'action and force of the proletariat' is for Gramsci embodied in a State of Councils (thus modifying Engels's and Lenin's prognosis that the State shall die out as unnecessary), built up by means of 'the organisation of workers and peasants on the level of production units (factory, agricultural enterprise, village, city, region, nation) *aiming to train the masses for self-government simultaneously in the industrial and in the political field*' (*Ordine* 104, emphasis mine; cf. a more detailed articulation in

---

and 'Brecht'. The relationship between people's various social roles requires further central articulation (as begun in Elson and Horvat, see in particular Chapter 10), including the use of gender theory.

752–3). In other words, socialism is (becoming) classless insofar as it is a *society of empowered producers*: 'Economic decisions ... are not controlled by a market but through a political process and reflect producers' rather than consumers' preferences as to what constitutes ... "socially useful" production' (Comisso, *Workers'* 13). Gramsci represents that rare stance which insists on class conflicts yet, as Hobsbawm encapsulates, fully recognises that *politics involve more than class repression*: that is, social *production*, in which politics is the articulation of how to go about deciding it. In States not having undergone a full bourgeois revolution, such as Italy, this entailed 'the creation of a people, the realisation of a nation' (Hobsbawm, *How* 330) – as it did in more complex, multinational ways in SFRY.

No doubt, socialist societies lagged behind the bourgeois attention to power through political framework and mechanisms because at first they had to concentrate on keeping power and on planning the economy. However, even the classical means of production (factories, land, etc.) are not really socialised unless they are managed and determined by a genuine self-government of all the working people concerned. This applies to micro-decisions in each enterprise but then, crucially, also to the economic macro-decisions – setting up the rules of accumulation, organisation, taxation, etc., for the economy as a whole. The first part was attempted in SFRY, the second not really (though it was clearly sketched in the astounding horizon of Kidrič's); therefore the whole could not succeed. Yet the alienating contradictions between individual workers and the social tasks of production can only be overcome by a thoroughly political feedback between the self-managers and the State executive. This entails 'a genuine democratisation of the system for the exercise of State power' (Brus, 'Commodity' 66, and cf. *passim*) – a giant step toward the famous withering away of the State's oppressive command. But this can only come about by strong political pressure from below.

The self-management concept in USSR after the October Revolution consisted of three prongs of spontaneous working-class governmentality: the Workers' Councils or Soviets as organs of territorial rule; the Trade Unions; and the Factory Committees. These comprised all factory employees in procedures of direct rather than representative democracy, and were thus an excellent possibility of reducing not only the deep physical misery of the manual workers but also the wider 'moral and civic' misery of *all* the salaried people within authoritarian and hierarchical organisations (Supek 139, see also 60–1 and 141). However, the last two prongs foundered in heroic but frustrated efforts to cope with the economic macro and micro-decisions, soon usurped by the central government first for civil war and survival necessities, and then for the interests of the new ruling class being born. Simultaneously, the Soviets were first backgrounded and then hollowed out by the etatised Party. Yet the USSR Factory Committees and the Yugoslav Workers' – and other working people's – Councils were the needed way for meshing the bourgeois-democratic revolution (capturing State power) with the communist revolution (giving power to the direct producers and their organisational systems). Politically and epistemologically speaking, *the interests of the working people are in the long run incompatible with a management of the economy which is still dominated by the mechanism of capital reproduction, and with the management of social life still dominated by secrecy and monolithism.* Capital means the power of command over labour and its products, wrote Marx in many variants (for example *Capital 1*: ch11.htm; this is well argued by Horvat, *Essay* 134): the emancipation of labour, the centrepiece of disalienation, means that *labour (the proletariat) commands itself.* To that end, any national community or State must have sovereign decisions at its centre – a matter sorely lacking in SFRY after 1965.

A kind of market, I have argued, was indispensable in a subordinate role: as Trotsky had envisaged, 'the plan is checked and, to a considerable degree, realised through the market'; the 'economy of the transitional period' requires 'the interaction of ... State planning, the market, and Soviet democracy' (Samary, electronic p. 19, citing his 1932 article 'The Soviet Economy in Danger'). The market is no panacea: it does not favour anything requiring long-run estimates of collective needs, such as the building of lodgings, sewers, communication networks, schools, parks, hospitals, child-care centres or even hydroelectric stations. On the contrary, today we desperately need a 'demarketisation of subsistence' (McNally 202); I mentioned Polanyi's arguments in that vein in Part 3, and he remains a needed beacon.[6] Non-market solidarity in highly developed forms of social security, including *de facto* compensations for the still inevitable inequalities of income, is decisive for the long-term growth of a socialist economy and for elementary social cohesion (cf. the argument in Brus, 'Commodity' 61–4). I agree with Samary's conclusion that the 'socialist project' requires (among her other items) 'rejecting the rule of capital markets' in favour of 'human control over daily life and the future' (electronic p. 27). Or as Stojanović, somewhat despairingly, hoped: 'Cannot one have ... *the fully self-governed society, that considers social development, including the market, that plans, controls, and guides?*' (*Kritik* 213–14).

---

6   Today however, in the Post-Fordist regime of accumulation dominated by globalised finance and in a different political climate, Nancy Fraser's suggestion that we return to emancipation rather than State protection as our basic principle seems better suited, and I regret I read her too late for more articulated embedding into my argument.

True, both democracy and communism, the two great attempts at collective power, have led to violent catastrophes, as Jacques Rancière noted in a recent interview (Belgrade, April 2010). I believe this is because democracy and communism were sundered instead of fused, both in the civic and economic sub-systems. The first of these domains is political (about power), and I shall pursue it in the rest of this Conclusion. The second is anthropological (about labour), and I cannot fully develop it. But beside the brief vectors in my book, it can be identified by one of the central orientations within the plebeian upsurge between Babeuf and Allende: William Morris's 'Useful Work *versus* Useless Toil'. He demolishes the argument 'that all labour is good in itself – a convenient belief to those who live on the labour of others', and posits a division announced in his title:

> [O]ne [that is, useful work] has hope in it, the other [that is, useless toil] has not ... What is the nature of the hope which, when it is present in work, makes it worth doing?// It is threefold, I think – hope of rest, hope of product, hope of pleasure in the work itself; and hope of these also in some abundance and of good quality; rest enough and good enough to be worth having; product worth having by one who is neither a fool nor an ascetic; pleasure enough for all for us to be conscious of it while we are at work [...]

> [...] But a man at work, making something which he feels will exist because he is working at it and wills it, is exercising the energies of his mind and soul as well as of his body. Memory and imagination help him as he works. Not only his own thoughts, but the thoughts of the men of past ages guide his hands; and, as a part of the human race, he creates ... All other work but this is worthless; it is slaves' work – mere toiling to live, that we may live to toil.

Thence Morris proceeds into a whole small overview of commodity production by and for different classes, into which all my conclusions should be inserted had we but world enough and time.

This book does not discuss the future, in particular the misanthropy of 'post-communism', yet the lessons of the past are to be learned in view of a better future. Both the past and the future have beyond a 'really existing' aspect (historical in the first case and imaginary in the other) also a 'being in possibility', Aristotle's *dynamei on*. I shall therefore turn to what the SFRY object-lesson can illuminate about why and how this key, indispensable fusion should and probably could have come about.

14.3 The Communist Party and Plebeian Democracy: Power and Value

14.3.0

Some readers might feel too much space is devoted in this book to the communist party. No doubt, this has to do with the writer's life experience. But beyond it, in the rich and contradictory system that was SFRY social life, the CPY/LCY was the system-driver.

14.3.1 *Lessons from the SFRY Communist Party Trajectory*

The pivot is here Lenin's invention of *a vanguard party for the revolution* (cf. Suvin 'On the Concept'). In Chapter 7 I approached its functioning and some central problems. Yet I believe the conundrum it poses – *nec tecum nec sine te*, I cannot live either with or without you* – is both crucial and quite unsolved. If one is assuming the need of a liberating revolution for a chance at disalienation, as I am, then it ought to be faced explicitly.

There are today two inescapable questions about Lenin's great Fordist invention. *First*, is the invention a long-duration one, coterminous with and indispensable for all revolutions (Leninist or not) needed to dispossess capitalism, or a short-duration one, indispensable for economically backward States and within the Fordist phase of competing imperialisms?

Most people on the Left would today plump for the second answer. Yet all the alternatives – the social democrats, the anarchists, and their cousins of the 'Seattle movements' – have failed just as badly and are continuing to fail, without any signs of redemption. More precisely, we have to ask then: indispensable for what? My answer would be, for radical collective emancipation from war and ecocide brought about by capitalism, from the untold psychophysical miseries of hundreds of millions – who are if not 99% then surely 95% of human kind. Industrial capitalism offends grievously reason and values, it either destroys or perverts cognition and ethics; financial capitalism multiplies this by the speed of light. 'On all levels, on all scales, everything is permitted: speculation, extortion, provocations, destabilisations, blackmail, massive deportations, genocide ... The ferocious will to a "death of politics" is nowhere more dominant than in the Ice Palaces of power' (Guattari & Negri 61 and 36, and cf. also 37, 47–50, 60–1, and 145). Therefore, we must return to the roots, which Robespierre brilliantly posed in his speech of 2 December 1792:

> What is the first aim of society? To maintain the inalienable rights of man. What is the first among these rights? The right to exist.// The first law of society is therefore to guarantee all of its members the means to exist; all other laws are subordinated to it; property has been instituted or

guaranteed only in order to strengthen it ... Any commercial speculation that I engage in at the expense of my fellow man's life is not trafficking, it is brigandage and fratricide.
227

And in his speech of 24 April 1793, he proposed four articles to codify the above stance, of which I cite the last three:

II. The right to property is limited, as all other rights, by the duty to respect others' rights.
III. It cannot harm the safety, nor the freedom, nor the existence, nor the property of our fellow men.
IV. Any possession, any traffic that violates this principle is illicit and immoral.
246

Even more urgently, today an efficient antagonist is indispensable against the quickly advancing moulting of capitalism into a combination of the worst traits of class societies: slavery, neo-feudalism based on corporation lordship, and constant warfare, all fuelled by unceasing pursuit of unnecessary profit for parasites; serfdom and social collapse are back on the social horizon, hunger and other epidemics are looming. Time is fast running out for inverting such a kidnap of history before habitat destruction of geological proportions and a split of humanity into perhaps genetically engineered overlords and a squalid mass of literal proletarians (and many other horrors we do not yet conceive of) bring centuries of a bloody, cybernetic and nanogenetic, Iron Heel. My answer depends, then, on two factors. I consider the dangers as overwhelming and a confrontation with them as urgent; no Fabian tactics apply. I further consider that the communist parties' moment between the successful revolution and their core constituting itself into a new ruling class was a largely emancipatory and fertile one, indicative of major potentials for a firm alliance of plebeian classes in feedback with a responsive and renewable vanguard. As Merleau-Ponty noted, this is the essence of the revolution and – citing Michelet about the French Revolution – 'the moment ... when one glimpses "a revolution within the revolution" ... unknown depths, abysses of future' (289).

For such reasons, I plump for the other answer: we have to investigate the hypothesis that the invention of the vanguard party might be a long-duration one. There is no alternative.

Second however, in that case another question becomes mandatory: Given that Lenin's early model was well attuned to the social stall before 1905 (cf.

Preve, *Filo* 187–8), but itself changing with the situations between 1903 and 1923 – how far must such a model be renewed in order to be still useful as a leader (a party and a movement) in very different societies? On the one hand people and political movements are caught in a much more effective vice of global warfare, turbocapitalism, and huge immiseration of all below the top, on the other hand they are in some cases at a higher rung of economic development and complexity, and in opposition to encroaching Leviathans in much greater and more pressing need of free choice and information for it. The question is, still more precisely: how can involution of the vanguard – that is, of the permanent core of a mass post-revolutionary communist party – into an oligarchy be continually counteracted in practice? A key answer is: communism needs today to insist on its *difference from capitalism* by resolutely endorsing a disalienation of what the latter suppresses or marginalises, which is – beside economic justice, ecological care, and disarmament – also effective political democracy:

> [The] social relations [of capitalism] have both advanced and strictly limited democracy, and the greatest challenge to capitalism would be an extension of democracy beyond its narrowly circumscribed limits. It is at this point that 'democracy' arguably becomes synonymous with socialism.
> WOOD 15

Unfortunately, Marxist thought does not possess a theory of revolution, in the sense of a lengthy process towards a classless society, but only a first step in *The Critique of the Gotha Programme*; Lenin's invention of the Party and then his enthusiasm for the Soviets (councils) was a theory of seizure of power. Almost all the rest – Lenin himself, Tito, Mao, Ho, Castro and all others – is improvisation with theoretical explanations of this or that isolated element (sometimes, as in Lenin, Trotsky, Mao, and Kidrič, of great interest). But 'if one resolutely eliminates the concept of an end to history, ... [then] the revolution is creative imbalance [a concept much favoured also by Mao – DS], and there will always be new oppositions to transcend ...' (Merleau-Ponty 285). Within it, Lenin's pithy slogan 'Electrification and rule of Soviets' indicated the proper orientation: toward the highest technology and direct associational democracy. The latter means also an open field for non-antagonistic *politics*, infringing '[Marx's] mythical idea of communism as a mode of production *without relations of production*' (Althusser, *Philosophy* 37).

To the contrary, it is clear from the brief indication in 1.1 here (see much longer ones in Appendix 1 and in Suvin 'On the Concept') that the civil war in Russia set the tone for the USSR as a State organised on the lines of military hierarchy and obedience, a mindset anyway near to, and of proven efficiency for, a successful revolutionary Party, which was in some ways both an Army – as Stalin liked to recall – and a Church.⁷ This salvational monolithism was bequeathed to the Third International and all of its parties. Problems of directing civil life and society as if it were an army (with a Church core, and a double mystique of militancy and triumphalism) were to return with a vengeance in more peaceable and more complex times.

In SFRY after 1950 a combination of need for popular support and of sincere revulsion against Stalinism by a part of the Party top brought about an attempt at a rethought praxis unconsciously echoing Gramsci, and therefore best explained through his formulations and horizon (I remember vividly his impact at the beginning of the 1960s, I was telling the Party cell at the Zagreb Faculty of Philosophy we should be a 'collective intellectual' …). For him, beyond Lenin's *State and Revolution*, the central problem and goal of the revolution is 'how to make a hitherto subaltern class capable of hegemony, believe in itself as a potential ruling class and be credible as such to other classes. – Here lies the significance for Gramsci of the ***party*** – "the modern Prince"' (Hobsbawm, *How* 324). But his strategy 'has at its core a permanently organised class movement' *not so much as institutionalised organisation but as emancipative 'forms of political leadership'* (idem 328 – emphasised DS). The party is therefore, as in Marx rather than Lenin, 'not to take part directly in "State life" but to create conditions for others to do so … [as] a "collective intellectual"':

> [I]ts task is to speak for the proletariat as a producer in the "universal" sense … from the overall historical perspective of advancing the interest of the producers as a collective whole. The party's role, then, is viewed by

---

7   See for example Stalin's characterisation of the Party in the 1920s being composed of 3–4,000 'generals', 30–40,000 'officers', and 100–150,000 'NCO's' (Waller 48–9). It should be added that at the same time Michels thought all mass parties were 'warfaring parties', needing centralism and 'militantism' (38 ff.). Althusser identifies as military the 'absolute vertical barrier' to upward initiatives from the Party basis, while horizontal relationships are considered factional (*Quel* 65–6); I mention such militarism and the attendant monolithism in Chapter 7, and discuss the latter further in Part 3, especially Chapter 13. For the Church aspect, an institutionalised community of belief that inevitably produces martyrs, priests, heretics, and inquisitors – also Jesuits and dogmatists – see Preve, *Filo* 187–91, also the sobering reminder by Badiou that not every such community is necessarily pathological, and that 'sacralisation' of artists (and in a few cases, of scientists) is today culturally accepted, so that if politics has an inalienable creative aspect it might warrant the same claims (22–3).

> Gramsci as one of analysis more than of ruling, of persuasion and leadership rather than of coercion ... The centrepiece of workers' democracy is, then, the factory council, designed to exercise political as well as economic power. Above it stands the rest of the State, a hierarchical system of producers' councils, elected by and responsive to the factory councils at the base, replacing the competitive market as well as the liberal democratic State. And at its side is a political party, committed to the hegemony of the producers and to the further evolution of workers' control over political and economic life.
> COMISSO, *Workers'* 14–15

Two linked sets of measures present themselves as indispensable. The *first* set is a really operating, democratic centralism *inside* the wannabe vanguard, that is, constant feedback between the momentary top and the basis. To foster emancipative forms of political leadership it could start with Gramsci's adoption of democratic centralism on condition that it be 'a "centralism" in movement', which does not congeal into a bureaucracy. He opposes to it

> bureaucratic centralism in the State [which] indicates that the leading group is saturated, that it is turning into a narrow clique which tends to perpetuate its selfish privileges by controlling or even by stifling the birth of oppositional forces – even if these forces are homogeneous with the fundamental dominant interests ... Democratic centralism ... consists in a critical pursuit of what is identical in seeming diversity of form and on the other hand of what is distinct and even opposed in apparent uniformity ...
> *Selection* 188–9

Gramsci's examples here are from bourgeois politics, but this is a red herring as the target is squarely Stalinism, or monolithic centralism with one-way traffic from top to bottom – a parodic distortion of Marxism and communism, which can also be seen as their perfectly alienated form (cf. Petrović 219). This inner organisation is, as Lazić wittily notes, an image and allegory of the very structure of the oligarchy as a collective ruling class (42). Monolithism without supple mediations leads to despotic suppression of contradictions and simultaneously to ad hoc compromises trampling on principles.

The only truly democratic and fertile mediation is to allow for what the Polish Communist Party dissidents around 1980 (belatedly) asked for: 'horizontal contacts', that is, discussions between individuals and groups without the intervention of the State or the Party top. These can only mature into coherent proposals when minorities with a continuous organisation of their own – finally fractions – are allowed and the idea of monolithism repudiated, as befits a living, changing political institution (cf. Stojanović 85 and *passim*).

The *second* set is an ungrudging, though discriminating, fostering of a critical civil society of professional and other organised groups *outside* such a vanguard, interacting cognitively and politically with it, and re-incorporating the consciousness gained into material practices. One could perhaps think of this as an institutionalised and polyarchic version or supersession of Mao's 'mass line' (cf. Selden 274–6 and Schram 30–1 and 53–4), later theorised in his speech on contradictions among the people; or as Martin Buber's structurally rich society. By the nature of things this would be a competitive and sometimes conflictual – but in a healthy society not antagonistic – interaction (cf. Rus 824–5, Arzenšek 85–91 and 97). Indeed, Hegel's realistic dialectics expressly tie a Subject's growth to determinate division and specific opposition 'until we come out on the other side – a requirement that seems to me to distinguish this dialectic from the more absolute skepticism of deconstruction' (Jameson 85). The motto for such fertile opposition should to my mind be Nietzsche's maxim 'What doesn't kill me, strengthens me' (*Was mich nicht umbringt, macht mich stärker*). Commanding attitudes can only be suggested by the vanguard to the State executive after real clarifying discussions with such allies and if faced with real inimical threats. This would be a system of *articulated democracy from below*, building on the initial basic self-management in the production and service enterprises. Attempts at it failed in SFRY, most clearly and finally in the clever elimination of the 1968 student protests and then the purge of the Serbian LC Central Committee in 1972 (see for these Kanzleiter-Stojaković eds. and Perović). The two souls of the Communist Party, posited in my Chapter 6, were reduced to the earthbound one, power: coercion rather than consensus. Yet the only chance of ensuring economic development and disalienation in SFRY, and finally its survival in whatever form, lay in mass politics 'articulated around a party nucleus within a constellation of autonomous institutions and organisations …, [with] a party rigorously democratic and creative in each of its militants' (Magri 1076). As I suggested earlier, the prerequisite for this was overcoming by intense theoretical and practical learning the epistemological gap between Stalinism and a quite new deal to be based on the *Communist Manifesto*'s fundamental insight that the proletariat cannot liberate itself without simultaneously liberating the whole society. Contrariwise, stopping halfway in de-Stalinisation means that, against Sartre's pious wish in 'The Ghost of Stalin', it will not 'destalinise the destalinisers' (251).

This stance can, I hope, draw further clarity and sustenance from Hegel's early arguments about the politics of religion. For Hegel, Greek polytheism, where gods were a more powerful and immortal species in the same world with humans, was a religion consubstantial to free *polis* citizens, while early Christianity 'is appropriate to and arises because of man's social and political subjugation ... Hegel writes [in *The Positivity of Christian Religion* that] "The despotism of the Roman emperors had chased the human spirit from the earth and spread a misery which compelled men to seek and expect happiness in heaven; robbed of freedom, their spirit ... was forced to flee to the deity"' – itself seen as a transcendental Master in 'another world' above Nature (Forster 216–17). There was a fragility to the *polis* between the absolute demands of the human State and the divine principle of freedom and solidarity, canonically explained by Hegel's consideration of *Antigone* as an insoluble contradiction destroying both parties (cf. Jameson 79). In the twentieth century, this is matched by the fragility of even the best post-revolutionary situation, caught in what I have posited as **the central communist contradiction** of emancipative disalienation and power alienation – which turns emancipation into a heavenly pie in the sky by and by, into a 'fatalistic ... ideological aroma ... rather like religion or drugs ...' (Gramsci, *Selections* 336). Yet obversely, the tensile strength of the Athenian *polis* also managed for quite some time to contain its constitutive and irresolvable historical conflict, and to give rise to a golden age of at least semi-popular democracy and cultural flowering. In the intervening 25 centuries or so economic justice and emancipation has grown feasible with modern productivity, and there is at least a hope that forces working for disalienation have grown more conscious and potentially stronger. To articulate them initially, I shall factor in the findings of my Chapter 6, which seems to me quite isomorphic to the *Antigone* situation.

In it, I call the original Marxian project and horizon Communism 1, and the official Party and State horizon and actuality I call Communism 2. The best recent economic definition I know of C_1, by Resnick and Wolff, runs: 'A communist class structure exists if and when the people who collectively produce a surplus are likewise and identically the people who collectively receive and distribute it' (9). In the key of political epistemology, I defined it in Chapter 6.2 as 'a horizon of full social justice and disalienation, politically implemented through free self-determination of every person in independent working and territorial communities with no State'. A partizan war communism with direct democracy existed in Yugoslavia during the heyday of the post-1941 liberation struggle, and a plan for carrying it over into post-war life in Lenin's *State and Revolution*. If we are to investigate (as a little mental experiment akin to Schrödinger's one about the quantum cat who both is and is not alive) the possibility of a different outcome to SFRY contradictions, this would have necessitated openly introducing into the real society of C2 permanently operating and viable – that is, institutionalised – ways of arriving nearer to the C1 horizon of a concrete utopia.

This would have meant adopting a number of radical innovations modifying Lenin's Model T to something of use today (personally, I liked the comfortable Peugeot). First, their orientation should be directly opposed to the assault on civic liberties and self-determination characteristic of capitalist technocracy and politocracy in this worldwide age of warfare and globalisation from the top down, with its hugely inflated reliance on the State, in favour of a firm committment to helping the working people and their creativity. Second, the innovations must take seriously Lenin's conclusion in *The State and Revolution*, mentioned in Part 3, that in the socialist transition period 'there remains for a time not only bourgeois law, but even **the bourgeois State – without the bourgeoisie**!' (ch05.htm#s4). From this follows that the (no doubt in many ways necessary) State is a two-faced Janus where strong bourgeois remnants of inequality and oppression readily interact with the social forces of patriarchy, authoritarianism, and capitalist misanthropy. I have also argued that Trotsky's 'law of combined development' after a revolution in backward countries leads to a coexistence and reciprocal maiming between the most advanced communist forms and the huge queue of vastly backward patriarchal, petty-capitalist, and autocratic relationships between people. While the latter get pulled vertiginously forward, it is an open question how much they contaminate and pull backwards the socialist relations of equality and fraternity, not to mention liberty. Using the State as a direct administrator of economy strengthens the backwards pull by stifling the democratic initiative from below – the only force that can make for the revolution's success (prominently including Trade Unions which would, as for Lenin and against Trotsky and Stalin, **not** be the State's transmission belt). As a first consequence, the central Party bodies must be disentangled from the immediate interests of the State, which yet the Party continues to lead. This was understood and partly theorised in the 1950s' SFRY, but no clear Party stance and function outside State power was found. To my mind, it should comprise at least the following elements.

First, a knowledge of the real contradictions, one that cannot be arrived at without free debate with all groups of people working to clarify them, including direct producers and vanguard intellectual groups in various professions and sciences (cf. Gorz 102–3 and 149, and Lefebvre 24 on yoking together direct democracy and cybernetics). *Second*, the resolute abandonment of the clerical pretence of Party omniscience, that is, the dismantling of the triune monolithic monster State-Party-Ideology (cf. Althusser, *Quel* 122), which grows especially pernicious in the syndrome of bureaucratic optimism, when official Party theory is supposed to be identical to reality.[8] This would include expunging from the communist party all traces of a monotheist Church as guardian of a static Truth and inquisitor into heresies. Knowledge and learning wilts under authoritarian methods and quickens in a polyphony of voices, a friendly competition. As H.G. Wells once put it, modern technology, especially the military one, puts on the world agenda the race between education (or better: self-governing consciousness) and catastrophe: a good example is Lenin's 1921 relegation of self-management to a time when Russia would be at least 50% urbanised (Supek 335). Therefore, in Marxian language, the educators also have to be educated. *Third*, the jettisoning of militarism within 'the [Party] organising structures, copying those of the [bourgeois] State' (Althusser, *Quel* 123). This leads to very costly mistakes, and also to a souring and haemorrhage of often the best activists – in Yugoslavia there must have been by the 1970s by my rough calculation half a million ex-Party members compared to the one million in the Party (and where the Party was not in power and bolstered by police and status pressure, the attrition ratio was probably worse).

Such a renovated Party model and stance would change from commander to a trainer and educator for the most useful consensus and to an enabler of the plebeian emancipation (see further below). It would have much less command based on State force and violence but not necessarily less power, of a consensual rather than coercive kind – a power that interacted with an encouraged political as well as economic democracy going from the ranks upwards. And to begin with, in the Party itself. In Tripalo's bold words from the late 60s:

> The stagnation about which we talk all the time is not only one in industrial production – but also a stagnation of stances ... We even have an in my opinion negative tendency to close our discussions off from public opinion. If we then at least discussed, ... let us say, in the Central Committee of LCY, and if we said: here are two stances, let us confront them, and

---

8 Cf. Bettelheim 2: 546 and 548; I have probed this à propos of the exemplary Kardelj in earlier chapters. I have found the best diagnosis of the diffuse Bolshevik, later Stalinist, mindset – according to which no central rethinking is necessary after major defeats and the Party must always be right – in the brilliant works of Victor Serge. To cite only one passage, from his 1944 diary: 'The psychological phenomenon of the [Bolshevik] Politbureau repeats itself *ad infinitum*. At root: idealists caught by the sclerosis of doctrines, of circumstances, and dominated by their convictions and their emotional attachments, in short by fanaticism' (50).

then we go public to the LCY, so that the whole of it and the whole people participate in the discussion. But no, the matter is blocked, and decisions are not reached.

337

To conclude in chess terms: a *partita di re* is a game in the open, where the king comes out from behind the defensive wall. It is an enforced and dangerous move – for once the king (Gramsci's Modern Ruler, *Principe*) is taken, the game is over – but also in the endgame often the only way to win. If only the LCY had adopted such a new twist on Gramsci's manoeuvre vs. position warfare! It would have made for a power stemming, as in the revolutionary war, from prestige in struggling with and finding a way out of central contradictions, without class privileges and only to a small and temporally limited part nested in cushy State apparatus.

The type of power introduced with the local and then vertical People's Liberation Committees was officially called *narodna vlast*, people's or popular power. The emancipatory point of this direct translation of the term 'democracy' is, however, that this power should be not only of and from but also permanently *by* the people (*vlast naroda*). Since 'the people' was during and after the Liberation War clearly conceived as the population minus the ruling classes, in my terms this would be a ***plebeian rule and power***.

However, the spectre of losing ruling-class status, inextricably interwoven with the fear of losing all 'socialist' power, is exactly why a sea-change of the communist party everywhere failed. Spinoza's *Ethics* (IV.67) pose the fulminant insight, important also for Marx, that 'the wisdom [of the free person] is a meditation on life rather than on death'; following which in his *Tractatus Politicus* the multitude led by hope 'cultivates life', the one yoked by fear 'only flees death' (v.6, cf. Lordon 199). The forward-looking wing of the Yugoslav partitocracy cultivated life until the early 60s, and then spent a dozen years stymied by ignorance and compromises; after 1972, it simply fled death. The courage of choosing the Novum and experimentation gave way to phrase-mongering. As an endangered, small, and in global terms rather powerless ruling class, it fell prey to the Post-Modernist malaise of forsaking the horizons of hope and no longer borrowing its solutions from the plebeian future, in favour of brief muddling through. Another Italian proverb says that 'when the game is over, the king and the pawn are put back into the same box' – when this very serious power game ended, the Party/State ruling class also lost, not to speak of the people: all recolonised by world capitalism.

14.3.1 Overviews of Power-Value Relationships

How can the lesson of Chapter 1, on the actantial system of the Yugoslav liberatory insurrection of 1941–5, be generalised? In it the Protagonist of the action had shifted from the Marxist-Leninist proletariat to the People, as opposed to the fascist invaders and their quisling helpers, including the supporters of oppressive prewar monarchy. The Mandator, obviously a 'god-word', is – as usual after the French revolution – History as a process guaranteeing popular sovereignty; while this preserves more than a dash of theological inevitability, entrusted to determinist evolution, the People-Protagonist was most actively relying on its own forces and thus turning reified History into palpable Liberation. The main Helper of the Protagonist was officially the partizan army, the armed part of the people practising self-help, but behind this spearhead was the Communist Party. The Value is Power, which politically means an integral self-government for the People but to my mind is strongly imbued with lay salvation, as in Roman *salus rei publicae*. The line from P to V in this scheme is thus one of emancipation/salvation. The Helper, literally a fighting vanguard, awakens the consciousness of the main Protagonist (the people) that it is its own highest value – politically speaking, that it doesn't need king, god or master but can govern himself by himself. Thus it might be better to call it here an Enabler, which I would gloss as a technical or pragmatic Helper who has some traits of the transcendental and legitimating Mandator (historical necessity). Behind the momentarily decisive but contingent wartime partizans, the Party comes openly to the fore in what I am calling the Yugoslav actantial system no. 2, for the years 1950–65, after the Party top decides to defy Stalin and then to introduce a soon burgeoning system of Workers' Councils. However, this also institutes a hesitation as to who is the principal bearer of History's mandate – the Party or the Working People; this becomes the crucial watershed of SFRY conflicts:

Catholic Actantial System

God — Humanity — Devil
　／＼　　／＼
Church　　　Evil forces
　　＼　／
　　Salvation

Marxist-Leninist Actantial System

History — Proletariat — Rulers
　　　／＼　　／
　　Party　＼／
　　　　Power

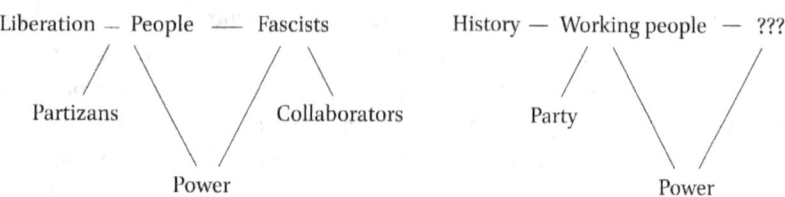

Yugoslav Actantial Sys I (1941–1945)   *Yugoslav Actantial Sys II (1950–1965)*

In both SFRY periods, it is remarkable how complexly articulated is the left side of the scheme, the Protagonist wing. To the contrary, in system II it is also remarkable how unclear it gets who is the Antagonist, after the wartime victory and the takeover of the urban economy. That wing cannot be represented by the Stalinist bugaboos of capitalist remnants or foreign spies, so that for communist party regimes there is a real temptation to say (as the Chinese one does for the last decades) that the above actantial scheme, based as it is on radical social conflict, no longer applies in a harmonious community of allied working classes: we are at the threshold of Arcadia or utopia. However, amid the SFRY economic problems after 1965 – and more acutely from the 70s on – this no longer holds water, nor does a congeries of faceless allegorical Antagonists sometimes proposed, such as economic and cultural backwardness (without identifying its class bearer). A flurry of concern for the Party top was in the late 60s occasioned by a rising class fraction of 'technocrats', but it soon settled down as a junior partner of the oligarchy. Thus, the monocratic force responsible for the State, that is the Party, becomes a prime candidate for being simultaneously a fading Helper-Enabler and a rising oligarchic Antagonist. This means it was being internally split into the forces in favour of self-government from below upwards and those opposing it in the name of Party power from the top down, into forces trusting plebeian classes and those clutching an exclusive historical mandate. The plebeian actantial logic applying (a retrospective ascription by me rather than a real force at the time, though well represented by the 'loyal opposition' in the intelligentsia) would then be:

SFRY Plebeian Actantial System

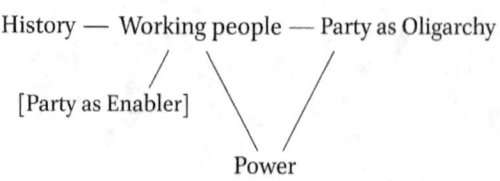

This is what I believe was happening, and by 1972 or so the monocrats clearly won out. Thus we pass, as I argue, from the 20 glorious post-war years to the 20 inglorious and finally disgraceful years of SFRY.

The Communist Party was thus being transmogrified from Protagonist to Antagonist, so that the latter was an aspect of the former, as Hyde was of Dr. Jekyll. Since in order to defeat the Antagonist, the Protagonist had first to see and identify it – give it a name and a local habitation – and the Party could neither recognise nor admit the monster in itself (Lenin could, cf. his writings in 1922 cited in Appendix 1), it was unable to save its original Protagonist-wing function.

Instead, C2, the really existing communist rule, with its monolithism and non-transparency of Stalinist origin, was fencing in and fossilising C1 – its emancipatory roots and reason for existing. As I concluded, Yugoslavia was lurching into an exploitative class society. As of 1972 civic repression accordingly rose sharply.

14.4 A Credo

I am writing this section concluding about SFRY as a kind of Credo, which I hope will be of general value though it is also quite personal.

I have throughout argued that hypothetical questions about Aristotle's alternative possibilities or potentialities (*dynamis*, cf. *Metaphysics* Book IX 1045b–1049a, in *Selections* 324–32) – concerning, for example, a social form that has come into contradiction with its founding horizon and forces – are not only epistemologically allowable, but even indispensable insofar as they allow open argumentation about the evaluation criteria for this form, which would otherwise remain unspoken.

Further, I postulated in 'Communism and Yugoslavia' (see in *Darko Suvin*, 331–40) that this experience shows how 'the blocking of a social conflict is always the prelude to a catastrophe' (from the splendid Cortesi, 151) – that is, how **both civic pressure groups from society at large as well as a co-ordinating and centralised power agency are necessary** for a modern society. For modern radical democracy to exist, forceful and enforced guarantees of associational and individual rights are necessary; yet the suspicion that civic pressure groups would destabilise a socialist power monolith has remained a crucial sterile aspect of Bolshevik tradition down to Tito (see the precise Kuljić 48, 51–2, 55, and *passim*). The turn to oligarchy, begun in the 60s and intensified after the failure to draw lessons from the political upheavals in 1968 and 1971, can be even legally seen in the failure to generalise self-management from the basic 'Organisations of Associated Labour' upward to all levels of political decision-making, at the expense of bourgeois parliamentarism and an uncontrolled executive. This made of self-management largely a sham instead of an integration factor. As Marx noted about the Paris Commune, 'The political rule of the producer cannot coexist with the perpetuation of his social slavery' (index.htm).

Tabooing *diversity in unity* (where a poor One splits into Two in order to become a rich One) practically amounts to the loss of active and informed proposals from below for adjusting, and if need be changing, the course. Intraparty democracy outside of a tight oligarchy as well as associational and direct democracy in the citizenry at large were disallowed, the latter by marginalisation and finally by repression (even if most other 'democratic' States achieve much the same, as apparently open struggles are kept within an undoubted consensus); and yet plebeian democracy remained the indispensable component and motivator of social well-being, the ideal horizon and *raison d'être* of a communist movement and revolution. The fixating on domination was a heritage from Lenin's reluctant but in particular from Stalin's wholehearted recourse to the suppression of democracy. Such heritage foreclosed social dialectics and brought about unmitigated ideological, economic, and finally political disaster. Ideologically, the descent into disaster began with the failure to recognise and conceptualise new forms of class struggle about economic and civic life in a socialist society, which were to my mind not necessarily insoluble – on condition that there were real economical and political democracy (including planning) from below upward as well as from up downward, a feedback.

In other words, Acton was right for all societies: power (twinned with violence) corrupts, and absolute power corrupts absolutely. Since power (but not violence!) is quite indispensable, it therefore always must be tamed from below, by checks and balances through various measures but certainly including open debate: *politics*.

The recent historical alternatives have been:

TABLE 14.1 *Forms of class and economic hegemony*

	Of plan	Of market
From lower classes upward	Marx's Communism	Early Capitalism
From upper classes downward	Welfare/Warfare State	19th C Capitalism

This is a redoing of Table 11.1 in Chapter 11 arrived at by the following operators: first, an insistence on classes; second, a splitting of Burawoy's original 'Market Despotism' into 'Early' and '19th Century Capitalism' – in order to make the point that Enlightenment is valuable and must be defended at all costs, in a properly sublated form; while '19th Century Capitalism' is reborn out of hi tech in the post-1970s' Gadarene rush backwards. Third, I call his 'Collective Self-management' rather 'Communism' in Marx's original sense. The latter translates my conclusion that, in the present-day collapse of capitalism into unproductive savagery and violent coercion, we must go back to the roots and clarify the only alternative horizon left. True, the garment is much bloodied and dirtied by history, in places also badly torn, but I believe one must bet on some analogue of it being cleansed and renewed for reuse.

The horizon to be striven for is *a marriage of work and poetry* – that is, freedom as creativity (cf. Kosík 67–8 and 124–5).

And what about communism through the State, my Janus with two foreheads or orientations? I mentioned how one of his heads lends itself readily to inequality and oppression. But we should not forget that *Ianus Geminus* or *Bifrons* is also the god of all **beginnings**, of openings, transitions, passages – all of which imply also an ending in time or space, before or after: Janus is a god of time, looking to the past and to the future. If not a dialectical god, his union of opposites was a solid presupposition of dialectics. He is the great initiator, in particular of planting and harvest times, and of new historical ages. As *Ianus Consivius*, he is the god of all insemination, that is, of biological beginning. Pleasingly, his youthful or bearded maleness opening the doors is paired with Juno, who presides over childbirth and the menstrual cycle and protects the young (*iuvenes*). Thus his beardless opening face counteracts all permanent closure. His kin are the Vedic and Iranian Vayu, and particularly the Zoroastrian Mainyus who 'stands at the opening of the drama of moral history of the world' (Dumézil – data for this paragraph are from en.wikipedia.org/wiki/Janus). As eternal as oppression is the rising of life against oppression.

Finally, however, I must in honesty note that factoring the underlying potential of the SFRY situation into my equation as criterion for what was not accomplished and for estranging judgement, as I attempt in several places of the book, can only lead to an ambiguous conclusion, of the counterfactual, better either-or, kind.[9] In other words, the borderline between Bloch's abstract and concrete

---

9   This seems logically akin to the fact it deals with a possible future that the past could have been, to which Aristotle's insight applies that about the future status of x one can only say

FIGURE 29   Ianus
FROM B. DE MONTFAUCON, L'ANTIQUITÉ ... EN FIGURES, 1722

utopianism is at times unclear. He interprets Hegel as arguing that the adequacy of the thought-object relation (*Begriff vs. Gegenstand*) can be tested in two ways: not only whether thought corresponds to the object, but also, more mysteriously, whether the object manages to correspond to what it potentially could be. (This would hold in spades for Marx.) And I read Bloch as concluding that the second correspondence is most valuable and most neuralgic when it is lacking, and yet remains the measure for any realisation, 'which is not yet' (14). Did the SFRY have a potential tendency and latency of corresponding to its furthest emancipatory horizon? If yes, what I am postulating here is a concrete (possible, useful) utopianism. If not, it is an abstract (impossible, useless) one. I disbelieve the hypothesis that communist revolutions were simply a force-

---

that it will either come about or not come about, as he explicates with the example of the sea-battle tomorrow (*De Interpretatione* Book IX 18b, in *Selections* 19).

feeding way to create non-existent bourgeoisies and capitalisms in 'backward' places, but I must acknowledge that in much of the decolonised Third World, as Hobsbawm notes, the main function of the new State apparatus was exactly this (*Revolutionaries* 252). Moreover, Fanon reserved his most acerbic disgust for its monocratic form: 'The single party is the modern form of the dictatorship of the bourgeoisie, unmasked, unpainted, unscrupulous and cynical' (165). While most of these ruling apparati did not originate in mass movements or social revolutions as SFRY did, in the capitalist *reconquista** these parody ruling classes turned into comprador ones in both cases. In sum: the proof of the pudding is in the eating, yet equally a bad pudding does not preclude making a good one – possibly by varying the recipe. I hope my utopianism may be concrete and of use, but I can neither prove nor be sure of it: it is not yet.

Thomas More ends *Utopia* with his protagonist saying he rather hopes than believes that commonwealth can be followed. I would invert the terms: I rather believe it can, than harbour the hope it will be (in the lifetime of my readers). Perhaps it is meet to end with the final wisdom of the tragic Sophocles, discerning the fall of his City: 'What is loved turns bitter, and bitterness becomes beloved' (*Oedipus on Colonus*, v. 615).

Glossary

in statu nascendi = being born

sui generis = of a particular kind

nec tecum nec sine te = [I can live] neither with nor without you – originally a proverb, used by Latin poets for a frustrating beloved, most memorably by Ovid in *Amores*:

> sic ego nec sine te nec tecum vivere possum,
> et videor voti nescius esse mei.
> aut formosa fores minus, aut minus inproba, vellem ...
> (Thus I cannot live either without or with you,
> And no conclusion seems in sight.
> O that you were either less beautiful or less perfidious!)

reconquista = recapture (the term was coined for the Spanish reoccupation of the Moslem Iberia or al-Andalus)

APPENDICES

The Socialist/Communist Discourse about Bureaucracy

∴

The philosopher [Wittgenstein] speaks no other language but the one he finds in his cognitive object.
GUNTER GEBAUER, 2011

APPENDIX 1

Bureaucracy: A Term and Concept in the Socialist Discourse about State Power (Upstream of Yugoslavia)

0   Introduction to Both Appendices

This essay is the first part of a discussion focusing on historical semantic lineaments of the term and concept 'bureaucracy', and its epistemological implications, in the nineteenth-century socialist movement and the two paradigmatic European socialist States, Russia and Yugoslavia. My aim here is limited: to provide the background and premises indispensable for understanding, in a second essay, the discourse about bureaucracy and State power in post-revolutionary Yugoslavia. This aim excludes an exhaustive account of this theme in the nineteenth century or in revolutionary Russia, as well as a critical account of the strengths and weaknesses of these semantic usages (which shall be dealt with in the following second part on Yugoslav discourse). I wish only to delineate a discursive universe which will be used after 1945 both by the Party/State and the oppositional discourse in SFR Yugoslavia.[1]

Lenin and his Bolshevik Party collaborators inherited the term of bureaucracy from the tradition represented on the one hand by Marx and Engels, and on the other hand by the experience of the Second International and its main pillar, the German Social-democratic Party. They fused it with the experiences of the tsarist officialdom and ranking system (*činovniki*), whose key executive role Lenin excoriated from his beginnings – for example in the polemic with

---

1   I write in this particular Appendix 'soviet' when referring to the various local councils and their system but 'Soviet' when referring to the USSR; also 'party', 'communist', and 'revolution' in lower case, except for quotes and specific cases such as 'October Revolution', 'Bolshevik Party', or the Party/State nexus. 'CP' means 'communist party', which was in the USSR at the beginning called 'Russian (and later the All-Federal) Communist Party (bolshevik)', acronym VKP(b), in Yugoslavia translated as SKP(b).

   In section 2 I draw heavily on Lenin's *Collected Works* in English, where possible checked against his *Polnoe sobranie sochinenii*, 5th edn., on his *Izbrannye proizvedeniia*, and on Bettelheim's *Class* (though I disagree with the latter's insufficient dichotomy between bourgeoisie and proletariat in socialism); they are cited as CW, IP, and B. I cite the internet texts of Marx's as WAMW, and the 1972 *Marx-Engels Reader* as Tucker ed.

Struve of 1894. In all of his programmatic writings about the Russian Social-democratic Party he insisted that all public functionaries must be elected and recallable; when Lenin wrote against the Kerensky government before the October revolution, he blamed its 'reactionary bureaucratic ways' (IP 81) which harked back to the old regime. I cannot here do justice to this important Russian context (for which see somewhat more in Suvin, 'From the Archeology'). The essay deals only with the Marx-to-Lenin tradition in the socialist and then communist movements and its perversion by Stalinism in the USSR.

'Bureaucracy' was from Marx to Lenin used in the discourse about – always class-derived – State power and its revolutionary replacement. In the USSR after Lenin it began to mean, confusingly, both a subordinate part of the State totality and a *pars pro toto* for it; while under Stalin it principally came to mean what impeded the centralisation, expansion, and smooth work of the hierarchical State machinery, with perhaps a demagogic hint to the workers and peasants that the Powers That Be were their allies against this oppressive excrescence. In Yugoslavia it advanced to the privileged key-word for an apparatus standing above civil society and implying a separate social group (possibly class), in the discourse criticising or indeed opposing socialist State power. It represented there the emergence of the understanding that in absolutism and capitalism the bureaucracy was, together with the army, an important part of the ruling class hierarchy; however, after the communist revolutions (which annihilated the other functions of the ruling hierarchy), the bureaucracy – the army was not considered further – became the whole of the hierarchy. In the USSR and Yugoslavia, it came to stand for the banished discourse about a new, Thermidorean ruling class.

As to 'socialism', I shall use it in the first Appendix to cover the political movement loosely organised in the Second International as well as the power constellations in the USSR during its formative period, roughly from 1917 to 1929; and in the second Appendix the power constellations in the Federative Republic of Yugoslavia, roughly from 1945 to the early 1970s.

I am aware that this endeavour is a kind of archaeological excavation into discourses and semantics (with very practical equivalents in social life) certain versions of which were familiar in 'socialist' States, and are therefore well-known to specialists, but are quite buried under the rubble of intervening events for most, including those who would wish to look at them anew. It cannot pretend to originality but only to helpfulness. I have decided to run the risk of unnecessary repetition rather than of omission of relevant matters and texts.

I shall avoid confrontation with the non-Marxist discourse on bureaucracy – by the ineffable Spencer and scores of anti-socialist polemicists during the rise of the German and French Social-democratic parties (see for the latter Angenot 65–7), then Weber, Michels, Merton, and so on – until it might naturally arise, in the second part, through its repercussions in SFR Yugoslavia. Certainly the militant tradition of Lenin's successors (including the pioneering Trotsky, who is here also not represented) had no time to enter into substantial confrontations with that discourse. This was understandable in view of their overriding necessities and of the fact that they had some once excellent tools. But after the 1920s, and especially the 1940s, this exclusive concentration turned sectarian, and the rapidly changing times demanded a much refurbished toolbox.

1 Marx, Engels, and the German Social-democratic Party as Sources

Bureaucracy was always considered by Marx as a mainstay of the State system, and in particular of the one begun in Absolutism and maturing after the French Revolution, when capitalism needed a powerful State, even at the price of strong monarchic and landowning elements – as in Germany and the U.K. The role of bureaucracy depended thus on one's views about the State, which in Marx crystallised after the Paris Commune of 1871.

However, from his earliest *Notes for a Critique of Hegel's Philosophy of Right* he identified the central characteristic of bureaucracy as 'founded on [the] separation [of the State and civil society]'. Further, 'The general spirit of the bureaucracy is the secret, the *mystery*, preserved within it by means of the hierarchy and externally as a closed corporation. To make public the mind and the disposition of the State appears therefore to the bureaucracy as a *betrayal* of its mystery. Accordingly, *authority* is the principle of its knowledge and being, and the deification of authority is its *mentality*' (WAMW/1843/critique-hpr/ch03.htm). Bureaucracy is '*an estate* in the medieval sense ..., where civil and political positions are immediately identical' (WAMW/1843/critique-hpr/ch05.htm). Hegel's 'civil society' (*bürgerliche Gesellschaft*) as private economic life is in Marx inverted as the presupposition for the State, and in *The Jewish Question* evolves to stand for the economic and ideological aspects below the political State (Tucker ed. 33), or below the power structure of the ruling class. Marx treats both as alienations of human possibilities: the State is an empty idealism of societal unity, civil society a petty materialism of individualist egotism (ibidem 32, 40–2, and in the 10th *Thesis on Feuerbach*, 109). At least since 1847–8 Marx and Engels always write about 'the army and the bureaucracy' as pillars of the State. And in Chapter 7 of *The 18th Brumaire* we find a first sketch of both the history and the function of bureaucracy in a modern autocratic State. As to history:

> This executive power with its enormous bureaucratic and military organisation, with its wide-ranging and ingenious state machinery, with a host of officials numbering half a million, besides an army of another half million – this appalling parasitic growth which enmeshes the body of French society and chokes all its pores sprang up in the time of the absolute monarchy ...

Then the French Revolution, Napoleon, and all successive governments added to and strengthened it: 'All revolutions perfected this [State] machine instead of breaking it'. This diagnosis was to be repeated and brought to a head in *The Civil War in France*.

As to social role:

> An enormous bureaucracy, well gallooned and well fed, is the 'Napoleonic idea' which is most congenial to the second Bonaparte. How could it be otherwise, considering that alongside the actual classes of society, he is forced to create an artificial caste for which the maintenance of his regime becomes a bread-and-butter question? Hence one of his first financial operations was the raising of officials' salaries to their old level and the creation of new sinecures.
>
> WAMW/1852/18th-brumaire/ch07.htm; TUCKER ed. 514 and 520

Bureaucracy is here something approximating a separate class, though not founded on economy but on politics and therefore somewhat curtly called 'an artificial caste'.[2] Marx is here backgrounding the point which was to worry communist heretics from the time of Trotsky to that of the *Praxis* writers: just how is bureaucracy situated in the class system?

I shall further confine myself to two key texts which were to be cited again and again in debates within socialist countries about their economic system and State apparatus: Marx's admiring analysis of the Paris Commune in 1871 and his critique of the German Social-democratic Party four years later. Engels's work in the *Anti-Dühring* and elsewhere is almost equally important but will be mentioned through his influence on Lenin.

Chapter 3 in *The Civil War in France* describes the workings of the Paris Commune. It wanted 'to abolish that class property which transforms the labour of

---

2 Marx took this meaning of 'caste' from the bourgeois Enlightenment polemic against a parasitic and unproductive aristocracy, e.g, in Sieyès: 'A class of people without function or use who enjoy personal privileges because they exist' (39).

the many into the wealth of the few. It aimed at the expropriation of the expropriators. It wanted to make individual property a truth by transforming the means of production, land and capital, now chiefly the means of enslaving and exploiting labour, into mere instruments of free and associated labour' (Tucker ed. 557). The Commune substituted the 'armed people' for the standing army and 'revocable agent[s] of the Commune ... serv[ing] at **workmen's wages**' for a closed civil-service group administering public affairs (ibidem 554). The horizon was: 'While the merely repressive organs of the old governmental power were to be amputated, its legitimate functions were to be wrested from an authority claiming pre-eminence over society itself ... The Commune type of constitution would have restored to the social body all the forces hitherto absorbed by the parasitic excrescence of "State", feeding upon and clogging the free movement of society' (ibidem 555–6). And further, quite prophetically for socialist States:

> [The Commune] was essentially *a working-class government*, the result of the struggle of the creating against the appropriating class, the finally discovered political form under which to work out the economic emancipation of labour.// Without this last condition, the Commune type of constitution would have been an impossibility and a delusion. The political rule of the producer cannot coexist with the perpetuation of his social slavery ... With labour emancipated, every man becomes a labourer, and productive labour ceases to be a class attribute.
> ibidem 557

The marginal glosses to the programme of the German Workers' Party, translated as the *Critique of the Gotha Programme* and for a long time forgotten, were popularised mainly by Lenin's *State and Revolution*, but deserve to be treated on their own. I shall bracket out here the economic aspects of the future 'emancipation of labour', immensely influential for example in Yugoslavia, and focus on his famous division of post-capitalist society and its road toward communism into two phases. The *first* phase is 'a communist society ... just as it emerges from capitalist society; which is thus in every respect, economically, morally, and intellectually, still stamped with the birthmarks of the old society from whose womb it emerges. Accordingly, the individual producer receives back from society – after the deductions [for the common funds] have been made – exactly what he gives to it' (Tucker ed. 386–7). What obtains is still regulated by an 'exchange of equal values', that is, this phase is subject to an ideal '*bourgeois right*' (*Recht* means right, law, and even jurisprudence):

[T]his *equal right* is still burdened by a bourgeois limitation. The ... equality consists in the fact that measurement is made with an *equal standard*, labour ... This *equal* right is an unequal right for unequal labour ... it tacitly recognises unequal individual endowment and thus performance capacity as natural privileges. *It is, therefore, a right of inequality in its content, like every right.* // [T]hese defects are inevitable in the first phase of communist society ... Right can never be higher than the economic structuring and its entailed cultural development of society.

    TUCKER ed. 387

In a *second*, 'higher phase of communist society, after the enslaving subordination of the individual to the division of labour ... has vanished ... – only then can the narrow horizon of bourgeois right be entirely overstepped and society inscribe on its banner: From each according to his ability, to each according to his needs!' (Tucker ed. 388)

What transformation will the State undergo in communist society? Marx's even more famous answer is that between capitalism and full communism, in a 'political transition period' corresponding to 'the period of revolutionary transformation of the one into the other', the State in the sense of a specialised ruling apparatus 'can be nothing but *the revolutionary dictatorship of the proletariat*' (Tucker ed. 395 and 396).[3]

Finally, the theoretical toolbox of Bolshevism and Lenin himself was in good part inherited from the Second International (cf. both books by Lih). Though harbouring a spread of attitudes, its parties came to be modelled on bourgeois parties and eventually got to be strongly institutionalised, that is, bureaucratised. Its pillar, the German Social-Democratic Party, practised a from top down relationship of the leadership to the lower echelons, whose local secretaries and other organisers were in great part appointed by and paid from the central instances. In 1907, the party's apparatus comprised 20,000

---

[3] I cannot enter here into the semantic confusions occasioned by the Roman-derived term 'dictatorship', possibly larger than even for 'proletariat', except to say that Lenin from his earliest writings on – say, *Two Tactics* – always explained it as Marx's dictatorship of a whole class, and not of a party or smaller group (see Draper and Balibar). True, having lost the core of the working class in the Civil War epoch, he fell back on the communist party as a temporary expedient. This imposed necessity became the precondition for, but cannot justify, Stalin's autocracy. In the lengthy Russian debates about which class should lead the revolution Lenin used (as everybody else did) the better term of 'hegemony', and at times its synonym *glavenstvo* (B 1: 127); from him it passed into the proclamations of the Third International and thence to the different stress of Gramsci (see Anderson 15–19).

people, and the number was rising (in the Weimar Republic it grew to between 100,000 and 300,000 paid functionaries, of which 7,500 were paid about triple the income of a small entrepreneur or the salary of a high German State functionary – Bricianer 123). Little democratic centralism remained, it was becoming centralism *tout court*, so that Lenin's recipe of that time even for the illegal organisation to fight tsarism was considerably more democratic (the practice under the Russian police onslaught limped behind).

It should also be noted that Lenin unreservedly admired the efficiency of the 'Prussian' (German) bureaucracy and State organisation, especially the post office and railways but then also the wartime centralisation of all economic life, and wished for such a 'culture' in the USSR as the basis of socialism (see, among many examples, IP 159 and 432).[4]

2   Lenin's Fight against Bureaucracy and the State Machine

My thesis is that 'two lines' coexisted in the USSR views on bureaucracy and the State machine up to Stalin's triumph: the horizon of instituting a radical proletarian democracy from below, with Marx's vanishing point of a non-State association of communes without a permanent army and bureaucracy, and the horizon of a strong centralised State apparatus, due in Lenin's time to the pressing needs of the revolution's survival and later used to justify full dictatorship by a small group in the Party-State personal union. Adding to the Maoist parlance the Blochian one (1: 240–2), we can also call them the warm and the cold streams within Soviet theory and practice.

Paradoxically, both of them have had their strongest as well as most intelligent and articulated defender in Lenin, in different periods. Leaving aside his work before World War I (his supposed mania for centralisation of the underground party has been misinterpreted by kremlinologists eager to establish a full continuity between him and Stalin – see their demolition in Lih, *Lenin Rediscovered*) the two periods are 1915–17 and 1918 to end (practically 1922). To anticipate, I believe his heart was in the full democracy of the Soviets on the model of the Commune, but as a statesman whose overriding aim was to save revolutionary power in the unprecedented Civil War and total economic and biopolitical catastrophe, he had to retreat to what he in the NEP debate called the 'commanding heights' of State power. The immediate task of avoiding the fate of the Paris Commune had to take precedence over the final horizon.

---

4   His other paragon was the US technology, trust organisation, and educational system.

2.1 The Theory of Revolution, 1915–17

Lenin took to heart Marx's (and then Engels's) lessons learned from the Commune of Paris. He did not know of Marx's early philosophical writings or the *Grundrisse*, but in *The State and Revolution* of 1917 he analysed, while in the underground hiding from the Kerensky government, their accessible documents, including letters, most thoroughly and on the whole fairly, though interpreting (as his subtitle shows) the 'Marxist Teaching on the State' with fierce concentration on 'The Tasks of the Proletariat in the [Impending] Revolution': the strength, and no doubt limitation, of Lenin's theorising is that it was for him always a phase of practice. He placed his readings into the overwhelming context of the monstrous growth of imperialist armed forces, as evident in World War I just going on, which were realising Engels's warning that they could 'devour the whole of society and even the State' (IP 132). The only way out was for him a violent revolution superseding such a State. From this vantage point, he cited the conclusion of Engels's *Origin of the Family, Private Property, and the State*:

> The State is therefore ... a product of society at a particular stage of development; it is the admission that this society has involved itself in insoluble self-contradiction and is cleft into irreconcilable antagonisms which it is powerless to exorcise. But in order that these antagonisms, classes with conflicting economic interests, shall not consume themselves and society in fruitless struggle, a power, apparently standing above society, has become necessary to moderate the conflict and keep it within the bounds of 'order'; and this power, arisen out of society, but placing itself above it and increasingly alienating itself from it, is the State.
> WAMW/1884/origin-family/cho9.htm

His somewhat one-sided gloss runs: 'The State arises when, where, and to the extent that class antagonisms objectively cannot be reconciled. And conversely, the existence of the State proves that the class antagonisms are irreconcilable' (IP 129). And further, 'the liberation of the oppressed class is impossible ... without the destruction of the apparatus of State power which was created by the ruling class and which is the embodiment of this "alienation"' (IP 130).

Two further specifications in Engels's argument, indicated by Lenin, are:

> [The State] ... is normally the State of the most powerful, economically ruling class, which by its means becomes also the politically ruling class, and so acquires new means of holding down and exploiting the oppressed class ... The ... modern representative State is the instrument for exploit-

ing wage-labor by capital. Exceptional periods, however, occur when the warring classes are so nearly equal in forces that the State power, as apparent mediator, acquires for the moment a certain independence in relation to both. [...]

[...] The State, therefore, has not existed from all eternity ... [It] became a necessity because of [the cleavage of society into classes]. We are now rapidly approaching a stage in the development of production at which the existence of these classes ... becomes a positive hindrance to production. They will fall as inevitably as they once arose. The State inevitably falls with them. The society which organises production anew on the basis of free and equal association of the producers will put the whole State machinery where it will then belong – into the museum of antiquities, next to the spinning wheel and the bronze ax.
   WAMW/1884/origin-family/ch09.htm

Lenin then highlights Engels's discussion in *Anti-Dühring* of the proletariat's seizing political power and 'turning the means of production into State property':

But in doing this, it abolishes itself as proletariat, abolishes all class distinctions and class antagonisms, abolishes also the State as State ... When at last it becomes the real representative of the whole of society, it renders itself unnecessary. As soon as there is no longer any social class to be held in subjection; as soon as class rule, and the individual struggle for existence based upon our present anarchy in production, with the collisions and excesses arising from these, are removed, nothing more remains to be repressed, and a special repressive force, a State, is no longer necessary. The first act in which the State really constitutes itself as the representative of society as a whole – this is, at the same time, its last independent act as a State ... The government of persons is replaced by the administration of things and the direction of processes of production. The State is not 'abolished', it *withers away*.
   cited from the very slightly emended form used for *Socialism: Utopian and Scientific*, TUCKER ed. 635

Lenin clarifies and updates: 'Engels speaks here of the proletarian revolution "abolishing" the *bourgeois* State, while the words about the State withering away refer to the remnants of the *proletarian* State *after* the socialist revolution' (IP 136). In between there would exist '*the State ... of the proletariat organised as the ruling class*', as Lenin approvingly cites (and underlines) from the *Communist Manifesto* (IP 140). Seizing on Marx's letter to Weydemeyer of 5 March 1852, he focuses on its words 'that the class struggle necessarily leads to the dictatorship of the proletariat; [and] that this dictatorship itself only constitutes the transition to the abolition of all classes and to a classless society'. Mindful of both the tsarist and the World War legacy facing him, Lenin adds: '... this period [of transition] is inevitably a period of unprecedented violent class struggle in unprecedented acute forms, and consequently, the State must inevitably be a State that is democratic *in a new way* (for the proletariat and the propertyless in general) and dictatorial *in a new way* (against the bourgeoisie) ... The dictatorship of a *single* class is necessary ... for the entire **historical period** which separates capitalism from "classless society", from communism' (IP 147–8).

Taking up Marx's distinction between a first phase of communism and a higher one, Lenin believed that in the first or lower phase, ending private property of the means of production means 'the exploitation of man by man will have become impossible', but that there will persist 'the other injustice, which consists in the distribution of articles of consumption "according to the amount of labour performed" (and not according to needs) ... the inequality of "bourgeois right"'. He optimistically believed that injustice and the sway of bourgeois right will be ended by '[converting the means of production] to *common* ownership', while they will persist 'in the distribution of products and the allotment of labour among the members of society' (IP 189). Having explained that socialism is an incomplete communism, he boldly stated that 'It follows that under communism there remains for a time not only bourgeois right but even the bourgeois State – without the bourgeoisie!' (IP 192). And *for the first time* – though relying on probable precedents in German debates – Lenin noted that this phase is 'commonly called "Socialism"' (IP 188), and he proceeds to use it without the quotation marks; Stalin then, with his penchant for scholastic clarity, simplified and flattened this historical scheme into the two phases of 'socialist society' and 'communist society' (none of which has any bourgeois earmarks except, early on, the remnants of bourgeois property), whence it passed to all other CPs.

It should be clear from the cited arguments and from Marx's *Civil War in France* (also discussed at length, together with Engels's 1891 Preface to it, IP 175–9) what happens in such circumstances to the State mainstays, the armed forces and the bureaucracy. This is briefly summed up in Marx's letter to Kugelmann at the time of the Commune: 'the bureaucratic-military machine [should be] *broken*, and this is the preliminary condition for every real people's revolution on the continent' (IP 150) – a statement which Lenin foregrounds as 'the principal [task] of the proletariat during a revolution in relation to the State'. To replace these twin pillars of class rule, 'Instead of the special institutions of a privileged minority (privileged officialdom, the chiefs of the standing army), the majority itself can directly fulfil all these functions ...' (IP 153–4). The workers' expropriation of the capitalists 'must be exercised not by a State of bureaucrats, but by a State of *armed workers*' (IP 190 – reality showed Lenin then, after 1918, that this was too hasty a jump). His summation is twofold, beginning with a quasi-Rousseauist vision of bureaucratic alienation:

> Under capitalism democracy is restricted, cramped, mutilated, disfigured by all the conditions of wage slavery, of the masses' distress and misery. This and this alone is the reason why the functionaries of our [social-democratic] political organisations and trade unions are corrupted – or more precisely, tend to be corrupted – by the capitalist condition, and betray a tendency to become bureaucrats, that is, privileged persons losing touch with the masses, standing *above* the masses.
>
> IP 205

> The workers, having conquered political power, will smash the old bureaucratic apparatus, they will shatter it to its very foundations, they will destroy it to the very roots, and they will replace it by a new one, consisting of the very same workers and office employees, *against* whose transformation into bureaucrats the measures specified in detail by Marx and Engels will at once be taken: 1) not only election but also recall at any time; 2) pay not exceeding that of a workman; 3) immediate introduction of control and supervision by all, so that *all* shall become 'bureaucrats' for a time and, therefore, *nobody* may be able to become a 'bureaucrat'.
>
> IP 200

To sum up, Lenin confidently believed in 1917 that the 'large-scale production, factories, railways, the postal service, telephones, etc.' created by capitalism has 'so simplified [the great majority of the old "State power" functions that they] can be reduced to such exceedingly simple operations of registration, filing, and checking [as are] easily performed by every literate person ... for ordinary "workmen's wages" ...' (IP 154). This is true even when the revolution is made 'by people as they are now, people who cannot dispense with subordination, control, and 'foremen and bookkeepers'.// But the subordination must be to the armed vanguard of all the exploited and toiling people, that is, to the proletariat. A beginning can and must be made at once, overnight ...' (IP 158).

His confidence was sorely tested after 1918, but he might today wax even more optimistic in view of the PC, the internet, possibly two-way television, and similar communication tools.

However, Lenin shared Marx's scathing dismissal of a 'free State'. He cited approvingly Engels's observation that freedom obtains when 'the State as such ceases to exist' (IP 185). No doubt, after the experiences of Hitler, Stalin, Pinochet, Pol Pot, and quite a lot of others in the century after *The State and Revolution* even Marxists should undertake some additions to this very general long-range position, beginning with Lenin's own later additions.

2.2 *Illuminating the Revolutionary Practice, 1918 on*

Soon after the 1917 October revolution, Lenin began to note with growing dismay the tendency of the necessary, and rapidly growing, State apparatus (*gosapparat*) to evolve modes of conduct incompatible with the revolutionary horizon. In particular, while acknowledging and strongly stressing the need for centralisation of all efforts in order for the revolution to survive, he inveighed against the de facto dispossession of the soviets of the working people, which were theoretically supposed to run the new country on all levels as the real power-holders or dictators. At his instigation, and probably with a good deal of support from the ranking cadres and even more by the file of the Bolshevik party, many supposedly binding resolutions of the CP congresses and decisions of its leading bodies were passed, but then in practice disregarded. '[T]he general tendency [of the party centre] was to bureaucratisation – which would later increase its "monolithic" character ... The process was that of the transformation of a political party into a State apparatus' (Lewin, *Lenin's* 126, cf. also 22–3). Lenin bitterly fought 'the metamorphosis of the soviets into State organisations' (IP 361), remarked how such a united party/State machine was acquiring an independent and dominant momentum, yet for all his frequent denunciations admitted that no remedy for this evil was at hand.[5]

From the very beginning in 1918, at the Seventh CP Congress and the struggle against financial collapse, Lenin noted that the State power as then consti-

---

5 In 1951 Boris Kidrič, the best Yugoslav CP theoretician, noted that, after the October Revolution, 'there began the great drama of Lenin's ceaseless conflict with bureaucratism, which he was objectively unable to eradicate, but he had in his quality of revolutionary and Marxist on the one hand to fight them and on the other – in the given situation – to strengthen them; this drama of the Russian revolutionaries ended in a tragedy' (140–1).

In the incipient age of mass organisation, the bureaucracy already in 1891 numbered 0.75 million members in the USA, 1.5 million in France and 1 million in the U.K. (Bukharin and Preobrazhensky 183), and these numbers swelled hugely in all major States up to, and especially during, World War I and after it.

tuted was not truly proletarian but exercised by a vanguard party, so that it was necessary 'to protect the material and spiritual interests of the ... proletariat from that very same State power', allotting this role largely to the trade unions (CW 32: 20–4, B 1: 98–9). In his important speech at the Eighth CP congress in 1919 (CW 29: 182–3, B 1: 330), Lenin rightly coupled the 'bureaucratic deviation' (*uklon*) or 'bureaucratism' with the absence of 'mass participation from below into Soviet rule', attributed it to the infiltration of the indispensable tsarist and 'bourgeois-exploitative' specialists, and lamented both their low level and the lack of 'cultured forces' that would enable us to kick them out (IP 431 and 432). A deviation means, in the imaginative geography of this discourse, a serious wrong turning, which can nevertheless still be rectified (Trotsky's post-exile diagnosis is based on this concept). The party programme adopted at that congress devoted a paragraph to the 'struggle ... for the complete eradication of this evil', in three points: '1. Every member of a soviet must undertake some definite work in the administrative service'; 2. There must be continuous rotation in that work; '3. By degrees, the whole working population must be induced to take turns in the administrative service' (in Bukharin and Preobrazhensky 383).

However, as the Civil War practically pulverised the Russian working class, and reduced the city population of Moscow by half and of Petrograd by two thirds, in mid-1920 new accents began to appear. Lenin had a confidential survey conducted in a major Soviet institution: from its 1,500 employees there were 900 from the old intelligentsia, 250 from the working class, and ca. 300 from the quondam bourgeois, landowners, clerics or high tsarist officials (Lewin, *Storia* 227–8). At the Ninth CP congress, Lenin boldly reiterated that the Soviet State was not a proletarian one but a workers' and peasants' State with a bureaucratic distortion. In the booklet against *'Left-Wing' Communism, an Infantile Sickness*, he underlined that the 'human material made by capitalism', including the proletarians, imported 'its own petty-bourgeois prejudices' into the administration and into the communist party: 'Within the Soviet engineers, within the Soviet teachers, within the privileged, that is the most qualified ... **workers** in Soviet factories, we see constantly reborn all the negative traits of bourgeois [careerism, vulgar philistine routine ..., national chauvinism, etc.]' (IP 623–4). Towards the end of 1920, he harked back to his radical anti-State proposal of 1917 by declaring, 'It is the task of the Soviet government to completely destroy the old machinery of State, as it was destroyed in October [1917] and to transfer power to the soviets' (CW 31: 421, B1: 331).

Thus, when, in *On the Tax in Kind* of May 1921, he asked what were the economic roots of bureaucracy, he found no real answer beside pointing to pre-capitalist peasant backwoods, economic collapse, and grave lack of cultural know-how (IP 701–2 and 705; CW 32: 335ff.). Or, three months later, to 'the trivial round (*obydenshchina*) of economics in a country of smallholders ... and the elementary petty-bourgeois force (*stikhiia*) which surrounds us like air and mightily penetrates into the ranks of the proletariat' (IP 722–3).

By January 1922, his theses on the new role of the trade unions identified the existing power as a 'transitional type of proletarian State', in which a proletarian class struggle, including strikes, had to obtain against both the capitalist appetites and 'all sorts of survivals of the old capitalist system in the government offices' (CW 33: 187; B 1: 330); regardless of the old, somewhat oversimplified tag of 'capitalist system', that meant the class enemy was now partly inside the government apparatus! All through the year, he poured his most acerbic scorn on the 'Soviet bureaucrat'. Thus in a letter to Sheinman in February 1922 he acidly noted: 'At present the State Bank is a bureaucratic power game. There is the truth for you, if you want to hear not the sweet communist-official lies (with which everyone feeds you as a high mandarin), but the ***truth***. And if you do not want to look at this truth with open eyes, through all the communist lying, you are a man who has perished in the prime of life in a swamp of official lying' (CW 36: 567). And in his March report to the Eleventh CP Congress he emphasised that the economic dangers were much stronger than the past military ones 'because the difficulty lies within ourselves ... This difficulty consists in the fact that we do not want to acknowledge this unpleasant truth imposed upon us, we do not want to get into the unpleasant position which is yet indispensable: start learning anew'. He concluded by taking the example of the Moscow communists in the administration and asked whether they led the bureaucratic machine for which they were responsible: 'To tell the truth, they do not lead, they are led' (IP 765 and 774).

Lenin sketched two mutually reinforcing explanations for this danger, which was for him on a par with the foreign encirclement and the internal petty bourgeoisie (mainly peasant). One was cultural backwardness, and the other remnants of the tsarist past. At the end of 1922, addressing the Fourth Congress of the Comintern, he largely identified the Bolshevik 'machinery of State' with the old tsarist one:

> We now have a vast army of government employees, but lack sufficiently educated forces to exercise real control over them. In practice it often happens that here on the top, where we exercise political power, the machine functions somehow, but down below, the government employees have arbitrary control, and they often exercise it to counteract our measures ...
>
> IP 805, CW 33: 428–9, and see also CW 36: 605–6; B1: 330–1, and B1: 490–3

But furthermore, he began to complain that the coercive apparatus of the supposedly proletarian dictatorship and its core CP members were themselves transformed by the exercise of power in the ruthless circumstances of economic collapse and civil war 1917–21. The best contemporary short approach to Lenin concludes that 'The new enemy acquired a bitterly ironical label: the "soviet bureaucrat" ...', and that he found the reason for this grave devolution 'the cultural deficit of the proletariat and (even more) of the [people]', by which he meant 'literacy, elementary habits of organisation, and other basic skills of modern "civilisation"' (Lih, *Lenin* 182–3). Discussing at the Eleventh CP Congress some émigré circles who believed the Soviet rule was sliding toward a bourgeois rule, he even warned: 'Let us talk openly, such matters are possible ... [T]he struggle with capitalist society has become a hundred times fiercer and more dangerous, because we do not always clearly see whether in front of us there stands an enemy or a friend' (IP 773). Lenin was thus, before his incapacitation and then death, haltingly coming to approximate Rosa Luxemburg's 1918 critique of the Russian Revolution – which she supported – as too Jacobin and dictatorial in the bourgeois sense, so that eventually, with the fading vitality of the soviets and other public or plebeian institutions, 'only the bureaucracy remains as the active element' (Luxemburg 47).

I have not been proposing here to give a balanced assessment of Lenin's theory, especially of his exile and underground phase culminating in *The State and Revolution*, since my main aim is to identify the parts which were to remain in the tradition as mediated by Stalinism and handed down to the Yugoslav CP. It remains a fact that grave economic and then political difficulties caused Lenin to veer back to State power, however restricted its actual class basis was. In particular, the prohibition of factions in the CP at its Tenth Congress in 1921 (originally for one year) proved to be a grave mistake, opening the door for a slide to Stalinist autocracy. It would be fair to retroactively note that he had not yet understood the danger, but only the advantages, of monolithism. Furthermore, his fear from 1922 on that an open split in the leadership might lead to the break-up of the CP means that he kept the struggle secret and only within the Politbureau (for a long time Trotsky would do this too). Thus, Marx's idea that the radically anti-State Paris Commune type of institution provides 'the ... medium in which the class struggle can run through its different phases in the most rational and humane way', because it 'begins **the emancipation of labour** ... by doing away with the unproductive and mischievous work of the State parasites' (*On the Paris* 149–50), vanished after 1922 from the USSR agenda.

The resulting tradition arose as a balancing act by Stalin, who was in a cleft stick in dealing with Lenin's legacy (see the excellent passage in Kidrič 153–

4). On the one hand, given the continuing prestige, at home and abroad, of the founder of the Communist Party and State, he necessarily had to continue propagating Lenin's work. He draped himself in the mantle of his faithful disciple and indeed only continuator (the rest, from Trotsky and Bukharin on, were killed and their work in part tacitly appropriated by Stalin and fully expunged from the official doctrine). Furthermore there were large swatches in Lenin, beginning with the theory and establishment of the party and culminating in his insistence on a strong central State, which could, with suitable extrapolation out of the original situation and misinterpretation, be used in the Stalinist vulgate. On the other hand some of his work did not fit and was subjected to various types of falsification, from a number of outright suppressions (cf. Medvedev 556), as in the case of his anti-Stalin 'Testament', to editorial tricks, for example muddling the horizon of his copious notes on Hegel, which stressed that contradiction reigns in every process and there is no final victorious harmony, by adding to it some other unimportant writings on various philosophers so that the volume could then be called *Philosophical Notebooks*, rather than *Notes on Hegel* or *Notes on Dialectics*. Most important, the unsuitable works were backgrounded, edited late and in small numbers, and expunged from any official syllabus for the communist parties of the USSR or of the Third International. Characteristically, in *A Short Course of the CPSU/b/ History* – which was, together with Stalin's *Questions of Leninism*, as it were the New Testament of the world communist movement – all the major works by Lenin are glossed, except *State and Revolution*!

In this complex negotiation, however, beside a cold-stream Lenin dominant after 1918 and usable for Stalinism there remained an irreducible core with the horizon of a radical soviet or council democracy, that had already been published in the first 10 years of the USSR and could not now be censored outright. Read with discerning and interested eyes, as in the Yugoslav post-1948 debates – the translation of *The State and Revolution* was published there by Winter 1947–8 – this 'warm stream' horizon of Lenin's testified to his difference from official, crudely hierarchical Stalinism not simply by the quality of his texts but also by its liberatory, plebeian Marxism.

3 Stalin's Unavowed Thermidor

In this section I shall follow the USSR developments between roughly 1922 and 1929, by which time the Stalinist social system had, for all the subsequent convulsions in the countryside and the upper reaches, acquired its permanent lineaments.

The most cruel Civil War

> brought about a deep trauma in the history of bolshevism and communism ... The Civil War was the triumph of a most terrible and primitive violence of arms and men, a flagrant contradiction of the fundamental ideas from the October Revolution, and it perpetuated what those ideas were supposed to bury forever ... Having barely survived this ordeal, the CP came out of it exhausted, the soviets were emptied out, the working class of the two 1917 revolutions dispersed. And there clearly appeared a gap between the movement from below and the decimated and bureaucratised vanguards; revolutionary discipline had largely been supplanted by war mentality, by the conditions of dire need, by corruption.
> CORTESI 303–4

The CP and State apparatus grew more and more powerful to cope with the huge demands of war and the accompanying economic breakdown. As an example, in 10 months between April 1920 and February 1921, the Uchraspred, a non-elected body assigning CP members to important tasks, made 40,000 assignments to important bodies (B 1: 304 citing Shapiro 253). Stalin was elected general secretary of the CP central committee (further CC) in March 1922, and during Lenin's ensuing illness proceeded to a full-scale top-down reorganisation of the Soviet party and State apparatuses, practically merging and hugely inflating them, and rigidly subjecting them not to the CC nor its elected Organisation Bureau, but directly to the Secretariat. This hugely increased the powers and material privileges of the apparatus members, giving them a strong incentive for clientelism: compared to the average monthly salary of under 7 rubles, it instituted an official minimum of 30 roubles while CC members received 43 roubles; with a bonus of 50% for CP functionaries with a family of three, and another 50% for extraordinary work, the lowest *apparatchik* (professional CP functionary) had a standard of living which I would calculate as 8 times the average. All of them had also free housing, clothing, medical aid, and in the higher echelons transport (eventually to become office limousines). On top of it, at that time of dearth such functionaries received regular distribution in kind of meat, sugar, rice, tea, cigarettes, etc. The criterion, as formulated by Stalin at the Twelfth CP congress in 1923, was to select such cadre so that 'posts will be taken by people capable of following the [party] line'; beside this new Stalinist shibboleth, even more important became his obsessive catchword of 'monolithism', extolled in a key speech on industrialisation in 1928 (B2: 539) and fully enunciated in 1931, when he had achieved it by eliminating open and rather vigorous intra-party currents. By 1923, the number of functionaries paid by the

Secretariat was over 20,000, with 40,000 further 'technical staff', also with special emoluments (the CP had then 400,000 members).[6] Perhaps as important, the 'CC instructors' to the provincial CP committees were given almost unlimited powers to steer the work of and elections to those bodies, so that by that year about half of the provincial secretaries were already elected on 'recommendation' of the Secretariat. Lenin's ideal practice of a democracy from below upward was thus erased, the soviets were practically powerless after 1921, and elections in the CP were in most – later all – important cases rigged in advance (all data in this paragraph from Podsheldolkin).

During Stalin's rise to dominance his calls for 'reconstructing the State apparatus' zigzagged between ritual repetitions of tags from Lenin and anodyne calls 'to make [the apparatus] sound and honest, simple and inexpensive' (B2: 367–8). In the speech to the Eighth Congress of the Communist Youth League, Stalin called for mass control from below, especially against 'the new bureaucrats, ... and finally, communist bureaucrats', and for the party's 'ruthless struggle against bureaucracy' (B2: 224–6). The Sixteenth CP Conference of April 1929 even put on its agenda 'the fight against bureaucratism', and passed a resolution criticising the 'bureaucratic perversion of the State machinery', asking that this machinery be improved in order to accomplish the Five-Year Plan, stressing 'precise execution of their respective tasks by each link in the chain' and 'overcoming inertia, red tape, bureaucratic suppression, mutual "covering-up" and indifference to the need of the working people' (B2: 435–6). The theme was soon buried by a management counter-offensive (B2: 230), even if it was to periodically recur. Confusingly, Stalin's purges, and later recurrent police persecutions, at times also cut into the bureaucracy, probably because it still had many members from Lenin's time, and then because no group should feel safe (Lewin, 'Alle prese' 32–3). The situation is well characterised by an anecdote about Brecht's attitude to it: he struck a penitent pose, squinted, and said (impersonating the State), 'I know I should die out' ... However, Stalin's preferred means, increased violence by the State, issued in a new doctrine of 'intensified class struggle', justifying most cruel and sweeping repressions: it was announced in a speech in July 1928 (see Davies 598–9), repeated in 1933, and led eventually, after his complete victory, in 1939 into a head-on denial of the 'rotten' anti-State axiom of Marx's and Engels's (see McNeal 62).

---

6   At that time, Trotsky began to speak of the danger of 'bureaucratic degeneration', later his central diagnosis; in exile, he called the ruling bureaucracy a caste and not a class, while finally acknowledging that it is an imprecise term (cf. Bongiovanni ed. 309). Important as this pioneering if insufficient insight is, it was edited out of the Stalinist tradition and I do not deal with it here.

In spite of oscillations and manoeuverings, bureaucracy thus principally meant in Stalinism what impeded the further centralisation, expansion, and smooth work of the oligarchic and despotic State machinery, that is, paper-pushing or what the French call *la paperasserie*, and this remained its official meaning until the end of the Soviet regime. Nonetheless, it was useful not only for disciplining subordinates in the apparatus but also in giving a hint to the workers and peasants that the top was aware of their oppression and working against its bearers. However, this last factor was closely watched so as not to give too much scope to the 'culturally and technically backward' masses, and never allowed to coalesce except as a movement for 'socialist emulation' and Stakhanovite work productivity. True, Bukharin was as late as 1929 still allowed to criticise the distended State apparatus, which he linked with increasing pressure on the peasants, and to call for 'all possible forms of association by working people so as, at all costs, to avoid bureaucratisation'. Since all this hinged on the role of the Bolshevik party, he also took aim at its blind discipline, exhorting members, in the critical tradition of Lenin, 'to take not a single word on trust ... to utter not a single word against their conscience'. But this was the swan-song of the original Marx-to-Lenin line: soon, Bukharin was to be denounced by the Stalinists for bowing to 'the backwardness and discontent of the masses' and infringing the necessary 'iron discipline' in the party (B2: 424 and 486, Cohen 304), and definitely silenced.

A further rough indication about bureaucracy could be gleaned from the composition of the CP. In its 1927 census it had one million members, of whom the 'office workers and others' – the latter were mainly students – occupied fully 60% as against 30% of the workers (B2: 334–5 and 350–1). True, later a huge drive was launched to get a 'workers' majority' in the party; but the definitions of social provenience were vague and mainly based on unchecked declarations by the members who had an incentive to claim virtuous working-class ascendancy. It seems that in most cases membership in the CP was in personal union with the official or 'bureaucratic' post one filled. The bureaucracy grew into 'a social stratum which led a life different from that of the workers in the factories and the fields, arrogated privileges to itself, and was unaware of the real problems faced by the masses' (B2: 336). The 1939 USSR census found that, including families, 14 million people were clerical workers or professionals employed by the State, 3.5 times as many – 10 million more – than in 1926 (McNeal 59–60). At the time, Stalin claimed that, of the almost 3.5 million CP members, there were 3–4,000 'superior' leaders or executives, 30–40,000 middle ones, and 100–150,000 members of 'the lower party leadership' (McNeal 46; the first two were usually called *krupnyi gosudarstvennyi deiatel'* and *otvet-rabotnik* – Lewin, 'Alle prese' 32).

It is therefore not too surprising that in the backward USSR Stalin's course was not without mass support in the CP and the country, including the reconstituted industrial workers (of whom 8% were CP members – see B2: 338–40). He appealed first to stability, a modest but clear rise of the overall living standard in comparison to the years of collapse, the longing for peace which dominated a people that had gone through seven years of war and civil war, and later to the interest of the new dominant class to build 'socialism in one country' – that is, industrialisation and modernisation which would preserve the existing oligarchy – in the USSR. The social system of ripe Stalinism from the 1930s on was 'a hierarchy, but with ample opportunities of upward mobility' (McNeal 57). The price to pay for this was to become very high: it began with 'the confiscation *sine die* of the elementary liberties of political expression, of gathering, of knowledge, of travel, of personal adventurous freedom' (Cortesi 725) as well as of strikes, and ended in mass assassinations and/or incarcerations of entire social groups. Politically, it consisted in the rise of a ruling stratum or class no longer in feedback with the masses: concerning the peasants, this disjuncture was true from the October Revolution on and moderated only by Lenin's insistence on safeguarding their interests and their monopoly on food production; concerning the industrial working class it became largely true since its reconstitution in the roughly five years after Lenin's death, after the old revolutionary core had been decimated and the workers in the party 'very quickly absorbed into the various apparatuses, so that they left the working class' (B2: 517). Economically, it was based on rapid industrialisation and a scarcity of consumer goods. As Trotsky satirically remarked:

> The basis of bureaucratic rule is the poverty of society in objects of consumption, with the resulting struggle of each against all. When there is enough goods in a store, the purchasers can come whenever they want to. When there is little goods, the purchasers are compelled to stand in line. When the lines are very long, it is necessary to appoint a policeman to keep order. Such is the starting point of the power of the Soviet bureaucracy. It 'knows' who is to get something and who has to wait.
> *Revolution*, cho5.htm

This meant that the 1919 1:5 ratio of minimum to maximum incomes grew in the 1930s to between 1:10 and 1:25 (Nove 212, Bettelheim, *Planification* 62), not counting the top apparatus, while in 1950 it was 1:40 (Ossowski 130). At the peak of this High Stalinism, the bureaucratic material privileges, superadded to those of authority and prestige, were huge: top people (including privileged artists) could use secret special shops with generally unavailable goods: the lowest bureaucrats had to pay for them, the middle ones paid only half, while the top echelons had unlimited free drawing rights (Mandel 8). To the contrary, the living standard of the workers, in particular, was subject as of the beginning of five-year plans to a sharp reduction in favour of State accumulation, only partly due to the great influx into towns and industries (see Cliff in cho4-a.htm#so). As to the intelligentsia, when Gorky urged Lenin to institute an alliance of the workers with the intellectuals, he is reported to have replied 'This is not a bad idea, not at all. Tell the intelligentsia it should join us' (Fischer 1: 415). But the majority remained inimical; the powerfully creative humanist minority which did join in was a tolerated epicycle, as of the end of the 1920s subject to strong control by bureaucratic organisations and then beheaded in the 1930s. However, natural sciences and a streamlined educational system were as of the first five-year plans strongly fostered. A new, subservient intellectual class became the subordinate administrative and technical elite (Stalin, as usual, called it a 'stratum' – McNeal 58).

The upshot of this complex involution was that the State apparatus grew into the principal ruling lever: isolated from the masses, 'Bolshevism acquired a social basis it did not want and did not immediately recognise: the bureaucracy' (Lewin, *Storia* 114). What is the CPSU, asked Tito in his most dissident phase of 1949–53? Its five million members were nothing else but the police, army, and administrative State apparatus: '[it] in no way represents the rank and file workers and peasants' (Banerji, electronic p. 8)

4   Summing Up

To sum up sections 2 and 3 about the USSR, I shall use citations from two of the most important books in the field.

A general conclusion would be Cortesi's take, in the best and richest survey to date, that the Thermidor 'shaped an autocratic State, with a growing distance from the 1917 revolutionary ideas' (737).

On bureaucracy in particular, Bettelheim's conclusion is:

> Lenin too used the expressions 'bureaucracy' and 'bureaucratic distortion,' but what is important is that he did not rest satisfied with these elements of analysis or of description, but strove to relate them to class relations and the class struggle. For almost all the CP members, including the leaders, however, the expressions 'bureaucracy' and 'bureaucratic distortion' served as substitutes for class analysis ... Consequently, the fight

against these phenomena seemed not to be primarily a question of class struggle, but to depend exclusively on the development of the productive forces, of education, or of repression.

B1: 516–17

APPENDIX 2

The Discourse about Bureaucracy and State Power in Post-Revolutionary Yugoslavia 1945–72

> How those who deemed themselves competent in matters of power have analysed the situation belongs to research about the situation.
> MOSHE LEWIN, on the discussions in Soviet 1920s

> [The problems of 'bureaucracy'] are problems, partly of the apparatus of administration, planning, administrative and political decision, etc., which any complex modern society must possess, and especially one of economic and social planning and management ...
> ERIC HOBSBAWM, 'Notes on Class Consciousness'

∴

0   Introduction

Was the discourse about bureaucracy in SFRY endogenous or exogenous: sparked by inner problems or the clash with Cominform, that is, with Soviet Stalinist practice?[1] The most pertinent hypothesis seems here that 'bureaucracy' was the clearest sign and confluence of two factors. The first and basic one was a smouldering unease felt more and more strongly by many professional Party cadres, most of all the top ones, when their revolutionary-democratic impulses and ideals began to wane in the practice of ruling which often mandated despotic forms of commanding – not only against the dispossessed bourgeoisie but also against peasantry, the Party's mass basis during the war, which had willy-nilly to feed the growing needs of village and town. A second and sparking factor was the conflict with the unacceptable practice of the USSR based on total subjection to the rulers, which was being imposed in

---

1   I refer to the periodical Praxis in italics and to the informal group of its collaborators as Praxis without italics. As explained at the beginning of the book, I write 'Party' with caps for the CPY/LCY.

all available ways by its government and emissaries and in a bare three years led to an open attempt at dispossession of the Yugoslav Party and revolutionary power in the Cominform 1948 Resolution (http://en.wikipedia.org/wiki/Informbiro_period). This clash '"rehabilitated" the self-managing and democratic forms born at the time of the revolution' (Kardelj, R 241); not only did it mean a quantum leap in sobering up of a decisive part of CPY, most of all its top, but it also gave them by way of Lenin and Stalin the term 'bureaucracy', with all its advantages and snares.

I shall arrive at a judgement about the notion and term of bureaucracy at the end, but the conclusion of Appendix 1 is that it can cover a heterogeneous field of negative stances – Brecht's *Haltung* or Bourdieu's *habitus* – in postrevolutionary power that runs from loss of efficiency and poor understanding of reality outside the official or placeholder bureaus (Stalin) all the way to the growth of a separate 'caste' as a pillar of that power (Marx), and then to incipient suspicion (pioneered by Trotsky, while in Yugoslavia such stances go from Kidrič, Djilas, and Kardelj to the Praxis group and other loyal socialist intellectuals) that this group is growing into a counter-revolutionary class usurping decision about the use of surplus from labour. 'Bureaucracy' became what Lewis Carroll called a portmanteau word, into which different meanings flowed whose negativity was symmetrical to the positivity of its diametrically contrary pole and field of plebeian democracy from below.

What other brief terms might have been suitable at the time for a wide-ranging discussion? 'Hegemony' was too mild for the Stalinist horrors which had to be articulated, called by Kidrič 'the most perfidious counter-revolution known to history up to now' (141); perhaps it is not without significance that in the documents of CPY I found 'hegemony' invoked only by Ranković, leader of the 'strong-arm' faction, at the third plenary session of the Central Committee (*Sednice* 513). 'Dictatorship' (of the proletariat) was quite unusable since it was, first, a positive concept in Marx and Lenin, second, in the practice of the wartime liberation struggle as a popular front of all patriots tabooed and therefore theoretically quite neglected, and third, the standard bourgeois bugaboo against any form of socialism and communism. To the contrary, bureaucracy was a term that could be embraced equally by those ideologically – though not practically – three quarters Stalinists, as were for the first year or two after the 1948 break almost all the Party leaders, and by those who were beginning to think if not about Trotsky (who remained taboo in SFRY) then about the radically democratic aspect of Lenin and Marx that they had intimately experienced in the practice of the Liberation War 1941–5. After them, the term was picked up within theoretical delving into the problems of socialist society by independent smaller groups, such as the one around the periodical *Praxis*, and a wide spectrum of other articles and finally books. However, the stance and discourse of the two principal groups, the 'Party/State' and the 'loyal opposition' one, were different, and finally incompatible. Therefore I shall discuss them separately.

The development periods of SFRY, I have argued in this book, were roughly 1945–52, 1952–65, 1966–72 and 1972–89. By the mid-1970s all was mainly decided, so that there were no further discursively significant debates but a Yugoslav 'Brezhnevist' stasis came about, accompanied by growing ideological and economic decay. I see no use in following the convoluted, mainly legal, discussions in the degeneration after 1972, when SFRY grows into an apathetic periphery of the capitalist world system: the cognitive paradigm of 'bureaucracy' had been exhausted.

1 The Party-State Discourse

1.0

All the semantic and ideological rethinking and revisions up to about the mid-50s took place within and were sparked exclusively by the leadership of CPY, the only organisation which de facto had the right of public and permanent discussion about the horizons and meaning of the revolution. The later, somewhat different and more or less opposed stances of the 'civil sphere' in public opinion were strongly co-determined by a permanent interpellation directed toward the discourse of the leaders. In this context an undoubted axiom for all was that the Leninist vanguard had after the armed revolution also to take care of the general societal interests. Beside the ongoing tutelage of Yugoslavia's independence, this primarily meant proceeding with the country's industrialisation and modernisation.

In this spread of approaches the best articulated ones were those by Kidrič, Kardelj and Bakarić, and I shall induce from a selection of their works, with briefer reviews of Tito and Djilas. As far as method is concerned this means following their terms and horizons as they evolved, limiting my explanations to the most needed ones but giving by the way an explicit or implicit indication of how I evaluate them.

1.1 Boris Kidrič

Kidrič was early after the war given the toughest job of directing SFRY economy (see Chapter 5.2), which involved complex and time-consuming operational problems of application and control, and he died early. Thus his discussions of bureaucracy are fewer than Kardelj's, but his contribution seems to me conspicuous in theoretical clarity and richness.

His first significant statement about 'the struggle against bureaucracy' is found in the 'Exposé on Reorganizing the Management of Economy' ('Ekspoze o reorganizaciji upravljanja privredom') at the beginning of 1950, which immediately focussed on a differentiation of the two semantic poles – discussed in his Introduction – of 'bureaucracy and bureaucratism'. The term of 'bureaucratism' signals immediately that one is talking about a system and not only singular or even group bad habits, and it was rarely used by the 'cold stream' or 'strong-arm tactics' supporters. Further, Kidrič explicitly refuses to consider 'secondary phenomena which are in fact a result of bureaucratism, such as slow decisions, loss of documents, etc. etc. We have to do here above all with *the social phenomenon of bureaucracy ... in socialism*', which means that 'the people's democracy, based on widespread human initiatives and conscious cooperation of the largest possible popular masses, is being replaced by a growing and growingly specialised (*sve kompetentnija*) bureaucracy, which simultaneously *gets ever more separated from the production process and looms above it as its tutor and parasite*' (59, italics mine). Kidrič thus immediately fused politics with economics and, refusing the insufficiently differentiated organic discourse about 'wens' (Marx) and 'excrescences' on an otherwise healthy body, opted for vertical dichotomy and opposition between 'the production process' (by metonymy a working-class matter) and a 'tutor' outside and above it. 'Parasite' itself is a term marking the moment of transition from organic discourse to class opposition; it is the 'middle term' of an organic enemy incompatible with the organism, adopted into the Marxist tradition from Saint-Simon and Adam Smith – for whom (but not really for Marx, see Suvin, *Defined* 439–42) all non-producing strata or classes are parasites. A bit further Kidrič formulates it thus: 'The point is that the apparatus ... should not mean a growth of bureaucracy at the expense of the productive population ...' (65). He thus formulated most clearly the polarisation between an efficient popular democracy from the partizan tradition and bureaucratism, which was shared by other Party leaders (Kardelj, Tito, and Djilas) because they were spontaneously drawn to it.

In the same speech, Kidrič shapes this opposition as a zero-sum game: 'do the positions of a true popular democracy in managing the State and the economy grow stronger and those of bureaucracy grow weaker, or do the latter ones, on the contrary, grow stronger and proliferate' (60). He is postulating here a frontal collision analogous to Marx's class struggle.

Some months later, in his speech at the federal Popular assembly (Parliament), socialist democratism is embodied in the Workers' Councils which he was then legally introducing. He divides the history of post-war Yugoslavia into 'a first period of State socialism', with a tendency toward growth and bureaucratisation of the central 'administrative apparatus', and an incipient second period in which the apparatus is being significantly diminished and changed from a command-giver to 'primarily planning preparatory and analytical functions. The command prerogatives in the State management of economy are being more and more reduced to those functionaries who are directly nominated by the presidiums of popular assemblies or by the executives of local councils'. The antagonist is identified with the important category of **monopolism**, which is for Kidrič not at all synonymous with planned economy but derives from 'the blind empiricist acceptance of USSR practice', and even deeper from 'monopolistic capitalism ... brought to its culmination by USSR bureaucratic centralism'. It is not only politically most dangerous for socialism but it also harms the quality, range, and development of production (all 70, and on monopolism – cf. 229). I assume monopolism has been borrowed in part from Marx but primarily from Lenin's *Imperialism*, where it is important not only as characterising this phase of capitalism but especially as a source of arrest and decay in the economy. Therefore Kidrič, as the supreme State manager of Yugoslav economy, also announced 'an essential restriction of the budgetary bureaucratic centralism in favour of the republican and self-governing [that is, local government] budgets as well as of the budgetary calculations (*privrednih računa*) of the single enterprises ...' (72).

However, soon thereafter, in 1951, Kidrič had to note 'a tendency to bureaucratise the Workers' Councils' within the top federal economic bodies (115), and one year later 'especially within the apparatus in the republics and districts which covets a return to administrative methods' (227), and where 'bureaucratic disposal of surplus labour' is the material basis of local chauvinisms (236)! Therefore he summarises in 1952 the new economic system of SFRY as 'carrying fully out ... the historical process of the fight against monopolies', monopolism being the diametrical contradiction of socialist democracy (198 and 200). He believed that in SFRY the phase of State monopoly was brought to an end 'before it could bring about and strengthen a bureaucratic caste by bureaucratising ourselves' (205). This belief was buttressed by the drastic restrictions he was directly introducing on the federal level, so that he calculated the salary of the highest officials was much lower than in the prewar Kingdom of Yugoslavia, while the salary of enterprise managers was about one third (*Sednice* 619).

In Chapter 5.2 I have written about the theoretical culmination of this phase, Kidrič's 'Theses on the Economy of the Transitional Period in Our Country' from the end of 1950. In it he summarised: as the USSR example shows, 'State socialism', after its initial necessity immediately after the revolution, necessarily grows into 'the strengthening of a privileged bureaucracy as a social parasite, the throttling ... of socialist democracy, and a general degeneration of the whole system', so that there comes about 'a restoration of a specific kind ... a vulgar State-capitalist monopoly' (84). To the contrary, his own inital 'Theses' start from a definition of 'a socialist *enterprise* (*poduzeće*) ... within the socialist *commodity exchange*' (79, italics mine). This founding step is a decisive notional breakthrough since it, first, starts inductively from the working collective (that is, upwards from below), as opposed to the Soviet starting from federal ministries and their branchings downward; and second, it affirms the existence of commodity production, in full rejection of the Soviet model. From then on he most sharply attacks 'the bureaucratic counter-revolution and exploitation of the working people', fully grown in USSR and latent in the old Yugoslav 'bureaucratico-socialist' [sic] way of organising (119), that 'counter-dialectically denies that within the socialist economic sector itself ... there necessarily exist contradictions and a struggle between ... elements of the capitalist past and of the communist future' (128). In his most caustic statement, Russian extreme backwardness found 'its own people, people of average or below average education, very agile only in intrigue, in organising a limitless rule of bureaucratic self-will (*stihije*) and State monopoly as well as in a falsely "revolutionary" presentation of the real processes' (141). He allowed that in the first phase of Yugoslavia, the State also 'functioned in the economy as the owner, albeit in the name of a society of working people, but still ... as a comprehensive and all-powerful economic monopoly administered by an apparatus of officials' (136).

In his article 'On the Drafts on the New Economic Laws' ('O nacrtima novih ekonomskih zakona') Kidrič reached the central problem which will haunt Yugoslavia as a spectre as long as it existed, and gave it an optimist outcome. He postulated that the new laws solve, 'in favour of the direct producers ... who create surplus of labour' –

> the basic question about the possibility or impossibility of exploitation of man by man in the economical and social system born from the socialist revolution, that is the question of who manages the surplus of labour – and behind that question sooner or later there appears the even more fateful question of who really appropriates the surplus of labour ...
> 122

The essay 'On Some Theoretical Questions of Our Economic System' ('O nekim teorijskim pitanjima našeg privrednog sistema'), inspired by Marx's *Critique of the Gotha Programme* and by Lenin's analyses from the Soviet period, postulates that three possibilites are dormant in the deeply contradictory production relationships: a return to capitalism, a consistently socialist upbuilding by means of fast industrialisation and a widening socialist democracy, and a bureaucratic tendency. The latter is characterised as 'the State form of social ownership (or the administrative way of managing economy)' (170–2). For all of Kidrič's optimism, he clearly saw –

> that today [written in mid-1951] bureaucratism has nested in the heads of local Party officials, also in the republican ministries, trading and other enterprises in the districts, etc. There is a stealthy bureaucratic resistance precisely against those new measure of ours that lead to rule-driven behaviour (*automatizam*) ...

– and he identified the root of this resistance as the fear of losing a position of authority (*Sednice* 560–1). In 1952, near the end of Kidrič's life, he even posits that 'the economic-cum-societal role of the Soviet bureaucratic caste is quite similar to the role of the capitalist class', unless it is even worse because of its omnipotence (230). Such radicalness was rather rare in SFRY, and it was totally forgotten at the top of the Party after the 1957 reconciliation with Khrushchev.

The limits of Kidrič's brief trajectory of only four years were perhaps reached in his claim that, as different from 'the class or caste rule by bureaucracy in the USSR' (136), the Yugoslav 'socialist commodity exchange certainly creates opposed interests, but does not necessarily lead to class antagonism' (82–3). This cautious hypothesis was in my view tenable at that time, but 20-odd years later became blindness in Kardelj or Bakarić.

1.2   Milovan Djilas

Djilas's talents as a historical writer did not include political practice or theory. His sincere and magnanimous indignation is to be seen in his stance against the monopoly of the administrative apparatus and despotism in Party practice, and particularly in his rage against 'the practice of conquest and exploitation by the USSR' as well as against the Party ideological monopoly that leads to a material and social monopolisation (*Sednice* 288–9, 559, 590–1). He should be given credit for being in 1950, together with Kidrič, the pioneer of a somewhat articulated approach to 'the creation of a privileged bureaucratic stratum, of bureaucratic centralism', which had in the USSR made the State a 'force above society' (*Borba* of 19 March 1950, cited from A.R. Johnson 101). In so doing he oscillated between 'a crisis of socialism' and 'a *sui generis* counter-revolution' that leads to 'a State (in fact capitalist) property' (Djilas, *Savremene* 14–15, and cf. 16–24). He gained world fame in the Cold War period after his exclusion from CPY with the book *The New Class*, rewritten by CIA specialists and translated into many languages as anti-communist propaganda with its funds (cf.

Bogdanović, also Stonor Saunders). He should be remembered not only for his civic courage and consistency despite repeated jailings but also as a pioneer of the radical stance that a 'new class' is in power in Yugoslavia. However, flashes of insight are in his book submerged in journalistic improvisation, so that it today reads as rather parochial. Its main theoretical point, then new in Yugoslav discourse but mainly taken over from outside sources, is the differentiation between 'bureaucracy as a stratum' and a separate 'nucleus of Party and political bureaucracy' which he called a new class (42–3). Whether there really was in Yugoslavia already in 1954 a new ruling class or – as I assume – some initial transitional forms towards it is a matter of further discussion by historians.

Djilas had a large following within the Party. Retrospectively, Bakarić confirmed that 'this was a very wide movement of critique in 1952–53, ... which contained a series of positive critical remarks against the existing system that was clearly out of date' (2: 276). Between 1953 and 1955 nearly half the CPY membership – that is, 378 out of 790,000 (Rusinow 96–8, and cf. Filipi and my Chapter 7) – was ejected or left of its own accord; since the 'Djilas affair' erupted at the very beginning of 1954, one should perhaps subtract from this number one third, and of the remaining quarter of a million a majority was probably not kicked out for 'djilasism', as at that time a large discouragement of village Party cadres came about after the failure of the campaign for cooperative production (cf. Denitch 100): yet the number of Djilas sympathisers still remains large. Of those erased from the Party rolls 25% were workers and 54% peasants, while the largest part of the newly admitted 234,000 members were somewhat older office employees. This rather sudden turn of the Party from a worker-peasant-intellectual to white-collar membership plus some workers could be taken as a confirmation of Djilas's horizons, were they less hasty and better articulated. I remember well that Party intellectuals I knew at the time opined Djilas had stymied democratisation for at least five to six years.

1.3   *Edvard Kardelj*

Since Kardelj industriously wrote about the problems of SFRY for a third of a century, I shall confine myself to the most characteristic samples of how he discussed bureaucracy. I shall follow their chronology, though thematics will enforce minor deviations, and divide them into roughly the phases of 1945–51, 1957–66, and 1966–ca. 1972. In 1952–7 – the beginnings of self-management and economic boom – he repeated the opinions of the first phase and began testing them based on the experience both of the successes and resistances within the Party monolith; I stop before the last phase (1972–89), when the blockade of self-management was set in stone despite surface curlicues.

1.3.1 Phase of Centralised Postwar Economic and State Build-Up 1945–51

The 1948 shock of Stalin's attempt to take over Yugoslavia forced its leaders, both on moral and practical grounds, to an 'agonising reappraisal' of the roots of Stalinism. The conclusions to which the top Party leaders arrived were: 'any communist party that identifies itself with the State and the police apparatus gets deformed', while 'the working masses in USSR were kept far away from governing' (R 122). What Yugoslavia should do is the contrary. The attack on 'bureaucracy', Soviet and increasingly also Yugoslav, was a decision to go for a mass popular democracy led and supervised by the Communist Party. At an end of the 1949 Central Committee meeting, Kardelj stated that the policy of USSR is based on a powerful and omnipresent bureaucratism opposed to socialist democracy, that as far as distance from the latter goes there was no important difference between Soviet-type and social-democratic party leaderships, and concluded that CPY 'must above all struggle against bureaucratism' to stop it from evolving into a Soviet-type system (*Sednice* 470, 477, and 480). At that point conflicts within SFRY power-holders began to take shape. Much later, Kardelj was to formulate them as 'the dilemma should we strive for a *State paternalism* (a good government which would take care of the good but "stupid" people) or for a true *socialist self-managing system* (laying the foundation of ... such material conditions and democratic forms in which the working people could take care of themselves)' (R 245). In 'Ten Years of the People's Revolution' ('Deset godina narodne revolucije'), an essay of the early 50s, he claimed that 'bureaucratism is the last and mightiest fortress of *remnants of a class system*, and thus the most dangerous enemy of socialism' (PSI 1: 103, italics mine). In his mid-1950s speech in the federal Assembly introducing the new law on the local People's Committees, which was a first major step toward local democracy, Kardelj attacked the bureaucratic 'caste' in USSR, where the arbitrariness of rulers is bigger than in the bourgeois West, and stressed: 'No bureaucratic apparatus can build socialism. Socialism can only grow out of the initiative of millions of common people together with the leading role of the proletarian party ... by means of their rising participation in the State apparatus from its lowest to its highest forms ...' (R 233, PSI 1: 430) And in a 1951 meeting on the legal and security system in the country he talked about the danger of a system of arbitrariness coming from bureaucrats, instancing in particular 'Party members in leading positions' and pleading for 'many changes in the minds of people within our leading bodies, including the Central Committee' (*Sednice* 562).

I believe that Kardelj's sincere horizon, at least for many years to come, was the formulation from his 1954 article 'Four Years of Experience' ('Četiri godine iskustva', *SDS* 85–93): that in the Workers' Councils the working class is growing '*independent from the State administrative apparatus, in other words it is really fully and directly changing this apparatus into its own tool*' (89). In this respect he was, with Kidrič, one of the loudest critics of bureaucracy, and he remained the most articulate one.

1.3.2   Phase of the First Political and Economic Waverings, a Moderate Expansion of Self-management with State Control of Investments, and the Appearance of 'Market Socialism', 1957–65

About this probably decisive and still promising epoch, Kardelj confessed in his speech at the Eighth Party Congress in 1964 that after 1956 the elements of the old system of 'administrative management in the economy' persisted (*PSI* 7: 473). Institutionally, they included high taxation of the enterprises' accumulations and a State disposal of thus created investment funds; politically, '*a strong influence of subjective measures and political wishes in their distribution*' (*R* 244–5, italics mine).

And in the 1970 speech looking backward from the twentieth anniversary of Workers' Councils, he somewhat contradictorily claimed that 'CPY as a whole strongly stimulated and helped their introduction … However, opposition to them even within the Party, was very strong', especially 'among many communists filling administrative positions in factories and State administrations, even among some who had leading positions in the Party, trade unions, etc …' (*R* 244–6). I shall dwell a bit more on this speech.

I find that Kardelj's laudable sincerity, nearer to Lenin than to Stalin, is accompanied by an imperfect system of causal explanation for the 'subjective measures and political wishes', since they finally came from a powerful and large segment of the Party. This perhaps diplomatic way of dealing with opposed political stances as subjective aberrations, as if subjectivity and wishing were a characteristic only of these anonymous enemies of self-management, refuses an open confrontation which would have been the only, if thorny, way out. In Kardelj's Collected Works, the fifth and final volume is titled 'Subjective Forces [sic] in the Self-managing Society' (*Subjektivne snage u samoupravnom društvu*). Though 'forces' for currents within the Party is a bad Stalinist fossil, I have nothing against talking about subjectivities; however, it is an ABC of both Marxism and political realism that they cannot be properly grasped unless anchored in societal *interests*, thence in *classes* or analogously 'strong' groups. If in the above speech for Kardelj, the Party 'as a whole' is identical with the will of the top leadership, this was already an anachronism: as of the 60s the decisions of federal authorities had to be to a large extent shared by other centres, such as republican and local ones. And

FIGURE 30 *Edvard Kardelj at UN (1951)*

the publicly not expressed but strong opposition of a good part of the Party cadre – from enterprise managers to the level just below the Politbureau (later Executive Committee) – steadily grew and never ceased, produced as it was by material class interests.

Very significant is also the permanent, and finally fatal, tendency of Kardelj's (and of almost all other top leaders) to fold over the furthest utopian horizon of a given legal or political measure onto its practical realisation. This is a direct consequence of the Stalinist deformation of Marxism and of Leninism, in which the ruling Party theory of the moment – in fact, the theory of a very small number of top leaders, and from 1928/29 only of the topmost one – is proclaimed and acclaimed as fully corresponding to reality (cf. Bettelheim II: 546–7), as a kind of Borgesian map fully matching the territory or Orwellian Newspeak. In fact, theoretical stances and legal measures cannot, of course, do anything else but *begin* a movement toward given horizons, that in practice may often move slowly or not at all, stymied by what Kardelj called strong oppositional pressures. Writing against the horizons of the Chinese Communist Party which downplayed the dangers of new megawars, Kardelj rightly concluded: 'Only that policy is truly revolutionary that unites a clear revolutionary orientation with a realist analysis of the objective conditions and all factors of social dynamics' (*Socijalizam* 25). Yet his 1970 overview of Workers' Councils in Yugoslavia is a clear example of how a given 'truly revolutionary policy' was neutralised by the lack of a realist analysis of the pertinent social dynamics. The horizon of his writings, as a rule laudably democratic, was therefore more and more sadly polluted by the pretence (or self-deception) that it is already reached, or is at least within the hand's grasp. When practice then denied some legal-cum-institutional measure, to admit a dozen or half a dozen years later that the horizon necessitates a further series of measures in order to be reached was at any rate better than pretending omniscience, but in time turned into a less and less believable ritual.

1.3.3   Phase of Blocked Self-management due to Monolithic Rule of the Party/State, and of Growing Economic Problems, 1965–early 70s

After 1965, opposition to the ambitious mega-reform turn of that year, discussed at length in this book (for the background and some conclusions see my Chapters 5, 8, and here especially 10), as well as opposition to the Workers' Councils grew into the decisive, if hidden, political factor. After years of backstage struggles, Kardelj attempted for the first time to identify its social roots in the long article of 1967, 'The Working Class, Bureaucratism, and the League of Communists of Yugoslavia' ('Radnička klasa, birokratizam i Savez Komunista Jugoslavije', *sss* 9–66). It manoeuvres again between sincerity and a refusal of class struggle, as a weak imitation of Marx's and Lenin's overviews.

On the one hand he pens a quite frank statement identifying 'bureaucracy' as a lawful phenomenon of an epoch in which the revolution had broken the bourgeoisie but the working class was too weak to impose self-management: 'Hence in the early phases of socialism the State appears as a force above the working class and the society, with all the contradictions ... which flow from this. Hence there had to come about *a very independent and politically very powerful managing stratum* [sic] *that could strongly* [*or essentially – bitno*] *influence the regulation of inner societal relationships and contradictions* ... Because of such political power, this stratum may come and comes into collision – sometimes in a progressive and sometimes in a conservative sense – with the central mass of the working class or with its single parts'. On the other hand, Kardelj claims that the bureaucracy is *not* a class, though it is difficult to say what else to call this 'stratum' in the phrase which I emphasised above: 'But because of such a position, the bureaucracy in a professional sense does not grow into a new class that would be the principal obstacle to the societal influence of the working class' (47–8). Somewhat earlier, this claim was better articulated: there is no bureaucratic class, but 'thereby I do not claim there are no elements of class relationships and class contradictions', connected 'with tendencies that are born in those societal groups which are nearer to the dining table of the State-property monopoly than to the workers' self-management ... This is not a struggle of class against class because in the final instance the long-term interests of all these strata are the same. Therefore the class struggle is in such conditions expressed ... primarily in ideological and political struggle ...' (45–6)

Such an apodictic *petitio principii* (the elementary logical error by which the basis of an argument is supposed to have been proved when it is only presupposed) wrapped into multiple evasions adds up to a refusal to think the matter to the end. Namely: (1) there exists a very strong and independent societal stratum that has 'essential' (*bitno*) political power in determining relationships between people, and is composed of 'societal groups' whose economic interests are shaped by the State monopoly in managing the forces of production; yet (2), this does NOT lead to a class struggle because Kardelj, without further argumentative ado, claims that 'in the final instance the long-term interests' of such 'strata' – as for example the working class and a not further dissected State bureaucracy – are identical. To sufficiently harmonise these interests, the essay argues, it is enough that there exist both the Workers' Councils at the then (1967) level – that is, without the vertical extension of their power up to and including a control or at least veto of federal economic decisions, as proposed at the very beginning by Kidrič (see Chapter 5.2) – as well as the top leadership of the SFRY State and Party.

The ruling 'forces' of SFRY concluded thus, as all the ruling classes in the world, that there can be no central dangerous contradictions in *our* society.

It is useful to complete this argumentation of Kardelj's with other texts in his deep commitment to the 1965 reform about which he wrote voluminously (as he did later about the much crazier 1974 constitutional reform). I shall use his ambitious report at the Second Congress of Yugoslav Self-managers in May 1971, 'Economic and Political Relationships in the Self-managing Socialist Society' ('Ekonomski i politički odnosi u samoupravnom socijalističkom društvu', *SDS* 213–80). It noted that after 1965 the State seizure of the surplus in production was not returned to associations of producers but 'flowed over' into the newly formed banks, insurance companies, wholesale and export companies as new forms of alienation of surplus labour from the working people and self-managing enterprises: the share the enterprises kept, in industry and mining, for investment into basic funds or capital (which was supposed to rise from 30 to 70%, see Part 3 of the book) fell after the reform, while their share of ongoing working capital (*obrtna sredstva*) stagnated in 1965–70 at one third (264)! Similar matters obtain for foreign trade and a part of wholesale commerce (264–7). Should the means of such independent economic centres continue to grow, concluded Kardelj, their financial and 'technocratic management monopoly' would also grow, and with it 'the economic and political conflict between these independent centres of economic plus financial power and self-managing labour' (266).

In this report Kardelj for the first time, I believe, broached not only a discourse on class struggle (in order to deny it) but also a discourse on capital, though neither clearly nor systematically. He defined State capital as 'a part of societal accumulation which up to 1965 the State kept and directed into the central investment funds'. A law in 1971 (six years after the reform!) transferred the federal State's capital from the disbanded federal banks to the constituent republics (240). In a booklet prepared in 1972 for translation into Italian he concluded that 'this spontaneous (*stihijski*) development in the relationship of forces bears a possibility of societal differentiations, that is, tendencies toward a restoration of State, group or private property [over means of production]' (*Proprietà* 51). And in a 1974 article he further concluded: there came about 'given forms of a "capital relationship" that influenced the society and the LCY', but we cannot return to one of the most dangerous forms of a 'capital relationship', that is 'the "socialist" primitive accumulation [of capital], based on a simple seizure of income from the workers' through laws or administrative acts and relationships (*sss* 314–15; see more about this in Chapter 10.4).

Kardelj's 1974 article 'For Democracy within Socialism, Not against Socialism' ('Za demokratiju u socijalizmu ne protiv socijalizma', *sss* 301–42) is written following the same structural scheme, which Barthes's *Mythologiques* called, after Marx, *petty-bourgeois ni-nisme*: neither this nor that, or: on the one hand – but on the other hand. Kardelj again started by using a perspicuous and unsparing identification of the successes and failures after 1965: *on the one hand*, 'it struck a heavy blow against the State bureaucratic centralisation by abolishing State [namely federal – note DS] investment funds and included the whole ... enlarged reproduction into the system of self-managing associated labour ...' *But on the other hand* it left open some essential questions, which enabled the 'techno-bureaucratically oriented parts of the political structure in the republics ... to maintain a very strong role in disposing of societal capital', even augmenting it through the credit and banking system, wholesale commerce, and other relationships supposed to further 'the association of labour'. What was earlier a conflict among the republics over sharing the federal funds is now being fought as 'a competition between banks, commercial and other economic organisations'. This is 'the economic basis for the links between our economic technocratic structure' with bourgeois nationalism (this was written after the dismissal of Party and State leaderships in Croatia and Serbia accused of nationalism). Even further, the 1965 reform was, Kardelj now confesses, 'barely a half step on the road of a self-managing transformation for the system of societal reproduction'. We did not succeed to bring about a timely 'new concept of societal planning ... partly because of a lack in experience and knowledge but in good part because of disagreements within the League of Communists', so that the reform did not prove efficient enough (312–13: I shall add that the 1960s are a beginning of a downturn in the postwar economic boom and of growing protectionism in markets, and on the horizon was the crisis of the whole Fordist production system; see the very stimulating Močnik, Intervju).

What can we conclude from this examination of Kardelj? To adopt his dichotomising: his sincere and tireless devotion to a quite abstract idea of self-management has its limit in the refusal that opposed class interests are here decisive (see Chapter 4.1.2, 'An Excursus on Classophobia'). Yet it is striking how he lacked a feeling for an intimate and inherent, spontaneous contradictoriness of any process, constitutive for Marx and the mature Lenin. In place of dialectics, his discourse conscientiously and exhaustively, even pedantically, lists elements divided into positive and negative (a proceeding well satirised by Marx in his attack on Proudhon, /cho2.htm); Kardelj then as a rule, especially before his half-turn to alarmed gloom in the 70s, ends up in a bureaucratic optimism (I expand on this in Chapter 10.4). This is the proceeding of bourgeois Positivism, perhaps with some kindred hints from Austro-Marxism, and with the horizon of unstoppable progress in spite of all obstacles, *per aspera ad astra**. It is better than Stalin's theological deductivity, but it cannot deal with sudden jumps or turns (except for the starry end-of-war moment when he was theorising the new People's Liberation Councils). His discourse therefore often arrives at top-heavy jargon and wooden constructions, insufficiently attentive to a quickly changing reality. The epistemological revolution after World War II, announced by post-Einsteinian physics but also by Marxist heretics like the early Lukács or Benjamin (not to dwell on the cognitions in art, in poetry say from Rimbaud to Brecht and further, or in narrative art at the time of Joyce, Dos Passos, and Kafka), passed Kardelj totally by.

1.4 *Josip Broz Tito*

As secretary general of the Yugoslav Communist Party from the later 1930s to his death and as the undoubted supreme authority of Yugoslavia from the war on, Tito had the final word in vetting and realising attitudes toward 'bureaucracy'. In 1949 he approved the introduction of Workers' Councils and a full revision of the Soviet 'command economy' model run by a gigantic and centralised State apparatus. I think one of the principal reasons for this decision was his realisation that, in conditions of hostility against Yugoslavia both by capitalism and by Stalinism, the only certain support for power lay in the widest possible backing by 'the working people', especially the workers. But it seems he was not much interested in formulating such stances but left it to his leading associates – Djilas, Kidrič, and most permanently Kardelj. Having read, for a sample, volumes VII–IX of his collected works that cover 1953–4, I find that in ca. 1,100 book pages tendencies toward bureaucratism or bureaucratic elements are mentioned seven or eight times; when in an interview his US interlocutors pressed him about its class content, he reached for Marx's 'bureaucratic caste', arising out of State centralism (*Djela VIII*: 177).

An exception is a section of Tito's report to the Sixth Congress of CPY in 1952, titled 'The Conflict between Yugoslavia and the USSR'. This section seems never to have been reprinted but was, scandalously, erased from his Collected Works; I report it from the 1962 documents ('Borba' 25–38, alerted by the ample excerpts in Lalović, 'Program'). At this culmination of High Stalinism, when the danger of military attack by the USSR was acutely present, Tito identified this conflict as a reaction to the USSR's abandonment of socialist principles in favour 'of an overt imperialist expansion' (25). Its deeper cause lies 'in the whole inner structure of that country, economic, political, and cultural. The USSR has long since deviated from a socialist development to the path of ***State socialism with a hitherto unseen bureaucratic system. Bureaucratism is in the USSR ... turning into an exploitative power above society ...***' (28, italics mine). The situation of workers in the USSR is worse 'than in the most regressive capitalist countries' (29). To this reality and to the horizons of 'the all-powerful Soviet ***bureaucratic caste***' (30, italics mine) there corresponds the anti-Marxist theory about the necessity of strengthening the State and its functions: 'Stalin wishes to strengthen the State towards the inside, for keeping under his thumb the wage labourers and in general the exploitative system, and towards the outside for carrying out his imperialist policy' (32). Therefore the CPY is defending Marxism and socialism from the attempts of the Soviet revisionists 'to use this revolutionary science for masking their imperialist and counter-revolutionary theories and practice. Thus our Party ... has posed and in practice shown ... that it is possible to develop socialism even in a small and backward country. It has in practice shown that humane methods in societal change work ...' (35–6)

As far as Yugoslav development was concerned, Tito then considered the problem on the whole solvable by a decentralisation and a permanent stress on the monolithic nature of the Party and the whole state, in his opinion still faced with huge economic and political dangers, so that he turned to a large extent toward foreign policy, and intervened only during crises.

As a final datum, in the voluminous document about Party work under Tito's leadership from 1958 on, submitted to the 1964 congress (*Izveštaj*), there is little or no talk about bureaucratism.

1.5 Vladimir Bakarić

After Kidrič's death, Bakarić – the perennial head of the Croatian CP – was the most important figure within Kardelj's 'centre-left' orientation toward self-management at the top of the CPY, to which he contributed both expertise in economics and the incisive mind of an intellectual. Perhaps paradoxically, he combined (as Kardelj too did) a consistent orientation to the ideal of 'direct producers' and to a strong-hand or even monolithic Party policy as far as keeping power goes; a case in point for the latter attitude is his total refusal to take the *Praxis* group's positions seriously.

1.5.1

Examining his four voluminous collections of speeches and articles, I found the first significant reflexion about bureaucracy relatively late, in the period of an already stymied self-management. Towards the end of 1964 he saw in bureaucracy the principal factor blocking self-management, since advocates of the governmental 'administrative allocation' of funds saw their own reason for existing only in extensive investments and in so-called 'political factories' which had no economic justification. This gave rise to the vicious circle of 'production with low productivity, closure into regional boundaries, request for more administrative solutions ...' (2: 22). The social basis of the political oscillations after the end of the 1950s was that 'a mass of people was in a relatively privileged position, for their emoluments were guaranteed', and 'some projects for further development of their regions seem safer if the old system is left standing'. Therefore the struggle in CPY lasted for many years – 'I won't say from 1950 on, but surely from 1960 to 1964', the reason being '*we did not immediately see the social roots of this process, that is, we kept discussing it as an ideological question*' (2: 134, italics mine). However, 'the system in which State authority represents social ownership [of means of production] opens the possibility for the existence of a bureaucratic stratum which can cut loose from the people ... and grow into an independent class or stratum ...'. The rise of a new stratum keeps resisting 'an establishment of direct democracy and direct [workers'] rule over economy ...' (2: 142, cf. also 285–6). From the context it is clear that Bakarić was referring both to the central federal administration and to local authorities. Yet he held that 'in face of all our measures, it is impossible that such a [bureaucratic] stratum could maintain itself. This would be Djilas's theory that we are creating a new class which rules and shall rule in socialism' (2: 151–2).

However, in mid-1967 Bakarić found that 'a considerable part [of the active Party membership] is divided. Some are ... practically, in their lives, in a different situation. They are not direct producers, they live objectively from the cleavage between the Party and the direct producers'. Thence the struggle in the 1960s on reforming the CPY; and therefore in 1967, as different from 1945, '[*Etatism*] *is no longer a dictatorship of the proletariat but an ossification of the bureaucratic power*' (2: 392 and 394, italics mine). At a seminar about the working class at the end of 1967 he asserted that 'a considerable part of the [Party] cadre is by education and social position relatively conservative', so that 'the great power of bureaucracy really hindered further development of forces of production [and of a progressive line within the working class]'. Three further statements (together with the statement italicised above, indicating that the leadership understood the struggle within the Party as an ideological and not a class political question) validate my hypothesis in section 1.6 below. In the first quotation, Bakarić states that in the Party there dominate 'those who represent the interests of our proletariat ..., but in the CPY there is quite a number of other elements. Thus there came about a whole period in which we simply missed a series of measures [pending] and allowed discussion to continue. *We did not wish the revolution to eat its children, we did not wish to have such social earthquakes* ...' (2: 451, italics mine). In the second quotation, 'However, there always must exist a social stratum which is not directly inside production, that we can conditionally call a bureaucracy. If we declare it to be a new class, the consequence is: *strike the bureaucrat wherever you can, annihilate him* .... This thesis, which did not follow Djilas to the end but reminded one of his views, was very present ...' – and Bakarić disagrees with it (2: 477, italics mine; cf. also 2: 486). But in the same text he allows that, because of this avoidance of crucial decisions, 'we came at the beginning of the 1960s to an acute crisis of State power. We could not solve a whole series of questions [concerning the division of funds] ... This was a first symptom that we no longer always represent this working class ... *Here this State apparatus – and thus the Party leadership and its middle strata – started separating from the* [*working*] *class*'. And this in turn comes from a situation where 'we do not yet have a self-manager that would have influence up to the top. Therefore, this [a certain dispossession of the CPY] would have meant leaving matters in the hands of that middle stratum or upper stratum which had separated itself from the self-manager' (2: 481 and 483, italics mine).

Finally, remembering retrospectively the situation around 1968, he added: '*at the time, we had great difficulty in talking about the enemy* ... If anyone mentions nationalism, then he has to mention separatism too ... and thus, no concrete fight against an enemy danger was possible' (4: 123, italics mine)!

Nonetheless, Bakarić stuck to the conception that 'the bureaucracy is fully dependent on social structure. It rules ... only insofar as it has the confidence of the class bearing this society' (2: 485) – which for him always meant the working class represented by the CPY. I shall return at the end of this essay to the aporias of such a divergence between the real and the ideal working class, in other (Lukács's) words, between its real and ascribed consciousness.

In mid-1971, Bakarić started addressing more often 'a stratum that is prominent today ... and does not live only from normal work but primarily from income outside it' – meaning by this the well-known burgeoning of non-State capital-holders in the new banks, insurance and trade companies. He calculated this stratum at about 5 % of those normally employed (that is, about one quarter of a million people), who yet have 'relatively huge incomes', and represent a danger for socialism. He then identifies 'the material interests of [such] people at given commanding points within our life' as the antagonist 'in the struggle for further development of self-management', since they are able to put into question 'the material situation of some working collectives'; thus they are a new variant of bureaucracy. Therefore, in the same text Bakarić finally identifies the resistances to self-management in 'bureaucratic elements – both in the CPY [cadre] and outside of it' (3: 304 and 306). Some months later, he finds that beginning in about 1960 the surplus value taken from workers has been less under the control of the central State apparatus but increasingly of 'banks and other credit institutions': 'not of the direct producers nor even working people, but ... of a series of organisations relatively independent from the direct producer and CPY ...' He sees the role of the working class weakening, and the antagonistic element he identified 'beginning to tread the path of a bureaucratic State with a certain support in the working class or ... even without it' (3: 339–40). In mid-1972 he reiterated that 'the banks are left uncontrolled, so that a financial stratum here came about that in fact commands the enlarged social reproduction' (3: 417). In other words, the place of decisive Party instances is on the verge of being taken by political forces which were habitually called 'technocratic' – though technics here did not mean an application of natural sciences but rather techniques of applying politico-economic power through financial levers. At the end of the same year, in a longish speech at a commission of the Party Presidium, this new element was more precisely identified: 'Beside our own bureaucracy there began developing a new ... techno-bureaucracy, techno-management, a techno-managerial segment that liaised with the State and used it for their own programs' (3: 492). Somewhat later, Bakarić characterised this 'technocratism' (that is, an ideological profile rather than a social class) as a 'professional cadre, which also wants to rule' by dominating enlarged economic reproduction (3: 522). By March 1972, as part of preparations for a new CPY Congress and State Constitution, he noted: 'before the Amendments to the Constitution, the State started to rely more and more upon those same bureaucratico-technocratic elements' and upon that part of the CPY whose behaviour was yoked to theirs; 'thus, the State organisation started separating from the working class' (3: 499). This also meant that 'the old organisational structure of the CPY ... more or less ideologically fused with those elements ... Therefore we had to reorganise it ...' (3: 509). And finally, using the strongest terms: 'this is a class struggle, one that could take acute forms' (3: 511). Or, speaking of the years after 1971, he used a paradox: 'It could be said in a series of matters that the CPY was in a minority within its own organisation' (3: 518). This sentence becomes intelligible if we presuppose that for Bakarić the 'real' CPY was the leadership to which he belonged – let us say the Kardelj current – which was in a minority not so much within the CPY as a whole but within the politocracy and the new technocracy of a major part of the rising professionals.

In Spring 1974 Bakarić drew some conclusions: the Party had 'broken the barrier of poverty', for Yugoslavia, but the effort to do so, and the maximal tension of all forces created by it, also gave rise to the phenomenon of interest and profit, which strengthened 'the tendency toward creating new classes' (4: 14). This 'tendency toward the modern capitalist concept of techno-managerialism weakens the positions of the working class', heightens social inequality, and disrupts relationships among the Yugoslav national groups (4: 22). The techno-managerial 'political group' opposed to socialist self-management tends towards 'privatisation ... of business, a privatisation of societal income' (4: 24); thus, though it is not an opposed class, the ideology of these 'elements' is born out of commodity production. Finally, in his late writings from the 1980s (he died in 1983), Bakarić notes that 'instead of behaving as a middling developed country', we do not adopt a more rational behaviour (it seems both economics and politics are meant here) when foreign credit ends (4: 418). Under a more articulated techno-structure, which reaches from republican centres to the enterprises and the credit institutions, and now 'more or less commands everything, ... the [Yugoslav] society is growing increasingly bourgeois (*sve gospodskije*), while the worker should go down into the pit and to live there' (4: 425 and 423) – a disconsolate trailing off.

1.5.2

A conclusion about the stances of this careful and certainly professionally best prepared viewer within the SFRY leadership from the 1960s on, who followed both the economy and the newer international developments, say in Galbraith, could be as follows:

– in the phase of preparing the 1965 economic reform, Bakarić immediately pinpointed a great, financially privileged group in important central and local positions in the CPY, that was, since 1950 and the rise of productivity, the enemy of both direct democracy and direct rule of producers. He called it a stratum, thus using the Positivist vocabulary to downplay any danger that it was or could become a ruling class inimical to the workers.
– in the phase of serious resistance to the reform, he noted that a good part of CPY cadre had interests contrary to those of 'the direct producer', so that their etatism meant ossified bureaucratic power. He persisted in denying that this was a new class and a ruling class in order to avoid an overt fight inside the Party and State, where in huge societal earthquakes 'the revolution would eat its children' (as in the French and Russian cases).
– after the 1968 student demonstrations and, when these were defeated, amid the growth of regional nationalism in 1971–3 and afterwards, Bakarić's 'stratum' of 250,000 people – an 'element' dangerous for socialism and tending toward a bureaucratic State – prominently included a newly created powerful and rich 'stratum' in banks and other credit institutions, which he gropingly called techno-bureaucracy or some similar term. This stratum he characterised as a 'professional cadre that also wants to rule' by appropriating enlarged societal reproduction in the economy, in increasing alliance with a good part of the State apparatus and CPY cadre. This capital without declared capitalists clearly started to act in synergy with nationalist tendencies and elements from outside Yugoslavia. However, Bakarić never let go of the basic doctrinal axiom that in Yugoslavia all societal income (except for private peasants and artisans) in fact pertains 'to one category ..., the class of producers and participants in social build-up' (4: 151). Thus for him the utmost consequence of realising that a gulf was appearing between the State power and the working class was a cautious, hypothetical possibility that this unthinkable 'class struggle' could, but in his opinion cannot and will not, take an acute turn. The one and unique category cannot split into two. The 'counter-class' cannot be named: *quod non est in libris, non est in mundo* (what's not found in the [holy] books does not exist in the world). In the last instance, despite his wider imagination, this is a horizon identical to Kardelj's.

What will remain fatal for SFRY is: 'our technocratic bureaucracy has begun to liaise with the remnants of the past and return to elements of capitalism and the remnants of the defeated bourgeoisie. A link was coming about here which was not at all insignificant' (3: 541). I would say that, except for possible links with the anti-communist emigration, there were no remnants of the pre-war bourgeoisie in SFRY; however, there clearly were first sprouts of new capitalist relationships and attitudes – that is, of a new ruling class (or class fractions) analogous to the bourgeoisie and conveying the attitudes and ideologies of the world bourgeoisie. Bakarić's conclusion, during the planning of constitutional changes at the beginning of the 1970s, was: 'this is capital, there is no doubt, ... that was formed in the banks and other credit institutions, that is independent, that is uncontrolled, and that is renewing capitalist relationships amongst us wherever it appears, and it appears everywhere' (3: 604). In the same sentence he states both that 'there are no capitalists in SFRY', but obviously there are 'everywhere' functional equivalents to capitalism which, he allows, need only political and military power to become a classical capitalist bourgeoisie. Thus his quoted statement that this was a class struggle was correct, and the self-proclaimed representatives of the working class of SFRY (who in part did protect some workers' interests) were in this struggle finally defeated.

1.6   *The Limit of the Party-State Discourse*

Karl Korsch noted three quarters of a century ago that Marxism in general, from the founder on, had two descriptive discourses, in alternation or combination: class struggle and capital accumulation (228–9). The SFRY Party-State discourse after, say, the mid-50s grew instead increasingly into an improvised combination of 'objective' structuralism and tags of ideology from the weakest Lenin about understanding or misunderstanding it 'subjectively': not dialectics but ad-hoccery.

Thus an overview of the Party/State discourse must note that the apodictic denial of opposed class interests within the struggle for self-management leads in Kardelj to the absence of class as a narrative agent (on agents see Chapters 1 and 14 of this book). Therefore his discourse is reduced to often improvised, at any rate usually unargued, entities: beside the State there is (a socialist!) Capital, an undifferentiated Working People promoted to Self-managing Producers, and then The Techno-Bureaucratic Structure into which financial means 'overflow' as if they were natural forces, say swollen rivers. All in all, it amounts to a faceless, fairly insane structuralism. Marx would have said that the dance is led by *Monsieur le Socialisme, Madame la Relation du Capital et Madame la Techno-Structure.*

From Bakarić's discourse there follows that, in this monolithic (Kidrič would have called it monopolistic) view of Yugoslav society, in the revolutionary years following World War II there were to begin with no classes, and somewhere around the early 1970s there was only one class, the working class as basis and incarnation of the CPY's mandate for power. The other groups were kinds of semi- or quasi-classes or 'strata'. Here and there Kardelj, and more so Bakarić, allows that in an acute crisis an 'ossified' class opposed to the workers could come to power, when even a class conflict would be possible, but this remains a momentary threat against opponents inside the LCY which is never seriously envisaged. Bakarić's dance is led, in Marx's terms, by *Madame la Classe Ouvrière* (meaning really the Party top) *et Monsieur Techno-Bureaucratie*, while around the corner there loom *les Bourgeois* (*Gospoda*) who strive for privatisation and liaise with nationalists and world capitalism, but are no class. Except for invoking the Bourgeois, this too is a deficient analysis.

2 The Discourse of the Socialist 'Loyal Opposition'

2.0

I have induced the term for the following grouping of two professionally different discourses from a perusal, first, of the almost complete set of Branko Horvat's general socioeconomic overviews in books plus some of his most important articles, and second, of about one quarter of the contents of the Zagreb periodical *Praxis*. The latter was chosen according to the articles' titles, and with a stress on and knowledge of the most important books of its characteristic and representative members: Petrović, Supek, Marković, Vranicki, Kangrga, and a few others. I shall here suggest only two justifications for my category of 'loyal opposition'. One Western critic (Ward), semi-ironical and semi-amazed, called the economico-political theories of Horvat 'marxism-horvatism'. As to *Praxis*, founded in 1964, its editors declared in the midst of the 1968 turmoil: 'We believe that outside or beside the Marxist-communist basis of ideas and horizons, outside or beside the programme of LCY [the League of Communists], there exists today no ideational or political force which could safeguard the integrity of this country' (no. 4 [1968]: 449–58).[2] This term of mine thus points

---

2 By 'programme of LCY' is certainly meant the one adopted at its Seventh Congress of 1958, that ends with the words: 'Nothing that has been created should be so sacred to us that it cannot be transcended and superseded by something still freer, more progressive, and more human' (*Programme* 270) – which was not realised.

   I trust it is allowable to add here my personal insights from the years 1959–65 when I had the occasion to frequently meet the Zagreb Praxis members, some of them at meetings of the Faculty of Philosophy Party cell. There is no doubt that authors like Petrović and their Zagreb comrades were ethically and intellectually upright, so that their written stances can be taken as fully sincere.

to both of these variants of unofficial discourse being together something like 'Her Majesty Socialism's loyal opposition'. However, their bearers were never publicly accorded this status, but on the contrary, they were at points of political tension attacked and after the first half of the 1970s cut off from subsidies, so that they could not pursue as a group further influence on the formation of public opinion. I shall arrive at a brief judgment about their strengths and limits at the end of this essay.

I assume that before my cut-off date of 1972 there were further interesting insights from similar horizons outside of these two groupings, especially in Slovenia, but I know little or nothing about them. It would be a service to justice and history to recover knowledge of what influence these, here slighted, individuals or groups had in Yugoslavia as a whole. My hypothesis is that the influence was small, outside of scattered Serbo-Croatian translations.

2.1   Branko Horvat

Horvat (1928–2003) was a prominent economist, from 1958 on member and at times director of the central planning institute of the SFRY federal government, who however frequently got into conflict with the State leaders, and after other hiatuses had to leave public service from 1972 to 1981. His deep behind-the-scenes insights into Yugoslav economics and politics are the basis of his share in the SFRY discourse about bureaucracy. His writing reworks stimuli by both the State discourse (Kidrič and Kardelj) and the 'Praxis school' discourse – in which he at times participated, for example by coediting a book about the history of the Workers' Councils concept – but Horvat primarily relied on his own experiences in economic practice. The title of his first, very optimistic book in 1961 was *An Economic Theory of a Planned Economy* (probably based on his 1958 doctoral dissertation, and more modestly entitled in the English 1964 translation *Towards a Theory of a Planned Economy*). In this work Horvat attempts to build a complete – even mathematised – theory of socialist planned economy, beginning with a discussion of categories such as capital and interest and ending with a definition of societal product and the role of planning. In the first part he deals with 'economic categories' (which are however also deeply political) and in the second he proposes a theory of an ideally possible process to move toward such a system. He calls it 'associational socialism', and defines it on 92–8, mostly from Marx as interpreted by the 'warm current' within Marxism, from Lenin's *State and Revolution* to Kidrič and the introduction of Workers' Council in SFRY. Towards the end of the first part Horvat discusses aspects of such self-management in Yugoslavia up to and including 1957, during their *Sturm und Drang*. He identifies the epoch-making role of associations of producers as a remedy against the principal societal illness of bureaucratism (83–92).

Horvat uses Max and Alfred Weber but he promotes bureaucracy to a meta-phenomenon that characterises principal societal processes of the present age in all social systems. He constructs 'a pure type' of bureaucratic pyramid organising and controlling the complete social system of a country, where the central principle is *obedience*, whence flows arrogance directed from above downwards and poltroonery directed from below upwards. In this system interests are polarised, for the top possesses a maximum and the bottom a minimum of choice. There follows a maximisation of social conflict, as testified by the historical differentiation between the ruling and the exploited class. The rulers buy the loyalty of bureaucracy through economic privileges and differences in status, as seen in ranks, uniforms, and exclusive social clubs or holiday resorts. The bureaucracy also unavoidably comes to identify itself with national superiority, ascribing all the successes of the nation to itself.

This meta-theory was coined principally to talk about socialism, which is clearly expressed in the claim that post-revolutionary society, while it substitutes for the old State apparatus members of the whilom exploited class, does not necessarily result in a classless society. '*If the principle of bureaucratic organisation, hierarchy, is allowed to operate, in time two societal classes with conflicting interests will be formed again*' (92). This may only be avoided if, as Engels says, the State withers. The conclusion is: 'For, the coming about of class antagonism and of a ruling class does not hinge on the [legal] property over means of production *by individual members* of that class but on class *control* over those means insofar as it makes it possible that this class exercise political control based on its power' (ibidem). This resolute conclusion much exceeds Kardelj's (though not Kidrič's) limits.

Since a return to the liberal capitalism of a really free competition, as the economist Horvat well knows, is impossible in the age of huge monopolies, associational socialism is the only efficient way to overcome the horrendously violent aspects of such 'State capitalism' (Stalinism would at the time come to mind as a prime example). Such violence is probable to the extent that a society is backward, a country economically less developed, and its tradition nearer to feudalism than to capitalism (93); here Horvat's views are close to some Belgrade Praxis members discussed in 2.2.1–2.2.2 below (Marković and Mićunović), but I don't know which way the vector of influence runs.

The second book I shall discuss from Horvat's 30-odd ones is his *An Essay on Yugoslav Society*, first published in 1967. It is an anatomy of Yugoslav society, also with an ambitious horizon. Of its six chapters, the first one repeats the text about associational socialism; I shall briefly comment only on parts of two other chapters.

The end of Chapter 4 deals with 'structures of Yugoslav society', and pinpoints these 'vertical strata', differentiated by wealth and power, in percentages of the 'active population':

1. the leading cadre, that is 'managers' in the government and in other highest economic and extra-economic positions, *0.7%*;
2. intellectuals, as a rule with a university degree, divided into three groups: 'technologico-economic ("technocrats"), higher administrative ("bureaucrats"), and ... humanist intelligentsia', *2.1%* (number increasing);
3. routine white-collar workers, *10.1%*;
4. manual workers, including 'peasant workers', *30%*;
5. artisans, *3.5%* (number falling);
6. peasants, *53.6%* (number falling) (147–8).

'Active population' numbered in 1961 around 8,350,000 people (*Statistički*), so that the absolute numbers of the above categories were as follows:

TABLE 1 *Active population of* SFRY
         B. HORVAT 1961

Leading cadre	0.7%	60.000
Intellectuals	2.1%	175.000
White-collar workers	10.1%	845.000
Manual workers	30%	2,500.000
Artisans	3.5%	260.000
Peasants	53.6%	4,480.000

Chapter 5 speaks to the role of the League of Communists, and its section 'on the genesis of bureaucratic mentality out of a revolutionary party' hypothesises that the development of the bureaucratic mentality is the cause of the LCY's lack of operational efficiency and of its ideological maladjustment to societal currents which it had initiated and to a large extent organised (193). 'The centralised and hierarchical organisation of communist parties is a potentially bureaucratic structure', especially after the stormy revolutionary years, when party and government fuse. The original necessity of a dictatorship of the proletariat then easily changes from temporary means into permanent goal, and grows into a dictatorship over the proletariat (196–7). As far as self-management is concerned, Yugoslav practice, starting from individual factories or plants, had shattered the Stalinian principle of *odinonachalie*, that is, of autocratic monarchism valid for all levels, but it is still far from real democratism; following the researches of Veljko Rus, Horvat calls this practice oligarchic (238). It should be apparent how much my book owes to these and other insights of his.

Under strong attacks, which include his removal from public positions at the beginning of the 1960s as well as for a long stretch after 1972, Branko Horvat did not develop further and apply to SFRY his principle that for the formation of a class it is enough to have *control* over the means of production, and he returned to the terminology of Positivist but safe 'strata'. But unlike the Party/State discourse, he saw not only the downfall of economic reforms after 1961 but also considerable problems in the very structure of the LCY; as one of the very few, he analysed these problems at length and with radical criticism. Unlike the Praxis group, with whom he shared the horizon of socialist democratisation, his work as an inside fellow-traveller of power in the more open periods and his top professional knowledge allowed him to see better the intersection of power and economics. Since this intersection is to my mind the key to SFRY history, Horvat is often referred to in this book.

2.2   *Praxis*

The group around the periodical *Praxis* was composed of strong and autonomous personalities. Since we have at our disposal only first overviews about it (the pioneering works of Marković and Cohen, Sher, MacBride, and Jakšić), it would be dangerous to draw generalising conclusions. One would first, for example, need detailed consideration of the relatively homogeneous stances of the Zagreb initiators and the looser cohesion of the Belgrade group, more interested in problems of immediate political power, as well as the different paths taken by groupings and individuals after the repression and downturn at the beginning of the 1970s. But one has to begin, so I shall here analyse some selected articles which talk directly about bureaucracy or consider it within a wider political or philosophical framework.

2.2.1   Mihajlo Marković

I found two direct discussions of bureaucracy of substantial length, one of which is the essay 'Socialism and Self-management' ('Socijalizam i samoupravljanje') by Mihajlo Marković from 1964 (I deal with the second one in 2.2.3). Here is his definition:

> the political bureaucracy is a durable and coherent societal group that [*1.*] *is professionally engaged in politics, that* [*2.*] *has rid itself of control by the masses, and that* [*3.*]*, thanks to its unlimited power of distributing past and reified labour, secures for itself larger or smaller material privileges.* Each of these conditions is a *necessary* but only all of them together are a *sufficient* condition for the existence of a bureaucracy.
>
>> 59, I have added the numbers; 'past and reified labour' is an awkward way of using Marx to avoid saying 'capital'

I shall discuss only the main lines of this somewhat awkward definition – based on politics but with tags from Marxist political economy and philosophy – while remarking that 'unlimited power' seems to me rather angry than precise, I would say 'very significant power'.

For Marković, condition 1 is 'the first step toward the formation of an isolated, closed, and, in relation to the rest of society, very solidary societal stratum'. Since after the revolution the interest of all other societal strata is 'that political activity should become a common, public activity accessible to all', the rule of bureaucracy means that politics remains alienated. Condition 2, the independence of bureaucracy from mass control, means that elections become an empty formality and that this stratum is responsible only to higher Party committees. This bureaucracy is the subject of history, while 'a great majority [of people] is in the permanent position of objects'. Taking into account the growing influence of mass media and other forms of propaganda, a majority of people can be very successfully manipulated. Condition 3, 'the full monopoly' of bureaucracy over distribution and use of past and present 'reified labour' (properly, surplus labour), means that it moves, after accession to power, from unconscious to conscious and cynical exploitation. In brief, bureaucracy is the bearer of a triune principle of alienation, reification, and exploitation (ibidem 59–60). Its actions are voluntaristic as far as the future is concerned (all it commands is possible) and deterministic as far as the past is concerned (all it has done is fully justified), thus excluding 'the key concept of *real possibility*' (63), and any scientific analysis – which it mistrusts. In particular, while it likes to use dialectical formulas and uncontrollably invents programmes and institutional forms, often '"sublated" before they could be practically realised' – the bureaucracy decisively denies essential aspects of dialectics: 'The dialectical unity in difference is reduced to "monolithic unity". Contradictions are denied and hidden' (64).

The bitter resistance by many so-called Marxists and socialists (meaning: by most politocracy in the Party core) against self-management – which Marković hails as the next phase of transition towards communism and a lasting thorough revolution – explains why basic enterprises had in the mid-60s rights of disposal only over 30% from national income (and as discussed earlier in the book, this proportion did not sensibly change later). The root of the resistance lay in an undeveloped, still mainly rural society that did not manage to create 'a sufficient number of rational, socialised, and humane personalities led by universal human ideals'. Such a society must therefore pass through a phase where 'an elite, in the best case truly revolutionary, shall create – by means of a maximal mobilisation of the masses, but also by compulsion – all such preconditions: an industry, a working class, an intelligentsia, a school system, a mass culture ... However, the key question is: will the elite, having realised these preconditions, find in itself sufficient moral force and fidelity to its original revolutionary ideals to voluntarily ... bring about a realisation of self-management, and thus by degrees eliminate itself as an elite of power ...' (54–5). Marković concludes correctly that bureaucracy may only be sublated if the self-management system is built up to the summit of the pyramid of power, so that the central State organs become organs of self-management while important political functions grow deprofessionalised and subject to real elections. But in 1964 he sees instead the bureaucracy attempting to strike a balance between self-management in the basic enterprises and the State apparatus; in practice this means that the bureaucracy keeps deciding about fundamental societal relationships while giving somewhat larger financial stimuli to the direct producers. This gives rise to an opposition between self-management and local bureaucratic cliques of techno-managers and professional politicians, who may even draw in co-opted representatives of Workers' Councils. The way out is in the development of education and workers' class consciousness, stimulation of initiative by workers, open public criticism with a higher accountability of the managers, and finally in thinking '*how to coordinate self-management with commodity and money relationships*' taken over from capitalism (68–70).

A brief comment: this interesting and courageous articulation of Marković's is laudably Left-humanist but not particularly Marxist, as it mixes in a 'universally human' fashion philosophical, ideological, and politically pragmatic criteria with some far-off indications that some class interests may here be involved. I remember that time well, and maybe nobody in Yugoslavia then really had better tools, that is, a consciousness that conflicts of class interests permanently continue and it is therefore necessary to explore the confrontation of politics and economics rather than of politics and morality: however (in Brecht's aphorism), the stone does not excuse the fallen.

Seven years later, after a failed attempt at a major economico-political reform, Marković added to these considerations, in an issue of *Praxis* having for its theme 'Equality and Freedom', what the Yugoslav revolution contributed to these two tenets. He began with a critique of bourgeois revolution, that where successful only managed to realise equality before the law and equality of opportunity. However, bourgeois revolutions also introduced a series of Enlightenment freedoms which represented an epoch-making liberatory breakthrough, without which a socialist programme, though it has so far slighted it, cannot be realised: 'the right of thought/opinion (*mišljenja*), of self-expression, of unhindered economic activity, and of choosing representatives in the institutions of political power' (11). He then concentrates on the category of *status*, neglected by all socialist revolutions. The Lenin-type party's great efficacy in carrying out revolution was after it accompanied by four main difficulties for the long-range revolutionary programme: 'inequality in the status of leading cadre, normal members, candidates, and sympathisers'; lack of consciousness about this inequality; stress on maximal self-abnegation and subordination to the movement's directives; and a society that, lacking bourgeois liberalism in the past, 'has not liberated itself from the typically feudal habit to relate to people of high status without any criticism, with vassal loyalty' (12). Inequality of status led in Yugoslav circumstances to inequality of power, and then to 'restoration of certain already overcome class differences', first based on State capital in the power of bureaucracy, and later also on financial capital (my term) in the power of the managerial techno-structures. Behind a façade of self-management, 'we find before us the class of "socialist big capitalists" *in statu nascendi* ... [being born]'. Marković thinks this process could probably still be stopped, but 'no sufficiently strong forces are visible that would be struggling with determination toward this goal' (13). A second problem was 'how to stop in its tracks the newborn petty bourgeoisie which got rich in these last years by speculating with land and weekend houses, by loot, and by unprecedented corruption'. His conclusion is that the socialist movement must be democratic, 'otherwise it will never bring about socialism ...' (14). In other words, I would conclude today, in this movement the hesitant forces from above that really were in favour of self-management should be joined by forces pressuring in the same direction from below.

Thus, Marković had in this while arrived to a somewhat improvised class analysis and to a political diagnosis that – in spite of lacunae and exaggerations typical for him, and perhaps for the intellectual opposition as a whole – seems stimulating for further discussion today.

2.2.2 Dragoljub Mićunović

The article by Dragoljub Mićunović 'Bureaucracy and Publicness' ('Birokratija i javnost') deals with this key element of *javnost*, a pleasing ambiguity that means – as in the German *Öffentlichkeit* – both publicness or openness of political activity and public opinion about it. It starts with three questions. The first one is: '*What makes the existence of bureaucracy possible?*' Answer: the need to carry out in an organised fashion *society's general affairs*. Max Weber affirms that bureaucracy (of the efficient German type, I would add) is technically superior to all other forms just as the machine production is to non-machine production; but in the words of Wright Mills, bureaucracy possesses perfect rationality without reason (642–3). The second question, '*What is the essence of bureaucracy?*' is answered: it is a perversion of the *representativity* necessary for the efficiency of any large organisation. This led Hegel to justify bureaucracy philosophically as against the particular interests of estates, and Marx to pen, in his critique of Hegel's philosophy of right, the most radical critique of that illusion, and to define bureaucracy as a separate closed body, directly opposed to the interests of publicness and civil society. The conclusion is that, 'since bureaucracy represents the State or something general, its particular interests will acquire a semblance of general interests' (643–5).

Mićunović answers the third question: '*Wherein lies the power of bureaucracy?*', by citing Marx: 'The general spirit of the bureaucracy is the secret, the *mystery*, preserved within it by means of the hierarchy and externally as a closed corporation. To make public the mind and the disposition of the State appears therefore to the bureaucracy as a *betrayal* of its mystery' (cited more fully in my Appendix 1). Weber agrees: '[B]ureaucratic administration is always one that excludes publicness ... The concept of the official secret is a specific invention of bureaucracy'. Therefore Mićunović concludes 'that the lack of informing the mass ... about the work of a managing body is almost always directly proportional to the bureaucratic power of that body' (646–7). In general, for him 'publicness is ... the negative correlation of bureaucracy'. But what is public opinion (*javnost, Öffentlichkeit*)? Following closely Marx's approach that it is civil society as opposed to State apparatus, the article poses that public opinion is 'the ensemble of all citizens who evince an interest for general and common questions of organising the social community, which entails also the right and possibility of participating not only in political activity and control but also in State authority/power and societal management'. And the pillar of this possibility is 'the free expression of opinions' of all those interested: Mićunović's ideal example is Zola's voice in the Dreyfuss affair, and he, again in the wake of Marx, pleads at length for the 'dignity and independence' of press and other media in socialism, which should be forums and instruments of *javnost*, in both of its senses (648–9). The article culminates by quoting Marx:

> The question is: is freedom of press the privilege of some people or the privilege of the human spirit? And Marx answers: 'Just as everybody learns to read and write, so everybody *must be permitted* to write and read'.
> 649

At the beginning, Mićunović stressed that he is not claiming to fully clarify what bureaucracy and publicness might be, but to deal only with what might be useful to say about their confrontation. I believe his article is in that sense, regardless of some tangents I left out, clear and efficient. The young Marx later supplemented what was cited here with class and politico-economic analyses, but never let go of the emancipatory dichotomy directed against the State and its bureaucracy (I argue this at length throughout this book and in Appendix 1). Thus Mićunović found in him a solid basis for defining ways of 'de-bureaucratising society' by means of publicness and direct democracy: 'for publicness is that free flame that melts the veil of bureaucratic secrecy and thus erodes bureaucratic power' (652).

2.2.3   Gajo Petrović

Petrović, co-editor of *Praxis*, was philosophically and politically in all probability the most prominent member of the group. A second most important article in the periodical directly confronting bureaucracy was his '*"Bureaucratic Socialism"*' in 1971. This phrase was often used in discussing the USSR and sometimes, in oppositional discourse, about SFRY too, and his scare quotes indicated doubt. He begins with a correct indication of the danger inherent in Stalin's scheme by which there are separate phases after the socialist revolution, namely: dictatorship of the proletariat → socialism → communism. For Marx (and Petrović) a dictatorship of the proletariat exists 'only if it is already the beginning phase of socialism and communism, if it is already achieving a humanist society'. This holds also for 'the usual distinction according to which the essential difference between socialism as a "lower" and communism as a "higher" phase lies in distribution (in socialism according to work, in communism according to needs)', since in Marx's conception already in the first phase 'the cleavage of society into "spheres" and the domination of economics' is overcome – sublated in Hegel's sense of *aufheben*, that includes both abolition and subsumption (B 484). Both a sharp division into phases and a reduction of the first phase to economic measures are for Petrović entirely mistaken.

Asking what is the essence of communism, his article reaches for Marx's early works, where it is defined as 'repeal of man's self-alienation', and posits that 'Communism is communism insofar as it is humanism', that is, 'the appropriation of human life in its fullness' (B 485).

As far as distribution is concerned, the claim that in the first phase 'all distribution must be done according to work done' is a caricature of Marx's and Engels's conception that distribution according to work was a temporarily needed use of bourgeois right, which is essentially unjust because it applies an equal measure to different people (and situations). The quoted principle 'may be relatively "progressive" ... only if it is applied to those who have the necessary preconditions for work', but it becomes 'inhuman if it is applied to the elderly, sick, invalids, pregnant women, children, and others who cannot work or who have ... no occasion to work' (that is, the unemployed – B 486); from the SFRY experience I would add to this list all those whose local or enterprise context is not equal to other such contexts (see my Chapter 10.4.2). It becomes clear that the so-called distribution according to work is a cruel fiction unless accompanied by inbuilt systemic corrections for all those who do not, in strict economic terms, 'produce'.

Thence Petrović gets to direct discussion of what is bureaucracy, using in his approach Marx and Weber. He finds that the meaning of the first component, 'bureau', ranges from a piece of furniture (*bureau*, writing desk), through the room in which the desk stands to the office, enterprise or institution which uses that room, and finally to 'the totality of people employed in a bureau'. Already this component, I would add, is a multiple trope that contains consecutive metonymies, *pars pro toto* synecdoches, and a strict metaphor by which a non-living element (the space of a societal institution) stands for a living element (people who work there). In that sense, Petrović distinguishes two meanings of bureaucrat: he is a person 'belonging to that societal stratum whose "objective" position is determined by its relation to a "bureau"; but one could also think of a person who ... in his individual behaviour shows certain traits that are deemed to be bureaucratic' – thus a German dictionary says 'Buchstabenmensch, Pedant', that is, a person who is 'in all matters excessively precise and keeps to the letter' (B 487). This second meaning is to my mind derived from the objective meaning of the societal function; though secondary, it is as a phenomenon much better known to the clients of bureaucratism, and it can also be applied to people in other professions or societal groups as an ensemble of traits, discussed in this article at length. Petrović adds that the confusion in meaning is augmented by mixing up the primary and secondary meaning (frequent from Lenin and Stalin on), as well as by reduction of all 'bureaus' to State ones, though they exist in all large organisations, from industrial enterprises through churches to hospitals, scientific institutes, etc (B 488).

However, the end and reason for the existence of bureaucrats is to act on other people, whence the article proceeds to the second component of 'bureaucracy', derived from *kratein*, to rule or possess power. If the stress is on ruling,

FIGURE 31   *Walter Crane*, The Angel of Socialism (*1885, as reused by Russian émigrés 1902*) *awakens labour lying prostrate under the vampire of capitalism; the body of the vampire is Capital, left wing Autocracy, right wing Bureaucracy and Church*
IMAGE REPRODUCED FROM L. LIH, LENIN 47

the meaning shifts from petty and middle white-collar workers to 'the highest functionaries with the greatest power', to the – also polysemous – concept of *bureaucracy*. It is articulated analogously to the concept of bureaucrat: first, 'the societal stratum of bureaucrats', and second, 'the totality of traits and behaviours proper to bureaucrats', meaning 'formal procedures using much paper, with unnecessary complexities and without much understanding for people'. A third sense is 'bureaucracy as a form of political rule in which the office ... and office people have a decisive role' (B 488–9). Except for an analogy to 'democracy' or 'aristocracy', Petrović does not explain how he arrived at this third sense from his previous analyses. I would say that the first, 'objective' sense was a hyperbole, since in States of absolute or even constitutional monarchies, where this concept arose, bureaucracy still was, in the best case, the third violin, after the ruling core (king and/or parliament) and the armed forces, possibly also after the clergy or the bourgeoisie; however, in the new situation where the other class powers have been neutralised, what was whilom hyperbole has been raised to relevant reality.

Petrović adds (again using my terms) that further polysemy exists also in the term 'bureaucratism' (B 489), which can be a synonym of the above three meanings, but it can also weaken them into 'a tendency of development' rather than a fixed state, or strengthen them into a closed societal system, stressing the '-ism', by analogy to capitalism or communism. He then parses at length Max Weber's approach, which amounts to understanding officialdom or bureaucracy as a societal stratum serving 'the ruling power'; however, 'there also exists a tendency that a means of ruling should become the ruler, a tendency which we have seen to a large extent realised'. Petrović pleads for differentiating between 'officialdom' that serves a power and 'bureaucracy' as a ruling societal stratum (while allowing there exist links and gradations between the two). Such a bureaucracy was brilliantly sketched by Marx: 'The bureaucracy counts itself as the final purpose of the State ... State aims turn into the bureau's aims or the bureau's aims into State aims' (B 492).

This 'officialdom come to power' is defined in three points, as:

> an officialdom that (1) constitutes and organises itself without a significant influence 'from below' or 'from above', ... and (2) adapts its organisation in order to fulfil a given function in all the most important areas of societal life, and (3) this is done according to rules and laws which it gives to itself according to its own interests.
> B 493

Unlike such full-blown power, run-of-the-mill white-collar officialdom 'is constituted "from below" or "from above", at any rate from the outside', it decides matters only in some societal domains, and sometimes does not give a final decision. To the contrary, the bureaucracy can use 'directly terrorist methods, but it can also "play at democracy"'. The Stalinist apparatus in the USSR is an instance of the former, while the latter is not identified but the allusion to the

Yugoslav case seems clear (B 493). A conclusion is that 'socialism ... as a free community of free personalities is incompatible with bureaucratism. In other words: *bureaucratic socialism is in principle impossible*' (B 494).

To my mind this is perhaps correct in a philosophical *longue durée*, but I doubt it must be so in the short duration of pragmatic social history, where loose forms like 'market socialism' and 'bureaucratic socialism' may be helpful short formulas for the implied situation, which Lenin would have called *dual rule* (*dvoevlastie*). Petrović allows in his further presentation for the possibility of 'a bureaucratic structure with subordinate elements of socialism' and of 'a socialist structure with subordinate elements of bureaucratism', but insists that the former case is not socialist: 'if we do not understand this, we shall not be able to orient ourselves in the contemporary world ...' (B 494). I have much sympathy for this stance, but logically I would hold that the latter variant could and can be called socialist. The article segues into a consideration of Lenin's stances on bureaucracy, which I find treated in an oversimplified way (cf. my Appendix 1).

At the end, the usual SFRY denial that etatisation of economic production equals socialisation is not only taken up but considerably radicalised in an anti-bureaucratic sense: 'The fact that behind and above the officialdom who administer enterprises there are no capitalists is of course important for the officials who have in this way become bureaucrats and rulers, but not for the workers, who have remained an object of rule'. This could have been an introduction to an openly class-oriented philosophical analysis, which was however in that historical moment impossible for reasons of both outer official and inner personal censorship. Therefore many passages seem to oscillate between a thorough analysis and direct political indignation; Petrović's essay as a whole is shaped by this oscillation, which leads to a discrepancy between claims to apodictic conclusions and insufficient thoroughness of analysis. To give only one important example, the aspect of 'representativity' needful for any bureaucracy that rules is not mentioned at all. However, he ends with a very appropriate differentiation between understanding bureaucratism 'as bad functioning of State apparatus' (which was a hobby-horse of Stalin's) and 'as the dominant role of this apparatus in the life of society' (B 498). He counts this distinction as a great merit of 'the Yugoslav Marxists and communists', but he also points to 'a fierce resistance of bureaucratic structures' against the development of self-management – which will be possible '*only by getting rid of the ruling bureaucracy and by constituting society from bottom to top as a league of self-managing units*'; anything else 'can only be false adornment by which the bureaucracy attempts to hide the true nature of its rule' (B 499 – italics DS).

It would be useful to read together with this argument Petrović's general approach to revolution, explicated in two articles from *Praxis* 1969–70 as well as in numerous other essays and books throughout his opus. Most interesting as a foil to the above attack on bureaucracy is perhaps the essay 'The Philosophical Concept of Revolution' ('Filozofski pojam revolucije') two years later. I shall refer here quite briefly to those parts that discuss bureaucracy and State power, though they are integrated into an ontological and 'metaphilosophical' approach to Being which I shall neglect, mostly because it leads Petrović to an extremist refusal of any thought about politics and the human condition that starts from a different professional position (sociological, anthropological, etc).

This second essay rehearses the meanings of the term 'revolution', starting with putsch and transfer of power from one class to another, up to 'building up a new societal order, and thence from the acceptation of revolution as a change in Man to the acceptation of revolution as the essence of Being (*bivstvovanja*)' (F 156–8). Therefore Petrović reproves 'vulgar Marxism', expressly Stalinism, which – as different from Marx and Lenin – strictly distinguish 'the revolutionary conquest of power ... from so-called "post-revolutionary development" ... as two mutually independent matters' (F 159), and advocates revolution 'as that activity in which man simultaneously changes both the society in which he lives and himself'. Socialist revolution is thus understood 'as the repeal of man's self-alienation', an endless process (F 162), and further as 'the radical denial of the whole inhuman class history', which ought to represent freedom, 'a development of human creative force that radically eliminates violence and cruelty' (F 165). The conclusion is: 'Any understanding of revolution as an exclusively societal change ... hides the danger of its separating from change in man', which leads us 'far from truth and revolution' (F 166). It leads also – I add here – to that rule of bureaucracy which Petrović discusses in the main article considered above.

2.2.4   Others

To these writings one could, if searching for more thoroughness, add many others, for example the article by Ljubomir Tadić 'Bureaucracy – Reified Organisation' (Marković and Petrović eds. 289–301); in it, the writer, after an exegesis of Weber, pleads for subjecting techno-bureaucratic administering to public control by citizens and producers. I find important the harsh stance of Milan Kangrga, in whose 1970 dialogue the 'Philosopher' *persona* states: 'I do not consider bureaucracy a vanguard of working class and socialism but their class enemy' (129), and especially condemns bureaucratic ethics and mentality (144–7). Though only Marković speaks directly about bureaucracy in SFRY (and probably also Jakšić, in the censored issue of *Praxis* to which I did not have access), I believe tackling bureaucracy in conjunction with State power always had the goal of understanding the situation in Yugoslavia. Marković and Kangrga are the only ones to mention 'class', everybody else uses (as does the official discourse) 'stratum' or 'societal group'. It is today difficult to judge to what extent the cause of this avoidance lay in scruple caused by insufficient information about the political statistics of power, in self-censorship or in avoiding repression.

A significant context was that the Praxis group was from time to time harshly attacked in the press, and grew into a favourite whipping-boy especially after the political tempests in 1968 (when Bakarić opined that the periodical 'largely expresses a modern American anti-communist stream' – 2: 532, see also 278, 547) and in 1971. This culminated in the banning of two articles in no. 3–4 of 1972 as well as the sentencing of author Božidar Jakšić to two years of jail – later suspended – 'for inimical propaganda' because of a 1971 article and lectures in which (I paraphrase the court decision as reported in *Praxis* 1973: 255–72) he criticises the bureaucratic and police mentality of the CPY as a new bourgeoisie that dominates over workers and peasants. What was persecuted here were some public lectures and articles, that is, a thought crime. This is in peacetime a black spot on the society legally allowing it – the young Marx reserved for it his most venomous sarcasms – and an indication of the probability of the criticism persecuted. Jakšić, a young instructor from Sarajevo, was more vulnerable than famous professors from Zagreb and Belgrade. Finally, however, after lengthy tos and fros, eight professors were forbidden to teach at the Belgrade University (including Marković and Mićunović), and *Praxis* was denied all funding and folded in 1975.

This was the sorry end of all public chances for a loyal socialist opposition, after which the anti-socialist opposition began to grow luxuriantly. What the impossibility for fertile confrontation between discourses of the Party/State and of the loyal socialist opposition implied and entailed is discussed in the body of the book.

3 A Conclusion

3.1 *The Split SFRY Marxism*

Judging by these limited soundings into the discourse on bureaucratism, I would propose the following, somewhat simplified, dichotomy within Yugoslav Marxist epistemology and semantics in 1945–72, as a contribution to our understanding today.

The Party theoreticians read little if at all Marx's *Early Works* and *German Ideology*, where he propounded his thesis about human alienation in class society. The *Praxis* writers certainly read Marx's *Grundrisse* and *Capital*, but cared little about them. The former limited themselves to political organisation of power and labour, forgetting about humanist de-alienation; the latter limited themselves to criticism of the former, forgetting about commodity fetishism. Both sides rather analogously simplified Lenin: the former group stressed the statesman who had to strengthen his most endangered State and, driven by necessity, to employ armed defence of the revolution against inner enemies; the latter stressed the defender of the plebeian power of *soviets* and critic of bureaucracy. If we today want to recover an integral, effective, still useful Marx and Lenin, we shall not find them in either group – though we shall in each recover some important, but often diluted aspects of a Marx and Lenin split down the middle. For official Party/State discourse, socialism was Lenin's 'first phase' of advancing toward communism, leaving out his insistence that elements of communism have to be continually and as quickly as possible introduced, even if piecemeal. For the discourse of the loyal opposition, socialism was Marx's transitional period toward communism, leaving out his deep sense that for this historical age destiny is located in political economy. Putting it very simply: the first group specialised in a power that ought to develop the economy, the second group in an ethics that ought to regulate power. This amounts to a fateful division into basis and superstructure.

Of course the leaders of LCY (in the best cases) sincerely held that their path to a true revolutionary humanism was the best one, and the Praxis group knew about fetishism. The polarities I find above do not pertain to personal knowledge and wishes but to effects that collectively flow from given approaches, their stresses and horizons.

The two sides and discourses in this Appendix may be to a degree, though not fully, identified with Ernst Bloch's image of the ocean of Marxism in which warm and cold currents coexist (if I were to supplement this image, Stalin would be the Aral Lake of Marxism, the salt desert of a dried up sea). Bloch himself was – together with, say, Brecht, Benjamin, Gramsci or Goldmann – a good example of how the largest, in fact enormous fertility of sea flora and fauna may be found where the cold Newfoundland and the warm Gulf stream meet and permeate, the place where nets are cast by the fishing fleets that feed the world (unless profit-hungry capitalism forces them to destroy the swarming life by over-utilisation).

This division might probably, if we had more data, obtain in regard to the important matter of rejuvenating Marx and Lenin by means of a critical incorporation of new insights. I am speaking here about writers after Marx rejected by Stalin (Kropotkin, Luxemburg, Trotsky, the young Lukács ...) and about writers after Lenin within Marxism, such as those named in one paragraph up; but also, within the vicissitudes of very fast changes of twentieth-century capitalism, not to forget the rise of Stalinism, about people on the margins or fully outside Marxism (for example Polanyi). Within 'cultural' discourse, who among those discussing bureaucracy in this Appendix had tackled Dewey, Wittgenstein, Vygotski, Wallon, Brecht, Merleau-Ponty, the later Sartre ...? (To the contrary, the Zagreb philosophers had a finally unfortunate fixation on Heidegger.) And within politico-economic discourse: Bakarić laudably delved into Galbraith, the *Praxis* writers into Weber and sometimes into Gorz, Marcuse, and Goldmann, and we have no idea what, if anything, new was being read by Kardelj. However, I find in the whole Yugoslav discourse about bureaucratism very little trace of the deep epochal changes as well as continuities within capitalism after 1945 (or perhaps better, after 1924, when the meaning of the rise of fascism came to the fore), that were in Western Marxism and near it widely debated. The exceptions would be the encyclopaedic economic erudition of Horvat – also his intimate knowledge of the problems of and debates about SFRY economics, see for an example his 'Yugoslav' – and the sociological and psychological erudition of Supek.

Still, in order to avoid falling into the neither-nor-ism (*ni-nisme*) which I excoriate in 1.3.3, I should add that after the collapse of SFRY the argumentation of the best among the Party/State wing (Kardelj and Bakarić) is out of date. An exception is clearly Kidrič, whose radical democratism remains untranscended, and was in a way inherited by Horvat and the best in Praxis. On the contrary, the critique of the 'loyal opposition' has not only proved correct – though today understandably insufficient – but it has also kept a certain degree of cognitive suggestiveness, and is to that degree still alive. For example, my book fully agrees with Gajo Petrović's conclusion on how self-management could and should get rid of bureaucracy (see the brief passage emphasised in B 499, above).

Finally, both groups much underestimated the maniacal though subtle aggressiveness of capitalist States and institutions: the inebriation with the revolution's victory equally gave the two Yugoslav groups wings and hobbled them. Both groups understood that in socialism – and in the massified world in general – politics included economics. The top of Party/State power attempted to deal with this by way of a sincere and courageous swerve from Stalinist centralism toward a (quite wrongly understood) decentralisation, but also toward the excellent key of self-management, which was however never given access to the lock that urgently needed unfastening – the vertical build-up of associative democracy to the power top. The loyal opposition of intellectuals attempted to deal with the huge concentration of oligarchic power as best it knew, by means of interesting and often correct arguments. But the Party/State power never allowed such arguments to gain full public rights, which would have been only possible in a direct plebeian democracy – for which a solid basis of classical civic rights was indispensable. In consequence, that part of the ruling class sincerely worried about socialism gradually but surely grew naked unto their onrushing enemies from the local bureaucracies and technocracies, that unavoidably came to ally themselves with nationalist particularisms. Thus the ruling power dug its own grave, and large parts of it, by the 1980s fully corrupt, were born again as dwarfish separatist classes that decided they did not need a federative Yugoslavia (see in the book, especially chapters 3–4 and 13).

Of course, in each of my two groups exceptions to this simplified account could be found. In the Party/State group, Kidrič surely hit the most balanced fusion of keeping and innovating power, while Tito understood supremely well all menaces to Yugoslavia's independence; in the 'loyal opposition' I would find most prominent by depth and coherence Petrović and Kangrga in philosophy, Supek in sociology, and Horvat in economy, while Marković's forte was current political analysis, and Vranicki was the meritorious and most learned historian of Marxism whose role was significant for my whole generation. Any trope, and especially my dichotomy here, has limits of pertinence.

I am also aware of a mountain of other writings in SFRY that more or less significantly mention bureaucracy. They are either, to a minor degree, to the right of Kardelj, that is on crypto-Stalinist – usually masked – positions, or somewhere between my two groupings. I mention as a sample the Zagreb symposium of 1967 *Communists and Self-management*, a title that laudably focussed on the relationship of these two abstractions. It might have been interesting to analyse, say, one quarter of the 39 speakers, but I shall mention only two reasonably articulate and representative ones: Nerkez Smailagić and Miroslav Pečujlić. Smailagić, a Zagreb University political science professor, somewhat nearer to the 'critical' wing, advocated a critical distance both from bureaucracy 'as an exploitative stratum whose goal is to reduce society again to thralldom with a small number of potentates', and from what he called utilitarian self-management, which he saw as spontaneously moving towards a petty-bourgeois view of society (Fiamengo et al. ed. 354). Pečujlić, a Belgrade sociologist and at times a high functionary in LCY and editor of the officious journal *Sociologija*, quite near to the 'official' wing, sharply disputed the contribution of *Praxis* collaborator, the philosopher Svetozar Stojanović,[3] that a bureaucracy

---

3 See Stojanović's book in Works Cited, which integrates his sharp and radical views before 1969, especially 50–4 and 125–6.

which administers all societal property was a separate class, insisting that 'it possessed no personal economic basis. Its position is based ... on delegation, on representing'; beside this legal argument, his second, even feebler (though interesting) one, was that 'institutions produced by a revolution against owning classes could not function [had bureaucracy become wholly independent]' (Fiamengo et al. ed. 628). My impression is therefore that such a 'swamp', sociologically rather interesting, did not supply cognitive arguments that would go beyond the horizons of the two groups I have discussed.

3.2   The Term 'Bureaucracy'

What in fact was the 'bureaucracy' debated here? The answer goes beyond the scope of my Appendix title which aims only at the discourse about bureaucracy. Yet discourses are, no doubt, deeply co-determined (*pace* Derrida) by various deformations of an extra-discursive reality, however protean: my take on that reality is in Chapters 3 and 4, on the SFRY classes. My hypothesis there is that this bureaucracy was a **proto-class** (term from Lenin's *Agrarian Programme of the Social-Democracy*), that finally constituted and differentiated itself into sub-classes sometime after the middle of the 1960s. A class coming into being increasingly takes on lineaments of exploitative rule, only counterbalanced in this case by an attempt at introducing a consistent workers' self-management – which however finally failed. In this conclusion I shall only attempt to determine what to call this proto-class.

The upshot of the debates in this Appendix seems to be that the term 'bureaucracy' rather obscures than clarifies. First, as Petrović found, officialdom in general (white-collar pen-pushers) ought to be sharply differentiated from the class holding power: thus the 'bureau' element is shown to be useless. As for the 'cracy' (power or rule) element, if we assume that its numerical strength on the federal level was in 1961 best approximated by Horvat's State 'managing stratum' of 155,000 people (plus families; see his *Essay* 205), and that within these no more than, say, 50,000 were its commanding top with powers of final decision, then I would – again following Horvat – call it a 'politocracy', a sub-category of oligarchy or rule of a small group based on political power, in this case fused with economic power. The term 'bureaucracy' at first helped to defer deciding whether this was a class or not. However, it gradually grew from a facilitation of public discussion, with reference to the prominent Marxists who had in the past or present used it and to the critique of Stalin's USSR, to sterile prevarications about 'strata' entailing the absence of deeper societal antagonism. Gramsci's sarcasm about a ruling unique party was here clairvoyant:

> For, even if no other legal parties exist, other parties in fact always do exist and other tendencies ...; against these, polemics are unleashed and struggles are fought as in a game of blind man's buff. In any case, it is certain that in such parties ... political language becomes jargon. In other words, political questions are disguised as cultural ones, and as such grow insoluble.
>> 149, and cf. 212–13; see for a similar appraisal of 'bureaucracy' HOBSBAWM 29

In the last decade of SFRY, when it increasingly becomes a periphery dependent on global capitalism, there matured the treasonable defection of three ruling oligarchies (now classes beyond a doubt) in Serbia, Slovenia, and Croatia.

Thus, paradoxically, bureaucracy was literally, as a term, quite useless. But the concept (and the state or condition) which was aimed at by this crooked arrow was crucial.

Glossary for the Appendices

tout court = simply
per aspera ad astra = through thorns to the stars

References

Works Cited in Foreword

Bloch, Ernst. '*Entfremdung, Verfremdung*: Alienation, Estrangement', in Erika Munk, ed., *Brecht*. Transl. A. Halley and D. Suvin. New York: Bantam, 1972, 3–11. [original in his *Verfremdungen I*. Frankfurt: Suhrkamp, 1963, 81–90]

———. *Subjekt-Objekt*, enlarged edn. Frankfurt: Suhrkamp, 1962.

Calic, Marie-Janine. *Geschichte Jugoslawiens im 20. Jahrhundert*. München: Beck, 2010.

Calvez, Jean-Yves. *La Pensée de Karl Marx*. Paris: Seuil, 1956.

Divjak, Slobodan. *Roba i revolucija: Marks, kritika političke ekonomije i socijalizam*. Beograd: SIC, 1982.

Dunayevskaya, Raya. *Marxism and Freedom*. New York: Columbia UP, 1988.

Elson, Diane. 'Market Socialism or Socialisation of the Market?' *New Left R* no. 172 (1988): 3–44.

Goldmann, Lucien. 'La Réification', in his *Recherches dialectiques*. Paris: Gallimard, 1959, 64–106.

Hamilton, Ian F.E. *Yugoslavia: Patterns of Economic Activity*. New York: Praeger, 1968.

Hrženjak, Juraj ed. *Rušenje antifašističkih spomenika u Hrvatskoj, 1990–2000*. Zagreb: Savez antifašističkih boraca Hrvatske, 2002.

Jameson, Fredric. *Representing 'Capital'*. London & New York: Verso, 2014.

Kidrič, Boris. *Sabrana dela*, vol. 2. Beograd: Komunist, 1985.

Kosík, Karel. *Dialectics of the Concrete*. Transl K. Kovanda and J. Schmidt. Dordrecht & Boston: Reidel, 1976. (original *Dialektika konkrétního*, 1961)

Kuljić, Todor. *Tito*, 3d edn. Zrenjanin: Gradska biblioteka 'Zrenjanin', 2010.

Marcuse, Herbert. 'Cultural Revolution', in his *Towards a Critical Theory of Society. Collected Papers*, vol. 2. Ed. D. Kellner. London & New York: Routledge, 2001, 121–61.

———. 'The Foundation of Historical Materialism', in his *From Luther to Popper*. Transl J. De Bres. London: Verso, 1988, 1–48. [original 1932]

Marx, Karl. *The Civil War in France*. www.marxists.org/archive/marx/works/1871/civil-war-france/

———. *Critique of the Gotha Program*, in *The Marx-Engels Reader*. Ed. R.C. Tucker. New York: Norton, 1972, 383–98. [original 1875]

Mészáros, István. *Marx's Theory of Alienation*. London: Merlin, 1970.

Mills, C. Wright. *Power, Politics, and People*. New York: Oxford UP, 1963.

Moore, Barrington, Jr. *Soviet Politics – The Dilemma of Power*. New York: Harper & Row, 1951.

Ollman, Bertell. *Alienation*, 2nd edn. Cambridge UP: Cambridge, 1976.

Petrović, Gajo. *Mišljenje revolucije*. Zagreb: Naprijed, 1978.
Skocpol, Theda. *States and Social Revolutions: A Comparative Analysis of France, Russia and China*. Cambridge: Cambridge UP, 1979.
Rusinow, Dennison. *Yugoslavia: Oblique Insights and Observations*. Ed. G. Stokes. U of Pittsburgh P, 2008.
Suvin, Darko. 'Locus, Horizon, and Orientation: The Concept of Possible Worlds as a Key to Utopian Studies', in his *Defined by a Hollow*. Oxford: P. Lang, 2010, 124–36.
———. 'Marksizam: nauka ili komunizam?' 'Aktiv no. 2', *Novosti* [Zagreb] of 26.XI 2010, p. 3, www.novossti.com/2010/11/marksizam-nauka-ili-komunizam/.
———. 'On the Horizons of Epistemology and Science'. *Critical Quarterly* 52.1 (2010): 68–101.
———. 'Two Cheers for Essentialism and Totality: On Marx's Oscillation and its Limits ...' *Rethinking Marxism* 10.1 (1998): 66–82.

Works Cited in Part 1: Fundaments

Chapter 1

Ali, Tariq. 'On Mao Zedong'. *New Left R* no. 66 (2010): 141–51.
Auty, Phyllis. *Tito*. London: Longman, 1970.
Bakarić, Vladimir. *Socijalistički samoupravni sistem i društvena reprodukcija (1958–1982)*, vols. 1–3. Zagreb: Informator et al., 1983.
Bilandžić, Dušan. *Historija SFR Jugoslavije: glavni procesi*. Zagreb: Globus, 1978.
Bobrowski, C[zesław]. *La Yougoslavie socialiste*. Paris: Colin, 1956.
Buden, Boris. 'Još o komunističkim krvolocima ...' *Prelom* 3.4 (2003): 51–7.
Davis, Mike. 'Marx's Lost Theory: The Politics of Nationalism in 1848'. *New Left R* no. 93 (2015): 45–66.
Denitch, Bogdan Denis. *The Legitimation of a Revolution: The Yugoslav Case*. New Haven: Yale UP, 1976.
Đilas, Milovan. *Vlast i pobuna*. Zagreb: Novi Liber & EPH, 2009.
Engels, Friedrich. 'Persia – China'. *New York Daily Tribune*, June 3, 1857. WAMW 1857/06/05.htm
Fejtö, François. *Histoire des démocraties populaires*, 2 vols., 2nd edn. Paris: Seuil, 1979.
Hobsbawm, Eric. *How To Change the World*. London: Abacus, 2011.
Jancar-Webster, Barbara. *Women and Revolution in Yugoslavia 1941–1945*. Denver: Arden P, 1990.
Johnson, Chalmers A. *Peasant Nationalism and Communist Power: The Emergence of Revolutionary China, 1937–1945*. Stanford: Stanford UP, 1962.
Kardelj, Edvard. *Reminiscences ... 1944–57*. London: Blond & Briggs, 1982.
———. *Tito and Socialist Revolution of Yugoslavia*. Beograd: STP [Socialist Thought and Practice], 1980.

Kirn, Gal. 'Conceptualisation of Politics and Reproduction in the Work of Louis Althusser: Case of Socialist Yugoslavia'. Ph.D. Diss. U of Nova Gorica 2012.

———. 'From the Primacy of Partisan Politics to the Post-Fordist Tendency in Yugoslav Self-management', in idem ed., *Postfordism and Its Discontents*. Maastricht: Jan van Eyck Accademie, & Ljubljana: Mirovni inštitut, 2010, 253–305.

Kržan, Marko. ['Nacrt historije samoupravnog socijalizma u Jugoslaviji'.] Lecture in Belgrade, Oct. 2012, electronic attachment of 9/12/2012.

Lenin, V.I. *The State and Revolution*. www.marxists.org/archive/lenin/works/1917/staterev/

Mann Borgese, Elisabeth. 'The Promise of Self-Management', in eadem and Ichak Adizes eds. *Self-management: New Dimensions to Democracy*. Santa Barbara: Clio P, 1975, ix–xxvii.

Melville, Herman. 'Letter to Nathaniel Hawthorne, [April 16?] 1851'. www.melville.org/letter2.htm.

Pupovac, Ozren. 'Projekt Jugoslavija: dialektika revolucije'. *Agregat* 4.9–10 (Dec. 2006): 108–17

———. 'Why Is the Experience of Yugoslavia Important Today?' Unpublished article, electronic attachment of 19/7/2011.

Suvin, Darko. 'How Can People Be (Re)Presented in Fiction? Towards a Theory of Narrative Agents', in *Darko Suvin: A Life in Letters*. Ed. Ph.E. Wegner. Vashon Island WA 98070: Paradoxa, 2011, 53–71.

Tito, Josip Broz. 'Development of the Liberation Struggle of the People of Yugoslavia in Relation to International Events' [speech to AVNOJ 1943], in his *Selected Works on the People's War of Liberation*. Bombay: Somatya, 1969, 142–56.

Chapter 2

See also Auty, Buden, Denitch, and Fejtö in Chapter 1.

Amin, Samir. *Accumulation on a World Scale*. New York: Monthly RP, 1974.

Benanav, Aaron, and *Endnotes*. 'Misery and Debt'. *Endnotes* 2, endnotes.org.uk/en/endnotes-misery-and-debt, 7 electronic pp.

Bilandžić, Dušan. *Ideje i prakse društvenog razvoja Jugoslavije 1945–1973*. Beograd: Komunist, 1973.

CIA. 'Economic Situation in Yugoslavia, 1 Sept. 1950', in US National Intelligence Council. *Yugoslavia: From 'National Communism' to National Collapse: US Intelligence Community Estimative Products on Yugoslavia 1948–1990*. NIC 2006–004. Washington DC: Government Printing Office, 2006.

Cohen, Stephen F. *Bukharin and the Bolshevik Revolution*. New York: Knopf, 1973.

De Angelis, Massimo. *The Beginning of History: Value Struggles and Global Capital*. L: Pluto P, 2007.

Dedijer, Vladimir. 'Istorijsko značenje jugoslovenske revolucije', in I. Božić et al. *Istorija Jugoslavije*. Beograd: Prosveta, 1972, 555–66.

Erlich, Alexander. 'Stalinism and Marxian Growth Models', in R.C. Tucker ed., *Stalinism*. New York: Norton, 1977, 137

Foa, Lisa ed. *L'accumulazione socialista*. Roma: Ed. Riuniti, 1969.

Harvey, David. *A Companion to Marx's Capital*. London & New York: Verso, 2010.

Heuser, Beatrice. *Western 'Containment' Policies in the Cold War: The Yugoslav Case, 1948–53*. London & New York: Routledge, 1989.

Hoffman, George W., and Fred Warner Neal. *Yugoslavia and the New Communism*. New York: 20th C Fund, 1962.

Lampe, John R. *Yugoslavia as History: Twice There Was a Country*. Cambridge and New York: Cambridge UP, 2000.

Löwenthal, Richard. 'Development vs. Utopia in Communist Policy', in Chalmers A. Johnson ed., *Change in Communist Systems*. Stanford: Stanford UP, 1970, 33–116.

Meillassoux, Claude. *Maidens, Meal, and Money: Capitalism and the Domestic Community*. Cambridge: Cambridge UP, 1981.

Močnik, Rastko. 'Nismo krivi ali smo odgovorni'. [Interview with O. Pupovac.] *Up& Underground* [Zagreb] no. 17–18 (2011): 139–55.

Rusinow, Dennison I. *The Yugoslav Experiment 1948–74*. Berkeley: U of California P, 1977.

Samary, Catherine. *Le marché contre l'autogestion: l'expérience yougoslave*. Paris: Publisud/La Brèche, 1988.

Woodward, Susan. *Socialist Unemployment: The Political Economy of Yugoslavia 1945–90*. Princeton: Princeton UP, 1995.

Works Cited in Part 2: Class Interests and Politics

Chapters 3 and 4

Adler, Max. *Die Staatsauffassung des Marxismus*. Wien: Wiener Volksbuchh., 1922.

Aronowitz, Stanley. *How Class Works*. New Haven: Yale UP, 2003.

Arzenšek, Vladimir. *Struktura i pokret*. Transl. from Slovene M. Đorđević. Beograd: Centar za filozofiju i društvenu teoriju, 1984.

Badovinac, Tomislav. 'Hrvatska u Drugome svjetskom ratu', in idem ed., *Titovo doba*. Zagreb: Savez društava 'J.B. Tito' Hrvatske, 2008, 53–71.

Bakarić, Vladimir. *Socijalistički samoupravni sistem i društvena reprodukcija*, vols. 2 and 3. Zagreb: Informator et al., 1983.

Barton, Allen H., Bogdan Denitch, and Charles Kadushin eds. *Opinion-Making Elites in Yugoslavia*. New York & London: Praeger, 1973.

Batinić, Jelena. *Women and Yugoslav Partisans: A History of World War II Resistance*. New York & Cambridge: Cambridge UP, 2015.

Bensaïd, Daniel. *Marx (Mode d'emploi)*. Paris: La Découverte, 2009.

Bilandžić, Dušan. *Historija SFR Jugoslavije: glavni procesi*. Zagreb: Globus, 1978.

———. *Ideje i praksa društvenog razvoja Jugoslavije 1945–1973*. Beograd: Komunist, 1973.

———, and Stipe Tonković. *Samoupravljanje 1950–74*. Zagreb: Globus, 1974.

Božinović, Neda. *Žensko pitanje u Srbiji u XIX i XX veku*. Beograd: Pinkpress, 1996.

Calic, Marie-Janine. *Geschichte Jugoslawiens im 20. Jahrhundert*. München: Beck, 2010.

Cvjetićanin, Vladimir, Josip Defilippis, Edhem Dilić, Alija Modžić, Vlado Puljiz, and Maja Štambuk, *Mješovita domaćinstva i seljaci-radnici u Jugoslaviji*. Zagreb: Inst. za društvena istraživanja Sveučilišta, 1980.

Debray, Régis. *Le Pouvoir intellectuel en France*. Paris: Ramsay, 1979.

Dedijer, Vladimir. 'Istorijsko značenje jugoslovenske revolucije', in I. Božić et al. *Istorija Jugoslavije*. Beograd: Prosveta, 1972, 555–66.

Denitch, Bogdan Denis. *The Legitimation of a Revolution: The Yugoslav Case*. New Haven: Yale UP, 1976.

Draper, Hal. 'The Principle of Self-Emancipation in Marx and Engels'. *Socialist Register* 8 (1971): 81–109.

Ehrenreich, Barbara. 'The Professional-Managerial Class Revisited', in B. Robbins ed., *Intellectuals*. Minneapolis: U of Minnesota P, 1990, 173–85.

———, and John Ehrenreich. 'The Professional-Managerial Class', in P. Walker ed., *Between Labor and Capital*. Boston: South End, 1979. 5–48.

ELZ4 = 'Jugoslavija', entry in *Enciklopedija Jugoslavije*. Zagreb: Leksikografski zavod, 1960, 4: 567–651.

ELZ5 = 'Jugoslavija', entry in *Enciklopedija Jugoslavije*. Zagreb: Leksikografski zavod, 1962, 5: 1–154.

Engels, Friedrich. 'The Principles of Communism'. www.marxists.org/archive/marx/works/1847/11/prin-com.htm

Erikson, Erik H. 'Youth: Fidelity and Diversity', in idem ed., *The Challenge of Youth*. New York: Anchor, 1965.

Fiamengo, Ante, et al. eds. *Komunisti i samoupravljanje. Zbornik radova učesnika naučnog savjetovanja ...* Zagreb: Fakultet političkih nauka, [1967].

Filipi, Slavko, comp. 'Statistički pregled razvoja KPJ-SKJ ...,' in M. Nikolić ed., *Savez komunista Jugoslavije u uslovima samoupravljanja*. Beograd: Kultura, 1967, 746–88.

Golubović, Zagorka. 'Novije teoretske paradigme za uporedno istraživanje "aktuelno postojećeg socijalizma"', in eadem ed., *Teorija i praksa 'realnog socijalizma'*. Beograd: Višnjić i Inst. društvenih nauka, 1987, 9–40 and 77–84.

Gramsci, Antonio. *Selections from the Prison Notebooks*. Ed. and transl. Q. Hoare and G. Nowell-Smith. New York: International Publ., 1975.

Gurvitch, Georges. *Le Concept des classes sociales de Marx à nos jours*. Les Cours de la Sorbonne. Paris: CDU, 1954.

Hamilton, Ian F.E. *Yugoslavia: Patterns of Economic Activity*. New York: Praeger, 1968.

Hegedüs, András. 'Towards a Sociological Analysis of Property Relations', in his *Socialism and Bureaucracy*. London: Allison & Busby, 1976, 93–125.
Hegel, G.W.F. *Philosophy of Right*. Transl. T.M. Knox. Oxford: Oxford UP, 1942.
Hirszowicz, Maria. *The Bureaucratic Leviathan*. Oxford: Robertson, 1980.
Hobsbawm, E.J. *Worlds of Labour*. London: Weidenfeld & Nicolson, 1984.
Horvat, Branko. *An Essay on Yugoslav Society*. White Plain NY: IASP, 1969.
———. 'Jugoslavenska agrarna teorija i politika u poslijeratnom razdoblju'. *Pregled* no. 7 (1975): 745–92 and no. 8 (1975): 972–1002.
Jancar-Webster, Barbara. *Women and Revolution in Yugoslavia 1941–1945*. Denver: Arden P, 1990.
Jovanov, Neca. *Radnički štrajkovi u SFRJ od 1958. do 1969. godine*. Beograd: Zapis, 1979.
Kardelj, Edvard. 'Radnička klasa, birokratizam i Savez Komunista Jugoslavije', in his *Subjektivne snage u samoupravnom socijalističkom društvu*. Sarajevo: Svjetlost, 1985, 9–66.
Kerševan, Marko. 'K vprašanju o razrednosti socialističnih družbenih sistemov'. *Teorija in praksa* 22. 12 (1985): 1467–86.
———. 'Razredni boj in družbena formacija', in his *Razredna analisa in marksistična družbena teorija*. Ljubljana: Delavska enotnost, 1980, 109–45.
Kontetzki, Heinz. *Agrarpolitisches Wandel und Modernisierung in Jugoslawien*. Nürnberg: Nürnberger Forschungsberichte Bd. 7. Nürnberg: V. d. Nürnberger Forschungsver., 1976.
Korošić, Marijan. *Jugoslavenska kriza*. Zagreb: Naprijed, 1988.
Kovačević, Dušanka, et al. *Borbeni put žena Jugoslavije*. Beograd: Sveznanje, 1972. http://www.afzarhiv.org/files/original/b5a58b7f3ad7beca75665c900324ca24.pdf.
Kovač, Bogomir. '"Socialistična" blagovna produkcija in diskretni šarm (njenega) akademizma'. *Teorija in praksa* 24. 3–4 (1987): 445–56.
Kurz, Robert. *Der Kollaps der Modernisierung*. Frankfurt a/M: Eichhorn, 1991.
Lampe, John R. *Yugoslavia as History: Twice There Was a Country*. Cambridge and New York: Cambridge UP, 2000.
———, Russell O. Prickett, and Ljubiša S. Adamović. *Yugoslav-American Economic Relations since World War II*. Durham & London: Duke UP, 1990.
Lazić, Mladen. *Čekajući kapitalizam*. Beograd: Službeni glasnik, 2011.
———. *Sistem i slom*. Beograd: Višnjić 1994.
———. *U susret zatvorenom društvu*. Zagreb: Naprijed, 1987.
Lenin, V.I. *Izbrannye proizvedeniia v dvukh tomakh*, vol. 2. Moscow: Gosizdat politicheskoi literatury, 1946.
Lewin, Moshe. 'Alle prese con lo stalinismo', in E.J. Hobsbawm et al., *Storia del marxismo*, vol. 3.2. Transl. E. Basaglia, Torino: Einaudi, 1981, 3–39.
Lukács, Georg. *Geschichte und Klassenbewusstsein*. Neuwied & Berlin: Luchterhand, 1971.

Macesich, George. *Yugoslavia: The Theory and Practice of Development Planning*. Charlottesville: U of Virginia P, 1964.
Marx, Karl. *Capital*, Vol. III. WAMW/1894-C3.
———. *The 18th Brumaire of Louis Bonaparte*. WAMW/1852/18th-brumaire.
———, and Friedrich Engels. *Werke*. Berlin: Dietz, 1962 ff. [cited as MEW with volume number].
Mills, C. Wright. *Power, Politics and People: The Collected Essays* ... Ed. I.L. Horowitz. New York: Oxford UP, 1963.
Moore, John H. *Growth with Self-Management: Yugoslav Industrialisation, 1952–75*. Stanford: Hoover Institution P, 1980.
Novaković, Nada. *Propadanje radničke klase: Materijalni i društveni položaj radničke klase Jugoslavije od 1960. do 1990. godine*. Beograd: Inst. društvenih nauka, 2007.
Ollman, Bertell. *Dialectical Investigations*. New York & London: Routledge, 1993.
———. 'Marx's Use of "Class"'. *The American J of Sociology* 73 (1967–8): 573–80.
Ossowski, Stanisław. *Struktura klasowa v społecznej świadomości*. Wròcław: Ossolineum, 1963 (cited from *Struttura di classe e coscienza sociale*. Transl. B. Bravo. Torino: Einaudi, 1966).
Petranović, Branko, and Momčilo Zečević eds. *Jugoslavija 1918–1988: Tematska zbirka dokumenata*. Beograd: Rad, 1988.
Polanyi, Karl. *The Great Transformation*. Boston: Beacon P, 2006. [original 1944]
Poulantzas, Nikos. *Classes in Contemporary Capitalism*. London: New Left Books, 1975.
———. *Pouvoir politique et classes sociales*, vol. 1. Paris: Maspéro, 1978.
Puljiz, Vlado. *Eksodus poljoprivrednika*. Zagreb: Inst. za društvena istraživanja Sveučilišta, 1977.
Ramet, Sabrina P. 'In Tito's Time', in eadem ed., *Gender Politics in the Western Balkans: Women and Society in Yugoslavia and the Yugoslav Successor States*. University Park: Pennsylvania State UP, 1997, 89–105.
Resnick, Stephen, and Richard Wolff. *Knowledge and Class: A Marxian Critique of Political Economy*. Chicago: U of Chicago P, 1987.
Ritsert, Jürgen. *Soziale Klassen*. Münster: Westfälisches Dampfboot, 1998.
Roemer, John. *A General Theory of Exploitation and Classes*. Cambridge MA: Harvard UP, 1983.
Roggemann, Herwig. *Das Modell der Arbeiterselbstverwaltung in Jugoslawien*. Frankfurt: Europäische V.sanstalt, 1970.
Rusinow, Dennison. *The Yugoslav Experiment 1948–1974*. London: Hurst, for the R. Inst. for International Affairs, 1977.
Schierup, Carl-Ulrik. 'Quasi-Proletarians and a Patriarchal Bureaucracy: Aspects of Yugoslavia's Peripheralisation'. *Soviet Studies* 44.1 (1992): 79–99.
Schleicher, Harry. *Das System der betrieblichen Selbstverwaltung in Jugoslawien*. Berlin: Duncker & Humblot, 1961.

Schrenk, Martin, et al. *Yugoslavia: Self-management Socialism and the Challenges of Development*. Baltimore & London: Johns Hopkins UP for the World Bank, 1979.
Simić, Andrei. *The Peasant Urbanites: A Study of Rural-Urban Mobility in Serbia*. New York & London: Seminar P, 1973.
Simon, György, Jr. *An Economic History of Socialist Yugoslavia*. Rochester NY: Social Science Electronic Publ., 2012.
Singleton, Fred. *A Short History of the Yugoslav Peoples*. Cambridge: Cambridge UP, 1985.
The Situation and Problems in Internal and Foreign Policy [of Yugoslavia]. Ed. Dragoljub Đurović. Beograd: SFRY Assembly, 1976.
Sklevicky, Lydia. 'Antifašistička Fronta Žena: kulturnom mijenom do žene "novog tipa"', in her *Konji, žene, ratovi*. Ed. D. Rihtman Auguštin. Zagreb: Ženska infoteka, 1996, 25–62.
———. 'Emancipacija i organizacija: uloga Antifašističke Fronte Žena u postrevolucionarnim mijenama društva (NR Hrvatska 1945–53)', in her *Konji ...* (see above), 63–152.
Statistički godišnjak Jugoslavije 1981. Beograd: Savezni zavod za statistiku, 1981. [further SG 81]
Ste. Croix, Geoffrey de. 'Class in Marx's Conception of History, Ancient and Modern'. *New Left R.* no. 146 (1984): 94–111.
———. *The Class Struggle in the Ancient Greek World*. London: Duckworth, 1983.
Stipetić, Vladimir. 'The Development of the Peasant Economy in Socialist Yugoslavia', in R. Stojanović ed., *The Functioning of the Yugoslav Economy*. Armonk NY: Sharpe, & Nottingham: Spokesman, 1982, 166–99.
Stojaković, Gordana. 'Vida Tomšič – Zašto je ukinut AFŽ'. http://pravonarad.info/?p=25
Šuvar, Stipe. 'Radnička klasa i razvoj jugoslavenskog društva', in Žuvela, Mladen, et al. eds. (see below), 23–65.
———. *Sociološki presjek jugoslavenskog društva*. Zagreb: Školska knjiga, 1970.
———. '"Srednji slojevi" ili "srednje klase" u jugoslavenskom socijalističkom društvu'. *Marksističke sveske* no. 1–2 (1972): 277–95.
Suvin, Darko. 'Living Labour and the Labour of Living', in his *Defined by a Hollow*. Oxford: P. Lang, 2010, 419–71.
———. 'On the Concept and Role of the Communist Party: Prehistory and the Epoch of October Revolution', in his 'From the Archeology of Marxism and Communism'. *Debatte* 21.2–3 (2013): 290–311.
———. 'Terms of Power, Today'. *Critical Quarterly* 48.3 (2006): 38–62, available at www.blackwell-synergy.com/
———. 'Where Are We? How Did We Get Here? Is There Any Way Out?' in his *Defined by a Hollow*. Oxford: P. Lang, 2010, 169–216.
Thompson, E.P. *The Making of the English Working Class*. Harmondsworth: Penguin, 1976.

Tomasevich, Jozo. 'Immediate Effects of the Cominform Resolution on the Yugoslav Economy', in W.S. Vucinich ed., *At the Brink of War and Peace: The Tito-Stalin Split in Historical Perspective*. Brooklyn NY: Brooklyn College P, 1982.

———. *Peasants, Politics, and Economic Change in Yugoslavia*. Stanford: Stanford UP, 1955.

Tomšič, Vida. *Žena u razvoju socijalističke samoupravne Jugoslavije*. Beograd: Jugoslovenska stvarnost, 1981.

Tonković, Stipe. 'Kako se živjelo u Socijalističkoj Republici Hrvatskoj', in Badovinac ed. [see above], 415–56.

Tozi, Đoko, and D. Petrović. 'Politički odnosi i sastav skupština društveno-političkih zajednica'. *Socijalizam* no. 12 (1969): 1590–5.

Trotsky, Lev D. *The Revolution Betrayed*. www.marxists.org/archive/trotsky/1936/revbet/index.htm

Woodward, Susan L. 'The Rights of Women: Ideology, Policy, and Social Change in Yugoslavia', in S.L. Wolchik and A.G. Meyer eds., *Women, State and Party in Eastern Europe*. Durham NC: Duke UP, 1985, 234–56 and 405–9.

———. *Socialist Unemployment: The Political Economy of Yugoslavia 1945–90*. Princeton: Princeton UP, 1995.

Wright, Eric Olin. *Classes*. London: Verso, 1985.

Žena u društvu i privredi Jugoslavije. Statistički bilten no. 788. Beograd: SZS, 1973.

Žuvela, Mladen, et al. eds. *Klasna borba i socijalna diferencijacija: prilog istraživanju socijalne strukture jugoslavenskog društva*. Zagreb: Centar SKH & Delo & Globus, [1984?].

Chapter 5

Bakarić, Vladimir. *Socijalistički samoupravni sistem i društvena reprodukcija (1958–1982)*, vols. 1–3. Zagreb: Informator et al., 1983.

Bavčar, Igor, Srečo Kirn, and Bojan Korsika. *Kapital in delo v SFRJ*. Ljubljana: Krt, 1985. [original 1983]

Bilandžić, Dušan. *Historija SFR Jugoslavije: glavni procesi*. Zagreb: Globus, 1978.

Bobrowski, C[zesław]. *La Yougoslavie socialiste*. Paris: Colin, 1956.

Boffito, Carlo. 'Introduzione', in his *Socialismo e mercato in Jugoslavia*. Torino: Einaudi, 1968, 11–49.

Brus, Wlodzimierz. *Socialist Ownership and Political Systems*. Transl. by R.A. Clarke. London and Boston: Routledge & K. Paul, 1975.

Coates, Ken. 'Democracy and Workers' Control', in Jaroslav Vanek ed., *Self-management: Economic Liberation of Man*. Harmondsworth: Penguin, 1975, 90–109.

Dallemagne, Jean-Luc. *Autogestion ou dictature du prolétariat*. Paris: UGE, 1976.

Divjak, Slobodan. *Roba i revolucija: Marks, kritika političke ekonomije i socijalizam*. Beograd: SIC, 1982.

Hamilton, Ian F.E. *Yugoslavia: Patterns of Economic Activity*. New York: Praeger, 1968.
Harvey, David. *A Companion to Marx's Capital*. London & New York: Verso, 2010.
Horvat, Branko. *Jugoslavensko društvo u krizi: kritički ogledi i prijedlozi reformi*. Zagreb: Globus, 1985.
———. 'Der Markt als Instrument der Planung', in K. Wessely ed., *Probleme zentraler Wirtschaftsplanung*. Wien: V. für Geschichte und Politik, 1967, 107–16.
———. *The Political Economy of Socialism*. Armonk NY: Sharpe, 1982.
———. *Towards a Theory of Planned Economy*. Beograd: Yugoslav Inst. of Economic Research, 1964 [revised transl. of *Ekonomska teorija planske privrede*].
Kalecki, Michał. *Socialism: Functioning and Long-term Planning. Collected Works* 3. Transl. B. Jung. Oxford: Oxford UP, 1992.
Kerševan, Marko. 'K vprašanju o razrednosti socialističnih družbenih sistemov'. *Teorija in praksa* 22. 12 (1985): 1467–86.
Kidrič, Boris. *O izgradnji socijalističke ekonomike FNRJ: Referat na V Kongresu KPJ*. Beograd: [Borba?, 1948].
———. *Socijalizam i ekonomija*. Ed. V. Merhar. Zagreb: Globus, [1979].
Korošić, Marijan. *Jugoslavenska kriza*. Zagreb: Naprijed, 1988.
Lenin, Vladimir I. *The State and Revolution*. www.marxists.org/archive/lenin/works/1917/staterev/
Lipovec, Filip. 'Nastanek dohodkovne mere v Kidričevem sistemu stopenj akumulacije'. *Ekonomska revija* no. 3–4 (1979): 265–79.
Marcuse, Herbert. *One-Dimensional Man*. Boston: Beacon P, 1964.
———. *Reason and Revolution*. Boston: Beacon P, 1960. [original 1941]
Markuš, Đerđ. 'Ekonomska i društvena struktura', in Feher, Ferenc et al., *Diktatura nad potrebama*. Transl. I. Vejvoda. Beograd: Pečat, 1986, 19–200. [original *Dictatorship over Needs*. Oxford: Blackwell, 1983]
Milenkovitch, Deborah. *Plan and Market in Yugoslav Economic Thought*. New Haven: Yale UP, 1971.
Polanyi, Karl. *The Great Transformation*. Boston: Beacon P, 2006. [original 1944]
Puharič, Krešo. 'Boris Kidrič o pomenu izumiteljstva in novatorstva'. *Ekonomska revija* no. 3–4 (1979): 325–30.
Samary, Catherine. 'L'Autogestion yougoslave'. E-mail attachment of 19/04/2011.
———. *La déchirure Yougoslave*. Paris: L'Harmattan, [1995?].
———. 'Du Juin 1968 yougoslave aux impasses du titisme'. www.contretemps.eu/archives/archives-revue-contretemps-telecharger
———. *Le marché contre l'autogestion: l'expérience yougoslave*. P: Publisud, 1988.
Suvin, Darko. *Darko Suvin: A Life in Letters*. Ed. Ph.E. Wegner. Vashon Island WA 98070: Paradoxa, 2011.
———. 'Death into Life: For a Poetics of Anti-Capitalist Alternative'. *Socialism & Democracy* 26.2 (July 2012): 91–105.

———. *Defined by a Hollow: Essays on Utopia, Science Fiction, and Political Epistemology*. Oxford: P. Lang, 2010.
———. *In Leviathan's Belly: Essays for a Counter-Revolutionary Time*. Baltimore MD: Wildside P for Borgo P, 2012.
———. 'Pogled unazad is krize na komunizam i SFRJ'. *Up&Underground* [Zagreb] no. 17–18 (2010): 86–95.
Tripalo, Miko. *Bez kompromisa u ostvarivanju samoupravnog socijalizma*. Zagreb: Naprijed, 1969.
Unkovski-Korica, Vladimir. 'Workers' Councils in the Service of the Market'. *Europe-Asia Studies* (2013): 1–20, dx.doi.org/10.1080/09668136.2013.855020.
Woodward, Susan. *Socialist Unemployment: The Political Economy of Yugoslavia 1945–90*. Princeton: Princeton UP, 1995.
Yugoslavia's Way: The Program of the League of Communists of Yugoslavia. Transl. S. Pribichevich. New York: All Nations P, 1958.
Žvan, Antun. 'Ekstaza i mamurluk revolucije'. *Praxis* no. 3–4 (1971): 455–65.

Chapter 6
Bobbio, Norberto. *Which Socialism?* Transl. R. Griffin. Minneapolis: U of Minnesota P, 1987.
Kouvelakis, Stathis. *Philosophy and Revolution: From Kant to Marx*. Transl. G.M. Goshgarian. London: Verso, 2003.
Labica, Georges, and Gérard Bensussan. *Dictionnaire critique du marxisme*. Paris: Quadrige/PUF, 1999.
Marx, Karl. *The Civil War in France*. WAMW/1871/civil-war-france/index.htm
———. *Critique of the Gotha Programme*. WAMW/works/1875/gotha
[Marx, Karl, and Frederick Engels.] *The Marx-Engels Reader*. Ed. R.C. Tucker. New York: Norton, 1972. [cited as Tucker ed.].
Marx, Karl, and Friedrich Engels. *Briefe über 'Das Kapital'*. Berlin [DDR]: Dietz V., 1954.
———. *Werke*. Berlin DDR: Dietz, 1958 ff. [cited as MEW with volume number].
Miller, Robert F. 'Civil Society in Communist Systems', in idem ed., *The Development of Civil Society in Communist Systems*. N. Sydney: Allen & Unwin, 1992, 1–10.
Rehmann, Jan. '"Abolition" of Civil Society?' *Socialism and Democracy* 13.2 (1999): 1–18.
Rousseau, Jean-Jacques. *Du contrat social*. Ed. B. Bernardi. Paris: GF Flammarion, 2012.
Suvin, Darko. 'Communism Can Only Be Radical Plebeian Democracy'. *International Critical Thought* 6.2 (2016): 165–89.
———. 'Inside the Whale, or *etsi communismus non daretur*', in his *Defined by a Hollow: Essays on Utopia, Science Fiction, and Political Epistemology*. Oxford: P. Lang, 2010, 473–502.

———. 'Living Labour and the Labour of Living', in his *Defined by a Hollow: Essays on Utopia, Science Fiction, and Political Epistemology*, Oxford: P. Lang, 2010, 419–72.
Zolo, Danilo. *La teoria comunista dell'estinzione dello stato*. Bari: De Donato, 1974.

Chapter 7
Section 7.1

Barton, Allen H., Bogdan Denitch, and Charles Kadushin. *Opinion-Making Elites in Yugoslavia*. New York: Praeger, 1973.
Bilandžić, Dušan. *Historija SFR Jugoslavije: glavni procesi*. Zagreb: Globus, 1978.
Carter, April. *Democratic Reform in Yugoslavia: The Changing Role of the Party*. London: F. Pinter, 1982.
Cohen, Lenard J. *The Socialist Pyramid*. London: Tri-Service P, 1989.
Comisso, Ellen T. 'Can a Party of the Working Class Be a Working-Class Party?', in J.F. Triska and C. Gati eds., *Blue Collar Workers in Eastern Europe*. London: Allen & Unwin, 1981, 70–87.
Dedijer, Vladimir. 'Istorijsko značenje jugoslovenske revolucije', in I. Božić et al. *Istorija Jugoslavije*. Beograd: Prosveta, 1972, 555–66.
Filipi, Slavko. 'Statistički pregled razvoja KPJ-SKJ u periodu 1946–1966 i struktura članstva', in Nikolić ed. (see below), 746–89.
Horvat, Branko. *An Essay on Yugoslav Society*. White Plain NY: IASP, 1969.
Izveštaj o radu CK ... do VIII Kongresa SKJ. Beograd: Komunist, 1964.
Lazić, Mladen. *U susret zatvorenom društvu? Klasna reprodukcija u socijalizmu*. Zagreb: Naprijed, 1987.
'Nedovoljno rasvetljeni događaji'. [Edited excerpts from the enlarged session of the Executive Committee of the CC of LCY, March 14–16, 1962.] Eds. R. Đurić and S. Dautović. *Politika* Nov. 17, 1998, p. 23, Nov. 18, 1988, p. 27, and Nov. 19, 1988, p. 27.
Nikolić, Miloš ed. *SKJ u uslovima samoupravljanja*. Beograd: Kultura, 1967.
Petranović, Branko, and Momčilo Zečević eds. *Jugoslavija 1918–1988: Tematska zbirka dokumenata*. Beograd: Rad, 1988.
Petrović, Gajo. 'Umjesto zaključka: Zašto sam marksist?' in his *U potrazi za slobodom*. Zagreb: Hrvatsko Filozofsko društvo, 1990, 209–23.
Pregled istorije Saveza Komunista Jugoslavije. Ed. Rodoljub Čolaković et al. Beograd: Inst. za isučavanje radničkog pokreta, 1963.
Rusinow, Dennison. *The Yugoslav Experiment 1948–1974*. London: Hurst, for the R. Inst. for Int'l Affairs, 1977.
The Situation and Problems in Internal and Foreign Policy [of Yugoslavia]. Ed. Dragoljub Đurović. Belgrade: SFR Yugoslavia Assembly, 1976
Statistički godišnjak Jugoslavije 1981. Beograd: Savezni zavod za statistiku, 1981. [as SG81]

Section 7.2

See also Carter, Cohen, Horvat, Nikolić ed., Rusinow, and *Statistički* in Section 1.

Auty, Phyllis. 'Yugoslavia's International Relations (1945–1965)', in W. Vucinich ed., *Contemporary Yugoslavia*. Berkeley, U of California P, 1969.

Bakarić, Vladimir. *Socijalistički samoupravni sistem i društvena reprodukcija*, vol. 2. Zagreb: Informator, 1983.

Baučić, Ivo. *The Effects of Emigration from Yugoslavia and the Problem of Returning Emigrant Workers*. The Hague: Nijhoff, 1972.

Bavčar, Igor, Srečo Kirn, and Bojan Korsika. *Kapital in delo v SFRJ*. Ljubljana: Krt, 1985.

Bićanić, Rudolf. *Economic Policy in Socialist Yugoslavia*. Cambridge: Cambridge UP, 1963.

Buden, Boris. 'Još o komunističkim krvolocima ...' *Prelom* 3.4 (2003): 51–7.

Bukharin, Nikolai. *Historical Materialism*. Transl. unknown. Ann Arbor: U of Michigan P, 1969. [original 3d edn. 1925]

Calic, Marie-Janine. *Geschichte Jugoslawiens im 20. Jahrhundert*. München: Beck, 2010.

Četvrti plenum CK SKJ. Beograd: Komunist, 1966.

Comisso, Ellen T. *Workers' Control under Plan and Market: Implications of Yugoslav Self-Management*. New Haven: Yale UP, 1979.

Cvjetičanin, Veljko. 'Uloga i struktura SK u sistemu diktature proletarijata', in Nikolić ed. (see Section 1), 254–69.

Denitch, Bogdan Denis. *The Legitimation of a Revolution: The Yugoslav Case*. New Haven: Yale UP, 1976.

Deutscher, Isaac. *Stalin*, 2nd edn. London: Oxford UP, 1967.

Divjak, Slobodan. *Roba i revolucija*. Beograd: SIC, 1982.

Dyker, David. *Yugoslavia: Socialism, Development, and Debt*. London: Routledge, 1990.

Fejtö, François. *Histoire des démocraties populaires*, 2 vols., 2nd edn. Paris: Seuil, 1979.

Kardelj, Edvard. *Reminiscences ... 1944–57*. L: Blond & Briggs, 1982. [original *Sećanja ... 1944–57*: 1980]

———. 'Snaga narodnih masa', in his *Samoupravljanje i društvena svojina*. Sarajevo: Svjetlost, 1982, 23–45. [Vol. 1 of his works in 5 volumes]

———. *Subjektivne snage u samoupravnom društvu*. Sarajevo: Svjetlost, 1982.

Kuljić, Todor. *Tito*. Zrenjanin: Gradska narodna biblioteka, 2010.

Lalović, Dragan. 'Program SKJ – koncepcijski razlaz sa staljinskim totalitarizmom?' in *1948: Povijesni razlaz sa staljinskim totalitarizmom*. Ed. T. Badovinac. Zagreb: Savez društava 'J.B. Tito' Hrvatske, 2009, 137–61.

Lampe, John R., Russell O. Prickett, and Ljubiša S. Adamović. *Yugoslav-American Economic Relations since World War II*. Durham & London: Duke UP, 1990.

Lilly, Carol S. *Power and Persuasion: Ideology and Rhetoric in Communist Yugoslavia, 1944–1953*. Boulder: Westview P, 2000.

Lukács, Georg. *Lenin: A Study on the Unity of His Thought*. Cambridge MA: MIT P, 1974 [orig. 1924].
Michels, Robert. *Political Parties*. Transl. E. and C. Paul. New York: Dover, 1959 [orig. 1911].
Milosavlevski, Slavko. *Revolucija i anti-revolucija*. Beograd: Revija, 1971.
Ranković, Aleksandar. 'Izveštaj o organizacionom radu KPJ ...' Beograd: Borba, 1948.
Robespierre: Écrits. Ed. C. Mazauric. Paris: Messidor/Éd. Sociales, 1989.
Rus, Veljko. 'Institutionalisation of the Revolutionary Movement', in G. Petrović and M. Marković eds., *Praxis: Yugoslav Essays in the Philosophy and Methodology of the Social Sciences*. Dordrecht: Reidel, 1979, 273–87.
Sednice Centralnog Komiteta KPJ (1948–1952). Eds Branko Petranović et al. Beograd: Komunist, 1985.
Šuvar, Stipe. 'Srednji slojevi ili srednja klasa u jugoslavenskom socijalističkom društvu'. *Marksističke sveske*, no. 1–2 (1972): 77–95.
Woodward, Susan. *Socialist Unemployment: The Political Economy of Yugoslavia 1945–90*. Princeton: Princeton UP, 1995.
Yugoslavia's Way: The Program of LCY. Transl. S. Pribichevich. New York: All Nations P, 1958.

Section 7.3
See also Cohen in Section 1.
Althusser, Louis. *Ce qui ne peut plus durer dans le Parti communiste*. Paris: Maspero, 1978.
Anderson, Perry. *In the Tracks of Historical Materialism*. Chicago: U of Chicago P, 1984.
Bahro, Rudolf. *The Alternative in Eastern Europe*. Transl. D. Fernbach. London: Verso, 1984.
Gorz, André. *Le Socialisme difficile*. Paris: Seuil, 1967.
Magri, Lucio. 'Per un nuovo realismo'. *Problemi del socialismo* 9.21 (Aug. – Sept. 1967): 1059–94.
Medvedev, Roy A. *On Socialist Democracy*. New York: Knopf, 1975.
Merleau-Ponty, M[aurice]. *Les Aventures de la dialectique*. Paris: Gallimard, 1955.
Montesquieu, Charles Secondat de. *De l'esprit des lois*, vols. 1–2. Paris: GF Flammarion, 2001.
Moulier Boutang, Yann. *Cognitive Capitalism*. Cambridge: Polity P, 2011.
Suvin, Darko. *Defined by a Hollow: Essays on Utopia, Science Fiction, and Political Epistemology*. Oxford: P. Lang, 2010.
Wang, Hui. *The End of the Revolution*. London: Verso, 2009.

Works Cited in Part 3: Self-Government vs. Alienation

Chapter 8

Bajt, Aleksander. *Samoupravni oblik društvene svojine*. Zagreb: Globus, 1988.

Bakarić, Vladimir. *Socijalistički samoupravni sistem i društvena reprodukcija (1958–1982)*, vols. 1–3. Zagreb: Informator et al., 1983.

Bavčar, Igor, Srečo Kirn, and Bojan Korsika. *Kapital in delo v SFRJ*. Ljubljana: Krt, 1985. [original 1983]

Bićanić, Rudolf [with M. Hanžeković]. *Economic Policy in Socialist Yugoslavia*. Cambridge: Cambridge UP, 1973.

Bilandžić, Dušan. *Historija SFR Jugoslavije: glavni procesi*. Zagreb: Globus, 1978.

Bobrowski, C[zesław]. *La Yougoslavie socialiste*. Paris: Colin, 1956.

Brus, Wlodzimierz. *Socialist Ownership and Political Systems*. Transl. by R.A. Clarke. London and Boston: Routledge & K. Paul, 1975.

CIA. 'Economic Situation in Yugoslavia, 1 Sept. 1950', in US National Intelligence Council. *Yugoslavia: From 'National Communism' to National Collapse: US Intelligence Community Estimative Products on Yugoslavia 1948–1990*. NIC 2006–004. Washington DC: Government Printing Office, 2006.

Comisso, Ellen T. *Workers' Control under Plan and Market: Implications of Yugoslav Self-Management*. New Haven: Yale UP, 1979.

Dirlam, Joel, and James Plummer. *An Introduction to the Yugoslav Economy*. Columbus OH: Merrill, 1973.

Drulović, Milojko. *Self-management on Trial*, rev. edn. Nottingham: Spokesman Books, 1978.

Dyker, David A. *Yugoslavia: Socialism, Development and Debt*. London & New York: Routledge, 1996.

Estrin, Saul. *Self-management: Economic Theory and Yugoslav Practice*. Cambridge: Cambridge UP, 1983.

Fejtö, François. *Histoire des démocraties populaires*, 2 vols., 2nd edn. Paris: Seuil, 1979.

Gnjatović, Dragana. *Uloga inostranih sredstava u privrednom razvoju Jugoslavije*. Beograd: Ekonomski institut, 1985.

Hamilton, Ian F.E. *Yugoslavia: Patterns of Economic Activity*. New York: Praeger, 1968.

Hoffman, George W., and Fred Warner Neal. *Yugoslavia and the New Communism*. New York: 20th C Fund, 1962.

Horvat, Branko. *An Essay on Yugoslav Society*. White Plains NY: IASP, 1969. [original *Ogled o jugoslavenskom društvu*. [Beograd:]: Jugoslavenski inst. za ekonomska istraživanja, 1967]

———. *Jugoslavensko društvo u krizi: kritički ogledi i prijedlozi reformi*. Zagreb: Globus, 1985.

———. 'O socijalnoj diferencijaciji u našoj zemlji', in Atlagić and Milanović eds. (see Chapter 10 below), 52–9.
———. *Towards a Theory of Planned Economy*. Beograd: Yugoslav Inst. of Economic Research, 1964.
Kanzleiter, Boris, and Krunoslav Stojaković eds. *1968 in Jugoslawien: Studentenproteste und kulturelle Avantgarde zwischen 1960 und 1975: Gespräche und Dokumente*. Bonn: Dietz Nachf., 2008.
Kardelj, Edvard. *Integration of Labour in a Society of Self-Management*. Beograd: STP, 1981.
———. *Reminiscences ... 1944–57*. London: Blond & Briggs, 1982.
———. *Samoupravljanje i društvena svojina*. Sarajevo: Svjetlost, 1982.
Kornai, János. *Anti-Equilibrium: On Economic System Theory and the Tasks of Research*. Amsterdam: N: Holland, & New York: American Elzevier, 1971.
Korošić, Marijan. *Jugoslavenska krisa*. Zagreb: Naprijed, 1988.
Lampe, John R. *Yugoslavia as History: Twice There Was a Country*. Cambridge and New York: Cambridge UP, 2000.
———, Russell O. Prickett, and Ljubiša S. Adamović. *Yugoslav-American Economic Relations since World War II*. Durham & London: Duke UP, 1990.
Macesich, George. *Yugoslavia: The Theory and Practice of Development Planning*. Charlottesville: U of Virginia P, 1964.
Marcuse, Herbert. *Reason and Revolution*. Boston: Beacon P, 1960. [original 1941]
Milenkovitch, Deborah. *Plan and Market in Yugoslav Economic Thought*. New Haven: Yale UP, 1971.
Milosavljević, Olivera. '"Centralizam" i "republikanizam"'. *Sociologija* 34.3 (1992): 359–70.
———. 'Država i samoupravljanje 1949–1956'. Diss. Beograd Univ. 1987.
Močnik, Rastko. 'Workers' Self-Management in Yugoslavia – Possible Lessons for the Present'. E-mail of Dec. 8, 2012 (forthcoming).
Novaković, Nada. *Propadanje radničke klase: Materijalni i društveni položaj radničke klase Jugoslavije od 1960. do 1990. godine*. Beograd: Inst. društvenih nauka, 2007.
Pervan, Ralph. *Tito and the Students: The University and the University Students in Self-Managing Yugoslavia*. Nedlands: U of W. Australia P, 1978.
Petranović, Branko, and Momčilo Zečević. *Jugoslavija 1918–1988: Tematska zbirka dokumenata*. Beograd: Rad, 1988.
Pregled istorije Saveza komunista Jugoslavije. Eds. Rodoljub Čolaković et al. Beograd: Inst. za isučavanje radničkog pokreta, 1963.
Prout, Christopher. *Market Socialism in Yugoslavia*. Oxford and New York: Oxford UP, 1985.
Rusinow, Dennison I. *The Yugoslav Experiment 1948–74*. Berkeley: U of California P, 1977.

Samary, Catherine. *Le marché contre l'autogestion: l'expérience yougoslave*. Paris: Publisud/La Brèche, 1988.

Schleicher, Harry. *Das System der betrieblichen Selbstverwaltung in Jugoslawien*. Berlin: Duncker & Humblot, 1961.

Simon, György, Jr. *An Economic History of Socialist Yugoslavia*. Rochester NY: Social Science Electronic Publ., 2012.

Stipetić, Vladimir. *Poljoprivreda i privredni razvoj*. Zagreb: Informator, 1987.

Tonković, Stipe. 'Kako se živjelo u Socijalističkoj Republici Hrvatskoj', in T. Badovinac ed., *Titovo doba*. Zagreb: Savez društava 'J.B. Tito' Hrvatske, 2008, 415–56.

Tyson, Laura D'Andrea. *The Yugoslav Economic System and Its Performance in the 1970s*. Berkeley: U of California P, [1981?].

Unkovski-Korica, Vladimir. 'Workers' Councils in the Service of the Market'. *Europe-Asia Studies* (2013): 1–20, dx.doi.org/10.1080/09668136.2013.855020.

Vanek, Jan. *The Economics of Workers' Management: A Yugoslav Case Study*. London: Allen & Unwin, 1972.

Woodward, Susan. *Socialist Unemployment: The Political Economy of Yugoslavia 1945–90*. Princeton: Princeton UP, 1995.

Yugoslavia's Way: The Program of the League of Communists of Yugoslavia. Transl. S. Pribichevich. New York: All Nations P, 1958.

Chapter 9

See also Bakarić, Bićanić, Comisso *Workers'*, Drulović, Estrin, Horvat *Jugoslavensko*, Macesich, Milosavljević 'Država', Tonković, and Vanek from Chapter 8.

Adizes, Ichak. *Industrial Democracy: Yugoslav Style*. New York: The Free P, 1971.

Bettelheim, Charles. *Class Struggles in the USSR*, 2 vols. Transl. B. Pearce. Hassocks: Harvester P, 1976 and 1978.

Bilandžić, Dušan, and Stipe Tonković. *Samoupravljanje 1950–74*. Zagreb: Globus, 1974.

Blackburn, Robin. 'Gunboat Abolitionism'. *New Left R.* no. 87 (2014): 143–52.

Bošković, Blagoje, and David Dašić eds. *Samoupravljanje u Jugoslaviji 1950–76: Dokumenti razvoja*. Beograd: Privredni pregled, 1977.

Bourdet, Yvon, and Alain Guillerm. *L'Autogestion*. Paris: Seghers, 1975.

Brinton, Maurice. *The Bolsheviks and Workers' Control, 1917 to 1921: The State and Counterrevolution*. London: Solidarity, 1970.

Carr, Edward Hallett. *The Bolshevik Revolution 1917–1923*, 3 vols. London: Macmillan, 1950–3.

Comisso, Ellen Turkish. 'Can a Party of the Working Class Be a Working-Class Party?', in J.F. Triska and C. Gati eds., *Blue Collar Workers in Eastern Europe*. London: Allen & Unwin, 1981, 70–87.

Dubey, Vinod, ed. *Yugoslavia: Development with Decentralisation*. Baltimore: Johns Hopkins UP, 1975. [Report of a World Bank Mission]

Duda, Igor. *U potrazi za odmorom i blagostanjem*. Zagreb: Srednja Europa, 2005.
Dunlop, John T. *Industrial Relations Systems*. New York: Holt, 1959.
Gerškovic, Leon. *Društveno upravljanje u Jugoslaviji*, 2nd edn. Beograd: Savremena administracija, 1959.
Gould, Carol C. *Rethinking Democracy: Freedom and Social Cooperation in Politics, Economy, and Society*. New York & Cambridge: Cambridge UP, 1988.
Hadžistević, Vojin, Husein Kratina, and Firdus Džinić. *Tendencije i praksa neposrednog samoupravljanja radnika u ekonomskim jedinicama*. Beograd: Inst. društvenih nauka, 1963.
Horvat, Branko, Mihailo Marković, and Rudi Supek eds. *Self-governing Socialism*, 2 vols. White Plains NY: IASP, 1975.
Hunnius, Gerry. 'Workers' Self-Management in Yugoslavia', in idem et al., *Workers' Control*. New York: Random House, 1973, 268–323.
ILO. *Workers' Management in Yugoslavia*. Geneva: ILO, 1962.
Janevski, Ana. '"We Can't Promise To Do More than Experiment": On Yugoslav Experimental Film and Cine Clubs in the Sixties and Seventies'. *Quaderns portátils* Macba [Barcelona] no. 27, 2012, www.macba.cat/en/quaderns-portatils-ana-janevski
——— ed. *As Soon as I Open My Eyes I See a Film*. Chicago: U of Chicago P for Museum of Modern Art, Warsaw, 2011.
Jovanov, Neca. *Radnički štrajkovi u SFRJ*. Beograd: Zapis, 1979.
———. *Sukobi*. Nikšić: Univerzitetska riječ, 1990.
Kirn, Gal. 'A Few Notes on the History of Social Ownership in the Spheres of Culture and Film in Socialist Yugoslavia from the 1960s to the 1970s'. *Etnološka tribina* 44.37 (2014): 109–23.
Kolaja, Jiri T. *Workers' Councils: The Yugoslav Experience*. New York: Praeger, & London: Tavistock, 1965.
Korošić, Marijan. *Ekonomske nejednakosti u jugoslavenskoj privredi*. Zagreb: Liber, 1983.
Lenin, V.I. 'The Immediate Tasks of the Soviet Government'. Transl. C. Dutt. *Collected Works*. Moscow: Progress, 1972, 27: 235–77, www.marxists.org/archive/lenin/works/1918/mar/x03.htm
Mandel, Ernest ed. *Contrôle ouvrier, conseils ouvriers, autogestion*, 3 vols. Paris: Maspero, 1970.
Mann Borgese, Elisabeth, and Ichak Adizes eds. *Self-management: New Dimensions to Democracy*. S. Barbara: Clio P, and Oxford: Oxford UP, 1975.
Marcuse, Herbert. *One-Dimensional Man*. Boston: Beacon P, 1964.
Marković, Mihailo. *From Affluence to Praxis*. Ann Arbor: U of Michigan P, 1974.
Meister, Albert. *Où va l'autogestion yougoslave?* Paris: Anthropos, 1970.
Močnik, Rastko. 'Nismo krivi ali smo odgovorni'. [Interview with O. Pupovac.] *Up& Underground* [Zagreb] no. 17–18 (2011): 139–55.

Ness, Immanuel, and Dario Azzelini eds. *Ours to Master and to Own: Workers' Control from the Commune to the Present*. Chicago: Haymarket Books, 2011.

Pannekoek, Anton. *Workers' Councils*. Oakland & Edinburgh: AK P, 2003. [original 1946?]

Pateman, Carole. *Participation and Democratic Theory*. Cambridge: Cambridge UP, 1970.

Robinson, Gertrude Joch. *Tito's Maverick Media*. Urbana. U of Illinois P, 1977.

Roggemann, Herwig. *Das Modell der Arbeiterselbstverwaltung in Jugoslawien*. Frankfurt am Main: Europäische V.sanstalt, 1970.

Rosenstein-Rodan, P.N. 'Problems of Industrialisation of Eastern and South-Eastern Europe'. *Economic J*. 53 (1943): 202–11.

Samary, Catherine. 'L'autogestion yougoslave'. E-mail attachment of 19/04/2011.

Seibel, Hans Dieter [and Ukandi G. Damachi]. *Self-Management in Yugoslavia and the Developing World*. London: Macmillan, 1982.

Singleton, Fred, and Anthony Topham. *Workers' Control in Yugoslavia*. Fabian Research Series 233. London: Fabian Society, 1963.

Statistički godišnjak Jugoslavije 1973. Beograd: Savezni zavod za statistiku, 1973.

Supek, Rudi. 'Problems and Perspectives of Workers' Self-management in Yugoslavia', in M.J. Broekmeyer ed. *Yugoslav Workers' Self-Management*. Dordrecht: Reidel, 1970, 216–41.

———. 'Some Contradictions and Insufficiencies of Yugoslav Self-Managing Socialism', in G. Petrović and M. Marković eds., *Praxis: Yugoslav Essays in the Philosophy and Methodology of the Social Sciences*. Dordrecht: Reidel, 1979, 249–71. [original in *Praxis* no. 3–4 (1971): 347–71]

Tornquist, David. *Look East, Look West: The Socialist Adventure in Yugoslavia*. New York: Macmillan, 1966.

Tripalo, Miko. *Bez kompromisa u ostvarivanju samoupravnog socijalizma*. Zagreb: Naprijed, 1969.

Vranicki, Predrag. 'Theoretical Foundations for the Idea of Self-Management', in G. Petrović and M. Marković eds., *Praxis* [see under Supek above], 229–47. [original in *Praxis* no. 3–4 (1972)]

Wachtel, Howard. *Workers' Management and Workers' Wages in Yugoslavia*. Ithaca: Cornell UP, 1973.

Žilnik, Želimir. 'Die Sechzigerjahre waren die kreat ivste Periode', in Kanzleiter and Stojaković eds. (in Part 1.2), 153–9.

Zukin, Sharon. 'Beyond Titoism'. *Telos* no. 44 (1980): 5–24.

———. 'The Representation of Working-Class Interests in Socialist Society: Yugoslav Labor Unions'. *Politics 6 Society* 10.3 (1981): 281–316.

Županov, Josip, and Arnold Tannenbaum. 'The Distribution of Control in Some Yugoslav Industrial Organisations ...', in A. Tannenbaum ed., *Control in Organisation*. New York: McGraw-Hill, 1968, 91–112.

Chapter 10

See also Bakarić, Bavčar et al., Bićanić, Bilandžić *Historija*, Brus, Comisso *Workers'*, Dirlam & Plummer, Drulović, Dyker, Gnjatović, Horvat *Jugoslavensko* and *Towards*, Kardelj *Integration*, *Samoupravljanje*, and *Subjektivne*, Korošić *Jugoslavenska*, Lampe, Milenkovitch, Močnik 'Workers'', Samary *Marché*, Simon, Tyson, and Vanek from Chapter 8; Adizes, Bettelheim, Bošković & Dašić, Bourdet & Guillerm, Brinton, Comisso 'Can', Horvat et al., Lenin 'Immediate', Mandel ed., Marković *From Affluence*, Supek 'Problems' and 'Some', Tripalo, Wachtel, and Zukin 'Beyond' from Chapter 9.

Allcock, John B. *Explaining Yugoslavia*. London: 2000.

Atlagić, David, and Vladimir Milanović eds. *Kritika socijalnih razlika*. Beograd: Komunist, 1972.

Bachelard, Gaston. *La formation de l'esprit scientifique*. Paris: Vrin, 1989. [original 1938]

Barthes, Roland. *Mythologies*. Paris: Seuil, 1957.

Begić, Kasim I. *Jugoslovenski 'sjever' i 'jug': međurepublička finansijska solidarnost*. Sarajevo: Oslobođenje, 1989.

Best, Michael H., and William E. Connolly. *The Politicised Economy*, 2nd edn. Lexington: Heath, 1982.

Bilandžić, Dušan. *Ideje i prakse društvenog razvoja Jugoslavije 1945–1973*. Beograd: Komunist, 1973.

Buden, Boris. 'Gastarbajteri, glasnici budućnosti'. Transl. M. Ćaćić. *Zarez* no. 338–9, July 5, 2012, p. 36.

Calic, Marie-Janine. *Geschichte Jugoslawiens im 20. Jahrhundert*. München: Beck, 2010.

Černe, France. *Jugoslovansko samoupravno gospodarstvo v teoriji in praksi*. Ljubljana: Delo, 1989.

———. 'Raspodjela dohotka prema radu u teoriji i stvarnosti'. *Ekonomist* [Z] no. 2 (1968): 283–305.

Chavance, Bernard. *Le Capital socialiste … (1917–54)*. Paris: Le Sycomore, 1980.

Cliff, Tony. *State Capitalism in Russia*. London: Pluto P, 1974.

Denitch, Bogdan Denis. *The Legitimation of a Revolution: The Yugoslav Case*. New Haven: Yale UP, 1976.

Dimitrijevic, Dimitrije, and George Macesich. *Money and Finance in Contemporary Yugoslavia*. New York: Praeger, 1973.

Divjak, Slobodan. *Roba i revolucija: Marks, kritika političke ekonomije i socijalizam*. Beograd: SIC, 1982.

Elson, Diane. 'Market Socialism or Socialisation of the Market?' *New Left R* no. 172 (1988): 3–44.

——— ed., *Value: The Representation of Labour in Capitalism*. London: CSE Books, 1979.

Golubović, Zagorka. 'Novije teoretske paradigme za uporedno istraživanje "aktuelno postojećeg socijalizma"', in eadem ed. (see below), 9–40 and 77–84.

———. *Staljinizam i socijalizam*. Beograd: Filozofsko društvo Srbije, 1982.
——— ed. *Teorija i praksa 'realnog socijalizma'*. Beograd: Višnjić i Inst. društvenih nauka, 1987.
Graeber, David. *Toward An Anthropological Theory of Value*, New York: Palgrave, 2001.
Hobsbawm, Eric. *How To Change the World*. London: Abacus, 2011.
Hodgson, Geoff. *The Democratic Economy*. Harmondsworth: Penguin, 1984.
Horvat, Branko. 'Der Markt als Instrument der Planung', in K. Wessely ed., *Probleme zentraler Wirtschaftsplanung*. Wien: V. für Geschichte und Politik, 1967, 107–16.
Jameson, Fredric. *Valences of the Dialectic*. London: Verso, 2009.
Jerovšek, Janez, Veljko Rus, and Josip Županov eds. *Krisa i perspektive*. Zagreb: Globus, 1986.
Kardelj, Edvard. *Proprietà sociale e autogestione*. Milano: Teti, 1975 [first edn. 1972].
Lazić, Mladen. *U susret zatvorenom društvu*. Zagreb: Naprijed, 1987.
Lenin, V.I. 'Five Years of the Russian Revolution and the Prospects of World Revolution'. Transl. D. Skvirsky and G. Hanna. www.marxists.org/archive/lenin/works/1922/nov/04b.htm
———. *The State and Revolution*. Transl. unknown. www.marxists.org/archive/lenin/works/1917/staterev/
Lowy, Michael. *Dialectique et révolution*. Paris: Anthropos, 1973.
———. *La pensée de Che Guevara*. Paris: Maspero, 1970.
Markuš, Đerđ. 'Ekonomska i društvena struktura', in Feher, Ferenc, et al., *Diktatura nad potrebama*. Transl. I. Vejvoda. Beograd: Pečat, 1986, 19–200. [original *Dictatorship over Needs*. Oxford: Blackwell, 1983]
Marx, Karl. *Notes on Adolph Wagner*. WAMW1881/01/wagner.htm.
McNally, David. *Against the Market*. London: Verso, 2003.
Močnik, Rastko. 'Od historičnega materializma k sociologiji kulture', in K. Vidmar Horvat and A. Lešnik eds., *Včeraj in danes*. Ljubljana: Odd. za sociologijo, 2010, 137–59.
Neumann, Franz L. *Behemoth*. London: Gollancz, 1942.
Nove, Alec. *The Economics of Feasible Socialism Revisited*, 2nd edn. London: HarperCollins Academic, 1991.
Parkin, Frank. 'Yugoslavia', in M.S. Archer and S. Giner eds., *Contemporary Europe: Class Status and Power*. London: Weidenfeld & Nicolson, 1971, 297–316.
Petrović, Gajo. '"Birokratski socijalizam"'. *Praxis* no. 3–4 (1971): 483–99.
———. *Filozofija i revolucija*. Zagreb: Naprijed, 1973.
Pienkos, Andrew. 'Socialist Transition in the Capitalist World Economy: The Yugoslav Experience'. *Critical Sociology* 12 (1984): 57–69, //crs.sagepub.com/content/12/57.
Polanyi, Karl. *The Great Transformation*. Boston: Beacon P, 2006. [original 1944]
———. *Primitive, Archaic, and Modern Economies: The Essays of Karl Polányi*. Ed. G. Dalton. Garden City NY: Doubleday Anchor, 1968.
Pusić, Eugen. 'Kriza pravnog sistema', in Jerovšek et al. eds. (see above), 261–99.

Rus, Veljko. 'Institutionalisation of the Revolutionary Movement', in G. Petrović and M. Marković eds. *Praxis: Yugoslav Essays in the Philosophy and Methodology of the Social Sciences*. Dordrecht: Reidel, 1979, 273–87.
Schrenk, Martin, Cyrus Ardalan, and Nawal A. El Tatawy. *Yugoslavia: Self-management Socialism and the Challenges of Development*. Baltimore & London: Johns Hopkins UP for the World Bank, 1979.
Singleton, Fred. *A Short History of the Yugoslav Peoples*. Cambridge: Cambridge UP, 1985.
Stojanović, Svetozar. *Kritik und Zukunft des Sozialismus*. Transl. F. Wagner. München: Hanser, 1970. [original *Izmedju ideala i stvarnosti*. Beograd: Prosveta, 1969]
———. 'Social Self-Government in a Socialist Community'. *Praxis* no. 1–2 (1968): 104–16.
Supek, Rudi. *Arbeiterselbstverwaltung und sozialistische Demokratie*. Transl. E. Prager. Hannover: SOAK-V., 1978. [original *Participacija, radnička kontrola i samoupravljanje*. Zagreb: Naprijed, 1974]
Suvin, Darko. 'Introductory Pointers toward an Economics of Physical and Political Negentropy', in his *In Leviathan's Belly: Essays for a Counterrevolutionary Time*. Baltimore MD: Wildside P for Borgo P, 2012, 331–50.
———. 'On the Concept and Role of the Communist Party: Prehistory and the Epoch of October Revolution', in his 'From the Archeology of Marxism and Communism: Pt. 2'. *Debatte* 21.2–3 (2013): 279–311.
Sweezy, Paul M., and Leo Huberman, 'Peaceful Transition from Socialism to Capitalism?' *Monthly R* 15 (March 1964): 569–90.
Tablada Pérez, Carlos. *El pensamiento economico de Ernesto Che Guevara*. La Habana: Casa de las Americas, 1987.
Waterston, Albert. *Planning in Yugoslavia: Organisation and Implementation*. Washington DC: International Bank for Reconstruction and Development, & Baltimore: Johns Hopkins UP, 1962.
Zović-Svoboda, Zorka. 'Ekstenzivni razvoj Jugoslavije i njezin opstanak ...' *Politička misao* no. 3 (2012): 92–115. [on Bakarić's views]
Županov, Josip. *Marginalije o društvenoj krizi*. Zagreb: Globus, 1983.
Žvan, Antun. 'Etatistički paternalizam ili samoupravljanje'. *Praxis* no. 6 (1971): 939–47.

Chapter 11

See also Horvat et al. eds. from Chapter 9; Hobsbawm from Chapter 10.
Aristotle. *Selections*. Ed. and transl. T. Irwin and G. Fine. Indianapolis: Hackett, 1995.
Burawoy, Michael. 'Terrains of Contest: Factory and State under Capitalism and Socialism'. *Socialist R* 58 (2981): 83–124.
Feenberg, Andrew. *Transforming Technology*. Oxford & New York: Oxford UP, 2002.
Gramsci, Antonio. *L'Ordine nuovo*. Torino: Einaudi, 1955.

Lukàcs, Georg. *Geschichte und Klassenbewusstsein*. Neuwied & Berlin: Luchterhand, 1971. [original 1923]

Marcuse, Herbert. *From Luther to Popper*. Transl J. De Bres. London: Verso, 1988.

———. 'Űber die philosophischen Grundlagen des wirtschaftswissenschaftlichen Arbeitsbegriffs', in his *Kultur und Gesellschaft II*. Frankfurt: Suhrkamp, 1965, 11–47 +173–5. [original 1933]

Marx, Karl. *Grundrisse*. Transl. M. Nicolaus. Baltimore: Penguin, 1973. [original 1851–61]

Morris, William. 'Useful Work *versus* Useless Toil'. www.marxists.org/archive/morris/works/1884/useful.htm

Petrović, Gajo. 'Marx's Theory of Alienation'. *Philosophy and Phenomenological Research* 2.3 (March 1963): 419–26, //thecommune.co.uk/ideas/marxs-theory-of-alienation-gajo-petrovic/

Chapter 12

See also Bakarić, Bavčar et al., Brus, Comisso *Workers*', Horvat *An Essay* and *Jugoslavensko*, Kardelj *Reminiscencesii*, Milosavljević 'Država', Močnik 'Workers'', Novaković, Prout, and Samary *Marché*, from Chapter 8; Bourdet & Guillerm, Comisso 'Can', Dunlop, Mann Borgese & Adizes eds., Močnik 'Nismo', Seibel, and Tripalo from Chapter 9; Atlagić & Milanović eds. and Golubović 'Novije' from Chapter 10; Burawoy from Chapter 11.

Arzenšek, Vladimir. *Struktura i pokret*. Transl. from Slovene M. Đorđević. Beograd: Centar za filozofiju i društvenu teoriju, 1984.

Braverman, Harry. *Labor and Monopoly Capital: The Degradation of Work in the Twentieth Century*. New York & London: Monthly RP, 1974.

Broekmeyer, Marius J. 'Self-Management in Yugoslavia'. *Annals of the American Academy of Political and Social Sciences* 23 (May 1977): 133–40.

Cvjetičanin, Veljko. 'Die Entwicklung der Selbstverwaltung in Jugoslawien', in B. Bošnjak and R. Supek eds., *Jugoslawien denkt anders*. Transl. E. von Steiner and R. Kaufmann. Wien & Frankfurt: Europa V, 1971, 237–54.

Flaherty, Diane. *Self-Management and Requirements for Social Property: Lessons From Yugoslavia*. biblioteca.clacso.edu.ar/ar/libros/cuba/if/marx/documentos/22/Self-Management%20and%20....

Gregory, Mary B. 'Regional Economic Development in Yugoslavia'. *Soviet Studies* 25.2 (1973): 213–28.

Jenkins, David. *Job Power: Blue and White Collar Democracy*. New York: Doubleday, 1973.

Kržan, Marko. ['Nacrt historije samoupravnog socijalizma u Jugoslaviji']. Lecture in Belgrade, Oct. 2012. Electronic attachment of Dec. 9, 2012.

Lazić, Mladen. 'Radništvo i samoupravljanje'. Zagreb: University Inst. for Social Research, 1981. Unpublished typescript.

Lebowitz, Michael A. *Build It Now*. New York: Monthly RP, 2006.
Lowinger, Jake. 'Economic Reform and the "Double Movement" in Yugoslavia: An Analysis of Labor Unrest and Ethno-nationalism in the 1980s'. Diss. Johns Hopkins U, 2009.
Mann Borgese, Elisabeth. 'The Promise of Self-Management', in eadem and I. Adizes eds. *Self-management* [see Chapter 9], ix–xxvii.
Marković, Mihailo. 'Struktura moći u jugoslovenskom društvu i dilema revolucionarne inteligencije'. *Praxis* no. 6 (1971): 811–26.
Marx, Karl, and Friedrich Engels. *Gesamtausgabe*. Berlin: Dietz V, 1975 ff. [as MEGA]
Tinbergen, Jan. 'Does Self-management Approach the Optimum Order?' in M.J. Broekmeyer ed., *Yugoslav Workers' Self-management*. Dordrecht: Reidel, 1970, 117–27.
Vidaković, Zoran. 'L' autogestion et la lutte des classes', u *Participation and Self-management: Conference in Dubrovnik*. Ur. E. Pusić. Zagreb: Inst. za društvena istraživanja Sveučilišta, 1972.

Chapter 13

See also Brus, Denitch, Horvat *Essay* and *Jugoslavensko*, Milosavljević 'Država', Močnik 'Workers'', Rusinow, Woodward, and *Yugoslavia's Way* from Chapter 8; Bettelheim, Mandel ed., Supek 'Problems' and 'Some' from Chapter 9; Elson, Lazić *U susret*, Pienkos, Suvin, 'Introductory', and Žvan from Chapter 10; Burawoy, Kržan 'Nacrt', and Marcuse 'Über' from Chapter 11; Cvjetičanin, Lebowitz, Lowinger, from Chapter 12.
Badiou, Alain. 'Must the Communist Hypothesis Be Abandoned?' in his *The Meaning of Sarkozy*. London: Verso, 2008, 97–103.
Carter, April. *Democratic Reform in Yugoslavia: The Changing Role of the Party*. London: F. Pinter, 1982.
Davidson, Cathy N. *Now You See It*. New York: Viking, 2011.
Dimitrijević, Branislav. 'Utopijski konzumizam'. Diss Univ. of Beograd, 2011.
Erlich, Vera St[ein]. *Family in Transition: A Study of 300 Yugoslav Villages*. Princeton: Princeton UP, 1992. [original 1964 from pre-1941 materials]
Groethuysen, Bernhard. *Die Entstehung der bürgerlichen Welt- und Lebensanschauung in Frankreich*, 2 vols. Halle: Niemeyer, 1930.
Kidrič, Boris. *Socijalizam i ekonomija*. Zagreb: Globus, [1979].
Kouvelakis, Stathis. *Philosophy and Revolution: From Kant to Marx*. Transl. G.M. Goshgarian. London: Verso, 2003.
Lenin, V.I. 'Draft Resolution on Freedom of the Press'. Transl. Y. Sdobnikov and G. Hanna. www.marxists.org/archive/lenin/works/1917/nov/04.htm
Löwith, Karl. *From Hegel to Nietzsche*. Transl. D.E. Green. New York: Columbia UP, 1991.
Magri, Lucio. *Il sarto di Ulm*. Milano: Il Saggiatore, 2011.
Marcuse, Herbert. *Counterrevolution and Revolt*. Boston: Beacon P, 1972.

Marković, Mihailo. 'Self-governing Political System and De-Alienation in Yugoslavia (1950–1965)'. *Praxis International* 6.2 (July 1986): 163–74.
Marx, Karl. *Capital*, vol. 3. WAMW 1894-c3/
———. *Critique of the Gotha Program*, in *The Marx-Engels Reader*. Ed. R.C. Tucker. New York: Norton, 1972, 383–98. [original 1875]
———. *The Poverty of Philosophy*. WAMW/1847/poverty-philosophy/
——— [and Friedrich Engels]. *Manifesto of the Communist Party*. Transl. S. Moore. WAMW/1848/communist-manifesto/cho2.htm
Moore, Barrington, Jr. *Soviet Politics – The Dilemma of Power*. New York: Harper & Row, 1965.
Perović, Latinka. *Zatvaranje kruga*. Sarajevo: Svetlost, 1991.
Rabinbach, Anson. 'The Aesthetics of Production in the Third Reich'. *J of Contemporary History* 11 (1976): 43–76.
Robespierre. Ed. C. Mazauric. Paris: Messidor/Éd. sociales, 1989.
Rus, Veljko. 'Participativna i reprezentativna demokratija'. *Praxis* 8.5 (1971): 697–717.
Schierup, Carl-Ulrik. 'Quasi-Proletarians and a Patriarchal Bureaucracy: Aspects of Yugoslavia's Peripheralisation'. *Soviet Studies* 44.1 (1992): 79–99.
Senjković, Reana. *Izgubljeno u prijenosu: Pop iskustvo soc kulture*. Zagreb: Inst. za etnologiju i folkloristiku, 2008.
Šuvar, Stipe. *Politika i kultura*. Zagreb: Globus, 1980.
Treći plenum CK SKJ. Aktuelni problemi borbe SKJ za sprovođenje reforme. Beograd: Komunist, 1966.
Wallis, Victor. 'Ecological Socialism'. *Capitalism Nature Socialism* 12 (2001): 127–45.

Works Cited in Conclusion

Chapter 14

Adler, Max. *Die Staatsauffassung des Marxismus*. Wien: Wiener Volksbuchh., 1922.
Althusser, Louis. *Philosophy of the Encounter: Later Writings 1978–1987*. London: Verso, 2006.
———. *Quel che deve cambiare nel partito comunista*. Transl. F. Fenghi. Milano: Garzanti, 1978. [French original 1978]
———. *Sur la reproduction*. Paris: PUF, 2011.
Anderson, Perry. *Considerations of Western Marxism*. London: Verso, 1987.
Aristotle. *Selections*. Ed. and transl. T. Irwin and G. Fine. Indianapolis: Hackett, 1995.
Arzenšek, Vladimir. *Struktura i pokret*. Transl. from Slovene M. Đorđević. Beograd: Centar za filozofiju i društvenu teoriju, 1984.
Badiou, Alain. *L'hypothèse communiste*. S.l.: lignes, 2009.
Benanav, Aaron, and *Endnotes*. 'Misery and Debt'. *Endnotes* 2, endnotes.org.uk/en/endnotes-misery-and-debt, 7 electronic pp.

REFERENCES

Bettelheim, Charles. *Class Struggles in the USSR*, 2 vols. Transl. B. Pearce. Hassocks: Harvester P, 1976 and 1978.
Bloch, Ernst. *Subjekt-Objekt*, enlarged edn. Frankfurt: Suhrkamp, 1962.
Bobbio, Norberto. *Which Socialism?* Transl. R. Griffin. Minneapolis: U of Minnesota P, 1987.
Bongiovanni, Bruno ed. *L'antistalinismo di sinistra e la natura sociale dell'URSS*. Milano: Feltrinelli, 1975.
Brus, Wlodzimierz. 'Commodity Fetishism and Socialism', in his *The Economics and Politics of Socialism: Collected Essays*. Transl. A. Walker. London & Boston: Routledge & K. Paul, 1973, 45–68.
———. *Socialist Ownership and Political Systems*. Transl. by R.A. Clarke. London and Boston: Routledge & K. Paul, 1975.
———, and Kazimierz Laski. *From Marx to the Market*. Oxford: Clarendon, 1989.
Buber, Martin. *Pfade in Utopia*. Heidelberg: Schneider, 1950.
Bukharin, Nikolay I. *Imperialism and World Economy*. www.marxists.org/archive/bukharin/works/1917/imperial/index.htm [also New York: Monthly RP, 1973].
Burawoy, Michael. 'Terrains of Contest: Factory and State under Capitalism and Socialism'. *Socialist R* 58 (2981): 83–124.
Calic, Marie-Janine. *Geschichte Jugoslawiens im 20. Jahrhundert*. München: Beck, 2010.
Carr, Edward Hallett. *The Bolshevik Revolution 1917–23*, 3 vols. London: Macmillan, 1950–2.
Černe, France. *Jugoslovansko samoupravno gospodarstvo v teoriji in praksi*. Ljubljana: Delo, 1989.
Comisso, Ellen T. *Workers' Control under Plan and Market: Implications of Yugoslav Self-Management*. New Haven: Yale UP, 1979.
Cortesi, Luigi. *Storia del comunismo*. Roma: manifestolibri, 2010.
Dirlam, Joel, and James Plummer. *An Introduction to the Yugoslav Economy*. Columbus OH: Merrill, 1973.
Đurek, Danijel. 'Tehnologija borbe za dohodak'. *Naše teme* 25.12 (1981): 1966–71.
Fanon, Frantz. *The Wretched of the Earth*. Transl. C. Farringdon. New York: Grove P, 1968. [original 1961]
Forster, Michael N. *Hegel and Skepticism*. Cambridge MA: Harvard UP, 1989.
Fraser, Nancy. 'A Triple Movement? Parsing the Politics of Crisis after Polanyi'. *New Left R* no. 81 (2013): 119–32.
Godelier, Maurice. *Perspectives in Marxist Anthropology*. Transl. R. Brain. Cambridge: Cambridge UP, 1977.
Gorz, André. *Le Socialisme difficile*. Paris: Seuil, 1967.
Gramsci, Antonio. *l'Ordine nuovo 1919–1920*. Torino: Einaudi, 1987.
———. *Selection from the Prison Notebooks*. Ed. and transl. Q. Hoare and G. Nowell-Smith. New York: International Publ., 1975.

Guattari, Félix, and Toni Negri. *Communists Like Us*. Transl. M. Ryan. New York: Semiotext(e), 1990.

Harding, Neil. 'Socialism, Society, and the Organic Labour State', in idem ed., *The State in Socialist Society*. London: Macmillan, 1984, 1–50.

Hobsbawm, Eric. *How To Change the World*. London: Abacus, 2011.

———. *Revolutionaries*. London: Abacus, 2008.

Horvat, Branko. *An Essay on Yugoslav Society*. White Plains NY: IASP, 1969.

———. *Business Cycles in Yugoslavia*. Transl. H.M. Kramer. White Plains NY: IASP, 1971.

Jameson, Fredric. *The Hegel Variations*. London & New York: Verso, 2010.

Kanzleiter, Boris, and Krunoslav Stojaković eds. *1968 in Jugoslawien: Studentenproteste und kulturelle Avantgarde zwischen 1960 und 1975: Gespräche und Dokumente*. Bonn: Dietz Nachf., 2008.

Korošić, Marijan. *Jugoslavenska kriza*. Zagreb: Naprijed, 1988.

Kosík, Karel. *Dialectics of the Concrete*. Transl K. Kovanda and J. Schmidt. Dordrecht & Boston: Reidel, 1976. [original *Dialektika konkrétního*, 1961]

Kuljić, Todor, *Tito*, 3d edn. Zrenjanin: Gradska biblioteka, 2010.

Kuzmanić, Tonči. *Labinski štrajk: paradigma začetka konca*. Ljubljana: Krt, 1988.

Lazić, Mladen. *U susret zatvorenom društvu*. Zagreb: Naprijed, 1987.

Lefebvre, Henri. 'O nekim kriterijima društvenog razvoja i socijalizma', in *Smisao i perspektive socijalizma*. Transl. S. Popović-Zadrović. Zagreb: Hrvatsko filozofsko društvo, 1965, 13–24.

Lenin, Vladimir I. 'The Impending Catastrophe and How to Combat It'. www.marxists .org/archive/lenin/works/1917/ichtci/index.htm

———. *The State and Revolution*. www.marxists.org/archive/lenin/works/1917/ staterev/

Lordon, Frédéric. *Capitalisme, désir et servitude: Marx et Spinoza*. Paris: La Fabrique, 2010.

Löwy, Michael. *The Politics of Combined and Uneven Development*. Chicago: Haymarket, 2010 [full edn. London: NLB, 1981].

Magri, Lucio. 'Per un nuovo realismo'. *Problemi del socialismo* 9.21 (Aug.–Sept. 1967): 1059–94.

Mann Borgese, Elisabeth, and Ichak Adizes eds. *Self-management: New Dimensions to Democracy*. S. Barbara: Clio P, and Oxford: Oxford UP, 1975.

Marković, Mihajlo. 'Socijalizam i samoupravljanje', in D. Pejović and G. Petrović eds. [see Lefebvre above], 54–71.

Marx, Karl. *The 18th Brumaire of Louis Bonaparte*. Transl. S.K. Padover. WAMW/1852/ 18th-brumaire/index.htm

———. *Capital*, vol. 1. WAMW/1867-c1

———. *Capital*, vol. 3. WAMW/1884-c3.

———. *The Civil War in France*. WAMW/1871/civil-war-france/

———. *Grundrisse*. Transl. M. Nicolaus. Baltimore: Penguin, 1973. [original 1851–61]
McNally, David, *Against the Market: Political Economy, Market Socialism and the Marxist Critique*. London: Verso, 1993.
Merleau-Ponty, M[aurice]. *Les Aventures de la dialectique*. Paris: Gallimard, 1955.
Michels, Robert. *Zur Soziologie des Parteiwesens in der modernen Demokratie*, 2nd edn. Ed. W. Conze. Stuttgart: Kröner, 1957. [original 1911]
Montesquieu, Charles de Secondat. *De l'esprit des lois*, vols. 1–2. Paris: GF Flammarion, 2001.
Moore, Barrington, Jr. *Soviet Politics – The Dilemma of Power*. New York: Harper & Row, 1951.
Morris, William. 'Useful Work *versus* Useless Toil'. www.marxists.org/archive/morris/works/1884/useful.htm
Ocić, Časlav. *Integracioni i dezintegracioni procesi u privredi Jugoslavije*. Beograd: CK SKS, 1983.
———. *Ekonomika regionalnog razvoja Jugoslavije*. Beograd: Ekonomika, 1998.
Parkin, Frank. 'Yugoslavia', in M.S. Archer and S. Giner eds., *Contemporary Europe: Class Status and Power*. London: Weidenfeld & Nicolson, 1971, 297–316.
Perović, Latinka. *Zatvaranje kruga: Ishod političkog rascepa u SKJ 1971–1972*. Sarajevo: 1992.
Petrović, Gajo. *U potrazi za slobodom*. Zagreb: Hrvatsko filozofsko društvo, 1990.
Preve, Costanzo. *Il filo di Arianna*. Milano: Vangelista, 1990.
———. *La passione durevole*. Milano: Vangelista, 1989.
Resnick, Stephen, and Richard Wolff. *Knowledge and Class*. Chicago: U of Chicago P, 1989.
Robespierre. Ed. C. Mazauric. Paris: Messidor/Éd. sociales, 1989.
Rosenstein-Rodan, P[aul] N. 'Problems of Industrialisation of Eastern and South-Eastern Europe'. *Economic J* 53 (1943): 202–11.
Rus, Veljko. 'Samoupravni egalitarizam i društvena diferencijacija'. *Praxis* no. 5–6 (1969): 811–27 [also as 'Self-Management Egalitarianism and Social Differentiation'. *Praxis* international edn. 6.1–2 (1970): 251–67].
Samary, Catherine. 'Mandel's Views on the Transition to Socialism'. 27 'electronic pages'. E-mail attachment of April 2013.
Sartre, Jean-Paul. *Situations VII*. Paris: Gallimard, 1965.
Schierup, Carl-Ulrik. 'Prelude to the Inferno: Economic Disintegration and the Political Fragmentation of Yugoslavia'. *Balkan Forum* 1.2 (March 1993): 89–120.
———. 'Quasi-Proletarians and a Patriarchal Bureaucracy: Aspects of Yugoslavia's Peripheralisation'. *Soviet Studies* 44.1 (1992): 79–99.
Schram, Stuart R. 'Introduction', in idem ed., *Authority Participation and Cultural Change in China*. Cambridge: Cambridge UP, 1973.
Selden, Mark. *The Yenan Way in Revolutionary China*. Cambridge: Cambridge UP, 1971.

Serge, Victor. 'Mexican Notebooks'. Transl. R. Schwartz and T. Selous. *New Left R* no. 82 (2013): 31–62.
Skocpol, Theda. *States and Social Revolutions: A Comparative Analysis of France, Russia and China*. Cambridge: Cambridge UP, 1979.
Spinoza, Baruch. *Ethics* ... Transl. S. Shirley. Indianapolis: Hackett, 1982.
———. *Tractatus politicus*, in idem, *Trattato politico*. Ed. P. Cristofolini. Pisa: ETS, 2011.
Stojanović, Svetozar. *Kritik und Zukunft des Sozialismus*. Transl. F. Wagner. München: Hanser, 1970. [original *Između ideala i stvarnosti*. Beograd: Prosveta, 1969]
Strpić, Dag. 'Obrazovanje, tehnološki i društveni razvoj i društvena infrastruktura'. *Naše teme* 32.1–2 (1988): 24–42.
Supek, Rudi. *Arbeiterselbstverwaltung und sozialistische Demokratie*. Transl. E. Prager. Hannover: SOAK-V, 1978. [original 1974]
Suvin, Darko. 'Brecht: Bearing, Pedagogy, Productivity'. *Gestos* 5.10 (1990): 11–28.
———. 'Communism Can Only Be Radical Plebeian Democracy'. (unpublished).
———. 'On the Concept and Role of the Communist Party: Prehistory and the Epoch of October Revolution', in his 'From the Archeology of Marxism and Communism'. *Debatte* 21.2–3 (2013): 290–311.
[———.] *Darko Suvin: A Life in Letters*. Ed. Ph.E. Wegner. Vashon Island WA 98070: Paradoxa, 2011.
———. *Defined by a Hollow: Essays on Utopia, Science Fiction, and Political Epistemology*. Oxford: P. Lang, 2010.
———. 'How Can People Be (Re)Presented in Fiction? Towards a Theory of Narrative Agents', in his *Darko Suvin* [above], 53–71.
———. 'Living Labour and the Labour of Living', in his *Defined by a Hollow* [above], 419–72.
Tamás, G.M. 'Words from Budapest'. *New Left R* 80 (2013): 5–26.
Tripalo, Miko. *Bez kompromisa u ostvarivanju samoupravnog socijalizma*. Zagreb: Naprijed, 1969.
Trotsky, Leon D. *La révolution permanente en Russie*. Paris: Maspero, 1969.
———. *The Year 1905*. www.marxists.org/archive/trotsky/1907/1905/index.htm
Vušković, Boris. 'Social Inequality in Yugoslavia'. *New Left R* no. 95 (Jan–Feb. 1976): 26–44.
Waller, Michael. *The Language of Communism*. London: The Bodley Head, 1972.
Wood, Ellen Meiksins. *Democracy against Capitalism*. Cambridge: Cambridge UP, 1995.
Zukin, Sharon. 'The Problem of Social Class in Socialism'. *Theory and Society* no. 6 (1978): 391–427.

Works Cited in Appendices: The Socialist/Communist Discourse about Bureaucracy

Appendix 1

Anderson, Perry. 'The Antinomies of Antonio Gramsci'. *New Left R* no. 100 (1976): 5–78.

Angenot, Marc. *L'utopie collectiviste*. Paris: PUF, 1993.

Balibar, Etienne. *Sur la dictature du prolétariat*. Paris: Maspero, 1976.

Banerji, Kalamalesh. 'Interview with Marshal Tito'. *Janata* Oct. 1, 1950. www.marxists .org/history/etol/newspape/fi/vol11/no06/banerji.html

Bettelheim, Charles. *Class Struggles in the USSR*, 2 vols. Transl. B. Pearce. Hassocks: Harvester P, 1976 and 1978.

———. *La planification soviétique*. Paris: Rivière, 1945.

Bloch, Ernst. *Das Prinzip Hoffnung*, 2 vols. Frankfurt: Suhrkamp, 1959.

Bongiovanni, Bruno ed. *L'antistalinismo di sinistra e la natura sociale dell'URSS*. Milano: Feltrinelli, 1975.

Bricianer, Serge, ed. and transl. *Pannekoek et les conseils ouvriers*. Paris: EDi, 1969.

Brus, Wlodzimierz. *Socialist Ownership & Political Systems*. Transl. R.A. Clarke. L & Boston: Routledge & Kegan Paul, 1975.

Bukharin, Nikolay, and Evgeniy Preobrazhensky. *The ABC of Communism*. Transl E. and C. Paul. Ann Arbor: U Michigan P, 1966.

Cliff, Tony [Yigael Gluckstein]. *The Nature of Stalinist Russia*. www.marxists.org/archive/cliff/works/1948/stalruss/

Cohen, Stephen F. *Bukharin and the Bolshevik Revolution*. New York: Knopf, 1973.

Cortesi, Luigi. *Storia del comunismo da Utopia al Termidoro sovietico*. Roma: manifestolibri, 2010.

Davies, R.W. 'Le scelte economiche dell'Urss', in E.J. Hobsbawm et al., *Storia del marxismo*, vol. 3.1. Torino: Einaudi, 1980, 581–601.

Draper, Hal. *Karl Marx's Theory of Revolution*, vol. 3: The 'Dictatorship of the Proletariat'. New York: Monthly RP, 1986.

Fischer, Louis. *Das Leben Lenins*, 2 vols. München: dtv, 1970.

Kidrič, Boris. *Socijalizam i ekonomija*. Ed. V. Merhar. Zagreb: Globus, [1979].

Lenin, V.I. *Collected Works*, 4th edn. Moscow: FLPH, 1960–70.

———. *Izbrannye proizvedeniia v dvukh tomakh*, vol. 2. Moscow: Gosisdat politicheskoi literatury, 1946.

Lewin, Moshe. 'Alle prese con lo stalinismo', in E.J. Hobsbawm et al., *Storia del marxismo*, vol. 3.2. Transl. E. Basaglia. Torino: Einaudi, 1981, 3–39.

———. *Lenin's Last Struggle*. Transl. A.M. Sheridan-Smith. London: Pluto P, 1975.

———. *Storia sociale dello stalinismo*. Ed. [and transl.?] A. Graziosi. Torino: Einaudi, 1988.

Lih, Lars T. *Lenin*. London: Reaktion, 2011.

———. *Lenin Rediscovered*. Leiden & Boston: Brill, 2006.
Luxemburg, Rosa. *The Russian Revolution*. New York: Worker's Age, 1940.
Mandel, Ernest. *On Bureaucracy: A Marxist Analysis*. London: IMG Publ., [1968].
Marx, Karl. Works in www.marxists.org/archive/marx/works/ [cited as WAMW].
[———, and Frederick Engels.] *The Marx-Engels Reader*. Ed. Robert C. Tucker. New York: Norton, 1972.
———. *On the Paris Commune*. Moscow: Progress, 1971.
McNeal, Robert. 'Le istituzioni della Russia di Stalin', in E.J. Hobsbawm et al., *Storia del marxismo*, Vol. 3.2. Transl. E. Basaglia, Torino: Einaudi, 1980, 39–68.
Medvedev, Roj A. 'Il socialismo in un solo paese', in E.J. Hobsbawm et al., *Storia del marxismo*, vol. 3.1. Torino: Einaudi, 1980, 550–80.
Nove, Alec. *An Economic History of the USSR*. Harmondsworth: Penguin, 1982.
Ossowski, Stanisław. *Struktura klasowa v społecznej świadomości*. Wrocław: Ossolineum, 1963 (cited from *Struttura di classe e coscienza sociale*. Transl. B. Bravo. Torino: Einaudi, 1966).
Podsheldolkin, Alexander. 'The Origins of the Stalinist Bureaucracy'. Transl. M. Jones. www.marxists.org/history/etol/revhist/supplem/podsheld.htm [ca. 1989?]
Rusinow, Dennison. *The Yugoslav Experiment 1948–1974*. London: Hurst, for the R. Inst. for Int'l Affairs, 1977.
Shapiro, Leonard. *The Communist Party of the Soviet Union*, 2nd edn. London: Methuen, 1970.
Sieyès, Emmanuel. *Qu'est-ce que le Tiers-état?* Paris: Flammarion, 2013.
Suvin, Darko. 'From the Archeology of Marxism and Communism: Pt. 1 "Phases and Characteristics of Marxism/s"', Pt. 2 'On the Concept and Role of the Communist Party: Prehistory and the Epoch of October Revolution'. *Debatte* 21.2–3 (2013): 279–311.
Trotsky, Lev D. *The Revolution Betrayed*.
www.marxists.org/archive/trotsky/1936/revbet/index.htm

Appendix 2

Bakarić, Vladimir. *Socijalistički samoupravni sistem i društvena reprodukcija*, 4 vols. Zagreb: Informator et al., 1983.
Bensaïd, Daniel. *Marx (Mode d'emploi)*. Paris: La Découverte, 2009.
Bettelheim, Charles. *Class Struggles in the USSR, Second Period: 1923–30*. Transl. B. Pearce. Hassocks: Harvester P, 1976.
Bilandžić, Dušan. *Ideje i praksa društvenog razvoja Jugoslavije 1945–1973*. Beograd: Komunist, 1973.
Bogdanović, Mira. *Konstante konvertitstva*. Beograd: C. za liberterske studije, 2013.
Denitch, Bogdan. 'Mobility and Recruitment in Yugoslav Leadership', in Barton, Allen H., et al., *Opinion-Making Elites in Yugoslavia*. New York & London: Praeger, 1973, 95–119.

REFERENCES

Divjak, Slobodan. *Roba i revolucija: Marks, kritika političke ekonomije i socijalizam*. Beograd: SIC, 1982.

Djilas, Milovan. *The New Class: An Analysis of the Communist System*, corrected edn. New York: Praeger, 1963. [first English edn. 1957]

———. *Savremene teme*. Beograd: Borba, 1950.

Fiamengo, Ante, et al. eds. *Komunisti i samoupravljanje*. Zagreb: Fakultet političkih nauka, [1967].

Filipi, Slavko. 'Statistički pregled razvoja KPJ-SKJ ...', in M. Nikolić ed., *Savez komunista Jugoslavije u uslovima samoupravljanja*. Kultura: Beograd, 1967, 746–88.

Gramsci, Antonio. *Selections from the Prison Notebooks*. Ed. and transl. Q. Hoare and G. Nowell-Smith. New York: International Publ., 1975.

Hobsbawm, E.J. *Worlds of Labour*. London: Weidenfeld & Nicolson, 1984.

Horvat, Branko. *Towards a Theory of Planned Economy*. Beograd: Yugoslav Inst. of Economic Research, 1964. [written by 1961]

———. *An Essay on Yugoslav Society*. Transl. H.F. Mins. White Plains NY: International Arts & Sciences P, 1969. [original *Ogled o jugoslavenskom društvu*. [Beograd:]: Jugoslavenski inst. za ekonomska istraživanja, 1967]

———. 'Yugoslav Economic Policy in the Post-War Period'. *The American Economic R* 61.3 (1971), Part 2, Supplement 71–169.

———, Mihajlo Marković, and Rudi Supek eds. *Self-Governing Socialism*, vol. 1. White Plains NY: Int'l Arts & Sciences P, 1975.

Izveštaj o radu CK i Centralne revizione komisije od Sedmog do Osmog Kongresa SKJ. Beograd: Komunist, 1964. [Author/s unknown]

Jakšić, Božidar. *Buka i bes*. Požarevac: Braničevo, 2005.

Johnson, A. Ross. *The Transformations of Communist Ideology: The Yugoslav Case, 1945–1953*. Cambridge MA: MIT P, 1972.

Kangrga, Milan. *Razmišljanja o etici*. Zagreb: Praxis, 1970.

Kardelj, Edvard. *Pravci razvoja političkog sistema socijalističkog samoupravljanja*, 2nd edn. Beograd: Komunist, 1978. [original 1977, cited as *PR*]

———. *Problemi naše socijalističke izgradnje*. Beograd: Kultura, 1954 ff. [cited as *PSI*]

———. *Proprietà sociale e autogestione*. Transl. M. Zega. Milano: Teti, 1975.

———. *Reminiscences ... 1944–57*. L: Blond & Briggs, 1982. [original *Sećanja ... 1944–57*. Beograd & Ljubljana: Radnička štampa, 1980, cited as *R*]

———. *Samoupravljanje i društvena svojina*. Sarajevo: Svjetlost, 1982. [cited as *SDS*]

———. *Socijalizam i rat*. Beograd: Kultura, 1960.

———. *Subjektivne snage u samoupravnom socijalističkom društvu*. Sarajevo: Svjetlost, 1985. [cited as *SSS*]

Kidrič, Boris. *Socijalizam i ekonomija*. Ed. V. Merhar. Zagreb: Globus, [1979].

Korsch, Karl. *Karl Marx*. New York: Russell & Russell, 1963. [original 1938]

Lalović, Dragan. 'Program Saveza komunista Jugoslavije – koncepcijski razlaz sa staljinskim totalitarizmom?' in *1948: Povijesni razlaz sa staljinskim totalitarizmom*. Ed. T. Badovinac. Zagreb: Savez društava 'J.B. Tito' Hrvatske, 2009, 137–61.

MacBride, William L. *From Yugoslav Praxis to Global Pathos*. Lanham: Rowman & Littlefield, 2001.

Marković, Mihajlo. 'Jednakost i sloboda'. *Praxis* no. 1–2 (1973): 3–18.

———. 'Socijalizam i samoupravljanje', in Danilo Pejović and Gajo Petrović eds., *Smisao i perspektive socijalizma*. Zagreb: Hrvatsko filozofsko društvo, 1965, 54–71.

———, and Robert S. Cohen. *Yugoslavia: The Rise and Fall of Socialist Humanism: A History of the Praxis Group*. Nottingham: Spokesman Books, 1975.

———, and Gajo Petrović eds. *PRAXIS: Yugoslav Essays in the Philosophy and Methodology of the Social Sciences*. Dordrecht & Boston: Reidel, 1979.

Marx, Karl. *The Poverty of Philosophy*. WAMW/1847/poverty-philosophy/

Mićunović, Dragoljub. 'Birokratija i javnost'. *Praxis* no. 4–5 (1965): 642–52.

Močnik, Rastko. Interview with Jerko Bakotin of May 21, 2008, www.h-alter.org/vijesti/europa-regija/zivot-u-istom-camcu/print:true

———. 'Od istoričnega materializma k sociologiji kulture', in K. Vidmar Horvat and A. Lešnik eds., *Včeraj in danes*. Ljubljana: Odd. za sociologijo, 2010, 137–59.

Petrović, Gajo. '"Birokratski socijalizam"'. *Praxis* no. 3–4 (1971): 483–99. [cited as B]

———. 'Filozofski pojam revolucije'. *Praxis* no. 1–2 (1973): 155–67. [cited as F]

The Programme of the League of Yugoslav Communists. Beograd: Jugoslavija, 1958 [also as *Yugoslavia's Way: The Program of LCY*. Transl. S. Pribichevich. New York: All Nations P, 1958].

Rusinow, Dennison. *The Yugoslav Experiment 1948–1974*. London: Hurst, for the R. Inst. for International Affairs, 1977.

Sednice Centralnog Komiteta KPJ (1948–1952). Eds B. Petranović et al. Beograd: Komunist, 1985.

Sher, Gerson S. *'Praxis': Marxist Criticism and Dissent in Socialist Yugoslavia*. Bloomington: Indiana UP, 1977.

Simmel, Georg. *Conflict*. Transl. K. Wolff. Glencoe NY: Free P, 1966.

———. *Soziologie*. Leipzig: Duncker & Humblot, 1908.

Statistički godišnjak Jugoslavije 1981. Beograd: Savezni zavod za statistiku, 1981.

Stojanović, Svetozar. *Kritik und Zukunft des Sozialismus*. Transl. F. Wagner. München: Hanser, 1970. [original *Izmedju ideala i stvarnosti*. Beograd: Prosveta, 1969]

Stonor Saunders, Frances. *Who Paid the Piper: The CIA and the Cultural Cold War*. London: Granta, 1999.

Suvin, Darko. *Defined by a Hollow: Essays on Utopia, Science Fiction, and Political Epistemology*. Oxford: P. Lang, 2010.

Tito, Josip Broz. 'Borba komunista Jugoslavije za socijalističku demokratiju', in *VI Kongres KPJ*. Beograd: [Komunist, 1962], 7–116.

———. [*Djela*] *VIII: Borba za mir i medunarodnu suradnju*. Zagreb: Kultura, 1957.

Index of Proper Names of Historical Persons

Prepared by Mary Wickizer Burgess

Names not cited but found only in the Bibliographies at the end are not listed, with the exception of multiple authorships or substantial textual input by translator or by editor, marked by *.

Acton, Lord (John Dalberg-Acton)   316
*Adamović, Ljubiša S.   393, 400, 403
Adizes, Ichak   181, 185–6, 189, 196, 198, 200–3, 223, 225, 238, 256, 258, 260, 295
Adler, Max   47, 288
Aganbegian, Abel   51
Ali, Tariq   24
Allcock, John B.   228
Allende, Salvador   302
Althusser, Louis   106, 152n4, 284, 305, 306n7, 311
Amin, Samir   37, 162, 273
Anderson, Perry   152n4, 298, 328n3
Angelus Silesius (pseud. of Johann Scheffler)   279
Angenot, Marc   xvii, 325
*Ardalan, Cyrus   409
Aristotle (Aristotelian)   12, 216, 250, 267, 280, 302, 315, 317
Aronowitz, Stanley   48
Arsovski, Mihajlo   xiii, xvi, 192 (graphic)
Arzenšek, Vladimir   60, 259, 308
Asimakopulos, Athanasios (Tommy)   156
Atlagić, David, and Vladimir Milanović   235, 263
Augustine of Hippo   119n3
Auty, Phyllis   34, 39n2, 139
Azzelini, Dario   180n1

Babeuf, François-Nöel Gracchus   14, 110, 234, 302
Bachelard, Gaston   237
Bacon, Francis   9
Badiou, Alain   14, 28, 266, 306n7
Badovinac, Tomislav   57
Bahro, Rudolf   152n4
Bajt, Aleksander   177
Bakarić, Vladimir   31, 50, 52, 57–8, 61, 65–6, 75, 77, 91, 103, 144, 146–7, 170, 175–6, 193, 207, 210, 214, 219, 222–4, 230, 234, 238, 244, 259, 262n1, 269, 347, 351–2, 361–7, 382, 384
Bakhtin, Mikhail M.   14
Balibar, Etienne   72, 328n3
Banerji, Kalamalesh   343
Barsky, Robert   181n1
Barthes, Roland   237, 358
Barton, Allen H.   55, 57, 129–31, 133, 135, 137
Baslé, Louis   214n3
Batinić, Jelena   68n2
Bavčar, Igor, Srečo Kirn, and Bojan Korsika   77, 148, 179, 214, 223–4, 236, 244, 261
Bebel, August   256
Beckett, Samuel   ix, 247
Begić, Kasim I.   207
Benanav, Aaron   37, 294
Benjamin, Walter   vii, xiii, 3n2, 5–6 (photo), 7, 238, 282, 359, 383
Bensaïd, Daniel   44, 54
Bensussan, Gérard   109
Bentham, Jeremy   294
Bernstein, Eduard   16
Bertolucci, Attilio   5
Best, Michael H.   219
Bettelheim, Charles   180, 215, 218, 219n4, 231, 269, 311n8, 323n1, 342–3, 355
Bićanić, Rudolf   142, 168, 170, 175–7, 196, 225
Bilandžić, Dušan   34, 40, 54–5, 57–9, 63, 65, 87n2, 93, 93n6, 133, 164n1, 166–9, 176, 178, 184, 223, 229
Bismarck, Otto von   38
Blackburn, Robin   181n1
Blanqui, Louis Auguste (Blanquism)   xxi
Bloch, Ernst (Blochian)   vii, xiii, 1–2, 3n2, 6–7 (photo), 7n4, 8, 16, 16n9, 82, 90, 232, 249, 265, 280, 317–18, 329, 383
Blumenberg, Hans   105n1
Bobbio, Norberto   105n1, 299
Bobrowski, Czesław   26, 94, 163, 166, 171–2
Boffito, Carlo   98n7
Bogdanović, Mira   352

Bongiovanni, Bruno   284n1, 340n6
Borges, Jorge Luis   231–2, 355
Bošnjak, Branko   105
Bošković, Blagoje, and David Dašić   194, 225, 236
Bourdet, Yvon, and Alain Guillerm   181n1, 209n1, 257
Bourdieu, Pierre   346
Božinović, Neda   68, 70
Bracke, Wilhelm   119n3
Braverman, Harry   254
Brecht, Bertolt   vii, xiii, xx, 3n2, 3n3, 9–10 (photo), 11–14, 83, 180, 206, 238, 279, 281, 298, 298n5, 299n5, 340, 346, 369, 373, 383–4
Brešić, Vjekoslav   xiv, xvi, 240 (map)
Brezhnev, Leonid I. (Brezhnevist)   85, 96, 215, 347
Bricianer, Serge   329
Brinton, Maurice   180n1, 216
Broekmeyer, Marius J.   256
Broz, Josip   *See*: Tito
Brus, Wlodzimierz   98, 100, 164, 164n1, 207–8, 210, 212, 234–5, 254, 256, 260–1, 266, 269, 274, 284, 293–4, 297–8, 300–1
Buber, Martin   308
Buden, Boris   xvii, 11, 27, 37, 105, 141, 212
Bukharin, Nikolai I. [Nikolay]   36–7, 149n3, 218, 287, 287n2, 334n5, 335, 338, 341
Burawoy, Michael   248–50, 254, 270, 317

Cabet, Étienne   110
Calic, Marie-Janine   5, 55–6, 140, 238, 296–7
Calvez, Jean-Yves   16n9
Carr, Edward Hallett   180n1, 282
Carroll, Lewis (pseud. of Charles L. Dodgson)   346
Carter, April   134, 136–8, 141–2, 144–5, 147, 268n2
Castro, Fidel   219n4, 305
Černe, France   232n7, 234n8, 237, 296
Cervantes, Miguel de   156
Chavance, Bernard   222
Cliff, Tony (pseud. of Yigael Gluckstein)   234n8, 343
Coates, Ken   101
Cohen, Lenard J.   119, 131, 134, 137n1, 138, 140, 150, 153n5
Cohen, Robert S.   145, 371

Cohen, Stephen F.   37, 254, 304, 341
Columbus, Christopher (Kristofor Kolumbo)   xiv, 286 (illustration)
Comisso, Ellen Turkish   134, 145n2, 165, 169, 176–8, 182, 184, 187, 190, 195–6, 198, 203–4, 207, 209n1, 211, 217, 220, 223–4, 235, 250, 259, 261, 262n1, 300, 307
Connolly, William E.   219
Cortesi, Luigi   xvii, 315, 339, 342–3
Crane, Walter   xiv, 378 (drawing)
Crvenkovski, Krste   147
Curtius, Ernst Robert   105n1
Cvjetičanin, Veljko   105, 147, 259, 265–6
Cvjetićanin, Vladimir   56–8

Dallemagne, Jean-Luc   99
Damachi, Ukandi G.   190, 193
Dante Alighieri   ix, 2
Dašić, David   *See*: Bošković
Davidson, Cathy N.   268
Davies, R.W.   340
Davis, Mike   26n1
Davis, Ronnie (R.G.)   xvii
De Angelis, Massimo   37
Debray, Régis   66
Dedijer, Vladimir   54, 78, 133
*Defilippis, Josip   392
Deng Xiaoping   96
Denitch, Bogdan Denis   129, 141, 150, 224, 236, 276, 352
Derrida, Jacques   14, 386
Descartes, René   9
Deutscher, Isaac   146
Dewey, John   384
Dickinson, Emily   280
*Dilić, Edhem   392
Đilas, Milovan   *See*: Djilas, Milovan
Dimitrijević, Branislav   277n3
Dimitrijevic, Dimitrije   222
Dirlam, Joel, and James Plummer   169, 179, 223, 297
Divjak, Slobodan   17, 97, 148, 232n7
Djilas, Milovan   5, 31, 75, 86n1, 133, 143, 167, 346–8, 351–2, 360–2
Dobrović, Petar   xiii, 32 (painting)
Dos Passos, John   359
Dostoievsky, Fyodor M.   156
Draper, Hal   72, 328n3
Dreyfus, Alfred   375

INDEX OF PROPER NAMES OF HISTORICAL PERSONS 423

Drulović, Milojko   176, 185–6, 188, 191, 223, 228
Dubey, Vinod   183, 191n2
Duda, Igor   197
Dühring, Eugen   326, 331
Dumézil, Georges   317
Dunayevskaya, Raya   16n9
Dunlop, John T.   196, 254
Đurek, Danijel   296
Dyker, David   148, 150, 176, 221, 225
*Džinić, Firdus   405

Ehrenreich, Barbara, and John Ehrenreich   66
Einstein, Albert   238, 359
Eisenstein, Sergei M.   238
*El Tatawy, Nawal A.   409
Elson, Diane   17, 212n2, 213–14, 214n3, 220, 266, 270, 299n5
Engels, Friedrich   vii, 27, 45, 47, 50, 54, 59, 119n3, 141, 208, 248, 256, 294, 299, 323, 323n1, 325–6, 330–4, 340, 369, 377
Epicure   7
Erić-Suvin, Nevenka   vii, xvii
Erikson, Erik H.   69
Erlich, Alexander   36
Erlich, Richard D.   xvii
Erlich, Vera Stein   277
Estrin, Saul   176, 183

Fanon, Frantz   319
Feenberg, Andrew   248
Fejtö, François   22–4, 39, 139–41, 143, 146, 163
Ferguson, Adam   109
Feuerbach, Ludwig   106, 111
Fiamengo, Ante   65, 385–6
Filipi, Slavko   67, 71, 131, 133, 135–6, 138, 352
Fischer, Louis   343
Fitzgerald, F. Scott   156
Flaherty, Diane   261
Foa, Lisa   36
Ford, Henry   51, 85, 106, 151, 194, 249, 301n6, 303, 359
Forster, Michael N.   309
Foscolo, Ugo   ix
Fourier, Charles   7, 110
Fraser, Nancy   301n6

Frederick William IV (king of Prussia)   106
Freud, Sigmund   76
Fried, Morton   285
Furet, François   xix
Fusi, Gabriella   2822

Galbraith, John Kenneth   364, 384
Gavrović, Milan   225
Gebauer, Gunter   322
Gebhardt, Richard   xvii
Gershwin, George, and Ira Gershwin   ix
Geršković, Leon   190, 193
Gini, Corrado   169
Gnjatović, Dragana   176, 225
Godelier, Maurice   285
Goldmann, Lucien   16n9, 383–4
Golubović, Zagorka   79, 209, 209n1, 233, 260, 264n1
Gorky, Maxim (pseud. of Alexei Peshkov)   343
Gorter, Herman   284n1
Gorupić, Drago   174
Gorz, André (pseud of Gérard Horst)   152n4, 153n5, 310, 384
Gould, Carol C.   181n1
Graeber, David   214n3
Gramsci, Antonio   xiii, 3, 31–2, 45–6 (photo), 47, 49–50, 75, 88, 110, 181n1, 207, 209n1, 210, 217, 238, 248–51, 266, 270, 276, 287, 299–300, 306–7, 309, 312, 328n3, 383, 386
Gréco, Juliette   281
Gregory, Mary B.   262, 262n1
Greimas, Algirdas Julien   26n3
Groethuysen, Bernhard   271
Guattari, Félix   303
Guevara, Che (Ernesto)   218, 219n4
Guillerm, Alain   See: Bourdet
Guizot, François   275
Gurvitch, Georges   44–7, 50, 63, 75, 210n1

Hadžistević, Vojin   200
Hamilton, Ian F.E.   19, 56, 91n5, 171, 173 (map), 174, 176
Hanžeković, Marijan   177, 225
Harding, Neil   287, 287n2
Harvey, David   37, 100
Heidegger, Martin   384
Hegedüs, András   74

Hegel, G.W.F. (Hegelian)   ix, xxi, 2, 12, 28, 43, 74, 77, 79, 82, 105n1, 106, 108–13, 124, 217, 264, 271, 280, 308–9, 318, 325, 338, 375–6
Herder, Johann Gottfried   27
Heuser, Beatrice   39n2
Hillel, Rabbi (the Elder)   279
Hirszowicz, Maria   79
Hitler, Adolf   32, 234, 334
Ho Chi Minh   305
Hobbes, Thomas   110–11
Hobsbawm, Eric J.   28, 31, 43, 45–7, 58, 64, 81, 219, 250–1, 299–300, 306, 319, 345, 387
Hodgson, Geoff   212n2
Hoffman, George W.   39n2, 143, 163
Hogarth, William   59
Horvat, Branko   xiii, xvi, 53, 55, 58–9, 61–2, (photos), 63–7, 75, 86, 98–100, 130, 136, 138, 142, 147, 153n5, 165, 167, 174–5, 177, 197, 207, 209, 209n1, 222, 226, 248, 253, 255, 257–8, 262–4, 268–71, 273, 295, 299n5, 301, 367–71, 384–6
Horvat, Srećko   10
Hrnjez, Saša   xvii
Hrženjak, Juraj   18
Huberman, Leo   212n2
Hughes, Langston   281
Hunnius, Gerry   198
Husserl, Edmund   7

Ibsen, Henrik   27n4
Iveković, Rada   xvii

Jakšić, Božidar   xvi–xvii, 226, 371, 382
Jameson, Fredric   xi, xix–xxi, 4, 230, 282, 308–9
Jancar-Webster, Barbara   25, 67–8, 68n2, 70–1
Janevski, Ana   191
Jefferson, Thomas   209
Jenkins, David   257
Jerovšek, Janez   228–9
Jesus Christ (Christianity)   30, 116, 119n3, 120–3, 247, 309
Johnson, A. Ross   351
Johnson, Chalmers A.   24
Jovanović, Andrea   xvii
Jovanov, Neca   57, 60, 198
Joyce, James   359

Kafka, Franz   359
Kalecki, Michał   98–9, 156
Kangrga, Milan   105, 367, 381–2, 385
Kant, Immanuel (Kantian)   267, 268n2
Kanzleiter, Boris   179n2, 308
Karamanić, Slobodan   xvii, 11, 26
Kardelj, Edvard   xiv, xxi, 23–4, 31, 33, 40, 75–7, 91, 97, 125, 140–1, 143–9, 164, 175, 206–7, 210, 210n1, 224–5, 230–2, 232n7, 233–4, 234n8, 235–40, 259, 261, 267, 269, 271–2, 275, 293, 311n8, 346–8, 351–4, 355 (photo), 356–61, 364–9, 384–5
Kaštelan, Jure   30
Katunarić, Vjeran   xvii, 10
Kautsky, Karl   16
Kerensky, Alexander F.   324, 330
Kerleroux, Jean-Marie   iv (drawing), xiii
Krševan, Marko   74–7, 102
Keynes, John Maynard (Keynesian)   272, 297
Khrushchev, Nikita S   90, 143, 145, 351
Kidrič, Boris   xiii, xxi, 15n8, 31, 40, 86, 86n1, 87, 87n2, 88–9, 89n3, 89n4, 90–1, 91n5, 92–3, 93n6, 94 (photo), 95–8, 98n7, 99–100, 118, 141, 144, 164, 166, 209, 219, 268, 292, 296, 299–300, 305, 334n5, 337, 346–51, 354, 357, 360, 366, 368–9, 384–5
Kirn, Gal   xvii, 11, 26, 191
Kirn, Srečo   See: Bavčar
Kolaja, Jiri T.   188–9
Konstantinović, Radomir, 19
Kontetzki, Heinz   55–6
Korać, Miladin   97
Kornai, János   164
Korošić, Marijan   56, 99, 164n1, 197, 234, 295
Korsch, Karl   249, 366
Korsika, Bojan   See: Bavčar
Kosík, Karel   12, 282, 317
Kouvelakis, Stathis   105n1, 111, 268n2
Kovač, Bogomir   51
Kovačević, Dušanka   67–8, 71
*Kratina, Husein   405
Krivak, Marijan   10
Krleža, Miroslav   vii, xiii, 30, 32 (portrait), 286
Kropotkin, Pyotr A. (Peter)   384
Kržan, Marko   xvii, 11, 33n5, 259, 262, 273
Kugelmann, Louis (Ludwig)   332

INDEX OF PROPER NAMES OF HISTORICAL PERSONS 425

Kuljić, Todor   xvii, 5, 141, 149, 315
Kurz, Robert   51n1
Kuzmanić, Tonči   291

La Rochefoucauld, François de   123, 290
Labica, Georges   109
Lafargue, Paul   271
Lalović, Dragan   xvii, 143, 148–9, 360
Lampe, John R.   39n2, 51n1, 56, 141, 163, 170, 176, 211, 222
Lange, Oskar   87n2, 98, 177, 212n2, 218n4
Laski, Kazimierz   293–4, 297
Lazić, Mladen   xiv, xvii, 11, 45, 49, 63–4, 73–4, 138, 243–4, 246, 261, 268, 291, 307
Le Guin, Ursula K.   x
Lebowitz, Michael A.   254, 272
Lefebvre, Henri   50, 152n4, 310
Leibniz, Gottfried Wilhelm von   216
Lenin, Vladimir I. (pseud. of V.I. Ulyanov; Leninian; Leninism; Leninist)   vii, xiii, xxi, 3, 16, 24–5, 27–8, 31, 36–8 (drawing), 45, 47, 49, 54, 75–8, 87, 89, 94, 96, 100, 113–14, 123–4, 129, 136, 139, 144–5, 152–3, 180, 180n1, 207, 209, 214n3, 215–16, 219, 225, 237, 249, 265, 267, 269, 274–5, 282, 284, 284n1, 285, 287, 287n2, 298–9, 303–6, 309–11, 313, 315–16, 323, 323n1, 324–8, 328n3, 329–34, 334n5, 335–43, 346–7, 349–50, 354–6, 359, 366, 368, 374, 377–8, 380–1, 383–4, 386
Leoncavallo, Ruggero   1
Lewin, Moshe   78, 334–5, 340–1, 343, 345
Lih, Lars T.   38, 328–9, 337, 378
Lilly, Carol S.   140–1, 144
Lincoln, Abraham   57
Lipovec, Filip   88, 95, 98
Löwenthal, Richard   36n1, 162
Löwith, Karl   105n1, 271
Löwy (Lowy), Michael   218, 219n4, 297
Lorde, Audrey   218
Lordon, Frédéric   312
Louis Bonaparte (Napoleon III)   326
Lowinger, Jake   261, 274
Lucian from Samosate   1
Lucretius (Titus Lucretius Carus)   128
Lukács, Georg   45–6, 50, 139, 249, 359, 363, 384
Lummis, C. Douglas   xvii

Luxemburg, Rosa   xiii, xvii, 37–8 (photo), 126, 298, 337, 384, 418

MacBride, William L.   371
Macesich, George   50, 168, 176, 183, 222
Machiavelli, Niccolò   5, 128
MacMillan, Gloria   xvii
Magri, Lucio   xvii, 152n4, 264n1, 292, 308
Makavejev, Dušan   5
Mandel, Ernest   180n1, 212n2, 218, 219n4, 232, 270, 280, 343
Mandel'shtam, Osip   280
Maniscalco Basile, Giovanni   xvii
Mann Borgese, Elisabeth   33, 181, 256, 258, 295
Manzoni, Alessandro   19
Mao Zedong (Maoist),   27, 89n4, 114, 124, 143, 219n4, 276, 287, 305, 308, 329
Marat, Jean-Paul   27
Marcuse, Herbert   4, 12, 15, 82, 85, 162, 181, 217, 238, 248–9, 271–2, 384
Marković, Goran   xvii
Marković, Mihailo   185, 191, 209–10, 259, 265, 292n4, 299, 367, 369, 371–4, 381–2, 385
Markuš, Đerđ (György Márkus)   99, 219
Marx, Karl (Marxian; Marxism; Marxist)   vii, xi, xiii, xxi, 1n1, 2, 2n1, 3, 3n2, 3n2, 7, 7n4, 8, 11–13 (drawing), 14–16, 16n9, 17, 25n1, 26n1, 27, 31, 36, 39–40, 44–50, 54, 60, 63, 65, 67, 72–6, 81–2, 96–7, 100–1, 105, 105n1, 106–19, 119n3, 121–2, 24–6, 141, 147, 152n4, 153, 166, 180, 207, 209n1, 212n2, 213, 214n3, 215–17, 219n4, 223, 230, 232, 232n7, 234–5, 238, 247–51, 254, 266, 268, 268n2, 269, 271–2, 275, 283–5, 287–9, 294, 297–8, 298n5, 299, 301, 305–7, 309, 311–13, 316–18, 323, 323n1, 324–6, 326n2, 328, 328n3, 329–30, 332–4, 334n5, 337–8, 340–1, 346, 348–50, 354–6, 358–60, 366–8, 372–3, 375–7, 379–86
*Mazauric, Claude   401, 412, 415
McNally, David   164, 212n2, 301
McNeal, Robert   340–3
Medvedev, Roy (Roj) A.   152n4, 338
Meillassoux, Claude   37
Meister, Albert   195, 198, 212, 256
Melville, Herman   28
Merleau-Ponty, Maurice   ix, 152n4, 304–5

Merton, Robert K.   325
Meštrović, Matko   xvii, 10
Mészáros, István   16n9
Michelet, Jules   304
Michels, Robert   17, 149, 149n3, 306n7, 325
Mićunović, Dragoljub   268n2, 369, 374–6, 382
Mihajlov, Mihajlo   5
Milanović, Vladimir   See: Atlagić
Milenkovitch, Deborah   98n7, 174, 208, 212, 220–3
Mill, John Stuart   158
Miller, Robert F.   110n2
Mills, C. Wright   13, 77, 375
Milosavlevski, Slavko   147
Milosavljević, Olivera   xvii, 18n10, 163, 170, 193, 254, 267
Milošević, Slobodan   225
Milton, John   11
Mo Di (Mo Zi)   ix, 279
Močnik, Rastko   xvii, 11, 38, 165, 194, 232n7, 239, 244, 258, 262n1, 276, 359
*Modžić, Alija   392
Molière (pseud. of Jean-Baptiste Poquelin)   6
Momčilović Ivana   xvii, 11, 26n2
Montaigne, Michel Eyquem de   9
Montesquieu, Charles Secondat de   152, 156, 297
Montfaucon, Bernard de   318
Moore, Barrington, Jr.   6, 9, 264, 289, 289n3
Moore, John H.   51
*Moore, Samuel   412
Mora, Alberto   218, 218n4, 219n4
More, Thomas   1n1, 285, 319
Morris, William   248, 302
Moses   36, 275
Moulier Boutang, Yann   151
Moylan, Tom   xvii
Možina, S.   255

Nancy, Jean-Luc   14
Napoleon Bonaparte   xix, 6, 19, 326
Neal, Fred Warner   39n2, 143, 163
Negri, Toni   303
Ness, Immanuel   180n1
Neumann, Franz L.   234n8
Nietzsche, Friedrich   308
Nikolić, Miloš   137, 147
Novaković, Nada   58, 70, 178, 186, 198, 261
Nove, Alec   214n3, 342

Occam, William of   64
Ocić, Časlav   295
Ollman, Bertell   16n9, 44–5, 50, 63, 77
Orwell, George (pseud. of Eric A. Blair)   355
Ossowski, Stanisław   44, 46–7, 50, 342
Ovid (Publius Ovidius Naso)   319
Owen, Robert   181n1

Pannekoek, Anton   181n1, 249
Parkin, Frank   228n6, 291
Pascal, Blaise (Pascalian)   273
Pateman, Carole   181n1
Pavičević, Borka   11
Pečujlić, Miroslav   74, 285
Perović, Latinka   264n1, 308
Pervan, Ralph   179n2
Pessoa, Fernando   278
Petranović, Branko   68, 132, 179n2
Petrović, Asja   xvi, 282
Petrović, D.   396
Petrović, Gajo   xiv, xvi, 8, 57, 97, 105, 139, 219, 233 (photo), 234, 247, 367, 367n2, 376–7, 379–81, 384–6
Picasso, Pablo   238
Picelj, Ivan   xiv, xvi, 241 (photo)
Pienkos, Andrew   212, 225, 270
Pijade, Moša   xiii, 29
Pinochet, Augusto   334
Plato (Platonic)   7, 128, 287
Plekhanov, Georgi   267
Plummer, James   See: Dirlam
Podsheldolkin, Alexander   340
Pol Pot   334
Polanyi, Karl   46–7, 75, 101, 212n2, 221, 272, 301
Poulantzas, Nikos   44
Preobrazhensky, Evgeniy A.   36, 218n4, 334n5, 335
Preve, Costanzo   298, 305, 306n7
Prévert, Jacques   281
Prickett, Russell O.   393, 400, 403
Propp, Vladimir   26n3
Proudhon, Pierre-Joseph (Proudhonist)   110, 181n1, 208–9, 209n1, 210n1, 359
Prout, Christopher   169, 176, 223, 260, 262n1, 263
Puharič, Krešo   92
Puhovski, Žarko   97
Pulig, Srećko   xvii, 10
Puljiz, Vlado   56, 58

INDEX OF PROPER NAMES OF HISTORICAL PERSONS 427

Pupovac, Ozren   xvii, 11, 28, 31
Pusić, Eugen   239

Quisling, Vidkun   24, 30, 35, 313

Rabinbach, Anson   234n8
Radek, Karl   276
Ragon, Michel   iv
Rancière, Jacques   118, 302
Ranković, Aleksandar   12, 142, 146, 210, 346
Rehmann, Jan   109
Resnick, Stephen   44, 309
Rimbaud, Arthur   359
Ritsert, Jürgen   44, 48, 74
Robespierre, Maximilien   27, 27n4, 81, 150, 269, 303
Robinson, Gertrude Joch   191
Robinson, K.S. (Stan)   xvii
Roemer, John   44
Roggemann, Herwig   71, 183–4, 186, 188–91
Roosevelt, Franklin D.   250
Rosenstein-Rodan, Paul N.   184, 297
Rousseau, Jean-Jacques   27, 42, 101, 110, 113, 126, 209, 333
Rus, Veljko   147–8, 150, 228–9, 232n7, 255, 264n1, 308, 371
Rusinow, Dennison   4, 12, 39n2, 57, 65–6, 138–9, 144, 144n2, 145–6, 148, 169–70, 174, 239, 277, 352

Saint-Simon, Henri de   110, 208, 348
Samary, Catherine   xvii, 36, 102, 176, 191, 211, 212n2, 237, 254, 259, 261, 262n1, 301
Sartre, Jean-Paul   308, 384
Schierup, Carl-Ulrik   55, 268, 295–6
Schleicher, Harry   58, 70, 166, 184, 188, 195
Schram, Stuart R.   308
Schrenk, Martin   56, 221, 228
Schrödinger, Erwin   309
Seibel, Hans Dieter   184–5, 190, 193, 198, 256–8
Selden, Mark   308
Senjković, Reana   277n3
Serge, Victor   311n8
Shakespeare, William   vii, 156
Shapiro, Leonard   339
Sheinman, Aron L.   336
Shelley, Percy Bysshe   2
Sher, Gerson S.   371

Shoup, Paul   170
Sieyès, Emmanuel   326
Simić, Andrei   58
Simmel, Georg   13
Simon, György, Jr.   51, 168, 176–7, 211, 222
Simonides of Ceos   86
Singleton, Fred   4, 54, 183, 185, 187–8, 193, 195, 227, 227n5
Sklevicky, Lydia   53, 68, 70
Skocpol, Theda   4, 289, 289n3
Slapšak, Svetlana   x
Smailagić, Nerkez   385
Smith, Adam   51–2, 106, 109, 216, 273, 298, 348
Šnajder, Slobodan   xvii
Sophocles   319
Souriau, Étienne   26n3
Spencer, Herbert   324
Spinoza, Baruch   87, 106, 267, 317
Stalin, Josif V. (pseud. of Soso Djugashvili; Stalinian, Stalinism; Stalinist)   xxi, 8, 24–5, 26n2, 31–2, 37–40, 50, 52, 76–7, 83, 85, 87n2, 88–9, 89n3, 90, 99–100, 114, 116, 119–20, 124, 126, 128, 133, 139–46, 149–50, 153, 162–3, 165–6, 180, 207–8, 210–11, 215–18, 220, 230–3, 234n8, 236, 238–9, 247, 250–1, 264n1, 269, 287–8, 293–5, 297, 306, 306n7, 307–8, 310, 311n8, 313–16, 324, 28n3, 329, 332, 334, 337–40, 349n6, 341–3, 345–6, 353–5, 359–60, 369, 371, 376–7, 379–81, 383–6
*Štambuk, Maja   392
Ste. Croix, Geoffrey de   45, 77
Stiglitz, Joseph E.   221
Stipetić, Vladimir   55–6, 168
Stőppler, Michael   xvii
Stojaković, Gordana   xvii
Stojaković, Krunoslav   xvii, 68, 179n2, 308
Stojanović, Branimir-Trša   xvii, 1
Stojanović, Svetozar   208, 212, 217, 301, 308, 385, 385n3
Stonor Saunders, Frances   352
Strpić, Dag   xvii, 295
Struve, Pyotr B.   324
Supek, Rudi   xiii, xvi, 105, 188–9, 191, 209n1, 210n1, 225, 226 (photo), 234, 236, 265–6, 298, 300, 311, 367, 384–5
Sutlić, Vanja   97
Šuvar, Mira   xvii

Šuvar, Stipe   xvii, 53, 56, 58, 60, 74, 76, 148, 277n3
Suvin, Miroslav   vii
Suvin, Truda   vii
Sweezy, Paul M.   212n

Tablada Pérez, Carlos   218
Tadić, Ljubomir   97, 381
Tamás, Gáspár Miklós   290
Tannenbaum, Arnold   185, 255
Taylor, Fred M.   177
Taylor, Frederick W. (taylorism)   257
Thatcher, Margaret   99
Thompson, E.P.   44–5
Ticonius   119n3
Tinbergen, Jan   256
Tito, Josip Broz (Titoism; Titoist)   5, 11, 23–4, 25n1, 28, 30–2, 34, 39, 68, 73, 85, 118, 134, 136, 139, 141, 143–6, 151, 162, 194, 217, 225, 236, 264, 267, 305, 315, 343, 347–8, 359–61, 385
Todorović, A.   255
Todorović, Mijalko   138
Tomšič, Vida   56, 68n2, 70
Tonković, Stipe   58–9, 168, 184, 196–7
Topham, Anthony   183, 185, 187–8, 193, 195
Tornquist, David   198–9
Tozi, Đoko   57
Tripalo, Miko   100, 182, 232, 262n1, 311
Trotsky (Trotskyist; Trotskyite), Lev D. (Leon)   36, 74, 78, 99, 219n4, 284n1, 287, 301, 305, 310, 325–6, 335, 337–8, 340n6, 342, 346, 384
Tucker, Robert C.   124, 323n1, 325–8, 331
Tudjman, Franjo   18, 137
Tyson, Laura D'Andrea   178, 221

Unkovski-Korica, Vladimir   xvii, 99, 164

Vanek, Jan   168, 182–3, 186, 197, 221, 227, 239
Vaništa, Josip   xvii, 286 (drawing)
Veljak, Lino   xvi–xvii
Vidaković, Zoran   261
Virgil (Publius Vergilius Maro)   128
Visković, Velimir   75

Vlahović, Veljko   143
Vranicki, Predrag   105, 181n1
Vukmanović Tempo, Svetozar   147
Vulpe, Milan   xiv, xvi, 242 (drawing)
Vušković, Boris   291
Vygotski, Lev   384

Wachtel, Howard   168, 188, 194–5, 203, 239
Wagner, Adolph   214n3
Waller, Michael   306n7
Wallis, Victor   xvi, 272
Wallon, Henri   384
Wang Hui   152, 152n4
Ward, Benjamin   367
Waterston, Albert   220
Weber, Alfred   369
Weber, Max   13, 44, 47, 64, 74–6, 325, 369, 375, 377, 379, 381, 384
Webster   See: Jancar-Webster
Wegner, Phillip E.   3n3
Wells, H.G.   311
Weydemeyer, Joseph   332
Wittfogel, Karl August   285
Wittgenstein, Ludwig   322, 384
Wolfe, Thomas   156
Wolff, Richard   44, 309
Wood, Ellen Meiksins   283, 285, 305
Woodward, Susan L.   36n1, 37, 40, 51, 54, 59, 70–1, 102, 148, 164, 177, 223, 225, 227, 229–30, 266, 273
Wright, Eric Olin   44
Wright Mills   See: Mills

Zaslavskaia, Tatyana   51n1
Zečević, Momčilo   68, 132, 179n2
Žilnik, Želimir   191
Zlatić, Ivan   xvii
Zola, Émile   375
Zolo, Danilo   105, 111–12
Zović-Svoboda, Zorka   214, 222
Zukin, Sharon   181, 194, 197–8, 222, 225, 233–4, 260, 288, 290, 292
Županov, Josip   185, 244, 255
Žuvela, Mladen   56, 75
Žvan, Antun   102, 207, 277

www.ingramcontent.com/pod-product-compliance
Lightning Source LLC
Chambersburg PA
CBHW071144070526
44584CB00019B/2655